7.

Autobiography of

MAXIM GORKY

Autobiography of

MAXIM GORKY

MY CHILDHOOD

IN THE WORLD

MY UNIVERSITIES

Translated by

ISIDOR SCHNEIDER

THE CITADEL PRESS SECAUCUS, NEW JERSEY

Second paperbound printing, 1973

Copyright 1949 by The Citadel Press

Published by The Citadel Press
A division of Lyle Stuart Inc.
120 Enterprise Avenue, Secaucus, N.J. 07094
In Canada: George J. McLeod Limited
73 Bathurst St., Toronto 2B, Ontario
Manufactured in the United States of America

Translator's Preface

O F ALL THE RUSSIAN MASTERS GORKY HAS FARED POOREST AT THE hands of his translators. The early Russian writers were translated, in most cases, by people who had at least a scholarly interest in their task and, for whom, often, it was a labor of love. In any case it had the virtue of conscientious care even where it exhibited meager literary endowments. By the time Gorky appeared, however, Russian 19th century literature was established in the great place it has held ever since and Gorky became immediately a figure of world interest. Publication of his work was hurried through the presses. The rush, unfortunately, showed itself in most of the translations.

This was so with what is generally considered the greatest of his works, the autobiographical trilogy *My Childhood, In the World* and *My Universities* (first translated as *My University Days*). As it reached its English reading public, it had only a dim resemblance to the original. In the case of one of the volumes, chapters were interchanged and sections dropped out of others. For this reason I was delighted when the project of a one volume edition in a new translation was broached.

In my rendering I have preferred to be free rather than meticulously "correct" where correctness might involve stiff "translation English." Gorky is outstandingly fluid and colloquial and such "correctness" would in itself be a mistranslation. I have also sought to mitigate unnecessary strangeness in the Russian names by using English equivalents, wherever possible, even at the sacrifice of the "quaintness" that some readers profess to enjoy. The names, of course, have no "quaintness" in the original. Generally I have dropped diminutives where they might stand in the way of the reader's immediate identification of the character as, for the same reason, I have dropped the middle patronymic. The usage is essential in Russian social intercourse but is an anomaly in English, and on test, has proved confusing to the reader. I have felt that any new step that would make so great a work more accessible to English-speaking readers was worth taking.

ISIDOR SCHNEIDER

Contents

My Childhood

Chapter One

ON THE FLOOR, UNDER THE WINDOW, IN A SMALL, SHUTTERED ROOM, lay my father, dressed in a long white garment I had never seen him in before. His feet were bare and the toes were strangely distended, while the fingers of his hands, resting on his breast, were curled in. The blackened disks of two copper coins covered his eyes, shutting out their accustomed, cheerful gleam. All the light had gone out of his still face. But what scared me most was the snarl his open mouth showed with the teeth bared.

Beside him, on her knees, was my mother, in an undergarment. She was combing his long, fine hair back from his forehead to the nape of his neck. The comb she was using was the one with which I scraped edible shreds from watermelon rinds. As she combed away, she talked to him without stopping, through tears that fell without stopping, until it seemed that they must finally flood her eyes out of their sockets.

I saw all this holding on to the hand of my grandmother, whose dark head and eyes and nose looked enormous—the nose shapeless and pitted like a sponge—but a gentle, yet vividly interesting, woman. She, too, wept with sobs that were like cadences to my mother's. Shuddering herself, she pushed me toward my father, but I was too terrified to let go and clung to her.

This was the first time I had ever seen grownups cry, and I could not understand her repeated bidding, "Say good-by to your father. You'll never see him again. He's dead before his time."

I, myself, was just out of sickbed after a long, hard illness. It was still fresh in my mind how my father had done all he could to amuse me; and then how his place at my bedside had suddenly been taken by that old woman, then a stranger to me, my grandmother.

I asked her where she came from, using the verb form which implies coming by foot.

"From up north, from Nizhny,"[1] she replied, "but I didn't walk it;

[1] Nizhny Novgorod (Lower Novgorod). Colloquially only the first part of the name was used.

3

I came down by boat. You don't walk on water, you little scamp."

This made no sense to me at all. Upstairs there lived a gaily-dressed Persian who wore a beard; and downstairs, in the cellar, there lived a withered, yellow Kalmuck who dealt in sheepskins. And I got up to one and down to the other by way of the banisters; and if I had a fall, I just rolled down. But there was no place for water. So her "down" from "up north" on water could not be true; but it was a delightful muddle.

"Why do you call me a little scamp?" I asked.

"Because you make so much noise, that's why," she said, with a laugh.

Her voice was sweet and her words were merry and I made friends with her at once.

Now, clinging to her, all I wanted was for her to hurry and get me out of the room.

My mother caught me to her with a burst of weeping and moaning that frightened me. I had never seen her so before, this strong, composed, reserved woman, always so glowing and neat, strongly-framed like a horse and with tremendous power in her arms. Now, quivering and puffy, she looked utterly stricken. Her hair had shaken out of its gaily-trimmed cap and out of the usual tidy coil around her head and was streaming over her shoulder; and the part of it that remained in braid tracked across my father's still face. All this time she had not given me even a look, unable to tear herself away from her grief-stricken combing of my father's hair.

Then a policeman and some grave-diggers appeared at the door. "Get a move on!" bellowed the policeman.

A draft had filled the shawl that curtained the window, filled it like a sail. That picture came to me because my father had taken me sailing, once, and the sail had filled out the same way, in a sudden gust. With it had come a clap of thunder and my father had pulled me to his knee to reassure me and, laughing, had said, "It's nothing; don't let it frighten you."

All at once my mother dropped to the floor and immediately turned over, her hair in the dirt. Her mouth came open on her now-livid face so that her teeth were bared like my father's. In a terrifying voice she ordered me out, and the door to be shut.

Pushing me aside, grandma rushed to the door crying out, "Friends, there's nothing to be alarmed about; it's not the cholera; she's giving birth. For the love of God, leave us! Good people, go away."

Hidden behind a big box in a corner I saw my mother moving convulsively over the floor, panting through clenched teeth. Grandma hovered over her with soothing, cheering words, "Patience, Barbara . . . Holy Mother of God, be her protection!"

I shook with fright. In their frantic movements they bumped against my father, they groaned and shrieked into his unmoved, even smiling, face. For a long time this thrashing about on the floor went on. And all through it, rolling in and out like a big, black, woolly ball went grandma on her errands.

Suddenly there was a whimper of a child. "Thank God!" grandma called out, "it's a boy!" and got up to light a candle.

And at that point, I must have fallen asleep in the darkness behind the box, because that was all I remembered.

My next memory is a solitary spot in a cemetery, in the rain. Standing beside a muddy pile of earth, I looked down into the hole in which they had sunk my father in his coffin. Frogs splashed in the water that had seeped in, and two were perched on the yellow coffin lid. Beside me were grandma, the drenched sexton and a pair of grave-diggers with shovels.

The sexton ordered the grave to be filled and moved off. Grandma wailed into an end of her head-shawl. Bent nearly double, the grave-diggers shoveled lumps of earth over the coffin, kicking the frogs who were trying to hop out, back into the grave.

"Come, Alex," said grandma, her hand on my shoulder, but I was too absorbed and slipped away.

"What next, O Lord!" grandma complained, half to me, half to God, and stood there in silence, with a dejected droop of her head.

Not till after the grave had been filled and the diggers' shovels had clanged to the ground and a sudden scurry of breeze had spattered us with raindrops, did she stir. Then, leading me by the hand, she took me to a church some distance away, over a path bordered by occasional dim crosses.

As we left the graveyard, she asked me, "How is it you're not crying? You ought to."

"I don't want to," I replied.

"You don't? Well, you don't have to," she said, gently.

It was a surprise to me that I was expected to cry. My crying had been always more out of temper than sadness. Father had laughed my tears away and mother had forbidden them. "Don't you dare to cry!" And so I seldom cried.

Afterwards we rode down a broad, but filthy street in a drozhky [2] be-

---

[2] A small carriage.

tween rows of houses all painted a dark red. On the way I asked grandma, "Can those frogs ever get out?"

"Never, God bless them."

God came more frequently and familiarly into her conversation, it occurred to me then, than He ever did in my father's or mother's.

Several days later I found myself, together with mama and grandma, in a tiny steamboat cabin. On a table, in the corner, lay the corpse of my little brother, Maxim, in white trappings held together with red tape. The porthole had the appearance of a horse's eye; I climbed up our piled luggage to look through. All there was to see was muddy froth. It charged against the glass, at one moment, with such force that it splashed in, and I scrambled down to the floor.

"There's nothing can harm you," said grandma lightly, lifting me back upon the baggage in her caressing arms.

Gray and brooding over the water, the fog thinned, now and then, to let a distant bulk of the shore loom through like a shadow, only to be lost again in mist and spume. Everything seemed to be aquiver except mother. With her hands clasped behind her head she stood rigid against the wall, with a grim, iron-hard face. Mute and expressionless, she seemed far away from us, an utter stranger. Even her clothes looked unfamiliar.

Gently, now and then, grandma would say, "Barbara, have a bite to eat." Mama did not so much as stir.

To me grandma spoke in whispers; to mama she spoke aloud, but infrequently, and in a timorous manner. Her fear of my mother was something I understood and made me feel closer to grandma.

A sudden, harsh exclamation from mama startled both of us. "Saratov. Where's that sailor?"

Saratov. Sailor. New words to me.

The sailor turned out to be a broad-shouldered, gray-haired man in blue. He carried in a box in which grandma laid my brother's body. She could not get through the door with it, being too broad, and came to a perplexed and ludicrous halt.

"Oh, mama!" exclaimed mama angrily, and took the little coffin from her. Both disappeared and I was left with the man in blue.

"Well, matey," he said, "your little brother has left you."

"Who are you?"

"I'm a sailor."

"Who's Saratov?"

"Saratov's a city. You can see it through the porthole."

From the porthole, the land seemed to shimmer. Dim and crusty, as it steamed in the fog, it made me think of a slice of bread fresh off a hot loaf.

"Where's grandma?"

"She's gone out to bury the little fellow."

"In the ground?"

"That's right."

Then I told the sailor about the frogs that had been buried alive with my father.

Lifting me up he fondled me, "Poor kid, you don't understand. Pity your mother, not the frogs. You don't know what unhappiness is crushing her."

From above came a howl that I recognized as the voice of the ship, so I wasn't frightened. But the sailor put me down at once and left me, shouting, "I must be off!"

I had an impulse to get away. I looked out—the passageway was dark and empty. Nearby glittered the brass plates of steps. Looking up the stair, I saw passengers with valises and bundles, evidently leaving the boat. I thought this meant I must leave, too.

But, at the gangway, in the crowd of debarking peasants, I was met with yells, "Whose boy is he? Who do you belong to, boy?"

Nobody knew me, and I didn't know what to answer. I was hauled from hand to hand until the sailor came up, took hold of me and explained, "It's that Astrakhan [3] boy, the one in the cabin."

He brought me back there, sat me on the baggage and went off threatening me with his forefinger and the words, "I'll give it to you."

The ship's voice, overhead, quieted down; the vibrations of the boat and its movements in the water stopped. Dripping walls opposite the porthole shut off the air and the light, and the cabin grew stifling and dark. The bundles among which I had been placed seemed to grow larger and harder, and I began to feel crushed by them. A fear that I had been left all alone and for good in that empty ship possessed me.

I tried the door, but the metal handle was unbudging. I picked up a bottle of milk and put all my strength in the blow I gave it to make it turn; but all I accomplished was to break the bottle and spill the milk, which splashed over me and trickled down my legs. Sobbing with exasperation, I cried myself to sleep on the bundles.

I woke to find the boat in motion and the porthole round and glow-

[3] A city on the Lower Volga.

ing like a sun. Beside me sat grandma, combing her hair back from her knitted brows and muttering to herself. Her blue-black hair was remarkable for its abundance. It came below her knees and even reached the ground. She had to hold it up with one hand while, with the other, she drew an almost toothless comb through the heavy mass. The strain made her lips purse and brought an exasperated sharpness to her eyes. There was something almost bitter in her expression; yet, when I asked why her hair was so long, it was in her usual melodious words and with her customary tender intonations that she answered, "God must have given it to me to punish me. It's combed out but look at it! When I was a girl I was proud of that mane but now I curse it. But sleep, child. It's early yet. The sun's barely up."

"I want to get up."

"Well then, get up," she said. As she braided her hair she glanced toward my mother who lay rigid on her bunk. "How did you happen to break that bottle? Tell me, but be quiet about it."

That was her way. Her words were like music and like flowers. They bloom in my memory like everlasting blossoms. I remember her smile as a dilation of her large eyes and a cheerful flash of her white teeth that gave her face an inexpressible charm. Despite her wrinkles and her weathered complexion she looked young and even glowing. All that spoiled her appearance was her bulbous, red nose with its splayed-out nostrils, the result of a weakness for drink and her snuff-taking; her black snuff box was almost always in her hand. Outwardly she looked dark, but within burned a vigorous, inextinguishable flame of which the radiance in her eyes was a reflection. She was so stooped as to be almost hunchbacked, yet her motions were gliding and light like those of a great cat; and she was soft and caressing like a cat.

I felt that I had been asleep and in darkness until she came, and that then I woke and was led into the light. It was she who provided the threads with which my mind wove its multi-colored patterns. And by this she became my lifelong friend, the dearest and most understanding and the closest to my heart. Nourished by her wise love for every living thing, I gained the strength to face a hard life.

The river vessels of forty years ago were slow. It took us a long time to get to Nizhny, long, unforgettable days, almost overrich in beauty.

We had good weather and grandma and I were on deck, under the clear sky, almost from dawn to dark, as the ship glided indolently between the shores of the Volga, gay in autumn colors. Behind us, on a long towline, followed a barge that creaked with its every rise and dip in the blue-gray water. That gray barge had the appearance, to me, of a huge wood-louse.

The sun floated along with us over the Volga, unnoticed. Every hour brought fresh landscapes. Like folds in the earth's rich robe rose the green hills. Towns and villages bordered the river banks; and the current was gilt with a drift of autumn leaves.

Over and over grandma exclaimed, "How beautiful!" crossing from one side to the other, her face shining and her eyes round with delight. As she took in these river views she sometimes forgot all about me and stood, silent, at the rail, her hands to her breasts and tears of joy glistening above her smiling lips. Then I would give a tug at her skirt of coarse, dark linen. "Ah," she would say with a start, "I must have been dreaming."

"Why are you crying?"

"Because I'm happy and because I'm old," she would reply, with a smile. "Sixty years have passed over my head, you know."

Taking a pinch of snuff, she would tell me marvelous stories whose heroes were chivalrous bandits, saints, forest animals and demons. Her manner of story-telling evoked tenderness and mystery as she put her face close to mine and fixed me with her big, believing eyes. Thus was the strength that was developing in me directly infused from her. The longer she spoke—or rather, chanted—the more melodious became the flow of her words. Listening to her gave me inexpressible pleasure.

When she had finished I begged for another, and this is an example of what I got: "Now an old goblin lives in the stove. Once he ran a splinter into his paw. As he rocked back and forth with the pain, he whined, 'I can't bear it, little mice, it hurts so much!' "

And she lifted her own foot in her hands and rocked it, comically screwing up her face as if she actually felt the pain.

The bearded, good-natured sailors would listen, too, and applauding the stories, would urge, "Give us another, grandma." And in reward they would invite us to supper with them. There they plied her with vodka and me with watermelon. This was done in secret, for there was a man patrolling the boat, dressed like an official, who forbade the eating of fruit, confiscating whatever he found and throwing it overboard. Everybody kept out of the way of this man who, besides, was perpetually drunk.

Sometimes, but rarely, mama came on deck. She spoke to nobody and avoided us, as well. Mama was a large, compact woman with a sharp face. Her coil of glossy, unbraided hair emphasized her massive look. Yet, her solid figure seemed lost in a mist, or in a transparent cloud, from which she looked out with glowering, gray eyes as large as grandma's.

Once she berated grandma, "Mama, people are laughing at you!"

Grandma showed no concern. "God bless them," she said. "Let them enjoy themselves. Good luck to them!"

I will never forget with what childlike elation grandma pointed out the sights as we reached Nizhny. Pulling me to the rail, she exclaimed, "How beautiful! That's Nizhny! Look at that church! As if it had wings, no?" And with tears shining in her eyes she called to mama, "Barbara, come here, look! Have you forgotten it? Doesn't it do you good to see it again?" Mama frowned, then smiled sourly.

As the steamer approached the lovely city at the confluence of two rivers,[4] the harbor bristling with hundreds of slender masts, a small, crowded rowboat pulled up alongside and tied up to the gangway hook. The people in it climbed aboard and a withered stump of a man, dressed in black, with a golden, ruddy beard, a birdbill of a nose and green eyes, elbowed his way to the front.

"Papa!" a hoarse cry came from mama and she flung herself into his arms. Taking her face in his stubby, red hands and merely giving it a pat, he said, "What's the matter with you, silly!"

Spinning around the visitors like a top, grandma hugged them and kissed them all. She pushed me toward them with a rush of introductions, "Hurry, you. This is your Uncle Mike, and this is your Uncle Jake, and this is your Aunt Natalie; these two are their boys, both Saschas, and the girl is Katherine; all our family—how many we are!"

Grandpa asked her, "Are you well, mother?" And they kissed one another three times. Then he pulled me out of the crowd, laid his hand on my head and asked, "And who might you be?"

"I'm the Astrakhan boy from the cabin."

"What on earth is he babbling?" he asked mama, but not waiting for an answer, gave me a shake and said, "You're a chip off the old block. Get into the boat."

Grandpa and mama led the way. He was a head shorter and walked with fussy little steps. From her superior height mama seemed literally to float at his side. Dark, slick-haired Uncle Mike, behind them, looked quite as wizened as grandpa; then came fair, curly-topped Uncle Jake, some stout, flashily-dressed women and six children, all older than me and acting subdued.

[4] The Volga and the Oka Rivers.

I stayed with grandma and little Aunt Natalie. Pasty-faced, dumpy and blue-eyed, the latter stopped every few feet, gasping, "I can't go another step." And grandma muttered in reply, "What a stupid lot they are. Why did they make you come?"

I took to none of them, neither grownups nor children. I felt a stranger among them and even grandma became alien and remote. I liked Uncle Mike least of all, instinctively fearing him as my enemy, an enemy to whom I felt drawn by wary curiosity.

Here we came, at last, to the end of our journey—the first building on a street perched on a slope—a squat, dirty pink, one-story affair overhung by a narrow roof and swollen with bay windows. From the street it looked spacious but, cut up into many tiny rooms, it proved cramped within. Like the boat pier the house was overrun with irritable people, and saturated with a vile smell.

I took a look at the yard which offered nothing pleasant to see. It was littered with heavy, soaking cloths and tubs filled with all the same color liquid, in which more such cloths were steeped. In a corner stove, in a tumble-down shed, a log fire made a bright blaze. Something there was being boiled and baked and an invisible somebody was reciting strange words, "Santalin, fuchsia, vitriol!"

Chapter Two

THUS SET IN FOR ME A RAPID CURRENT OF INTENSE, CONFUSING, ASTONishing life. It all strikes me now like a raw tale, narrated by a goodhearted, but painfully truthful, genius. From this space of time, as I go back to it, I find it a strain to believe that such things actually took place. My impulse is to dispute and disown the reality—such dull savagery on the part of one's own tribe is too wounding to acknowledge. But truth outweighs pity. Besides, this is no mere autobiographical passage; it is a picture of the stifling, pent-in atmosphere in which the ordinary Russian lived—indeed, lives to this day.

An endemic plague of hostility festered in my grandfather's house. All the adults were fevered with it and even the children were infected. From what I had overheard from grandpa, I knew my uncles were insisting that grandpa divide the family property between them the very day mama arrived. Her unwelcome return had only strengthened their determination to have the property shared out at once. They feared mama would put in a claim for her dowry, withheld from her by grandpa because she had eloped with a man he had disapproved of. My uncles wanted the dowry withheld, to have that to share, as well. Another old rift between them was over which of the two was to open a second dyeshop, and whether in the town or in the nearby village of Kunavin, on the Oka River.

One of these disputes took place during dinner, a few days after our arrival. Snarling and tossing their heads like dogs, they leaped out of their chairs, leaned over the table and yelled at grandpa; and he, crimsoning, rapped the table with his spoon, and in a voice as raucous as a crowing cock's, cried, "I'll turn you all out!"

Grandma, her face distorted with anguish, pleaded, "Give them what they ask, father, if you want some peace."

"Hold your mouth, idiot!" grandpa shouted at her, his eyes flashing. It was extraordinary, considering his size, what deafening volume he could put into his voice.

Rising from the table and walking to the window with a calm step, mama turned her back on everybody.

Suddenly Uncle Mike slapped his brother hard across the face with the back of his hand, and with a yelp of rage, the other lunged at him. The two rolled on the floor, howling, panting and cursing each other. Pregnant Aunt Natalie let out a scream and the children began to cry. Mama took Aunt Natalie around, protectively, and led her out of the way. Eugenia, a chipper little nursemaid, shooed the children out of the room. After separating the wrestlers, thrashing about among upset chairs, Tsigan (Gypsy), the broad-shouldered, young shop assistant, sat on Uncle Mike's back while the foreman, Gregory, a bald-headed, bearded man with dark glasses, nonchalantly tied his hands in towels.

Horrible curses came from Uncle Mike, as he twisted his head, soiling his wispy, black beard in the dirt. Rushing around the table grandpa exclaimed with bitter scorn, "Brothers—blood relations! What a disgrace!"

When the quarrel started I was terrified and climbed up on the oven.[5] From there, with quaking astonishment, I watched grandma

[5] Russian ovens were a combination of heating furnace, baking oven and cookstove, all in one, and included compartments to keep dishes warm or simmering. The oven occupied one corner of the kitchen, which was usually the largest room of the house and generally served as the living room. Because of its corner location, it served to heat a wall of two adjoining rooms. The oven was very large, averaging nine by five feet, and four feet in height. The top was slept on, usually by the elder members of

wash Uncle Jake's bruised face with a cloth dipped into a small basin. Uncle Jake wept and stamped his foot while, in a sorrowful voice, grandma scolded, "Evil creatures, a family of wild beasts you are! When will you come to your minds?"

Hiking his ripped shirt over his shoulder, grandpa said to her, "It's wild beasts you've brought into this world, eh, old woman?"

After Uncle Jake had gone grandma went into a corner where, shuddering with anguish, she prayed, "Restore them to their minds, Holy Mother of God!"

Looking back at the disordered table, with everything spilled over and overturned, grandpa, who stood beside her, said in a low voice, "Think of them and Barbara's little one that they're so angry about . . . so, who has the better heart?"

"Oh, let's have some quiet, for Heaven's sake! That shirt needs mending; take it off!" When he leaned against her, his face touched her shoulder, so short he was, and she bent down to kiss his forehead and patted his head. "It's clear, mother," he said, "we'll have to share it out to them."

"That's so, father, it'll have to be done."

This was the amicable beginning of a long talk. But soon grandpa was scraping his feet on the floor like a cock preparing for battle. Shaking his finger in grandma's face he whispered fiercely, "I'm on to you! It's them you love, not me! What's your Mike—a Jesuit! And your Jake—an atheist! They feed on me; parasites, that's what they are!"

Making an uneasy turn on the oven top, I upset an iron which thundered to the floor. Grandpa ran over, stood on the oven ledge, pulled me down and stared at me as if he were seeing me for the first time in his life. "Who set you on the oven there, your mother?"

"I climbed up, myself."

"That's a lie."

"It's not. I climbed up myself. I was scared."

Giving me a light slap with the palm of his hand, he pushed me from him. "Another one like your father! Out of my sight!"

I ran out of the kitchen, glad enough to get away.

Grandpa's sharp, calculating, green eyes, which I realized were keeping watch on me, kept me in constant fear of him. How I wished I

---

the family, sometimes, in bitter frosts, by all the family. A ledge, about eighteen inches from the ground, helped the sleepers to get on and off and was also, sometimes, used as a bench.

could find a refuge from that pursuing glance. I dreaded his vindictiveness. His mocking tone gave offense to everybody and he sought
to provoke everybody into outbursts of temper. A frequent exclamation of his was, "Ekh, you!" Ever since, that drawn-out sound, "ekh,"
has revived in me a sense of chill and disquiet. When the shop took
an evening break, he led my uncles and the workmen into the kitchen
for tea, and as they sat down with weary sighs, their hands spotted
and scarred with santalin stains and sulphuric acid burns, and their
hair tucked under linen strips, their faces dark as icon images, in that
uneasy hour grandpa roused the envy of the other children against me
by sitting opposite me and giving me most of his attention.

Grandpa was an incisive and tidy man in everything. Though his
heavy, silk-embroidered, satin waistcoat was well-worn, though his
colored shirt was crumpled and showed the effect of many washings,
though his trousers were conspicuously patched at the knees, he had a
neater appearance and more refined look than his sons who sported
silk ties and starched shirt-fronts.

Soon after my arrival he had taught me prayers. The other children,
being older, were getting reading and writing lessons from the clerk
at the Uspensky church. My teacher was timid and soft-voiced Aunt
Natalie. Her face was child-young, still, and her eyes had such transparency that I had the notion that, with a deep look, I might actually
see what went on inside her head. Under my fixed gaze her eyes soon
began to flutter and, as she turned her head away she said, or rather,
whispered, "Enough now . . . Please say, 'Our Father, which art in
Heaven, hallowed be Thy name.'" And when I asked her, "What
does it mean, 'Hallowed be Thy name'?" she would throw a worried
glance around her and chide me, "It's wrong to ask questions. Just
say it after me, 'Our Father . . .'"

Such admonitions puzzled me. Why was it wrong to ask questions?
The phrase, "Hallowed be Thy name," took on mysteries and I played
with words, deliberately changing their order every which way. My
poor, pale aunt, tired but patient, cleared her ever husky throat and
repeated, "That's not it. Just say, 'Hallowed be Thy name.' That's
simple enough." But by that my tired and patient aunt only provoked
me to a resistance that kept me from properly memorizing the prayer.

One day I was quizzed by grandpa, "Well, Alex.[6] What have you
been at, all day? Playing? Those scratches on your forehead show it.

[6] Alex (Alexei) Peshkov was Gorky's real name. It was discarded after his pseudo-
nym, Maxim Gorky (Maxim the Bitter), had made him well known.

They're easy to get. But what about 'Our Father'? Have you got that in your head?"

"His memory isn't so good," my gentle aunt hastily explained. Grandpa looked pleased at that, smiling and twitching his sandy eyebrows. "That's nothing; he needs a whipping, that's all." Turning to me, he asked, "Did you ever get one from your father?"

Not knowing what he was talking about I did not answer, but mama replied, "Maxim never laid a hand on him, and he forbade me to beat him, too."

"Might I ask why?"

"Beating is no way to bring up a child, he said."

"Your Maxim, he was every kind of a fool," exclaimed grandpa, his words sharp with anger. "God forgive me for such thoughts about·the dead." Observing that what he had said had made me angry, he said, "What are you pulling such a long face about? Ekh—you!" And stroking his red hair that was flecked with silver, he went on, "Come Saturday and I'll give Sascha a whipping."

"What's a whipping?" I asked.

That made them all laugh and grandpa said, "You'll find out, just wait."

I brooded over that word "whipping." Evidently, it meant the same thing as beating. I had seen horses, dogs and cats beaten, and in Astrakhan I had seen Persians beaten up by the police, but only here had I seen little children beaten. Here I saw my uncles strike their own children over the head and the shoulders, the children showing no resentment, merely trying to rub the pain away and answering, when I asked if it hurt, "Nah, it's nothing!" And I remembered the famous thimble story.

In the early evening hours, between tea and supper, my uncles and the shop foreman, Gregory, used to sew pieces of dyed material together and pin on tickets. Meaning to play a trick on Gregory, who was going blind, Uncle Mike had his nephew, Sascha, heat Gregory's thimble red hot in the candle flame, which he did, holding the thimble with the snuffers. Then he put the red-hot thimble near Gregory's hand, and hid behind the oven to watch. At that very moment, however, grandpa walked in, sat down to work and put the burning thimble on his finger.

Hearing the commotion, I ran into the kitchen and I'll never forget the comical figure grandpa made as he hopped about with pain, waving the burnt finger and howling, "What idiot played this trick!"

Doubled up under the table, Uncle Mike snatched up the fallen thimble and blew on it. With the shadows chasing on his bald spot, old Gregory went on sewing, indifferently. Uncle Jake, who had rushed in, retired to a corner to enjoy a laugh by himself. Grandma kept herself occupied grating raw potatoes.

"Jake's Sascha did it," said Uncle Mike, suddenly.

"Liar!" cried Uncle Jake, springing out of his corner.

From behind the stove the boy wailed, "Don't believe him, papa; he made me do it; he told me to do it."

My uncles took up their running quarrels on this next tack. Everybody blamed Uncle Mike, so I asked would he get the whipping. "He ought to," said grandpa, giving me a sidelong look.

Banging his fist on the table, Uncle Mike yelled at mama, "Make that pup of yours shut his muzzle or I'll beat his brains out!"

"You just lay hands on him, go on!" said mama; and not another word was said.

That was mama's way; a few pointed words and she seemed to push people out of her way, made them appear insignificant, brushed them aside, so to speak. She clearly overawed them all. Even grandpa was less belligerent with her than with the others. This gave me great satisfaction and I boasted to my cousins, who didn't dispute it, "My mother's a match for the lot of them!" But what happened that Saturday took my pride in my mother down a peg.

By Saturday I had had time to get into mischief. My fascination with the way grownups changed the colors of cloths, from one to another, brought trouble upon me. They dipped a yellow cloth in a black liquid and out it came, a deep blue; a gray piece, dipped in a reddish liquid, turned mauve. It seemed simple, yet it was beyond explaining. I confided my longing to perform that magic to Jake's Sascha, a thoughtful and seemingly good-natured and obliging boy who curried favor with the grownups by obsequiously waiting on them. They all had a good word for his obedience and cleverness, all but grandpa, whose name for him was "That artful beggar!"

He was skinny and sallow and had bulging, spying eyes. He spoke in a low, convulsive voice as if the words were sticking in his throat; and in the meanwhile, his glance flickered from side to side, as if he were preparing to run and hide at the first alarm. The hazel pupils of his eyes seemed to be rigid, except under excitement, when they seemed to fuse into the whites. I didn't care for him, much preferring Mike's Sascha, who was looked down on as an idiot.

A quiet boy, his eyes were sad and his smile ingratiating, like his gentle mother's. His teeth, of which there were a double upper row, protruded unpleasantly. In his concern over this defect he had his fingers almost constantly in his mouth, trying to pry that superfluous back row loose. He tolerated people's curiosity about it, letting whoever wanted, have a look at his mouth. That, however, was the only thing of interest about Sascha. His life in that swarming household was solitary. He chose to sit in dark corners by day, and at the window by night, content to remain there for hours, without speaking, his face flattened against the pane, watching the flight of the daws as, black upon the ruddy evening sky, they soared and dipped and wheeled around the dome of the Uspensky cathedral till they were lost in an opaque, black cloud and, disappearing from sight, left a void. And all this, of which he had no desire to speak, beguiled him into a pleasant languor.

Uncle Jake's Sascha, on the other hand, had something to say about everything, and despite his cautious ways, spoke with the fluency and authority of an adult. And so, hearing of my desire to try out the secrets of the dyers, he suggested that I take a white tablecloth out of the cupboard, one of the best, and dye it blue. "White takes the color best," he said with authority.

I dragged the heavy tablecloth out into the yard, but before I could get more than an end of it into the tub of blue dye, Tsigan swooped down on me, caught up the cloth, wrung it out with his leathery hands and ordered my cousin, who had been looking on from a hiding place, "Quick, call your grandmother." And to me, with a foreboding shake of his head, he said, "You'll catch it for this!"

When grandma saw what had happened she was exasperated to tears and she scolded me in her absurd way, "You fresh pickle, you! I hope this gets you a spanking!"

But to Tsigan she said, "No need to tell grandpa. I'll manage to keep it from him. Something is bound to come up to distract him."

Wiping his hands on his multi-stained apron, and with a preoccupied look, Tsigan replied, "He won't hear anything from me, but you better look to it that Sascha don't blab."

"I'll keep him quiet," said grandma. Then she took me into the house.

On Saturday night, before evening prayers, I was summoned into the kitchen which was dark and silent. I recall, even now, that the doors to it, and the shed doors, were shut tight; and I remember the gray autumn mist that, nevertheless, seemed to seep through, and the sound of the rain. Before the stove, with a cross look such as I had never seen on him before, sat Tsigan. At the chimney corner grandpa was testing long switches that had been standing in a pail of water. He flourished each one in the air, making it whistle, and measured it, and bundled it with the others. In the shadows I could hear grandma loudly taking snuff and muttering, "Tyrant! Now you're in your glory!"

In the middle of the room sat Sascha, his knuckles to his streaming eyes. In a strange voice, like that of a decrepit beggar, he was whining, "For Christ's mercy, forgive me."

Beside the chair, with shoulders touching, stood Uncle Mike's children, brother and sister.

"When you've had your flogging, then I'll forgive you," said grandpa, trying the long, dripping rod along his knuckles. "Come on, down with your breeches!"

His manner was composed; and nothing seemed to jar the ceremonial stillness that filled the almost lightless room, up to the sooty ceiling; neither the sound of his voice, the creaking of the boy's chair as he fidgeted in it, nor grandma's feet scraping on the floor. Finally, Sascha, standing up, let his trousers down to the knees and, stooping to hold them up, he stumbled toward grandpa at the bench. I found it painful to look and my legs began to weaken.

What followed was far harder to look at. Submissively the boy prostrated himself on the bench, face down. Tsigan tied him down with a broad towel hitched under his arms and around his neck, then gripped the boy's ankles in his dark hands.

"Here, Alex," grandpa shouted across to me. "Come up closer, don't you hear me? Come on. You're going to see what a whipping is . . . one . . ."

With a dainty flourish he whipped the switch down on the bare back, drawing a shriek from Sascha.

"Trash," said grandpa. "That's nothing to howl over. Here's one you'll feel!" And he switched away until the boy's flesh swelled and became ridged with red wheals, while a continuous howling issued from the victim.

"Nice, eh?" asked grandpa, as his arm swung up and down. "Enjoying it, eh? That's for the thimble."

As the arm rose with a flourish my heart seemed to be torn up with it; and as he let it down again, everything inside me seemed to sink with it.

"I'll never do it again," moaned Sascha, in a frighteningly weak whisper, unnerving to listen to, "I told you about the tablecloth, didn't I?"

As composed as if he were reading from a book grandpa answered, "Tattling won't excuse you. The first strokes go to the informer. This is for the tablecloth."

Grandma rushed to me and took my hand. "I won't let you touch Alex. I won't let you, you monster!" And she yelled, "Barbara, Barbara!"

Grandpa charged upon her and knocked her over, grabbed me and hauled me to the bench. I hit him with my fists, kicked, scratched, pulled his beard and bit his fingers. He bellowed and his arms clamped me like a vise, then hurling me on the bench, he punched me in the face.

I'll never forget his savage howl, "Tie him up! I'll kill him!" Nor mama's bloodless face and staring eyes as she ran up and down beside the bench, screaming, "Don't, father! You mustn't! Give him to me!"

Grandpa beat me unconscious and I was sick for days. I lay on a big, smothering bed, in a tiny room which had only one window and was yellow and smoky from a lamp in the icon corner,[7] that was kept constantly lit before the holy pictures.

These were, perhaps, the decisive days of my life. They saw me through a rapid growth and I was conscious of changing. I developed a fellow feeling for others; I became alert to their hurts and mine, quite as if the lacerating of the heart had now rendered it sensitive.

Because of this, a quarrel between mama and grandma brought me greater pain. Looking huge in that narrow room grandma pushed mama into the icon corner and shouted at her, "Why didn't you get him away?"

"I was frightened."

"You—a strapping, healthy one like you? Aren't you ashamed to say that? I'm an old woman and I wasn't afraid. It's a disgrace!"

"Oh, cut it out, mother, I'm sick of the whole mess!"

"The trouble is you have no love for him. You have no feeling for that poor orphan."

In a loud, self-pitying voice mama said, "I've been an orphan all my life."

The two of them had a cry together, sitting on a chest in the corner.

[7] The corner in Russian homes where religious pictures were hung and before which prayers were said.

Finally mama said, "If it weren't for Alex, I'd go away. It's like living in hell, here. I can't take it. I haven't the strength, mama."

"My own flesh and blood!" moaned grandma.

All this sank deep in my mind. I understood that mama was weak, not strong. She was afraid of grandpa, like the rest of them. And, another misfortune, it was I who was keeping her here, in a house where it was impossible for her to live. And, soon after, mother did leave the house, supposedly on a visit.

And soon after that, as if he had dropped there from the ceiling, there was grandpa, his icy hands feeling my hot forehead.

"How goes it, young gentleman? Come on, answer me, no sulks. So, what have you got to say?"

My impulse was to kick him, but every movement hurt me. He wagged his sand-colored head from side to side in a worried way. His sharp eyes seemed to fix on something on the wall as he pulled a ginger-bread goat, a sugar horn, an apple and a cluster of purple raisins out of his pocket, and laid them on the pillow, right by my nose. "There. That's for you. A present."

He stooped and kissed me on the forehead. Patting me on the head with his cruel little hands, whose crooked, claw nails were ringed with yellow stains, he said, "So, I left my mark on you, my friend. You lost your temper and bit and scratched until you made me lose my temper, too. But there's no harm getting some licks more than you rated. It'll lighten your account next time. Better learn not to mind a beating when it's from the family. Then it's part of your upbringing. A beating by an outsider would be different, but coming from your own, it doesn't matter. Maybe you think, Alex, I never felt the stick. But even in your worst dreams you couldn't imagine such beatings as I got. Ah, it was so bitter, God, himself, would have cried to see it. But, you see, it did me good. Here I am, an orphan, son of a poor widow, risen to my position, a master craftsman and head of the guild."

And in vigorous, effective phrases, with skillfully-chosen words, he told me the tale of his childhood, bending his wizened, but sinewy, body over me. His green eyes sparkled, his sandy hair was in a rakish toss, his voice went a pitch higher, and his breath puffed in my face.

"You got here by steamer, boy. These days steam gets you anywhere you want; but when I was a boy I hauled a barge, by myself, up the Volga. The barge was there, in the water, and I was on the bank pulling it, barefoot, over the sharp stones. I kept at it from dawn to dark, with the sun broiling the back of my neck and my head bubbling as if it were a pot of melted iron. The torments piled on me. I had an ache in every little bone till I could hardly see straight, but I had to hang on; and the tears ran and I cried my heart out. It's torture, Alex, even to talk about it. And I hung on until I lost my grip on the towline and fell flat on my face. And a good thing, too. I got up revived. Without that bit of rest it would have killed me.

"And that's how we used to live, before God and the blessed Lord Jesus. Three times I took Mother Volga's measure, that way, from Simbirsk to Rybinsk, then to Saratov and from there all the way to Astrakhan and the Markarev Fair, a matter of over two thousand miles. Four years of it; and I was a master water man. The boss knew what I was made of."

And right before my eyes, as he spoke, he seemed to swell up like a cloud, changing from a withered, runty oldster into a man of legendary might. Hadn't he hauled one of those enormous, gray barges up the river, by himself? Several times he popped off the bed to show me how the barge took the towline, and how water was pumped out of it; and he sang scraps of a river chantey in his bass voice; then he popped back on the bed, agile as a boy, till I marveled at him; and, as he went on, his voice grew hoarse with excitement:

"Some summer evenings, Alex, when we'd camp at Zhiguliakh, or some other spot under the green hills, we'd laze around cooking our supper, and the boatmen from the hill country would start up their heart-breaking songs, and the whole crew would join in so that it would send a shiver through you to hear it, and you'd feel the Volga current was like a racing horse and that it was heading up to the clouds; and then troubles didn't matter any more than specks in the wind. The singing went on until the pot boiled over, and for that the cook got a slap with a wet towel. 'You can play only if you mind the pot,' he was told."

When anybody stuck his head in that day to call grandpa, I pleaded with him to stay; and then, with a laugh, he waved off whoever it was with, "It can wait."

He was at his story-telling best till it began to get dark, and then he parted from me affectionately; and I realized that he wasn't so evil and overbearing, after all. To think that it was he who had so heartlessly beat me brought tears to my eyes, but I couldn't get it out of my mind.

Grandpa's visit started a procession, and from then on, all day long, I had visitors sitting on my bed, doing their best to entertain me, not always to my satisfaction. My most frequent visitor was grandma, who shared the bed with me at night. But at that time it was Tsigan who made the deepest impression on me. The stockily-built, deep-chested, curly-headed young man made his appearances in the evening, dressed in his best, a shirt with gold thread embroidery, trousers of velveteen, and new boots that squeaked like a harmonica. Everything was aglitter, his slick hair, jolly eyes under bushy eyebrows, and teeth flashing white under the shadowy young moustache. The reddish light of the icon lamp wasn't too dim to be reflected on his shimmering shirt.

"See," he said, rolling up his sleeve to the elbow to expose red scars. "See how swollen it is! And yesterday it was worse. Yesterday it ached all day. I stuck my arm out when your grandfather started to flog you, hoping the switch would crack on it and then, while he was hunting out another, your mother or your grandmother would get you away and hide you. Boy, that's a game I know something about."

He laughed a gentle laugh, took another look at the inflamed arm and said, "I felt so bad I was choking. A shame . . . the way he lashed you!" As he went on he snorted and tossed his head like a horse and, drawn to him by his childlike directness, I told him how much I loved him. With a simplicity that remains fresh in my memory he replied, "I love you, too. That's why I let myself get hurt. Think I'd have done it for anybody else? I'm not such a fool."

Then, with furtive glances at the door, he gave me this whispered advice, "Next time don't try to wriggle away, don't resist; it hurts twice as hard when you struggle. Just let go, then he'll be easy on you. Be relaxed and limp and don't give him any hard looks. Just you remember that and you'll find it helps."

"He's not going to whip me again?"

"Of course he will," said Tsigan, matter-of-factly, "over and over."

"But why?"

"Because your grandfather has his eye on you." And he repeated his cautions. "When he gives a flogging he brings the switch down straight. If you lie quiet he might start the stroke lower so as not to break the skin; and if you hump yourself up to meet it the stroke will be still shorter and that will make it lighter still." And with a wink from his black, squinting eyes he went on, "In that department I know more than a cop, even. Boy, I've had such beatings on my bare shoulders the skin came off!" And the look on his bright face as he said this reminded me of the story grandpa told me of Ivan, Tsarevich and Ivan, Durachka.[8]

[8] Ivan, Tsarevich (Ivan the Crown Prince); Ivan, Durachka (Ivan the Fool).

Chapter Three

AFTER I RECOVERED I CAME TO UNDERSTAND TSIGAN'S IMPORTANCE IN the household. Grandpa never bawled him out as he did his own sons; half closing his eyes and nodding his head for emphasis, he would say of Tsigan, though never to his face, "A good workman, Tsigan. I tell you, he'll get somewhere, he'll make his pile."

Even my uncles made up to Tsigan, never baiting him as they did the foreman, Gregory, who was an almost daily butt of some cruel or humiliating practical joke of theirs. Sometimes they heated the handles of his shears; sometimes they put tacks on his chair; sometimes they mixed up the pieces of dyed cloth he was to stitch together, and, being nearly blind and unable to distinguish the separate pieces, he would sew up the wrong pieces and then come in for abuse from grandpa.

One day, napping off in the kitchen after a meal, his tormentors gave his face a coat of fuchsia dye; and for days until it came off, he was a frightening and ludicrous sight, his smeared spectacles overlooking his gray beard and his long, stained, dejected nose hanging down like a tongue.

Their barrel of such tricks was bottomless, but Gregory bore it with indifference, merely taking such precautions as spitting on his fingers before touching a metal object—scissors, thimbles, needles, iron handles, and so on. It became a reflex with him so that, at meals, he made the children squeal with laughter as he slobbered over his fingers before taking up knife or fork. When the practical jokers managed to hurt him his eyebrows would twitch and wrinkles rippled up his face to disappear, mysteriously, off his bald pate.

How grandpa regarded this horseplay of his sons I have no idea; but I remember that it infuriated grandma, who would shake her fists at them and berate them, "Evil beasts! Have you no shame?"

Behind his back my uncles ran down Tsigan, too, ridiculing him, belittling his work, calling him loafer and thief. I asked grandma why, and as always, her unhesitating explanation made it all clear to me. "You see, each one wants to take Tsigan with him when he sets up his own shop. So each one belittles him to the other, and complains about his work, without meaning a word of it. It's just their tricks. They're worried Tsigan won't go off with either of them but will stay with grandpa. Grandpa always manages to get his way and he might even set Tsigan up as a partner in a third shop, which would be bad business for your uncles. Now, do you understand?" And she gave a gentle laugh. "Such crafty ones; no thought of God; but grandpa sees through them and needles them. He keeps saying to them, 'I'll buy Tsigan's exemption from military service. What'll I do if they take him away?' And this infuriates your uncles; it's just what they're afraid of, grandpa wanting to keep him. Besides, exemptions cost money, and they can't bear to think of any money being spent that might make a nick in their share of the family property."

I was constantly with grandma now, as on the steamer; and again I had her wonderful tales at bedtime, fairy tales or stories of her life that she made as fascinating as her fairy tales. When she spoke of family matters, the sharing out of the family property among the children, for example, or grandpa buying a new house, it was in a curiously unconcerned manner, as if she was an onlooker, or at best a gossipy neighbor, rather than in the character of the second-in-rank in the household.

It was from her that I found out that Tsigan was a foundling. One rainy night in early spring he had been discovered on one of the porch benches. "There he lay," said grandma, making it sound sad and mysterious, "so numb with cold he could barely cry."

"Why do people leave their children?"

"Maybe the mother has no milk and no other way to feed the child. So she listens to the talk and when she hears of a house where a baby has died recently, she leaves hers there."

She paused to scratch her head, sighed, looked up at the ceiling and went on. "Poverty's always behind it, Alex; and there's a kind of poverty that can't even be talked about—because an unmarried girl who has a baby can't let it be known; she would be persecuted. Grandpa was all for turning over Tsigan to the police; but I said, 'Let's keep him to take the place of one of ours that are gone.' I've had eighteen, you know, and if they'd all lived they'd've had to have a street all to themselves, eighteen families! By then I'd borne fifteen children—I married at eighteen, you see—but God took a liking to my flesh and blood and took off most of them to be his angels; and that made me happy and miserable all at once."

Sitting on the edge of the bed in her blowsy nightgown, looking big and shaggy with her tumbled black hair, she reminded me of a bear brought into our yard, one day, by a bearded lumberman from Sergach. But her breast was spotless and snow-white, and crossing herself there she uttered a sigh, as ever, making light of her troubles. "They were taken to a better life, but it was hard to bear, their going, so it was a joy to get Tsigan. But to this day, oh, my little ones, I feel the pain of losing you. . . . Well, we held on to him, had him baptized and here he is, living happily among us. My first nickname for him was 'cricket'—really, there were times when you could positively hear him chirp—creeping in corners and chirping, just like a cricket. I want you to love him; he's a good soul."

That was a command I could obey. Tsigan had my unreserved love and admiration. On Saturdays, after grandpa had doled out the weekly whippings to the children and had gone to the church for the evening services, Tsigan and I had wonderful times in the kitchen. He would pick cockroaches off the oven, harness them with thread to a paper sleigh and soon two teams of coach horses were trotting over the shiny, slippery table. With a whip made of a thin wooden sliver, he drove them on, shouting, "Now they're off to the bishop's!"

Pasting a scrap of paper on another cockroach, he'd send him scurrying behind the sleigh, explaining, "We forgot to load on the bag and the monk has to run after them with it. Giddap, there!"

Tying the forelegs of another cockroach with thread, he clapped his hands as the insect hobbled off, its head bobbing, and said, "That's the deacon staggering out of the tavern to say the evening services."

After that he put on a show with a trained mouse, the little creature rising at his command and marching on its hind legs, its long tail dragging, and its lively black eyes glittering like jet beads, and blinking clownishly. Tsigan befriended mice, carried them in his blouse, fed them sugar and fondled them.

"Mice are clever little fellows," he said with assurance. "The house spirit is their patron and whoever is good to them will have his wishes come true."

Tsigan could also do tricks with coins and cards and was noisier at play than the children. The truth was you could hardly see any difference between us. One day he had a bad run of cards in the game of "fool," [9] being made fool several times in a row, and he began to sulk. He pouted and threw his cards down; and later he grumbled to

[9] A game in which the player left with a certain designated card after play is finished is the "fool."

me, his nose twitching irritably as he spoke, "They had the game fixed. They signaled to each other and changed cards under the table. Call that card playing? If the point is to cheat, there's some tricks I could show them!" Yet he was a young man of nineteen and bigger than all four children put together.

Particularly vivid are my memories of him on holiday evenings when grandpa and Uncle Mike went visiting; and curly-headed, rumpled Uncle Jake brought in his guitar, while grandma set out snacks to have with tea, and vodka in a square bottle, decorated around the bottom with a wreath of red glass flowers expertly molded around the base. In his gay, holiday getup, Tsigan was the life of the party.

Old Gregory sidled in, peering out of his colored spectacles; also Eugenia, the housemaid, her face raw and pimply, her pudgy torso round as a jug, her cunning eyes twinkling and her reedy voice piping. Among the guests was the hairy deacon from the Uspensky church. The rest had damp and slimy shapes in my memory, like fishes and eels. They guzzled and swilled and panted, and children got treats of wine glasses filled with syrup, all of which incited an odd and rather feverish gaiety. As he bent amorously over his guitar tuning it, Uncle Jake shouted, always the same, identical phrase, "Come on, get started!"

With a toss of his head he curled still more caressingly around the guitar, his neck elongating like that of a goose. A dreamy expression came upon his pouched, self-indulgent face; his shifty, sullen eyes were veiled in an oily film. Lightly fingering the strings, he plucked scattered chords which had the effect of involuntarily lifting him to his feet. Jake's music compelled absolute silence. It cascaded down like a torrent from a distant spring, lapping at the heart and penetrating it with a mysterious unease. Under its spell melancholy overcame us all, and the oldest there felt as helpless as children. In the perfect stillness everybody sat steeped in revery. Uncle Mike's Sascha, sitting beside Uncle Jake, acted bewitched, his eyes glued to the guitar, his mouth wide open and drooling.

And the rest of us sat as if turned into snowmen, or as if waiting for someone to come and break the spell. The only sound to be heard, beside the music, was the purr of the samovar in which tea was brewing, a not inharmonious sound.

A light from the kitchen reached the darkness outside through two small windows, on which passersby sometimes tapped. On the table two slender tallow candles brandished their lights like yellow spears.

Gradually Uncle Jake's body stiffened and his teeth clenched, and he seemed to have gone off into a trancelike sleep; but his hands moved as if they had a separate life of their own. The curled fingers of his right hand fluttered over the strings like agitated birds, while his left hand swooped up and down the neck of the instrument.

Nearly always, when he had some drink in him, he sang a certain interminable song, in an unpleasant, hissing voice, as if forcing it through his teeth.

In the song he compared himself to a hound howling over his weariness and the dreariness of the world, with its creeping nuns, its chattering crows, the monotonously chirping crickets, the crawling beetles, and beggars stealing their little from each other. Weariness and dreariness were the refrain words that ran through it. The song wrung my heart and when the singer got to the part where the beggars robbed each other I would break into an outburst of uncontrollable grief.

The music affected Tsigan like the rest of us. As he listened, he ran his fingers through his shaggy black hair and his sleepy stare would fix on a corner wall. Sometimes, startling everybody, he would sigh out, "If only the Lord had given me a voice, how I would sing!"

Grandma would sigh out, too. "Do you mean to break our hearts, Jake? Hey, Tsigan, suppose you give us a dance!"

Not always did she get her way immediately. But sometimes, with a final flourish over the strings and with a gesture as if he were casting something from him, he would say abruptly, "That's enough of sadness; up, Tsigan!"

Looking very dapper as he straightened his yellow blouse, Tsigan would make his way to the center, treading mincingly as if on tacks. His swarthy face simpering and reddening, he would ask, "Please, Jake, a little faster!"

The guitar twanged in a frenzy, heels tapped in spasms, dishes on the table and in the cupboard rattled, and Tsigan outblazed the kitchen fires, soaring like a kite, wheeling his arms like a windmill, and the motion of his feet was so rapid all you saw was an immobile blur. Then, crouching to the floor, he circled like a golden bird, the yellow silk of his blouse lighting everything around as it billowed and rippled, making him look like something aflame and afloat in the air. He was tireless and the dance made him oblivious of everything. Had the door opened, he would probably have whirled out, it seemed, through the street, through the town and out of sight.

"Let's have some room," shouted Uncle Jake, and he stamped and whistled piercingly, and in a grating voice recited the quaint old rhyme, "If I could bear to part from my shovel I'd leave the wife and kids in the hovel."

Those who sat at the table, looking on, nudged each other. Every now and then they let out yells as if a fire had scorched them. Bearded foreman Gregory smacked his bald head and contributed his growl to the hullabaloo. Once he bent over me, his silky beard tickling my shoulder, and confided in my ear, as one adult to another, "Ah, Alex, if only your dad was here; then you'd see the fun! What a cut-up he was, always full of tricks. Don't you remember?"

"No."

"No? Well listen to this. One time he and your grandma—but hold on—"

He stood up, looking, in his emaciated height, like the conventional figure, bowed to grandma, and, in a curiously croaking voice, made this request, "Akulina, be so kind as to cheer us up with a dance like you did that time with Alex's father."

"What are you asking me, my dear man? What are you after, Gregory?" but smiling and preening. "At my age? I'd be a laughing stock!"

But she sprang out, all of a sudden, shook out her skirts with a jaunty air, and holding herself erect and tossing her big head, skipped across the floor crying, "Come on, laugh if you like and may it do you good. Strike up, Jake!"

My uncle let go. He played in a slow, concentrated manner, his eyes shut. After an instant's hesitation, Tsigan leaped over to grandma, circled her in a squat dance while she skimmed soundlessly, as if on air, her arms out, her brows up, her black eyes fixed in space. I thought her comical and laughed, and this drew a stern forefinger from Gregory and disapproving glances from the other adults.

"Let her be," ordered Gregory, and obediently Tsigan stepped aside and took a seat by the door. Then Eugenia, the maid, her Adam's apple bobbing, began a song in a pleasing voice, about a lacemaker who sewed at her frame, her sight getting dimmer and her face getting lined, sewed till late in the night, every day in the week till the Sabbath.

Grandma now seemed to be dancing a story rather than a pattern of steps. Her motions were slow and reflective; she swayed; she looked sideways; her great body quivered through its whole length; her feet seemed to test each step. Then she stopped as if she had heard something alarming, and a tremor crossed her face and left her with a downcast look. But, directly after, her hearty smile lit up again. Backing away with gestures, miming a rejection of somebody's hand, her expression changed and her head drooped as if she were dying. But now, revived, she was giving eager attention to someone; she was smiling rapturously; and suddenly, as if someone were whirling her, her figure took on elegance, she seemed to grow taller and it was impossible to tear your eyes away, such a triumph of beauty and grace was hers in that amazing rejuvenation! And Eugenia sang on, how, after the Sabbath prayers, the lacemaker danced on and on till midnight, making the most of her brief holiday.

Her dance finished, grandma reassumed her place at the samovar. Everybody applauded, and putting her hair to rights, she said, "Stop. You haven't seen any real dancing. There isn't any like it now. Back home, in Balakaya, there was a girl—her name's gone from me with the rest of them—it brought tears of joy to your eyes to see her dance. It was enough just to see her, you couldn't ask for more. How this sinner envied her!"

"The world's best people are the singers and dancers," said Eugenia solemnly, and was off on a song about King David, while Uncle Jake, his arm around Tsigan, said, "You'd make a hit in a night spot with your dancing. You'd be the toast of the town!"

"If I only could sing!" mourned Tsigan. "If God had blessed me with a voice I'd have been at it all these ten years now. I'd be a singer even if I had to join a monastery to sing!"

Meanwhile the vodka ebbed as Gregory kept soaking it up. As she poured him glass after glass, grandma cautioned, "Easy now, that's no medicine for your eyes!"

"So what!" he replied. "What's left for me to use my eyes on?"

The drink didn't turn him tipsy; it only made him garrulous. He kept reminiscing to me about my father, "A big-hearted man he was."

Grandma confirmed it, sighing, "That he was, one of God's own!"

Such praises of my father entranced me, making a soothing sadness well up in my heart. For happiness and sorrow are neighbors within us; their interchange happens with such swiftness as to be imperceptible.

As Uncle Jake began to feel the vodka, he took to ripping his shirt and pulling at his hair, at his nose, his graying moustache and his hanging lips—then slapping himself on cheeks, chest and forehead, while the tears poured down, howling, "What am I doing here, abandoned, sinful creature, lost soul that I am?"

"Ai, so you are!" echoed old Gregory.

Grandma, a little touched by the vodka, too, took her son's hand and said, "Enough, Jake, God will guide us!"

Drink added to grandma's charm. Her eyes grew darker and gayer, radiating her heart's warmth on all. She slipped off her kerchief because it heated her cheeks, and cried in a tipsy voice, "Lord, how good everything is!" This, spoken from her heart, was the governing idea of her life.

My usually carefree uncle's tears and outcries left an impression on me and I asked grandma why he had cursed and struck himself. "Must you know everything?" she said, with a hesitancy strange in her. "You'll find out soon enough."

This only piqued my curiosity and I sought out Tsigan in the shop and tackled him on that matter, but got no answer from him. With a subdued laugh, and a sidelong look at Gregory, he hustled me out, "Let that rest; run along, run along now, or I'll dump you in one of the vats and dye you!"

In front of the low, wide oven, with dye vats cemented into it stood Gregory, stirring the colors with a long metal rod, which he lifted out, now and then, to inspect the liquid as it dripped off. The oven fires were reflected on his leather apron, which was as riotously colored as a priest's vestment. From the simmering vats rose an acrid stream clouding the room to the very door. Peering at me from under his glasses, from filmy, bloodshot eyes, Gregory said sharply to Tsigan, "They want you in the yard, don't you hear?"

When Tsigan was out, Gregory sat down on a bag of santalin and called me over to him. Pulling me to him, his warm, silky beard brushing my cheek, he said, as if in a revery, "Your uncle killed his wife with his beatings and torments; and now his conscience gives him no rest. Do you understand? Well, your head will be in a fine muddle if you try to understand everything."

Gregory was direct like grandma, but what he said was always disquieting; he seemed to see right through everybody.

"And how," Gregory went on, "did he kill her?" His manner was strangely matter-of-fact. "Why it was like this. They were in bed together and he pulled the quilt over her face and started beating her. And for what reason? He, himself, can't tell you."

And, ignoring Tsigan, who had brought in an armful of cloths, and was warming his hands at the oven, he speculated, "It might be because he saw that she was better than he and it aroused his fury. The Kashirins [10] have no liking for good people. They're envious of them; they can't abide them; they do all they can to get rid of them. Ask your

[10] The family name of Gorky's grandparents and his uncles.

grandma how they did away with your father. She'll tell you. Deceit is hateful to her; she can't understand it. They can count that woman among the saints even though she does like her mouthful of drink and her pinch of snuff. A grand woman. Stick to her; never let her go."

Then he prodded me to the door, and it was with a dejected and frightened feeling that I found myself in the yard. Before I got to the house, Tsigan had reached my side and whispered to me, "Don't let him get you down. He's all right. All you have to do it look him straight in the eye. He likes that."

But that didn't lift my lost and depressed feeling. I had little knowledge of any other way of life, but vague as my memories were, I knew that my mother's and father's life had not been like this. Their way of speaking to each other had been different; they had a different conception of happiness. Walking or sitting, they had always kept close to each other. They had laughed a lot and, in the evenings, they sat together at the window singing so cheerfully they often had a crowd in the street below looking up at them. I had an absurd memory of the upturned faces which had appeared to me like unwashed dinner dishes. But here laughter was a rarity; and the occasion for it was generally a mystery. They were often in a fury with each other and stood in corners mumbling secret threats. The children received attention only to catch abuse; they were subdued and flattened to the earth like dust by a rainstorm; I felt alien in the house; everything that occurred appeared to stab at me, and I became wary and took care to learn everything that went on.

My friendship with Tsigan flourished. Grandma's household chores kept her occupied day and night. So I hung around Tsigan most of the time. When grandpa beat me, Tsigan again stuck his hand under the switch and, showing me his swollen fingers the next day, he would mutter, "What sense does it make? It doesn't save you a stroke and this is what it does to me. It's the last time, I tell you." But at the next beating, he underwent the needless pain just as before.

I'd say, "I thought you weren't going to do it anymore."

"I made up my mind not to, but it happened without my thinking. I just stuck out my hand."

Shortly afterward, some new knowledge about Tsigan increased my affection and interest in him. Early on Fridays he would harness Sharapa, a bay gelding, a spirited, elegant, knowing animal, and grandma's pet, to the sleigh. Putting on his sheepskin, which came to his knees, and his fur cap, and buckling himself in with his green belt, he set out to market. It was sometimes late afternoon before he returned and then apprehension filled the house. Every second somebody would be at the window thawing a spot on the frozen pane to look through.

"Any sign of him?"

"No."

Grandma would be the most concerned and would rail at grandpa and her sons. "You've sent him and the horse to ruin, you creatures without souls. You ought to be ashamed of yourselves. A family of sots and fools you are. God will punish you!"

"Enough!" mumbled grandpa. "I tell you, this is the last time!"

When Tsigan got back, grandpa and my uncles scrambled out and grandma waddled after, like a bear, and because it was the allotted time for it, taking her pinch of snuff self-righteously. The children joined them, and the merry business of unloading the sleigh began.

"Got everything on the list?" asked grandpa, giving the load a quick, appraising glance.

"It's all there," answered Tsigan cheerfully, as he hopped up and down and clapped his mittened hands to warm them.

"Those mittens cost money. You'll wear them out," scolded grandpa. "Have you any change?"

"No."

Looking over the load, grandpa said in a low voice, "There's too much here again. You couldn't get it without paying for it, of course. But no more, understand?" And he stepped aside, frowning.

Greedily my uncles set about the unloading, whistling as they hefted poultry and calves' feet and great cuts of meat. "Well, that was a quick job of unloading," they cried in self-approval.

Uncle Mike's raptures were something special. He skipped about, sniffed the edibles and smacked his lips, his eyes fluttering with bliss. He took after his father; he had the same dried-out look and was taller and had darker hair. His chilled hands tucked into his sleeves, he asked Tsigan, "What did papa give you?"

"Five rubles."

"And this ought to come to about fifteen rubles' worth. What did you pay out?"

"Four rubles, ten kopecks."

"The other ninety kopecks are lining your pocket, eh? Haven't you noticed, Jake, how money rolls all over the place?"

In his shirt sleeves, despite the frost, Uncle Jake blinked in the cold blue light and laughed lazily, "You brought us a sip of brandy, didn't you?" he asked.

Grandma cooed to Sharapa as she unharnessed him. "There, there, little one, you spoiled child, you God's pet!" and the huge animal tossed his mane, nipped her shoulder, nuzzled his satiny nose into her hair, eyed her with a loving look, twitched the frost from his lashes and neighed softly.

"Bread, is that what you want?" And grandma gave him a big, salted crust and bunched her apron under his head, like a feed-bag, and watched him munch.

Tsigan, playful like a colt, trotted up to her. "What a horse he is, a real smarty!"

"Don't come near me, you!" cried grandma, and stamped her foot. "None of your tricks. You know I don't like you today."

Afterwards she gave me the explanation. Tsigan had stolen the greater part of what he had brought home from the market. "Let's say he gets five rubles from your grandpa; he spends three; and three rubles' more worth he steals. To him it's fun; he's like a child. He tried it once and he wasn't caught; and, instead of getting a scolding for it here, they laughed and applauded; and so they brought him into the habit of stealing. Your grandpa got his fill of poverty in his youth, but all he learned from it is greed, and money has become more precious to him than his own children's blood. He isn't ashamed to take presents. And Mike and Jake . . ." Her gestures spoke her contempt.

She mused over her snuff box, then went on plaintively, "All that, Alex, is a piece of work done by a woman, a woman with blind eyes . . . Lady Luck . . . She spins our fortune and doesn't consult us about the design. You see! . . . And if Tsigan's caught stealing he'll be flogged to death!" After another pause she went on drily, "Good sayings we have enough of, but living up to them, that's another matter."

Next day I pleaded with Tsigan to stop stealing. "If you don't they'll flog you to death!"

"They'll never lay hands on me. I'm quick as a frisky horse." He laughed then, but a minute later he had a downcast look. "I know well enough stealing's a sin and a risky business. I'm bored, so I do it for amusement. The money doesn't stick to me. In no time your uncles chisel it out of me. But what do I care? They're welcome to it; I've got all I want."

Suddenly he picked me up in his powerful arms and gave me a light shake. "You're going to grow into a champion; you're lean and springy, and you've got good bones. Why don't you learn the guitar? Ask your uncle to teach you. But perhaps you're too young yet; too bad. You're small, but you've got a will of your own. You don't care much for grandpa, do you?"

"I don't know."

"To hell with the Kashirins. The only one of them I like is grandma."

"How about me?"

"You're no Kashirin; you're a Peshkov, a different breed."

He gave me a sudden, petulant nudge, and in a sighing tone said, "If only I'd been born with a singing voice! God, what a name I'd have made in the world. Beat it now, old man, I've got to catch up on my work."

Putting me down on the floor he stuffed tacks in his mouth and stretched and tacked down pieces of damp, black cloth on a large, square wooden frame.

Soon after he met with his end in this manner:

Propped against the yard fence, near the gate, leaned a heavy cross made of oak logs, the crossarm thick and gnarled. I had first seen it when I arrived at the house, and then it had been clean and yellow. By now the autumn rains had weathered it black, but it still gave off the acrid odor of peeled oak. It took up needed space in that cluttered yard.

The cross belonged to Uncle Jake who had bought it to put over his wife's grave, and who had vowed to carry it there on his back, on the anniversary of her death, a Saturday in early winter. The day followed a snowfall and turned out chilly and windy. My grandparents with the three other children—I was kept home in punishment for some mischief—preceded my uncles in order to hear the requiem. My uncles, both in short fur coats, stood the cross up, and it was so tall the crossarm towered above them. Some neighbors helped Gregory lay the cross on Tsigan's broad back while my uncles held up the end. Even the powerful Tsigan staggered, his legs sagging.

"Can you make it?" asked Gregory.

"I don't know. It feels heavy."

"Shut up, you blind devil, and open the gate!" shouted Uncle Mike.

And Uncle Jake wheedled, "Aren't you ashamed to say that, when you're stronger than both of us put together?"

Opening the gate, Gregory kept cautioning Tsigan, "Take it easy; God be your protection!"

"Bald-headed idiot!" shouted Uncle Mike back from the street.

There was loud talk and laughter in the yard as if people felt relief at being rid of the cross. Gregory led me by the hand into the shop and said consolingly, "With all this going on maybe grandpa'll skip the licking tonight."

He sat me on a heap of woolens to be dyed, wrapped me in them up to the shoulders and then, reflectively, as he inhaled the vapors from the vats, he said, "Thirty-seven years I've known him, my boy. I saw the beginning of this business and I'll see the end of it. We began as friends, in fact the business was planned out as a partnership. But he's a clever one, your grandpa, and he meant to be the master, and he had his way. I didn't understand it, then. God is cleverer than them all. God smiles and the wiseacre blinks like an imbecile. You don't understand all that's going on, but you'll have to learn now. An orphan's cut out for a hard life. What a fine man your father was, and he had an education too. So your grandpa resented him and wouldn't have him around."

Such words about my father were pleasant to hear; and it was soothing to watch the play of the ruddy flames in the oven and the pearly vapor rising from the vats, that seemed to coat the slanting ceiling rafters with a blue frost darker than the blue ribbons of sky that were visible between the chinks. The wind had died down; the yard looked as if it had been sprinkled with ground glass. The sleighs passing on the street made a crunching sound; the smoke from the chimney looked blue; and the shadows gliding over the snow seemed to be writing a story.

Bearded, hatless, long-eared, cadaverous, stirring the cooking colors with his long arms, Gregory looked like an amiable sorcerer, as he gave me this advice. "Look straight in people's eyes, even when a mad dog's coming at you. If you do that, he'll stop and let you go." His heavy spectacles were ridged into his nose, which was tipped with purple like grandma's, and for the same cause.

"What's up?" he exclaimed suddenly, and stuck his ear out. Then, kicking the oven door shut with his shoe, he ran, or rather jumped, across the yard to the house with me hot after him. Stretched out on the kitchen floor lay Tsigan on his back, his body striped with bars of sunlight from the window. A strange moisture glistened on his forehead; from below his lifted eyebrows his squinted eyes were fixed on the smudged ceiling; from his livid lips bubbled a reddish foam and blood trickled from the corners, down his cheek and neck to the floor, while another stream of blood flowed from beneath his back. His legs forked out clumsily; his damp trousers lay soggily flat on the floor boards which had been rubbed to a polish with sand. The trickles of blood, intersecting the beams of light, made a vivid show as they flowed to the door sill.

Tsigan lay without a movement, except a weak, convulsive scratching on the floor with fingernails whose stains shone in the light.

Eugenia, crouching beside him, tried to fit a thin candle into his hands, which lacked the strength to hold it; the candle kept dropping to the floor, its flame quenching in his blood. Picking it up and wiping it off she kept making attempts to fix it in the agonized fingers. A whispering sound became audible in the kitchen and seemed to blow me like a breeze away from the door to which I clung.

"He slipped," Uncle Jake was explaining, in a toneless voice, shuddering and twisting his head. A haggard look had grayed his face and his eyes twitched as with a tic. "He slipped and the crossarm came down on him and got him in the back. It would have done for us, too, if we hadn't dropped the end in time."

Gregory said mournfully, "It's your doing!"

"What do you mean?"

"Your doing!"

The blood kept flowing, collecting near the door in an ever darkening and deepening pool. There was another jet of bloody froth from Tsigan's mouth; he made a sound like a man in a nightmare and then seemed to collapse, flattening out as if he were being glued to, or sinking through, the floor.

"Mike's gone on a horse to fetch father," Uncle Jake continued his whispering explanation, "I brought him here in a carriage. A good thing it wasn't me under the crossarm or this is what I'd be like, now."

Once more, Eugenia tried to get a candle into Tsigan's hand, dripping tears and melted wax over him.

"That's the way! Paste his head to the floor, you clumsy!" said Gregory gruffly. "Take off his cap!"

Eugenia pulled the cap off and it dropped with a damp thud.

When it was off his head, the flow of blood changed, coming now from only one side of the mouth but in a thicker stream.

All this took a frighteningly long time. My first thought had been, Soon Tsigan will sit up, give his familiar sighing yawn and say, "Whew! It's steaming hot!" which he always did after Sunday dinner. But not only was he not waking up, but he appeared to be melting into the ground. The sun had abandoned him now; its diminishing rays now reached only the window sills. His entire body was in darkness and the spasmodic clutching of his fingers had stopped; there were no more blood-flecked bubbles over his lips. Round his head three candles stood against the gloom, their little tips of light casting bright reflections on Tsigan's tumbled, blue-black locks and eddies of yellow light over his swarthy cheeks, and flashes of light on the tip of his nose and his blood-spotted teeth.

"Little dove," moaned Eugenia through her tears, as she threw herself at his side, "little bird, little consoler."

It grew freezing cold, and I had huddled into a new hiding place under the table when grandpa, bundled up in his raccoon coat, stormed in, followed by grandma in her fur-trimmed coat, Uncle Mike, the children and a crowd of neighbors.

Pulling off his coat and flinging it down, grandpa shouted, "You scum! Look what you've done to me, you two mindless ones! In five years he would have earned his weight in gold for me!"

Behind the barrier of coats I could no longer see Tsigan from under the table. Crawling out I bumped into grandpa. Pushing me aside, he made a fist with his stubby red hand at my uncles and called them "Wolves!" Then, sitting bowed on a bench, his elbows resting on it, he shrilled through his dry sobs, "It's plain enough to me! He was a bone in your throats, that's what bothered you. Poor foolish Tsigan, what they've done to you, eh? 'For the stranger's horse rotten harness will do.' Oh, mother, God's had no love for us this past year, eh, mother?"

Stooped over Tsigan on the floor, grandma was chafing his hands and his chest and blowing on his eyes. Knocking the candles over as she struggled to her feet, looking severe in her black silk dress and with her eyes wide in a terrifying stare, she ordered people out in a tense voice. "Go, you accursed!"

All but grandpa crowded out.

No fuss was made over Tsigan's funeral. Soon he was all forgotten.

Chapter Four

LYING UNDER FOUR FOLDS OF A HEAVY BLANKET, I LISTENED TO GRANDMA at her prayers. She was kneeling; one hand was on her breast and with the other, at intervals, she devoutly crossed herself. It was icy out-of-doors. The moonlight had a greenish cast as it filtered through the traceries of frost on the window panes. It lay a flattering ambience on her prominent nose and her amiable face, and touched off phosphorescent sparks in her black eyes. Her glossy, luxuriant hair seemed to reflect furnace flames; and on her rustling black dress ripples cascaded from her shoulder to the floor.

Her prayers over, grandma quietly disrobed, carefully folding each garment and laying it on a chest. When she got into bed, I lay curled up in pretended sleep.

"You're awake, you rascal," she said. "Stop that make-believe, little duck, and give me some of the cover!"

Anticipating the coming fun, I could not keep my smile back, seeing which she cried, "Playing tricks on your old grandma, eh?" With an adroit and powerful yank at the blanket, I went spinning over and over until I came to rest in the soft hollow of the featherbed, while she chuckled, "What's the matter, little jumping jack, did a mosquito peck you?"

But there were times when her prayers lasted so long, I nodded off and was fast asleep when she got into bed. Such extra-long prayers would usually come after a day of worries or family quarrels and were interesting to hear. She furnished God with every detail of what had occurred. At first, as it came from the bowed heap she made on the floor, the account was mumbling and indistinct; then it turned hoarse and loud. "You know we all mean it for the best, O Lord. The older one, Mike, ought to have his own shop in town, in that new section that's not yet overrun with competitors like the others. The place down the river isn't for him. But what's to be done? Jake is his father's pet. Should one child be favored above the other? Is that right? Teach him, Lord; he's such a stubborn old codger."

With a warm look at the bright-eyed, dark-browed icon, she suggested to God, "Show him in a nice dream how to deal with his children." Then, after bowing so deep her big forehead thumped the floor, she began coaxing God: "How about a bit of happiness for Barbara? Is she any the worse sinner than the rest? A fine, strapping young woman like her to have all that aggravation! And have a thought for poor old Gregory, dear Lord. Every day his eyes get worse. It would be terrible for him to go blind. He'll be sent packing. Sure, he's used himself up for grandpa, but what chance is there of grandpa taking care of him? Oh, Lord, Lord?"

Then, still kneeling, she would lapse into a long silence, her hands limp at her side, her head bowed, till you would have thought she had fallen asleep or been frozen to the ground. Then she would say, thinking aloud, her brows knitted, "Who's left? Oh, of course, Lord, save all the faithful! Forgive this accursed fool—but Thou knowest my sinning is through stupidity, not ill will." And, on a last deep breath, in a tone expressive of her affection and of the consolation she had received, she concluded, "Son of God, everything is known to Thee, all-seeing Father!"

I took to grandma's God, with whom she seemed so familiar, and I would sometimes ask her, "Tell me about God." She spoke about Him then in a special manner, her voice rather hushed, curiously lengthening out the words and keeping her eyes closed. And she took care, before she began, to sit up and straighten her kerchief.

"God sits in a place up in the hills, in the green meadows of Paradise. He sits on an altar of sapphires with ever blooming linden trees all around. You see, winter never comes in Paradise, not even fall, so the flowers never fade; everything is joyful, having God's favor. The angels fly around Him like snow; and, I think, bees are buzzing there, and white doves carry messages between heaven and earth, telling Him all about us and the other folks. And down here each of us has an angel to take care of him—you and I and grandpa. God provides for everybody alike. Take your angel: he'll fly up to God and report, 'Alex stuck his tongue out at grandpa.' 'All right,' says God, 'the old man can give him a whipping.' And that's the way it goes. People get from God what they've earned, some get sorrow, some get joy. What He does is always right and the angels celebrate all the time, they never fold their wings and they never stop singing, 'Glory, glory unto Thee, O Lord. Glory unto Thee!' And He smiles at them, and His smile alone is happiness enough for them and more than enough." And she would smile herself and wag her head.

"Did you ever see it?"

"See it? Lord, no. But that's known."

Speaking about God, heaven, or angels, she seemed to return to youthful slenderness, her face growing younger, and a sudden warmth radiated from her liquid eyes. Coiling her heavy, satiny braid around my neck with my hands, I listened quietly to her stories that had no end, yet never palled on me.

"It's not for human beings to look on God, their sight isn't pure enough. Only saints can look Him in the face. But I've seen angels, myself. When souls are in a state of grace angels may appear before them. Standing in a church at early mass, one time, I saw two of them floating over the altar like clouds. Their wings came all the way down to the floor; they were so light I could see everything through them brighter than before. They were helping old Father Elya at the altar, holding up his elbows when he raised his arms. He was very old and feeble and nearly blind, and he used to stumble when he performed the services; but that day he got through with the mass easily. I nearly burst with joy seeing them, my heart was so full, and my tears just ran down. How beautiful it was! Oh, Alex, dear heart, things go well wherever God is, in heaven or here on earth."

"But you can't mean here in our house?"

"Praised be Our Lady!" said grandma, crossing herself, "everything goes well."

I was bothered by this. I couldn't see how what was happening in our house could be said to be going well, when, to me, they were daily growing more unbearable.

One day, through the door of Uncle Mike's room, I saw Aunt Natalie, half-dressed, with her hands to her bosom, moaning desperately, as she paced up and down in a frenzy, "Shelter me, Lord, deliver me from here!"

The prayer struck a sympathetic chord, just as when I heard old Gregory muttering, "They'll turn me out as soon as I've gone blind. I'll be better off in the streets begging, than here."

For that matter, I wished he would go blind, soon, because I had made up my mind to go begging with him. I had already proposed it to him and he had smiled in his beard as he had answered, "Sure, we'll go together. I'll show myself around town shouting, 'Here's a grandson of Basil Kashirin's with me, his daughter's son.' Then, maybe he'll find something for me."

At times I saw blue swellings around Aunt Natalie's hollow eyes, or would notice her lips standing out swollen from her yellow face. "Does Uncle Mike beat her?" I asked grandma.

"Yes," she sighed, "that devil! But not very hard. Grandpa allows it only so long as he does it at night. He's a bitter one and she's—soft as a pudding. But," she continued, more cheerfully, "he doesn't go on the way he used to. Now, it's just a fist in the mouth, or a yank at her ear, or he drags her by the hair a bit. But there was a time when he used to torture her, beat her for hours at a time. One Easter day grandpa beat me from dinnertime till bedtime, on and on, stopped only to catch a breath. And with a strap, too!"

"What for?"

"I don't remember any more. Another time, he beat me till he saw

I was close to dying; and then he wouldn't allow food to be given to me for hours. When he was through with me that time I was barely alive."

I was appalled. Grandma was twice the size of grandpa; how could he have done that to her? "Is he stronger than you?" I asked. "Older, not stronger," she replied. "Besides, he's my husband, and he must account to God for me; my part is to endure with patience."

One thing I enjoyed particularly watching grandma do, was polishing and cleaning the icon, especially around the crusts of ornament. Its crown was lavishly studded with silver, pearls and other jewels. She held it lovingly, smiled at it, exclaimed feelingly, "What a sweet face!" crossed herself, then kissed it and said, "Holy Mother, prop of the Christians, joy of the faithful, we'll rid Thee of the dirt that has come on Thee." To me she said, "Alex, look what small writing, such teeney letters; yet it's all there and can be read. The name of it is The Twelve Holy Days. There's the Mother of God in the middle, whose purity was foreordained; and the writing here says, 'Mourn not me, Mother, that am soon to be laid in the grave.' " And, at times, her absorption in the icon seemed to me like my little cousin Katherine's play with her doll.

She saw devils at times, both singly and in groups. "Once on a clear, moonlit night in Lent, passing the Rudolfovs' house, I noticed something on the roof, and it turned out to be a coal-black devil sitting on the chimney. His head, horns and all, was bent over and he was sniffing up what was coming from the chimney. There he was, the big, ungainly one, with his tail hanging, sniffing and smacking his lips. I made the sign of the cross in front of him and recited, 'Christ is risen and His foes are scattered.' And did that scatter him! He tumbled off the roof head first! There must have been meat cooking on the Rudolfovs' oven that day, and he was giving himself a treat smelling it."

The picture of the devil scattering head-first off the roof made me laugh, and grandma laughed along as she continued: "Devils are as playful as kids. Once I was late finishing a wash in the laundry when all of a sudden the door flies open and in rushes a crowd of tiny red, green and black creatures. They were all sizes, and they swarmed like cockroaches, and in a minute they were all over the little room. I tried to get to the door, but couldn't; that swarm of imps kept me from lifting hand or foot. Such a crowd of them I couldn't even turn around. Over my feet they crawled, swung themselves from the hem of my dress, surrounded me so I didn't have elbow room to cross myself. The feel of them was hairy and cozy like a cat, but they walked upright.

They circled around me, took a peep into everything, their teeth showing like mice, their bits of green eyes blinking at me. They kept sticking me with their horns and they held their tails up—little things like pigs' tails. My dear, I thought I was going out of my mind! And how they jostled me! The candle was nearly put out; the water in the kettle was lukewarm; the wash was strewn all over the floor; and it was a pain and a bother to even breathe, I tell you."

Closing my eyes, I could see the little laundry with its gray cobblestone floor completely inundated by that spew of shaggy, motley-colored imps. I could see them puffing out the candle flame and sticking out their mischievous pink tongues. The picture was at once frightening and funny.

Grandma took a breath before she resumed, with a shake of her head, "I've seen demons, too. One winter night, in the snow, I was crossing the Dinkov causeway—remember, where your uncles tried to push your father under the ice. I was just about to turn out on the lower fork when I heard such a hissing and a racket! And there, as I looked up, came a team of horses, black as crows, racing at me. A big, chubby demon with protruding teeth, who had on a red nightcap, was in the driver's seat. The reins were made of iron chains and he had to stretch out his arms to hold them. There being no way around, the horses zipped right over the pond and were gone in a whirl of snow. The passengers in the sleigh were demons, too, and they were having a high old time, yelling and sputtering and tossing their nightcaps. Seven sleighs, all like that one, ripped past me, each with its load of the devil's breed, going like fire-engines. They exchange visits, you know, they ride off to their parties at night. What I saw, I imagine, was one of their weddings."

And so artless and convinced was grandma, as she told these stories, that you had to believe her. Her best story was the one about Our Lady going over the ravaged land seeking out the bandit woman, Engalicheva, and telling her to stop murdering and robbing Russians. I also liked the stories about Saint Alexei, the fighter Ivan, the sage Basil, the priest Kozha, beloved of God, and the hair-raising tales of Martha Posadnitsa, the robber chief Baba Ustia, and sinning Egyptian Mary and other women, mothers of bandits. Her store of fairy tales, legends and ballads was inexhaustible.

Though she had no fear of grandpa or devils, she could be put in a panic by black cockroaches, whose presence she could sense at a distance. She would sometimes rouse me out of sleep at night, "Alex, darling, there's a cockroach around, get rid of it, for heaven's sake." Half asleep, I'd crawl over the floor with a candle in my hand, stalking the enemy, sometimes, seemingly, in vain. "There isn't any," I'd insist, but she, all muffled up in bedclothes, would plead with me, "I know there is, please take another look, I know there's one of them crawling around."

And sure enough, sooner or later, far from the bed, I'd come upon the insect. Then, throwing off the blanket, she would sigh with relief, and, smiling at me, would say, "Thank God, you got it. Thanks, dear."

Should I fail to track it down it cost her the night's sleep. I could feel her trembling in the darkness and hear her whispering to herself anxiously, "It's got near the door; now it's crawling near the chest."

"Why are you scared of cockroaches?" I asked her.

"I don't know myself," she answered unconcernedly. "Maybe it's the way the loathsome things crawl about. God has made other vermin signify something. Wood-lice signify dampness; bedbugs are a sign of dirty walls; and everyone knows that when lice are seen they prophesy an illness; but these things! Who knows what their power is or even what they feed on!"

One day grandma was on her knees having one of her heart-to-heart talks with God when grandpa burst in, shouting, "Mother, God's hand is on us again! We're on fire!"

"What're you saying!" cried grandma, jumping up; and the two of them stamped about the parlor. With commanding authority grandma ordered, "Eugenia, take down the icons; Natalie, get the baby dressed." While all grandpa could do was to mutter ekhs.

I ran to the kitchen. Its window, looking out on the yard, was all a golden glow. Yellow reflections played on the floor and Uncle Jake, half-dressed, hopped and stamped on them as if they were actual flames scorching his feet. "This is Mike's work!" he shrieked, "He's set us on fire, then he cleared out!"

"Quiet, you dog!" said grandma, giving him such a push he nearly fell through the door.

The fire had reached the roof of the shop and flames were curling out of the open door and could be seen right through the webs of frost on the window panes. The night was still and smoke did not discolor the flames; while overhead hung a black cloud, but not low enough to blot out the silvery furrow of the Mlechna road. A livid brightness shimmered on the snow. The walls trembled and heaved as if about to leap into the flames, which sported rakishly through the widening red gaps, snapping out the bent and red-hot nails. Streamers of red and gold wreathed around the roof beams until they were all swathed in flame, with only the lean chimney with its spout of smoke standing erect. At our window the sound of the fire was gentle, like the rustling of silk. The flames kept spreading and adorning the shop, so to speak, until it all looked like an icon altar in the church; and the fire grew ever more fascinating to me.

In a big fur coat that covered me, head to foot, and with my feet in the first pair of boots that came to hand, I went out on the porch. There I was at first stunned and blinded by the brilliance, and then stunned again by the uproar made by grandpa and my uncles and Gregory, shouting together. I was still more alarmed to see grandma, a sack draped over her head and a horse blanket around her body, running straight into the fire. As she disappeared within, she cried, "The vitriol, you idiots! It'll explode!"

"Pull her out, Gregory!" yelled grandpa. "Ai, she's a goner!"

But grandma appeared, almost immediately, sooted over, half-fainting, doubled over the vitriol bottle she was carrying out.

"Father," she cried, "save the horse; and pull this thing off my shoulder! Can't you see it's on fire?"

Gregory pulled off the singed blanket and then, doing the work of two, shoveled snow into the burning doorway. Uncle Jake, brandishing an axe, hopped around him, while grandpa hopped around grandma, sprinkling snow over her. After burying the vitriol under a snow bank, grandma ran to the gate, outside which a crowd had assembled, and appealed to them, "Neighbors, help us save the storehouse. If the fire catches in the hayloft there, it'll burn us out entirely and spread to your houses. Pull down the roof and bring the hay into the garden. Gregory, pitch some of that snow up, not all on the ground. Jake, don't just hang around. Hand out axes and spades to these good people. Dear neighbors, act like our friends and God will return it to you."

To me grandma was quite as thrilling as the fire. In the glow of the flames, out of whose mouth she had so narrowly escaped, her dark form turned up everywhere, helping, directing; nothing eluded her attention.

Let out of the stable, Sharapa reared and nearly knocked grandpa down. The light shone into the panting animal's wild eyes and his forelegs pawed the air. Grandpa dropped the reins, jumped sideways and called out, "Mother, catch hold of him!"

Almost under the rearing hooves she stood, her arms outstretched, looking like a black cross. Neighing plaintively, the frantic animal let himself be led by her, twitching, aside from the flames.

"You're not frightened any more," grandma soothed him, patting his neck as she picked up the reins. "Think I'd leave you when you're so upset? Silly little mouse!"

And little mouse, several times her size, obediently followed her to the gate, glancing and sniffing at her reddened face.

Eugenia brought out the other children, all muffled up, from the house. A smothered bawling came from them. "We can't find Alex anywhere," she told grandpa.

Grandpa's answer was to order her away; and I hid behind the stair to escape being taken away by Eugenia.

By this time the burning roof had caved in, leaving the corner posts outlined against the sky, glowing and vaporing like coals of gold. With a howl and a bang, a red-blue-green tornado exploded inside; and, with new vigor, flames spurted out into the yard, and at the people spading snow into the fire.

In the heat the vats came to a furious boil, sending up a billowing, smoky steam and an uncanny smell that made the eyes water. Creeping out from behind the stairs, I stumbled in grandma's way, and she screamed at me, "Get away, or you'll be trampled; get away!"

Just then a brass-helmeted man rode into the yard on a frothing roan horse. "Make way!" he roared at everybody, threatening them with a whip.

And there followed an agitated, merry ringing of gongs, as delightful to me as a feast day.

Grandma pushed me to the steps of the house. "I told you to go away!"

This was no time for disobedience. Going back into the kitchen, I glued my face again to the window, but my view was blocked, now, by the crowd; all there was to see now were the firemen's helmets gleaming among the fur caps. The fire was got under control and died down. Policemen dispersed the crowd and grandma came into the kitchen.

"Who's this? Oh, it's you! Scared? There's nothing to be afraid of now. It's all over."

As she sat beside me I felt her shiver. It was a relief to have darkness and quiet back.

Grandpa called in the doorway, "Mother?"

"Yes."

"Did you get burned?"

"A little, nothing much."

He struck a light which gleamed on his soot-stained face, went to light the candle on the table and came back and sat beside grandma.

"The best thing for us now," she said, "is to wash up." She, too, was sooty and smelled of smoke.

"Sometimes," said grandpa, breathing heavily, "it's God's pleasure to endow you with good sense." He patted her shoulder and added, grinning, "but only now and then, and just for an hour or so; but it's there, all right."

Grandma smiled, too, and she started saying something, but was interrupted by grandpa who said, frowning, "Gregory'll have to go. All this came through his neglect. He's played out. His working days are over. Now you better go to that fool, Jake; he's sitting on the steps bawling."

She rose and went out, blowing on her scorched fingers. In a low voice and without looking at me, grandpa said, "You saw the whole fire from the beginning, didn't you? Then you saw what grandma did! And she's an old woman, bear that in mind, used up and going to pieces. And yet . . . Ekh, you!"

After a long pause he rose out of his huddled position, snuffed out the candle and asked, "Were you scared?"

"No."

"That's right. There was nothing to be scared about."

Then, pulling off his shirt with irritable jerks, he went to the wash basin. "A fire is a stupidity. A person who's to blame for starting a fire should be flogged out on the square! He's either a fool or a thief. If that was the penalty the fires would stop. Now off to bed with you! What are you hanging around for?"

I did as I was told, but there was no sleep for me that night. Hardly had I lain down when an inhuman cry seemed to come up from under my bed. I rushed back in the kitchen to find grandpa standing there in the middle, holding a candle that nearly went out each time he stamped his foot, crying, "Mother, Jake, what's that?"

I climbed to my hiding place on the oven, and once more the house was in a tumult. A prolonged, blood-curdling scream resounded from ceiling and walls, gathering volume every instant. What followed was like a repetition of the scene in the yard. Grandpa and Uncle Jake ran around not knowing what to do with themselves until grandma ordered them here and there. Gregory was fussy and noisy, putting wood on the fire and drawing water into the iron kettle. With his head bobbing up and down he looked like an Astrakhan camel.

"Get a fire going in the oven," grandma ordered. Climbing up to tend to the oven, Gregory tripped over my legs. "Who's there?" he cried out in alarm. "Whew! You gave me a scare. You're always where you don't belong."

"What happened?"

"Aunt Natalie's just had a baby," he explained, jumping down.

My mother, I recalled, had not screamed like that when she had had her baby.

Having put the kettle on the fire, Gregory climbed back on the oven. Taking a pipe out of his pocket, he showed it to me. "It's for my eyes," he said. "Grandma thought I ought to take snuff, but I think smoking will be better."

He crossed his legs at the edge of the oven and looked down at the feeble candle light. His face was coated with soot. Through a rip in his shirt I could see his ribs, broad as barrel staves. One lens of his spectacles was broken and the eye that peered through the gap was raw and red, like a wound.

Packing his pipe with coarse tobacco, he muttered ramblingly, like a drunkard, as he listened to the moaning woman in labor, "I'm sure I don't know what that grandmother of yours can do for that poor body with her hands burned so bad. Just listen to your aunt groaning! They forgot all about her, you know. As soon as the fire started her attacks came. Fright brought it on. See what pain it costs to bring a child into the world! And yet they look down on women. But you listen to me; women ought to be honored, they are the mothers."

At this point I dozed off quietly, only to be wakened by a new commotion, doors banging and Uncle Mike shouting drunkenly. Through it all I heard mysterious phrases, "They'll have to open the royal gates . . . rub her with sacramental oil and brandy, half a glass of each, and stir in about a tablespoon of soot . . ." And in the midst of it Uncle Mike repeating, like a nagging child, "I want to have a look at her," repeating it from where he was, sprawled out on the floor, where he kept spitting in front of him and hammering on the boards with his fists.

By this time, the oven having gotten uncomfortably hot, I slid down and Uncle Mike grabbed at my legs so that I took a fall backward on my head.

"Fool!" I shouted at him.

He made a lunge for me, yelling, "I'll crack your skull on the stove for you!"

Scrambling for safety to the icon corner in the parlor, I bumped against grandpa, who was on his knees, and was pushed aside by him. He was looking up and saying in a beseeching voice, "There's nothing can excuse any of us!"

The icon light gleamed above him, a candle was burning on a table in the middle of the room, and the windows were beginning to pale in the early light of a foggy winter morning.

After awhile grandpa turned toward me, "So what's the matter with you?"

Everything, I could have answered. My head felt damp; my body was aching all over with weariness. But I didn't want to say so, because everything around me was so unusual. In nearly every chair sat a stranger, a priest with lilac-colored vestments, a gray-bearded man with glasses, dressed in a military uniform, and a crowd of others, immobile in their chairs like wooden images or frozen people. They seemed to be waiting for something, and in the meanwhile listening to the only sound to be heard, water dripping nearby. Nearest to the door was Uncle Jake, standing bolt upright, his hands folded behind his back. To him grandpa said, "Take this child, here, up to bed."

My uncle motioned me to follow him and tiptoed before me up to my room. When I was under the covers he whispered, "Aunt Natalie's dead."

This was no surprise to me. For some time now I hadn't seen her, not even at meals.

"Where's grandma?"

With a vague gesture, he replied, "Down below," and, still tiptoeing, left the room.

I lay in bed straining, wide-eyed. Pallid, shaggy faces seemed to be staring at the windows; and though I recognized the shapes on the chest in the corner to be grandma's clothing, I had an obsession that something alive had ambushed itself under them. I covered my head with the pillow, leaving space for just one eye to keep watch on the door, and to hop off the bed and out of the room. It was stifling, and the reek in the air reminded me of the night of Tsigan's death and the blood on the floor.

In my head or my heart I felt a swelling outwards. Everything that had happened in that house seemed to pass before my mind's eye, like a procession of sleighs, and as each came up to me, to topple over me.

Very slowly the door came open and in crept grandma, using her shoulder to shut the door. Slowly she came forward and held out her hand to the bluish light of the icon lamp, sobbing plaintively like a child, "Poor little hand, it hurts me so!"

Chapter Five

THIS NIGHTMARE WAS SOON FOLLOWED BY ANOTHER. ONE EVENING after tea, while grandpa was reading to me from a prayer book and grandma was doing the dishes, Uncle Jake, at his sloppiest, looking all ends like a kitchen broom, rushed in. Dispensing with salutations and flinging off his cap, he burst out, waving his arms, "Mike's on the rampage! We were having dinner together and he began acting like someone out of his mind. He smashed dishes, ripped up an order we'd just finished, a wool dress, broke the windows, cursed me and Gregory; and now he's on his way here, for you, hollering, 'I'll have my father by his whiskers! I'll kill him! Watch out!' "

Grandpa rose slowly, his knuckles on the edge of the table. Beneath his scowl his face seemed to be tightening to an edge, cruel and sharp like an axe. "Hear that, mother?" he bellowed. "How does that strike you, your own son running here to kill his father! But it's the time, children, the time has come!"

Straightening his shoulders, he went to the door, slipping the big iron hook that latched it into its ring, and said to Jake, "It all comes from your greed to get your hands on Barbara's dowry; that's the thing." Grandpa laughed, contemptuously, in my uncle's face, when he replied, in a hurt tone, "Me? What would I want it for?"

"Ekh—you! I know you!"

Grandma put the dishes away in the cupboard in silent haste.

With a biting laugh grandpa said to Uncle Jake, "Very good, my son. Accept my thanks. Mother, hand this fox a pressing iron, or a poker, or whatever you wish. So, Jake, when your brother breaks in here, kill him before your father's eyes!"

Sticking his hands in his pockets, Uncle Jake went sulking into a corner. "All right, if you don't want to believe me!"

"Believe you!" raged grandpa. "No! Sooner some animal, a dog or even a rat, than you! I know your tricks! You got him drunk, then you put him up to it! Well, what's stopping you? Kill me right now—him or me, take your pick!"

Grandma whispered to me, "Hurry upstairs and watch at the window and when you catch sight of Uncle Mike run back and tell us. Hurry now!"

Apprehensive over this threatened invasion by my violent uncle, but proud of the trusted part I had just been given, I leaned out of the window which overlooked the street, now so thick in dust that the round tops of the cobblestones were barely to be seen through it. To the left the street was carried over the causeway on to Ostrozhny Square where, set solidly in the clayey soil, was a gray structure with a turret on each of its four corners, the old prison, a building possessed of a moody grace of its own. To the right, about three houses off, the street opened into Sienia Square, where the prison staff had their residence. This was a yellowish edifice surmounted by a leaden-colored watchtower where a lookout was kept for fires, with watchmen pacing around the parapet, looking like dogs on leash. The square was separated from the causeway by a green, bushy overgrowth, and off to the right, by the stagnant Dinkov Pond into which, as grandma told the story, my uncles had pushed my father, meaning to drown him. Almost directly opposite my window was a row of small houses, painted in different colors, ending up at the squat Church of the Three Apostles, whose roof, if you stared at it, assumed the shape of a capsized boat riding the green waves of the garden, bottom up. Discolored by the autumn rains and the winter snows, the houses had the new, seasonal affliction of a coat of dust. With half-lidded eyes they seemed to prey on each other like beggars on church steps. And they seemed, with their open windows, to be casting suspicious glances, as if they were on the watch for someone, like I was.

A few people were perambulating on the street like meditative cockroaches on an oven; a smothering heat wafted in along with the stench of meat pies with carrots and onions, baking, an odor that, for some reason, has always depressed me. I felt absurdly, but unbearably, dejected. Warm lead seemed to be loading my breast, pressing against and percolating through my ribs. It seemed to be swelling me up like a balloon, yet I was stuck here in this tiny bedroom with the ceiling arching over me like a coffin lid.

And there, peering from behind one of the gray houses, was Uncle Mike! He tried to get his cap to pin down his ears, but they sprang out again. He was in a brown jacket and dusty top boots. He had one hand in a pocket of his checked trousers, the other in his beard. I couldn't see his face, but he was in a crouch as if about to jump across and grab up our house in his grimy, calloused hands. I should have hurried down to give warning, but I stayed glued to the window until my uncle, shuffling nervously, raising the dust around his feet, started across the road; and I stayed on until I heard the tavern door creak, its glass panels tinkling as he charged in. Then I ran down and knocked at grandpa's door.

"Who's there?" he asked in a gruff voice, hesitating to open up until he recognized me. "Oh, it's you. Well, what?"

"He went in the tavern."

"So. Well, run along."

"I'm scared up there."

"Can't be helped."

Once more I took my post at the window. Night was coming on. The dust seemed to thicken and grow black; streams of yellow light dripped from neighboring windows; from the house across the way drifted string music, soothing but melancholy. Singing came from the tavern, too, every time the door swung open, songs in a quavering voice that I recognized as the crippled Nikitushka's. The decrepit beggar had one eye of glass and kept the other tightly closed. Every time the door banged shut, it seemed to cut off his song like an axe.

Grandma was envious of the beggar, Nikitushka. After listening to a song of his, she would sigh, "What a talent! How many ballads he has by heart! He's got the gift!"

Sometimes she called him into the yard where, perched on a step, he sang or yarned away, while grandma, listening beside him, broke in with such questions as, "You don't mean to tell me Our Lady came to Ryazan?" To which Nikitushka would reply, with quiet conviction, "She's been everywhere, through all the provinces."

A narcotic languor seemed to rise from the street below and to descend heavily upon my heart and my eyes. If only grandma or even grandpa would come up! What sort of man, I pondered, had my father been that he had made himself so hated by grandpa and my uncles, whereas grandma and Gregory and Eugenia spoke of him with such warmth and respect? And where had mama gone to? She grew in my thoughts day by day. She became mixed up with grandpa's fairy tales and legends. Her refusal to live here raised my opinion of her. I thought of her as living in a cross-roads inn among bandits who held up the rich and shared the booty with beggars; or in a forest cave, again, of course, in such a Robin Hood company, keeping house for them, and taking care of their hoard. Or she roamed about as did the bandit, Engalicheva, looking over the world's treasures, with the madonna for traveling companion, who exhorted her not to steal, as She had exhorted Engalicheva, to sate the lusts of the body. And in reply mama, like Engalicheva, would beg the madonna's pardon and explain that it was for her young son's sake that she stole. And the madonna, who was good-natured, like grandma, would pardon her and tell her that it was for her, too, though she had Tatar blood, that She had stood under the cross; and the madonna absolved her from any sin for the robbery of infidel Kalmucks and Mongols, but forbade her to rob Russians.

I was daydreaming over this story, virtually living it, when I was roused by brawling below, in the yard and around the shed. Looking down I saw grandpa, Uncle Jake and Melian, the clownish bartender from the tavern, hustling Uncle Mike through the gate. He was hitting out at them and getting blows and kicks in return. And then he went sailing through and landed in a heap in the gutter. The gate banged shut and the bolt scraped into place; the only sign of the melee was a battered cap near the gate, and all was quiet.

After awhile, Uncle Mike staggered up, all tousled and torn. He pried a cobblestone out of the street and heaved it at the gate, on which it made a hollow clang like a barrel pounded on the bottom. It brought dim shapes out from the tavern; they let loose with shouts, curses and raised fists. Heads popped out of the windows. The street began to fill with people turning out to enjoy the show. To me it was like a story you had to hear the end of, but that gave no pleasure, that left you disquieted. Then, suddenly, it all seemed to be blotted out; the voices dropped away; and the people drifted out of sight.

I saw grandma sitting, bowed, on a chest near the door, scarcely appearing to breathe. I went up to her and patted her damp cheeks, but she seemed insensible to the touch, and only murmured repeatedly, in a hoarse whisper, "Have you no pity left for us, O Lord, for me and my children? Have mercy, Lord!"

Though, apparently, grandpa had moved into the house on Polevoi Street only a year ago that spring, it had proved time enough to achieve an embarrassing notoriety. It was a rare Sunday that the neighborhood kids were not dancing around our door gleefully blaring, "The Kashirins are fighting again!"

It was worst in the evenings that Uncle Mike generally made his appearance, and kept us in a state of terrorized tension, as if under siege. At times he had partners along, two or three ugly-looking rowdies. They would steal in by way of the causeway, into the garden, where they gave full vent to their destructive drunkards' caprices, trampling and stripping the berry bushes; now and then, they extended their forays into the bathhouse where they got at everything breakable, smashing stools, benches, kettles, stoves, ripping out floor boards, dismantling the door frame.

Grim, but silent, grandpa listened at the window to the havoc made by these despoilers of his property, while grandma went out to the garden and could be heard in the dark, pleading, "Oh, Mike, Mike, what's got into you?"

The answer was a stream of filth, as horrible as the delirium of a lunatic; the brute was clearly too drunk to understand the sense or the effect of the obscenities he spewed forth.

I knew better than to run after grandma then, but I was afraid to be alone, and came into grandpa's bedroom, only to have him curse me and order me out. So I climbed up to the garret to station myself at the gable window overhanging the garden, trying to see grandma. Fearful lest she be killed, I shrieked down to her, but she did not come up; but my uncle, hearing me, made mama the target of his rage and his obscenities.

On one such night grandpa, who was ailing, kept rolling his head, which was swathed in towels, over his pillow, lamenting, "So for this have I lived a sinful life to gain riches! If it were not for the scandal, I'd call the police and have them hauled to court tomorrow. But the scandal! Parents having their own children arrested! So there's nothing you can do, old man, but bear it in silence."

But suddenly he staggered out of bed and over to the window. Grandma, who was tending him, pulled at him. "Where are you going?"

"Put on a light!" he commanded, panting.

Taking the candlestick with the lit candle from grandma, and holding it against him like a soldier shouldering a gun, he bellowed loud gibes at my uncle from the window, "Hi there, Mike, you bandit, you mangy, mad dog!"

A broken brick instantly shivered the upper window and landed near grandma, on the table.

"What's the matter with your eye?" shrieked grandpa, deliriously.

Taking him up in her arms, as she might have taken me, grandma put him back in bed, repeating in a horrified tone, "What's come over you? What can you be thinking of? God forgive you! Siberia lies ahead of him, I can see that; but in his madness he doesn't realize what Siberia means."

With convulsive kicks as he lay there, and shaken with dry sobs, grandpa said, in a choking tone, "Let him kill me!"

From without the howling, the trampling, the thudding at the walls continued. Snatching the brick from the table I jumped to the window, but grandma intercepted me and, throwing it into a corner, screamed, "Little devil, you!"

Once my uncle came equipped with a heavy post to ram in the door; but grandpa was in the vestibule, waiting for him, armed with a club, and reinforced by two tenants also carrying clubs, and the tavern keeper's tall wife, wielding a rolling pin. Behind them grandma pleaded, in a low voice, "Let me see him; just for one word with him."

Without answering, grandpa, standing poised, with one foot forward, like the hunter aiming the lance in the painting called "The Bear Hunt," jolted her aside with his elbow and his knee. The stance of the four was formidable, but the flickering light of the lantern, hanging above them on the wall, gave their faces a ludicrous appearance. I saw it all from my perch at the head of the stairs, and how I wished I could coax grandma up there with me!

My uncle's ramming operation was energetically and successfully carried out. The door, wrenched out of the lower hinge, was creaking out of the upper hinge. Grandpa instructed his comrades-in-arms, in a rasping voice, "Please keep your clubs down, off his addled head; aim at the arms and legs."

In the wall beside the door was a tiny window through which one could barely get his head. Uncle Mike had broken it, and within its jagged, splintered frame, it looked like a black eye. Grandma ran over to it and, waving her hand through it, cried, "Mike, go away, for Christ's sake! They'll tear you to pieces. Go away!"

He struck her. Some broad object could be seen, distinctly, crossing the window and descending upon her hand. And grandma fell down; but even from the ground she continued to warn him, "Mike, Mi-i-ke! Run!"

"Where are you, mother?" called grandpa in a frantic voice.

The door was wrenched away, and there, in the shadowed frame, stood my uncle, but only for a moment. Like a spadeful of dirt he was thrown down the steps.

The innkeeper's wife carried grandma to grandpa's room, to which he followed soon after, asking grimly, "Any broken bones?"

"Akh, they must all be broken," said grandma, her eyes shut. "What have they done to him; what have you done to him?"

"Be sensible," replied grandpa angrily. "Am I a wild beast? He's down in the cellar, tied up, and we've cooled him off, good, with a pail of cold water. Sure, that's not nice, but who started all the trouble?"

There was a groan from grandma.

"I've sent for the bone-setter," said grandpa. "See if you can hold out until she gets here." And he sat beside her on the bed. "They're making short work of us, mother, rushing us into ruin," he said.

"Oh, let them have what they want."

"How about Barbara?"

And there was a long discussion, back and forth between them, grandma's manner soft and sympathetic, grandpa's loud and harsh.

Then a tiny old woman hunchback came in, whose gaping mouth stretched from ear to ear, the lower jaw wagging like the maw of a fish, and a sharp nose peering over her upper lip. I could not see her eyes. There was barely any movement of her feet as her crutches creaked over the floor, and the parcel in her hand made a rattling sound.

In my excited imagination she seemed to be bringing death to grandma, and I rushed at her, and with all my might I yelled at her, "Go away!"

Grandpa, with none too gentle hands, and giving me a wrathful look, picked me up and carried me into the attic.

Chapter Six

IN THE SPRING MY UNCLES SET UP SHOPS OF THEIR OWN, UNCLE JAKE IN town and Uncle Mike down the river, while grandpa purchased a big and interesting house on the same street, the ground floor of which was used for a tavern. There were comfortable little rooms on the upper floors; and the garden reached to the causeway, which was spiked with willow boughs not yet in leaf.

"Spanking switches," remarked grandpa with a jovial wink, when, after a look in the garden, he took me for a stroll over the muddy road. "Soon I'll be teaching you to read and write, and they'll come in handy."

Roomers filled the house except for the top floor, where grandpa had his bedroom and a room where he received guests, and the attic where grandma and I were accommodated. Our window looked out on the street, and from the sill we were treated, every evening and holidays, to such sights as drunkards staggering out of the tavern and lurching and shouting up the road. Sometimes they were pitched out like sacks of rubbish; and then they would try to get back into the tavern. The door would slam, the hinges squeal, the uproar of a fight would follow. I found it very interesting.

In the morning grandpa visited his sons at their shops, to help them over the difficulties of getting started; and he returned at night fatigued, discouraged and irritable.

Grandma kept herself occupied cooking, sewing and puttering around in the kitchen and the garden; there was always something to keep her spinning, like an enormous top set off by an invisible cord. Perpetually at her snuff box, she would sneeze and wipe her sweating face and congratulate herself, "Bless the good old world. Well, Alex, my dear, haven't we come to a snug, quiet life at last? Thanks to you, Queen of Heaven, everything's turned out well."

But her notion of the quiet life did not accord with mine. What a running in and out and up and down of the lodgers, by way of being neighborly—always running and always late—making unending complaints and requests of the ever obliging, "Akulina!"

And Grandma Akulina, tirelessly accommodating and accessible to all, would reinforce herself with a pinch of snuff, dry her nose and fingers on a big, red-checked handkerchief, and then give her advice, "You'll have to wash yourself oftener, my friend, if you want to be rid of lice. Take mint-vapor baths. If the lice have got under the skin, rub on some of this mixture: a tablespoonful of goose-fat, rendered as pure as you can get it, a teaspoonful of sulphur, and three drops of mercury, stirred in an earthenware vessel seven times, with a piece from a broken pot. That's best, because with a wood or bone spoon you'll get no good out of the mercury; and if you use a spoon of brass or silver, it will even do you harm."

At times, after pondering a problem, she'd say, "On this, good woman, I don't know how to advise you. Better see Asaph the druggist."

She served families as midwife, and as peacemaker in their quarrels, helped to heal sick infants, taught women to recite the "Dream of the Madonna," whose verses were considered charms, and had a word of advice handy for anybody's housekeeping problems.

"The cucumber, itself, shows when it's time to pick it. When it drops off the vine and gets its peculiar smell, that's the time to pick it. *Kvass* needs rough handling; sweetness is not the thing for it, so use raisins when you prepare it; and as for sugar just a pinch to the pail. There are different ways of making curds—the way they do it on the Don, and the Kuban region, and the Caucasus—each for its own flavor."

Wherever she was, in the garden or the yard, I tagged after her; I went with her to the neighbors, where she would sit over tea for hours, regaling her hosts with stories of every description. I was like something that had grown onto her and become a part of her. No memory from this period of my life is so vivid as my memory of this energetic old woman tirelessly giving people comfort and help.

"Are you a witch?" I once asked her.

"So! And what notion will pop into your head next?" she exclaimed, with a laugh. Then she became thoughtful and said, "I a witch? Witchcraft, you know, is a science; and I have no learning; neither reading nor writing—not even the alphabet. Now, grandpa, he stuffs himself like a cormorant with learning; but the Madonna never saw fit to make a scholar out of me."

And then another side of her life was presented to me. "You know, I was an orphan child, too, like you. My mother was a poor peasant woman—and crippled. A gentleman seduced her when she was hardly more than a child; and one night, overcome by the miseries she foresaw, she jumped out of the window. Some of her ribs were broken and her shoulder was injured in such a way that her right hand, which she needed most in her work—she was a lace-maker and well known in the craft—began to wither. Naturally her boss had no more use for her and fired her, to get along any way she could. But without hands, who can earn his bread? So she begged, and kept us alive on the charity of others. But in the old times people were better off and they had kinder hearts. The Balakhana carpenters, too, like the lace-makers, were famous; and they all liked to make a show.

"We sometimes stayed in the town, mama and I, all through the fall and winter, but at the first wave of the archangel Gabriel's sword, when he drove out the winter and brought back green spring, we took to the roads again, following our eyes—to Murom, to Urievitz, along the upper Volga, and the peaceful Oka. Wandering over the world in spring and summer, when the earth is so cheerful everywhere and the grass feels like velvet—that was pleasant; and God's Holy Mother strewed the way with flowers, and everything spoke straight to the heart and the heart answered with joy. Sometimes, in the hills, mama shut her blue eyes and sang. Her voice wasn't very strong but it was bright like a bell; and, it seemed to me, as I listened to her, that she lulled everything around to easy sleep. God, how good it was to be alive those days!

"But when I was nine mama thought people would blame her for still taking me begging on the roads, and for being a wandering beggar herself, so she settled down in Balakhana and begged there from door to door, and on the church steps on Sundays and holidays, while I stayed indoors and learned lace-making. I was so eager to be a help to mama that I cried any time I didn't do a thing right. But I really had a knack for it, and in two years, though still a child, I had mastered the trade, and became known all over town, so that people who wanted the finest lace would come and say, 'Akulina, start your bobbins whirling.'

"And that made me happy. Those were grand days for me. But mama really deserves the credit, not me; not for any work of her hands—she had only one, and it was useless—but for teaching me so well. A good teacher is more valuable than ten workers.

"In my pride, I said to her, 'Now, little mother, I'm earning enough for both of us and you must stop begging.'

" 'Nonsense,' she said, 'What you're earning goes toward your dowry.'

"And it wasn't long before your grandpa came into the picture. What a lad he was, only twenty-two and already a master river man. His mother had been keeping her eye on me. She appreciated me as a good worker, but being only a beggar-woman's daughter, she must have thought she'd be able to keep me under her thumb. A tricky, ill-willed creature she was, but we'll let that rest. . . . Why keep the evil in remembrance? God watches them, sees how they act; and the devils pick them for their own."

And she disposed of that with a hearty laugh that wreathed her nose in absurd wrinkles, and the caresses for me in her gentle eyes were even more expressive than her words.

One quiet evening, as I remember, I came for my tea with grandma in grandpa's room. He was sick, and had a towel wrapped around his shoulders, and was panting and in a sweat. His green eyes were bleary, his skin livid and baggy, his small, pointed ears inflamed almost to purple. It was pitiful to see him shaking as he reached out for his tea. He had become mild, quite unlike himself; and the tone of his voice, when he complained, "Why don't you give me some sugar?" was pettish like that of a child.

"I've put in honey instead," said grandma in a kind, but firm, voice, "it's better for you."

With a loud inhalation of breath, that sounded like a duck quacking, he drank the tea in one swallow. "You'll see," he said, "this time I'm going to die."

"Don't fret yourself. I'll see you through."

"So you say; but if I die now, everything will go to pieces; I might as well not have lived."

"Hush. Lie quiet, will you?"

But he couldn't stay silent more than a minute. Even with his eyes shut, his discolored lips made smacking sounds and he kept knotting his thin beard in his fingers. Suddenly, as if he had been stuck with a pin, he gave himself a shake and was again spilling what was on his mind.

"Jake and Mike should find themselves new wives, right away. With new ties they're more likely to take a new hold on their lives, don't you think?" And he began naming the eligible women he could think of.

But grandma kept drinking her tea in silence; and I stared at the reddening evening sky, and its rosy reflections in the windows across the way. As a punishment for something or other, grandpa had forbidden me the garden and the yard. I heard beetles making a chirring sound as they circled the beech trees in the garden; in one of the neighboring yards a cooper was at work on his barrels; in another knives were being sharpened on a grindstone. The sounds of playing children rose from the bushes in the garden and along the causeway, in which they were hidden. I was magnetized by it, while the moodiness of twilight seeped into my heart.

Grandpa broke into my revery by displaying a crisp new book, smacking it sharply on the palm of his hand, and calling to me briskly: "Come here, you little scamp! Sit down! See those letters? This one is *Az*. Repeat after me: '*Az, Buki, Viedi*.' [11] What's this one?"

"*Buki*."

"Right. And this?"

"*Viedi*."

"Wrong—*Az*. And these are *Glagol, Dobro, Yest*. What's this one?"

"*Az*."

"Right. And this?"

[11] First letters of the Russian alphabet.

"Father, you ought to be lying quiet, you know that," said grandma.
"Stop nagging me. This is just what I need; it distracts me. Go on,
Alex."

Putting his clammy arm on my shoulder he clocked off the letters
there with his fingers. A powerful reek of vinegar and onions came from
him and almost suffocated me; but when he felt me recoil and lag, he
raged at me, bellowing the letters in my ears, "*Zemlia! Ludi!* . . ."

I already knew the sounds, but the shapes in the Slavic script looked
wrong for them. *Zemlia* (З) wriggled like a worm; *Glagol* (Г) was
round-shouldered like old Gregory; *Ya* (Я) looked like Grandma and
I standing alongside each other; while something of grandpa seemed
to appear in all the letters.

He put me through it over and over, sometimes in order, sometimes
skipping around, and some of his heat seemed to be conducted into
me; I, too, was sweating and shouting—which amused him. He felt
his chest, after a violent cough, and wheezed to grandma, as he threw
the book down, "Just listen to him bawling, Mother. What's all this
commotion for, you little Astrakhan lunatic!"

"You're the one who's been making the commotion."

It was nice seeing him so gay and grandma smiled at us from the
table where she sat, resting her elbows, and chided us with a gentle
laugh, "You'll both split up the sides, laughing that way."

Grandpa explained to me, quite amiably, "I shout out of irritation
because I'm ill, but what's eating you?" And, turning to grandma, he
said, "Poor Natalie was wrong to say his memory's poor," and shook
his moist head. "There's nothing wrong with his memory, thank the
Lord. It's like a horse's memory. On with it, snubnose!"

And when he finally pushed me off the bed, it was with a playful
nudge, and he said, "That's enough. Take the book, and tomorrow,
if you can get through the whole alphabet without a mistake, I'll give
you five kopecks."

When I reached for the book he pulled me to him and said, a little
hoarsely, "That mother of yours doesn't seem to care what becomes of
her lad."

"Oh, father!" exclaimed grandma. "How can you say such a thing!"

"I shouldn't, but I couldn't control myself. What a wayward one
that girl is!"

He pushed me off roughly. "You run along. You can go out—in the
garden or the yard—but not in the street!"

I chose the garden into which I was drawn by a special lure. No sooner did I show myself on the slope there, than I became the target for the boys on the causeway with whom I exchanged volleys of stones. "Here comes sissy," the cry would go up, immediately. "Let's paste him!" and began picking up stones.

Not knowing what they meant by "sissy," I took no offense; I felt proud to be standing off the lot of them, all by myself, especially when a good shot made them take to the bushes. We entered into these skirmishes without bad feelings and we usually came out of them without a scratch.

Reading and writing came easy to me. Grandpa spent more time on me and spankings became rarer, though, as far as I could see, more were coming to me since, with growth and increasing vigor, I found more occasion to break his rules and defy his orders; but this drew no more from him than scoldings and flourishes of his fist. Because of this I had the temerity not only to think that his past beatings had been without cause, but to tell him so.

He took me lightly by the chin, pulled my face up toward his, winked and said, "Wha-a-at's tha-a-at?" and, almost laughing, added, "Heretic! How on earth could you tell what's your proper portion of spankings? Who's to judge if not me? Go on, scoot!"

But the moment he said this he yanked me back by the shoulder and asked, "What was that—a trick or a piece of simple-mindedness, I wonder?"

"I don't know."

"You don't? Let me tell you—be tricky—you'll win that way. The simple are fools. Remember it's the sheep who are simple beasts. All right. Now off with you."

I was soon spelling out the Psalms. After evening tea was the time generally allotted to it, my stint being one Psalm. "B-l-e-s-s, Bless, e-d, Blessed," I read, pointing my way over the line with a little stick, "Blessed is the man—"

"Would that mean Uncle Jake?" I asked for a diversion.

"Maybe a box on the ears will teach you who's blessed!" grandpa snorted; but I felt his wrath was only put on, because he thought he ought to show anger. And this was borne out by his forgetting all about it a minute later, when he commented, "It's a fact, King David doesn't show up so well in some of those songs of his, and that business with Absalom. Ah, you chirper of songs, you word monger, you clown—that's you!"

Absorbed in the brooding, perplexed expression on his face, I stopped reading. And his somewhat wandering eyes seemed to penetrate me and a warming, moody brightness came from them, to be replaced soon enough, I knew, by their customary hard look. His skinny fingers drummed spasmodically on the table, sending flashes from his stained nails; and his yellow eyebrows twitched up and down.

"Grandpa."

"Yes?"

"Tell me a story."

"Come on, you loafer, get your reading done!" he scolded, but rubbing his eyes as if he had been jarred out of a nap. "Stories are what you fancy, not the Psalms!"

That was also his preference, I guessed. He had virtually memorized the Psalms, having read them through nightly before going to bed, in fulfillment of a vow, and the reading had become a chant, like a deacon's rendering of the breviary. And the old man, whose hardness was gradually weathering away, yielded to my plea. "All right, then; soon God will be haling me up for judgment, but you'll always have the Psalms at hand "

Sunk back in the upholstery of an old armchair, his head turned up so that his eyes were on the ceiling, he told me stories of his youth. His father had been killed by highwaymen who had broken into Balakhana to rob its local magnate, the merchant Zayev. Rushing up the belfry to ring the alarm, he had been overtaken by the marauders, cut down by their swords and his body cast from the tower.

"Being only an infant when it happened, I remember nothing about it. The first person I can recall is a Frenchman. I had just that day turned twelve. Soldiers brought three groups of prisoners—small, dried-up people they were—into Balakhana. More ragged some of them were than beggars, and others so numb with cold they could hardly stand up. A mob of peasants wanted to kill them, but the soldiers of the escort saved them. They scattered the peasants, and after that the Frenchmen were safe enough. We got used to them and they turned out to be handy and clever and a jolly sort—they sang so often. Important people drove down from Nizhny to question them. Some were rude to them, shook their fists in their faces, and even hit them; but there were others who spoke to them very civilly in their own language, and even gave them money. One old gentleman put his hands over his face and cried for them, saying the scoundrel, Napoleon, had been their ruin. You see? He was a Russian and a gentleman, but he had a kind heart—he could feel for those foreigners."

He paused for a moment, and, with his eyes closed, ran his fingers through his hair; then he continued, careful to make his recollections precise. "Winter had its grip on the streets; all the huts were snowbound. Sometimes the Frenchmen stood under our window—my mother baked rolls for sale—and knocked on the glass, shouting and hopping up and down. Mother wouldn't let them in, but she let them have the rolls, throwing them out to them through the window. They were hot out of the oven, yet the Frenchmen put them next to their bare skin—how they stood it is more than I can imagine. The cold killed a lot of them, for they were not used to it—theirs is a warm country. We had two of them living in our bathhouse, an officer and a man named Miron, his orderly.

"The officer was tall and so lean you could see the bones through his skin. He was good-natured, but he drank, and mother sold him home-brew on the quiet. With drink in him he sang. When he learned enough Russian he aired his impressions—'Your country not white; it is black—bad.' His pronunciation was bad, of course, but we could follow him, and what he said was true enough. The upper Volga country is no paradise, though it gets warmer farther south, and they never see snow around the Caspian Sea. There's no word said about snow or winter in the Gospels, or the Acts, or the Psalms . . . or where Christ lived. . . . When we're through with the Psalms we'll read about it, together, in the Gospels."

He went into another sleeplike silence. His thoughts had gone wandering, and his eyes, casting sidelong glances out of the window, looked tiny and hard.

"Some more," I begged, to remind him, as inoffensively as I could, of my presence.

With a start he resumed. "Oh, we were talking about the French . . . human beings, no worse sinners than us. Sometimes they would buy flour from mother, calling her 'Madam'; that means 'My Lady'; and she would fill their sacks with flour—five poods [12] in each. She had phenomenal strength for a woman. Even when I was twenty—and I was no featherweight then—she had no trouble lifting me up by the hair. Now this orderly of the officer's, this Miron, had a passion for horses; he'd stand in the yard making signs offering to groom the horses. At first there was wrangling over whether he should be allowed to or not; but in time he had his way. 'Hi, Miron,' a peasant would call out, and Miron would come running, grinning and nodding.

[12] A pood is approximately forty pounds.

His hair was sandy-colored, almost red; his nose was big and his lips were thick. He knew a lot about horses and could cure their diseases. He settled down in Nizhny as a veterinary; but he went mad and died in a fire. Toward spring it was clear that the officer was fading away and one day, in early spring, he came quietly to his end, sitting at his window, in a revery, with his head bent down.

"That was how he passed away, and I grieved for him, even weeping for him, when I wasn't seen. He had acted so kindly. He used to pat me and say affectionate things to me in his language. I didn't understand them but it gave me pleasure to hear them—human kindness is not a commodity you can pick up in the market. He began teaching me French, but mother wouldn't have it and sent me to the priest, whose prescription was a beating for me, and a talking to to the officer, which he, himself, undertook. We got rough treatment in those times, boy. You haven't had anything to match it, yet. What you've gone through is nothing, remember that. . . . Take me and what I went through!"

It was growing dark. In an odd way grandpa seemed to enlarge in the half-light and his eyes to brighten like a cat's. In exchanges of opinion he was usually measured and thoughtful in his speech; but, talking about himself, his words would come in a rush, he was self-pitying or boastful; and it was not pleasant to listen to him; and his frequent interjections, "Now remember this, take care not to forget it!" annoyed me.

Many of the things I was so peremptorily bidden to remember, I didn't want to remember; but they were a morbid matter that festered in my memory and infected my heart.

None of his stories were fictional; they were always about actual happenings. Observing that questions annoyed him, I persisted in asking, "Who are better—the French or the Russians?"

"How do I know? I never saw the French at home," he muttered irritably, adding, "In his own hole there's nothing wrong with a skunk."

"But how about the Russians—are they good?"

"In many respects, yes; but under the rule of landlords we Russians were better. Now people are at each other's throats and it's hard to make a living. It's the gentry's fault because they have the advantage of intelligence; though you can't say that for every gentleman—in fact, only a few have shown intelligence. Most are as simple as mice—you can put anything over on them. We have heaps of nutshells but no kernels;

the kernels have been eaten up. Boy, learn a lesson from that! It's something we should have learned by now, and sharpened our wits on it; we're still too dull."

"Aren't the Russians stronger than other people?"

"There are some pretty strong fellows among us; but it's not strength that counts, but handiness. If things went according to strength the horse would be our master."

"Why did the French make war on us?"

"War is the Emperor's business. We're not expected to understand it!"

When I asked what kind of man Napoleon was, grandpa replied musingly, "A wicked one. He set out to beat the whole world; and then he wanted to abolish the proper differences between people—no rulers or Emperors—everybody the same, one set of rules, one religion for everybody, nothing to distinguish one man from another except his name. Sheer idiocy. Among all creatures except lobsters, one can be distinguished from the other. Fish have their classes; the sturgeon keeps apart from the catfish, and the sterlet [13] won't mix with the herring. We have had Napoleons of our own—there was Stenka Razin and Pugachov. [14] Some other time I'll tell you about them."

At times grandpa's silences would last quite a time, and his eyes would roll over me as if he were seeing me for the first time—hardly a pleasant experience. And he avoided any reference to my parents. Occasionally grandma would glide in without a sound, while these talks were going on, sit down in a corner and would remain unheard and unseen until, suddenly, she would put a question in her fondling voice, "Remember, father, how nice it was on that pilgrimage we took to Murom? Do you recall what year that was?"

Grandpa would mull it over, then say, picking his words, "Exactly what year I couldn't say. I know it came before the cholera epidemic; it was the year we tracked down those escaped convicts in the woods."

"Ah, so it was. How scared everybody was!"

"True."

I asked about the escaped convicts, what were they and why were they hiding in the woods? Grandpa didn't seem to relish making the explanations. "They're just some men who've stolen out of prison—who've run away from the work they were given to do."

"How did you track them down?"

[13] A smaller kind of sturgeon famous for the superior quality of its caviar.
[14] Leaders of peasant uprisings.

"How? It's like your boys' game of cops and robbers—some run and the others chase them. They were caught; then they were flogged and their nostrils were slit and a mark was burned on their foreheads to show that they were convicts."

"Why?"

"To that question I have no answer. And who's in the wrong, he who runs or he who chases him?—that's a question, too."

"And, remember, father," continued grandma, "how after the big fire we . . ."

Grandpa, who made a fetish of being precise, asked primly, "Which big fire?"

When they retraveled their past this way, I was forgotten. Words and voices blended so harmoniously it sounded, at times, like elegies commemorating plagues, conflagrations, massacres, sudden deaths, swindlers, mad saints, rapacious landlords. And grandpa would mumble reflectively, "How much we've lived through; how much we've seen!"

"It's not been such a bad life, has it?" said grandma. "Remember how well it was with us that spring after Barbara was born?"

"Yes, that was the year of the campaign in Hungary, '48; and right after the christening they drove out Tikhon, her godfather."

"And he was never seen again!" sighed grandma.

"True, and from then on, God's blessings have slid off our house like water off a duck's back. That Barbara—"

"Enough, father!"

"What d'ye mean 'enough,'" he exploded. "Our children haven't turned out right, look at them any way you want. The hope and strength of our youth—where have they gone? We imagined we were keeping our youth fresh and whole in our children, like things well wrapped up and put away in baskets; but look, God has wrought his changes, and all we have in our hands is a riddle and no answer."

He groaned like an invalid, then he hopped about the room, yelping as if he had been scalded, and turned on grandma, vilifying the children to her, brandishing his wizened little fist in her face and shouting, "You're to blame for it all, you hag; you spoiled them, you were always on their side." The climax came in tears and howls as he prostrated himself beneath the icon, and penitentially pounding away with all his might on his skinny chest, he complained, "Lord, have I sinned beyond the rest? Then why?" And he shuddered all over, and his tearful eyes gleamed with indignation and rancor.

Crossing herself in silence, in her corner, grandma waited awhile before coming to him. Her approach was wary and she tried to soothe him. "Why fret yourself? It's God's doing and He knows. You think others have better children? Look around you, father, don't you see it's all the same—arguments, quarrels, scenes everywhere? We're not the only parents who cleanse their sins with their tears."

With such words he would sometimes let himself be pacified. He would begin undressing for bed, and grandma and I would glide out and up to our attic. Once, however, he met her attempt to comfort him with a punch in the mouth delivered with all his strength. Grandma staggered and almost fell. Recovering her balance she wiped her lips, soberly called him, "Fool," and spat blood at his feet. Two long, drawn-out howls came from him, and threatening her with both fists he cried out, "Get away or I'll murder you!"

"Fool!" she said again, and started to go. Grandpa lunged after her and she slammed the door in his face. Grandpa clawed at the door frame, his face livid with hatred as he yelled, "Old hag!"

I sat trembling on the oven, feeling faint, and looked on, unbelievingly. He had never before struck grandma in my presence, and this newly-revealed side of him I found unforgivable; it filled me with such loathing that it choked me. There he stayed, gripping the door frame, his face turning dry and gray as though sprinkled over with ashes.

All at once he came to the middle of the room, dropped to his knees, bent over and put his hands on the floor, then straightened up again and pounded himself on the breast—"Oh, Lord—"

Sliding off the warm tiles of the oven I tiptoed out as warily as if I were treading floating ice. Upstairs grandma was pacing the room, stopping now and again to rinse her mouth.

"Are you hurt?"

Her reply, after she spat some water into the basin, was calm, "Nothing to worry about. No teeth broken; only bruised lips."

"Why did he do that?"

With a glance toward the window, she replied, "He just loses his temper. And he's having a hard old age; everything is going badly for him. Now get to bed, say your prayers and forget about it."

I persisted in my questions and, with an asperity strange in her, she cried me down: "What did I tell you? Go to bed immediately. Such impudence!"

Then she sat at the window nursing her lip with a handkerchief. Still looking toward her, I undressed. Over her black head and through the blue square of the window, I could see the stars. The street below was still, and it was dark in the room. After I was in bed she came to me, stroked my head, and said, "Sleep sound, sweetheart. I'm going down to him but there's nothing to worry about. I was to blame, really. Sleep."

She kissed me and went out, leaving me overwhelmed with anxiety. I could not stay in the big, warm comfortable bed. I went to the window where, numb with misery, I stared down at the empty street.

Chapter Seven

IT DID NOT TAKE ME LONG TO REALIZE THAT GRANDPA'S GOD WAS different from grandma's. This difference was forced on my attention too persistently for me to escape it.

Some mornings grandma sat on the bed combing her wonderful hair. Holding her head back she drew the gap-toothed comb through every silken, black strand, muttering in a low voice to keep from waking me, "Plague you. You're all stuck together, devil take you!"

When her hair was unsnarled, she rapidly braided it, washed hastily with irritable jerks of her head, the fretfulness remaining, like stains, on her big face, which still showed the creases of sleep. It was before the icon that her real ablutions began, bringing immediate refreshment to all her being.

Straightening her bowed back and lifting her head, she adored the round face of Our Lady of Kazan, before whom she devoutly crossed herself, and whom she invoked in a fervent whisper, "Most Glorious Virgin! Take me this day, Dear Mother, under Thy care!" Prostrating herself, and then with much effort creaking back into position, she resumed her rapturous whispering, "Fountain of our happiness, beauty without blemish, blossoming apple tree!"

New expressions of loving praise welled up from her every morning, and in order not to miss them I strained to hear every word.

"Pure, dear Celestial Heart; my Guardian and my Heaven. My Golden Sun. Mother of God. Keep me from temptation; let me harm no one this day, and let me take no offense for any thoughtless thing done to me."

With her dark-eyed smile and a rejuvenated air, she again crossed herself with her ponderous hands. "Jesus Christ, Son of God, for the sake of Thy holy Mother have mercy on this sinner."

There was little of the liturgical in her devotions; they were simple and her praises were heartfelt. And these first prayers were brief because she had to tend to the samovar. Grandpa would keep no servants, and should his tea not be ready the instant he wanted it, he would go into a tantrum.

Occasionally, he would be the first one up; then he would come up to us. As he would listen to her praying, his sharp, dark lips would assume a derisive twist. Later, over his tea, he would berate her, "You booby! Over and over again I've told you how to say your prayers. And you keep drooling that foolishness of yours, heretic! It's more than I can tell how God stands for it!"

With quiet assurance grandma would say, "He understands even what we can't tell Him; He has His eye on everything."

"Accursed dolt! Ekh—you!" was all his reply.

Grandma's God was beside her all through the day; even to animals she spoke of Him. Her God was glad to serve all His creatures—men, dogs, bees—even the grasses in the field; all on earth could come to Him and could count on His grace.

A cat, a pet of the tavern keeper's wife, a cunning, ingratiating pretty animal with cloudlike fur and golden eyes, once brought down a starling in our garden. Grandma got the nearly dead bird away and spanked the cat, admonishing her, "Wretch! Have you no fear of God?"

When the tavern keeper's wife and the porters laughed at that, she chided them, "Think animals have no knowledge of God? You heartless ones, they know more about Him than you!"

Harnessing Sharapa, who was entering an obese and fretful old age, she would have a chat with him. "Why so moody, you God's laborer? Eh? Getting old, my dear, that's it." And the horse would seem to nod his head and sigh.

Nevertheless, the name of God was not as frequently in her mouth as grandpa's. Her God was no mystery to me; I knew it was wrong to lie when He was around; I would feel ashamed. That sense of shame was so strong that I couldn't lie to grandma. I felt that nothing could be hidden from this good God; and even the wish to hide something never came to me.

In a scene with grandpa the tavern keeper's wife once extended her curses to grandma, who had not been involved in the quarrel, and even threw a carrot at her. "You're a fool, my good woman," said grandma, but kept her temper. I felt outraged, however, and plotted vengeance.

For some time I could not decide on the best punishment for this drab-haired, bloated, double-chinned and almost eyeless woman. From what I recalled of feuds between neighbors I knew that revenges included chopping off the tail of an enemy's cat, driving away his dog, raiding his barnyard and killing some of his chickens, breaking into his cellar and pouring kerosene into his sauerkraut and pickle tubs, opening the spigots of *kvass* barrels and letting the liquor run out. None of these appealed to me. I sought a revenge both more refined and more terrifying.

Finally an idea came to me. Keeping watch on the tavern keeper's wife I waited until she went down into the cellar, then locked the trapdoor, did a dance on it, tossed the key up on the roof, and ran to grandma's kitchen bubbling with ecstasy. As soon as she learned the cause she spanked me on the part of the anatomy adapted to that purpose, hauled me out into the yard and ordered me up the roof to fetch the key. Reluctantly I handed it to her, puzzled by her behavior. From an observation post in a corner, I watched her liberate the prisoner, and I saw them enjoying a friendly laugh together.

"I'll see that you're paid for this!" said the tavern keeper's wife, flourishing her lumpy fist at me; but a good-natured smile creased her eyeless face.

"Why did you do that?" grandma demanded as she hauled me back into the kitchen by the collar.

"She threw that carrot at you."

"So it's for me you did it? And what will I do for you? I'll give you a good taste of the horsewhip, and let you have the mice for company under the oven. So that's the kind of guardian you are! 'Just look at a bubble and it bursts.' Grandpa would skin you if I told him. Up to the attic, to your lessons!"

She wouldn't talk to me all day, but before her prayers that night, she told me in a grave voice something that has clung in my memory. "Alex, darling, better keep out of the affairs of grownups. They have obligations and they have to account to God for them; but you can still live according to a child's conscience. Wait, and in time God will take command in your heart and reveal to you what you are to do and what way you are to go. Understand? It's not for you to concern yourself over who's at fault. God is the judge; it is for Him to punish; that's His part, not ours."

After a moment's pause for snuff-taking, and with her right eye half-shut, she continued, "God, Himself, doesn't always know where to put the blame."

Astonished, I asked, "Don't God know everything?"

"If he did some of the things that go on wouldn't. It's as though the Father, He looks down from above and sees us on earth moaning and weeping so much, and He says, 'Poor dear folks, I'm so sorry for you!' "

She, too, wept as she said this; and wiping her tears, she went to the icon corner to pray.

And, from then on, I felt closer to her God. I felt I understood Him even better.

In his teaching grandpa also declared God to be All-pervading, All-knowing, All-seeing, Who helped people in their troubles; but his prayers were different from grandma's. On rising it took him some time before he took his stand under the icon; he spent time over his washing and dressing, carefully combing his sandy hair and brushing his beard, taking repeated looks in the mirror, tucking his shirt in, and knotting his tie; and after all this, he approached the icon corner warily, virtually stealing to his place there. There was one chosen board in the parquet flooring that he prayed on. He prayed with an empty expression that gave his eyes a bovine look. He stood, head bowed and silent a minute or so, his hands straight to his sides like a soldier at attention. Then, straightening up, stiff as a nail, he began in a grave tone, "In the name of the Father, the Son and the Holy Ghost . . ."

With this phrase an amazing stillness seemed to settle on the room; the very flies seemed to mute their buzzing.

In an imperious manner, with his head so far back his golden beard stuck out horizontally, and his bristling eyebrows arched high, he said his prayers in an even, distinct voice, as if he were reciting a lesson.

"It will be of no avail before the Judge when every deed is unbared . . ." After a perfunctory thump upon his chest, he went on, with rising fervor, "To Thee alone may sinners turn . . . Avert Thy face from my faults . . ."

He used only the prescribed form when saying the Credo. Through it all his right leg shook rhythmically, as if noiselessly clocking his prayers. As his body strained up to the icon, it seemed to elongate and become even more spare and neat—a spruce, persistent, demanding suppliant he was.

"Celestial Healer, purge the ingrained passions from my soul. From my heart I appeal to Thee, Holy Virgin. Devoutly I offer myself to Thee." And with tears welling from his green eyes he loudly entreated, "Judge me, God, by my faith, not by my works, which surely could not weigh in my favor."

And from there on, at frequent intervals, he crossed himself, jerked his head as if he meant to butt somebody, and his voice became screechy and broken. Happening to enter a synagogue, in later years, I was struck with the resemblance of his type of prayer to that of the Jews.

By then the snorts of the samovar and the smell of pancakes would be filling the room. Grandma would be pacing to and fro, her face lowered and frowning. The cheerful eye of the sun would be looking in from the garden. The dew on the tree would gleam like pearls. The morning air would carry the fragrances of dill, currants, and ripening apples. And still grandpa would squeal up to God, "Quench the passions burning in my soul, for sorrow overwhelms me; I am accursed."

I knew these morning prayers by heart and in my very dreams the proper words would succeed each other. When I listened to him it was for a mistake or a slip, a rare occurrence. But when it happened, I got a vindicated thrill. Then, after he was finally through and had greeted us and taken his seat at the table, I would say, "You missed a word this morning."

"No!" grandpa would exclaim, incredulous, but uneasy.

"Yes, where you should have said, 'My faith reigns supreme,' you left out 'reigns.'"

"Indeed!" he would exclaim and would sit back vexed, his eye twitching with mortification. He would take reprisals on me, later, and cruelly; but these moments of triumph, watching his perturbation, were sweet to me.

Once grandma kidded him, "Your prayers must bore God by now; the same items over and over."

"How's that?" he replied in a slow, menacing voice. "Nagging again? What about, now?"

"From what I hear you aren't offering God one measly word from the heart."

White and trembling with rage, he jumped up, and hurled a plate at her head. "You old she-devil. Take that!" A buzzing whine came from him like a saw through wood.

In reference to God's omnipresence he always dwelt on its punitive aspects. "Man sinned, and the flood overwhelmed him; again he sinned and fire consumed his cities; with famines and plagues God repaid the sinning people; and right now His sword hangs over the world, ready to cut down sinners. Misfortune and ruin will befall everyone who knowingly breaks His commandments." And for emphasis, he rapped his knuckles on the edge of the table.

Such vindictiveness on the part of God was hard for me to believe, and I had a suspicion that grandpa was inventing it to make me fear him, rather than God. I was frank with him and asked, "Aren't you saying all this to frighten me and make me obey you?"

Equally frank, he acknowledged: "Maybe I am. Are you plotting new disobedience?"

"How about what grandma says?"

"Don't listen to the old fool!" he ordered. "She's always been an illiterate, a dope, a being without reason, even in her youth. I'll forbid her to speak to you on matters like these. Now, tell me, of the companies of angels, how many are there?"

I gave the correct answer, then asked, "Are they incorporated?"

"You grasshopper brain! What relation have corporations with God? Corporations are of this earthly life. They're established to get around the laws."

"What are laws?"

"Oh, laws? They actually develop out of people's customs," began the old man at once, eager to exhibit his knowledge, a pleased sparkle in his intelligent, probing eyes. "In order to live together, people have to come to agreements. 'This is the best thing for us to do; let it be our custom— our rule!' In the end it becomes a law. Take, for instance, children playing a game; before it starts they decide how they are going to play it, what are to be the rules. That's also how laws come to be made."

"What have corporations to do with the laws?"

"Oh, they're like the chaps who do whatever they like . . . They come along and turn the law into a joke."

"Why?"

"That's more than you can understand now," he said, wrinkling his brow; but later, as though to explain it, he told me, "Whatever man does only carries forward God's plans. Man aims at one thing but by God's will it comes to something else. There is nothing permanent in the institutions of men. God's breath upon them is enough to scatter them in ashes and dust."

My curiosity about corporations had a certain point. I went on, "What does Uncle Jake mean when he says . . ." and I repeated a quatrain whose gist was that the angels fought on God's side, while the corporations took their orders from the devil.

Grandpa's hand shot into his beard to cover his mouth; he closed his eyes and his cheeks heaved and I knew he was repressing a laugh.

"Your Uncle Jake ought to be tied hand and foot and ducked into the water," he said. "He oughtn't to have sung those verses and you oughtn't to have listened. It's a gag that's going the rounds in Kaluga; such nonsense is popular with heretics and schismatics." And staring as if he were seeing through me and beyond, he ended with his inevitable, "Ekh—you!"

But far above mankind as he set God, as a Being of dread, he too, as did grandma, called upon God in everything he did.

The saints grandma knew were the humane and sympathetic Nicholas, Yury, Frola and Lavra, who shared the life of the people in hamlet and town, and concerned themselves with the cares of people; while grandpa's saints were generally those who had pulled down idols or defied the emperors of Rome and suffered torture, burning at the stake or being flayed alive.

On occasion grandpa would muse aloud, "Now if only God were to help me dispose of that house at only a modest profit, I'd make a donation in the name of St. Nicholas."

Grandma's laughing comment to me would be, "Isn't that like the old fool? As if our little Father Nicholas had nothing better to do than bother with the sale of a house."

For a long time I kept a church calendar of grandpa's marked up in his handwriting. One of the inscriptions was in red ink and rigidly vertical letters, marking the day of Saints Joachim and Anna: "My benefactors who shielded me from a calamity."

I well recall that "calamity." Anxious about supporting his wasteful children, grandpa became a money-lender without bothering to take out a license, carrying on the transactions *sub rosa*. Someone informed on him and the police made a search at night. There was a great commotion but it didn't end badly. Grandpa prayed all through the night and before he sat down to breakfast I saw him write that inscription.

It was his custom to read the Psalms with me, or the prayer book, or the heavy tome on religion by Ephraim Sirin, before the evening meal. Immediately after, he was at his prayers again, and the sombre, penitential phrases resounded through the quiet of the evening. "What can I bring Thee, O Gracious God, or how can I gain Thy forgiveness, great King of Kings . . . Guard us from thoughts of evil . . . Guard me, O Lord, from certain people . . . My tears pour like the rain at the recollection of my sins . . ."

Grandma, on the other hand, would sometimes say, "I'm all worn out, I'll skip prayers tonight."

It was grandpa who took me to church—to Saturday vespers and mass on Sundays and holy days. Even there, when God was being invoked, I made a distinction as to whose God it was, grandpa's or grandma's. What the priest or deacon intoned was to grandpa's God; but the choir sang to grandma's. Naturally, of this difference, discerned by a child's mind, I can now give only a rough approximation, but I recall that it set up a violent emotional conflict in me, and that when grandpa's God held my mind I was troubled and fearful. Unloving, He kept His stern eyes upon us, prying out any unseemly speck of sin; He appeared to distrust people, was always imposing penances, and took pleasure in punishing people.

Thoughts about God was my soul's food those days, and as much of beauty as life allowed. Whatever else I met with has left an impression of noisome squalor and inhumanity, to which I reacted with disgust and hostility. Of the beings I lived among, God—that is, grandma's God—was the brightest and best, the Good Companion of all creation. Naturally, I could not escape being distressed by the question, Why can't grandpa see the Good God?

Running around in the street was forbidden to me, because I was too wrought up after it. The impressions it left in me acted like intoxicants. Almost inevitably it ended in a scene. I had no playmates. To the neighbors' kids I was the enemy. Seeing that I resented being dubbed "the Kashirin this or that," they made it a rule, the moment they sighted me, to yell, "There's that Kashirin brat, get him!" and the fight would be on.

I was husky for my age and knew how to use my fists. Having learned this, my enemies never took me on singly. Always having a mob against me, I came home beaten, with a scratched nose, gashed lips, a face mottled with bruises, clothes ripped to shreds, and discharging puffs of dust at every step.

"What was it this time?" grandma would greet me with mingled sympathy and alarm. "Another brawl, you young scamp! What's the matter with you?" And as she washed my face and salved my bruises, she went on, "What's all this fighting about? At home you're as mild as anything; but let you out of the door, who knows what you turn into? It's a disgrace! I'll tell grandpa to forbid you to go out."

But my bruises never drew any full scale scolding from him; he merely chuckled and exclaimed, "Decorated again! Listen, my young cavalier, while you're living in my house, I'll not have you running wild in the street! Understand?"

There was no lure for me in the street when it was empty; but no sooner did I hear the cheerful clamor of the children than I forgot grandpa's admonitions and bolted out of the yard. It was not the blows and the jeers I suffered that distressed me, but the cruelty in their play, a cruelty I already knew too much of and that brought me, at times, to a feeling of desperation. I could not restrain my fury when I saw the children pestering roosters and dogs, torturing cats, untying and driving off goats belonging to Jews, tormenting helpless drunks and baiting, "Igosha, death in his pocket."

This last was a tall, wizened man with a complexion like smoked meat, his hollow, rusty face stubbled with bristling hairs. He stumbled and stooped over the streets in a dragging sheepskin, speaking to no one, his eyes fixed to the ground. The metallic look of his face and its little, suffering eyes, made me feel a troubled respect for this man who, I thought, was engrossed in something important, a man on a quest who should not be interfered with.

The boys pursued him, pelting his broad back with stones. For some time he ignored the blows as if he were insensible to pain; then he would stop, raise his head, and take a spasmodic pull at his tattered cap, looking as if he had just been aroused from sleep.

Immediately the boys would yell, "Igosha, death in his pocket! Where are you going, Igosha? Look! Death in your pocket!"

He would stick his hands in his pocket, then dart down to pick up a stone or a dry lump of earth and, waving his long arms, he cursed them, always in the same few, foul words. The boys had a vastly richer vocabulary of abuse. When he chased them, his long sheepskin would trip him; then he would rest on his knees and, with his grimy hands on the ground, he looked like a gnarled branch fallen from a tree. Meanwhile the boys shied stones at him from behind and from the sides, and the biggest ventured near enough to sift dust on his head.

Most painful of all was to see Gregory, our former shop foreman, still straight and handsome, but now quite blind, on his begging rounds. A tiny, gray woman led him by the arm. She would stand under a window, and without looking up, beg in a piping voice, "Something for the poor blind, for Christ's sake!"

Gregory himself never spoke. His lips were pressed tight together, and his broad beard touched his stained, folded hands. Wall, window, or passing face, his dark glasses were turned on them in the same steady stare. As often as I saw him I never heard a murmur from those sealed lips, and the thought of that silent old man lay on my mind with a torturing weight. I couldn't bring myself to come near him, and the moment I saw him, I dashed in to grandma, crying, "Gregory's out in the street."

"Oh, is he?" she would say anxiously. "Go back and give him this."

Annoyed and brusque, I would refuse and she would go out, herself, and spend a long time with him, and he would laugh and stroke his beard, but what little he said was in monosyllables. Sometimes she called him into the kitchen and served up some food, and always he asked for me.

Grandma would call me, but I would stay in hiding out in the yard. I simply could not face him; I felt unbearable embarrassment in his presence and I knew grandma suffered as well. Only once did we speak of it when, after leading Gregory to the gate, she came back, her face lowered and in tears. As I took her hand, she asked, "Why do you avoid him? Such a good man; and you know how fond he is of you!"

"Why did grandpa send him away?"

"Grandpa?" She paused, then, hardly audibly, she made this prophecy: "Remember what I'm telling you—God's grievous punishment will come upon us for it. God's punishment . . ."

And her words were not amiss. Ten years later, after she had gone to her death, grandpa was making the beggar's rounds himself, his mind broken, whining under windows, "Show kindness, cooks, just a morsel of meat pie, a little morsel. Ekh—you!"

Along with Igosha and Gregory, there was a woman called the Voronka, who also gave me some bad moments. She had a bad reputation, which people thought a justification for having the police hound her off the streets. It was on holidays that, huge, blowsy and drunk, she made her appearance, in a sort of floating motion, like a cloud, her feet seeming not to move or to touch the ground, as she carolled her lewd ditties. Whoever was then in the street got out of her way, ran around corners, or into alleys, or into shops; she made a clean sweep. Her face was quite blue, the cheeks distended like balloons; she had big, gray eyes that were always wide open in a frightening stare; and at times, she groaned, "Little children mine, where are you?"

I asked grandma about her. "It's nothing you ought to know," she replied, but she gave me the story briefly, nevertheless. "This woman's husband, Voronov, was in the government service. Seeking a promotion, he sold her to his chief, who took her off somewhere, and kept her away from home for two years. When she got back her two children, a boy and a girl, were dead, her husband was in jail—he had embezzled money and gambled it away. In her misery she took to the bottle and that's how you happen to see her in the streets, making scenes. Every holiday she has to be picked up by the police."

Home was indeed better than the street. My favorite time of day came after the midday meal when grandpa went off to Uncle Jake's workshop, and grandma sat at the window and told fairy stories and legends and talked about my father.

The rescued starling had had its broken wing clipped; and a wooden leg, skillfully fashioned by grandma, replaced the one ripped off by the cat. Grandma tried to get it to talk, sometimes spending a full hour at its cage in the window, looking like a big, good-natured animal herself. She would hoarsely repeat to the bird, whose feathers were coal black, "Come, my pretty starling, ask for some food."

With his pert little eyes upon her, he would rap on the thin metal floor of his cage with his wooden leg; thrusting out his neck he would mimic the warble of the finch, the mocking cuckoo call, and even essay the mewing of a cat or the barking of a dog; but human speech was beyond him.

"Stop fooling!" and grandma would be quite serious. "Now say, 'Give birdie some food!' "

Having managed a sound that might be taken for "grandma," the little, black-feathered ape would be fed by the blissfully smiling old woman who said, "I'm on to you, you faker! There's nothing beyond you, you're so clever!"

And she succeeded in imparting to the starling words enough for him to make his wants known; and he delighted grandma by learning to greet her, "Go-od mor-ning, my good woman," in a genteel drawl.

From his first home in grandpa's room, he had been evicted after he had learned to mimic grandpa at his prayers, squawking when grandpa was going through them, "Thou, thee-thee, thou!"

Grandpa lost his temper, and finally he interrupted his prayers to shout, as he stamped with rage, "I'll kill that devil if you don't take him away!"

Much that went on in the house was diverting, but there were times when I was overcome with an inconsolable melancholy. I seemed to be all eaten up by it. The house seemed to be a deep pit from which light and sound and feeling were absent, in which I lived a blind and almost lifeless existence.

Chapter Eight

QUITE SUDDENLY GRANDPA DISPOSED OF THE HOUSE ABOVE THE TAVERN and took another in Kanataroi St.—a sprawling place, with grass up to the walls, but otherwise neat and quiet. The end one of a row of small houses, done in different colors, it seemed to spring right up out of the field.

It was tidy and pretty, our new house. It was painted on the outside in a pleasing shade of raspberry, against which the three lower window shutters and the single, square attic shutter—all done in sky blue—were brightly set off. The roof was picturesquely overhung, on the left side, by big elms and limes. Paths went winding through yard and garden, as intricately as if laid out for games of hide and seek.

Especially lovely was the garden—not large, but with good trees and pleasingly varied. The little bathhouse at one end looked like a toy hut. In another corner was a weedy pit with a chimney protruding, all that was left standing of an older bathhouse. On one side the garden ended at the wall of Count Ostianikov's stables; and, on the other side, at the wall of the Betlenga establishment. The far end adjoined the meadow of the dairy woman, Petrovna, stout—she was shaped like a bell—and loud, and red-faced. Her hut in the hollow was dingy, tumbledown and moss-grown; its two windows seemed to peer amiably at the field, the ravine and the forest, which, at this distance, looked like a dense blue cloud. Soldiers drilled all day in the field, their bayonets catching the slanted autumn rays like white lightning flashes.

The boarders who filled the house seemed to me quite remarkable people. There was a round Tatar soldier and his plump little wife who giggled, clattered noisily, or sang all day long in a high, lilting voice, accompanying herself on an ornate guitar. Her favorite song advised lovers not to lose heart if a girl rejected them, but to seek out another, and the search would be rewarded by one who was not only ready for kisses, but seven times as desirable as the first. At the window sat her rotund husband, his bluish cheeks puffed out, his red eyes dancing waggishly from side to side, his pipe seldom out of his mouth, and emitting an occasional cough and a curious half-bark and giggle that sounded something like "Vukh—Vukh!"

The tenants of the comfortable room above the basement and stable were a moody, long-legged Tatar named Valei, an officer's orderly, and two wagoners, runty, grayish Uncle Peter and his dumb nephew, Stephen, a good-humored chap whose face made me think of a round copper tray. They were all sensations to me, "great unknowns." But I was still more intrigued by a lodger nicknamed "Good Idea" who occupied a long room in the rear adjoining the kitchen. It had two windows, one looking out on the yard, the other on the garden. He was skinny and hunched over; spectacles covered his kind eyes; and his pale face receded into a forked beard. He was shy and laconic. Called in to meals or to tea, he invariably replied, "Good idea." And grandma got to calling him that, even to his face. It would be, "Alex, call Good Idea," or "Good Idea, you haven't touched a thing on your plate."

His room was cluttered and almost walled up with chests and cases full of weighty books that looked odd, though they were in Russian. There were also bottles of vari-colored liquids, and metals in lumps and bars— iron, copper and lead. All the long day, looking disheveled in a reddish leather jacket and smeared and evil-smelling checked trousers, he fused lead, soldered unidentifiable brass objects, weighed bits of things on fragile scales, cried out when he scorched his fingers, and then blew on them, uncomplainingly. Sometimes, with a stumbling gait, he would come up to some tracing pinned up on the wall; polishing his glasses he would eye it very close, as if he were sniffing it, his strange, pale, pointed nose almost touching the paper. Or he would suddenly go immobile in the middle of the room, or before the window, his head up but his eyes closed, as in a trance.

Climbing to the roof of the shed from which I could see into his open window, I would look at the blue flame of his Bunsen burner on the table; and I could watch his shadow-like figure, as he made entries into a crumpled notebook, his spectacles giving off blue glints, like reflections from ice. I was sometimes held absorbed for hours by the seeming sorcery of his activities, my curiosity mounting to an almost agonized tension. There were times when he would go to the window, stand there as if framed, his hands behind his back, his eyes fixed on the roof where I was. Yet he seemed unaware of my presence, and this offended me. Suddenly he would dart back to his table and, almost bent double, would resume his puttering there.

Had he been better dressed and looked rich, I imagine he might have scared me; but I could see the soiled shirt collar above his coat collar, I could see that his pants were smeared and patched; and that the slippers on his bare feet were practically trodden through; I saw that he was poor and there is no danger from the poor. This was an unconscious piece of learning acquired from grandma's pitying consideration for the poor, and grandpa's scorn.

Good Idea had no friends in the house; everybody derided him. The soldier's vivacious little wife called him "Chalk-Nose"; Uncle Peter's name for him was "The Apothecary" or "The Sorcerer"; and grandpa veered between "that Voodoo Man" and "that Free-Mason!"

I asked grandma, "What is he doing?"

"Shush! It's none of your business!"

One day I ventured to his windows, and barely overcoming my agitation, I stammered out, "What do you do?"

He gave a start, stared at me over the rim of his glasses, motioned me up with his hands which were seamed with scars left by burns, and said, "Climb up!"

His bidding me come in through the window, instead of the door, magnified my respect for him. He sat on a crate, had me stand before him, then asked, "Where are you from?"

This was odd, considering that I was his neighbor at the kitchen table four times a day. "I'm the landlord's grandson."

"Ah—so you are," he said, looking down at his hands.

That was all he said and I felt impelled to explain, "But I'm not a Kashirin. My name's Peshkov."

"Peshkov?" he said, wonderingly. "Good idea."

He stood up and went to the table, bidding me, "Sit still."

I sat a long time watching him filing a piece of copper, then putting it in a sort of press from which the filings dropped like golden grains, upon a strip of cardboard. Scooping them into the palm of his hand, he sifted them into a retort, adding a white powder that looked like salt from a bowl, and some liquid from a dark bottle. The mixture at once emitted jets of smoke, angry snorts, and an acrid odor that started me off on a fit of coughing.

"Nasty smell, eh?" said the sorcerer, rather boastfully.

"Yes."

"But that's good. It means that it has turned out right, my lad."

What's he bragging about? I wondered to myself. Aloud I said, "If it's nasty, how could it have turned out right?"

"So? That doesn't follow necessarily," he said. "But—do you play knuckle bones?"

"You mean jacks?"

"Jacks, then?"

"Yes."

"Would you like me to make you a jack?"

"All right."

He came over to me with the steaming retort in his hands into which he peered with one eye, and said, "I'll make you a jack if you'll promise to stay away from me—is that a bargain?"

Deeply offended, I cried out, "You'll never, never see me again!"

Fuming, I went out into the garden where grandpa was puttering about, giving the base of the apple tree its autumn ration of manure. It had already been stripped of its leaves.

Grandpa handed me the shears. "Go prune the raspberry bushes."

"What sort of work does Good Idea do?" I asked him.

"Work! What he's doing is wrecking the room! The floor's scorched; the curtains are ripped and full of stains. I'm going to tell him he'd better move on."

"Yes," I said, as I trimmed the dead twigs off the raspberry bushes. "That's what he ought to do." But I spoke too soon.

On rainy evenings, if grandpa happened to go out, grandma got up jolly little tea parties in the kitchen for the roomers and the neighbors. The wagoners, the orderly, the fat dairy woman, Petrovna, sometimes the Tatar soldier and his lively little wife would come, and Good Idea would show up, take his corner spot by the stove and stay there, without sound or movement. A card game would get underway between the Tatar orderly, Valei, and Dumb Stephen. Valei would rap the deck on the deaf mute's splayed nose and yell, "You deal!"

The wagoner, Uncle Peter, brought a big slab of white bread and a pot of jam and handed generously spread slices around, making a bow as he presented them in the palm of his hand, and saying, "Oblige me!" And when the bread had been picked up, he would inspect his stained hand and proceed to lick off jam drips.

Petrovna's contribution was a flask of cherry brandy; the hearty little soldier's lady passed around candy and nuts. With all this, added to what the dear, stout hostess provided, the jollity would proceed to her satisfaction.

Almost immediately after Good Idea's attempt to bribe me to keep out of his way, grandma held one of these at-homes. Outside there was a chill autumn drizzle, and a howling wind tossed the trees and knocked their boughs against the walls; inside it was warm and genial, and the guests sat close together in cozy amiability, listening to grandma's yarns, each better than the last. She sat on the edge of the oven, with her feet on the ledge, the light of a small tin lamp on her face. This was her chosen position whenever she felt like telling stories. "When I'm looking down," she explained, "the words seem to come out easier."

I took my perch at her feet on the broad ledge which brought me almost on a level with the head of Good Idea. Grandma was reciting the ballad of Ivan the Warrior and Miron the Hermit.

"Once upon a time there was an evil man named Gordion, a black-souled one with no more conscience than a stone, and an enemy of truth. Ah, what suffering he caused, keeping people in chains and torturing others. He was like an owl who falls upon his prey from a hidden perch in a hollow tree. And that's how he lived, his sins covered up. But no one provoked him to such fear and hatred as did Miron the Hermit, beloved by the people, a man who was kindly and peaceful but fierce in defense of the truth.

"Planning death for Miron, Gordion ordered his most trusted warrior, Ivan, to do the killing, though Miron was not only guiltless, but unarmed. Gordion said, 'Ivan, that Miron with the scheming brain shall stand up against me no more. That stiff-necked monk has earned his death. The time has come for him to say his farewell to the world. He has afflicted it long enough. Go take him by his gray bread and bring me the head that has frightened so many cowards. This head, that grudged me my power, shall become meat for my hungry dogs.'

"Obediently Ivan went about that task, but muttering to himself, 'The guilt of this murder won't be on me. I'm only carrying out orders.' But, aloud, he said no word of that, so that nothing should be guessed of what he was about. Coming to the monk he hailed him, hypocritically, 'I rejoice to see you in health. Give me your blessing, father, and may God bless you.'

"The monk answered with a curt laugh, and curt words: 'Hold your lies, Ivan; you can't deceive me. Now you'll understand that God knows everything; and nothing, good or ill, is ever done against His will. You see, I know very well what is your mission here!'

"Shamefaced before the monk stood Ivan, trembling before the man he had come to kill. He pulled out his sword from its leather scabbard and polished the blade till it shone. Then he said, 'I meant to take you by surprise and kill you before you could say your prayers; but now I dare not; now I will leave you time to pray to God, as long as you want, to pray for yourself, for me, for everyone already born and everyone to be; but after that you'll follow the prayers to the place you sent them.'

"The hermit knelt under an oak, and the tree bowed to him. Smiling, he said to the warrior, 'Think it over, Ivan. How long I'll be at my prayers I can't tell. Perhaps you'd better kill me right away, than wait till I weary you and you act in anger.'

"Ivan frowned in annoyance and said, 'I've given you my word. You can take a century but I'll still be here waiting; go on, pray in peace; don't restrain yourself.'

"The shadows of dusk fell on the monk praying; and he prayed through that night and all the next day and night; and through all the golden summer and the bleak winter; and through year after year. And Ivan did not dare to interrupt. The oak sapling became a tree whose branches reached into the sky; while from its acorns an oak forest grew; and still the holy prayer went on; and goes on to this day. Quietly the old man prays to God and the madonna, the Universal Mother, for aid to the men and women who falter, who are weak and in need; for a little happiness to comfort the afflicted.

"And Ivan the Warrior stands at his side. Dust has tarnished his glittering sword; and his armor, rusted to pieces, has fallen from him and left him naked; a coat of mud has taken its place. Heat does not warm him; it only burns. His fate would freeze any heart. Furious wolves and savage bears run when they see him. Snowstorm and frost do not touch him. He has no strength to move from the spot, or to lift his hands, or to speak a word. Let his miserable fate be a warning to us. Let us not make obedience an excuse for sin. When commanded to do evil our duty is to stand firm.

"Still the hermit prays for us sinful ones, still his prayer flows to God, even now, like a flashing, beautiful river flowing down to the sea."

Before grandma came to the end Good Idea was seized with agitation that became quite noticeable. He fidgeted with his hands, put his glasses on and off, or swung them in time with the cadence of the verses, nodding, rubbing his eyes, stroking his brow and his temples as if wiping off sweat. At any one who coughed or creaked in his chair, he hissed, "Sh-h!" and the moment grandma had finished and was drying her damp face on her sleeve, he jumped up, held out his hands as if he were suffering a dizzy spell, and raved, "Marvelous! I tell you, you ought to have it written down. And how true . . . Our . . ."

We all could see now that he was weeping, and with such a welling-up of tears that his eyes were swimming—a startling and touching sight. He made such a ludicrous spectacle pacing, or rather, hopping around, dangling his glasses before his nose, unable in his agitation to fix the ear pieces properly over his ears, that Uncle Peter laughed and everybody else sat stiff in embarrassed silence.

"Write it down if you want to," said grandma, brusquely. "I see no harm in it. I know a lot more of that sort."

"No, only this one," cried Good Idea. "It's so terribly Russian." Stopping dead in the center of the kitchen, he began a loud tirade, his right hand sweeping through the air, his left hand clutching his glasses. He went on for some time, in a frenzy, his voice pitched high in his excitement, stamping his feet and repeating some phrases, especially, " 'When we are commanded to do evil, our duty is to stand firm.' How true!"

There was a sudden crack in his voice; the tirade was cut short; he glanced around him and without another sound, and with his head lowered guiltily, he left the room. The others laughed and exchanged embarrassed glances. Grandma leaned back into the shadows, and we heard her sigh deeply.

Stroking her luscious red lips, Petrovna said, "He seems to be all wrought up."

"Nothing out of the ordinary," said Uncle Peter. "He's always like that." And, as grandma stepped down from the oven to prepare the samovar, he added, "Some the Lord makes that way—freaks."

"Silly bachelors—they're all daft," said Valei censoriously, getting a laugh from the rest. But Uncle Peter said meditatively, "He was really crying."

Their comments irritated me, for the incident had left me with a heartache. His behavior had startled me, but had also touched me. His swimming eyes kept revolving in my mind.

That night he slept away from the house, returning the following night after dinner—subdued and shamefaced. Like a contrite child he said to grandma, "About that scene last night, you're not annoyed with me, are you?"

"Why should I be?"

"Because I interrupted you, and chattered away."

"No one took offense."

But I sensed a certain uneasiness in grandma. She avoided his eyes, spoke in a constrained tone, wasn't herself at all.

He approached close to her and, with astonishing candor, said, "It's my fearful loneliness. I'm so shut up and then, suddenly, my soul erupts as though it had been ripped apart; and then I could talk to stones and trees."

Grandma edged away from him. "Suppose you were to get yourself a wife?" she suggested.

"What?" he exclaimed, his arms flung out in a panic and his face twitching, and he ran out. Grandma aimed a frown after him, took a pinch of snuff and warned me, "Keep away from him, you hear me? God knows what that man is!"

But the attraction I had felt toward him revived. I had seen the change and the dejection in his face when he had mentioned his "fearful loneliness." For those words I had a sympathetic understanding; they touched me to the heart. I sought him out.

Standing in the yard, I looked in at his window. He was out, and the empty room looked like a cellar where unwanted stuff had been tossed in—unwanted and bizarre like its tenant. I went on into the garden and there he was, at the edge of the pit. From an uncomfortable seat on the tip of a half-burnt plank, he was bending over, his elbows on his knees and his hands behind his head. The better part of the plank was imbedded in earth, and this end, gleaming like coal, protruded out of the pit, which was all overgrown with briars.

Somehow the very discomfort of his position was a point in his favor to me. He did not seem to see me, looking beyond me with his half-blind, owlish eyes; then suddenly, in a fretful voice, he asked me, "Is there anything you want me for?"

"No."

"Then what are you doing here?"

"I don't know."

He took off his glasses, wiped them with his red and black polka dot handkerchief, and called me over, "All right, climb up."

When I was perched beside him, he put his arm around me, gave me a squeeze and said, "Settle down. Let's sit still and be quiet. Is that all right with you? It's all the same . . . Are you a stubborn one?"

"Yes."

"Good idea."

A long silence. The evening was still and mild, one of those brooding, late summer evenings when, in the midst of the still abundant flowering, there are forewarnings of dissolution, when every hour leaves the earth a little poorer; and, its riotous summer fragrances gone, exhales only a cool dampness; when the air is weirdly translucent and the aimless flights of daws across the reddened sky make one melancholy. In the reigning silence the slightest sound, like the beating of a bird's wings or the rustle of falling leaves, is enough to make one start and shudder; but the shudder itself ebbs quickly into the stagnant stillness which appears to cover the earth and bind the heart in a spell. In such moments perceptions of a rare purity arise, transparent and insubstantial as a cobweb, eluding expression in words. They are evanescent, like falling stars, and sorrow is kindled in the soul, soothing and disquieting at the same time; and the malleable soul takes on, in the melancholy heat, enduring impressions.

Warmed by his body to which I snuggled close, I peered with him through the black apple branches at the darkening red sky, followed the slow flights of the jackdaws, watched the withered poppy heads on their stems shaking out seeds in every stir of wind; and I gazed at the purpling clouds, whose livid, ragged edges dipped over the fields, and at the weary, low-flying rooks on their way to their nests in the cemetery.

It was entrancing, and particularly so that evening, with my feelings so attuned. Now and then, with a deep sigh, my companion would say, "This is it, eh, boy? You don't feel any dampness or a chill?"

Then, as the sky clouded over and the dewy dusk blanketed everything, he said, "It's no use. We'll have to go in." And at the garden gate, he stopped briefly to say in a low voice, "Your grandma's a wonderful woman, a pearl!" And with his eyes shut, but a smile on his lips, he repeated quietly, but distinctly, " 'Let his miserable fate be a warning to us. Let us not make obedience an excuse for sin. When we are commanded to do evil our duty is to stand firm!' " and added, "Keep that in mind, boy." And, as he sent me in ahead of him, he asked, "Do you know how to write?"

"No."

"Learn it, my boy, so you can write down your grandma's stories. It'll prove worthwhile, my boy."

And so our friendship began; and from then on, whenever the inclination took me, I visited Good Idea. Perched on a crate or a heap of rags I watched him smelt lead and fire copper to a red heat and shape sheets of iron over a little anvil, using a tap-hammer with an ornamented handle; or a fine-toothed file or an emery saw that had a blade like a taut thread; or weighing articles—and he weighed everything—on his sensitive copper balance. After he had filled the retorts he would wait until an acrid smoke rose and filled the room; then his face would wrinkle and he would probe through a heavy tome, chewing his lips or huskily humming, "Rose of Sharon."

"What're you doing now?"

"Making something, boy."

"What?"

"It's hard to explain it to you; you couldn't understand."

"Grandpa says it wouldn't surprise him if you were a counterfeiter."

"Your grandpa says that? So? He just says that to have something to say. My boy, money's a delusion."

"Could we get bread without it?"

"Of course we have to have money for that."

"And meat, too."

"Right, for meat, too."

With a forbearance that astonished me, he smiled and tweaked my ear, and said, "It's no go debating with you; you win every point. I better keep my mouth shut."

At times he quit work and, with me at his side, stared out of the window, watching the rain drumming down on the roof, noted how the grass was overgrowing the yard, how leafless the apple trees were getting. Good Idea was sparing of words, but they were to the point. When he wanted to call my attention to something he would let a nudge or a wink serve rather than words. I had never found much in the yard to attract me, but his proddings and laconic words changed its appearance for me until everything to be seen in it acquired interest.

A playful kitten might stop before a pool, and seeing its reflection, lift its little paw as though to rap it. "Cats," observed Good Idea, "are self-centered and suspicious." Or the russet-gold rooster Mamai, hopping up on the hedge, would spread out his wings only to unbalance himself, nearly fall, and in annoyance, thrust his neck out and sputter with anger. "There's a general for you," Good Idea would say, "and not overburdened with brains." Or clumsy Valei would cross the yard, plodding through the mud like a tired horse. His high-cheekboned face looked bloated as he blinked at the sky, whose pale autumn light fell in straight rays on his chest, glinting on his brass coat-buttons. Stopping still, the Tatar fondled them with his hooked fingers. "As if," remarked Good Idea, "they were military medals he had won."

My affection for Good Idea grew stronger day by day and I found his company equally necessary to me in times of hurt or grief, and in times of joy. Taciturn himself, he never checked me, letting me voice anything that came to mind; whereas grandpa always stopped me with his brusque, "Stop chattering, you mill of Satan!"

Grandma was not a good listener either, being too full of her own notions; but Good Idea paid careful attention to everything I said, merely stopping me sometimes with a smile, to say, "That's not so, my boy; you made that up." These terse comments were always interjected at the proper moments. He seemed to have the power to penetrate the outer coating of heart and mind and see within, so that he could halt futile or misunderstanding words before they reached my lips—driving them back with a gentle blow, "Not true, my boy."

To test this sorcerer-like perception I would sometimes fabricate and narrate my fabrication as an actual occurrence; but before I had finished, he would interrupt, "Not true, my boy," and shake his head.

"How did you know?"

"I can sense it, my boy."

When grandma went to haul fresh water from the pump on Sienia Square she would take me along. On one of these trips we saw five townsmen beating up a peasant. They knocked him down, trampled him, and dragged him as dogs might drag another dog. Ordering me to "Run away," grandma dropped her pails and used the yoke on which they hung upon the assailants.

I didn't dare leave her and did my bit by firing pebbles and stones at the men while she went at their heads and shoulders with the yoke. Other people came up and the men took to their heels, and grandma tended to the victim. He had been kicked in the face and it was sickening to see him hold to his torn nostrils muddy fingers through which blood spurted into grandma's face and breast, along with retching groans and coughs. Grandma, herself, could not repress an outcry of horror and a fit of convulsive trembling.

As soon as we were home I hurried to tell Good Idea. He stopped his work, gave me a pained and concerned look from beneath his glasses, and cut me short with a gravely spoken, "Fine doings, those, fine doings!"

I was so engrossed by what I had seen that I did not understand the intent of his gestures and his words, and went on with my story. He put an arm around me, then broke away and began agitatedly pacing the room. "Enough," he said. "I don't care to hear any more. You've told me all that's necessary, boy, understand?"

I was hurt and gave no reply. Thinking it over afterwards, I realized, and I can still remember how startled I was by the realization, that he had stopped me at exactly the right moment, when, in fact, I had already told all there was. "Don't dwell on it, my boy," he told me. "It's not a good thing to keep in the mind."

Some of his remarks, made impromptu, have clung in my memory. I remember telling him about my adversary, Kliushnikov, from New Street, a big-headed, fat boy. Neither he nor I could get the better of the other. Good Idea, listening concernedly to my troubles, said, "Nonsense; his sort of strength is of no account; real strength is in movement; the swifter is the stronger. Understand?"

And in my next encounter with Kliushnikov I had that in mind, relied on agility and had an easy victory; and after this, I listened with added respect to Good Idea's remarks.

"Learn to really get hold of things, understand? It's not easy to learn how to get a real hold on things." I did not understand this at all, but, unconsciously I kept this in mind, together with other of his sayings, because there was something intriguing in its mystifying simplicity. It did not seem to call for any extraordinary wisdom to get a real hold upon a stone, or a slice of bread, or a cup or a hammer.

Among the others, however, the dislike of Good Idea steadily grew. Even the jolly lady's companionable cat would not as readily hop on his knee as on others, and would not come to his kind-voiced call. That got her a spanking and a tweak of her ears from me; almost weeping, I ordered her not to avoid him.

"It's because of the acids in my clothes," he explained. "She doesn't like the odor." But everybody else, even grandpa, gave other explanations—false, unkind and hurtful to him.

"What are you hanging around him for?" grandma would demand irritably. "What he has to teach you is bad—you'll see!" And I got a savage smack from grandpa whenever he saw me return from a visit to Good Idea, who, he was positive, was up to no good.

Of course I kept it from Good Idea that I had been forbidden his friendship; but I let him know what they were saying about him in the house. "Grandma's scared of you. She says you practice black magic. And grandpa says you're an enemy of God and it's a risk having you here."

Then his hand would hover about his head as if he were waving off flies; and a sad smile would flush over his chalk-white face, and my heart would contract and a haze would seem to form around my eyes.

"I see," he would say meekly. "What a pity, eh?"

"Yes."

"Yes, it's a pity, my boy."

At last he received an eviction notice. On one of my customary, after-breakfast visits to him I found him on the floor packing his stuff in crates, and humming "Rose of Sharon." "It's good-by, my friend," he told me, "I'm leaving."

"Why?"

After a long fixed look at me he said, "Can it be that you don't know? They want my room for your mother."

"Who said that?"

"Your grandfather."

"He lied."

Good Idea drew me toward him and, as I sat beside him on the floor, said gently, "Don't let it upset you; I thought you knew and wouldn't tell me; and I felt disappointed in you." And that explained his preoccupied and vexed manner toward me. "Remember," he went on, in a voice barely above a whisper, "when I asked you to keep away from me?"

I nodded.

"You were hurt, weren't you?"

"Yes."

"But I didn't mean to hurt you, child. I realized, you see, that friendship with me would make trouble for you with your folks. And isn't it so? Now you can see why I did it."

All this was spoken as if he were a child my own age, and this gave me an almost delirious joy. It seemed to me I had known this all along and I said so. "I realized that a long time ago."

"Well, that's that. It's happened just as I said, little dove."

The ache I felt in my heart was almost more than I could bear. "Why are they all against you?"

He put his arm around me and drew me to him, and said, with twitching eyes, "I'm not their kind—don't you see? That's the trouble. I'm not as they are."

I just pressed his hand, knowing nothing to say, unable, indeed, to say anything.

"Don't let yourself get upset," he repeated, and bending to my ear, whispered, "And no crying, either," while his own tears were running down beneath his splashed glasses.

Then, as we always did, we sat in a prolonged silence, broken at intervals by a word or two. That evening he left, bidding everybody a gracious farewell and hugging me fondly. I went with him to the gate, to watch him jolted away, as the cart bounced over ridges of frozen mud.

Grandma lost no time cleaning and scrubbing the mess in the room, and I purposely walked in her way. "Get out!" she exclaimed, as she stumbled over me.

"Tell me why you sent him away."

"Keep out of matters you can't understand."

"You're all fools," I said, "all of you."

She smacked me with an end of the wet mop and exclaimed, "Are you out of your mind, you little beast!"

"I didn't mean you, I meant the others," I said, to pacify her; but her anger held.

At the evening meal grandpa said, "Thank God, he's out. It wouldn't have surprised me, seeing what I saw, to have found him one day with a knife in his ribs. Ekh! Good riddance!"

In retaliation I broke a spoon; and then returned to the morose indifference I had become accustomed to. Thus ended the first of a chain
of friendships with the best people of my land.

Chapter Nine

I SEE MY CHILDHOOD AS A HIVE TO WHICH, AS BEES BRING THEIR HONEY,
various plain, inconspicuous people came to me with their understanding and impressions of life, a contribution of great spiritual riches.
Sometimes the honey was muddy, sometimes it had a bitter strain, but
always it was a combination of wisdom, and, therefore, honey to me.

Peter, the carter, took the place of the departed Good Idea. He resembled grandpa in his wizened appearance and neat habits, but was
even shorter and in every way a smaller man. He gave the impression
of a youth who had not yet reached full development, masquerading as
an old man. The delicate creases in his skin made his face look like a
piece of fine-grained leather, and his quick, humorous, yellowish-white
eyes skipped among these wrinkles like finches in a cage. His graying
hair, once raven-black, was curled; his beard, too, was all curls; and the
smoke from his pipe, of the same color as his hair, uncoiled in similar
ringlets. He had a flamboyant way of speaking, studded with quaint
sayings, and spoken with a rapid voice. Despite his frequently genial
mood, I felt that he was ribbing everybody.

"The first time I came to the lady, that Countess Tatiana, she said
to me, 'You'll be the blacksmith.' But then I'm sent out to assist the
gardener. I don't mind, really, but I didn't hire out as a laborer, and it's
not right to make me. Later, it's 'Peter, you'll have to catch us some
fresh fish.' All one to me, fisherman or gardener, but I decided to bid
the fish 'good-by, my dears' and came to town as a carter, and here I
am. I haven't profited by the change as yet; my only property is the
horse, which brings my countess back to mind."

This aged horse of his had started life white; but once a drunken
painter had begun to do him in other colors and had left off in the
middle. Its legs looked as if they had been broken and set wrong; and
it could be best described as rags sewn together in the rough shape of a
horse. The gaunt head, with its dim, downcast eyes, was precariously

attached to the cadaver by swollen veins and aged, worn skin. Uncle Peter tended this creature, whom he had named Tanka,[15] with great respect.

"What did you give the beast a Christian name for?" grandpa once asked.

"Nothing of the sort, Basil," replied Peter. "In all humility I say it. There's no Christian name such as 'Tanka,' though there is a Christian name 'Tatiana.'"

Uncle Peter had had some education and had done some reading. He and grandpa had arguments over the comparative sanctity of the saints; and together they sat in judgment, each more Draconian than the other, on the sinners of history. Most harshly dealt with, of all classic sinners, was Absalom. Sometimes the argument took a grammatical turn, grandpa insisting that the proper ending for certain prayer words was *khom* and Uncle Peter insisting that it was *sha*.

"So I say it my way and you say it another," grandpa would shout, his face livid with anger, and wound up jeering, "Vasha! Shisha!"

And Uncle Peter, behind his curls of smoke, asked provocatively, "And what use are all your *khoms*; think God gives a hoot for them? God listens to our prayers and says, 'Pray any way you like.'"

Peter was a very tidy little man. When he went into the yard he'd scrape aside with his shoe any wood-shavings, or broken glass, or old bones on the path, remarking caustically, "This serves no purpose; it's only in the way."

Generally an easy-going, cheerful, loquacious sort, he would sometimes slink into a corner and sit there, hunched up, as mute and torpid as his nephew, while his eyes turned bloodshot and set into a stare as fixed and empty as that of a corpse.

"What's the trouble, Uncle Peter?"

"Leave me alone," he would reply, morosely.

A neighbor of ours, a man with a warty forehead, had this eccentricity: on Sundays he sat at his window with a shotgun and fired at dogs, cats, chickens, rooks, whatever came within range, that happened to displease him. Once Good Idea became his target. The pellets didn't go through the leather of his coat and some dropped into his pocket. I'll never forget his absorbed expression as he looked at the little, bluish balls. Grandpa tried to work him up into filing a complaint, but he threw the little balls in a corner, saying, "Not worth the trouble." When the marksman, however, put some shot in grandpa's leg, his career on our

---

[15] A diminutive for Tatiana.

block was over; grandpa got other victims and witnesses on the street to sign a petition to the authorities, and nothing further had to be done; the dead-shot disappeared.

But Uncle Peter, whenever he was home, and the gun began popping, would toss on his shiny Sunday cap, with the dangling earlaps, over his iron-gray skull, and rush to the gate. There he would fit his hands under his coat-tails so that he could shake them like a rooster; and would then parade almost up to the marksman's window, and back, over and over again. Watching at the gate we could see the purpling face of the marksman and the blond head of his wife over his shoulder, and the people of the Betlenga establishment at the gate of their yard— only the gray, inanimate façade of the Ovsianikov mansion took no interest.

Sometimes, Uncle Peter paraded in vain, the hunter seeming to disdain such game as unworthy of his marksmanship; but sometimes, thoroughly provoked, he would fire volley after volley in fury. Boom, boom! went the double-barreled gun while Uncle Peter, without quickening his pace, would come to report, delightedly, "Every shot went wild!"

Once, however, he got some pellets in his shoulder and neck and, while grandma was probing them out with a needle, she lectured him, "Why must you encourage that animal? One of these days he'll blind you!"

"No chance, Akulina," said Uncle Peter, with a contemptuous drawl. "He can't shoot."

"But why encourage him?"

"Encourage him! I get fun teasing that gentleman." Glancing at the extracted pellets in his hand he went on. "He's no shot at all . . . But at my lady's, the Countess Tatiana's place, there was a real officer, Marmont Ilyich. Matrimonial occupations took up most of her time—husbands were just a sort of footman to her; she kept them on duty around her. Now there was a marksman for you! Only he used bullets; he wouldn't fire anything else. He'd tie a bottle to the belt of Ignatz, the Idiot, and stand him forty paces off, or so, and with Ignatz standing there, with his idiotic grin, his legs apart and the bottle dangling between them, Marmont Ilyich took aim—bang!—and the bottle dropped to pieces. Only once, Ignatz had the misfortune to have a gadfly or something crawl into his grinning mouth; and he moved and the bullet got him in the knee, right in the kneecap. The doctor came out and cut the leg off—it took a minute in all—and they buried the leg."

"What happened to the idiot?"

"Did him no harm. Legs and arms aren't so necessary to an idiot. It's his idiocy brings him his food and drink—and more than enough. Who doesn't love an idiot? They do no harm. You know what they say: 'The more fools the lower classes are, the better; they can do less harm.' "

Such talk didn't startle grandma; she had heard enough of it; but it made me uneasy. I asked Uncle Peter, "Couldn't that gentleman kill somebody?"

"Of course—why not? Once he fought a duel. A Uhlan paid Tatiana a visit, and Marmont and the Uhlan got into a quarrel. Right away they had their pistols in their hands and they went out into the park and on the path to the pond they stopped and banged away at each other, and the Uhlan plugged Marmont right through the liver. They sent Marmont to the cemetery, and the Uhlan to the Caucasus—and the whole business blew over in no time. That's how they managed for themselves. The peasants and the others there don't even talk about him. They don't miss him; not for himself, anyway. But they did feel sorry— about the property."

"Not much," said grandma.

"That's so. His property wasn't worth much, either."

Toward me Peter was well disposed, spoke affably, looking me in the face, as if I were a grownup; nevertheless something about him made me uncomfortable. But he gave me jam; and whatever was left on the knife he would spread again on my bread; and he'd bring me cookies from the market; and in his conversation with me his manner was never patronizing.

"Well, young gentleman," he asked me, "what are you aiming to do when you grow up—the Army or the Civil Service?"

"The Army."

"Fine! Nowadays a soldier doesn't have a hard time of it. A priest has it easy, too . . . a bit of chanting and praying to God . . . doesn't take up too much time . . . I'd even say a priest has it easier than a soldier . . . But a fisherman's job's the lightest of all. You get into the habit—and that's your apprenticeship."

He went into an amazing piece of mimicry—a fish warily approaching the bait; and then the different ways different kinds of fish have, when caught, of trying to get off the hook.

"Why get into a temper when your grandfather gives you a whipping?" he would say, to mollify me. "There's no point to it, young gentleman; whipping goes with education. And the whippings you get

aren't anything. You should have seen my lady, Tatiana, having somebody flogged. She had it done right! She had a man named Christopher,
just for that work; and he was good at it. Sometimes neighboring gen-
tlefolk would send to the countess, 'Please send Christopher over to
whip the footman.' And she'd always oblige them."

Then followed a description, in artless detail, of how the countess,
in a white muslin gown, and a lacy, sky-blue handkerchief over her
head, would sit in a red armchair on the porch, beside a pillar, watching Christopher flog the serfs, men and women.

"This Christopher came from Ryazan and he looked like a Gypsy or
a Ukrainian, and his moustaches stuck out beyond his ears, and he'd
shaved off his beard, leaving his face blue. He might have been, or he
just made believe he was, a fool, so as not to have to bother answering
questions. He used to catch flies and cockroaches, which are a sort of
beetle, in a cup of water and put them on the fire to boil."

Of that sort of story I had had my fill, from both grandpa and
grandma. However else they differed, they had one common trait—
somebody being tormented or humiliated or cast out. Wanting no more
of them I asked the carter, "Tell me a different sort of story."

His wrinkles would seem to run together around his mouth, then
radiate toward his eyes, and he said, indulgently, "A greedy one you
are, all right. Well, once we had a cook——"

"Who had a cook?"

"The Countess Tatian."

"Why do you say Tatian instead of Tatiana? Was she a man, then?"

A piping laugh. "Of course not. She was a lady, but she had whiskers,
too. She was dark-colored—came of a dark breed of foreigners—they're
a Negro type of people. So, as I was telling you, this cook—this is a
funny one, young gentleman."

And in this "funny one" the cook spoiled a fish course and was forced
to eat it all as his punishment, and had taken violently ill.

"That's not funny," I complained.

"Well, what's your idea of something funny? What do you think is
funny, eh?"

"I can't say."

"Then shut your mouth!" and he would start on another dreary yarn.

On some Sundays or holidays my cousins paid us a visit, Uncle Mike's
indolent and moody Sascha and Uncle Jake's neat know-it-all Sascha.
On one of these visits we climbed up on the roof, and from there, look-

ing into the Betlenga yard, we saw some puppies and, seated on a wood-pile against the wall, a gentleman playing with them. He was dressed in a green coat, trimmed with fur, but his head was bare, and it was little and yellow and bald. One of the Saschas proposed that we steal a puppy, and they soon had it all schemed out. They were to go down to the Betlenga yard gate and wait there till I did something to distract the gentleman, when they would dash in and make off with one of the puppies.

"But what'll I do to distract him?"

"Spit on his bald spot," was the proposal.

Wasn't it a sin to spit on a person's head? But how often I had heard and, myself seen, far worse things done! So I carried out my part of the venture—and with my customary luck.

There was an immediate commotion. A virtual army of men and women, led by a handsome young officer, charged from the Betlenga mansion into our yard. Since, at the moment of the outrage, my two cousins were promenading innocently down the street and denied any knowledge of the crime, I alone caught the whipping which mollified the Betlenga-ites.

Lying in the kitchen, aching all over, I received a visit from Uncle Peter, all dressed up and looking very chipper. "A bully idea that was, young gentleman," he confided. "Just what that goat of a silly old man deserves—to be spat on! Next time break his filthy head with a rock!"

I could see, again, the blank, shaven, childlike face of the gentleman, and I recalled his feeble, outraged squeal, so like that of his puppies, as his little hand went to his yellowish pate; and I was overcome with remorse and resentment toward my cousins. But all this vanished as I looked at the carter's seamed face, twitching with the same mixed expression of revulsion and anxiety that I saw in grandpa's face when he flogged me.

Kicking and striking out at him I screamed, "Go away!" He went out, tittering and winking at me.

From then on I lost all taste for his company and I avoided him. But I kept a watch on his movements, vaguely suspecting him.

Another disagreeable occurrence followed soon after the Betlenga House affair. I had long been intrigued by the Ovsianikov mansion whose gray façade, in my fancy, concealed something romantic and mysterious.

The Betlenga establishment was lovely and gay. Its tenants were lovely ladies who had many visitors, officers and students. Consequently

it was an unending source of music, singing and laughter. With its sparkling clean windows, the house itself seemed to have a fresh and merry
face.

But grandpa saw nothing good in it, and its occupants, he said, were
all "heretics, people without God!" particularly the ladies, to whom he
gave a vile name which Uncle Peter defined for me in terms as vile.

For the gloomy, silent Ovsianikov mansion, however, grandpa was
all reverence. This one-story, yet impressively high, building stood on
a well-tended lawn, bare except for a well in the center, which had a
roof supported by two posts. As if it sought seclusion, the structure
seemed to retire from the street. Two of its three windows had carved,
arched frames, set rather high in the wall, upon whose grimy panes the
sun, as it fell, struck off oily rainbows. A storehouse, a replica of the
mansion, except that its windows were not real and their simulated
sashes and frames were outlined in white paint, stood opposite the mansion, with the gateway in between. The blind windows had a sinister
look, and the storehouse reinforced the general Ovsianikov impression
of looking for cover and isolation. Everything about the establishment
suggested disdainful withdrawal down to the noiseless stable, and the
vacant coach-shed with its wide doors.

A tall old man without a beard, but with a moustache whose bristles
stood out like needles, was sometimes seen hobbling around the yard.
Sometimes another old man, bearded and hook-nosed and lame, limped
from the stable leading out a gray, long-necked mare, a hollow-chested,
thin-legged beast whose bowing and scraping, when she was brought out
into the yard, made her resemble a begging nun. The lame groom
slapped his palms over her side, whistled and loudly sucked in his
breath; and then the mare was again sent into her cell in the dim stable.
In my fancies the lame old groom meant to run away but he was bewitched and couldn't.

Almost every afternoon three boys came out to play in the yard.
They were all dressed alike, in gray coats and trousers, and identical caps;
and all were round-cheeked and gray-eyed, and so closely resembled each
other that I, watching them through a crack in the fence, could tell
them apart only by their height. I looked on, unseen, but yearning to
make them aware, in some way, of my presence. Their games were unfamiliar to me, but I liked them for the gay and amiable spirit in which
they were played. Their clothes seemed attractive to me, too, and I
admired them for their consideration toward each other, particularly
marked in the attitude of the older boys to the youngest, a lively, com-

ical little chap. They laughed at his falls—it being a universal reaction to laugh at anyone who trips—but there was no gloating in the laughter and they hurried over to help him up; and if he had soiled his hands or knees they wiped him off with their handkerchiefs or leaves, and the middle-sized boy would scold, good-naturedly, "Now, clumsy!" I never saw them wrangle or take advantage of each other. They were all strong lads, nimble and tireless.

Climbing up a tree one day, I whistled to them. They stopped, looked at me, then came together in a huddle. Imagining that they were going to stone me, I dropped down for ammunition. With my pockets and the front of my blouse bulging with stones, I climbed back to my perch, but they had gone off to a far corner of the yard, where they played as if they had forgotten I was there. This experience ended in two disappointments: I didn't want to be the one to start a fight with them; and at that moment they were summoned from a window, "Time to come in now, children." And obediently, but unhurried, they went in, one behind the other, like geese.

Again and again I took that post in the tree overhanging the fence, in the hope that they would invite me to play with them; but the invitation never came. In my mind, however, I always joined in their games, and with such absorption that I would sometimes laugh or cry out, and that would again, after a look at me, bring them together in a huddle, while I, embarrassed, would scramble down and out of sight.

In a game of hide and seek one day, the middle brother was "it." Dutifully shutting his eyes, he stood in the corner counting, while his brothers hid. The agile oldest brother climbed speedily into a rickety sleigh that stood in a shed alongside the storehouse; but the youngest kept stumbling around the well, unable to find a hiding place. Suddenly, as the counting was coming to an end, he climbed up the well and into the bucket, which, making just one muffled sound as it scraped the side of the well, immediately descended out of sight. I was paralyzed to see with what speed and how soundlessly the well-oiled wheel spun around; but, immediately recovering myself, I jumped into their yard, crying, "He fell in the well!"

The middle brother and I got to the well at the same instant. He grabbed the rope, but finding himself being yanked up, let go. I caught the rope just in time and the older brother, arriving at that moment, helped me pull up the bucket, saying anxiously, "Careful, please."

In a minute we had the little fellow up and out. He was thoroughly scared. His right hand was bleeding a little, and a cheek was rather badly scraped. Wet to the waist, the chill put a bluish pallor on his face. But he smiled, shivered, shut his eyes tight, smiled again, and asked, in a chattering voice, "How d-did I f-fall?"

"That was a crazy thing to do!" said the middle brother, wiping the boy's bleeding face and clasping him around. The oldest brother frowned and said, "We'd better go in. We couldn't hide this, anyway."

"Will you get a whipping?" I asked.

He nodded, then held out his hand to me. "You were so quick!" he said.

I was pleased at his compliment, but before I could take his hand, he had turned to his brothers. "We'd better go right in or he'll catch a cold. We'll say he fell; let's not say anything about the well."

"No," said the youngest, shivering. "Let's say I fell in a puddle, right?" And they went in.

All this had taken so little time that when I turned back to the tree, the branch I had jumped down from was still swaying and yellow leaves were fluttering down from it.

I didn't see the brothers again for about a week; but when they came back it was with greater zest than before. Seeing me in the tree, the oldest brother called out, "Come down and play with us."

We sat together in the old sleigh in the shelter of the overhanging storehouse roof, looked each other over, and had a long talk.

"Did you get a whipping?" I asked.

"I should say!"

I found it hard to believe that such boys were whipped just as I was, and I felt indignant in their behalf.

"Why do you snare birds?" the youngest asked me.

"I like to hear them sing," I replied.

"It's not right to snare them; why shouldn't they be allowed to fly around, free?"

"I don't want to, that's why," I said, stubbornly.

"Will you catch one for me?"

"For you? What kind?"

"One that hops around in the cage."

"A finch is what you want."

"The cat would kill it; and anyway, papa wouldn't allow it."

"No, he wouldn't," agreed the oldest brother.

"Have you got a mother?" I asked.

The oldest said "no," but the middle one said, "We have, only she's not really ours; ours died."

"And the other's called a stepmother?" I asked. "Yes," and the oldest brother nodded.

The faces of all three darkened into a brooding look. From grandma's stories I knew what stepmothers were like, and I knew the meaning of the boys' preoccupied look. There they were, huddled together, looking as like each other as peas in a pod; and I thought of the witch who had become a stepmother, supplanting the real mother, by a spell.

"You'll get your real mother back," I assured them, "You'll see."

The oldest one said, with a shrug, "Such things can't happen. How can they when she's dead?"

"Can't happen? But lots and lots of dead people, even when they've been cut in pieces, have come alive when they're sprinkled with the water of life. And over and over again, death hasn't come from God, and isn't real, but an enchantment by a sorcerer or a witch."

With excited haste I began telling some of grandma's stories. At first the oldest laughed at them, "Fairy tales! We know all about that!"

But the others listened, absorbed; the smallest one with pursed lips, the middle one with his elbows on his knees, holding his brother's hand which was around his shoulder.

Evening was approaching, and the clouds over the roof had turned red, when suddenly the old man with the spiky moustache stood beside us. His cinnamon-colored cloak was long, like a priest's, and he had on a shaggy fur cap.

"And who may he be?" he asked, pointing at me.

The oldest boy, standing up, nodded toward grandpa's house, "He's from there."

"Who invited him?"

The boys climbed down the sleigh, in silence, and trooped into their house, giving me a still stronger impression of a flock of geese.

With a hand that closed on my shoulder like a vise, the old man gripped me and pushed me before him, over the yard to the gate. I would have cried out in terror but his strides were so long and rapid, that before an outcry could escape from me, I was out in the street and he was standing at the gate, shaking a warning finger at me, "Don't you ever come near me again!"

Enraged, myself, I shouted, "I never wanted to come near you, you old devil!"

Once more the long arm shot out and I was hauled over the pavement, while his voice struck like a hammer on my skull, "Is your grandfather home?"

Unluckily for me, he was; and with his head back and his beard projecting outward he looked into the bulbous, dim, fish-eyes of the menacing old man, and explained, agitatedly, "You see, his mother's away; and I'm busy, and there's nobody to see what he's up to; won't you overlook it this time, Colonel?"

The colonel paced about the room, raving like a lunatic. Then, almost before he was gone, I had got my beating and been flung into Peter's cart. "In disgrace again, young gentleman?" the carter remarked, unharnessing his horse. "What about, this time?"

When he heard he rasped indignantly, "And what do you want to make their friendship for? The little snakes! This is what it got you! Now, you can get even and tell on them; that's what you ought to do."

He went on in this way for a long time; and at first, aching from my beating, I was inclined toward his suggestions of revenge; but the way he wagged his wrinkled face became more and more repulsive to me; I reminded myself that the boys would also get whippings, and with no more cause than I.

"They shouldn't get a beating," I cried out. "They're good kids; and what you're saying, every word's a lie!"

He gave me a mean look and ordered me, suddenly, out of his cart. As I jumped out I yelled "Fool!" at him.

He chased me, unsuccessfully, around the yard, screeching, "So! I'm a fool! So, I tell lies! Wait till I catch you!"

Grandma popped out of the kitchen and I ran to her.

"I get no peace with this little scamp! Old as I am he has the gall to curse at me . . . to insult my mother and everybody."

Stupefied by this brazen lie, all I could do was stand and gape at him. But grandma gave it to him. "You're lying now, Peter, that's clear. He'd never curse you or anybody." Grandpa would have believed the carter.

From then on there was a tacit, but implacable, war between us. In manipulating his reins he would try to flick me with them, without seeming to. He set my bird cages open, and some of my birds were caught and devoured by the cat. And he found occasion after occasion to tattle on me to grandpa, who believed everything. My first impression of him, as a boy no older than I in the guise of an old man, was confirmed.

On my part I unraveled his bast shoes; that is, I ripped them inside a little way, so that they began to go to pieces on the way. One day some pepper I shook into his cap set him off on a fit of the sneezes that lasted all of an hour, and he nearly lost the day's work.

On Sundays, especially, he kept watch on me, and more than once caught me in the forbidden act of meeting the Ovsianikov boys—and ran off to tell grandpa. Yet this dangerous acquaintance with the boys prospered and gave me increasing gratification. There was a little winding footpath between our house and the Ovsianikovs' fence. It was overgrown with elms, linden trees and elderberry bushes. Under their shade, as cover, I cut a hole through the fence; and the brothers visited me in turn, or sometimes two at a time. Crouched about that hole we held long conversations, in muted voices, while one of the brothers kept watch to prevent our being surprised by the colonel.

I learned what a miserable existence they led, and was sorry for them. We talked about my caged birds, and other boys' concerns, but I do not recall hearing a word from them about their father or stepmother. More often than not they wanted a story, and, as precisely as I could, I repeated grandma's; and if I was uncertain about a detail, I had them wait, while I went to her to get it right. Grandma was always pleased.

They heard much from me about grandma, and once the oldest brother commented, with an envious sigh, "It seems your grandmother is good in every way. We used to have a good grandmother, too."

Reminiscing sadly, like this, about the past, he could sound like a centenarian and not an eleven-year-old boy. I remember his hands as being slender, with fine, delicate fingers, and his eyes as having a gentle glow, like church lamps. His brothers were also lovable boys, whom you felt you could trust and for whom you wanted to do favors; but I liked the oldest best.

Our conversations so absorbed me that once Peter was right upon me before I noticed him; and his exclamation, "Again!" sent us all flying.

I observed that Peter was becoming moodier and less talkative, and I soon could tell, at a glance, what his mood was from the way he returned from work. When he was feeling right, the gate creaked open with a long, lazy sound; but when he came in, feeling out of sorts, there was a quick, sharp squeal from the hinges, as if in pain.

His dumb nephew had married and gone off to the country with his wife and Peter was now alone in the stable, in a low stall with a broken window that had a foul mixture of smells—leather, tar, sweat and tobacco—enough, by itself, to keep me away. It had become his habit to keep the lamp burning when he went to sleep, to which grandpa violently objected, "You'll burn me out, yet!"

"No, I won't," he would reply. "Don't let it worry you. I set the lamp in a pan of water." As he said it he gave us a sidelong glance. He seemed to look at everybody sidelong, now. And for a long time he had been absent from grandma's evenings, he and his jam pot. His face seemed to be shriveling up, each wrinkle deepening, and his walk had become dragging and uncertain, like that of an invalid.

One mid-week morning after a night of heavy snow, grandpa and I were clearing a path in the yard, when, suddenly, the gate banged and a policeman entered, shutting the gate behind him by leaning his weight against it. Having eased himself there, he raised a fat, gray forefinger and beckoned grandpa over.

When grandpa stood before him he bent down till his pointed nose seemed to be engraving something on grandpa's brow, and spoke in a voice so low I couldn't hear the words.

Grandpa started and exclaimed, "Here? Good God! When?" And then, hopping grotesquely, he cried out, "Bless the dear Lord! Can that be possible?"

"Pipe down!" warned the policeman.

Looking around grandpa saw me and ordered, "Put the shovel down and go inside."

I hid in a corner and saw them go into the carter's stall. I saw the policeman pull the glove off one hand and slap it on the palm of the other, and heard him say, "He knows we're on his tail. He's left the horse wandering in the street and he's hiding out here, somewhere."

I ran into the kitchen to tell grandma. She was preparing dough for bread, and her flour-dusted head bobbed rhythmically to her movements as she listened to me without excitement, and remarked matter-of-factly, "He's probably stolen something. Run along now. What business is it of yours?"

When I went back into the yard grandpa was at the gate; his cap off, and with eyes up to heaven, he was crossing himself. Nevertheless, his face was contorted with anger; everything about him expressed anger, and one of his legs was shaking. He stamped his foot at me and shouted, "I told you to go inside." But he accompanied me into the kitchen and called out, "Come here, mother."

They went into the next room where they talked in whispers; and when grandma came back into the kitchen her expression told me at once that what had happened was dreadful.

"Why do you look so scared, grandma?" I asked.

"Keep still," she said, but not impatiently.

And for the rest of the day, something ominous hovered over the house. I noticed a frequent exchange of uneasy glances between grandpa and grandma; and their conversation was in muted whispers that deepened the disquiet.

Grandpa coughed as he ordered, "Light the lamps all over the house, mother."

We rushed through our meal, eating without relish, hastily, as if expecting a visitor. Grandpa looked tired, and his voice had a rusty sound as he mumbled, "What a power the devil has over men! . . . everywhere . . . even among the clergy . . . Why, eh?"

Grandma didn't answer except to sigh.

That silvery winter's day dragged out its hours of anxiety and depression. Before evening another policeman arrived, a ruddy, stout fellow, who took a cozy seat on the oven and began dozing. When grandma asked, "How was it found out?" he answered in a smug voice, "We find out everything; don't worry."

I recall that I sat at the window with a large copper coin in my mouth, to warm it so it would leave a print of its St. George-and-Dragon image on the frosted pane. Suddenly, terrifying sounds came from the vestibule; and our neighbor, the fat dairywoman, Petrovna, burst in, shrieking hysterically, "Come and see what's out there!"

When she caught sight of the policeman she tried to run away, but he caught hold of her and in an overbearing voice, demanded, "Hold on, there! Who are you? What's there to see out there?"

Brought to a sudden stop by the policeman's grip, she fell to her knees and, with a voice choked by struggling words and sobs, she screamed, "When I went to milk the cows there it was . . . What's that thing there, in the Kashirins' garden, that looks like a boot? I thought . . ."

But grandpa roared at her, stamping his foot, "You lying fool! You couldn't see into our garden. The fence is too high and without a crack. There's nothing in our garden, you liar!"

"Little father, it's the truth," cried Petrovna, holding one hand out to grandpa and the other to her head. "It's the truth, little father; who'd lie about a thing like that? I followed the foot prints right to your fence and there was a spot where the snow was all trampled and I looked through and there *he* was . . ."

"Who? Who?" but no matter how many times that question was repeated, she couldn't reply. On a sudden, simultaneous impulse, everybody made a mad dash into the garden, each elbowing the other, as if in a delirium. Beside the pit, with snow already drifted over him, lay

Peter, his back propped up on the charred beam and his head bowed on his chest. A deep gash gaped under his right ear, red like a mouth, with bits of flesh projecting jaggedly, like teeth.

I closed my eyes to shut out the horror; but through my trembling eyelashes I could see his familiar harness-maker's knife clasped in his smudged right hand; and both resting on his knee. His other hand, which had been cut off, was half sunk in the snow. He himself was sinking as the snow thawed under him, so that the diminutive body appeared to be nestled in a soft, glistening down, and had an even more childlike look than in life. To the right of the corpse an eerie red shape had formed, something like a bird; but to the left the snow was unruffled, smooth and dazzlingly white. The bowed head looked strikingly penitent, with the chin, fringed by the bulge of his thick, curly beard, pressed to his bosom, and over the blood frozen upon it gleamed a large brass cross. The noises all around me made me feel dizzy. Petrovna screamed without stopping and the policeman roared orders, and to Valei, hurrying to do the policeman's bidding, grandpa yelled, "Careful; don't step in his footprints!"

Suddenly, wrinkling his brows, grandpa looked down at the ground; but it was in a sharp, angry voice that he said to the policeman, "Look here, officer, what are you kicking up such a fuss about? This is in God's hand . . . God's judgment, you hear! . . . and you stirring up all this nonsense . . . eh!"

And at these words a hush fell over the garden. Everybody stood still now, took deep breaths, and crossed himself. Passersby and neighbors began streaming into the garden from the yard. Climbing over Petrovna's fence some took a fall, and cried out in pain, but the crowd was decorously quiet; suddenly grandpa said, in an anguished voice, "Have you no consciences, neighbors! You're trampling my raspberry bushes!"

Grandma, shaking with sobs, took me by the hand into the house.

"What did he do?"

"Couldn't you see?"

All that night, into the small hours, the house reverberated with trampling feet and loud voices. The police had taken charge, and a man who strutted like a deacon quacked, "What? What?"

Grandma served them tea; at the kitchen table sat a roly-poly, bearded man, with a face stippled by smallpox, who reported in an affected voice, "His real name is not cleared up yet . . . he was born in Elatma, that's all that's been established up to now . . . and Dumb Stephen . . . a nickname, that's all . . . wasn't deaf and dumb . . . Knew all about it . . . And there's a third partner . . . Haven't tracked him down yet . . . Robbing churches . . . that was their racket."

"Lord!" Petrovna cried out, flushed and perspiring.

And, lying on the oven ledge, I looked down on them and thought how squat and obese and repulsive all of them were.

Chapter Ten

A ROBIN-SNARING EXPEDITION TOOK ME, ONE EARLY SATURDAY MORN-ing, into Petrovna's vegetable patch. The agile redbreasts would not be tempted into my snares, and kept me there a long time. Provocatively beautiful, they skipped cheerfully over the silver snow, and flying from branch to branch of the frost-laden bushes, scattered bluish snow crystals at every flight. It was all so enchanting I felt no annoyance over my failure. The truth is I was not much of a sportsman, taking more delight in the incidents of the chase than in the bag it brought me. Watching and contemplating the ways of the birds gave me the keenest pleasure. It was enough for me to sit by myself, a snow-covered field before me, enjoying the singing of the birds in the crystalline, icy stillness and the distant, evanescent sounds of sleighbells, like the melancholy notes of the lark lost in Russia's wintry vastness.

Numb from my long session in the snow, and feeling the frost getting at my ears, I gathered together snare and cages, and, climbing over the wall into our garden, went toward the house. Through the open street gate, a colossus of a man, whistling cheerfully, was leading out three steaming horses, pulling a big, covered sleigh. My heart skipped a beat and I asked, "Whom did you bring?"

He looked at me from under his arms, which held the reins, and took his seat in the coach-box before answering, "The priest."

I wasn't quite convinced; for if it were the priest, he must have been visiting one of the boarders, not us. "Giddap!" roared the driver, then resumed his jovial whistling as he gave the horses a cut of the reins, and soon had them tearing over the fields. I stood there awhile, watching them, then shut the gate.

On coming into the kitchen, the first thing I heard was my mother's vibrant voice saying, very clearly, "Now, what! Do you want to kill me?"

Throwing down my paraphernalia, and not waiting to pull off my outer clothes, I plunged into the vestibule where I ran into grandpa, who gripped my shoulder, gave me a frenzied stare, gulped and said hoarsely, "Your mother's back . . . go on to her . . . but wait!" and gave me such a shake I nearly fell and reeled toward the door. "Go on!"

I knocked at the door, which was muffled with weather-stripping and a felt and oilcloth pad, and my hand, numb with cold and shaking with nervousness, had difficulty finding the latch. When I was in, at last, I halted in the doorway in dazed bewilderment.

"Here he is!" exclaimed mother. "Heavens! He's got so big! What's the matter, don't you recognize me? What a way to dress him! Look, his ears are going white; hurry, mama, get some goose-fat!"

Stooping over me in the center of the room, she helped me off with my outer clothes, spinning me around as if I were no more than a ball in her hands. Her statuesque figure was made striking by a softly draped, warm red gown, full like a man's cloak, fastened by a diagonal row of black buttons running from shoulder to hem. I had seen nothing like it before.

Her face seemed somewhat more pinched than I remembered it, and the eyes larger and hollower, and her hair a darker gold. Her red lips curled with disgust as she threw each garment she pulled off into the doorway, demanding, "Say something! Aren't you happy to see me? Pugh! What a filthy shirt!"

Then she rubbed goose-fat on my ears and made them sting; but the odor which came from her while she bent over me was so pleasant that it eased the pain. Too overcome to speak, I pressed against her and looked mutely into her eyes. Through it all I could hear grandma saying plaintively, "He's so contrary . . . nobody can control him . . . hasn't any fear of grandpa, even. Oh, Barbara, Barbara!"

"Stop whining, mother, for heaven's sake; that's no help."

And beside mother, everything appeared meagre and pitiful and old. I, myself, felt as old as grandpa.

Holding me to her knees and stroking my hair with her firm, warm hand, she said, "He needs someone over him with a strong hand. And it's time he began school. You'll like to study, won't you?"

"I've studied all I want."

"But you'll have to study a little more. My, how strong you've grown." And she played with me, and resonant, contralto laughter welled up from her.

As grandpa came in, his face ashen, his eyes bloodshot with fury, she led me aside, and in a loud, challenging voice, asked, "Well, what have you decided, papa? Want me to go?"

He stood at the window in silence, picking at the ice on the panes with his nails. In the painful tension, as always at such moments, my body seemed to be hearing and seeing on every inch; and something seemed to swell in my breast to the point of bursting, producing an agonized desire to scream.

"Get out, Alex!" grandpa ordered gruffly.

"What for?" mama asked, pulling me toward her. "You're not to leave this room; I forbid it!" She then rose, and gliding over like a rosy cloud, behind grandpa, said, "Papa, listen to me."

With a shriek he turned upon her, "You shut up!"

With cool composure mother said, "I won't have you shouting at me!"

Grandma got up from the couch, and waving an admonishing finger, said, "Now, Barbara."

And grandpa sought a chair, mumbling, "Hold on. I have to know. Who was it, eh? How did it come about?" And, in a changed voice that made it sound like a stranger's, he roared, "You've disgraced me, Barbara."

"Go out of the room," grandma ordered me, and I went to the kitchen, where, feeling that I was suffocating, I climbed on the oven, from which I could hear everything. Their talk rose and fell, from tumults in which they were all interrupting each other, to long silences, like sleep. They were talking about a child recently born to my mother and turned over to someone else to bring up. The puzzle to me was whether grandpa was mad at mother for having a child without his permission, or for not bringing it here.

Later he came into the kitchen, looking disheveled and exhausted, and his face ashen. Grandma, wiping her eyes with the hem of her blouse, followed him in. Grandpa sat on a bench, bowed, his hands gripping the edge, spasmodically chewing his pallid lips; and grandma went down on her knees to him, pleading in a low but intense voice, "Forgive her, father! You can't throw her off like this. Haven't you heard of such things happening in noblemen's families and millionaires? You know how women are! Come, forgive her! Nobody's perfect, you know."

Propped back against the wall, grandpa looked at her, emitted a bitter laugh that was half-sob, and growled, "So, and what next? If it were up to you anything would be forgiven; ekh—you!" He bent over, gripped her by the shoulders, and shook her, whispering rapidly, "Good Lord, don't aggravate yourself. Forgiveness—not from me! Here we are, practically in our graves, and retribution catches up with us. No peace, no happiness for us, now or to come. What's more, let me tell you, before it's all over we'll be beggars—beggars!"

Grandma took his hand, settled herself at his side, and with a soothing laugh, said, "Is that what's worrying you, poor thing, being a beggar? What if we do? All you'll have to do is wait home for me. I'll do the begging. They'll be good to me, don't worry. We'll have plenty, so don't let that worry you."

That set him off laughing, and jerking his head like a goat. He embraced her, looking tiny and crumpled in her arms.

"Ah, you fool, you blessed fool!" he said. "You're all that's left to me. There's no worry in you because there's no understanding. But think back, think how we slaved for them, you and I, the sins I committed for them, and for all this, now . . ."

At this point I was overcome. My tears overflowed all restraints; and hopping from the oven, I rushed upon them, sobbing with joy to hear them talking so lovingly, sobbing also out of pity for their sorrows, sobbing with relief to have mother back, sobbing with contentment that they embraced me, moist as I was, and wept with me; grandpa saying, with a low chuckle, "There you are, you little imp! So your mother's back and now you'll be tagging after her. That poor old devil, grandpop, can go hang now, eh? And grandma, too, eh, for all she's pampered you so? . . . ekh, you!"

Pushing both of us away, he straightened up and shouted angrily, "They're all abandoning us, turning their backs on us . . . Go call her in; what are you standing around for?"

Grandma left the kitchen and grandpa bowed his head, in the icon corner, his fist thumping his breast, and praying, "See, All Merciful Lord, how things are with us!"

I always found his doing this distasteful. In general, all his dealings with God were distasteful to me; as if he were God's chief concern.

Mother's red dress illuminated the kitchen as she came in. She sat between grandma and grandpa, and its full sleeves draped their shoulders. In a composed, quiet voice, she spoke to them, and they listened with submissive attention, as if they were her children, not once interrupting her. I, exhausted, dropped off to sleep on the couch.

That evening, my grandparents, all dressed up, went to vespers. Grandma winked playfully toward grandpa, who was strutting in his guildmaster's regalia, under his long, raccoon cloak, and she remarked to mama, "Take a look at your father, isn't he something! Chipper as a young goat!" And mama laughed happily.

When I was at last alone with her, in her room, mama called me over to her side, on the couch, on which she sat with her legs crossed under her, and said, "So, tell me, do you like it here? Not much, I suppose."

"I don't know."

"Grandpa whips you, eh?"

"Not so much any more."

"Tell me about it, tell me anything you want. Go on."

I didn't care to make grandpa the topic of our conversation, choosing instead, the kindly former occupant of this room, whom nobody had liked and whom grandpa had put out. It was clear she wasn't interested. "And what else?" she asked.

So I spoke about the three brothers and the colonel chasing me out of their yard; at which her grip on my arm tightened. Her eyes blazed. "What idiocy!" she exclaimed, and then looked down on the floor in silence.

"Why was grandpa mad at you?" I asked.

"He thinks something I did was bad."

"Because you didn't come with the baby?"

She gave a violent start, frowned, bit her lips, then laughed and hugged me tighter. "You little devil! About that you're to keep mum, understand? Not a word. Forget that you ever heard anything about it."

And she took a long time to tell me things I couldn't understand, speaking rather quietly, but very seriously; and then she rose and paced the room, her fingers drumming on her chin, and raising and lowering her heavy eyebrows. The mirror reflected the guttering candle on the table; dim shadows crawled across the floor; moonlight silvered the frosted windows. Mama began looking around as if she missed something on our bare walls. "When do you go to bed?"

"Let me stay up some more."

"Well, you've had a nap already," she said, as a reminder to herself.

"You're thinking of going away?"

"Where?" and she sounded surprised; then lifted my head and looked at me so long it brought tears to my eyes.

"What's wrong with you?" she asked.

"My neck hurts." And my heart, too, for I had a premonition that her stay here was to be brief.

"You're getting to be like your father," she remarked, kicking at a mat. "Has grandma told you about him?"

"Yes."

"She was very fond of him, and he of her."

"I know."

Mother frowned at the candle, then snuffed it out and said, "That's better." And it was; everything became fresher and clearer after it was extinguished. The dim shadows were gone; the frost crystals on the windowpane gleamed golden; and the moonlight lay in bright blue squares on the floor.

"Where did you live while you were away?"

She named some towns, as if she were recalling, with an effort, something long forgotten; and throughout, she darted soundlessly about the room, like a hawk.

"Where did you get that dress?"

"I made it. I sew all my own clothes."

I wanted mama to be different from the others, but not so taciturn. Unless I asked her something, she scarcely opened her mouth. After awhile she sat down again beside me, and holding each other close, we stayed there in silence until the old folks returned, solemn but gentle, and with a churchly smell of incense and wax. And, as if it were a holy day, our evening meal was ceremonious; few words were spoken, and those low-voiced, as if in consideration of some very light sleeper nearby.

Almost immediately and with energy, my mother began teaching me Russian. She got me some books, and in a few days I was reading, but, to our mutual discomfort, mama insisted on teaching me a verse by heart. It was this:

> *Bolshaya doroga, priamaya doroga,*
> *Prostora nie malo, beryosh ty ou Boga.*
> *Tebya nie rovniali topor y lopata*
> *Miaka ty kopitou y pyiliu bogata.*

(Broad road, straight road. You didn't ask God for much space; and it wasn't pick and shovel that leveled you, but hooves in the soft dust.)

But I read *prostogo* for *prostora* and *rubili* for *rovniali* and *kopita* for *kopitou*.

"Stop and think!" mother cried. "How could it be *prostogo*, you little scamp! *Pro-sto-ra*; do you get it now?"

I did, in fact; yet, to my own amazement, as well as hers, I continued to say *prostogo*.

She became annoyed and called me brainless and stubborn; and it was wounding to hear, because I made every effort to remember those cursed lines; and, in my own mind, I could say them without a hitch, but the moment I said them aloud my tongue tripped. I got to loathe them, and began deliberately to mix them up, running all the like-sounding words together, feeling triumphant when, under that magic, they were transformed into gibberish.

But this game soon brought its reckoning. One day, after a lesson that had otherwise gone very well, mama asked me had I learned the verse, and on the spur of the moment, I babbled,

"Doroga, dvoroga, tvorog, niedoroga,
Kopito, popito, korito."

(Road, doorway, curd, no road,
Heap up, perplex, blame.)

I stopped, but not in time. Mama rose, gripped the edge of the table, and very emphatically demanded, "What's that you're saying?"

"I don't know," I replied sullenly.

"You know very well!"

"Just something."

"What something?"

"Something funny."

"Go stand in the corner."

"Why?"

"Go stand in the corner." Her tone was quiet, but her manner menacing.

"Which corner?"

She made no reply, but her gaze was so unsparingly steady, I became confused; I had no notion just what she wanted me to do. If it was the icon corner, a little table holding a vase with aromatic dried grass and flowers, barred the way; a covered trunk and the bed barred access to two other corners; and there was no fourth; the door came right up to the wall.

Despairingly, I said, "I don't understand. What do you mean?"

Relaxing a little, she smoothed her brow, "Didn't grandpa ever send you to a corner?"

"When?"

"I'm not asking when; did he *ever* send you to a corner?" and she rapped on the table, twice.

"Never—as far as I can remember."

"Pugh! Come here!" and she sighed.

I came to her and asked, "Why are you so mad at me?"

"Because you deliberately made a mess of that verse."

I did my best to explain to her that I could say it, word for word, in my mind, but that when I tried to say it aloud, the words came out different.

"You're not making that up, are you?"

I told her I was; but on afterthought I wasn't quite so certain, and suddenly, to my amazement and confusion, I heard myself saying the verses without a mistake. Flushed with embarrassment I stood before my mother, and my face seemed to swell, my ears tingled, and my head knocked with disagreeable noises. Through my tears I saw her face clouding with annoyance; I saw her scowling and gnawing her lips.

"What does all this mean?" she asked, in a strange voice. "So you were making it up."

"I can't say. I didn't mean to."

"You're a trial!" she said, with a droop of her head. "Go away."

She persisted in teaching me poetry, and my capacity to retain the easy, running lines lessened daily, while my mad impulse to tamper with them strengthened in proportion. I even substituted new words, sometimes to my own surprise; and a sequence of words that had no relation to the subject would be mixed in with the words of the text. At times an entire line would blot out and no effort could summon it back. I had got into trouble with that deeply felt verse of Prince Biazemskov—I never got the first three lines straight: "At dawn and dusk, the orphan, the widow and the old man beg for alms in Christ's name—yet the fourth line, "Under the window, moaning," always came out right. Mystified by this, mama discussed it with grandpa who said grimly, "It's a trick. His memory's fine. I taught him the prayers by heart and he learned them. Its a trick, that's what it is. He needs a whipping."

Grandma joined in, "You can remember the stories and ballads, and ballads are poems, too, aren't they?"

All this I could see and it made me feel guilty; nevertheless, all I had to do was try to memorize verses, when other words, from God knows where, would crawl in like cockroaches.

> "To our doors came beggars, too,
> Old men and orphans, not a few;
> But the food we give to make them well,
> They bless and take it—and then sell,"

to which I added,

> "to Petrovna, for her cows,
> And then on whiskey they carouse."

At night, lying beside grandma, I would say over, to exhaustion, what I had learned that day, and what I had composed of my own. Verses like those sometimes made her giggle, but more often she reproached me. "It's wrong to ridicule beggars, God bless them. Christ and all the saints lived in poverty."

Then I might murmur:

> "On paupers, pugh!
> And grandpa, too.
> Pardon me, Lord,
> For that crime;
> But grandpa socks me
> All the time."

"What's that! May your tongue fall out!" grandma would exclaim. "If grandpa heard you—!"

"He can if he wants."

Then, patiently, and sympathetically, grandma would say, "It does you no good being so perverse. It only vexes your mother who has enough troubles without that."

"What troubles?"

"Never mind. It's nothing you could understand."

I had a bad time of it, for I was desperately seeking a kindred spirit; but, in fear of rebuff, I masked my quest by being rebellious and contrary. My lessons with my mother grew more and more disagreeable and hard. Arithmetic came easy, but I was impatient with writing, and grammar was beyond me. But the most depressing thing, which I quickly sensed, was that mother was finding life tedious at grandpa's. Every day she grew more morose, seemed to see everything with an alienated eye. For hours together, she would sit at the window, facing the garden in silence; and the glow that had characterized her had dulled.

During lessons her deep-set eyes seemed to go through me, to wall or windows; her questions came in a listless voice, and my answers often went unheard; and she was quicker with anger, which wounded me, for mothers ought to be sweeter than anybody else, as they are in fairy tales.

Now and then I would say, "You don't like it here?" and she would fly into a rage, "Mind your own business!"

It dawned on me, gradually, that some plan of grandpa's was worrying both mama and grandma. He often closeted himself with mama, in her room, and squeals and tootings would issue from him that reminded me of the nerve-wracking pipings of Nikanor, the stoop-shouldered shepherd. During one of the sessions mama could be heard all through the house, screaming, "No! I won't!" And I heard the door bang and grandpa howl.

It was at night when this happened. Grandma was in the kitchen sewing a shirt for grandpa and muttering to herself. When the door banged, her muttering stopped; she raised her head to listen, and she said, "Good Lord! She's gone up to one of the boarders!"

And grandpa burst into the kitchen, and gave her a punch in the head and shouted and shook his bleeding fist at her, "That's for tattling about things you should keep quiet about, you old witch!"

And grandma calmly retorted, as she put her messed hair to rights, "And you're an old fool! Think I'll keep quiet? I'll always warn her when I know what you're scheming!"

Lunging at her again he beat her about the head with both fists; and she, making no attempt to fend him off or hit back at him, said, "Go on, you silly fool, beat me. Go on, hit me!"

I stripped the couch of blankets and pillows and threw them at him; and I picked up and threw at him all the boots standing around the stove; but he took no notice, he was in such a fury. He knocked grandma down and kicked her in the head, then tripped, spilling a pail of water in his fall. Snorting and sputtering, he picked himself up, gave a frantic look around, and dashed out to his own room.

Grandma picked herself up and, sighing, sat on the bench and fixed her hair. When I jumped off the oven to go to her, she said sharply to me, "Get those cushions and things back where they belong! The idea of throwing them at people! Was it any of your business? The old one is out of his mind, the fool!"

Then, with an almost sobbing inhalation of breath and a tightening of her face, she called me over, bent her head and said, "Take a look; something's hurting me there. What is it?"

Parting her hair I saw a hairpin imbedded in her scalp. Having extracted that one I found another, but with that my fingers became limp and I said, "I'm scared; let's call mama."

Waving me away, she said, "What for? Call mama! I'll call you! Thank the Lord she's seen nothing of this. And you—go on, you're in my way!"

And with her agile, lace-maker's fingers she explored her heavy mane and found two more of the imbedded hairpins, which I summoned up the strength to help her pull out.

"Does it hurt?"

"Just a bit. Tomorrow I'll heat some water and wash my head and everything will be all right."

Then she coaxed me, "Darling, don't tell mama he beat me; promise! It would only add to the bad feelings between them. Promise?"

"Yes."

"Don't forget! Now let's straighten up here. Any marks on my face? Good, we'll be able to keep it quiet."

She mopped the floor and with all my heart I said, "You're just like a saint! You bear all the tortures; you don't mind anything they do to you!"

"Such nonsensical chatter! Saints? Did you ever see any?"

And, crouched on her knees, she mumbled to herself, while at the oven I planned vengeance on grandpa. Never before, in my presence, had he abused grandma in such an atrocious and revolting way. Like an apparition in the dusk, I could see his inflamed face and his tossing red hair again; and my heart seethed with anger; and I was annoyed with myself for not being able to hit upon a fitting retaliation.

A few days later, bringing him something in his room, I found him squatting on the floor at an opened chest, going through some papers. On a chair, at his side, was his favorite calendar, twelve gray, cardboard oblongs; and in the square for each day was a picture of its saint. Grandpa treasured this calendar, and a look at it was a privilege accorded me only for exceptional good conduct; and then I had always been inexpressibly captivated by that huddle of charming images. I knew tales about a number of them, among them Cyril and Ulita, and the noble martyr, Barbara, and Panteleimon; but above all, the tragic Alexis, man of God, about whom there were such beautiful ballads, which grandma frequently, and with deep feeling, recited for me. It was comforting to realize that there were hundreds of such martyrs.

Now, however, I resolved to tear up that calendar, and when grandpa went to the window with a dark paper, for better light to read it by, I snatched up some of the sheets, ran downstairs with them, got grandma's scissors, and began snipping off the saints' heads. When one row had been decapitated, I began to feel qualms about destroying the calendar and decided only to cut out the squares; but before I could finish my job on the second row, grandpa appeared in the doorway thundering, "Who told you you could take my calendar?"

Then, seeing the bits of paper on the table, he picked them up, one after the other, closely and incredulously scrutinizing one, to put it down and pick up another. His jaw sagged, his beard quivered, and his breath came in stormy gusts, that blew all the papers off the table.

"What did you do?" he screamed, as he finally found words. Catching at my leg, he dragged me to him over the floor.

Grandma came in and caught at me, and I went somersaulting. Grandpa punched her and screamed, "I'll kill him!"

Mama entered just then, and I hid in the stove corner while she pushed grandpa away, catching his hands which he was brandishing in her face. "What a way for a man to behave! Pull yourself together!"

Grandpa flung himself on the window bench and yelled, "You're out to murder me. You're all against me, all of you!"

"It's a disgrace," said my mother, but her voice was low and full of concern. "What an exhibition!"

Grandpa kept up his tantrum, howling, kicking at the bench, his eyes shut tight and his beard pointing grotesquely at the ceiling. I had a feeling that he really was embarrassed before mother, but helpless to stop himself, and for that reason kept his eyes closed.

"I'll back the sheets with cloth and glue the pieces back and the calendar will look even nicer than before," mama said. "It was cracked and ripped, anyway."

She spoke to him commandingly, as she used to speak to me when I was slow with my lessons; and he got up, patted his shirt and vest straight, spat, and said, "But get it done today. I'll bring you the other sheets."

On his way to the door he halted at the threshold to crook his finger at me, "And he's got to get a beating!"

"Of course," mama said, and turning to me, asked, "Why did you do that?"

"I wanted to. He'd better not beat grandma again; I'll cut off his whiskers."

Grandma, pulling off her ripped blouse, shook her head at me, reproachfully. "Hush, now, keep your promise. May your tongue swell up if you don't!"

Mama turned from her to me, "When did he beat her?"

"Now, Barbara, aren't you ashamed to be questioning him? What business is it of yours?"

Mama went up to her and put her arm around her, "Ah, little mother mine."

"Oh, let me be, you and your 'little mother'! Go away!"

In heavy silence they looked at each other. Outside in the vestibule, grandpa could be heard pacing.

Right after her return, mama had become friends with the lively little soldier's wife. She visited with her every evening, mingling with other guests who included visitors from the Betlenga establishment, some of its beautiful ladies and their officer friends. Grandpa disapproved; and once, in the kitchen, he waved his spoon at mama and said, "Back to your old ways, accursed one! No sleep for us anymore until morning!"

And he turned out the lodgers, bought some loads of furniture for the empty front room, which he padlocked. "We don't have to have roomers," he announced. "From now on I'll do the entertaining."

And from then on we had visitors. Sundays and holy days, grandma's sister, Matrena, a large-nosed, nagging laundress who had blondined her hair, arrived, dressed in a gown of striped silk. Her sons came along, Basil, a draughtsman, who dressed quietly in gray, but who had a lively and agreeable nature, and Victor, who ran to gaudy colors in his dress, had a narrow horse-shaped face, peppered with freckles, and who gave me a start, while he was still in the vestibule removing his rubbers, by piping out, in a screechy voice like the carter Peter's, snatches from a current hit tune, "Daddy Andy."

Uncle Jake also turned up with his guitar, accompanied by a bald, stooped man, a watchmaker, in a black dress suit. His manner was ingratiating, reminding me of a monk. He had a cleft chin, which, after he had taken his accustomed seat in the corner and cocked his head, he would tap with his finger. He had only one eye, and the stare it fixed upon us was disconcerting. He was dark in complexion, and he said very little, usually, "Please don't disturb yourself; it's of no consequence whatever."

My first sight of him brought instantly back to mind an incident I had forgotten. There was an ominous and insistent drumming outside the gate, and we saw a crowd of soldiers, and people dressed in black, walking before, behind and on the sides of a cart being driven from the jail to the public square. On a bench, in the cart, sat a chained man of medium height, wearing a woolen cap. Over his breast hung a placard with large white lettering on a black background; and the man's head hung strangely down as if he were trying to decipher it; and he shuddered so that his chains clashed. With this picture in my mind, when mama said, "My son," and presented me to the watchmaker, I backed away in fright and hid my hands behind my back.

"Please don't disturb yourself," said he, and his mouth went into a terrifying, sideward gape that reached to his right ear, and he pulled me to him by my belt, spun me around with ease, and then set me free. "He's all there; a solid little fellow."

I retreated to the corner to curl up in a leather upholstered armchair, so ample one could stretch out on it, a bragged-about treasure of grandpa's who called it Prince Gruzinsky's armchair. From its depths I surveyed the grownups, and concluded that they had a tedious way of enjoying themselves, and that it was odd and suspicious how the expression on the watchmaker's face kept changing. It was a viscid face that was in constant, jelly-like motion. When he smiled his thick lips moved up his right cheek and his nose moved with it, like a little meat ball sliding over a plate. His big, protruding ears also moved in strange ways, one rising with the eyebrow of his seeing eye, whenever he lifted it, and the other coordinating with the movements of his cheekbone. And when he sneezed, it seemed as if it would be as simple for him to use them to cover his nose, as to use his hands. At times he vented a sigh, and his dark tongue, cylindrical like a pestle, rolled over his thick lips as he licked them. The sight did not amuse me; but I could not resist staring at that phenomenon.

They drank tea spiked with rum that gave off an odor like burnt onions; they sipped cordials brewed by grandma, some a golden yellow, some pitch black and some green. They snacked on cheese, on butter biscuits, on eggs and on honey, over which they sweated and gulped, while they sang grandma's praises. And having stuffed themselves, they settled back in their chairs with bloated and flushed, but polite, looks, and made languid calls upon Uncle Jake to give them a tune.

And, bowed over his guitar, he plucked out a repellent song of the period, about how a group of revellers, each in turn, told his life story to a lady of Kazan. I disliked it, and grandma said, "Play something else, Jake, a real song. Remember, Matrena, the songs we used to sing!"

Flouncing her noisy silk, the laundress replied, "They're out of fashion now."

Uncle Jake blinked at grandma as if he were seeing her from a distance, and stubbornly kept twanging out lugubrious notes and idiotic words.

Grandpa confabbed, in a mystifying way, with the watchmaker, gesturing, and getting him to look in mama's direction, whereupon his plastic face assumed some inexplicable new shape.

Mama sat between Matrena's sons, talking in a serious manner to Basil, saying with a sigh, "Yes, that's something to consider"; while Victor, with the sated smile of one who has eaten his fill, tapped his shoe on the floor and suddenly burst into his "Daddy Andy!" And in the surprised silence, the laundress made the proud explanation, "He came home with it from the theater. That's what they're singing now."

After some three such evenings the watchmaker appeared in daylight, one Sunday after mass. I was with mama in her room helping her mend a torn piece of bead embroidery, when the door swung open and grandma rushed in, looking frightened, and whispered loudly, "He's here, Barbara!" and rushed out again.

Mama didn't stir, not even an eyelash. Then the door opened again and grandpa appeared on the threshold. "Get dressed, Barbara; we've got to get going."

She remained seated and without a glance at him, asked, "Where?"

"Get going, for God's sake! Let's have no arguments. He's a decent, quiet man; he's well-fixed; and he'll be a good father to Alex."

His manner was unusually formal and his hands kept patting his sides; but his elbows shook as they crooked back, as if he were repressing an impulse to stretch his arms out.

Calmly, mother broke in, "I tell you it can't be."

Grandpa went over to her, his arms before him like one who is blind, and stooping over her, sputtering with rage, he said, "Will you come, or will you have to be dragged over by the hair?"

"So you'll drag me over to him, will you!" said mama, turning white. She stood up; very swiftly she undressed, down to her chemise. Then she said, "Now. Begin dragging!"

He gnashed his teeth, brandished his fist at her, and shouted, "Barbara, get dressed immediately!"

Mama pushed him aside, went to the door, and, with her hand on the knob, said, "Well? Aren't you coming?"

"Curse you," replied grandpa, in a whisper.

"I'm not coy, come!" and she opened the door; but grandpa caught at her chemise and dropped to his knees, whispering, "Barbara, you devil, want to ruin us? Have you no shame?" And he called out, plaintively, "Mother, mother!"

Grandma was already barring mama's way, waving her hands at mama as if she were a hen, drawing her back into the room, and hissing between her clenched teeth. "You lunatic, you shameless one, where are you going? Get back in your room!"

Having driven mama in and latched the door, she bent over grandpa, raising him with one hand and shaking the other in his face, "Pugh! You old demon!"

When she got him on the couch, he collapsed in a heap, as limp as a rag doll, his mouth agape and his head hanging.

"And you, get dressed immediately," ordered grandma.

"But I'm not going to him—is that understood?"

Grandma pushed me off the couch. "Hurry; get a basin of water!" Her voice was unagitated, so low as to be almost a whisper, and spoken in her usual, sure manner.

In the hallway I could hear someone pacing heavily in the guest room, while from mama's room I heard her say, "I'll go away tomorrow!"

In the kitchen I sat down at the window as in a dream. I heard grandpa groaning and screaming; I heard grandma mumbling; I heard a door bang. And then all froze into depressing silence.

Recalling my errand, I ladled some water into a brass basin and brought it into the hallway. The watchmaker was leaving the guest room, his head bent, his hands on his fur cap, smoothing it down, and cackling something. Grandma, with folded hands, was bowing behind him and saying, placatingly, "You understand how it is, yourself; affection can't be forced."

After a halt on the threshold he went on into the yard; and grandma, with a shudder, crossed herself, and seemed to be as ready to laugh as to cry. I ran to her and asked, "What's the trouble?"

She snatched the basin from me, and the water doused my legs. "So this is where you come with it. Bolt the door!" And back she went to mama's room; and back I went to the kitchen, where I heard them moaning and groaning and mumbling; and it was as if they were shifting a burden that they found too heavy, from place to place.

A bright day. The rays of the winter sun came in aslant through the frosted windows. The table was laid with a pewter dinner service. A subdued glow came from a decanter of red *kvass* and another of dull green vodka brewed by grandpa from mint and other herbs. Where the ice on the window had thawed, the snow could be seen in broad, gleaming expanses on roofs, and shimmering like silver on fence posts. In their cages, hanging from the arch of the window, my birds enjoyed the sun; the finches sang, the robins twittered, the canary reveled in its bath.

But this glittering, resplendent day, in which every sound rang, brought me no happiness, seemed mistimed—everything out of order. I had an impulse to free the birds, and was on the point of unhooking their cages when grandma ran in, slapping herself on her hips, and calling herself names. Rushing to the stove she berated herself, "Curse you, Akulina, for being an old fool!" Taking a meat pie out of the oven, she felt the crust, and spat on the floor in vexation. "All dried up! There it is; and all your fault. Akh! Devil take you. A plague on you! Keep your eyes open, you owl! You're a bad luck penny!"

And, weeping, she blew on the pie, turned it over on all sides, tap ping the horny crust, big tears splashing on her worrying fingers.

When grandpa and mama came into the kitchen, she slammed the meat pie down on the table and the dishes bounced. "Look at it! That's your work! It's all crust!"

Mama, looking calm and quite happy, kissed her and told her not to upset herself about it; and grandpa, looking exhausted and utterly crushed, sat down, opened his napkin, blinked from the sun in his eyes, and said, "Enough. It's no matter. We've had our share of good meat pies. When you have dealings with the Lord He pays for the year in minutes, and no interest. Sit down, Barbara. That's the last of it."

He sounded as if he had gone out of his mind, and rambled on about God and the sinful Ahab and about a father's hard lot, until grandma broke in angrily, "Eat your dinner. That's what's left for you to do."

Her bright eyes shining, mama joked all through. Giving me a nudge, she asked, "Were you frightened?"

The truth was I had not been frightened then; but now I was confused and uneasy. As the meal went through its customary dragging Sunday-and-holiday course, I felt, Can these be the same people who, a bare half hour ago, were screaming at one another, weeping and sobbing, and ready to tear each other to pieces? I could not believe in them,—that is, I could not believe they were not shamming, that they were not still on the verge of tears. Those tears and outcries, those tumults they inflicted on each other, how often they flared up, how swiftly they died down; so that I was becoming used to them and no longer suffered palpitations or heartache.

In time I came to understand that out of the misery and murk of their lives the Russian people had learned to make sorrow a diversion, to play with it like a child's toy; seldom are they diffident about showing their unhappiness.

And so, through their tedious weekdays, they made a carnival of grief; a fire is entertainment; and on a vacant face a bruise becomes an adornment.

Chapter Eleven

Following THIS INCIDENT, MAMA TOOK COMMAND, AND SOON RULED the house. Grandpa became preoccupied and retiring, quite unlike himself, shrinking into insignificance.

Now he seldom went out, but sat in his room reading, in a curiously furtive manner, a book called *The Writings of My Father*. He kept it locked in his trunk, and one day I saw him wash his hands before he touched it. The squat tome had a red leather binding. On the blue flyleaf there was a scroll-like inscription in colored inks, "To the esteemed Basil Kashirin, in sincere remembrance and gratitude," under which were signatures of people I did not know. The decoration was a bird on the wing.

With great care grandpa would raise the ornate cover, put on his silver-framed glasses, peer into the pages, twitching his nose to get the lenses into focus.

When, as I sometimes did, I asked him about the book, he answered solemnly, "Bide your time. It will be yours when I die . . . I'm also leaving you my raccoon cloak."

When he spoke to mama he was gentler than before, but he spoke less frequently. As he listened to her, in turn, his eyes had a glitter that reminded me of the carter, Peter. Soon he would wave her away, muttering, "Enough; do as you please."

Many remarkable garments were heaped in that trunk of his . . . silk shirts, quilted satin jackets, long silk robes, silver lamé cloth, pearl-spangled headbands, jewel necklaces, colored handkerchiefs and lengths of colored goods. He sometimes piled them in his arms, and went, panting, with them, into mama's room, and laid them out on chairs and tables—mama had a passion for dress—and told her, "Dress was richer and more beautiful when I was young; and people got along better. But those days are gone; they can't be whistled back. There, take them, dress up."

One day mama slipped into her room to emerge, a little later, in a dark blue, sleeveless gown trimmed with gold embroidery, and over her brow a headband studded with pearls. And, bowing low to grandpa, she asked, "And how does my lord Father fancy this?"

Grandpa was wonderfully elated, chuckled, walked around her, waved his hands, and said thickly, as in a voice out of a dream, "Ekh, Barbara, if you had the money, the best people would be at your feet."

Mama had moved to the two best rooms and did a good deal of entertaining, her most constant guests being the Maximov brothers: Peter, a handsome, robust officer with a full, fair beard and blue eyes, the very man to appease whom grandpa had whipped me for spitting on the bald-head; and Eugene, tall too, but thin and pale, whose small beard came to a point, and whose eyes were big as plums. On his green coat gleamed a row of gold buttons, and gold lettering was braided over his narrow shoulders. He had a way of smiling genially as he gave his head a toss, to bring his long, silky hair back from his high, smooth brow. And his invariable husky-voiced beginning, when he told a story, was, "Let me tell you how it looks to me."

Mama's eyes sparkled as she listened to him, and she broke in frequently and laughingly, "You're a baby, Eugene, forgive me for saying so." And, slapping his knee, he would reply, "Some baby!"

There was noise and frolic throughout the Christmas week; almost every evening mama, beautifully dressed, received visitors; or, still more splendidly dressed, outshining everybody, she went out. Whenever she and her friends, in their finery, went out, the house seemed to empty and to sink into the earth, and a fearsome silence seeped into every corner. Grandma waddled around like an old goose, straightening up; and grandpa, warming his back on the tiles of the oven, muttered to himself: "So that may be the thing. Good enough. We'll see about the family."

After Christmas mama sent me and Uncle Mike's Sascha to school.

Uncle Mike had married again, and the stepmother had taken an instant dislike to the boy and was maltreating him; and, at grandma's entreaty, he had been taken in to live with us. We went to school about a month, and so far as I can remember, about all I learned was to answer, "My name is Peshkov," not merely "Peshkov," when I was called; and that I must not retort to my teacher, "Listen, old man, don't holler at me; I'm not scared of you!"

I had no fondness for school, but my cousin seemed to take to it at once, and to feel at home. However, he once dozed off during a lesson, cried out in his sleep, "I won't!" woke with a start, and bolted out without bothering about formalities, earning howls of laughter. The following day, in the approach to the square where the school building stood, he stopped, and said to me, "You go on. I'm not coming. I'm going for a stroll."

Bending down, he buried his books in the snow and was off. The January day was bright, filled with silvery sunlight, and I envied my cousin. But with an effort of will, resolved not to grieve mama, I went on. The next day, Sascha's buried books were not to be found, providing another excuse for staying away. On the third day, however, his truancy was brought to grandpa's attention and we were summoned for judgment.

In the kitchen, sitting around the table, were grandpa, grandma and mama, and we underwent a cross-examination. I'll never forget Sascha's ludicrous answers to grandpa's questioning.

"Why didn't you go to school?"

"I forgot the street."

"Forgot?"

"I looked and looked."

"But you went with Alex; he knew the way."

"But I lost Alex."

"Lost him?"

"Yes."

"How?"

Sascha took a moment to think, gulped, and replied, "It snowed and I couldn't see a thing."

This brought a smile; the atmosphere seemed to clear and even Sascha ventured a smile, too. But grandpa, with a cruel glint of his teeth, said, "Couldn't you have taken Alex' arm, or held on to his belt?"

"I did," explained Sascha, "but the wind tore my hand away."

His tone was listless and despondent, and I felt uncomfortable listening to this futile, clumsy lie, wondering at his persistence in it.

We got a beating and an ex-fireman, an elderly man with a broken arm, was hired to lead us to school and see that Sascha did not stray from the path of learning. But it was no use. No sooner did we reach the approaches to the school than my cousin, pulling off one of his boots, threw it one way, and then, pulling off the other, threw it, as far as he could, the opposite way, and ran off in his stocking feet. Panting, the old man salvaged the boots, and, terribly put out, brought me home.

That day grandpa, grandma and mama hunted the runaway all through the town, finding him at last in Chirkov's tavern, where he was dancing for the customers. They took him home and the shivering, mutely obstinate lad got away without a beating. But, lying beside me in the garret, his feet up and his soles scraping the ceiling, he whispered to me, "My stepmother doesn't care for me, neither does papa or grandpa. Why should I stay with them? I'll ask grandma where the bandits live, and run away and join them. . . . Then you'll all know why. . . . How about us running away together?"

But that I couldn't do, for I was preoccupied with another project, to grow up to be an officer with a full, fair beard, for which school was an essential. When I confided that project to my cousin, he reflected on it, then approved it. "Not a bad idea. By the time you're an officer, I'll be the chief of the bandits, and you'll have to go after me, and one of us will have to kill or capture the other one. I won't kill you."

"And I won't kill you."

On that we were in agreement.

Then grandma came up to us, and, sitting on the oven, she looked at us and said, "How is it, little mice? Ah, poor orphans, poor little ones!"

And, from pitying us, she went on to abuse Sascha's stepmother—fat Nadezhda, the tavern keeper's daughter, and stepmothers in general, apropos of which she chanted to us the ballad of the hermit sage, Iona, who, when he was but a boy, received God's judgment against his stepmother.

"Iona's father was a fisherman, who lived by the White Lake.

"By his young wife he was brought to ruin. A powerful drink, brewed of sleep-inducing herbs, she gave him. And, as he slept, she laid him in an oaken boat, dark and narrow as the grave. With oars of maple, she rowed him to the center of the lake. There she had dug a hole;

and, in that dark pit, she had planned to cover up her deed of evil sorcery. She overturned the boat, that evil witch wife! And down, deep, sank her husband.

"Swiftly the witch swam ashore, and, wailing, threw herself on the ground, in pretended lament. And all the good folk, believing her, lamented with her, as seemingly disconsolate, she cried, 'Alas, too short was your married life; too soon must you bear the widow's grief. But life is in God's hand and He sends death when it pleases Him.'

"But her stepson, Iona, had no faith in her tears. Grimly he put his hand to his heart, and he cried out to her, 'You, stepmother of doom, you crafty bird of night, born to deceive men! I put no trust in these lamentations of yours. What you feel is not anguish, but joy. Let's ask our Lord and the Saints above to give the proof. Take a knife, someone. Throw it high into this cloudless sky. If she is innocent, then let the knife strike me; if she is guilty, thus will she die!'

"The stepmother gave him a malignant look, and, her eyes blazing with hatred, she stood up. Vehemently she answered his charge, her words pouring forth. 'You senseless creature, you abortion, you piece of garbage! What do you think to gain by this scheme? What sensible answer have you to that?'

"The good folk stood around, sad and troubled, not knowing what to make of this dark business. Then they held council, and a dignified old fisherman came forward, bowed and said, 'Put a steel knife into my right hand, folks; I will throw it up and we'll see on whom it falls.'

"They put the knife in his hand; that was their reply. He threw it up, above his grizzled head, and high the keen blade went, up into the air, soaring like a bird. In vain they waited for its return. They peered into the crystal reaches of the sky, their hats off and standing, huddled together, in silence. Brooding night came and still the knife fell not.

"As dawn, like a ruby, flushed over the lake, the stepmother regained her composure, and there was a look of triumphant scorn upon her face. And, at that moment, darting down like a swallow, the knife pierced her heart.

"Down went the people on their knees, praising the God who governs all, praising His justice. And the old fisherman adopted Iona and made a hermit of him, and his shrine is far off by the Kerzhents River, a cell almost invisible from the town." [16]

[16] (Author's footnote.) In the year 1890, in Kolinpanovka Village in Tambov Province, I heard a variant version in which the stepmother is presented as guiltless, and the knife kills the stepson as punishment for calumniating her.

The following morning I woke, all spotted red, the beginning of smallpox. I was put away in the attic where I lay a long time, blind, hands and feet tightly wrapped in bandages, enduring ghastly nightmares, one of which nearly finished me. Only grandma came to me to feed me from a spoon, like a baby, and spun me stories, a new one each time, from her inexhaustible store.

Once, during my convalescence, with my bandages off, except those on my hands, retained to keep me from scratching, I lay waiting for grandma, who, for some reason, had not come at her usual time, causing me great alarm. Suddenly I saw her lying face down, her arms spread out, in the dust of the attic floor, just outside the door; and her neck was hacked half through, as I remember the carter Peter's. And out of the corner, in the grimy half-light, there stole toward her an enormous cat with greedy, green eyes wide open. I jumped out of the bed and out of the window, and landed in a snowdrift in the yard. This happened on an evening when mama was noisily entertaining; the broken glass and the cracking window frame went unheard; and I lay in the snow for some time. I suffered no broken bones; but I was severely lacerated by the glass, my shoulder was dislocated, and I could not move my legs, so that, for three months, I was confined to bed. Lying on my back with nothing to do but listen, I thought what a noisy place the house had become, how incessantly the door slammed downstairs, what a coming and going of what a mob of people!

I heard the sweep of snowstorms over the roof; the gusts of wind that thumped at the door and whined, funereally, down the chimney, setting the dampers clattering. By day I heard the crows cawing; in the night stillness the distant, mournful howling of wolves. Under that musical influence was my heart nurtured. Later came shy spring, peeping into my window with the radiant eye of the March sun, hesitant at first, but warmer and more venturesome, day by day. Then cats in heat called to toms from the roof. The rustling spring sounds permeated the walls themselves. Icicles snapped off; half-melted snow thudded down from the stable roof; and the bells, so crystal clear in winter, had a more muffled sound.

When grandma came to me now there was vodka on her breath, and the odor grew stronger, day by day, and finally she took to bringing it with her in a large white teapot, which she hid under my bed, winking to me as she said, "You won't say a word about it to grandpa, will you, darling?"

"Why do you drink?"

"Ah, that. You'll have to wait until you're grown up to understand."

She would take a sip from the spout, wipe her mouth on her sleeve, and, with a genial smile, would ask me, "So tell me, my little gentleman, what shall it be tonight?"

"Tell me about my father."

"Where do I start?"

I would recall to her where we had left off, and for a long time her voice flowed over me like a melodious stream.

This narrative about my father had been started some days back when, coming to me, nervous and depressed and weary, after a restless night, she told me, "I dreamed about your father. He was walking over the fields and whistling, and a spotted dog with his tongue hanging, followed behind him. I don't know why, but I've been dreaming about him, lately. Probably his soul is not at rest."

And starting then, and continuing for several evenings after, she gave me my father's biography, which proved absorbing, like all her stories.

My father's father was a soldier who had risen to be an officer. He practiced such cruelties on those under him that he was finally banished to Siberia, where my father was born. He had an unhappy childhood, and several times ran away from home. Once his father tracked him down by setting hounds on his trail; another time he beat the boy so inhumanly that neighbors took him and hid him away.

"Do they always flog children?" I asked, and grandma replied, matter-of-factly, "Always."

My father's mother died young; and he was only nine when his father also died. He was taken on as an apprentice by the maker of crosses in the town of Perm; but he ran away and earned his bread by conducting blind people to fairs. At sixteen he came to Nizhny and got a job with a carpenter who worked on contract for the Kolchin steamboats. At twenty he was a skilled carpenter and upholsterer in a workshop next door to grandpa's house on Kovalich Street.

"The fence happened not to be high, and certain people happened not to be shy," said grandma with a laugh. "One day Barbara and I were picking raspberries when, hop over the fence, came your father. I was a little put out, foolish as I was; but there he stood, under the apple trees, such a nice looking fellow, bareheaded and barefoot, but in a white shirt and velvet trousers, and leather headbands around his long hair. That's how he courted your mother. The first time I'd seen him from our window, I had said to myself, 'That's a likely lad!' So I said to him now, when he came up, 'What's this, young man, coming here in this fashion!'

"And he went down on his knees to me and said, 'Because my heart is here, all of it, with Barbara. For God's sake, help us get married.'

"It was such a shock, I couldn't unlock my tongue for awhile. I looked around and there was your mother, the hoyden, making signs to him from behind an apple tree. She was all red, as red as the raspberries, and her eyes were full of tears.

" 'You rascals,' I cried. 'However did it happen? Are you mad, Barbara? And you, young man,' I said. 'What are you about? Are you thinking of carrying her off by force?'

"Grandpa was quite a rich man then. He had already given the children their portions and he owned four houses besides, and had money, and was getting big eyes. Only a little while before he had been presented an embroidered hat and uniform for being the head of his guild nine years running. Oh, he felt high and mighty in those days. I told them what I was duty bound to tell them, trembling with fear and sorrow for them; the two of them had become so sad.

"Then your father spoke up. 'I know very well Mr. Kashirin won't give his consent, so we will have to elope; only we need your help.'

"I give them help! I couldn't help laughing at them. But your father wouldn't take 'no.' 'And if I get stones from you instead of help, I won't give up,' he said.

"Then Barbara went over to him and put her arm around his shoulder, and said, 'We've been planning to get married a long time—we *should* have been married in May.'

"What a turn that gave me, good Lord!"

And grandma began to laugh, and her whole body shook with it; and then she took snuff, wiped her eyes, sighed in a relaxed way, and continued, "That's something you can't understand yet; you have no notion what it means to be married; but this you do know, for a girl to have a baby before she's married is something awful. Keep that in mind, so that when you grow up you won't take advantage of a girl; you'd be committing a big sin. The girl would be cast out and the child would be a bastard. Never forget that. And be kind to women; love them for themselves, not for your pleasures. I'm giving you good advice."

She was silent and rocked herself in the chair; then she shook herself out of her revery, and continued, "But what was I to do? I slapped your father, and I pulled Barbara's braids; but your father, very sensibly, said, 'A quarrel won't settle matters,' and Barbara said, 'First, let's decide what to do and have our fight afterwards.'

"I asked him if he had any money. 'I had some money,' he replied, 'but it went for Barbara's ring.'

" 'How much for it?'

" 'About a hundred rubles.'

"At that time money happened to be tight, and prices high; I looked at the two, your mother and father, and thought, 'What infants, what little fools.'

" 'I hid the ring under the floor,' said your mother, 'so it shouldn't be seen. We can sell it.'

"Both of them were such children! However, we made plans to get them married within a week, and I promised to make the arrangements with the priest. But I was all on edge, and my heart fluttered; and so did Barbara's; we were in such terror of grandpa! But everything was arranged just the same.

"But one of grandpa's workmen had it in for your father. He guessed what we were up to and spied on us. I got together the best clothes I could for my only daughter, and dressed her up and took her to the gate and put her into a carriage, where your father was waiting. He gave a whistle and away they went. Coming back into the house, this workman stopped me and said in a wheedling voice, 'I'm a man with a kind heart; I have no wish to stand in the way of fate; only I must have fifty rubles to keep me out of the way.'

"Money I had none. I never craved it, and I never saved any when I had it. So, like a fool, I said, 'I have no money so I can't give you any.'

" 'But promise you'll give it to me later and I'll wait.'

" 'How can I?' I asked. 'Where'll I get money to keep my promise?'

" 'Is it hard to steal a little sum from a rich husband?' he answered.

"Oh, if I hadn't been such a fool I should have led him on; but I spat into his filthy mug, and off he rushed to shout what he knew in the yard."

She shut her eyes, and smiled as she went on. "To this day, I can remember it, just as it happened, this risky thing I did. Grandpa came roaring at me like a wild animal. Were they making fun of him, he wanted to know. As a matter of fact, he had been making his own plans for Barbara and bragging around that he was going to marry her off 'to a gentleman—the nobility.' And here was his nobleman, here was his gentleman! The Holy Mother of God knows best which persons are to be brought together.

"Grandpa chased around the yard as if his clothes were on fire, calling for Jake and Mike and the coachman, the last at the suggestion of that vicious workman. I saw grandpa take a leather whip tipped with a lead weight, and I saw Mike take his gun. Our horses, at that time, were the best, high-spirited, and they had a light carriage to pull. 'Surely,' I thought, 'they'll overtake them.' And at this Barbara's guardian angel gave me a hint. I got a knife and cut a shaft rope. 'That'll cause a breakdown,' I calculated. And so it did. The shafts came loose on the way, and grandpa and Mike and the coachman barely escaped with their lives, besides, of course, holding them up; so that, by the time the repairs were made and they got to the church, Barbara and your father were standing in the church porch, the wedding safely over, thank God!

"Our people picked a fight with your father, but he was a powerful fellow, and at that time, because of his youth and happiness, in a rare condition. Mike was pitched off the porch and got a broken arm; and the coachman, too, was hurt; and grandpa and that bad man took fright.

"Even in the heat of the fight your father didn't lose his self-control; he said to grandpa, 'Now, put down that strap and don't shake it at me. I'm looking for peace between us. I've only taken what God has granted to me, and what I'll give up to no man. That's all there is to say.'

"At that they left off and grandpa went back to the carriage, shouting, 'It's good-by, Barbara. You're no daughter of mine. I never want to see you again, alive or starved dead.'

"And when he arrived home he cursed me, and beat me; but I only groaned and kept mum.

"Everything blows over; what is fated comes to pass. He said to me, 'Understand, Akulina, you have no daughter any more. Remember that!'

"But I said to myself, 'Lie to yourself, you ill-natured sandy-head—tell me ice is hot!' "

I listened to all this with greedy absorption. Her story gave me some surprises, for grandpa had given quite another version of mother's wedding. He said he had forbidden the marriage, and barred the house to mama after it, but that it had been no secret, and he had attended the wedding in the church. I had no desire to question grandma as to which was the true version; hers was the more picturesque and I gave it my preference.

In telling stories grandma rocked from side to side as if she were in a boat. The sadder or more chilling the story was, the more violent her rocking became, and her hands would thrust in the air as if she were fending something off; and often she covered her eyes, and a gentle, unseeing smile nestled in her wrinkled cheeks. But seldom, through it all, did her thick eyebrows move. At times her indiscriminate kindness touched me to the heart; but at other times I could not bear it that she had not answered back and not asserted herself more.

"For the first two weeks," she said, "I didn't know where Barbara and your father were keeping themselves; then a little barefoot boy came from them to tell me. And, on a Saturday, when I was supposed to be at vespers, I went there, instead. They were living quite a distance away, on the Svetinsk Hill, in a room over a factory yard, a sooty, noisy place. But they didn't mind; they were like two happy kittens, purring and playing together. I brought them what I could, some tea, some sugar, some cereals, some jam, some flour, some dried mushrooms and even a little money . . . it's no sin to steal, you know, when it's not for yourself.

"But your father wouldn't take a thing. 'We're no beggars,' says he. And Barbara sings the same tune. 'What's this for?'

"So I gave them a talking to. 'You young fools,' said I, 'And what am I, I'd like to know? I'm the mother God gave you, and you, little fool, are my own flesh and blood; and do you think I'll let you insult me? Don't you know that when a mother is insulted on earth, God's Mother weeps in heaven?'

"So your father picked me up in his arms and toted me all around the room, and actually danced with me! What a bear he was—so strong! And Barbara, that little hussy, was so proud of her man, proud as a peacock, and couldn't keep her eyes off him, as if he were her new doll, and talked about her housekeeping so importantly, you'd think she'd been married a lifetime! It was fun just to listen to her. A wolf would have cracked his teeth on her cheese buns that she served with the tea!

"Well, so months went by, and the time for you to be born was coming close, and still not a word from grandpa—what a stubborn one he is, our old man! Of course he knew I was seeing them, on the sly, but he made out he didn't know. He'd forbidden the mention of Barbara in the house, and her name never came up, not even from me.

But I knew a father's heart would speak out, sooner or later. And the time came. It was a stormy night, that sounded as if bears were butting against the windows. The wind came howling down the chimney; all the devils seemed to be on the loose. Grandpa and I couldn't sleep.

" 'It's hard on the poor, on a night like this,' I commented, 'but even harder on people who have no peace of mind.'

"And Grandpa pops out with, 'How're they doing? Are they well?'

" 'Who d'you mean? Barbara, our daughter, and Maxim, our son-in-law?'

" 'How'd you guess it?'

" 'Leave off, father,' I said. 'Stop being such a fool. What satisfaction is there in it?'

"He sighed. 'Ekh, you devil, you old devil!' After awhile, speaking of your father, he said, 'I hear he's a fool. Is that true?'

" 'A fool,' I said, 'is a man who doesn't do his share, who hangs on others' necks. Jake and Mike, for example, don't they behave like fools? Who works in this house; who brings in the money? You. What use are they to you as assistants?'

"His answer was to curse me—I was a fool, a low creature, a whore and God knows what else; but I kept mum. And he went on, 'How could you let such a one take you in? Who knows what he is and where he comes from?' And still I said nothing; I let him tire himself out; and then I suggested, 'Why don't you go see them? They're not doing badly.'

" 'That's an honor they don't deserve! Let them come here!'

"This made me cry for joy, and he pulled my hair loose—he liked to play with my hair—and he said, 'Silly to let yourself get upset. Think I've got no heart?'

"There was a time, you know, when he was very good, until he got to thinking he was smarter than everybody; and then he got stupid and ill-natured.

"And so on a holiday they appeared, your father and mother, big and all slicked-up; and your father stood in front of grandpa, who put his hand on his shoulder, and he said to grandpa, 'I want you to know that I haven't come here to ask for a dowry; I'm here to pay my respects to my wife's father.'

"Well, that tickled grandpa and he laughed and said, 'So, you're a fighter, you bandit! Well for once we'll let that go. I want you to come here to live.'

"Your father wrinkled his brow. 'That's up to Barbara,' he said. 'Whatever she wants will go with me.'

"And so it started. They just couldn't get on together—at each other's throats all the time. I'd wink at your father, and give him a kick under the table, but it was no go; he wouldn't give way. His eyes were very fine, clear and shining; and his brows were thick and black; and when he knitted them together, you almost couldn't see his eyes; and his face got such an obstinate stony look! I was the only one he'd listen to. If that's possible, I loved him better than my own, and he knew it, and he loved me, too. How he used to hug me and lift me in his arms and carry me around the room, saying, 'You're my real mother; you're like the earth. I love you better than Barbara.' And your mother—when she was happy she was such a minx—she'd rush at him, 'Monster! Don't you dare say such a thing!' And there were the three of us, romping together. Ah, my dear, then we knew what happiness was! He was a marvelous dancer, and he knew wonderful songs that he'd picked up from blind people—there are no singers like the blind, you know.

"Well, they settled down in that outbuilding in the garden, and there, at noon on the dot, you were born. Your father came in for his lunch and there you were to welcome him. He was quite beside himself with joy, and tired your mother out; he didn't seem to realize how exhausting it is to bring a child into the world. He heaved me up on his shoulder and hauled me all the way across the yard to grandpa to bring him the news —that he had another grandson. Even grandpa laughed, 'What a devil you are, Maxim!'

"But he was no favorite of your uncles. He didn't drink, he was open in his talk, and he liked to play tricks—to his own cost. Once, during Lent, there was a strong wind, and suddenly, a weird wailing went through the house. It stunned us all. What was it? Even grandpa was in a panic, had all the lamps lit, and shouted at everybody, 'Let's all pray together!'

"And just as suddenly as it started, it stopped, which scared us worse. Your Uncle Jake guessed, 'I'll bet it's one of Maxim's tricks!' And later, your father admitted that the sound had come from the wind blowing in the necks of different sized bottles he'd set up in the gable window. 'Watch out,' grandpa threatened him, 'or your tricks will take you back to Siberia!'

"During an unusually hard frost one winter, the wolves came in from the woods; so there were dead dogs, and runaway horses and even some tipsy watchmen were devoured; and the town was in a panic. Your father went gunning for them on snowshoes and brought back two of them. He skinned them, hollowed out their heads, gave them each a pair of glass eyes—a very neat job altogether. Well, your Uncle Mike stepped out into the vestibule for something and bolted back, gasping, his eyes rolling, his hair standing, too paralyzed to speak. At last he got out a whisper—'Wolf!' Everybody picked up whatever came to hand that could serve as a weapon, and crowded into the vestibule, and shone their lights on a wolf's head raised above a box. They shot him and clubbed him—and guess what it was? Coming closer, all they saw was the hollowed-out head and the skin with the forepaws nailed down. This trick of your father's put grandpa in a real temper.

"Then Jake had to have a share in this horseplay. Your father made a cardboard falseface with flax strands glued on top, for hair, and a frightening nose, mouth and eyes; and he and Jake went through the street with it at night, and poked that fiend's face into people's windows, so that they ran about, screaming. Another time they promenaded at night in sheets, sent a priest running for his life into a sentry box, and the sentry, who was just as frightened, called the police. It was one such practical joke after another, and there was no stopping them. I begged them and Barbara begged them to stop their fooling; but they did as they pleased. Your father's answer was a laugh; it made him split his sides to see people run wild with fright and knock their heads together, because of his tricks. 'Talk to them!' he'd say.

"But he got a taste of his own medicine—and it nearly killed him. Your Uncle Mike was always around grandpa; he would flare up at anything and carried grudges. He worked out a plan to dispose of your father. It was early in winter and four of them were on their way back from a visit, your father, your two uncles, and a deacon who was later unfrocked for the murder of a cabman. Coming out of Yamsky Street your uncles got your father to go with them to the Dinkov pond, where they said they wanted to go skating. There they slid on the ice like children and edged him over to a hole, and pushed him in. But I've told you that."

"What made my uncles so bad?"

"It's not that they're bad," said grandma, calmly, taking snuff. "It's only that they're stupid. Mike is crafty as well as stupid, but Jake on the whole's a pretty decent sort. Well, they pushed him in but he caught on to the edge of the ice. Then they came down on his fingers with their heels. Luckily he was sober and they were drunk, and with God's help, he managed to keep his head out of the ice in the center of the hole, where they couldn't get at him; and they got tired and left him to drown or freeze in the ice. But he climbed out and went to the police station which, as you know, is nearby, in the market; and the officer there knew him and all the family, and wanted to know how it happened."

Grandma crossed herself and said in a grateful tone, "God rest your father's soul; he's earned it; the fact is he protected them. 'It's my own doing,' he said. 'I got drunk and strayed over to the pond and stumbled into a hole.'

" 'That's not the truth,' said the officer. 'You haven't been drinking.'

"No matter. They rubbed him down with brandy, dressed him in dry clothes, wrapped him in a sheepskin and an officer and two of his men brought him home. Jake and Mike weren't back yet; they'd gone to a tavern to toast their success. Your mother and I stared at Maxim. He wasn't like himself; his face was blue; his fingers were cut and caked with dried blood; and his hair looked as if it had been snowed on; only this snow didn't thaw! His hair had turned white!

" 'What did they do to you?' Barbara screamed.

"The officer smelled that something was wrong and started to ask questions, and I knew, inside me, some evil had been done.

"I left Barbara with the officer and tried to find out, on the quiet, from your father, what had happened.

" 'The first thing to do,' he whispered, 'is to head off Jake and Mike and tell them to say they left me at Yamsky Street, and went down Pokrovsky Street while I went on through Priadilny Lane. Don't get that mixed up or we'll have the police on our heads.'

"I went to grandpa and told him, 'Go keep the officer talking while I watch for our sons to let them know of the evil they brought on us.'

"He dressed himself, trembling all over, and grumbled, 'I knew this was coming. I expected it.'

"All bunk! He didn't know anything about it. Well, I met my sons with my hands covering my face. It frightened them sober at once; and Jake, the dear boy, spilled everything by blabbing, 'I don't know anything; it's Mike's fault. He's the oldest!'

"But we fixed it with the officer, who was a gentleman. 'I see,' he said. 'But take care. If there's any trouble in your house, I'll know who's to blame.' And leaving us that to think over, he went away.

"And grandpa went to your father and said, 'Our thanks to you. I know, in your place, others would have acted differently. And I'm grateful to you, daughter, for bringing such an honorable man into your father's house.' Grandpa could make nice speeches when he felt like it. But after this happened he turned foolish and kept his heart locked up as in a tower.

"Left alone with Barbara and me, your father began weeping; he almost got delirious. 'Mama, why did they do this to me? Have I harmed them in any way?' He always called me 'mama' like a child, and he really had a childlike character.

"I wept too, what else? I was grieved about my children. Your mother ripped the buttons off her blouse and sat, all disordered, as if she had been in a fight and she cried, 'Let's go away. My brothers are our enemies. What'll they do next to us? Let's go away!'

"I tried to calm her. 'Don't pile dirt on the fire; isn't the house smoky enough without that?'

"And it was at that moment that your fool of a grandpa had to send the two in to ask to be forgiven. Barbara sprang at Mike and slapped his face. 'That's how I forgive you!' And your father asked, 'Brothers, how could you do a thing like that? You might have made a cripple out of me. What kind of a workman would I be without hands?'

"Well, they were reconciled. But your father was sick; he lay around for seven weeks, getting no stronger, saying to me, 'Ah, mama, I'm sick of this town; let's go somewhere else.'

"Then an opportunity came to him to go to Astrakhan. The city was expecting a visit from the Tsar that summer, and your father was assigned the job of erecting a welcoming arch. They took the first boat down, and it broke my heart to see them go; and your father was sorry, too, and kept asking me to come to Astrakhan with them, but Barbara was happy to go, the minx, and didn't try to hide it, either! And so they left . . . and that's the end!"

She took a drop of vodka and a pinch of snuff and then, looking out of the window at the deep blue sky, she said, "True, your father and I weren't the same flesh and blood, but in our souls we were kin."

Now and then, when she was telling me these stories, grandpa would look in, his sharp nose in the air, sniffing, and giving grandma accusing looks, and saying, "That's a lie, that's a lie!" And sooner or later, without warning, he'd ask, "Alex, has she been drinking here?"

"No."

"You're lying; I saw her myself!" But he would leave, looking mystified.

And grandma would wink at his back and chuckle, and say something pleasant like, "Go on, only don't scare the horses."

One day, standing in the middle of the room, he looked down on the floor, and in a low voice called, "Mother."

"Yes."

"See what's going on."

"Yes."

"What do you think?"

"There'll be a wedding, father. Remember your talk of a nobleman?"

"Yes."

"Here's your nobleman."

"But he's got nothing."

"That's her lookout."

Grandpa went out and, filled with uneasiness, I asked, "What were you talking about?"

"You've got to know everything!" she complained, as she massaged my legs. "If you're to know everything now, as a child, you'll have nothing to ask about when you're grown up." Then she shook her head at me and laughed.

"Ah, grandpa, grandpa! You're only a speck of dust in God's eyes. Alex—not a word about this to anybody, but grandpa's ruined. A certain gentleman to whom he lent a big sum has gone bankrupt."

She went into a revery, smiling at first; but gradually her face wrinkled up and became gloomy.

"Tell me what you're thinking."

She came to with a start, and answered, "I'm just thinking of something to tell you. Shall it be the ballad of Evstignia? Well, here it is.

"There was a deacon named Evstignia, who thought he was the wisest of men, wiser than bishops or boyars [17] or the craftiest hunter. He held himself erect like a blade of spear-grass. So proud was he, he was always telling his neighbors, high or low, what to do. He complained about this, and found fault with that. When he looked at a church, 'Not tall enough!' When he went through a street, 'Too narrow!' When he picked an apple, 'Not ripe!' And the sun, itself, rose too soon for Deacon Evstignia. Nothing in the world was right enough to suit him."

Grandma plumped out her cheeks and rolled her eyes. A droll, deliberately witless expression came into her kind face as she continued in a drawling voice, " 'There's not a thing I couldn't fix up better, all by myself,' he said, 'if only I had the time.' "

She paused, smiled to herself again, and resumed, "Well, some devils paid a visit to the deacon one night. 'Having a dull time of it here, eh, deacon?' they said. 'Well, old fellow, we'll take you along with us to hell, and see if the fires there are hot enough for you.'

"Before that wise deacon could even get his hat on, they got hold of him with their paws, and, giggling and screeching, they pulled him down. A devil apiece sat on his shoulders, and smack in the middle of

[17] An old Russian title of nobility.

the fire they stuck him. 'Nice fire, eh, Evstignia?' they asked him. The roasting deacon was burned red hot, but he stood there, proudly, with his hands to his sides, and pouted, and said, haughtily, 'How terribly smoky it is, here in hell!' "

And in the same lazy voice, low and smooth, she explained with a quiet laugh, "He'd never give in, that Evstignia; stuck to his own notions to the end, obstinately, just like grandpa. That'll do now; go to sleep; it's late."

Mama seldom came up to see me; and her visits were brief, and she spoke in a hurried way. She looked more beautiful every day, and was dressed more gorgeously. I sensed a change in her; as I sensed a change in grandma. I felt that something was happening and it was being kept from me and I tried to puzzle it out.

Grandma's stories no longer held my interest, not even those about my father. They could not soothe my vague, but constantly increasing, forebodings.

"Why is my father's soul not at peace?" I asked grandma.

"How do I know?" and she covered her eyes. "It's in God's hands. It's supernatural. It's beyond human beings."

At nights, unable to sleep, I gazed through the dark blue blocks of the windows, at the stars already flowing across the sky. And a sad story formed itself in my mind in which my father was the hero, a lonely man with a stick in his hand, and a shaggy dog following him, over the roads of the world.

Chapter Twelve

WAKING AFTER AN AFTERNOON NAP ONE DAY, I FELT AWAKE IN MY legs, too. When I stuck them out of bed they still felt stiff; but it was a fact that my legs were healed and I would soon be walking again. At this electrifying news I raised a joyous shout, and tried to stand up. My legs couldn't yet bear my entire weight and down I went. So I crawled to the door and down the staircase, excitedly anticipating the surprise I would cause downstairs.

I got into mama's room on my hands and knees, how I can't recall; but she had guests, one of whom, a withered old lady in green, said authoritatively, in a sharp voice that silenced all others, "Let him have some raspberry tea and see that his head is covered."

She was all green, dress and hat and even her face, which had tufted warts under the eyes, the very hairs of which were like grass. Her upper lip rose and her lower lip fell, exposing green teeth; and she covered her eyes with a black-mittened hand.

"Who's that?" I asked, suddenly struck timid.

In an unpleasant voice, grandpa said, "Another grandma for you."

And, laughing, mama led Eugene Maximov over to me, saying, "Here's your father." Speaking very rapidly, she added something that I didn't catch, and Maximov, with a friendly twinkle in his eyes, leaned over me and said, "I'll get you a painting set."

The room was all lit up. Several five-branched candelabra were on the table, and among them stood the "Mourn me not, Mother" icon, grandpa's favorite. Its inset pearls gave off iridescent gleams in the flickering lights, and the radiance from the gems in the golden crown was dazzling. Outside the windows were staring faces like round pancakes, with noses flattened to the panes; and I felt everything afloat around me. With chill fingers the old green woman felt my ears and croaked, "Certainly, certainly!"

"He's fainting," grandma said, and carried me to the door. But I was not fainting. I had merely closed my eyes. As soon as, half-lifting me, half-dragging me, she had gotten me upstairs, I asked, "Why didn't you tell me?"

"Enough, you . . . watch your tongue!"

"You're all fakers!"

Putting me down on the bed, she herself buried her head in the pillow and began weeping, shaking convulsively all over. "Why aren't you crying?" she asked, in a choked mumble.

I felt no wish to cry. It was dark in the attic and bitterly cold. I shivered and the bed creaked; and the image of that old green woman did not leave my eyes. I made a pretense of sleeping and grandma left.

Monstrous days, one no different from the other, trickled out like a shallow stream. Following that betrothal, mama went off somewhere, and a heavy stillness burdened the house.

One morning grandpa came in to chisel away the putty around the winter windows. Grandma followed with a basin of water and a wash rag, and grandpa asked in a low voice, "Well, old woman, how does it strike you?"

"What do you mean?"

"Glad or not?"

And she gave him the same answer I had gotten, "Enough, you . . . watch your tongue!"

These days I gave the simplest words mysterious meanings, as if they covered over something significant and tragic, not to be mentioned, but known to everybody.

With care grandpa pried out the winter frame and carried it off, and grandma went to the window for a breath of air. From the garden could be heard the starlings' call and the sparrows' twittering; and there drifted in the exhilarating fragrance of thawing earth. The oven tiles, dark blue in color, seemed to have paled; it gave one a chill to look at them. I got out of bed.

"Don't you start running around barefoot," warned grandma.

"I'm going into the garden."

"Better wait. It's not yet dry enough."

But I paid no attention to her. The truth was that the very sight of adults had become repellent to me. In the garden the pale blades of new grass had already forced their way out; the full buds on the apple tree were about to open; on the roof of Petrovna's hut the new green on the moss made a pleasing sight; birds were everywhere; all sounds were cheerful; and the fresh and fragrant air made one joyously giddy. Around the pit where the carter, Peter, had slashed his throat, among remaining splashes of snow, grew a tall, reddish grass, that gave me no pleasure to look at, that I could not include with spring. With the dismal chimneys rearing out of it, the entire pit was a pointless eyesore. I had an angry impulse to root out that tall grass, to take the chimney apart, brick by brick, to get rid of this useless mess, and transform the pit into a clean place for myself, where I could get through the summer, away from adults. Immediately I put the thought into action, and, for awhile, the work took my mind off occurrences in the house, which often disturbed me, but lessened in importance from day to day.

"What are those sulks about?" both mama and grandma would ask me; and the question embarrassed me, since it was not anger toward them I was feeling, but a sense of alienation from everyone in the house.

At both the midday meal and supper and at tea, the green old woman was likely to appear, resembling nothing so much as a rotten post in a rickety fence. Her eyes seemed to be sewn to her face with unseen thread, and in danger of popping out of their bony sockets, as she rolled them around in swift, prying glances everywhere, taking note of everything, turning them up to the ceiling when she called on God, and directing them down her nose when the talk was of domestic matters. Her eyebrows looked like cutouts pasted on. She put things into her mouth with a ludicrous, sweeping gesture, the little finger pointing out; and she chewed noiselessly with her horselike teeth; and bones above her ears rolled like balls; and the hair from her warts wagged up and down, as if they were crawling over her yellow, withered, scrubbed, yet nauseating, skin.

True, she was very clean, as was her son, and I found it repellent to come close to either of them. There was such a strong whiff of yellow soap, mixed with incense, from the corpselike hand she offered to my lips that, from the very first time she presented it, I shrank from it and ran away. Over and over again she prodded her son, "Eugene, that boy badly needs disciplining. Understand, Eugene?" An obedient nod, or frown—then silence. In the green woman's presence frowns were the rule.

Toward that woman, and her son as well, my hatred was implacable, and many a beating did it earn me.

Once, at dinner, her eyes revolving in their ghastly way, she said, "Oh, Alex, why must you bolt your food? And such big pieces! Better give it up, my dear."

I took the morsel out of my mouth, fitted it back on the fork, and offered it to her. "Here, only, careful, it's hot."

Mama led me away from the table, and I was banished to the attic in disgrace; there grandma joined me, her hand over her mouth to smother her giggles, "Lord, but you're a fresh little ape—bless you!"

I was annoyed to see her holding her hand over her mouth, so I got away, climbed up the roof and sat by myself, leaning against the chimney for quite awhile. Indeed, I preferred to be insolent and to insult them all; and I didn't know how to cope with this feeling, though it was necessary to master it.

One day I smeared the chairs of my stepfather- and stepgrandmother-to-be, one with grease and the other with cherry sap, which stuck both of them to their seats—a comical sight. After the beating by grandpa, mama came to me in the attic, drew me close, held me against her knees and said, "Listen! What makes you so hateful? If you only knew what misery it causes me!" And, as she pressed my head to her cheeks, her bright tears flowed over me.

This affected me painfully. Indeed, I would have preferred a beating. I promised never again to be rude to the Maximovs, if only she stopped crying.

And affectionately she replied, "There now. Just be civil to them.

Soon we shall be married, and then we'll go to Moscow; and when we come back you'll live with us. Eugene is good-natured and clever and the two of you will get along. You'll go to primary school and later you'll be a student like him; then you can become a doctor, or anything else you choose. What you study for will be up to you. Now run along and play."

These "thens" and "laters" felt to me like steps leading down and away, far from her, into loneliness and darkness. There was no happiness for me where those stairs led. I wanted to tell her, "Please, mama, don't get married. I'll support you." But I could not get the words out. Mama never failed to arouse me to immediate tenderness, but I could never express it to her.

My building project in the garden was advancing. I tore off the tall weed grass or chopped it down with a pruning knife. Against the rim of the pit, upon the loosened earth, I laid a course of bricks, making a sort of stone bench, broad enough to sprawl on. In the cracks between the bricks I stuck shards of colored glass and pottery, which gave rainbow reflections when the sun peeped in, as in church.

"That's well planned," said grandpa one day, as he inspected my work, "but you've only snapped off the blades and left the grass roots. Let's have your spade and I'll dig them out for you."

I brought him the spade and, spitting on his hand and grunting, he stamped it into the earth with his foot. "Pitch these roots away. I'll put in some sunflowers here, for you, and raspberries. It'll be nice, real nice." Then, stooped over the spade, he stood there, dead silent.

I stared at him and observed a rain of small tears from his little, clever pig eyes. "Anything the matter?"

He gave himself a shake, brushed off the tears with his hand, and fixed a dim gaze upon me. "I was perspiring. Look—what a lot of worms!"

He returned to his digging but, after a while, he broke off saying, "All your work is for nothing. I'll soon be selling the house. It's got to be sold before the fall. I have to have the money for your mother's dowry. That's how it is. I hope it will bring her happiness, God bless her."

Throwing down the spade, he went off, with a resigned gesture, behind the bathhouse, to a forcing bed he had there. I set to digging, and almost with the first stroke of the spade, mashed my toes. This kept me from attending my mother's wedding at the church. I could only hobble up to the gate, from which I saw her, on Maximov's arm, her head lowered, tiptoeing fastidiously over the cobbles, over the grass, and across cracks, as if she were treading on spikes.

The wedding was quiet. On their return from church they sat around at tea, looking depressed. Mother, who had already changed from her bridal dress, went to her room to pack. Coming over to me, my step-father said, "I promised you a set of paints, but the ones you can get here are no good, and I need my own; but I'll bring you a set from Moscow."

"What'll I do with it?"

"Don't you like to draw?"

"I don't know how."

"Then I'll bring you something else."

Mama returned. "We'll soon be back," she said. "Your father has to take an examination, and when his studies are finished we'll be back."

It made me feel good to have them talk to me in this way, as if I were grown up, but it struck me odd to hear of a bearded man studying.

"What are you studying?" I asked.

"Surveying."

What surveying was I did not bother to ask. A heavy stillness seemed to pervade the house, broken only by a sort of woolen rustling and I wished night were not so slow in coming. Grandpa, his back to the oven, stared frowningly out of the window. The green hag, with signs and mutterings, was helping mama pack. Grandma was out of sight, shut up in the attic. She had got drunk by noon and kept to her room, ashamed.

Mama left early in the morning. In her farewell she lifted me off the ground and held me in her arms, and with eyes that had become a stranger's, she looked into mine, kissed me, and bid me "Good-by."

"Tell him he better mind me," said grandpa pettishly, looking up at the still rosy morning sky.

"Do as grandpa tells you," said mama, and made the sign of the cross over me.

I had anticipated her saying something else, and was furious with grandpa for interrupting.

Getting into the carriage, mama got into a temper trying to extricate her skirt from something it had caught on. "Help her, why don't you? Are you blind?" shouted grandpa at me. But I could not. I was too helpless with grief.

Maximov tucked in his long, blue-trousered legs, and grandma gave him some bundles, which he heaped up in his lap, keeping them put with his chin. His pale face puckered with embarrassment and he said, haltingly, "That's—enough."

In another carriage sat the green hag with her older son, the army officer, who scratched his head with his sword hilt and yawned.

"So you're off to the war?" asked grandpa.

"I have to."

"Well, it's a good thing. The Turks need a beating."

Then they were off. Several times mama turned to wave her handkerchief. Grandma, so overcome that she had to support herself against the wall, waved her hand. Grandpa wiped his eyes, and in a breaking voice said, "Nothing good—will—come of it."

Astride the gatepost I watched until the carriages turned a corner, and I felt as if a door in my heart had just been locked and bolted. It was very early; the shutters were still fastened over house windows; the street was still. Never before had I been so conscious of an absence of life. From afar could be heard the rasping tootling of the shepherd.

"Let's have some breakfast," said grandpa, his hand on my shoulder. "It appears to be your lot to live with me; and you've begun to leave a mark on me, like the striking of matches on a brick."

All day long we kept busy in the garden. He set out plants, he propped up the raspberry bushes, he scraped the moss off the apple trees, he squashed caterpillars, while I went on with the construction and adornment of my pit structure. Grandpa sawed off the protruding end of the burnt beam, and split it into sticks, which he stuck into the ground for me to hang my bird cages on. And I wove the dried grass and stretched it over my dwelling, like a canopy, to protect it from the sun and the dew, with quite satisfactory results.

"It's good for you to learn to rely on yourself," said grandpa.

I took what he said very seriously. At times he would lie down on the bench, on which I had spread a mat of turf, and give me counsel in halting phrases, as if it were hard for him to find the right words.

"Now you're really cut off from your mother. She'll have other children, and they'll mean more to her than you. And grandma's taken to drink."

After a silence in which he seemed to be listening for something, he resumed, his words seeming to come reluctantly. "This is the second time. She took to drink before, when Mike started his miltiary service. The old idiot coaxed me into buying his discharge. He might have turned out a different sort if he'd done his soldiering. Ekh—you! Soon I'll die—and that means you'll be all by yourself, on your own. You'll have to earn your own living. Understand? Good. So learn to depend on yourself, and don't let yourself be imposed upon! Live at peace with others, quietly and honorably. Whatever others have to say—listen to it, but do what will be to your own advantage."

Weather permitting, I lived in the garden all that summer, even sleeping there on warm nights, on a length of felt that grandma contributed. Quite often she joined me, spreading out hay alongside, for her bedding. Lying there, she would go on and on with her stories, interrupting herself to remark, "Look, a falling star! Some pure, suffering soul has remembered Mother Earth. It signifies that a good man or woman has just been born." Or she would point, "There's a new star just risen, like a great big eye; oh, you shining creature of the sky, you gem of God."

"Fool of a woman," grandpa would mutter. "You'll catch cold, or get a stroke, or robbers will break in and murder you."

There were sunsets, when what looked like rivers of flame ran down the sky, and golden cinders seemed to shower down on the garden's velvet green. Everything grew a shade deeper in hue, and a size larger, to swell out in the warm, enfolding dusk. Weary of the sun, the leaves hung limp, the grass was bowed, everything softened and mellowed, and gave forth gentle, fragrant exhalations that calmed like music. And music, itself, in fitful gusts, was wafted in from peasants or picnickers in the fields.

Night fell, and with it there entered one's heart something that freshened and invigorated it like the caress of a loving mother. With hard, but warming hands the stillness stroked the heart, and what was best forgotten, all the bitterness and dirt of the day, was scraped away. To lie with one's face upturned to the sky, to watch the stars burning in its infinite deeps, each high range opening upon a new, starry vista, was entrancing. You barely lifted yourself from the ground, and a marvel!—either earth dwindled before your eyes, or you grew gigantic, swelling out to merge with everything around you. And the dark and the stillness deepened, with every instant; yet sounds followed one another, tiny, drawn out, barely audible; each, whether it be a bird drowsily chirping in its sleep, or a hedgehog running, or a subdued human voice, differed from its daytime sound, had something individual that lovingly accentuated the sentient stillness.

The notes of an accordion somewhere, a woman's ringing laugh, a sword scraping over flagstones, a dog's bark—the sounds were no more than the last fluttering leaves of the dead day. You might hear a sudden cry and the stumble of a drunk out in the field, or in the street; but that, being common enough, went unregarded.

Grandma's sleep was short, and lying with her head pillowed on her arms, she would use any pretext to begin her stories, indifferent to whether I listened or not. She had a faculty of choosing stories that enhanced the beauty and the profundity of the night.

Lulled by the even flow of her words, I fell quietly asleep, and was up with the birds. With the sun looking me in the eyes, he seemed to wrap me, cozily, in his rays; there was a gentle morning breeze; dew was scattering from the apple boughs. With a faint mist hovering over it, providing a new, crystalline translucence, the wet grass looked more brightly, more freshly, green. Too high in the sky to be visible, a lark caroled. All the tints and sounds, freshened by the morning dew, fostered a happy good will, an immediate urge to rise and do one's work and live on good terms with every living thing.

In all my life I have known no quieter or more thoughtful time; and that summer there was implanted and grew in me a consciousness of my own powers. I became diffident and ingrown; I had no temptation to join them on hearing the Ovsianikov children at play; and I found the visits of my cousins an annoyance; the only feeling it evoked in me was fear for my refuge in the garden, the first work of my hands—fear lest they destroy it.

I lost all interest in grandpa's talk, which grew duller, more nagging, more self-pitying, day by day. It had practically become a habit with him to quarrel with grandma and forbid her the house; and then she stayed at Uncle Mike's or Uncle Jake's. Once she was away for a number of days and grandpa cooked for us. He burned his fingers, yelled, cursed, smashed dishes; and he became noticeably gluttonous. Coming to my little hut, now and then, he would take his ease on my turf bench and, after watching me for a time, would suddenly ask, "Why so quiet?"

"Because I prefer it. Why?"

And that would precipitate a lecture. "We're not upper crust. No one bothers about our education. We have to learn by ourselves. For them books are written and schools are built; but no time is thrown away on us. We have to get along by ourselves." And he lapsed into a preoccupied silence; he made me feel uncomfortable and tense, as he sat there inert and oblivious.

One morning at tea, not long before he sold the house, he made an abrupt announcement to grandma. "Mother, I've fed you and clothed you, and fed you and clothed you; now it's time for you to look after yourself."

Grandma took the news without a blink, quite as if she had been anticipating it. She calmly reached for her snuff box, took a pinch up her porous nose and said, "No matter. If it has to be, let it be."

Grandpa rented two dim cellar rooms in an old house at the bottom of a small hill. On establishing ourselves in these quarters, grandma put an old bast shoe under the oven and, taking a squatting position, summoned the hearth spirit. "Hearth spirit, here's your sleigh; join us in our new home; come and bring us luck."

Grandpa, looking in from the yard, shouted, "You pagan, you're trying to disgrace me. I'll let you have it for this!"

"Look out you don't bring harm down upon you, father," said grandma earnestly; but he was furious with her, and would permit no invocations to the hearth spirit.

The sale of his house furnishings and other goods took him three days of haggling and abuse with a Tatar second-hand dealer. Watching them from the window, grandma laughed at times and wept at others, and kept muttering, "That's the way! Pull and haul and smash everything!"

I was almost in tears, myself, grieving over my little house in the garden.

We moved in two carts; and the one I stood in, in the midst of loose house articles, jolted as if, any moment, I and part of the load would be pitched out. For some two years, almost till my mother died, I had an obsession that I had actually been flung out along the way.

We had just moved, and grandpa had just settled down in the cellar, when mama appeared, gaunt and pale, with a strange glitter in her large eyes. She looked at us, her own parents and her child, as if she were seeing us for the first time, in a long wordless stare, while my stepfather paced up and down, whistled guardedly, cleared his throat, his fingers working convulsively, where he kept them, behind his back.

"Lord, how you've grown," mama said, laying her hands on my cheeks. Her full, brown dress did not become her. She seemed swollen round the middle.

My stepfather held out his hand to me. "How're things, my boy? Getting along?" Then he sniffed and said, "It's quite damp down here, you know."

The two of them looked exhausted, as if they had run a long way; their clothing was untidy and stained, and all they asked for was a place to lie down. There was tension in the air as they had tea; grandpa, looking at the rain-streaked window, asked, "Hm, lost everything in the fire, eh?"

"Everything," my stepfather answered, emphatically. "We were lucky to get away with our lives."

"So! A fire's no joke."

Bending down, mama whispered something in grandma's ear, and grandma blinked as if under a strong light. The tension perceptibly increased.

Suddenly, in a cold, scornful tone, grandpa said, "But according to the word that reached my ears, my dear Eugene, the fire never happened; but it all went over the card table!"

In the ensuing dead silence, all that could be heard was the samovar whistling, and the rain pattering against the window. At last mama, in a coaxing voice, began, "Papa—"

"Don't 'papa' me," bellowed grandpa. "What now? Didn't I tell you it would be no go—a woman of thirty and a man of twenty? There's you and there's he, the conniving one, the aristocrat! So? What do you say now, little daughter?"

Then all four were at it, at the top of their voices, with my stepfather outshouting them all. I went out and sat on a woodpile on the porch, stunned to find mama so changed, so different from what she had been. This had not impressed me so strongly when I was with her inside, as here in the twilight, in which memory brought back her former self.

Some time after, under circumstances I have forgotten, I found myself in entirely new surroundings in Sormovo [18]—a house with bare walls, weeds growing through the cracks in the beams and cockroaches clustering in the weeds. My mother and stepfather lived in two rooms facing the street, and I lived with grandma in the kitchen, which had a window looking out upon a shed. Nearby rose factory stacks discharging a thick smoke, which the winter wind beat down over the whole village; there was always a burnt odor in our chill rooms. In the morning hours we heard wolves howling.

By standing on a stool I could see, through the top pane, beyond the shed, a factory gate, with lanterns at the sides, gaping open like a toothless old beggar's mouth, and a swarm of tiny people crawling in. At noon the gate reopened its black lips and the factory spewed out the chewed-up people who streamed darkly through the street, till a harsh, snow-driving wind came blustering down and chased them into the houses. The sky was a rare sight in Sormovo. Day after day, above the house roofs, loomed another roof, sombre and low, weighing down the mind, the eyes becoming almost sightless in its unrelieved drabness.

At nightfall a dingy, reddish light pulsated down above the factory and illuminated the stacks, giving them the appearance, not of rising from

[18] Industrial suburb of Nizhny Novgorod, where the shipbuilding works and other factories were located.

the ground into the sky, but of falling from that smoldering cloud and, in their fall, screeching and exhaling flames. All this was intolerably dreary and its tedium oppressed my heart. Grandma was maid-of-all-work from morning to night. She cooked, scrubbed, split firewood, kept the water pails filled; and when she came to bed she sighed with fatigue. At times, after her kitchen work was done, she would put on her short, quilted jacket and, with skirt lifted, sally to town. "I'll take a look to see how the old man is doing."

"Take me along."

"You'd freeze. See how it's snowing!"

And she'd walk the four miles to town, over the roads and the snow-covered fields.

Mama, pregnant, yellow, and chattering from the cold, went about in a worn, fringed, gray shawl, which I loathed because it deformed her statuesque figure. I could not endure the cords of the fringe and pulled them off. I abominated the house, the factory and the town. Mama walked in trodden-down felt boots; she was constantly coughing; her unsightly, big belly heaved; a hard light glittered in her gray-blue eyes; and she frequently leaned against one of the big empty walls as if stuck to it. For a full hour, sometimes, she would stare out of the window on a street which resembled a jaw, half of whose teeth were crooked and blackened with age, and the other half artificial.

"Why do we live here?" I asked.

"Oh, keep your mouth shut, can't you?" she replied.

She seldom said anything to me, and then it was to set me chores. "Come here . . . go there . . . bring this and that."

I was seldom allowed on the street, from which I invariably returned scarred; for fighting was my chief, in fact my sole, diversion, into which I threw all my energy. Mama strapped me, but punishment only provoked me to fight next time with greater fury, which brought me greater punishment. And so it went until the day I threatened to bite her hand next time, and escape to the fields to die by freezing. In astonishment she pushed me away, and, pacing the room, panting, said in an exhausted voice, "You've turned wild as an animal!"

The feeling called love bloomed in my heart, pulsating with life, and shimmering like a rainbow. Denied love, I yielded to more frequent outbursts of resentment, which discharged like smoky, bluish flame, and a choking irritation smoldered in my breast, a sense of being abandoned, alone, in that drab, senseless existence.

My stepfather was harsh to me and hardly ever spoke to mama. He whistled or coughed and, after meals, he stood before a looking-glass, meticulously picking his ill-spaced teeth with a wood sliver. He quarreled with mama more and more, insultingly addressing her by the pronoun used for children or inferiors, something which infuriated me. At such times he would take care to close the kitchen door to prevent me from hearing; but his deep bass rumbled through.

I heard him one day, stamping his foot and bellowing, "So I can't have any company here, because you're too stupid not to become pregnant— you cow!" This so astounded and enraged me that I jumped high enough to bump my head on the ceiling, and bite my tongue and make it bleed.

On Saturdays dozens of factory hands came in to sell him coupons, which they were supposed to exchange for food in the company store; for these coupons they received half-value from my stepfather. It was all transacted in the kitchen where, sitting at the table with an imposing air, he would pick up a coupon, frown, and say, "Ruble and a half."

"But, Mr. Maximov, for the love of Christ!"

"Ruble and a half!"

This confused, sordid existence lasted for me up to my mother's confinement, when back I went to grandpa's. He was then living in the village of Kunavin (on the outskirts of Nizhny Novgorod), in a small room heated by an oven. The room was in a two-story house, on a sandy lane that led to the Napolno graveyard, and its two windows faced the yard.

He met me with cackles of laughter. "What's up? It's the mother who's supposed to be the best friend; but now it looks like it's the old devil of a grandpa, eh? Ekh, you!"

I scarcely had time to take a good look at my new home, when grandma brought mama and the baby. My stepfather's shady dealings with the workers had finally brought about his discharge; but he had almost immediately gotten a new job in the railroad depot ticket office.

Then, after a monotonous time, I found myself again living with mama, this time in a warehouse cellar. Immediately after we moved in I was sent to school, to which I took an instant dislike. My school clothes were a pair of mama's shoes, a coat converted from an old jacket of grandma's, a yellow shirt, and trousers patched out to fit. This outfit made me a butt, and the yellow shirt got me the nickname, "ace of diamonds." Nevertheless, I won the boys' good will, though not that of the teacher and the priest.

The irritable teacher looked jaundiced, and suffered from nosebleeds. He came to class with cotton wads in his nostrils, and, from time to time, as he snuffled posers at us, he would pull out the wads, examine them and shake his head. His face was broad, and the color of copper, shading off to green in the creases, and its expression was disagreeable; but his most repulsive feature was his, literally, leaden-hued eyes that seemed to dwell so adhesively on my face that I had an urge to peel them off my cheeks with my fingers.

For days I was kept in front among the primary students, close to his desk, a situation I found intolerable. He seemed to see nobody else and kept snuffling at me, "Peshkov, a clean shirt!" "Peshkov, stop scraping your feet!" "Peshkov, tie your shoelaces."

I retaliated for his nagging by tying a hollowed-out half of a watermelon over the door, and suspending it by string and pulley in such a way that, when he let himself in by the door, the melon came down on his bald skull like a cap. I was paid for this on my skin by the principal, to whom I was escorted by the janitor with a note.

Another time I sprinkled snuff on his desk, which brought on a sneezing fit and sent him home. His substitute was his brother-in-law, an officer who passed the time conducting the class through the songs, "God Save the Tsar" and "O Liberty, My Liberty," laying his ruler over the heads of those who were off key. The sound it made was hollow and funny, but the effect was painful.

The priest was young and handsome—strikingly so, because of his fine head of hair. He gave us our religious lessons, and was annoyed with me for not having a Bible, and for making fun of his speech habits. As soon as he came in, he would ask me, "Have you brought the book, Peshkov, or not? Yes, the book!"

I replied, "No, I haven't brought it, yes."

"What do you mean—yes?"

"No."

"Then you may as well go home. Home, yes. I have no intention of teaching you. Yes! I have no such intentions."

To be dismissed was no hardship to me. Outdoors, I scrambled about in the dirty street and looked on at the noisy passing show, until he was through with the lesson.

The priest's face was like a beautiful Christ's, his eyes caressing like a woman's, and his hands dainty—like everything else about him. No matter what—book, ruler, pen—he handled it with care, as if it lived and could be hurt, as if he loved it and feared to injure it by his touch. Though he was not quite so tender with the children, they adored him.

Despite the fact that I was a tolerable student, I was soon given notice of imminent expulsion for bad behavior. I was depressed, anticipating a scene with mama, whose temper was worsening and who beat me more than ever before. But salvation came in a surprise visit to the school by Bishop Khrisanph.[19]

As I recall him, he was very small and a hunchback, and looked like a wizard. He seemed especially small in his full, black robes and the absurd hat, like a little black bucket, that covered his head. Shaking his hands free of his sleeves, he said, "Now, children, let's have a chat." And immediately warmth and brightness, an unprecedented cheerfulness, entered the room.

Calling me over in my turn, he asked, "How old are you? Is that all? How tall you are! Been out in the rain a lot, eh?"

Putting a withered hand with long, pointed nails on the table, and tugging his scraggly beard with the other, he brought his face, with its kindly eyes, quite close to mine, and asked, "Tell me, now, what's your favorite Bible story?"

When I explained that I had no Bible and hadn't been getting the scripture lessons, he straightened his robe and said, "How's that? That just has to be learned, you know. Perhaps you've learned something from what you've heard. Know the Psalms? Good. And the prayers? There you are! And the lives of the Saints? In ballads? Well, you seem to be up on the subject."

At this point our priest turned up, red-faced and panting. The bishop gave him his blessing, but when the priest started to explain about me, the bishop held up his hand. "Just a minute, please. . . . Tell me the story of Alexis, the Man of God."

When I halted, having forgotten one of the verses, he said, "Lovely verses, those, eh, my boy? Let's have some more, something about King David. Go on, I'm listening."

His attentiveness was noticeable, and he obviously liked the verses. After a while he stood up suddenly and asked abruptly, "And you've learned the Psalms? Who was your teacher? A good grandpa, eh? Bad? Is that so? But don't you misbehave?"

After some hesitation I admitted, "Yes."

Both the teacher and the priest were avid to confirm this admission, and he heard them out with troubled eyes.

"Hear what they say about you? Come here," he said, sighing, and put-

[19] (Author's note.) Author of *Religions of the Ancient World* and of many articles, among them "On Marriage and Women," which greatly impressed me when I read it in my youth. I have an impression that the title is not accurate; it was published in a theological journal in the seventies.

ting his hand, which carried an odor of cypress wood, on my head. "Why do you misbehave?"

"It's so dull in school."

"Dull. But that can't be so, my boy. Then, you'd be a poor student, which the teachers tell me you're not. So there must be some other reason."

He took a notebook from a breast pocket and wrote, "Peshkov, Alexis" in it, reciting the name as he wrote it. "So. But hold yourself in, my boy. Try to behave a little better. We'll allow just a little mischief. People are plagued enough without that, eh, children?"

Many voices merrily chorused, "Yes."

"But I don't think you misbehave much. Isn't that so?"

And laughing, the boys responded in chorus. "No. We misbehave very much."

The bishop drew me to him and surprised everybody, evoking a laugh even from the teacher and the priest, by saying, "The fact is, my brothers, at your age I, too, misbehaved very much. Imagine that!"

The children laughed. He began giving them trick questions and got them answering and confusing each other, until the class was in a cheerful uproar. At last he got up and said, "Ah, it's been so pleasant to be with you, but now I must go." And, lifting his hand and flipping his sleeve back, he covered us all with a sweeping sign of the cross, and blessed us, "In the name of the Father, the Son and the Holy Ghost, I bless you and your labors. Good-by."

And they shouted in unison, "Good-by, my lord. Come again soon."

"I'll come again," he replied with a shake of his robes, "and I'll bring some little books." And to the teacher, as he swung out of the classroom, he said, "Send them home now."

He took me by the hand, and on the porch he bent down and said, "So now you'll hold yourself in, won't you? That's settled, isn't it? I understand why you misbehave. Good-by, my boy."

I was deeply moved; new emotions possessed my heart when the teacher, keeping me in after the class was dismissed, said that from now on I ought to be gentler than water and humbler than grass. I heard this acquiescently.

Putting on his fur coat, the priest, in his gentle way, added, "And from now on you're to help me with the lesson. Yes, that's the thing for you to do. And be quiet, too; be quiet, yes."

But while things went better at school, something distressing happened at home. I stole a ruble from mama. The theft was unplanned. One evening mama left me to mind the baby while she went out. To pass the time I dipped into one of my stepfather's books, *Memoirs of a Physician* by Dumas père, and came upon two bills, one for ten rubles, the other one ruble, between the pages. The book proved too adult for me and I was putting it back, when it occurred to me that, with a ruble, I could buy not only the Bible, but a copy of *Robinson Crusoe*, of whose existence I had recently heard. One frosty day, at recess, I was entertaining some boys with a fairy tale, when one of them scornfully interjected, "Fairy tales are the bunk. *Robinson Crusoe* for me! That's a true story." Other boys who had read it, joined in its praises. Though I resented the snub to grandma's stories, I decided to get hold of *Robinson Crusoe* too, to be able to tell them that that was "the bunk."

And so I came to school next day, with a Bible, two tattered copies of *Andersen's Fairy Tales*, three pounds of white bread and a pound of sausage. In the dank little bookshop, near the Vladimir church, I could have picked up a *Robinson Crusoe*, too, a thin, little, yellow-backed book with a frontispiece showing a bearded man in a fur cap wearing an animal pelt over his shoulders. But it had not attracted me; I had preferred even the covers of the fairy tales, despite their tatters.

During the recess, I handed the bread and sausage around, and we began reading the wonderful story, "The Nightingale," which captivated us all.

"In China all the people are Chinese, even the Emperor." I remember how delighted I was with this direct, smiling, singing opening. Many other details impressed me as equally wonderful. But I was not to enjoy that book in school. I was not given time. When I got home, mama, who was at the oven, frying some eggs, asked in a strange, constricted voice, "Did you take that ruble?"

"Yes, from that book there."

She whacked me with the frying pan and took Andersen from me—a worse penalty. I was away from school for several days during which my stepfather must have gossiped about it to the parents of one of my schoolmates, for I returned to hear the new taunt, "Thief!"

This was a terse and vivid description of the act, but inaccurate, since I had not denied that I had taken the ruble. But my explanations were given no credence; and, on coming home, I told that to mama, and refused to return to school. She was sitting near the window, feeding my brother Sascha. She was pregnant again; her face was haggard and her eyes were taut with weariness and strain. She stared at me and her mouth fell open like a fish.

"You must be mistaken," she said, in a low voice at last. "How could anybody there know you took the ruble?"

"Come and ask them yourself."

"Then it must have been your own chattering about it. Admit it, didn't you tell them yourself? I warn you, I'll find out for myself, tomorrow, how that story got out in the school."

Then I told her my schoolmate's name and her face pitifully knotted up and she began to weep. I retired to the kitchen to stretch out, on my bed, a box behind the oven, and from there, I heard mama moaning, "Oh, my God!" No longer able to endure the nauseating smell of drying slop rags, I went out to the yard, but mama called out, "Where are you off to? Where are you going? Come here!"

We sat together on the floor, Sascha on mama's knee, pulling at the buttons of her dress, nodding his head and saying his baby version of pugolka (button), "boovooga."

I sat close to mama who kissed me and said, "We're poor, and every kopeck—every kopeck . . ." a sentence she never finished, for she suddenly tightened her hot arm around me and exclaimed, "What trash—what trash!" a phrase she had recently taken to. And Sascha echoed, "Tash."

He was an odd little misshapen boy with an oversize head. His beautiful, deep, blue eyes took in everything with a mild, expectant smile as if awaiting someone. He had started talking unusually early, and his life was one of continuous, passive happiness. He was feeble, barely strong enough to crawl. I was always welcome to him; he would want me to lift him up in my arms, where he took pleasure in crumpling my ears with his soft, tiny fingers which always, somehow, seemed to have a scent of violets. He died very suddenly, and without an illness. In the morning he had been his usual, gently happy little self; in the evening, as the vesper chimes were pealing, they laid out his little corpse on the table. This occurred soon after the birth of the new child, Nicholas.

Mama had kept her promise and straightened out things at school for me; but I was soon in new trouble. Coming in from the yard one evening at tea time, I heard mama pleading, "Eugene, I beg you—" and my stepfather answering, "Tommyrot!"

"You're off to her—I know!"

"So?"

A brief silence. Then mama coughed and said, "What unspeakable trash you are!"

I heard the sound of a blow, and, rushing in, found mama knocked to her knees, back against a chair, her head averted and a spasmodic sound coming from her throat, and a terrifying glaze over her eyes; while he, in a new coat and other finery, was kicking her in the breast. From the table I picked up a bread knife with a bone handle in a silver socket, the last of my father's belongings that mother had been able to hold on to and, with all my strength, I stabbed at my stepfather's side.

Fortunately mama pushed him away in time and the deflected knife merely grazed his skin as it slashed through his coat. My stepfather gasped and bolted from the room, holding his side, and mama lifted me up, then groaned and flung me to the floor. Returning from the yard, my stepfather pulled me away from her.

Later that evening, my stepfather having gone out, mama came to me behind the stove, embraced me and kissed me, and said through her tears, "I was to blame, forgive me. Darling, how could you . . . with a knife?"

I can recall how distinctly I told her I would kill my stepfather and myself, as well. I think I would have, or at least attempted to. To this day I can see that abominable long leg in its braided trousers, out in the air, kicking a woman in the breast. Years later I was to see that unlucky man draw his last breath in a hospital. By that time a curious attachment had sprung up between us, and it brought anguished tears to my eyes to see the light fading out of his handsome, restless eyes; but even in that tragic moment, though my heart was wrung by grief for him, this memory clung to my mind.

Often, recording such atrocious memories of our bestial Russian life, I wonder whether there is any point in recalling them. And, with revived assurance, I tell myself, "The point is that this continues to be the actual, loathsome fact to this very day, that this fact must be traced back to its source and uprooted from our memories, from the souls of our people, from our confined and squalid lives."

And there is another point in recording these brutalities. Repellent though they are, and though many beautiful souls are burdened and crushed to death by them, yet the Russian remains spiritually so young and sound that he can and does transcend them. In this extraordinary Russian life not only does our animal self thrive and fatten, but along with it, and triumphant despite it, grows a brilliant, creative, wholesome human type which encourages us to seek our regeneration, a future of peace and humane living for all.

Chapter Thirteen

BACK TO GRANDPA'S AGAIN.

"What are you after, bandit?" was his greeting to me, and he rapped on the table. "I'm through feeding you. Let grandma do it."

"Of course," said grandma. "What misfortunes! Think of it!"

"Go ahead, feed him if you wish," said grandpa; then, calming down, he explained, "She and I live apart now; we have nothing to do with one another."

Grandma was sitting at the window making lace. Her movements were very fleet, the shuttle made a gay, snapping sound; the pincushion looked like a golden porcupine in the spring sunlight. Grandma herself showed no change; it was as if she had been cast in bronze. Grandfather, however, had aged, had become dryer and more wrinkled; his sandy hair was graying; and a querulous petulance had replaced his confident, proud manner. In his dimming green eyes the expression of mistrust was constant. With a laugh grandma described the recent division of their possessions. Heaping up the kitchen utensils and tableware, he told her, "That's your portion and don't look for another thing from me."

And, putting together everything else, all her things, including her fur coat, he sold them for seven hundred rubles, which he lent, at usurious terms, to his Jewish godson, the fruit dealer. The disease of avarice took such hold of him as to obliterate all shame; he made the rounds of well-to-do acquaintances, one-time colleagues of his, giving them a sob story about being beggared by his children, and asking for money. This exploitation of their good will toward him paid off. He brought home notes which he flaunted in grandma's face. "See, fool! You wouldn't be given a hundredth part of that." And the money thus got, he invested with new acquaintances, Khlist (horsewhip), a tall, bald-headed furrier, and his shopkeeper sister, a stout, rosy-cheeked woman, whose brown eyes looked dark and sweet like wild honey.

The household expenses were meticulously apportioned. One day's meals were at grandma's cost; the next day's at grandpa's. His dinners were always the poorer. Grandma bought good meat, but he dished up liver and such, and meat scraps. They kept separate stores of tea and sugar, but they used the same teapot, and grandpa would say, "Hold on! Just a minute! How much did you put in?" And he would shake the tea leaves into his palm and measure them. "Mine's a larger leaf, so I ought to put in less."

He made sure grandma poured his tea and hers equally strong, and that, on refilling her cup, she refilled his. "How about the last cup?" she'd say, and grandpa would look into the pot and say, "There's enough there."

He even insisted on a separate supply of oil for the icon lamp—this, after fifty years of working together. I found these quirks of the old man funny, but repellent, too. But they only amused grandma.

She would try to allay my resentment. "Hush, now. He's just an old man, growing senile, that's all. He's eighty, or close to it. We must make allowance for a bit of silliness; what's the harm? Don't worry; you and I, we'll get along; I'll get some work."

I, too, made my contribution. On holidays and in the early mornings I went through the streets and the backyards with a sack, collecting rags, paper, bones and metal scraps. Junkmen paid me two greven[20] for a forty-pound bundle of rags, paper and metal junk, and eight to ten kopecks for the same weight of bones. I carried on my junk-collecting after school hours as well, and Saturdays. For specially lucky finds I got from thirty kopecks to half a ruble, and sometimes even more. When grandma accepted the money from me, she hastily stuffed it into her skirt pocket, looked down, and commended me, "Ah, thanks, darling. This will get us our food. You've made out well."

I saw her once, weeping as she gazed at a five-kopeck coin I had given her; a grimy tear wobbled on the tip of her grainy nose, that looked like a bar of pumice stone.

More profitable than ragpicking was stealing from the lumber yards on the banks of the Oka or on Pesk Island, where, during the Fair, the temporary booths where metal articles had been sold were dismantled at the end of the Fair, and the posts and boards stored on the piers, until the approach of the spring floods. A good board would fetch ten kopecks from cottagers, and one might make away with two such boards a day. But the job required bad weather, snow or a heavy rain that would send the watchmen to cover.

I got together a small gang; ten-year-old Sanka Vyakhir, son of a Mordvin[21] beggarwoman, a boy marked by serene good nature; Kostrom, a tall, skinny orphan with strikingly big black eyes who, at thirteen, was com-

[20] A greven was 10 kopecks.
[21] A Finnish people living in the middle Volga valley.

mitted to a reformatory for the theft of two pigeons; the Tatar boy Khabi, a twelve-year-old "giant," genial and frank; snubnose Yaz, eight-year-old son of a cemetery caretaker, wordless as a fish and an epileptic; and the oldest, Gregory Churka, a widowed dressmaker's son, an honest and judicious lad and formidable with his fists. We all came from the same street.

In our village stealing did not count as crime; it was a way of life, indeed, almost the only livelihood of villagers ever on the verge of starvation. The six-week Fairs did not bring enough to keep them through the year. Even "respectable citizens" engaged in a little "river work," that is, salvaging logs or finished timbers borne downstream by the current, securing them piece by piece, or in loads. But, in the main, this "river work" took the form of robbing barges or a general marauding along the Volga and Oka River banks, making off with whatever was not tied down. On Sundays adults bragged about their hauls; and the small-fry eavesdropped and learned.

During the hot spell before the Fair, children picked the pockets of tipsy factory hands, truckmen and other workers lurching through the village streets. This, too, went disregarded; children did it in sight of their parents. A carpenter might be stripped of his tools, a cabman of his keys; harness might be stripped from the cart horse and metal parts from axles.

Our gang did not do that sort of stealing. Churka declared, "I won't steal. Mama forbids me." And Khabi said, "I'm scared to." Kostrom loathed the child thieves; and he enunciated the word "thief" with scornful vehemence. When he saw a little thief at the pockets of a drunk, he interfered, giving the pickpocket a beating, if he caught him. This big-eyed, melancholy boy aped grownups, adopted the longshoreman's swaggering gait, spoke in the gruffest voice he could manage, and put on a taciturn, composed manner as if he were an old man. Vyakhir believed stealing was a sin.

However, we didn't consider it sinful to make away with lumber from Pesk Island. None of us had any twinges of conscience over that. Our chief concern was to so plan our forays as to make sure of success. At night, or by day in bad weather, Vyakhir and Yaz would openly cross the creek to Pesk over the thawing ice. This was done to divert the attention of the watchmen; the rest of us crossed unobserved, one by one. With the watchmen's eyes on Yaz and Vyakhir, who decoyed them out of range, we got to the timber, picked out what we wanted and made away with it. We each carried a small length of rope with a bent nail at the tip, which we hooked into plank or post, dragging it over the snow and ice. We were hardly ever seen by the watchmen, and then we were too far off for pursuit.

On disposal of our booty, we divided the money into six parts, about five to seven kopecks apiece. That provided for a satisfactory day's meals; but Vyakhir got a beating from his mother if he failed to bring something extra for a drop of liquor. Kostrom was putting his money by in order to start a pigeon coop. Churka's mother was an invalid, and for that reason he was always on the lookout for more work. Khabi, too, was saving his money—for fare back home. The uncle who had brought him to Nizhny had drowned almost immediately after their arrival. Khabi had forgotten the name of his home town; all he remembered was that it was on the Kama River, near its junction with the Volga. We chose to make fun of the town, making up a rhyme to tease him:

> "Oh, the town's on the Kama, there,
> But nobody knows where."

Khabi's first reaction was one of anger, but when Vyakhir, in his cooing voice which earned him his nickname, Dove, said, "Come on, now. You don't get mad on comrades," it so shamed the Tatar that, from then on, he joined in when the ditty was sung.

We favored ragpicking, however, to timber stealing. It was especially interesting in the springtime when the thaws and the rains washed the pavements. On the Fair grounds there were sure to be nails and other metal scrap; and our finds sometimes included coppers and even silver. The watchman had to be appeased either with bribes of a few coins or obsequious bows and salutations, or he would chase us and confiscate our sacks. All in all money was hard to come by. Just the same we boys kept on good terms, and despite occasional flareups, I cannot recall one serious dispute.

Vyakhir served as peacemaker. He was always ready with the disarming remark that startled or shamed us; and he himself uttered it as if it had taken him by surprise. He never took offense or let himself be tripped up by Yaz' biting comments. For him evil had no place; he rejected it, as a matter of course.

"What use can it be?" he would say, whereupon its uselessness would appear obvious.

He called his mother "my Mordvin"; and we would forbear laughing over it. "My Mordvin rolled in drunk again, last night," he'd say, good-humoredly, his round, golden eyes sparkling. "She sat in the doorway, on the step, squawking her songs like a chicken."

"What did she sing?" asked Churka, always in search of exact details.

Vyakhir slapped his knees and, imitating his mother's barnyard voice, sang a song urging a shepherd to tap on windows and call people out to dance away to his piping and to cast his spells upon the village. His store of such ardent songs was a rich one, and he sang them excellently.

"Right. And she went to sleep," he continued, "there on the doorstep; and it got so cold I shivered down to my toes and just about froze to death; and I couldn't get her in; she's so heavy. And in the morning I asked her, 'How could you get so pie-eyed?' And she answered, 'Put up with me just a little longer. I'll soon be dead.' "

"She will," said Churka. "She's got dropsy."

"Would you be sorry?" I asked.

"Of course I would," said Vyakhir, surprised. "She's all right."

We all knew that Vyakhir, though his Mordvin beat him, considered her "all right." Sometimes, when pickings had been slim, Churka would propose, "Let's chip in for a drink for Vyakhir's mother or she'll give him a beating."

Of the gang only Churka and I could read. Vyakhir envied us this accomplishment and would mutter, picking at his pointed, mouselike ears, "When my Mordvin's buried, I'll go to school, too. I'll beg the teacher, on my knees, to accept me, and when I graduate, I'll work in the archbishop's gardens, or maybe even the Tsar's."

That spring, Vyakhir's Mordvin and an old man who was collecting church-building funds, and a bottle of vodka, were all caught under a collapsing woodpile. When the woman was taken off to the hospital, the practical-minded Churka told Vyakhir, "Come live with us, and mama will teach you reading and writing." And in no time, Vyakhir, holding himself erect, would read *Bakaleiniye* (grocery store); however, he read it *Balakeiniye*, and Churka would correct him, "It's *Bakaleiniye*, pal," and Vyakhir would reply, "I know, but those letters just skip around. They're jumping with joy at being read."

He gave us continual surprises and amusement by his affectionate care for trees and grass. The village was on sandy soil, and its vegetation was sparse—just a sickly willow tree in a yard, or a dropping elderberry bush; or some dry, ashen grass blades shrinking back against a fence. If one of us should sit on them, Vyakhir would cry out, "Must you sit on the grass? Why not on the gravel? It makes no difference to you, does it?"

He saw no sense in breaking off willow branches, or picking the elder-

berry blossoms; and when we cut wands from the weeping willows growing on the Oka's banks, he would exclaim in reproachful surprise, as he
shrugged and waved his hands: "Why must you destroy everything? You
devils! Now see what you've done!" And his passion over it made us
ashamed.

We had worked up a jolly Saturday evening game for which we made
preparations the rest of the week by storing away all the cast-off bast [22]
shoes we could pick up.

On Saturday dusk when the Tatar stevedores plodded back from the
river where they had unloaded Siberian goods, we waylaid them on the
crossroads and pelted them with the bast shoes.

Irritated at first, they chased and cursed us. But soon they took to the
game themselves. Having learned what to expect, they came to battle
armed with similar ammunition, sometimes through tracking out our
stores and pillaging them. After our complaints of "No fair!" we took to
dividing the entire supply evenly; and the battle would be on. Generally
they took a position in the open, in the very hub of the crossroads; yelling, we would circle them, firing our ammunition. They, too, yelled; and
the laughter was deafening when a good shot caught somebody under-
foot and tripped him, head first, into the dust.

The game would go on briskly, sometimes till it was too dark to see.
The villagers gathered around to watch, or looked on from corners,
grumbling, because that was considered the civic thing to do. Like crows
in the humid air flew the shoes. Sometimes a hit proved painful, but the
fun outweighed it.

The Tatars enjoyed it as much as we did. Often, when we were through
playing, they took us along to their restaurant, where they treated us to
a peculiarly sweet fruit jam and thick, reddish tea, sweetened with candy.
We liked these big people, whose energy matched their dimensions; and
who were so childlike and trusting. I was struck by their mild natures,
their unfailing geniality and their dignified consideration for one another.

Their laughter was so hearty that the tears streamed down. One of
them, who hailed from the town of Kassimov, a chap with a broken nose,
was a celebrated strongman. Once, from a barge quite a distance from
the bank, he carried ashore a bell weighing twenty-seven poods (over a
thousand pounds), laughing and roaring out a string of rhymed nonsense,
"Voo, voo! Grass, sass, pennies, many, coin of gold, all sold, words, words!"

---

[22] Bast shoes were made of woven strips of bark by the peasants. They were easily
made but quickly worn out, and Russian roads would be marked by discarded bast
shoes.

Once he sat Vyakhir on the palm of his hand and raised him up, saying, "See where you're living now, all the way up in the sky!"

In bad weather we met in Yaz' hut in the cemetery. His father had protruding bones, long arms and a small head; and his facial hair was the color of mud. His skull was set on his thin neck like a burdock on its stalk. He amused us by half-shutting his yellow eyes and mumbling, "God rest us. Ai!"

We bought three *zolotniks* (about half an ounce) of tea, sugar for eight, bread, and some vodka for Yaz' father, whom Churka would order about, "Peasant, start the samovar!"

Our peasant would chuckle and start the tin samovar. While the tea was brewing we talked over our plans, and he contributed scraps of advice, "How about this? Day after tomorrow there's to be a celebration at Trusov's—a big feed—should mean a lot of bones."

"The cook collects all the Trusovs' bones," said Churka, the omniscient.

Vyakhir stared meditatively through the window at the graveyard earth, "Soon we'll be going out in the woods."

Yaz never spoke, merely gazing at us with his expressive, melancholy eyes. Silently he exhibited his playthings, wooden soldiers retrieved from a dump, legless toy horses, buttons and bits of metal.

His father laid the table—no two cups and saucers matched—and set down the tin samovar. Kostrom poured, and the elder Yaz, having tippled his vodka, climbed up the oven, stuck out his long neck, looked us over with alcoholic eyes, and muttered, "So, you carry on as if you weren't boys at all, eh? Akh, you thieves. God rest us. Ai!"

Vyakhir replied, "We're no thieves!"

"Junior thieves, then."

If the elder Yaz became a bore, Churka silenced him, "Quiet, you peasant scum!"

Vyakhir, Churka and I could not endure his enumeration of the houses where people were ailing, his speculations on when they might die. His comment was all calculation and without a grain of feeling; and, seeing our response, he baited us, "So it disturbs you, my young masters? Indeed! And soon, a certain fat one's going to croak. And long may he rot in his grave!"

He wouldn't stop for anything we'd say. "And you, too, will have to die; you're not too long for this cesspool!"

"Good enough!" said Vyakhir. "When we die we'll be angels."

"You!" exclaimed the older Yaz, with a gasp of astonishment. "You—

angels!" And he chuckled and returned to goading us with his nauseating undertakers' tales. At times, in such talk, his voice would drop and thicken into a peculiar mumble. "Hold on, kids, and listen to this . . . Couple of days ago, it was a female they buried. You know what the woman was?" Women figured a good deal in his chatter, and always salaciously.

Nevertheless there was something wistful and inviting in his stories in which he seemed to summon us to share his thoughts. His speech was ignorant and unintelligent, and broken by his own interrupting questions; yet these splinters, as it were, of his narratives stick in the memory.

"They grill her. 'Who was the firebug?' 'I was,' she says. 'Fool of a woman, how could you be? You weren't home, you were sick in the hospital.' 'I started the fire.' And that's how she went on. What for? Ai! God rest us!"

He had in his mind the biographies of virtually every woman interred by him in that gloomy, arid graveyard; and it sounded as though he held the housedoors open to us, so that we could see how they lived there; and this made us feel solemn and adult. He would have been good for the whole night, but, as dusk began to mist the window, Churka got up and said, "I'm going home or mama will start worrying. Anybody coming along?"

And we all left, then. Yaz escorted us to the fence, and having shut the gate, squeezed his sallow, bony face to the grating, and bid us "Good-by" in his muffled voice.

We called back "Good-by." It was always a wrench to leave him there in that cemetery. Once, with a backward glance, Kostrom said, "We'll look for him there, someday, and find he's dead."

"Yaz has it the worst of all," Churka often said, but Vyakhir would rebut, "None of us has a bad time!"

And looking back, I do not see it as a bad time. That free life, with all its variety, had many attractions for me; I was also drawn to my comrades, who stirred generous desires in me to serve them.

Life at school had once more turned hard for me. My classmates taunted me with "ragpicker" and "hobo." They complained to the teacher one day, after picking a quarrel with me, that they couldn't sit with me because I smelt like a sewer. I recall how deeply this wounded me, and what a trial it was to go to school afterward. The charge was a spiteful lie. I never wore my ragpicking clothes to school, and always gave myself a good scrubbing in the morning.

Despite all this I passed on into the third grade with honor certificates and prize books—a cloth-bound copy of *The Gospels*, a cloth-bound copy of Krylov's *Fables* and a paper-covered copy of a volume abstrusely entitled, *Fata Morgana*. I brought my gifts home, and grandpa expressed appreciation and wanted to take them from me and lock them up in his box. But grandma had been ill in bed for days without a kopeck, and grandpa had been tormenting her with his groans and plaints, "You'll eat me out of house and home, ekh, you!" So I took my prizes to a bookshop and got forty-five kopecks for them, which I turned over to grandma. Then I scribbled all over the honor certificates to spite grandpa, handing them to him folded. He stored them away, unaware of the vandalism, for which I had to pay, later.

When school recessed I returned to my life in the streets, finding even greater satisfaction in it than before. It was well on in spring and money came rather easy. Early, Sunday mornings, our whole gang took to the fields or the woods, lush with new foliage, and we did not get back till late, tired and happy, and in closer comradeship than ever.

But this cheerful life soon ended. My stepfather had run up debts, lost his job and gone off, and mama came back to grandpa's with my baby brother, Nicky, whom I had to tend, since grandma was living at a shroud-maker's shop where she worked.

Mama had become so anemic and feeble she could barely stand up, and fixed an unnerving stare on everything around her. The baby had scrofula and his skin was painfully ulcerated. He was too weak to cry out; hunger only brought a whimper from him. In his naps, after meals, his breathing had a curious sound, like a kitten mewing.

After a good look at him, grandpa said, "What he needs is lots of rich food; but I haven't enough to feed all of you."

From the bed in the corner mama sighed and said hoarsely, "It's little enough that he wants."

"A little here and a little there makes a heap." Then, to me, with a wave of his hand, he said, "Nicky needs the sun—keep him out in the sand."

I emptied a sack of clean sand in a spot that got the sun, and set my brother in it up to the neck, as grandpa advised. The little fellow loved it; he babbled affectionately and turned his glowing eyes upon me—remarkable eyes without whites—blue pupils circled with bright haloes.

I felt an immediate attachment to my brother. I felt he understood everything I was thinking when I watched him from my post under the window, from which I heard grandpa shrilling, "If he dies—and that he'll manage easy—it'll be your chance for life." Mama's answer was a prolonged coughing spell.

Freeing his hands, the little one held them out to me, with a shake of his little white head. His scanty hair was almost gray, and there was a sage and elderly expression in his diminutive face. Should a hen or cat approach, Nick would give it a long look, then turn to smile at me as if to communicate something significant. This troubled me. Could he sense that I was bored tending him and longed to leave him and get back to the street?

The yard was small, foul and confined. From the gate to the bath-house there was a continuous row of sheds and cellars. All the roofing was made of flotsam—timber out of old boats, and anything, from sticks to logs, salvaged from the drift brought down by the thawing ice and the spring floods on the Oka. The whole yard was unsightly with heaps of waterlogged wood which steamed in the sun and gave off sharp scents of decay.

Next door there was a place where small cattle were butchered; nearly every morning the bleating of sheep or the bellow of calves was succeeded by the odor of blood which, at times, was so concentrated, it seemed to hang in the air like a transparent, purple web.

When a beast bellowed as the ax-butt landed between its horns, Nick would blink; his lips would puff out in attempted mimicry; but all he could do was blow out a "phoo."

At noon grandpa, sticking his head out the window, would announce, "Dinner!"

He saw to the child's feeding. He took him on his knee, pushed bread and potatoes into the mouth of the child, and the dribble covered his thin lips and pointed chin. After the child had taken a little food, grandpa would raise the baby's shirt, prod the swollen abdomen, and consider aloud, "Has he had enough? Does he have to have any more?"

And from her dark corner would come mama's voice, "See how he's going after the bread."

"Little fool. How could he know how much he needs?" But he gave Nick another morsel.

This feeding made me ashamed; I always felt a sickening lump in my throat.

"That's all," grandpa would conclude. "Give him to his mother."

I lifted Nick, who whimpered and reached his hand toward the table. Mother, painfully raising herself, advanced toward me, holding out her dreadfully emaciated arms, dry and long and thin, like boughs off a Christmas tree.

She had become almost a mute, seldom uttering a word in that once ardent voice of hers, as her lingering death took its course on her corner bed. I knew, I felt she was dying, and all too often grandpa made death the subject of his droning talk, particularly in the evening shadows, when the odor of decay, with a kind of woolly smugness, like a sheepskin, worked in through the window.

Grandpa's bed was near the window, and almost under the icon; and he lay so that he faced them; and there for a long time he would mumble away in the dark, "So death is catching up with us. And how to face Our Maker, how to answer Him? After all our life's struggle what have we accomplished? And to what purpose?"

My bed was on the floor between the stove and the window. It was too short for my legs, which I had to stick under the oven, to be tickled by crawling cockroaches. I got some perverse fun from my post there, for I could watch grandpa at his cooking, and derive malicious satisfaction from his mishaps with the oven rake, the end of which he often poked through the window. It was a joke to watch it, and astonishing, I reflected, that so shrewd a person as grandpa had never thought of lopping off the end of the rake.

Once, in clumsy haste to take out a boiling pot, he broke the window sash and two panes, and upset and smashed the pot. In exasperation, the old man sat on the floor and howled, "Oh, Lord, oh, Lord!"

When he went out that day, I whittled down the oven rake with the bread knife, only to get a scolding from grandpa when he saw it. "Accursed devil. It should have been done with a saw. Rolling pins could have been made from the end, and sold, you imp of Satan!" He thrashed about wildly and then bolted out, and mama said, "Why did you have to butt in?"

The end came on a Sunday in August, about noon. My stepfather had just come back to town and gotten a job. Grandma had brought Nick to him in a new apartment he had rented near the depot. Mama was to be moved there a few days later.

That morning, in a voice brighter and more distinct than it had been for some time, she ordered me, "Go ask Eugene to come here." And, raising herself by pressing against the wall, she added, "Hurry! Run!"

And it seemed to me she smiled and her eyes had recovered their glow.

As it turned out, my stepfather was at mass; grandma sent me out for snuff; and the storekeeper had none ready and I had to wait while he prepared it. Returning to grandpa's I found mama at the table, in a fresh, lilac-colored dress, with her hair carefully done and looking quite like her old, splendid self.

"Feeling better?" I asked, frightened for some reason.

Glaring at me, she said, "Come here! Where have you been?"

She gave me no chance to reply, but clutched me by the hair with one hand and with the other brandished a long, flexible knife, shaped out of a saw, the flat of which she brought down on me. It slipped out of her hands and she commanded, "Pick it up; give it to me!"

I picked it up, but flung it on the table, and mama pushed me off. I sat on the oven ledge and in a trance of horror watched her movements.

From her chair she went painfully to her bed in the corner, lay down, and began wiping her sweating face with her handkerchief. Her movements became unsure; twice her hand mopped at the pillow instead of her face.

"Some water!"

I brought her a cup and, struggling to raise her head, she drank a little. With a hand that had become chill, she brushed mine aside and breathed heavily. After a glance at the icon her eyes returned to me; her lips moved as though to smile; and, slowly, her long lashes closed over her eyes. Her elbows held tight to her side, with feebly switching fingers her hands toiled over her throat. A shadow invaded her face, occupying every feature, yellowing her skin, silhouetting her nose. Her mouth fell open, as if to express amazement; but her breathing was no longer audible. How long I stood at my mother's deathbed, I don't know; I stood there, holding the cup, watching her face turn gray and cold.

Grandpa came in and I told him, "Mama's dead."

He threw a glance toward the bed, "What are you lying for?"

He went to the oven to take out a dish and made a racket with the dampers. I knew mama was dead and watched him, waiting for him to find out.

My stepfather came in, togged out in a short coat and a summer cap. Careful not to make a sound, he brought a chair over to mama's bed, only to let it down with a crash and to trumpet out, "Look, she's dead!"

Grandpa, holding a poker, shuffled away from the stove, stumbling, though his eyes were wide open, like a blind man.

Just a day or two after mama's funeral grandpa told me, "Alex, I can't have you hanging on my neck. There's no room for you here. You'll have to go out into the world."

And out into the world I went.

In the World

Chapter One

I
T WAS AS A DOOR BOY IN A SMART, MAIN-STREET SHOE STORE THAT I
went out into the world. The boss was a tubby little man with a coarse,
brownish face, greenish teeth, and moist, slime-colored eyes. I thought
he was blind, and, as a test, I made a face, at which he said with a rather
gentle severity, "Stop twitching!" I was irked at the thought of those
dead eyes watching me. Wasn't it more likely he had guessed I was
making faces?

"I told you to stop twitching!" he repeated, barely moving his grubby
lips. "Stop scratching," his dry whisper stole, as it seemed, upon me.
"You're working in a first-class store, just bear that in mind. The door
boy must stand straight as a statue."

I didn't know the meaning of the word "statue," and as for stopping
scratching, how could I when my hands were dotted with the bites of
vermin.

"What did you do for a living before?" asked my boss, after a look
at my hands. When I told him he wagged his round head, covered with
closely cropped gray hair, and exclaimed in a shocked tone, "Ragpicking! Why, that's even worse than begging or stealing!"

With a touch of pride, I informed him I had stolen, too.

At this, gripping the edge of his desk, he looked like a cat with its
paws up, and with an apprehensive glance, he barely breathed, "What?
You stole? How?"

When I explained he said, "Oh, that. I consider that only a prank.
But if you steal any shoes or money here, I'll have you locked up in jail
for life."

He said this with a frightening composure that ended any liking I
had for him.

In addition to the boss, the store staff included my cousin, Uncle
Jake's Sascha, and the efficient, wheedling, red-faced head clerk. Sascha,
decked out in long trousers, a brown frock coat, a dickey and a tie,
snubbed me. After grandpa had brought me in to the boss, he had asked
Sascha to give me help and advice. Sascha, with a big-shot scowl, had
stipulated, "But he'll have to do as I say!"

Grandpa put his arm on my neck in such a way as to force me to bow. "You're to do as he says; he's older than you and has more experience."

Sascha nodded and said to me, "Remember what grandpa said," and at once began exploiting his seniority.

"Stop looking so goggle-eyed, Kashirin," the boss would tell him.

"I-I'm looking right," Sascha would mumble, lowering his head.

"Ready to butt somebody? Want the customers to think you're a goat?"

The head clerk smiled obsequiously, the boss' mouth gaped to a repulsive grin, and Sascha, red-faced, took refuge behind the counter. I did not enjoy this repartee. And so many of their expressions were new; they might have been talking in a foreign tongue.

When a lady entered, the boss' hands would pop out of his pockets to give his moustache a pull; his face would compose into a sugary smile that gave his cheeks a new crease, but could not liven up the expression of his drab eyes. The head clerk would stand erect, with his elbows pivoted upon his ribs, and the wrists politely dangling. Sascha would blink diffidently, as if trying to cover his bulging eyes; and I, from my post at the door, would scratch surreptitiously and watch the rituals of salesmanship.

On his knees at the customer's feet, the head clerk would try shoes on with remarkably agile fingers. His touch on the woman's foot was tremulously light, as if he were fearful of damaging her solid enough leg which looked like an upturned bottle with a tapering neck.

Once a lady jerked her foot back, screeching, "You're tickling me!"

"Ah—but you have such sensitive skin," the head clerk hurriedly and flatteringly explained.

It was a joke to see him fawning on customers, and I had to turn away and stare through the glass door panels to hold in my laughter. But curiosity drew me back to follow the salesman through his fascinating maneuvers. Watching him, I thought I'd never achieve such a delicacy of touch, I'd never be so deft fitting shoes on the feet of others.

Frequently the boss would retire to a back room, calling Sascha in with him, and leaving the salesman alone with the customer. Once, fitting a red-headed woman, and toying over her foot, he suddenly took it up in his hand and kissed it.

"My, you're fresh," exclaimed the woman.

And he panted and sighed a prolonged, "O-o-oh!"

And this so convulsed me with laughter that, to stay on my feet, I grabbed the door knob, which turned open, propelling my head through a glass door panel. The head clerk stamped his foot at me, the boss rapped me on the head with a heavily ringed knuckle, and Sascha made a lunge for my ear. On our way home that night, he scolded me, "You'll get fired for things like that. What's there to laugh at, I want to know?" And he went on to explain, "It's good business to have ladies take a shine to the salesman. She mightn't need a new pair of shoes, but she might come in, anyway, just to have a look at him. But you—you're too thick-headed. We put ourselves out for you, and you——"

This made me angry. Nobody was putting himself out for me, certainly not Sascha.

Mornings I had to act as the cook's slavey. She was an unhealthy, unpleasant woman. At her orders I shined the shoes and brushed the clothes of the boss, the head clerk, and Sascha, started the samovar, hauled in firewood, and mopped up in the kitchen. My store chores included sweeping, bringing in tea, making deliveries to customers; then back to the kitchen to bring in meals, at which time Sascha tended door for me, a job he felt beneath him, so that he fumed at me, "Hurry up, slow-poke; making me do your work!"

It was a tedious, fatiguing existence for me, who had become used to the freedom of the sandy Kunavin streets and the banks of the slow Oka, or roaming the fields and woods all day. I had been separated from grandma and my gang. I had no companionship and life had turned its false and seamy sides to me.

When no sale was made, all three would behave as if the customer had swindled them. The boss would pack away his sugary smile; "Kashirin, put the stuff away," he would order, and he would rage, "Sow of a woman! The idiot got bored idling at home, so she has to come here and turn the store inside out. If you were my wife, you'd get it!"

But his wife, a juiceless creature, black-eyed and big-nosed, just stepped on him, ordering him around like a servant.

Or, after bowing a customer out with syrupy flatteries, they would run her down in a mean and conscienceless manner, till I had an impulse to run out and report it to her. I knew well enough that people generally slander others behind their backs; but these three did it in a peculiarly disgusting way, as if they were the elect chosen to indict all the rest. Tormented by envy, they had nothing good to say about anybody, and dug up scandals about everybody.

Into the store one day came a young lady with shining, rosy cheeks and radiant eyes, dressed in a fur-trimmed velvet cloak, her face emerging from the fur like an exotic flower. She was even more beautiful divested of her cloak, which she handed to Sascha. Her dress of blue-gray silk set off her fine figure, and diamonds glittered on her ears. She brought to mind "Vassillissa, the Beautiful," and I could well have believed her the governor's wife. My three superiors were markedly deferential, bowing to her as if she were a holy lamp, and almost choking as they slavered out compliments. They pranced about like madmen, so that their reflections did St. Vitus dances in the mirror. When she was gone, after having purchased an expensive pair of shoes, the boss whistled and jeered, "The tart!"

"An actress—the low creature," sneered the salesman. And they gabbed about her lovers and her luxuries. That day, when the boss took his siesta in the back room, I pried his gold watch open and squirted vinegar into the mechanism. I felt a happy sense of reward when, on awakening, he came rushing into the shop, holding up his watch, and raving, "What happened? My watch got all wet. It never happened before. It's all wet; it'll be ruined!"

More than once, in my depression, I thought of doing something to get myself fired.

The snow-covered passersby made no sound; they seemed to be hastening to a funeral, as if, having come late for the procession, they were scurrying to the cemetery by themselves. Horses, plodding through the drifts, shuddered with the strain. From a church belfry back of the store building came melancholy Lenten chimes, which my brain muffled like a pillow.

One day I was in the yard opening a crate of goods that had just been delivered at our back door, when the church watchman, a hunched old man as soft as a bundle of rags and as tattered as if he had just been set upon by a pack of dogs, sidled over to me and whined, "Won't you be so kind as to steal a pair of rubbers for me?"

I made no answer. Taking a seat on the empty crate, he made the sign of the cross over his yawning mouth and reiterated, "How about stealing me a pair?"

"Stealing is a sin," I said.

"Just the same, people steal. Old age must be given some consideration."

He was a pleasing change from the sort I was living among. I knew it was his conviction that I'd steal for him, and I agreed to hand him a pair of rubbers from the window.

"Good," he said matter-of-factly, exhibiting no excitement. "You're not fooling me? No, I see you're not."

After a momentary silence, during which he kept stamping his heels in the slushy snow, and lit up a pipe, he startled me by saying, "But how about if I'm fooling you? How about if I bring the rubbers to your boss and tell him I got them from you for half a ruble? What about that? They cost two rubles and you let me have them for half a ruble. A present, eh?"

I stared at him in stunned astonishment, as if it were already done; but he snuffled on, staring at his shoes, and exhaling bluish smoke. "Suppose your boss had asked me, 'Go test that boy; let's see if he's a thief!' Eh, what?"

"I won't give you the rubbers," I said, scared and angry.

"You've got to. You promised."

He pulled me to him by the arm, his icy forefinger on my forehead, and said, "How can you be thinking 'Here's this,' and 'Here's that.' "

"But you're the one who asked for them."

"I might have asked you anything. I might say, come rob the church! Would you? Think you can trust the whole world? Ah, you little fool!" He nudged me aside and rose. "I don't want any stolen rubbers. I'm no gentleman. I never wear rubbers. I was only fooling. But, because you're so simple-hearted, I'll let you into the belfry, come Easter, to ring the bells and have a look at the town."

"I know how the town looks."

"But it looks much better from the belfry."

Slowly dragging his patched boots through the snow, he turned the corner of the church, I staring after him, cast down and troubled, wondering whether the old man had really been fooling or had really been put up by the boss to test me. I was reluctant to return to the store.

Sascha stormed out into the yard. "What the devil's happened to you?"

With a sudden burst of anger I shook the pliers I had in my hand at him. I knew he and the salesman were stealing. They would stow away a pair of shoes or slippers in the oven flues. On leaving for the night they would tuck them into their overcoat sleeves. They made me nervous, for I had the boss' warning on my mind.

I once asked Sascha, "Do you take anything?"

"Not for myself," he explained, irritably. "I just help the head clerk. 'Do what I tell you,' he says to me, and I have to. If I didn't he'd fix me. The boss understands. He was a clerk himself. You just keep out of it."

When Sascha spoke to me he ogled himself in the mirror, and adjusted his tie with the identical, spread-finger gesture, suitable enough to his splayed hands, used by the head clerk. He was indefatigable in asserting his seniority rights over me, bawling me out and ordering me around in a deep, bass voice, and taking menacing attitudes. I had the advantage in height, but was rather scrawny and gawky, whereas he was compact and well-padded. In his long trousers and frock coat he looked rather imposing to me, yet there was something offensive and ludicrous in his appearance, as well.

He had a seething hatred of the cook, a puzzling old woman of whom it was hard to say whether she was good or evil. Her fiery black eyes would widen as she exclaimed, "A fight, that's what I enjoy more than anything—any sort, a cock-fight, a dog fight, or between men—it's all one to me." And if she heard cocks or pigeons battling in the yard she would drop what she was doing and, mute and immobile at the window, watch till the battle was over. In the evening she would bait Sascha and me, "Why do you kids sit here, doing nothing. How about a fight?"

This always infuriated Sascha. "I'm no kid, you idiot. I'm the junior clerk."

"Means nothing. Till you're married you're a kid."

"Idiot! Dope!"

"The devil's smart but God hasn't any use for him."

Sascha couldn't stand her chatter; he did his best to wound her with his sallies, at which, scornfully looking him up and down, she said, "Ekh, you cockroach! God slipped when He made you!"

Now and then Sascha would try to get me to smear shoeblack or soot over her face when she napped, put pins in her pillow, or some other trick. But she scared me. In addition, she was a light sleeper, getting up many times during the night. Then she would light a lamp and stare at something in a corner. Sometimes she came to my bed behind the oven, stirred me out of sleep, whispering huskily, "I'm restless. I'm not feeling right. Talk to me."

Drowsily I would spin some yarn, while she rocked herself and didn't say a word. Her body seemed to give off waves of heat and odors of wax and incense, and I expected her to die at any moment—pitch down on her face and die. And then fright would make me raise my voice and she'd halt me, "Hush, you'll wake everybody up and they'll think we're having an affair."

When she sat beside me she always took the same position, hunched-over, her hands between her knees and pressed to her skinny shanks. She was flat-chested, and right through the heavy linen of her night-gown, her ribs could be seen in outline, like the staves of a broken barrel. She would conclude her lengthy silences with, "And if I die, so what? Happens to everybody!" or, addressing some invisible auditor, "So what, I've lived, haven't I?" or she would cut me short with the command, "Sleep!" and, getting up, would shuffle soundlessly through the dark room.

Sascha would call her "witch!" but behind her back.

I challenged him. "Why don't you say it to her face?"

"Think I'm scared?" But he would follow that, frowning, with, "No, I wouldn't say it to her face. She *could* be a witch!"

With impartial scorn she was inconsiderate of everybody; she certainly never indulged me, dragging me out of bed at six, yelling, "Mean to sleep all day? Get the wood in; start the samovar; polish the brass sign on the door."

His sleep broken by her bawling, Sascha would complain, "What's the row about? I'll tell the boss nobody gets any sleep on account of you!"

With agile motions of her emaciated body, she would turn her smoldering insomniac eyes upon him, "Oh, it's God's mistake talking! What you'd get if you were a son of mine!"

Sascha would curse her, and on our way into the store he would propose, "Something's got to be done to get her fired. How about putting salt in all the pots, when her back's turned? If everything's over-salted, they'll fire her. Or kerosene. What are you staring at?"

"How about doing it yourself?"

"Coward!" he snorted.

The cook died right before our eyes. Leaning over for the samovar she fell down without a sound, as if she had been punched on the chest. On the floor she just turned over once, and blood oozed from her mouth. Sascha and I knew at once she was dead but, numb with fear, we just stared at her awhile, too stunned to move. Finally Sascha bolted out of the kitchen and I, not knowing what to do, stood at the window. The boss waddled in, squatted beside her and prodded her face.

"She's dead," he said. "No doubt of it. Wonder what from?" He went to the corner where a small icon hung, and crossed himself. After his prayer he ordered Sascha, "Kashirin, run out and call the police."

The police arrived, stamped through the place, took their tips and departed, to come back a little later with a wagon and its driver. Lifting the cook by the head and the legs, they carried her out. Watching them in the doorway, the boss' wife said to me, "Mop the floor."

The boss' comment was, "It's good she died at night." Why that was good I didn't understand.

Going to bed, Sascha, in a gentler tone than usual, said, "Don't put the lamp out."

"Scared?"

He pulled the blanket all the way over his head, and lay quiet for some time. The night was very still, as if watching for something. The next moment, it seemed to me, a bell clanged, there was a general alarm, and the whole town was out, shouting and jostling. Sticking his nose out of the blanket, Sascha wheedled, "Let's lie on the oven, together."

"It's too hot."

After a brief silence, "But didn't she pop off suddenly? She must have been a witch. I can't sleep."

"I can't, either."

He began telling stories about the dead, about corpses leaving their graves and staying out till midnight, hunting for the places where they had lived and for their kin. "All the dead remember is the town, not the houses and streets."

The stillness deepened and so did the darkness. Half-rising, Sascha asked me, "Want to see what I got in my trunk?"

What he had stored away in that small chest had long piqued my curiosity. He kept the box padlocked, and on opening it he looked around guardedly, and any attempt I made to peep was rebuffed with, "Hey, what are you after?"

When I said "yes," he sat up, keeping his feet in bed, and ordered me, quite imperiously, to bring the trunk over and set it at his feet. He kept the key around his neck together with his baptismal cross. Glancing around the dark kitchen, with a self-important look, he unlocked the trunk, blew on the lid as if to cool it, and after a dramatic pause, lifted out a covering layer of linen shirts. Underneath were cardboard boxes, colored tea wrappers, and old shoe polish and sardine cans.

"What's in them?"

"You'll see."

He put the trunk between his legs, and, bending down, hummed, "Tsaru nebesniu—" (heavenly Tsar).

What I expected to see was playthings. I had never owned any and affected scorn of them, but had always rather envied those who had them. It made me feel good to think that such a solemn personage as Sascha kept some, though he was shamefaced about them.

Opening a box, he took out the empty frame of a pair of eyeglasses, put them on his nose, and said with great gravity, "It don't matter that the glasses are out. This is a special sort."

"Let me try them on."

"They wouldn't fit you. Your eyes are light and these are for dark eyes." Then he mimicked the boss' wife nagging, but stopped himself short and gave a frightened look around the kitchen.

In an old shoe polish can he kept a collection of buttons, of which he boasted, "I picked them all up myself, in the street. I got thirty-seven here."

In a third box were a big brass pin, also picked up in the street, old nails, shoe buckles, metal doorknobs, bone cane-heads, girls' castoff combs, a copy of *The Dream Book and Oracle*, and a quantity of other objects of the same character.

In my ragpicking I could have accumulated a tenfold heap of such junk in a month. Those treasures of Sascha's were not only disillusioning; they moved me to embarrassing pity toward him. But Sascha looked at each with pride, fondly stroked it, his thick lips pursed out. His bulging eyes regarded them with a loving care, which, through his glassless spectacles, gave his childish face a ludicrous look.

Through these spectacles he now gave me a gracious glance, asking, "How would you like something here for a present?"

"I don't want anything."

I could see that this rejection offended him; his treasure trove had been scorned. After a moment's silence he calmly ordered me to "Get a towel and go over them. They're covered with dust."

When his treasures had all been wiped and stored away, he turned toward the wall. There was a pouring rain; we heard it drain from the roof, and the wind lashing it against the windows. With his face still averted, Sascha said, "You just wait. Soon as it's dry in the garden I'll show you something that'll make your eyes pop out."

I was dozing off and made no reply. In a few seconds he was at it again, scratching at the walls and saying feverishly, "I'm scared. God, how I'm scared! God Almighty, what's this?"

I felt a paralyzing terror. It seemed to me there stood the cook at the window, her back turned, her brow against the pane, just as she had done in life, taking in a cock-fight. Sascha moaned and kept clawing the wall. With a great effort, as if I were treading live coals, and not daring to look back, I made my way to him and lay down at his side. Exhausted, we finally got some sleep.

Several days later there was a holiday and the store closed at noon. After the midday meal, the boss dozed off and Sascha whispered to me, "Come on."

I supposed that I was to be shown the thing that would make my eyes pop out. He led me into the garden. On a strip between two buildings stood a row of lime trees, their thick trunks stained with moss, their black boughs protruding, stripped and lifeless, and not even a crow's nest in the branches. They affected me like gravestones. These trees were all that grew in the garden—no hedge, no grass. The path was black and trampled to an iron hardness; and the spaces beside it, that were clear of the mat of last year's leaves, were stamped flat and looked like stagnant pools.

Sascha took me to a corner where we were covered from the street by the fence; there he stood under one of the trees, rolled his eyes, and took cautious looks up at the grimy windows of the house next door. Squatting down, he lifted off a heap of leaves, uncovering a massive root, beside which were two bricks buried in the soil. Pulling these out I saw a strip of roofing tin, and beneath that a board which, lifted out, disclosed a tunnel under the root.

Sascha lit a candle end, and holding it to me, said, "Take a look down, only don't get scared."

He looked thoroughly scared himself. The candle end shook in his fingers; he had become pale; his lips sagged, his eyes dampened, and he hid his free hand behind his back. His fright was contagious, and it was with trepidation that I looked down into the tunnel under the root. It had been hollowed out like a vault, in the rear of which he had lit three little church candles, which threw a bluish light. Though it had no greater depth than a coal scuttle, it was much broader. Its sides were covered with bits of glass and pot shards. On a rag of red cloth, draped over a little mound in the center, was a tiny coffin decorated with strips of tin foil and half-covered with a scrap of cloth, which might have been ripped from a brocaded shroud. Under this protruded a tiny gray claw and the beak of a sparrow. Behind the coffin was a pulpit, on which reposed a brass cross and around it the three candles, in holders, made out of gilt and silvered paper taken from candy boxes.

The slender candle flames dipped outward. The little crypt was dimly dappled with spots of outer light, and tinted gleams within. From it exuded the mingled odors of wax, damp earth, and warm rot; it seemed to slap my face and it irritated my eyes, on which it impinged like a jagged, broken rainbow. Astonishment overcame my fright.

"Nice, eh?"

"What's it for?"

"It's a chapel. Isn't it just like a chapel?"

I shrugged.

"And the sparrow's a corpse," he continued; "they might use his relics because it was for no fault of his that he died."

"Was he dead when you found him?"

"No. He lost himself in the shed and I smothered him in my cap."

"What for?"

"Because I wanted to."

He looked me in the face and again asked, "Nice, isn't it?"

"No."

He bent down, laid the board across the tunnel, forced the bricks back, stood up, brushed himself, and asked me haughtily, "Why don't you like it?"

"I'm sorry about the sparrow."

With eyes that showed no motion, as if he were blind, he stared at me, and gave me a push with his hand on my chest, "Dope! You only say you don't like it because you're jealous. Maybe you think that thing you built in the garden on Kanatnoi Street was better."

Recalling my summer shed there, I said with assurance, "Of course it was better."

Sascha tore off his coat and tossed it on the ground, rolled up his sleeves, spat on his hands, and challenged me, "Is that so? Well, that means a fight!"

I had no desire to fight. The low state of my feelings had drained my combativeness. My cousin's wrathful face alarmed me. With a rush, he butted me on the chest and knocked me over. Straddling me, he shouted, "Shall we fight to the death?"

But I was the stronger and, by now, roused to wrath. In a minute or so it was he who was stretched out on the ground, his face in the dirt, his hands clasped around his head and a gurgle in his throat. Frightened, I wanted to help him, but he punched and kicked me off. Still more worried, I stood apart wondering what to do. He looked up and said, "You know what you got yourself into? When the boss and his missus aren't looking, I'll fix things so I'll have to complain about you and you'll get fired!"

On and on went his abuse and threats until, in a fury, I ran over to his cave, demolished it, and flung the coffin and its sparrow cadaver out into the street. I gutted his "chapel" and trampled everything down.

My frenzy had a strange effect on Sascha. Sitting on the ground, his eyebrows knit together, his hand to his mouth, he looked on in silence. When I was through he rose, without showing any agitation, fixed his clothes, put on his coat, and then said to me with ominous composure, "Now, you'll see! Just wait! I had all this planned out. Witchcraft. You're under a spell. Ha, ha!"

I dropped down as if the words were physical blows. I went cold inside. He did not even give me a backward glance, as he went off, and this heightened his menacing calm. I resolved to run away tomorrow, from the boss, from Sascha and his witchcraft, from this wasted, mindless existence.

Next morning the new cook, when she came to wake me, said, "Goodness, what have you done to your face?"

The witchcraft's beginning, I thought, and my heart sank. But her laughter was so hearty I had to smile, too, and I looked in the mirror. My face had a coat of soot.

"Did Sascha do it?" I asked.

"It might have been me," said the cook, laughing.

In the first shoe I took up in my shoe shining that morning, I ran a pin, which had been stuck in the lining, into my finger. "So this is his witchcraft!" He had fixed all the shoes that way, and so cleverly, that no matter how careful I was, I couldn't escape sticking myself. I got a bowl of icy water, and it gave me great joy to pour it over the wizard's head where he lay, still asleep or feigning sleep.

Nevertheless, I felt low. That coffin kept turning up in my mind, and that sparrow with its crooked, gray claws and its pale beak, outthrust so pathetically, those tinted beams vainly striving to fuse into a rainbow. My fancy magnified the coffin, and reanimated those claws until they reached out, tremulous and alive.

I decided to run away that same evening; but, just before dinner, warming up some food on a primus, I was negligent and it caught fire. Trying to put it out, I spilled burning oil over my hands, and had to be taken to the hospital. I remember that hospital nightmare. In what I recall as a grayish-yellow wilderness, there were herded together, muttering and moaning, gray figures in white robes like shrouds, while a giant on crutches, with eyebrows thick as whiskers, yanked at his black beard and bellowed, "I'll report this to His Eminence."

The cots made me think of the coffin, and the patients, with their noses conspicuously up, of dead sparrows. The yellow walls swayed, the ceiling bellied out like a sail, the floor rose and ebbed like waves under me. Everything about the place bespoke misery and despair, and tree branches tapped on the windows like hands with sticks.

In the doorway jigged a gaunt, red-headed corpse gibbering as he pulled his shroud over him with his emaciated hands. "Keep me away from madmen!" And the giant on crutches roared in his ear, "I'll report this to His Eminence!"

I had heard from grandpa, grandma and others that in hospitals people died of hunger, so I thought it was all up with me. A woman wearing glasses, and dressed in the shroudlike, white smock, came over to me and chalked something on a slate hanging from the headboard of the cot. The chalk broke and fell on me.

"Your name?"

"I haven't any."

"You must have."

"No."

"Stop fooling, or you'll get a whipping."

I felt that I could be sure of a whipping, and for that reason, I defied her. She hissed at me like a cat, and glided out, noiselessly, like a cat, too.

They lit two lamps, whose yellow globes swung from the ceiling like two eyes, winking and dazed, and swaying as if trying to come together.

In a corner someone mourned, "How can I play without my hand?"

"That's so. They've amputated your hand."

My conclusion was they cut off a man's hand for gambling! What would be done to me before I starved to death?

My burnt hands ached as if the bones were being torn out. I wept with the fright and the pain. I tried to squeeze back the tears by shutting my eyes, but they welled out through the lids and trickled down my temples into my ears.

Night came and everybody burrowed into their cots, secreting themselves beneath gray blankets. The silence deepened every moment. There was just the sound of someone mumbling, "What's the use. He and she, the both of them, are crooks."

I would have written to grandma asking her to come and abduct me from the hospital before they could kill me, but I couldn't use my hands. I pondered ways to escape.

The night silence grew more intense, as if it were the silence of eternity. Quietly slipping off the cot, I went to the double doors, one of which was ajar. In the hall, under a lamp, on a bench with a back, I saw a grizzled head wreathed in smoke, peering at me with hollow, dark eyes. I had no time to hide. "Who's that roaming about? Come here!"

But the voice was gentle, not severe. I went up to him. I saw a round face fringed with stiff hair. On the top of the head the hair was long, sprouted in all directions, and looked like a silver halo. From his belt hung a ring of keys. Had his beard and hair been fuller, he would have resembled Peter the Apostle.

"You're the one with the burned hands? Well, why are you traipsing about at night? Who gave you permission?"

He puffed smoke into my face, put a warm arm round my neck, and pulled me toward him. "Scared?"

"Yes."

"Everybody who comes here is scared, at first; but it's nothing. And of all people you've got no cause to be scared of me. I never hurt a soul. Care for a smoke? Don't, then. You've time yet; another year or so. Where's your parents? None? Well, they're not necessary; you'll get along without them. Just don't let anything scare you."

Not for a long time had I met with anyone whose words were so direct and kind and understandable, so that listening to him was an indescribable relief. When he led me back to my cot, I asked him to sit beside me, and he consented.

"Who are you?" I asked.

"I'm a soldier—a real one, a Cossack. And I've been in wars—you bet! That's what soldiers live for. I've fought against the Hungarians, and the Poles, and the Circassians, all you can think of. It's a great calling, war is."

I shut my eyes for a minute, and on opening them, instead of the soldier, there sat grandma in a dark dress, and he was standing beside her, she saying, "They're all dead? Oh, dear!"

The sun was frisking in the room, now plating everything with his gold, now going in hiding, now returning in lavish radiance, like a playing child.

Grandma bent over me and asked, "What did they do to you, darling? Mutilate you? I told off that old red devil!"

"I'll see to everything," said the veteran, leaving. Grandma, wiping her tears, said, "It appears our soldier hails from my home town."

Still thinking I must be dreaming, I said nothing. The doctor came, bandaged me, and behold! there I was with grandma in a carriage, driving through town. She said, "Oh, that grandpa of yours, he's losing his wits; he's sickening, he's got so miserly. A little while ago he made off with a hundred rubles from the office of his new friend, the furrier, Khlist. What a row there was!"

The sun was bright; the clouds soared like white birds. We crossed the bridge over the Volga. The breaking ice creaked underneath and between the bridge planks we could see patches of clear water; and over the distant cathedral's red dome gleamed the golden cross.

We passed a broad-cheeked woman with an armful of willow branches. Spring was approaching; soon it would be Easter. "How I love you, grandma!"

This did not startle her. She answered matter-of-factly, "That's because we're related. But—and I'm not bragging—others love me, too, and for that my thanks to Thee, O Blessed Lady." And, with a smile, she went on, "She'll be rejoicing soon. Her son will rise up. O, Barbara, my daughter!"

And that plunged her into silence.

Chapter Two

WHEN I ARRIVED, GRANDPA WAS ON HIS KNEES IN THE YARD, SHAPING A wedge with an axe; and his greeting to me was a gesture of aiming it at my head; then, doffing his cap in mockery, he said, "And how does your Holiness? Eh, your Highness? Your term of service is over? Well, now you can live as you please, eh? Ekh—you!"

"We know all about that, everything!" said grandma, waving him off. In her room, getting the samovar started, she told me, "Grandpa is practically ruined. What money he had he lent at high interest to his godson, Nicholas, but without papers. I don't know just how the matter stands; but he's practically ruined; the money's gone. And that's his punishment for not helping the poor or taking pity on the unfortunate. God said to Himself, 'Why bless the Kashirins?' And so He's stripped everything from us."

With a glance around the room she resumed, "I've been trying to persuade God to relent a little, not to be so hard on the old man; and I've been giving a little charity, on the quiet, at night, out of what I earn. You can come with me if you like; I've got a bit of money for tonight."

Grandpa came in, blinked and asked, "Going to have a snack?"

"It's not yours," said grandma, "but you can join in, if you want to; there's enough."

He sat down at the table and said, "Come on, pour the tea."

Everything in the room was in its accustomed place. Only there was the sad emptiness in mama's corner; and on the wall above grandpa's bed was pinned a sheet with the inscription in big letters, "Jesus, Life of the World. May Thy Holy Name accompany me every day and hour of my existence."

"Who lettered that?"

Grandpa offered no answer, but grandma, after a pause, said, smiling, "That piece of paper cost—a hundred rubles!"

"None of your business!" shouted grandpa. "I give to others."

"No harm in giving now, but there was a time when you didn't," said grandma, quietly.

"Shut up!" he shrieked. Which brought old times right back again.

In a basket, on a box in the corner, Nicky woke up, his faded blue eyes barely visible. He looked sallower and more frail and anemic than before. Failing to recognize me, he silently turned away and shut his eyes.

News from the street was somber. Vyakhir had died—had drawn his last breath before Easter week. Khabi had moved. Yaz' feet had been amputated—he would never walk again. Giving me this news, dark-eyed Kostrom said bitterly, "Boys die early."

"It's only Vyakhir who died."

"It's all the same. Leaving the street is like dying. As soon as we make friends and are getting along, the boys have to go to work in town or they die. There are new tenants in your old place at Chesnokov's. The name's Evsienko. They have a boy, Niushka, who doesn't amount to much. He's got a couple of sisters; one's too small; and the other's a cripple, uses crutches, but she's beautiful." After a pause, he added, "Churka and I are in love with her, both of us, and we fight."

"Fight? With her?"

"No, Churka and I fight. We don't fight with her—not often."

I realized of course that big boys and even men fall in love. I had heard my share of vulgarities on that topic. But the news disconcerted me. I felt sympathetic with Kostrom, but it made me uneasy to look at his gaunt figure and his sullen, dark eyes.

I met the girl cripple that very evening. Going down the stair to the

yard she dropped a crutch, and waited, helpless, on the steps, supporting herself on the banister, with small, frail, almost transparent, hands.
I did my best to pick up the crutch with my bandaged hands, and was
exasperated at not succeeding. From her position above me she watched
me, and laughed in a gentle manner.

"What did you do to your hands?"

"Burned them."

"And I'm lame. Do you live here? Were you in the hospital long? I
was there a long, long time," and added, sighing, "such a long time."

She was dressed in white and had on light blue galoshes, worn but
clean. Her hair was done in a thick, smooth braid that came down to
her breast. Her eyes were large and sober. From their still depths flamed
a blue light that illuminated her delicate, sharp-nosed face. Despite her
amiable smile, I didn't take to her. "Hands off, please!" seemed to be
written over her invalid body. What had made my friends infatuated
with her?

"I've been crippled for so long now," she said, voluntarily, and almost
with pride. "I was bewitched, out of spite, by a neighbor with whom
my mother quarreled. Were you scared in the hospital?"

"Yes," and I left her, feeling awkward.

It must have been midnight when grandma very gently roused me
out of sleep. "Coming with me? By doing good to others your hands will
heal quickly."

Taking my arm, like one who escorts the blind, she led me through
the dark streets. It was an overcast, humid night. A steady wind that
sped the river current, whipped cold sand over my legs. Warily approaching the lightless windows of the hovels, grandma would twice
cross herself, then lay a coin and three hard biscuits on the window sill,
and again cross herself. Raising her eyes to the black sky, she mumbled,
"O Sainted Queen of Heaven, succor these people. Dear Mother, in
Thy sight, sinners are we all!"

The stillness and the shadows deepened the farther we went. Pitch
black was the sky, impenetrable, as if stars and moon were gone for
good. A dog lunged at us, snarling; I saw the glitter of his eyes in the
blackness, and cravenly I sought refuge against grandma. "It's all right,"
she soothed me. "It's nothing but a dog. It's past the time when the
devil is about. The cocks have started crowing."

Calling the dog over, she patted him and rebuked him, "You mustn't
scare my grandson, pup."

The dog gave me an ingratiating rub on my legs, and the three of us marched on. Twelve such "secret alms" did grandma leave on windows. The first light appeared, and in it the gray houses emerged from the shadows; the white Napolny church belfry stood up like a sugar loaf; and you could almost see through the graveyard wall.

"This old lady is getting tired," said grandma. "It's time to go home. When the housewives get up they'll see that Our Lady has left something for their little ones. When there's never enough a scrap comes in handy. Oh, Alex, the folks are so poor and nobody cares!" And she sang this verse: "The millionaire forgets God, has no thought of Judgment Day, never thinks of the poor man as friend and brother. He only thinks of heaping up gold that will turn into coals of Hell."

"That's the way it is. But we ought to live for each other instead, the way God lived for all of us. I'm glad to have you back."

I, too, felt serenely happy, realizing dimly that what I had taken part in was something unforgettable. The brown dog at my side shivered; I saw his cold muzzle, and trusting eyes begging to be forgiven.

"Can I take him home?"

"If he'll come with us. Here's a biscuit for him. I have two left. Let's sit down on the bench. How tired I am!"

And we rested on a bench near a gate with the dog at our feet crunching the biscuit; and grandma told me, "There's a Jewish woman living here must have about ten servants. I asked her, 'Do you live according to Moses' commandments?' And she said, 'I live as if I and my family were in the presence of God; how else?' "

Snuggling against my warm grandma, I fell asleep.

Again the current of my life flowed swift, a stream of impressions bringing me something new each day, filling my soul with elation or unrest or pain, but at least challenging me to think. I, too, was soon resorting to everything to see the crippled girl, to sit with her, chatting or silent at the gate. In her company silence, too, was pleasant. She was a tidy person, and her voice was like that of a singing bird. Charmingly she would describe the life of the Cossacks on the Don, among whom she had lived with her uncle, an oil refinery worker. Now her locksmith father had settled down in Nizhny. "An uncle of mine works at the Tsar's palace."

On Sundays and holiday evenings all the people on the street came together here at the gate. The youths went to pet in the graveyard; the men flocked to the taverns; and the wives and the children stayed here, sitting on the bench or in the sand.

The children played ball, or bowled, or played other games; the mothers watched, cheering them on or laughing at misplays. It was gay, though deafening. Stimulated by the attention of the grownups, any trifle was sufficient to excite impassioned rivalry. But no game could so absorb Kostrom, Churka and me, but we found an occasion to break off to make a display before the girl cripple.

"Ludmilla, did you see me knock down five pins in that bowling match?" And for reward a nod and a sweet smile.

Formerly our gang always took the same side in games, but now Kostrom and Churka played against each other. They sought to outdo each other in feats of skill or strength, sometimes coming to blows and tears. In one fight they could not be pulled apart, and adults had to pour water over them as over fighting dogs. Ludmilla, on the bench, stamped on the ground with her good foot, and when the antagonists wrestled up to her, prodded them away with her crutch, commanding them in a terrified voice, "Stop that!" Her face was almost blue-white, and her eyes twisted and glittered in a frenzied way, like those of a person possessed.

Another time Kostrom, after losing to Churka in a bowling match, crouched behind an oat bin in a grocery store, and wept. I couldn't bear to see it. The sobs came through clenched teeth; his cheekbones seemed to strain through the skin. His bony face seemed to have turned to stone. Plump tears dropped from his sullen, dark eyes. To my efforts at consolation he replied with fierce threats, as he choked back his tears, "Wait. He'll get a brick on his head. You'll see."

In his conceit, Churka took to walking in the middle of the street like the marriageable youths, hands in pocket, cap at angle. He had learned to spit between his teeth like a sport, and boasted, "Soon I'll be smoking. I tried twice but it made me sick."

I was disturbed by all this. I saw my friends leaving me, and I put the blame on Ludmilla. One evening, in the yard, as I was sifting my pickings of bones, rags, and other scrap, she approached in a swaying walk, and waved at me. "How do you do," she said, with three little ceremonial nods of her head. "Have you seen Kostrom or Churka?"

"Churka isn't pals with us anymore. And it's your fault. The two of them have quarreled, because they're in love with you."

She blushed, but made a mocking reply, "And how am I to blame?"

"What do you want to make them fall in love with you for?"

"Do I ask them to?" And as she went off angrily, she said, "Oh, it's so stupid. I'm older than they are. I'm fourteen. Boys don't fall in love with older girls."

"So that's all you know!" I said, intending to hurt her. "How about Khlistov's sister? She's old and the boys run after her, in her store."

Ludmilla turned on me, dug her crutch in the sand, and said in a tearful voice, and with an excited gleam in her lovely eyes, "You don't know so much yourself. That storekeeper is a bad woman,—and me, I'm only a little girl. But you ought to read the novel, *Kamchadalka*, part two; then you'll be able to talk."

Next day, wishing to make up with Ludmilla, I brought her some barley sugar, which I knew to be her favorite candy. "Like to have some?"

"Go away," she replied angrily. "We're not friends!" Yet she soon accepted it, but with the comment, "You should have wrapped it in some paper. How dirty your hands are!"

"I washed them, but it don't come off."

She took my hand in her dry, hot palm, and looking at it, cried out, "My, but it's rough!"

"Yours is rough, too."

"That's from the needle. I sew a lot." Then, looking around, she proposed, "Let's go where we can be alone and read *Kamchadalka*. How would you like that?"

It took us a while to find a place; nothing seemed suitable; and we ended up in the bathhouse. Though it was dark, it had a window overlooking a littered spot, hemmed in by the shed and the adjoining shop where the small cattle were butchered. Seldom did anybody cast a glance there. Sitting there beside the window, her lame foot on a stool, her good foot on the floor and her face behind the tattered book, she agitatedly declaimed many tiresome or meaningless words. And yet I was enthralled. From the floor I could look up at her eyes, moving like two blue flames across the page. Now and then tears brimmed over, and her voice choked, and the rapid, unfamiliar words ran together unintelligibly. Nevertheless I retained some of the words, sought to fashion them into verses, putting them through all sorts of turns, and succeeded in making what she read completely incomprehensible to me.

My dog, whom I had christened "Wind" because he was long, shaggy, swift, and sounded like the autumn wind in the chimney flues when he howled, would lie on my knees, dozing.

"Listening?" Ludmilla would ask, and I would nod.

Arranging the words in my mind, to give them cadences as in a song, each word taking on its own shining life like a star in the dark—this grew into an obsession.

As the light failed, Ludmilla's white hand would drop across the book and she'd say, "Good, wasn't it?"

These readings in the bathhouse went on even when, to my great satisfaction, Ludmilla stopped reading *Kamchadalka*. It had been a trial being quizzed about the interminable book—there was a third part, following the second, which she had been reading to me, and she said there was a fourth to come. A rainy day suited us best, unless it was a Saturday, when the bath ovens were stoked. When it rained, the yard was soaked; no one ventured out; no one could spy on us.

Ludmilla dreaded our being discovered, as did I. We sat together, hours on end, talking of anything that came to our minds. I told her some of grandma's stories, and from her I heard of the life of the Cossacks on the Medveditza River.[1] "It was so lovely there," she would say with a sigh. "What is it like here? A land of beggars!"

Then the bathhouse became unnecessary to us. Ludmilla's mother took a job with a furrier and was away from the house all day. Since her sister went to school, and her brother to a tile factory, the house was all ours. On rainy days I went there and helped the girl at her housework. With a laugh she would say, "We're living together just like a married couple, and even better; husbands don't help their wives."

When I got some money I spent it on cookies, which we had with tea; and to keep her nagging mother from finding out that it had been used, we then cooled off the samovar with cold water. Grandma sometimes joined us, bringing her lace orders or other sewing, and spinning her wonderful yarns. On grandpa's excursions into town, Ludmilla visited us, and what carefree banquets we had! "How well we live!" grandma would say. "With money of our own we can do as we wish."

She abetted my friendship with Ludmilla. "It's good for a boy and girl to be friends—only no tricks!" And, in honest words, we were told what "tricks" were meant. What she told us had the beauty of an inspiration. I was given a full understanding of the mistake of picking the unripened flower and forfeiting, thereby, the fragrance and the fruit.

We were free of any urge toward "tricks," but we did not hesitate to discuss that tabooed subject. It was virtually forced upon us by the gross forms, offensive to us both, in which the sexual relationship was continuously and tediously exhibited.

Ludmilla's handsome father was about forty. His hair and his beard were curly, and he could overpower one with a lift of his eyebrows. A

[1] This river is a tributary of the Don.

peculiarly taciturn man, I cannot recall hearing a word out of him. When he petted his children, the sounds he made were inarticulate, like those of a mute; and he was silent, even when he beat his wife.

On Sundays and holiday evenings he would appear at the gate in a pale blue blouse, ballooning velvet trousers tucked into polished high boots, with an accordion strapped over his shoulder; and there he would stand, stiff as a military sentry. And soon there would be something like a military parade across the gate as girls and women would file past, giving Evsienko "the eye," under their lashes, or brazenly direct, while he, with his lower lip pouted out, took appraising glances with his black eyes. This communication through wordless ogling had a repellent, animal-like character. From the languid, tranced movement of the women in this processional, one could imagine that a commanding flick of his eyelid toward a chosen one, would send her fainting to the mucky ground.

"The sot; the showoff!" Ludmilla's mother would mutter. She looked like a worn broom, tall and thin, her face long and sallow and crop-haired from an attack of typhus. Ludmilla, beside her, would chatter away, in vain attempts to divert her attention. But, blinking in her agitation, her mother would exclaim, "Oh, you monster! Stop! Stop!" Her slitlike Mongol eyes had a glittering, rigid look, always focused on something and never moving.

"Mama, don't aggravate yourself. What does it matter?" Ludmilla would say. "Look how fancy the mat-weaver's widow has got herself up!"

"I'd be able to dress up, too, if not for the three of you. You've consumed me," said the mother, staring pitifully through her tears at the squat figure of the mat-weaver's widow. She was like a hut. Her bosom projected like a roof, and her red face, half-covered by her green kerchief, was like a gable window in the sun.

Evsienko, pulling his accordion around front, started it up, playing tune after tune which carried far, bringing children swarming and tumbling with ecstasy in the sand at his feet.

"You wait. I'll give it to you!" his wife threatened. He gave her a disdainful glance, but said nothing. The mat-weaver's widow took a seat on the Khlistovs' bench nearby, and gave him rapt attention. Sunset reddened the field back of the graveyard. Like lumps of flesh in their holiday colors, people bobbed through the street, as on a river current. The children were swift as gusts of wind. The air was excitingly warm and caressing. From the sun-heated sand steamed a curious pungency. Most penetrating was the oily, sweetish slaughter-house odor, the odor of blood, while from the furrier's yard came the acrid smell of curing skins. Chattering women, bellowing men, children chiming like little bells, the vibrant bass of the accordion, all merged into one great resonance, a mighty sigh of the ever-laboring earth.

Bare and brutal though it all was, it somehow inspired a faith, embracing and profound, in that harsh and frankly animal life. And above the din unforgettable, feeling words reached straight into the heart. "Each in his turn." "It's unfair to gang together against one." "If we cannot pity ourselves, where will we find pity?" "Did God make woman to be a laughing stock?"

The night began to close in; the air freshened; sounds grew faint. Draped in shadows the cottages seemed higher and broader. Children were carried away to bed, some already asleep under the fence, or in the laps or at the feet of their mothers. The darkness quieted the children and made them docile. Unobserved, Evsienko vanished as if he had melted away. Gone, too, was the mat-weaver's widow. The deep accordion notes reverberated from far off, behind the graveyard. Ludmilla's mother sat on a bench, bowed, her back humped up like a cat's. Grandma was taking tea with the midwife, an enormous, yet flat-chested, woman, whom the street feared as a witch. She had a nose like a duck's bill, and wore a gold "hero" medal on her curveless, mannish bosom. She was said to have carried out of a burning house the invalid wife and three children of a colonel. Grandma and she were friends; they smiled when they saw each other, no matter how far off, as if they were seeing something especially nice.

Ludmilla, Kostrom and I sat on the gate bench. Churka had challenged Ludmilla's brother to a wrestling match. Panting in each other's grip, they were furiously trampling the sand. "Stop it!" cried Ludmilla, anxiously.

With his black eyes in a sidelong gaze upon her, Kostrom told a ghost story about Kalinin, the hunter, a crafty-eyed, grizzled old man, ill-famed throughout the town, who had recently died, but whose body had not been interred in the earth. His black coffin stood on scaffolding, apart from the other graves. On its lid were painted in white, a cross, a spear, a stick and crossed bones. Every night at dusk, according to the story, the old man left his coffin and hunted for something all over the graveyard and didn't get back till cock-crow.

"Don't talk about such things!" pleaded Ludmilla.

"That's the bunk!" cried Churka, slipping out of his antagonist's hold. "Why do you have to lie? I saw them bury him, myself, in the ground; the one above is only a monument. And that story about the dead man walking, it was that souse of a blacksmith who started it."

Kostrom, not deigning to look at him, said, "Go sleep in the grave-yard, and you'll see."

Thus began their usual wrangle. With an unhappy shake of her head, Ludmilla asked, "Mama, do the dead walk at night?"

"Yes," her mother answered, as if recalled by the question from some-where far off.

A shopkeeper's son, Valek, a tall, plump, rosy-faced youth of twenty, came up, and hearing the dispute said, "I'll give three greven and ten cigarettes to any of you three boys who'll sleep on top of the coffin till morning."

We were stunned to silence by the challenge, and Ludmilla's mother exclaimed, "Such foolishness! What do you want to put children up to such foolishness for?"

"Hand over a ruble, and I'll go," said Churka.

Kostrom immediately taunted him, "Three greven makes you afraid?" He turned to Valek. "Offer him a ruble; he won't go anyway. He's just a blow-hard."

"All right. Here's the ruble."

Churka got up, and without saying a word, slowly, almost hugging the fence, slipped away. Kostrom whistled after him jeeringly, between his fingers. Ludmilla, in a troubled voice, however, said, "Why does he have to brag so!"

"Where are you off to, coward?" sneered Valek. "And that's sup-posed to be the champion of the street."

I could not bear his sneers. We wasted no affection on this paunchy youth who egged boys on to mischief, told them dirty stories, and incited them to tease girls. For doing what he told them, boys were continually getting into trouble. Something had made him take a dis-like to my dog, whom he used to stone, and to whom one day he gave bread with a needle in it. Still less could I bear to see Churka shrinking away, humiliated.

I told Valek, "Give me the ruble. I'll go."

At once he began making fun of me and doing his best to throw a scare into me. He asked Ludmilla's mother to hold the ruble, but she refused it, and said angrily, "Don't ask me to hold it. None of that!" And went off.

Ludmilla couldn't get herself to hold it, which set Valek off into more jeering. I was about to go off without the money, when grandma came along, and hearing about it, accepted the ruble. To me she said gently, "Wear your overcoat and take along a blanket. It turns chill at dawn."

What she said strengthened my confidence that I could expect nothing awful to happen there.

Valek made the condition that I should remain on the coffin, sitting or lying, all through the night, even if the coffin should heave while old Kalinin was getting out. If I jumped off, I would lose. "Remember," he said, "I'll have my eyes on you."

Grandma kissed me and made the sign of the cross over me as I set off toward the cemetery. "If you see anything, don't stir; just repeat 'Hail Mary.'"

I hurried on, eager to have the thing started and done with. Kostrom and another boy went with me as escorts. Climbing over the brick wall, I got tangled in the blanket and had a fall, but was up immediately as if the earth had pushed me off. I heard a low laugh, and my heart clenched and a shudder ran down my spine.

I stumbled on to the black coffin, against which sand had shored up on one side, though on the other, the stumpy posts on which it was supported were visible. It was as if someone had tried to raise it, only to let it fall askew. Sitting on the edge of the coffin, I looked around me. The hilly space was just heaped with crosses, and shadows trembled over the graves. Among the graves stood slender willows, their boughs uniting buried neighbors with their shade. Through their shadow tracery stiff grass blades rose.

The white church loomed up like a snowdrift, and the small, setting moon shone through the still clouds. I heard Yaz' "fool-of-a-peasant" father languidly ringing the bell in his hut. With each pull at the cord its tortured little creak could be heard, to be followed by the clang of the little clapper, a sharp, unhappy sound. I could almost hear him say, "God rest us. Ai!," and the memory was somehow smothering and hard to bear. Despite the night coolness I sweated profusely. Should I get into Yaz' hut in time if old Kalinin actually got out?

I knew the layout of the cemetery, having often chased among the graves with Yaz and other playmates. Mama's grave was near the church.

People were still up in the village, for snatches of their laughter and verses of songs drifted over to me. Perhaps from the railroad tracks to which sand was being carted, or from the adjoining village of Katizovka, there came the muffled strains of an accordion. And, as usual, Miachov, the drunken blacksmith, was staggering and singing. I recognized his song:

"Mama's one little sin is she loves nobody but papa."

It was pleasant to hear the day sigh itself out; but with each peal of the bell the silence deepened; it was like a river flooding a meadow, drowning and covering everything. The soul seemed to be floating up into the infinite, to go out like a match in the dark, absorbed in that sea of space where live only the bright, unattainable stars, while all on earth crumbles away, worthless and dead.

Wrapped in my blanket with my feet tucked under, I faced the church. With every movement I made the coffin creaked, and a gritty sound came from the sand beneath. Twice something fell close to me, and a lump of brick followed. A thrill of fear passed through me; but I realized that it must be Valek and his pals on the other side of the wall, trying to scare me. On the contrary, the presence of living beings bolstered my confidence.

Without wishing to, I began thinking about mama. Catching me with a cigarette once, she wanted to beat me, but I said, "Don't touch me; I'm suffering enough, I feel sick." And later, having been sent behind the stove for punishment, she had complained to grandma, "He is without feelings; he has no love for anybody."

I had been hurt by that. I felt sorry for mama when she beat me, because she seldom had cause. Altogether I had borne a heavy load of maltreatment. Now there were those on the other side of the wall, knowing I was terrified lying alone in the graveyard, yet doing their best to intensify my terrors.

I had an impulse to shout, "Go to the devil, you!" to them, but that was perilous. Who could tell what the devil, who might be around, would do about that? The mica in the sand glimmered in the moonlight, and I recalled how, lying on a raft, once, on the Oka, face down to the water, a sunfish almost grazed my face, then turned on its side, curved like a human cheek, glanced at me with its round, bird eyes, and dove down with a fluttering motion, like a falling maple leaf. And memory kept toiling for me, recollecting episode after episode, as if straining to fend off the fantasies born of fear.

A hedgehog bowled along, scraping the sand with its hard paws. It made me think of a hearth spirit; it was as tiny and tattered. And I remembered grandma, squatting before the oven, invoking the hearth spirit, "Good master of the house, rid us of the cockroaches."

Far away, beyond the town, too distant to see where, it began to grow light. The cold dawn wind ruffled my cheeks and my eyes. I snuggled in my blanket. I didn't care what came now.

Grandma woke me. Standing beside me, tugging at the blanket, she said, "Up now. Are you cold? Were you scared, eh?"

"I was. But don't let anybody know. Don't tell the boys."

"Why not?" she asked, astonished. "If you weren't scared, you'd have nothing to be proud of."

On our way home she said to me, "On this earth, darling, you have to learn from your own experiences. If you can't learn from yourself, you can't learn from anybody."

By nightfall I was the street hero. I was asked, "Could it be that you weren't scared?" When I replied, "Yes, I was scared," they wagged their heads and said, "You see!"

A shopkeeper buttonholed everybody to vociferate, "So that might only be nonsense about Kalinin walking about. And if he did walk would that boy have been scared? No, sir. He would have chased Kalinin out of the graveyard; and that would have been the last of him!"

From Ludmilla I got glances of tender admiration. Even grandpa showed his pleasure. Everybody made much of me, except Churka, who sneered, "That was nothing for him; his grandmother's a witch!"

Chapter Three

LIKE A STAR GROWING FAINT AT DAWN, MY BROTHER NICK FADED OUT. He slept, along with grandma and myself, on a bedding of rags on planks set up in a small shed. A chicken coop was on the other side of the wall, through whose chinks we could hear the fattened hens squawking and flapping during the night, and in the morning the brassy rooster crowing his alarm. "I could tear you to pieces!" grandma, wakened out of her sleep, would mutter.

I was up already, gazing fascinated at the rays of sunlight streaming through the chinks, and the silvery motes that danced in them. To me the motes were like the words of which a fairy tale was made up.

The planks on which we lay had been gnawed by the mice, and served as a playground for swarms of spotted red beetles.

At times, to get away from the infiltering stenches of the chicken coop, I stole out of the shed and took a perch on the roof, from which I watched the tenants as they woke up, bloated with sleep and almost eyeless. The shaggy pate of the boatman, Fermanov, a bad-tempered drunk, emerged, and I would see him blink at the sun with gummy, running eyes, and hear his bearish snorts. Next came grandpa, pattering across the yard to the bathhouse for his morning rinse in cold water. There would follow the landlord's talkative cook, a freckled woman with a pointed nose, who resembled a cuckoo, and the landlord himself, who resembled a plump old pigeon. All, in fact, seemed close to the animal world, bird or beast.

Cheerfully bright though the morning might be, I would feel depressed, longing to get away to the unpeopled fields, having learned by this time that the human presence manages to blight a beautiful day.

I was thus sprawled on the roof one day, when grandma called me, and when I stood beside her on the bed, she told me in a low voice, with a sad shake of her head, "Nick is dead."

The child had rolled off his pillow and was curled up, gaunt and blue, on the coverlet. His shirt had hiked up to his neck, baring his little bloated belly and his deformed legs. His hands were curled behind his back in a curious way, as if in an effort to raise himself; and his head was turned sideward.

"Thank God he's gone!" said grandma, as she combed her hair. "What could the unfortunate little creature have lived for?"

Mincing in, on what were almost dance steps, grandpa appeared, and warily touched his fingers to the child's closed eyes. Grandma turned on him. "What's the idea of touching him before your hands are washed!"

"You see!" grandpa mumbled. "It's born, it eats—but all for nothing."

Grandma cut in, "Still talking in your sleep!"

He gave her an absent look. On his way out into the yard, he said, "You can do what you like but I'm not giving him a funeral."

"You cheapskate!"

I left and did not come back till nightfall. Nick was buried the following morning, and while masses were being said, I sat with my dog over mama's reopened grave. Beside me was Yaz' father, who had done the digging at cut rates, and kept reminding me of it. "I only did it for friendship's sake. I would have charged anybody else so many rubles."

The yellow pit exhaled a strong, musty smell. Peering in, I saw damp black boards. No matter how lightly I moved, the sand around the edge cascaded down, leaving little gulleys in the heaped soil. My movements were deliberate. I wanted to cover those boards.

"None of your tricks," said Yaz' father, smoking.

Grandma carried the little coffin to the grave. The "peasant trash" jumped into the pit, set the coffin next to the boards, climbed out, and kicking and shoveling the earth back, he filled the grave, grandpa and grandma silently lending a hand. No priests; no beggars; only we four among the swarming crosses. As she paid him, grandma reproached him, "You moved Barbara's coffin."

"Couldn't help it. Otherwise I'd have had to dig into somebody else's plot. Don't worry about it."

Grandma knelt on the grave, lamented, and then went off, with grandpa after her, his cap over his eyes and his hands holding his shabby coat together.

"Seed sown in unplowed ground," he said, trotting ahead, like a crow hopping over the furrows during plowing.

"What does he mean?" I asked grandma.

She replied, "He gets ideas, God bless him."

It had grown hot. Grandma plodded, her feet sinking in the warm sand. She stopped often to mop her sweating face.

"The black thing in mama's grave," I asked, "was that her coffin?"

"Yes," she said bitterly. "Stupid dog that he is! Barely a year and Barbara's already decayed. It's this sandy soil; the water goes through. That being the case he should have——"

"Do we all have to decay?"

"All. The only exceptions are the saints."

"Then you won't decay."

She stopped, fixed my cap, and said to me earnestly, "Better not think about it, do you hear?"

But I did. How outrageous and ugly death was! How revolting! It made me feel bad.

By the time we got home grandpa had already heated the samovar and set the table. "Let's have some tea. I expect you're hot. My tea's in there, too. This is for all of us."

He patted grandma on the shoulder. "Well, mother?"

Grandma raised her hands. "What can be the meaning of it all?"

"It means God's offended with us; and he's stripping everything from us, piece by piece. If families lived in harmony, like the fingers of a hand——"

It was long since I'd heard him so gentle and amicable. In the hope that what the old man said might soothe my injured feelings, help me forget the dripping, protruding black boards, I listened to him. But grandma unceremoniously cut him short.

"None of that, father. You've been handing that out all your life, and I'd like to know, has it done anyone any good? Your whole life you've been eating into people like rust into iron."

Grandpa gave her a look, mumbled something under his breath, but ventured nothing audible.

That evening, talking to Ludmilla at the yard gate, I spoke of that melancholy morning's burial at my mother's grave. She was unimpressed.

"Orphans have advantages. If my father and mother died, I'd let my sister look out for my brother and I'd become a nun. Anyway, that's all there'd be for me to do. A cripple doesn't get married, and she can't work. And I wouldn't want to risk bringing other cripples into the world." She spoke practically, as did all the women on our street, and it was probably that evening that my interest in her began to fade. Besides, the turn my life took after that left me few occasions to see her.

Several days after my brother's death grandpa told me, "Go to bed early today, before dark. We'll be going to the forest for wood."

"I'll come along to pick herbs," said grandma.

There was a pine and birch forest on swampy ground about two miles off. On one side it stretched to the Oka; on the other to the Moscow road. It was full of dead and fallen trees. Nearby, on what was called Savelov Ridge, was a stretch of pine woods, whose bristly, black outline against the horizon looked like a shaggy black tent. Both were properties of Count Shuvalov, but were indifferently guarded, and were regarded by the people of Kunavin as a sort of village common. They trimmed off the dead branches, carted off the fallen trees and, on occasion, did not scruple to fell live trees. In the autumn people slipped into the woods, dozens at a time, with axes in their belts and ropes coiled around their waists, to bring out a supply of winter firewood.

And so it was that, at dawn, we three made our way over the dewy, silvery green meadows. On our left, beyond the Oka, ruddying the sloping Diatlov Hill, lighting up the white walls of Nizhny and its golden church domes, and brightening the garden, rose in its unhurried fashion our indolent Russian sun. Like a sleepy breath blew the soft wind from the sluggish Oka. Overweighted with dew, the golden buttercups seemed to stagger; little flower bells of a lilac hue bowed humbly to the earth; varicolored straw flowers stood serely on patches of dry sod; and the flower we call "belle of the night" opened its blood-red, starlike petals. Like a sombre army the forest advanced to meet us. The pines looked winged like gigantic birds; the birches looked like girls. The dank swamp odors floated over the fields. Beside me, his pink tongue lolling out, trotted my dog, stopping now and then to sniff and cock his foxlike head questioningly. Grandpa, wearing a jacket of grandma's and an old beret, winking and smiling over some secrets of his own, walked as furtively as if he were stealing something; while grandma, in a blue blouse, a black skirt, and a white kerchief over her head, waddled along serenely. You never need hurry walking behind her.

As we entered the forest grandpa livened up. He had his nose in the air and began to speak, at first brokenly and quite unintelligibly, then gaily and grandly, as if he had had something to drink.

"Forests are God's gardens. How were they planted, if not by His breezes, the sanctified breath of His mouth? In my youth, when I worked on ships, I made a trip to Zhegulia. I tell you, Alex, you'll never have the life I had. There are forests along the Oka, from Kasimov to Murom; and along the Volga they stretch all the way to the Urals. Ah, it's endless and wonderful."

Grandma gave him a sidelong glance and winked at me, while he, stumbling over the uneven ground, told me in dusty, rambling words, a tale that has fixed itself in my memory.

"We were freighting oil drums from Saratov to the Fair at Makara. Cyril of Porekha was our captain, and the mate was a Tatar called by some name like Asaf. At Zhegulia we had the wind head on, and in gale force, and since there was no point in being tossed around, we went ashore to cook a meal. It was May. The water lay all around the land. The waves swam over it like flocks of birds, like the swans that sail on the Caspian by the thousands. In spring the hills around Zhegulia are green, and the sunlight just drowns everything in gold.

"Resting there we became friends, we felt as one. On the river it was raw and gray; but on the banks it was cozy and smelled sweet. When night fell, our captain, Cyril, a tough old man, got up, pulled

off his cap and said to us, 'Children, from now on I'll command you
and serve you no longer. Get along on your own. I'm taking to the
woods!'

"We were stunned. What could he be saying? Somebody had to be
in charge. People, as you'll understand, can't get along without somebody to guide them, even on the Volga where it's straight ahead like
a road. Even there you can lose your way, because people without a
head are like brainless beasts—and no one cares what becomes of the
other! So we were alarmed; but that one—his mind was made up. 'I'm
tired of being your shepherd,' he said, 'I'm taking to the woods.'

"There were those among us who were ready to hold him back by
force, but the rest wanted to wait. Then the Tatar mate shouted,
'I'm going along!' And that meant quite a loss to him. The boss owed
him for the last two trips; and here he was finished with half of a
third. Quite a piece of money to be forfeiting! We argued it back and
forth through the night, and in the end seven of our crew left, about a
third of the crew. That's the pull the forest has on people!"

"Did they turn bandits?"

"Possibly; or hermits. That wasn't settled then."

Grandma crossed herself. "Mother of God! Just thinking about
people makes you sorry for them."

"The same reasoning power is given to us all. That's what the Devil
catches on."

Our path through the forest was a muddy one that wound between
damp mounds and slender pines. It seemed to me a good thing to do
to go live in the woods like Cyril of Porekha—no jabbering humans,
no quarrels, no drunks. It would be possible there to forget grandpa's
nauseating stinginess, mama's grave in the porous sand, which saddened me, which bore down on my heart like weights.

Coming to a dry spot grandma said, "How about a bite now? Let's
sit down."

In a cloth were bread, onions, salt, cucumbers and cottage cheese,
which she had carried all the way in a basket. Grandpa blinked at the
spread confusedly, and said, "But I didn't bring any food, mother."

"There's enough for all of us."

For a backrest we had a pine trunk that rose tall as a mast. The air
smelled resinous. A light breeze blew in from the fields, setting the
grass waving. Then grandma went, picking herbs in her dark hands,
telling me, as I went with her, what were the medicinal or occult powers
of the plants and ferns she was gathering. Grandpa went to cut up

the fallen logs. My part was to haul the hewn wood onto one pile; but I couldn't resist following grandma, who seemed to float between the rugged trunks, and to dive when she bent over to pick among the pine cones. All the while she kept talking to herself, "Too early, again, hardly a mushroom around. Lord, how badly you look after your poor. Mushrooms are the delicacy of the poor."

I tried to move noiselessly, to avoid attracting her notice, and to avoid distracting her from her chats with God, the plants and the frogs. But she caught sight of me.

"You've slipped away from grandpa?" And leaning over the dark earth, so splendidly arrayed in its flower embroidery, she discoursed of the time when God, furious with mankind, sent the flood that drowned all living things. "But the tender Mother of God had taken care to gather the seeds of everything in a basket which she hid away; and after the flood, she urged the sun, 'Dry the earth from top to bottom, and what praise you'll get from all the people!' After the sun dried the earth she planted the seed. God took a look. He saw the earth covered again with life—plants, people, animals. 'Who did all this against my will?' he demanded. And she confessed, and as it turned out, God Himself had regretted seeing the earth lifeless, so He gave Her His approval. 'That was well done.' "

I found this story to my liking, but I was confused by it. I told her, with some concern, "But did that really happen? Because the Mother of God wasn't born until long after the flood."

That startled grandma. "Who said that?"

"It's in the books at school."

Reassured by that, she advised me, "If it's only in books, you can forget it. They lie, those books." And with a quiet laugh, she said, "Think of it, little fool. God was; but not His mother? How was He born then?"

"I don't know."

"That's good. It's quite a piece of learning to be able to say, 'I don't know.' "

"The priest said the Mother of God was the daughter of Anna and Joachim."

That made grandma angry. She turned upon me with a sharp look. "If that's what you think, I'll smack you!" And, a little later, she went on to explain, "The Blessed Virgin came before everybody and everything. She gave birth to God and then——"

"But what about Christ?"

Grandma had no answer, shutting her eyes in perplexity.

"What about Christ?"

I realized that I had won; but it was not pleasing to me to have trapped her in religious mysteries.

We went deeper and deeper into the forest, into the bluish haze penetrated by the golden sunbeams, and pervaded by a soft hum, a dream sound that provoked one to dreaming. Through it could be heard the crossbills' song, the tinkle of the titmouse, the piping of the goldfinch, the chuckle of the cuckoo, the loud, insistent tune of the chaffinch, and the brooding note of that strange bird, the grosbeak. At every step we seemed to intrude upon emerald-green frog families. Like a sentry guarding the roots of a tree, an adder lay coiled, its golden head erect. We heard a squirrel crack a nut and saw its furry tail bobbing among the pine branches. The farther we went the more there was to see.

Seeming to play among the pine trees were gigantic airy phantoms that kept dissolving in the massed green, through which shone the blue and silver sky. And one walked on a luxurious moss carpet, dotted with bilberries; and the grass was flecked with moorberries as with drops of blood. And from everywhere rose the strong, appetizing odor of mushrooms. "Holy Virgin, glorious light of earth!" prayed grandma, breathing deeply.

In the forest, too, she conducted herself like the mistress of an establishment, at home among her brood. With a bearlike waddle she went on, giving everything an interested look, and a word of praise, and thanksgiving. It was as if she radiated warmth upon the forest; and it gave me particular satisfaction to see the moss after she had stepped on it, rear up again.

And as we went on, the life of the bandit appealed to me; to strip hoarders and give the loot to the needy; to bring contentment to all; no one envying his neighbor, nor abusing him; no more snapping at each other like snarling curs. It was good, then, to take it up with grandma's God, and her Holy Virgin; to let them know of the disagreeable way people live, how they entombed each other in heaps of abuse, like a burial under dirty sand. So much avoidable ugliness and torment had to be endured on earth! And I thought, If the Holy Virgin gives heed to what I tell her, let her endow me with the necessary understanding and I will reconstruct everything, and better our life. And what if I was not an adult? The wise men had taken the counsel of Christ when He was but a year older.

And thus, self-absorbed, I stepped into a pit, bruising my hip and the nape of my neck. Mired in the cold slime at the bottom, which was as gluey as tree-gum, it exasperated me to realize that I would not be able to get out by myself; and I wanted beyond everything not to call grandma and alarm her. But there was nothing else for me to do; and she soon had me out. Crossing herself, she said, "Lord be praised! What good fortune this bear pit was empty! Where would you be if the master of the house had been in?" But she wept through her laughter.

She led me to a stream, where she washed my bruises, poulticed them with healing herbs, and bandaged them with strips ripped from her chemise; and left me at a railway signal station, for I was too lame to walk all the way back. And from then on, almost every day, I proposed to grandma, "Let's go to the forest." She went willingly, and thus we passed through the summer and far into the fall, bringing back stores of herbs, berries, mushrooms and nuts, the sale of which gave us our living. "Lazy beggars, you!" shrilled grandpa, though we took not a crumb of his bread.

The forest gave me a relaxing sense of peace in which my grievances seemed to ebb, in which everything displeasing seemed to be dissolved. My senses seemed to sharpen, too; eyes and ears became keener, my memory more tenacious, my range of feeling widened.

And I gained new respect for my amazing grandmother. I had come to regard her as a higher being, the kindest and most understanding creature on earth, and what I saw her do continuously confirmed this judgment. Returning one evening from gathering white mushrooms, grandma sat down for a minute's rest, just as we emerged from the woods, while I cut back into the woods to look for more mushrooms. Suddenly I heard her admonishing a famished-looking gray dog, whose tongue was slavering, while she was calmly trimming a mushroom, "Now, go away, you! Go, and God be with you!"

Valek having recently poisoned my dog, I immediately thought of replacing him with this one, and ran after him. He hunched himself up in a peculiar way, seeming not to move a muscle of his neck; and after a glance out of his hungry green eyes, he lunged into the woods, his tail between his legs. He did not turn at my whistle, but scurried more frantically to cover; and in everything his movements were not quite a dog's.

"You saw him," said grandma, smiling. "I didn't realize it at first. I took him for a dog, until I gave him a second look and saw my mistake. He had the fangs and neck of a wolf. Gave me quite a scare. I said to him, 'If you're a wolf better clear out!' It's lucky wolves aren't dangerous in the summer."

She felt no fear in the woods and never lost her way. She could smell out the presence and type of a mushroom by the scent of the grass. At times she quizzed me in mushroom lore. "What kind of tree does this mushroom take to? How do you tell the safe from the poisonous kind?"

By hardly visible claw-marks in the bark, she would tell me in what tree a squirrel had his hollow, and climbing up, I would rob him of his winter supply of nuts, getting as much as ten pounds at a time. But once, despoiling a squirrel, a squirrel hunter's gun spoiled me, imbedding twenty-seven pellets in my ribs. Grandma probed out eleven of them with a needle; the rest lodged in my skin for years, gradually working out to the surface.

Grandma was delighted with me for making no fuss over the pain. "Brave lad," she said. "The patient one turns out the clever one."

Whenever the sale of her mushrooms and nuts left her something over, she put it on window sills as "secret alms," though she herself lacked a whole garment, even for Sundays.

"You're shabbier than the beggars," grumbled grandpa, in one of their increasingly frequent quarrels, "You make me ashamed of you."

"What concern is it of yours? I'm not your daughter. I'm not hunting a husband."

"I have no more sins on my head than others," complained grandpa. "Why must I bear a heavier punishment?"

And grandma needled him, "What you're worth is something only the devil can say." And she would tell me, in confidence, "My old man's scared of devils. How senile he's getting! It's fear that's aging him, the poor man!"

That summer in the forest had hardened me and turned me into something of a savage, taking away what interest I had in those of my own age, like Ludmilla, whose common sense I found a bore.

One day grandpa came back from town soaked through; the autumn rains had come. As he stood in the doorway, shaking himself like a sparrow, he announced with the tone of one who had scored a victory, "Look here, you young scamp, tomorrow you're going off to a new job."

"Where to?" asked grandma, annoyed.

"To your sister Matrena's son."

"You've made a bad mistake, father."

"Shut up, idiot! They'll make a man of him."

Grandma made no reply, but her head drooped.

That night I told Ludmilla I was going off to town. "I'm being taken there, too, soon," she said moodily. "Papa wants to have my leg amputated. I'll get well when it's off."

She had lost weight that summer; her complexion had turned bluish and her eyes looked larger.

"Are you frightened?" I asked.

"Yes," she answered, and fell into silent weeping.

My own gloomy anticipations of life in town left me too dispirited to console her. For a long time, in silent misery, we sat close together. Had it been summer I should have proposed to grandma that we go off as wandering beggars, as she had done when she was a child, taking Ludmilla, whom I would pull along in a hand cart with us. But summer was gone. Rainy winds blew through the streets; the sky was packed with storm clouds; the whole earth seemed to scowl, to have taken on a look of grimy misery.

Chapter Four

BACK IN THE CITY, IN A TWO-STORY, WHITE HOUSE, THAT GAVE ME the impression of a mass coffin. The house was new, yet it had a sick look, blown up like a beggar who had struck it rich and had overeaten. It stood at an angle to the street, had eight windows per story, but only four where its street face should properly have been. Those on the ground floor had the back yard and the narrow passage to it for a view; those on the upper floor were provided a view of a laundress' hut and a ravine.

There was no street, in any understandable sense of the word. Before the house ran an unkempt ravine, intersected by a narrow dam. On the left the ravine stretched to the jail. With its jumble of rotting wood and filth, it had the look of a public dump, with a pool of green slime at the bottom; a similar stretch on the right, terminated in a stagnant pond. The house stood exactly midway, opposite an expanse of litter and muck, overgrown with briars and weed grass, and a patch cleared as a garden by the priest, Pokrovsky, who had erected there a summer house of red-painted laths, so thin that a hurled stone could crack them. The place was unbearably dreary and degradingly filthy. Autumn had cruelly pounded this filth-laden earth till it had become a sort of red goo that dragged at one's feet. I had never before seen that much dirt in that little space; and, having grown used to the cleanly fields and woods, this littered nook roused my aversion.

Beyond the ravine were stretches of gray, sagging fences; I recognized the house, not far off, where I had stayed when I had worked as the door boy in the shoe store; and its proximity added to my depression.

I was already acquainted with my boss. He and his brother had once paid visits to mama; and it was his brother who had sung the comic tune, "Daddy Andy."

They showed no change. The boss, hook-nosed and long-haired, had the same friendly manner and seemed a kind man; his younger brother, Victor, retained his horse-length of face and his freckles. Their mother, grandma's sister, was an ill-tempered nag. The boss' wife was an imposing-looking creature with a skin as white as bread made of fine flour, and big dark eyes. The very first day she twice informed me, "I gave your mother a silk dress trimmed with jet."

I was reluctant, for some reason, to believe that she had given a present and that mama had accepted it. At the second announcement I told her, "So you gave it to her; all right; it's nothing to brag about."

She started from me, exclaiming, "What? Who do you think you're talking to?" And red spots blotched her face, her eyes rolled, and she yelled for her husband. He appeared in the kitchen with a pair of compasses in his hand, and a pencil stuck behind his ear; he heard his wife out, and ordered me to "Speak respectfully to her and to everybody here; no insolence!" Then he turned on his wife. "Don't bother me with nonsense!"

"Nonsense? What do you mean! If your relations——"

"To hell with my relations!" cried my boss, and rushed off.

It was disagreeable for me to think of these people as grandma's relations. I had learned from experience that relatives treat each other worse than strangers. Knowing more of their vices and follies, they can be more wounding in gossip; and they are quicker to quarrel.

I liked my boss. The gestures with which he tossed back his hair and tucked it behind his ears were graceful, and in some ways he recalled Good Idea. A cheerful laugh came easy to him; the look in his gray eyes was friendly; and his hooked nose nested within humorous wrinkles. "Eh, you wild geese," he would say to his mother and his wife. "Haven't you tormented each other long enough!" And his small, even teeth showed in an amiable smile.

Mother-in-law and daughter-in-law pecked at each other perpetually. It astonished me how readily they could slip into a quarrel. They were at it as soon as they were up; they would tramp through the house as if it were afire, before their hair was done or their dresses fastened; and they went on all day long, only stopping for a breath at meals. Even in the dining room, after stuffing themselves till they could cram in nothing more, they made food the theme of a languid debate, in preparation for the big quarrel. No matter what the mother-in-law had cooked, the daughter-in-law would complain, "It's not the way mother cooked it."

"Then it was badly cooked."

"Far from it; hers was much tastier."

"So, go back to your mother."

"I'm mistress in this house!"

"And what am I?"

And the boss would cut in. "Enough, you wild geese! What's the matter with you? Have you gone crazy!"

For no understandable reason, everything in that household was queer and ludicrous. To get to the dining room from the kitchen you had to pass through a closet, the only one in the house; and so, through that closet went the samovar and the food; and that, alone, gave rise to witty sallies and comical confusions. My bed was a couch between the entrance to that closet and the entrance to the cellarway. This exposed me, at the head, to the heat from the cook stove, and at the feet to the cold draft from the cellar stairs. On retiring I used to wrap around my feet all the floor mats I could pick up.

Peculiarly drab and depressing was the parlor, with its two full-length mirrors, its gilt-framed portraits, its set of card tables, and its dozen Vienna cane chairs. There was a smaller parlor, crowded with upholstered furniture, wedding gifts, silver plate and tea service. Among its adornments were three lamps, each of which seemed bigger than its two rivals. There was also a windowless bedroom furnished with an extra-size bed, and chests and closets which gave off scents of leaf tobacco and Persian camomile. These three rooms were left unused, the whole household crowding into the far from spacious dining room.

Immediately after breakfast, about eight o'clock, the boss and his brother set up their table and laid out sheets of drafting paper, drafting instruments, pencils and tiny bowls of India ink; and taking their places at the two ends of the table, set to work. The table, which almost filled the room, wobbled; coming out of the nursery, the boss' wife or the maid might bump a corner, and Victor would complain, "Don't come barging in here!"

"Basil!" the boss' wife would call out, indignantly, "tell him to stop shouting at me!"

"All right; but see you don't shake the table," he would reply, placatingly.

"How can I help it? I'm pregnant and the room's so crowded!"

"Then we'll work in the parlor."

To which she snorted, angrily, "Heavens! Think of using the parlor for a workroom!"

From the closet door emerged the wrathful face of the mother-in-law, reddened from the heat of the stove. She called out, "That's her! She must get in your way! The other four rooms aren't enough for her!"

As Victor enjoyed a laugh, the boss shouted, "That's enough!"

His wife slumped theatrically into a chair and moaned, "I'm dying! I'm dying!"

"Don't keep me from my work, damn you!" roared the boss, pale with exasperation. "Might as well be in a madhouse as here! And me wearing myself out to keep you, you wild geese!"

In the beginning these rumpuses alarmed me, especially the time the boss' wife, grabbing a knife off the table, locked herself in the closet and started shrieking hysterically. In a moment of calm the boss, who had failed to force the door, told me, "Climb up my back and unhook the door."

I mounted his back, broke the glass pane in the door, but when I put my head through the opening, the boss' wife gave me a cut on the head with the knife. Nevertheless, I managed to unhook the door and the boss tugged his wife into the dining room where, after a tussle, he retrieved the knife. In the meanwhile, sitting in the kitchen nursing my rapped head, I decided that all my sufferings had been wasted. That blunt knife could scarcely saw through bread, and could never have nicked the skin. Neither had there been any point in my scaling up the boss' back; I could as easily have smashed the glass from a chair; and in any event, the unhooking would have been simpler for one of the men, whose arm had a longer reach. After that commotion I was no longer upset by these scenes.

The brothers were in the church choir and they sang as they worked. The older brother, a baritone, would begin: "The maiden's heart was in the ring I threw into the sea"; and they younger brother, a tenor, joined in: "and with that very ring I wrecked her joy on earth."

From the nursery would come the peevish voice of the boss' wife, "Are you out of your heads? The baby's just fallen asleep"; or, "Basil, you a married man, singing a song like that! And any minute the vesper bell will ring!"

"What's the row now? This is a church tune!" To which the boss' wife gave answers implying that it was not seemly to sing church tunes any which place; and besides—pointing significantly at the little door.

"We'll just have to move, or what on earth will become of us!" And just as regularly he spoke of getting a new work table—spoke of it for three years running.

Hearing my bosses on the subject of other people reminded me of the shoe store, where I had heard the same sort of talk. Obviously here too they considered themselves the elect of the town; they knew the laws of proper behavior to the last punctilio; and, conforming to those laws, which were hazy to me, they dealt out ruthless judgments upon others. This passing of sentences on others engendered a fierce and resentful wrath in me toward the precepts of my employers; and it became one of my pleasures to break them.

I was kept well occupied. I did all the chores of a house servant; I gave the kitchen a thorough going over on Wednesday, mopping the floor, and cleaning the samovar and the pots; on Saturdays I washed the floors of the other rooms and the two staircases. I also split firewood and hauled it in; I cleaned and cut up vegetables; I helped the boss' wife at her marketing, carrying the basket home; and I ran errands to the drugstore and other shops. But my real taskmaster was grandma's sister, a loud, domineering, fierce old woman. She was up at six, hurriedly washed herself, and, still in her underwear, went to the icon corner to pester God with appeals and complaints concerning herself, her sons and her daughter-in-law. "Lord," she would whine, with her two index fingers and thumbs pressed to her temples, "I ask you for nothing; there's nothing I want, only a little rest, a little peace. Lord, let it be by Thy power!"

Awakened by her groans, and still half-asleep, I would watch her from under my blanket, hearing her impassioned prayers with a sort of terror. Through rain-streaked panes the autumn morning would look feebly in. In the cold half-light, her shadowy figure waved from side to side on the floor, and her arms thrashed about in alarming gestures. Her thinning hair whipped over her nape and her shoulders, out of the kerchief that kept slipping down, and which she replaced, with irritated proddings of her left hand, and irritated mutterings, "Nuisance!"

Slapping her forehead violently and thumping her breast and her back, she would plead, "And please, Lord, take my troubles into account and punish my daughter-in-law. Make her atone for the suffering she has caused me. And open my son's eyes, and Victor's. O Lord, give Victor help, be compassionate toward him!"

Victor also had his bed in the kitchen, and hearing his mother's moaning, would call out, "Tattling on the young wife again! Disgraceful!"

"It's all right; you go to sleep," the old woman would reply in a guilty whisper. There would be a minute or so of silence, and then the vindictive muttering would resume, "May their bones crack; may there be no roof over their heads on earth, O Lord!"

Not even grandpa's prayers had been so horrible. Her prayers over, she would rouse me, "Up with you! You'll never amount to anything if you don't get up early. Start the samovar! Bring in the firewood! Didn't you split some last night?"

To avoid hearing that foaming mumble of hers, I would speed through everything; but there was no satisfying her. Through the kitchen she would storm after me, "Quieter, you imp! You wake Victor up, and I'll give it to you! Hurry to the bakery!"

On weekdays, I would buy two pounds of white bread and some rolls for the boss' wife. When I came in with the package, the two women would look it over suspiciously, and heft it with their palms, and ask, "Didn't they put something in for good measure? No? Just open your mouth!" And they would crow triumphantly, "See! There's the pieces between his teeth! He's wolfed down what they put in for good measure. See that, Basil?"

I did my work with a will. The expulsion of dirt gave me some satisfaction as I mopped floors, scoured pots or polished doorknobs. From time to time, in the peaceful intervals, I heard the comments of the women upon me, "He's no shirker." "And he's clean." "But he's impertinent." "But, mother, what sort of education has he had?"

And both strove to educate me to accord them a respect I could not feel, since, in my estimation, they were morons. I disliked them, wouldn't obey them, and talked back to them. Apparently perceiving the small effect their tirades had, the boss' wife would interject, more and more frequently, "You should keep in mind what a poor family you come from. I gave your mother a silk dress trimmed with jet." To which I replied one day, "Do you want my skin in payment for that dress?"

"Heavens," she cried out in agitation, "he's likely to set the house on fire!"

This startled me. What made her say such a thing? Both women complained about me to the boss after this interchange, and he was quite severe with me. "Watch your step, my boy!" However, he took another occasion to reproach his wife and his mother. "What a pair you are! Is the boy a horse that you work him like that? Another lad would have cleared out of here long ago—that is, if you hadn't already worked him to death."

This stung the women to tears, and his wife had a tantrum and berated him. "Think of saying that in his presence, you long-haired idiot! How will I ever manage him now? And in my condition!"

As for his mother, she affected sadness, "May God forgive you, Basil. I warn you, you're spoiling him."

They went out fuming, and the boss remarked irritably, "See, you scamp, the scenes you get me into! Back you'll go to your grandpa and your ragpicking."

This slight was beyond my endurance, and I replied, "I was better off ragpicking. I was taken on as an apprentice, but what training have you given me? Emptying the slop pails?"

He grabbed at my hair, but without rancor; and looking straight in my eyes, he said in a wondering tone, "So, you're rebellious, huh? That won't go with me, my boy. No sir!"

And I thought I would be packed off. Instead, a few days afterward, he appeared in the kitchen with a roll of drawing paper, a pencil, a ruler and a square, and told me, "When you're through with those knives, copy this." And he pointed to a front projection of a two-story house, agape with windows, and grotesquely overdecorated. "And here's a pair of compasses. Put dots on the paper where you want your lines to end, and draw the lines with the ruler, the lines that go across, first—the horizontal lines —and then the lines that go up and down—the vertical lines. Now get going."

I was delighted with this change to clean work, yet I stared at the paper and the instruments apprehensively, knowing nothing about their use. However, I washed my hands and set to. I copied all the horizontal lines and compared them with those on the original and found them good enough, except that there appeared to be an excess, three extra to be exact.

Then after drawing in the vertical lines I was astonished to find that I had given the house quite another face. I had started a migration of the windows, one leaving the frame altogether suspended in the air. The entrance stairway had climbed up to the second story; a roof corner and a gable had got dislocated, one on the center of the roof, and the other tilted over the chimney.

Hardly able to keep back my tears, I stared at these prodigies of error, seeking the causes for their occurrence. Unable to locate them, I sought to compensate with flights of fancy. On the face of the house and along the roof-coping and over the cornices, I drew in crows, pigeons and sparrows; and on the street level, under the windows, I placed crippled passersby, who carried umbrellas which failed to cover their deformities. Then I ruled slanting lines over the whole and delivered the results to the boss.

He rumpled his hair, and with eyebrows raised in astonishment, inquired gruffly, "What's all this?"

"That's rain falling. In the rain the house looks slanting because of the slant of the rain. About the birds—all these are birds—they're getting in out of the rain. That's what they do when it rains. And these people are hurrying home. That lady there, she had a fall; and that peddler, he sells lemons."

"Much obliged for the explanation," said the boss; then, leaning over till his hair brushed the paper, he burst into laughter and cried, "Akh, you ought to be torn up and thrown into the wastebasket yourself, you wild one!"

The boss' wife came in and, taking a look at my work, told her husband, "Beat him!"

But the boss replied placidly, "Never mind. My own apprentice work was no better."

And crossing out my work with a red pencil, he handed me some more paper. "Try it again."

The second attempt was more successful, except for a window that supplanted the door. But not relishing a vacant house, I tenanted it. I sat ladies with fans and suitors with cigarettes at the windows. I had a non-smoking suitor "make a nose" at the others. I placed a cabman at the doorstep and a dog at his feet. But the boss demanded, "Why all these scrawls over it again?"

When I went into my feelings about a house without people, he said impatiently, "To hell with this fooling around. If you have a mind to learn, put your mind to it. This is nonsense."

When finally I succeeded in making a copy close enough to the original, he was delighted. "Now, see what you can do! It's up to you, now, let's go on." And he began instructing me. "Draw a plan of this house indicating the arrangement of the rooms, the locations of doors and windows and so on. I won't show you how. Work it out yourself."

I took the sheet to the kitchen, and pondered over it. How was I to go about it? And right there my studies in draftsmanship came to a halt. Wrathfully the boss' mother charged upon me, hissing, "So, you want to draw!"

Grabbing me by the hair, she banged my head on the table with such force as to bruise my nose and my lips; and she snatched up the sheet of paper, tore it into bits, grabbed up the drawing kit, and with her hands on her hips, in a stance of victory, she crowed at me, "Who could endure it? Giving this work to an outsider, while his own flesh and blood, his own brother, has to go hunting for work!"

In rushed the boss, his wife pell-mell after him, and what a scene followed! All three shrieking and spitting at each other, with the women in tears at the end, and the boss telling me, "Forget the idea for the time being. Look what it got us into!"

He had my sympathy, poor man, so overwhelmed and deafened by the shrieking women. It had already been obvious to me that the old woman resented my studying; she had done her best to prevent it. Before I sat down at my drafting paper, I had always asked, "Do you want me for anything?" And she had scowled and replied, "When I do, I'll let you know." And in a matter of a few minutes, she would find an errand for me to go on, or she would say, "Isn't that a beautiful job you did on the stairs today? Dirt in every corner! Go over there, and sweep it clean!"

I would find nothing to sweep, at which she would cry out, "How dare you contradict me?"

She spilled liquids over my drawings; one time it was *kvass*, another time oil from the icon lamp. The tricks she played on me were worthy of a child, as naïvely calculated, and with as naïve attempts to cover them up. Nowhere else have I seen a person so quick to boil up with rage, on provocations so trifling, or so joyously passionate in her complaints. Complaining is a common enough failing; but she went at it with such gusto you would think she were singing!

Her love for her son Victor was a mania. I could laugh at it, yet it also alarmed me by what can only be called its delirious intensity. There were times, after her morning prayers, when she would stand on the oven ledge, her elbows resting on the headboard of the bedding on the oven, and exclaim in feverish whispers, "My good fortune! My little god! Drop

of my own warm blood . . . diamond pure . . . light as an angel plume . . .
Ah, sleep, child, and dream yourself such a bride, the beauty who out-
shines them all . . . a princess, an heiress, daughter of a millionaire! And
your enemies, let them die at birth; and your friends, let them all live to
a hundred; let the girls flock after you like hens after the cock."

All of which I found insanely ludicrous. The vulgar loafer, Victor, had
a nose big and patchy as a woodpecker's beak, and the same dull obstinacy of character. If his mother's whispers awoke him, he would let go
in a surly, sleepy mumble, "The devil with you, ma! What's the idea,
snorting in my face! Life is unbearable with you around!" At which she
would sometimes sneak away, with an apologetic laugh. "So, sleep. Sleep,
you fresh boy!" But at other times she seemed to collapse, her feet clattering against the oven, and with panting exclamation, as if her tongue
were on fire, she hissed out, "How? Your own mother you're sending to
the devil! Ekh, you! You disgrace, you curse upon my heart! The devil
must have fastened himself in me at your birth, to see to your ruin!"

Obscenities streamed from her, the filth of the street corners, making
it a trial to listen to her. She slept poorly, nervously hopping off the oven
again and again at night, and crawling over and waking me.

"What's the matter?"

"Sh!" and staring at something in the dark, she would cross herself and
whisper, "O God, and the prophet Elias, and Barbara the Martyr, keep
me from a sudden death!"

With a shuddering hand she lit a candle, and her round, large-nosed
face showed up, swollen, tense, and her gray eyes turned alarmed blinks at
familiar things that looked unfamiliar in the dim light. The large kitchen
looked small, sectioned off by the shadowy trunks and cupboards. The
moonbeams lived their quiet life; the little icon light flickered; in their rack
on the wall, the knives glittered like icicles, while the black frying pans
on the floor turned up what seemed to be eyeless faces.

The old woman would let herself carefully down the oven, as if she
were wading off a river bank, and sliding along barefoot, would go to the
washstand in the corner, over which hung a wide-mouthed pitcher that
made me think of a decapitated head. Another pitcher on the stand contained water, which she drank, choking and gasping; afterward she stared
through the windows, right through the bluish frost traceries on the glass,
saying, "Mercy, oh Lord, mercy!" in whispered prayer. Then she snuffed
out the candle, knelt, and mumbled querulously, "Lord! Who has any
love for me, who has any need of me?"

Climbing back on the oven, she opened the chimney vent, felt for the

flue valve to see if it were in line, and got soot on her hand. The following moment, exactly, she dropped off to sleep as if felled by an invisible
fist. In moments of anger toward her, I thought, what a shame grandpa
hadn't married her. What a life they would have led each other!

Time after time she made me utterly wretched; but there were days
when sadness covered her bloated face, tears filld her eyes, and she said
plaintively, "Think I've got it easy? I brought children into the world,
raised them, put them on their feet and what for? To be their house servant! Think that's a blessing? My son takes a stranger, and strange blood
into the family. Think that suits me? Eh?"

"Of course not," I admitted.

"That's how it is, see?" And she would begin obscenely running down
her daughter-in-law. "When I went to the bath with her I saw what she
had. She's got nothing to brag about. Who'd call her a beauty?"

There was vulgarity in everything she said about the marital relation.
In the beginning my reaction was one of disgust; but becoming accustomed to it, I began to follow it with attentive interest, perceiving in it
some painful truths. "Woman has the power. She put it over on God,
Himself! That's a fact!" The old woman chuckled, slapping the table.
"Through Eve, we're all damned to Hell. How about that?" On the theme
of the power of a woman she could go on interminably, and I had the
impression that her talk was intended to be overheard and alarm somebody. The phrase, "Eve put it over on God," particularly stayed with me.

The wing of an apartment house overlooked our yard. Of its eight flats
four were tenanted by officers, and a fifth by the regimental chaplain.
The yard swarmed with orderlies and valets, with washerwomen, nurse-
maids and cooks trailing after them. Romantic dramas were enacted in
every kitchen to accompaniments of tears, tirades and squabbles. There
were fights between the soldiers, between the soldiers and workmen, and
a continual beating of women.

In the yard there was a constant babbling of so-called vice and depravity,
that is the overpowering appetites of robust youth. There were demonstra-
tions of brutal sensuality, of insensate tyrannizing, of the obscene swagger
of the "lady killers"; and they were all minutely gone over by my employers at their meals. Slavering over the miseries of others, the old woman,
up on all the tragedies of the yard, retold them with avidity. The boss'
wife listened absorbed, with smiles of pleasure on her full lips. Victor's
response was the belly laugh; but the boss would exclaim, frowning, "Let's
have an end to that, mama!"

"Lord, I'm not even permitted to speak, now!" complained the story teller, with Victor egging her on, "Go ahead, ma, who's stopping you? We're all your own here, aren't we?"

It never failed to puzzle me, how they could mouth such obscenities among themselves.

The boss shunned his mother, toward whom his attitude was one of pitying contempt. When she was with him, she either showered him with grievances against his wife, or with appeals for money, which he would meet by hurriedly stuffing a ruble note or some silver into her hand, saying, "I shouldn't; but take it. I don't grudge it to you, but it's not right."

"I'm going to church; I need it for alms and candles."

"There's nobody to give alms to. You use it to spoil Victor."

"You have no love for your brother. That's your great sin." And he would stalk away, waving her off.

Victor's attitude toward his mother was one of coarse derision. That glutton was always hungry. On Sundays, when the old woman baked custards, she would hide some in a pot under my couch. On leaving the table Victor would make for this cache, and as he devoured it, grumble, "Couldn't you have left me a couple more, you old dope!"

"Hurry up; get done before they see you."

"So I'll tell them you steal sweets for me behind their backs."

Once I rifled two of the custards and ate them, for which Victor short of murdered me. Our dislike of each other was hearty and mutual. I had to take his abuse. Several times a day he made me shine his shoes. When I slept in the attic he would pry up the trap door and spit through the crack, with my head for his target. Probably aping his brother, whose favorite expletive was "wild geese," Victor interlarded his conversation with catch phrases, but his were ludicrously inane: "Mama, you left wheel, where's my socks!" And me he tormented with idiotic quizzes, "Tell me, Alex, why do we write *sinenki*, but pronounce the word *finiki*? And why *kolokola*, instead of *okolokola*? And *k'derevou* instead of *gdye plachou?*"

I found the manner of speaking of all of them uncouth. Having been brought up to the harmonious diction of my grandparents, it startled me to hear contradictory words joined together, like "terribly funny" or "dying to eat" or "awfully happy." I wondered how anything funny could be terrible, how it could be awful to be happy, or how one could die of the desire to eat.

"Can you say that?" I asked, only to be jeered at: "Listen to the teacher! Want your ears plucked?"

The plucking of ears itself made no sense to me. You could "pluck" grass, flowers, fruit, but not ears. Their efforts to prove to me that ears could be plucked were without effect; I would exclaim victoriously, "Just the same, you've not plucked my ears."

All about me I saw cruel arrogance and conscienceless obscenity. I found it worse by far than the "disorderly houses" and the "street walkers" of the Kunavin streets. To account for the muck and coarseness of the latter, there was toil and a strained and famished life. But people here were overfed and comfortable, and their work was easy and unworried. Yet everything was overcast with a nervous, insidious exhaustion.

Hard as my life here was, grandma's visits made it harder. She would come through the back way into the kitchen, cross herself under the icon, and bow to her younger sister. That genuflection bowed me down as under a smothering burden.

"Is that you, Akulina?" was the hostess' coolly indifferent greeting.

Grandma was unrecognizable. Her lips humbly shut, her face a blank, she seated herself on a bench at the door and kept still, in guilty silence, until spoken to, when she answered her sister deferentially. This tortured me, and I would exclaim, bitterly, "What are you sitting there for?"

With a gentle wink at me, she replied, "Quiet, you. You're not the boss, here."

"He's always butting in where it's none of his business, no matter how many beatings and scoldings he gets," complained the old woman, off on her usual tirade.

How often the spiteful woman would throw it up to her sister, "So you've taken to begging?"

"That's my misfortune."

"It's no misfortune to those who feel no shame."

"Christ, they say, also lived on alms."

"Who says so?—dopes and heretics; and you, you old idiot, pay attention to them. Christ wasn't a beggar; he was the Son of God. He'll come, as it is said, in glory, in judgment on the quick and the dead—the dead, too, you understand. You won't get away from Him, not even if you were in ashes. You and your Basil are getting it now for your pride; for the way you treated me when you were rich and I came to you for help!"

"And I gave you all I was able to give," answered grandma, patiently. "And God, you know, He'll pay us back."

"It was a trifle you gave, just a trifle!"

Her sister's incessant tongue bored and wearied grandma. Hearing that nasty voice I wondered how grandma could endure it. At those moments I could not love her.

The boss' wife came out and nodded affably to grandma. "Come into the dining room. Come, please."

The boss always greeted grandma with pleasure. "Ah, there's Akulina, the sage. How are you? Is old Kashirin still about?"

And grandma would give him her sweet smile, "Still working hard?"

"Yes, always at it, like a convict."

The talk between them was good, and affectionate, but grandma took the tone of a senior. Sometimes their talk turned to my mother, of whom he would say, "Barbara, what a woman, a real heroine!"

His wife would interrupt to say to grandma, "Remember my giving her that dress—black silk with the jet trimmings?"

"Certainly, I remember."

"And it was in good condition."

"Yes," said the boss, "a dress, a palm; and life cheats you." [2]

"What do you mean by that?" asked his wife, dubiously.

"Nothing, my dear. Happiness and good souls are both soon gone."

"I can't tell what's come through you," said his wife, mystified.

Then grandma was shown the new baby, and while I was clearing off the table, the boss said to me, "A good old woman, that grandmother of yours."

Those words won my deepest gratitude. Alone with grandma I asked her, with a pang in my heart, "Why do you have to come here? Don't you see how—"

"Akh, Alex, I see it all," she replied, with a gentle smile on her wonderful face; and I had a twinge of conscience. Of course she saw it all; there was nothing she missed; not even what was agitating my soul that very moment. Looking around to make sure we were alone, she gave me a hug, and said with heat, "I wouldn't come here but for you. What do they mean to me? The truth is, grandpa's sick and I'm exhausted tending him. I haven't had a chance to do any work, so I haven't got a penny, and Mike has thrown out his son, your cousin, Sascha, and now I have him to feed, as well. They agreed to pay you six rubles a month; but I doubt if you've seen a ruble from them, and you started close to half a year ago." Then she bent down and whispered, "They tell me they have to talk to you and scold you, that you're disobedient; but, darling, stick it out. Have patience this short couple of years while you get your strength. Have patience, will you?"

I gave her my promise, but it was not easy to keep. The life there was so burdensome; it was so barren and depressing. Meals were the only

[2] A pun on the words, *talma* (cloak), *palma* (palm), and *shelma* (juggler).

events; and my life passed as in a sleep. At times I thought I must run away; but winter had taken its cursed hold. Snow storms howled through the night, the wind pounded over the house, and the timbers cracked in the grip of frost. Where could I go?

I was not allowed out, and in fact, who could go out in that weather? Household chores helped to speed through the brief winter day. But I had to go to church; on Saturdays to Vespers, and on Sundays to mass.

I enjoyed church. Standing in one of the less crowded and darker nooks I loved to look at the far-away icon stand, which seemed afloat in the candle light that flowed in profuse streams over the pulpit. The shadowy figures on the icon seemed to stir with a gentle motion, the gold embroidery on the priest's vestments rustled ecstatically, the candle flames in that bluish air seemed to buzz like golden bees, and the heads of women and children seemed to nod like flowers. And everything around seemed in harmony with the chanting choir. Everything seemed touched with legend; and the church seemed to rock like a cradle, swaying in the blackness of space.

There were times when, in my imagination, the church was submerged in a deep lake, where it carried on a hidden life of its own, alien to other kinds of life. I am now quite convinced that this fancy sprang from grandma's tales of the town of Kitezh; and often I found myself dreamily swaying, to and fro, as though in time with the rocking motion around me. Somnolent with the lulling hymns of the choir, the murmuring of prayers and the breathing of the worshippers, I dwelt on the sad and tuneful ballad,

> The accursed Tatars are closing in; aye, the unclean ones are closing in on Kitezh, the glorious; they enter at the holy hour of the morning prayer. Oh, Lord God, and His Holy Mother, protect Thy servants, preserve them to sing the morning services, to hear the sacred chants. Oh, let not the holy church be made the sport of the Tatars, let them not debase our wives and our maidens; let not our virgins become their toys; let not our sages be tortured to death.
>
> And the God of the Sabbath and His Holy Mother heard this human moan, these Christian entreaties. And to the Archangel Michael spoke the God of the Sabbath, "Go, Michael, give the earth under Kitezh a shake, so that Kitezh sinks under the lake!"
>
> And to this day the people remain at prayer, without rest,

yet unwearied, from matins to vespers, through all the services, forever and aye!

Grandma's ballads filled my head, in those months, as honey fills a hive. I even thought in cadences.

In church I said no prayers. I felt too embarrassed to recite the wrathful prayers and doleful psalms of grandpa's God in the hearing of grandma's God, Who, I was certain, could find as little to relish in them as I did, if for no other reason than that they were set down in books, and He had them all by heart, like all educated persons. And so, when some sorrows mellowed in my breast or the day's petty grievances harassed me, I made up my own prayers. And, at the thought of my drudgery, words of complaint seemed to link together, involuntarily.

"Lord, Lord, behold my misery; oh, let me grow up quickly, out of this unbearable existence. Forgive me, Lord, but I have no teaching to benefit from; since that servant of Satan, Matrena, stalks me like a wolf, and embitters my life."

Some of these prayers return to my mind even today. The workings of a child's mind are deeply engraved; and they can effect one's entire life.

For still another reason I enjoyed being in church. I could find repose there as I had found it in the woods and the fields. There my cramped heart, already shrunk with grief and fouled with the slime of a muddy life, could luxuriate in cloudy, soaring reveries. But I went to church only in times of hard frost, or when snow blasts stormed through the streets, when the very sky seemed ice, when the wind was like a moving sheet of snow, when the earth lay rigid under the drifts as if it would never come to life again.

But on mild nights I preferred to roam the streets, searching out the darkest corners. On such walks I sometimes felt winged and sailing like the moon above. Ahead of me crept my shadow, blotting out the reflections of light in the snow, and humorously bobbing up and down. I met the night patrolman, in his thick sheepskin, rattle in hand,[3] and a dog at his side. Out of the yards came the shadowy outlines of people, and as they wavered down the street, the dogs pursued. I also passed young ladies promenading with their swains; who, it occurred to me, were also truants from church. Sometimes, through an illuminated *fortochka*,[4] or ventilator, there drifted a peculiar odor, strange and barely perceptible,

---

[3] At night patrolling policemen in Russia carried rattles instead of whistles.
[4] A small, hinged window, set into the storm window.

but hinting at another kind of life unknown to me. There, under the window, I inhaled the scent, trying to sense the life people lived in such houses. It was the vesper hour, yet cheerful song came from them, laughter and the sounds of a guitar, whose deep twang reverberated out of the ventilator.

I was particularly drawn to the hunched-over, one-story houses at the corners of the bare Tikhonovsky and Martinovsky Streets. Standing there of a moonlit night, intent, I listened to weird sounds. They resembled musical notes hummed loudly, which floated out with the warm, indoor air, through the ventilator. I could make out no words, but the song sounded like something I knew and understood. When I followed it, I did not hear the indolent plucking which interrupted, rather than accompanied, it. I sat on the curb thinking what marvelous music that peculiar, unendurable sort of fiddle was playing—it proved to be a cello —unendurable because I heard it with a sort of ache. The sound swelled to such volume at times that the house seemed to quake, and the windows to clatter, and from the roof moisture dropped like tears, as they did from my eyes.

The night patrolman had come upon me, unawares, and he pushed me off the curb, exclaiming, "What are you loitering here for?"

"The music." I said.

"A likely story! Get moving!"

I circled the block to return to my post under the window, but the playing had stopped. From the ventilator came hilarious sounds, so different from the sad strains I had been hearing that I thought I was in a dream. I made this house my goal every Saturday night, but only once, in the spring, did I hear the cello again, when it played on and on until midnight, earning me a thrashing when I got home.

These night sorties under the winter sky through the empty streets were an enriching experience. Deliberately I picked streets on the outskirts where there were no lights, and where I might run into no acquaintances of the boss to inform upon me, that I had stayed away from church. No drunks or prostitutes or cops molested me, and I could see into rooms on lower floors when the windows were not frosted over or curtained.

Many and varied were those pictures framed in windows—people at prayer or at cards, kissing or quarreling, and absorbed in soundless talk all through. It was a free show for me, a panorama of mute, fishlike existence. Once, through a basement window, I saw two women at a table, and a student opposite, reading to them. The younger of the two sat back in her chair, listening with knitted brows. Suddenly the older woman, thin, but with magnificent hair, put her hands over her face, and her sobbing was apparent from her heaving shoulders. The student tossed his book from him; the younger woman rose and ran out; and he got down on his knees to the woman with the abundant hair and pulled down her hands and kissed them.

In another window I saw a woman in a red blouse on the knees of a huge bearded man, who was rocking her like a baby, and apparently serenading her, for his mouth was open wide and he was rolling his eyes expressively. Shaking with laughter, she leaned back and swung her legs. He straightened her out, started up his song again, and again she burst into giggles. I watched them a long time, going away only when I realized it was going to be an all-night game.

There were many such pictures to see, that endure in my memory; and their attraction was so strong as to keep me up late, arousing doubts in the two women, who questioned me, "What church were you at? What priest conducted the services?"

They knew all the priests, which of the gospels would be read from, in a word, everything. They could readily catch me in a lie. Both worshiped grandpa's God of wrath who preferred to be approached in fear. He was eternally on their lips. In their quarrels they menaced each other with Him, "Wait! God will give it to you for this; He'll plague you for this! You'll see!"

On the first Sunday in Lent the old woman burned some fritters. Ruddy with the heat of the stove, she exclaimed in anger, "The devil with you!" Suddenly, sniffing the pan, her face clouded with dismay, she threw the pan down and moaned, "It's been used for meat! It's unclean! The grease didn't all come off on Monday when I scalded it." She went down on her knees and wept as she pleaded, "Lord God, Our Father, grant forgiveness to this accursed one! In the name of Thy passion and Thy suffering, forgive me. Withhold Thy punishment from this old fool!"

The burned fritters went to the dog, and the pan to the garbage dump, but the incident, thereafter, served the boss' wife in her quarrels, "And you fried fritters, on Lent, in a pan used for meat!"

They pulled their God into all their affairs, into every hole of their trivial existence, to give their wretched lives some semblance of significance, pretending to devote every hour to the services of the Power Above. I found this pulling and hauling of God over this desert depressing. I found myself, involuntarily, peering into dark corners, sensing invisible eavesdroppers upon me; and by night a cloud of terror enveloped me, spreading over me from the icon corner with its incessantly flickering lamp.

Beside the icon was a big double window, separated by a center post. It offered a blue block of space, and a quick motion would give you the effect of everything fusing into it, and streaming up to the stars, and being submerged in its eternal silence, like a stone sinking soundlessly in water. I have forgotten just how I rid myself of these obsessions, but I did, and soon enough, I know it was grandma's good God to whom I turned for help, and it was then, I believe, that I came to these simple truths: that nothing evil threatened me; that I deserved no punishment when I was not at fault; that life knew no law requiring the innocent to suffer; that the sins of others could not be laid to my account.

I stayed away from mass, too, particularly in the spring, which held me back from church with an irresistible power. A seven-kopeck piece given to me to put into the collection was my ruin. I bought jacks with it, played all through the mass, and got home late, of course. And once I managed to lose the coins given to me for prayers for the dead and for the sacramental bread; and when the priest distributed it, I had to take some other person's share.

I developed quite a mania for gambling. I was equipped with skill and strength, and was soon renowned through the streets for my prowess at jacks,[5] billiards and bowling.

During Lent I was told to get ready for communion, and I went to confess to the neighbor priest, Father Pokrovsky. He impressed me as a stern sort, and many of my sins had been at his expense. I had stoned his flimsy summer house in the garden, and I had fought with his children. Such sins, if he chose, he could himself recall. This made me fearful; and standing in his poor little church, waiting my turn in the confession box, my heart skipped some beats.

But Father Pokrovsky gave me a cheerful greeting, "Oh, it's my neighbor. Kneel down, my boy, what sins have you committed?"

Over my head he laid a piece of heavy velvet. The odors of wax and incense reached my nostrils. I found it hard to speak, and I did so reluctantly.

"Have you obeyed your elders?"

"No."

"Say, 'I have sinned.' "

Then, startling myself, I came out with, "I stole."

[5] Played for money stakes, and in a form which made it an adult gambling game.

"How? Where?" asked the priest, slowly and reflectively.

"At the church of the Three Saints, at Pokrov, at Nikol . . ."

"So, in all the churches! That was wrong, my child; a sin, do you understand?"

"I understand."

"Say, 'I have sinned.' And why did you steal? For something to eat?"

"Sometimes; and other times it was because I lost money at games; and since I had to bring home some sacramental bread, I stole."

Father Pokrovsky said something in a tired and almost inaudible whisper; then, after a few more questions, he suddenly asked me, and his face was now very solemn, "Did you read any banned books?"

That question, of course, was beyond me, and I asked, "What books?"

"Banned books. Did you read any?"

"No. Not one."

"Rise; your sins are remitted."

I gave him an astonished glance. His look was abstracted, but kind, which intensified my bad conscience, and added to my uneasiness. By way of preparation for the confessional, my employers had stressed its terrors, and harped on the necessity of baring even the most trivial sin.

So I added to my testimony, "I threw rocks at your summer house."

Still looking past me, the priest raised his head and said, "That was very bad. You can go, now."

"I stoned your dog, too."

"Next!" Father Pokrovsky called, ignoring me.

And off I went, feeling cheated and neglected. To have been subjected to such apprehension over the confessional ordeal, only to discover that it was so harmless, even dull. The only thing about it that interested me was the matter of the banned books, of which I was entirely ignorant. I recalled the basement room reading scene, the student reading to the two women; and Good Idea's shelves of squat, black tomes with their incomprehensible diagrams.

The following day I was given fifteen kopecks and dispatched to my communion. Easter was late; the snow had thawed off sometime ago; I walked through dry streets; dust already blew over the highways; and the weather was bright and genial. Close to the church some workers were rolling jacks. I said to myself, "There's still time for communion," and asked to be let into the game.

"A kopeck's the ante," said a ruddy pock-marked man, cockily.

As cockily, I began with a three-kopeck bet. I had a run of luck; two tries by an adult player, at the pair of jacks I had bet on went amiss, which brought me six kopecks winnings from grown men, and I felt elated. Then one of the players said, "Keep an eye on that kid, or he'll scoot off with his winnings."

Taking this an an insult, I showed my defiance by placing a nine-kopeck bet. The players seemed unimpressed, except for a boy of about my own age who said, "What luck he's got, that little devil from Zvez-drinsky; I know all about him."

A thin man, a furrier by the reek from his clothes, said cuttingly, "A little devil? Good!"

With a careful throw, he won my nine kopecks and turned to me, "Howl, little devil!"

My reply was a three-kopeck bet, which he accepted and lost. By the rules of the game, one could not bet on the same jacks more than three times in succession. I picked another pair and garnered four more ko-pecks. But there my luck ran out, and I lost my next three bets. In the meanwhile mass had been finished, the church bells rang the close of services, and the congregation began pouring out.

The furrier asked me, "Are you married?" and made a grab at my hair, but I dodged and got away. I came to a boy, all dressed up in his holiday best, and asked him, very mealy-mouthed, "Were you at communion?"

"Suppose I was? What's it to you?"

I asked him to describe the communion rite, what the priest recited, and what my part in it would have been. He took hold of me, gave me a shaking, and terrified me with his yelling. "You heretic, staying away from communion! You won't get a thing out of me. I hope you get a thrashing from your father!"

I ran home, dreading a quizzing, certain that my truancy would be fished out of me. But after receiving their congratulations, all the old woman asked me was, "What did you give the clerk?"

"Five kopecks," I replied, brazenly.

"And three kopecks for the other; you got away with seven kopecks, you beast!"

It was spring; and each new spring, as it came, seemed to wear something new, and be gayer and more dazzling than the last. Heady odors came from the young grass, and the birches in their fresh foliage. Maddening desires surged up in me to roam the fields, to hear the larks, to sprawl on the warm earth; but I had to clean winter coats and store them away in chests, to shred leaf tobacco, to dust around, to spend the whole day on chores that seemed to me as purposeless as they were tedious.

Nor was there a thing for me to look forward to in my free time. There was nothing to do in that dismal street to which I was confined. Exhausted, irritable workers and greasy cooks and washerwomen filled the yard; and the night scenes offered to my eyes so disgusted me, that blindness seemed a blessing.

I took to my attic, with scissors and colored paper, and cut out paper lace with which I adorned the beams. At least in this I could somehow absorb my discontent. How I yearned to be somewhere where people did not seek to sleep out time, where there were fewer quarrels; where God was not so tiresomely beset with grievances, where people did not so constantly lay harsh judgments upon each other.

The first Saturday after Easter the miracle-working icon of Our Lady of Vladimir, from the Oransky monastery, was brought into town, whose guest it was through the middle of June. It was taken to bless the houses of all the members of the congregation, and it came our turn during the middle of the week. I was doing the pots in the kitchen, when the boss' wife cried out in an agitated voice, from the nursery, "Open the door; they're bringing in the Oransky icon!"

Sloppy from the kitchen, and with hands as gritty as a brick, I rushed down and opened the door. His own hands taken up with a lamp and a thurible, a young man grumbled good-naturedly, "Are you all in bed? Give us a hand!"

Two men carried the bulky, framed icon up the narrow stairs, with my shoulder and dirty hands adding a support at one of the corners. Behind me followed the monk, snuffling a lagging, perfunctory chant, "Holy Mother of God, pray for us!"

The frightening thought passed through my mind. "She must be mad at me for touching her with dirty hands; she'll make them wither!"

They stood the icon up in a corner, on two chairs which had been draped over with a clean sheet. At its sides were two handsome young monks with sparkling eyes, rapturous looks and beautiful hair, like angels.

There were prayers. "Oh, Celebrated Mother," chanted the big priest, but feeling under his long hair, throughout, at a swelling on the lobe of his ear. "Holy Mother of God, pray for us," droned the monks.

I knew from grandma that it was the Holy Virgin who, for the sake of the poor, had planted the earth with flowers, with all that gave joy, with all that brought blessings and beauty into life, and I loved Her. When the time came to kiss Her, taking no note of how the adults had performed the salute, I kissed Her lovingly on the cheeks, the lips. A powerful hand swept me all the way to the door. I do not recall the carrying out of the icon, but I have a vivid recollection of my employers holding a council around me, on the floor, debating my fate with tremulous anxiety.

"We'll have to talk with the priest about him," said the boss, whose scolding was free of rancor.

"Dope! How could you not know that the lips must not be kissed? You must have learned that in school!"

For some days, fearful, but resigned, I awaited divine punishment, wondering what it would be. I had put unclean hands on the icon and given it a forbidden kiss. I could not go unpunished. But the Mother of God evidently forgave the unmeant sin that proceeded from impulsive love; or perhaps Her penalty was too light to be noticed, among the punishments so generously awarded me by the good people of the house.

And, to provoke the old woman, I observed to her, now and then, "Seems the Holy Virgin has forgotten my punishment!"

"Just you wait!" the old woman replied, viciously.

While I festooned the beams in the attic, with laces cut out of pink crepe paper from tea-packets, and tin foil, and tree leaves and other ornaments, I sang whatever popped into my head, finding words to church tunes, like the Kalmucks singing on the roads:

> "Sitting in the attic, scissors in hand, I cut and cut the paper.
> I'm a dullard, I'm a dunce. I'd rather be a dog and run around
> where I like. Instead, I hear all day, 'Sit down, shut up, if you
> want to wear a whole skin!' "

When the old woman took a look at my work, she laughed uproariously and said, "Why not decorate the kitchen, too?"

And when the master paid me a visit to inspect my performance, he said, sighing, "You're a droll one, a devil! What will you turn out, I wonder, a magician? Who can guess?" And he gave me one of the big Nicholas [6] five-kopeck pieces. I wired the coin into a conspicuous position among my works of art. A few days later it was gone; and it must have been the old woman who made away with it.

[6] Minted in the reign of Nicholas I.

Chapter Five

THAT SPRING I RAN AWAY. GOING TO THE BAKERY FOR BREAD ONE MORN-ing, the baker, indifferent to my presence, abused his wife, finally smashing a weight down on her forehead. Running out, she collapsed in the street. A crowd collected, and the woman was put on a stretcher and taken to the hospital in a cab, behind which I ran, without looking where I was heading. I found myself, in the end, on the banks of the Volga, with two greven (twenty kopecks) in my hand.

So caressing was the spring sunlight, such a friendly breadth did the Volga have flowing beside me, so ample and harmonious did the earth seem here, that my own existence there seemed more than ever like life in a mouse trap. So I decided not to return, nor to go back to grandma at Kunavin, for shame at not keeping my promise to her, and for fear of grandpa's jeers.

For several days I roamed the shore, getting meals and shelter for the night from charitable stevedores, in their sheds. Finally one of them said to me, "No point hanging around here, boy, you can see for yourself. I hear they're looking for a mess boy on the steamer, 'Good'; go and take a look there."

I did and was interviewed by a tall, bearded steward who wore a black silk skull cap and glasses, through which dim eyes stared at me. "Two rubles a month," he said placidly, "let's have your passport."

I had none. After thinking it over the steward said, "Bring your mother here."

I ran to grandma, who approved what I was doing, and sent grandpa to the government labor bureau for a passport for me, while she accompanied me to the boat.

"Good!" said the steward, when he saw us. "Come with me."

He led me to the stern, where a giant of a chef, in a white apron and a white cap, sat at a little table drinking tea, without stopping, while puffing at a thick cigar. The steward pushed me toward him. "The mess boy," he said.

With an irritable toss of his close-cropped head, and a rounding out of his black eyes, he stretched himself, snorted and bellowed at me, "Who are you?"

I found him decidedly unprepossessing. He looked dirty despite his white outfit. What looked like wool seemed to grow over his fingers, and tufts of hair sprouted out of his big ears.

"I'm hungry," I replied.

With a blink, a change came over his face; his fierce expression gave way to a broad smile, that pulled his brick-red jowls all the way around to his ears, and made his mouth gape open on a display of horselike teeth. His moustache drooped and suddenly he looked like a stout, motherly woman.

Tossing the tea in his glass over the ship's side, he poured a fresh draught for me and pushed a French roll and a large cut of sausage my way. "Eat your fill. Have you got parents? Do you steal? Don't get upset. This place is full of thieves, as you'll soon learn."

His speech was like a succession of growls. His huge, bluish, clean-shaven face was knitted together around his nose with a close network of red veins; and the nose itself, bloated and purple, drooped over his moustache. His hanging lower lip was another disfigurement. From the corner of his mouth hung his smoldering cigar. He must have just emerged from a steam bath; he still smelled of the birch twigs,[7] and beads of sweat gleamed on his temples and the nape of his neck.

After I had finished my tea, he gave me a ruble bill, saying, "Buy yourself a couple of aprons. Wait, I better go with you."

Setting his cap straight, he joined me, shambling ponderously, his feet slapping on the deck like a bear's.

The moon was bright that night as it sailed above the boat toward the meadows on the left. The ancient red craft, with its stained funnel, took its time; and her wheel cut the silvered water in clumsy strokes. Floating toward her, as though for a meeting, the dark shore cast its shadow over the water; further back glimmered the pert little windows of peasant huts. From the villages came song; merrymaking lassies singing—and their *Ai, Ludi* (Ah, people) came over as "Hallelujah."

In the steamer's wake, on a long towline, bobbed a big barge, also painted red. Its rail was high, making the deck a cage, within which were penned convicts bound for exile or jail. Stationed on the prow was a sentry whose bayonet gleamed like a candle flame. No sounds came from the barge, which was adrip with moonlight, but against the black metal bars gray blots could be dimly seen—convicts taking a look at the Volga. The water now seemed to sob, now to chuckle diffidently. It was as still here as in a church, and there was a similar scent of oil.

[7] Used in the massage routine in Russian steam baths.

Gazing at the barge I recalled my earliest childhood, the voyage from Astrakhan to Nizhny, the rigid faces of mama and grandma, through whom I made my first acquaintance with this absorbing, though difficult, life among people. And, thinking of grandma, all that had seemed so evil and repugnant, vanished. In a sudden transformation everything grew interesting and attractive, and people acquired kinder and better selves.

I was almost stirred to tears by the loveliness of these Volga nights. I was deeply affected, too, by the coffin-like barge, looking so lost on the breadth of the flowing river, in the dreamy stillness of the warm night. The changing shoreline, now climbing up, now sloping down, was a pleasant stimulus to my imagination. There were roused in me yearnings after goodness, yearnings to serve others.

The people we had on board were a peculiar sort. Young and old, men and women, they all resembled each other. Busy people took fast boats. Ours being a slow boat, it attracted the slothful. Singing and eating all day long, they dirtied innumerable cups and plates, knives, forks and spoons, all day long. Cleaning the silver was my job, and it kept me occupied from six in the morning till near midnight, easing off in the late afternoon and toward midnight, when the passengers rested from eating and only imbibed tea, beer and vodka. My superiors, those who tended the buffet, were also free then. Smoury, the chef, had tea at a table near the hatchway, with his assistant, Jake, the kitchen man, Max, and Serge, a steward who was hunchbacked, whose face was pitted with smallpox, and who had oily eyes between high cheekbones. Jake told dirty stories, punctuating them with sobbing laughs that exposed his long, stained teeth. Serge's froglike mouth, grinning, spanned his face from ear to ear. Max frowned in silence, fixing his cold, colorless eyes upon the others.

"Asiatic! Mordvin!" interjected the old chef, from time to time, in his bass voice.

I did not take to these people. Bald and obese, Jake had only one subject, women, and only one attitude toward them—lustful. His vacuous face was studded with purplish pimples. On one cheek he had a mole with a tuft of red bristles, which he twisted out on the shaft of a needle. Let a woman passenger appear who was lively and not stand-offish, and he would wait on her in an odd, servile manner, like a beggar; he would make honeyed, solicitous remarks, licking her, you might say, with agile flickerings of his tongue. Somehow, it seemed to me that his sort of big, suety creature was the hangman type. "Learn how to get around women," he would tell Serge and Max, and they would take in his instructions with drooling lips and reddening faces.

"Asiatics!" Smoury would growl in disgust, and getting up heavily, he would give me my orders. "Peshkov, march!"

He would take me to his cabin, stretch out in a hammock strung up beside the ice-box, hand me a little, leather-covered book, and command me to "Read!"

Sitting on a chest, I would read, patiently: "The umbra pierced by a star means that the dreamer has good relations with heaven and is devoid of vice and profanity."

Smoury, puffing at a cigarette, emitted a cloud of smoke and rumbled, "The camels! They said—"

"Baring the left bosom," I went on, "indicates an innocent heart."

"Whose bosom?"

"It doesn't say."

"A woman's, of course. And a tart!"

He shut his eyes and lay back with his arms folded under his head. His cigarette, its light reduced to a spark, drooped from a corner of his mouth. He righted it with his tongue, made a movement that sent a whistling sound out of his chest and a discharge of smoke that almost obliterated his huge face. Thinking he had fallen asleep, I sometimes quit reading the wretched book that bored me to the point of nausea. Gruffly he would order me, "Go on; read!"

"The sage responded, 'See here, Brother Suvierin.' "

"Sevierin."

"It's printed here 'Suvierin.' "

'That's witchcraft, then. There's some verse at the end. Take off from there."

I took off: "Inquisitive ones, seeking to profane our secrets; never will your weak eyes penetrate them; never will you hear the music of faery."

"Stop," said Smoury, "that's no poetry. Give me that book." After irritably leafing through it, he put it under the mattress. "Get me another."

To my misfortune, he had a big stock of books in his ironbound trunk. They included, *Maxims of Peace, Memoirs of an Artillery Man, Letters of Lord Sydenhall, Harmful Insects, Their Extermination,* and *Advice About the Plague*—books seemingly without beginning or end. On some occasions he had me read off all the titles, interrupting me angrily, "What's it about? Why must you read as if you were spitting it through your teeth? Impossible to follow you. Who the devil's this Gervase? Gervase! And umbra, no less!"

Portentous words, tantalizing names, wearied my memory and pricked my tongue. I had a desire to repeat them over and over, thinking that thus, possibly, their meanings might come to me. And outside the port-hole the water indefatigably lapped and sang. I would have enjoyed going to the stern where the sailors and stokers sat among the crates, where the passengers sang, gambled or told stories. I would have enjoyed sitting with them, listening to clear, understandable conversations, gazing at the banks of the Kama, at pine trees spun out like wire, at meadows where ponds, still left by the spring floods, glittered like splinters of glass, re-flecting the sun.

We were sailing well offshore, yet we could hear the peal of bells too far away to see, that bespoke villages and people. Fishermen's dories had the appearance of crusts of bread as they floated past. Here a little village hove in sight; there a gang of boys swam along a beach; and men in red shirts walked along a sandbar. Seen from midstream everything looked diminished to multi-colored toys.

I had impulses to cry out friendly salutations toward shore and to the barge. The latter fascinated me. I could look at it endlessly, as its blunt nose dipped in the churning water. It was dragged by the steamer like a protesting pig. When the tow rope loosened, it thrashed in the water; then, tautening again, it once more tugged the barge by the nose. I de-sired intensely to see the faces of these people, caged like zoo animals. At Perm, where they were disembarked, I managed to get to the gangway; and gray people filed past me, in tens, with a dead tramp of feet and rattle of chains, their backs bowed under heavy packs. There was the same variety among them as among ordinary people; there were young and old, handsome and homely; their only difference was in their dress and the close shaves that disfigured their faces. Robbers, probably, but grandma has spoken well of robbers. Smoury looked much more the fierce bandit, as he glowered at the barge and growled, "Keep me, O Lord, from such a fate!"

I once asked him, "What's bothering you? You're a cook; but these are robbers and murderers."

"I don't cook; I prepare the food. The old women cook it," he said with a laugh. But after a moment's thought, he went on, "The difference in people is their wits. There's one who's clever, another who's less clever, and a third who's a plain fool. To get among the clever ones, you have to read the proper books—black magic and so on. Read all kinds of books and you'll come upon the proper ones." And he was incessantly pressing me to "Read. If you don't understand it the first go, read it again; read a book seven times if necessary, and if you still don't get it, a dozen times."

Smoury was gruff with everybody, the grim steward not excepted. With a disgusted sag of his lower lip and stroking his moustache, he stoned people with his words. Toward me he always showed consideration and concern, but something in his concern for me made me uneasy. There were times when I thought he was mad, like grandma's sister. He would order me, "Stop reading," and lie for quite a while with eyes shut, his breathing a series of snorts, his huge belly heaving. His hairy fingers, joined across his chest like those of a corpse, worked as if with invisible needles knitting invisible socks. Then a sudden growl would issue from him, "Look at you! You've got intelligence. Use it to live! Intelligence is handed out stingily. If the intellectual level was the same for all—but it isn't! One understands, another doesn't, and some lack even the desire to understand!"

With halting words he told stories of his soldiering days. I never got their drift, and found them dull. He would begin in the middle, wherever they happened to come into his mind.

"The colonel called his soldier over and asked him, 'What did the lieutenant tell you?' So he said exactly what happened—a soldier is sworn to tell the truth—but the lieutenant looked at him as if he was a wall, and then he turned away and bowed his head. Yes—"

Indignation overcame him, and puffing out volumes of smoke, he growled, "How was I to know what to say and what to hold back? So the lieutenant was shut up in a fortress and his mother said—Lord! There's no learning I've mastered."

We had hot weather. Everything seemed aquiver; everything sizzled. The water splashed against the iron hull; the wheel turned; the wide current of the river flowed on between columns of lights. In the distance, the waving line of the meadowy bank, the trees adroop. After one's ears became attuned to all the sounds, we seemed to sail in silence, despite the mournful call of the watch, "Sev-en! Sev-en!"

There was nothing I would have cared to join in. I neither wished to listen in, nor to work at anything. All I craved was to get away into the shadows, away from the greasy, odorous kitchen heat, to sit and stare, drowsily, at the still, slow slipping-away of life through the water.

"Read!" came the chef's harsh command.

Even the chief steward feared Smoury, and the dining room steward, who was mute as a fish, also feared him. "Hey, you, swine!" Smoury would call to him, "Come here, thief! Asiatic!"

The sailors and stokers were in awe of him, and waited on his favors. He gave them soup meat and asked after their relatives. The oily, smoke-withered stokers, Byelo-Russians, were accounted the lowest in the ship's social scale. They were all called "Yaks"; and to tease them people would say, "I shamble along the bank like a Yak."

On hearing this, Smoury bristled, his face filled with angry blood, and he bellowed at the stokers, "Why do you let them ride you, you dopes! Throw slop in their faces!"

The boatswain, a handsome but bad-tempered man, once said to him, "They're just like Ukrainians; they have the same religion."

The chef grabbed him up by the collar and belt and shook him, "Want to be knocked to pieces?"

There were frequent quarrels between these two; and when it roughened to fighting, Smoury never got the worst of it. His strength was superhuman; besides, the captain's wife, who had a man's face and hair like a boy's, took his side.

He drank staggering amounts without ever getting drunk. He started on awakening, his eye-opener a bottle of vodka, which he downed in four swigs; after which it was beer all day, till late in the evening. As he drank, his face seemed to darken and his eyes to widen.

Some nights, he sat in the hatchway for hours, looking enormous and white, sat there in unbroken silence, his eyes moodily fixed on the far horizon. That was the time he was most feared, and when I most pitied him. Jake would emerge from the kitchen, perspiring and radiating heat. Scratching his bald skull and gesturing with his arm, he would announce, careful to keep at a safe distance and under cover, "We've gone out of fish."

"Well, there's the sauerkraut."

"What if they order fish-soup or boiled fish?"

"It's waiting for them. They can cram themselves."

Sometimes I got the courage to go to him. He gave me a heavy stare. "What do you want?"

"Nothing."

"Good."

In one of these moods I asked him, "Why are they all scared of you, since you're a good man?"

Unexpectedly, he showed no anger. "I'm good only to you." But he went on, with thoughtful simplicity, "You're right. I'm good to them all, only I don't show it. It's no good showing it to people, or you'll have them on your neck. Kind people are swarmed and trampled over like a piece of dry ground in a swamp. Fetch me some beer."

Having drained the bottle, he sucked his moustache and remarked, "There's a lot I could teach you if you were a bit older. There are things

I could pass on to a man. I'm no fool. But you keep on reading. In books you'll come upon everything you need. Books aren't trash. Have some beer."

"I don't care for it."

"Good for you. Good, your keeping off it. Drinking is a calamity. The devil's behind vodka. If I had the money I'd get you to study. An uneducated man is an ox, only good under a yoke, or for meat. The best he can do for himself is wag his tail."

The captain's wife lent him a volume of Gogol. I read the story, *The Terrible Vengeance* with delight, but Smoury angrily dismissed it as "Trash! Just a fairy tale! I know them! There are better books."

Taking the book from me, he got another from the captain's, and gruffly ordered me, "Read Taras[8]—what-you-may-call-it. Go get it. It's good, she says; good for whom? For her, maybe; but maybe not for me? She bobs her hair; pity her ears aren't bobbed, too!"

When Taras challenged Ostap, the chef laughed aloud. "That's it! Certainly! You have learning, but I have strength! What do they say to that? Camels!"

He listened, absorbed, but with grumbling interjections. "Nonsense! Cutting a man in half from his shoulders to his hips; can't be done. Nor can you thrust a lance upward; it would break off. I've soldiered, myself."

Andrew's treachery disgusted him. "A low creature! Like a woman. Pugh!"

But when Taras killed his son the chef got half out of his hammock, bent over and wept. The tears splashed from his cheek to the floor as he snorted, "O my God, my God!" And he stormed at me, "Read on, you rib of the devil!"

But it brought on an even more violent fit of weeping when I read Ostap's dying cry, "Do you hear, father?"

"Ruined, completely ruined," exclaimed Smoury. "Is that how it ends? Ekh! A bad business, that! Taras, now that was a man! Don't you think? Yes sir, a man all right!"

He took the book from me, and handled it with deference, his tears dripping on the binding. "A fine book; that was a treat!"

Ivanhoe followed. Smoury approved of Richard Plantagenet. "A real king!" he said, with conviction.

I had found the book dry. As a matter of fact, our tastes differed. I enjoyed *The Story of Thomas Jones*, an old version of Fielding's *History of Tom Jones, Foundling*, but Smoury snorted, "Trash! Your Thomas

[8] Gogol's novel about the Cossacks. *Taras Bulba.*

means nothing to me. What good is he to me? Let's have some other books."

I told him, once, there were other books, banned books, that could be read only secretly, at night in cellars. His eyes came wide open. "What? What are you lying for?"

"I'm not lying. When I went to confession the priest asked me about them; and I, myself, saw people reading them and the books made them cry."

The chef gave me a hard look. "Who cried?"

"The lady who was listening; and the other one was so scared, she ran out of the room."

"You must have dreamed it," said Smoury, passing his hand over his eyes; then, after a pause, he muttered, "But there must be things I haven't seen. I'm not that old, and for a man of my sort—so, whatever it was—"

And for a whole hour he talked, and with real eloquence.

Without noticing how, I got the reading habit and found it a pleasure to pick up a book. What I read was such a pleasant change from a life which I was finding increasingly burdensome.

Smoury, too, found recreation in it, and often summoned me from my work. "Come, read, Peshkov."

"I've still got some dishes to do."

"Let Max do it."

Brusquely he bade the assistant to do my work and, in retaliation, Max broke glasses. On the quiet the steward warned me, "I'll have to get you off the boat."

Once Max purposely left glasses in a bowl of slop water; and when I threw the water overboard the glasses sailed with it. "It's my fault," said the head steward, "charge it to me."

I got nasty looks from the other dining room workers and nasty remarks, such as, "What were you hired for, bookworm!"

And they did their best to pile up work for me, deliberately dirtying dishes for me to wash. I had forebodings that I was in for a bad ending, and so it turned out.

One evening, in an alcove in the boat, there sat two women, the older one red-faced and blowsy, the younger one, a girl in a new rose-colored jacket and a yellow dress. Both were tipsy. The older woman smiled and bowed to everybody, and when she spoke she accented her "O's" like a deacon. "Pardon me, friends. I've had a drop too much. But I've been in court, and been acquitted, so I've been celebrating."

The girl also laughed, and stared with filmed-over eyes at the other passengers. She nudged the other woman and said, "Ah, we know you, you nuisance!"

They had berths in second-class, opposite the cabin occupied by Jake and Serge. When the older woman went off, Serge took her place beside the girl, his froglike mouth distended lasciviously.

That night, my work finished, I stretched out on the table for some sleep when Serge came in, grabbed my arm and said, "Come, we're marrying you off."

He was drunk. When I tried to free my arm, he hit me. "Come on!"

Max came in, drunk too, and they dragged me over the deck, past sleeping passengers, to their cabin. But there stood Smoury, and in the doorway, holding the door, stood Jake. The girl kept digging her elbow in his back and crying drunkenly, "Let me go!"

Smoury delivered me from Serge and Max, took them by the hair, cracked their skulls together, and left them where they fell.

"Asiatic!" he roared at Jake, and slammed the door on him. To me, as he pushed me ahead of him, he growled, "Out of here!"

I went off to the stern. It was a cloudy night, and the river was black. In the boat's wake, two seething furrows of gray water curled toward the unseen shore. Between them the barge dragged on. Now to the right, now to the left, swung blobs of red light that illuminated nothing. A sudden bend of the shore blotted them out and everything became darker and more awesome.

The chef came up and took a seat beside me. "So they tried to force you on that creature? Akh, the filthy beasts. I heard them!"

"Did you get her away from them?"

"Her?" After he had vilified her, he went on, moodily, "Everything's muck on this boat. Worse than a village. Ever live in a village?"

"No."

"In a village it's all misery—in the winter most of all."

He threw his cigarette overboard, mused, then resumed, "You've landed among a pack of swine; I'm sorry for you, kid. For them, too. Don't know what I'd have done another time. Maybe dropped on my knees and prayed, 'What's got into you, you sons of bitches? What are you at, you blind ones! Camels!'"

The steamer's whistle lengthily wailed, the towline plopped into the water, lantern lights bobbed up and down, guiding us into the harbor. More lights glowed out of the darkness.

"Piany Bor[9]—Drunk!" muttered the chef. "And there's a river named Pianaya; and I knew a captain named Pienkov and a clerk named Zapi-vokhin and another captain called Nepeipivo. I'm going ashore."

The strapping Kamska girls hauled furnace wood from the shore on long skids. Stooped under their harness, they trotted up in teams of two, and pitched their loads into the black stoke hold crying, "Wood!"

As they unloaded the wood, the sailors plucked at their breasts or legs and the women screeched, spat, and used their straps to parry slaps and pinches. I must have seen this a hundred times, the same thing everywhere the steamer stopped for fuel.

I felt as though I had grown old on that boat, lived on it for years, and could foretell what would happen a week from now, at the end of summer, by the end of next year.

Day had come. The outlines of a pine forest on a sandy butte above the harbor took shape. From the hills and the woods came laughter and singing from the women who trooped away like soldiers.

I had an impulse to weep; tears bubbled in my breast; my heart ran over with them; it was a pain to repress them, but a disgrace to be seen shedding them; and I went to give a hand to the sailor Bliakhin, who was washing the deck.

Bliakhin looked no-account—withered and faded; and he helped on the impression by retiring into corners, from which his sharp eyes glowed. "My real name's not Bliakhin—my mother, you see, lived a disreputable life. I've got a sister; and she, too. Happened to be their fate. Fate, brother, anchors everybody down. You're heading somewhere? Well, you'll find out."

As he swabbed the deck, he said in a low voice, "See what trouble comes from women? There you are! Damp wood may smolder a long time, but then it catches. I don't take to that sort of thing; it don't appeal to me. Had I been born a woman, I'd have picked a deep pool and drowned myself. Then I'd be safe with Jesus and no harm to anybody. But as long as you live you risk the fire. Take it from me, eunuchs aren't fools. They're wise; they know a bit of magic. They put aside vanities and serve God in purity."

The captain's wife passed us, lifting her skirts as she stepped through the slop water. She was tall, buxom, and had a fresh, candid face. I had

---

[9] The name of a pine forest. The word *piany* resembles the word for drunk, and the other names in the paragraph are related to the root word for drunk. *Nepeipivo* is close to the words meaning "don't drink beer."

a strong desire to follow her, begging her out of a full heart, "Speak to me; speak to me!"

Slowly the ship backed away from the pier. Bliakhin crossed himself and whispered, "We're off!"

Chapter Six

At sarapulia max was put off the ship. he left without a word of farewell to anyone, and in a dignified manner. Behind him trotted the gay woman passenger, and behind her followed the girl, bedraggled and swollen-eyed. For a long time, Serge kneeled on the threshold of the captain's cabin, bumping his head on the door, kissing it, and crying out, "Forgive me! It was Max's fault, not mine!"

Sailors, stewards and some passengers as well, knew he was to blame, but they interceded for him, "Come on, forgive him!" The captain kicked him out with such force that he sent him sprawling. Nevertheless he forgave him, and Serge promptly rushed on deck, toting a tea-tray around among the passengers, looking into their eyes with a hang-dog expression.

Max was replaced by a soldier from Viatka, a gaunt man with a small head and brick-red eyes. He was sent to kill some chickens, killed two, but let the rest get away. The passengers chased them, but three hens flapped overboard; and the soldier sat on a stack of stovewood near the chicken coop, and wept.

"What's up, you fool?" asked Smoury, enraged. "Imagine a soldier crying!"

"I'm only in the Reserves," confided the soldier, and that finished him. In half an hour he had become the universal butt. People came up to him, stared at him, and asked, "Is this the one?"

At the beginning he took no notice and seemed not to hear their giggles. He kept mopping at his tears on a cuff of his old shirt, in such a way as to make him appear actually to be hiding them up his sleeve. Finally, he became aware of his audience and his brown eyes blazed wrathfully, and in the rapid Viatka dialect, he shouted, "What're you looking at? You should be torn to pieces!"

This only furnished more entertainment to the passengers, who snapped their fingers at him, pulled at his shirt and apron, heartlessly baiting him like a goat, till dinner. Then someone put a squeezed lemon on a wooden ladle and tied it to his back with his apron strings. With every movement the ladle wagged, provoking general laughter, while he scurried like a trapped mouse, having no notion of the cause of their mirth.

Smoury, behind him, sat silent, his face like a woman's. Feeling sorry for the soldier, I asked Smoury, "Can I tell him?"

He nodded, without a word.

When I explained to the soldier why he was being laughed at, he tore off the ladle, threw it on the floor, and stamped on it; then with both hands he grabbed me by the hair. As we wrestled, the overjoyed passengers formed a ring around us. Smoury broke through it, separated us, gave me a cuff, and took the soldier by the ear. Seeing the little man writhing in the chef's grip the passengers yelled, whistled, stamped and laughed to split their sides. "To the attack, soldier! Butt the chef in the belly!"

Their savage glee made me yearn to come at them with a wooden club, and knock them all on the head. Smoury let go of the soldier, and with his hands clasped behind him, turned on the passengers like a wild boar, his back up and his teeth bared. "To your cabins! March!"

Again the soldier lunged at me, but Smoury took him around in one hand and carried him to the hatchway, where he held him under a water pump, spinning his frail body around as if it were a puppet.

The sailors came running up, along with the boatswain and the mate. The passengers crowded back. Standing a head taller than the rest was the chief steward, mute as ever.

Sitting on a stack of firewood near the kitchen the soldier took off his boots and kept wringing his dry socks, while the water dripped from his matted hair—another joke to tickle the passengers.

"Never mind," said the soldier, "I'll kill that boy!"

Smoury took me by the shoulder and spoke to the mate, and the sailors dispersed the passengers. Then Smoury asked the soldier, "What's to be done with you?"

The latter said nothing; but he stared at me with delirious eyes, yet seemed to be under restraint.

"Calm yourself, you breed of the devil!" said Smoury.

"Not being the piper, you can't give the tune," said the soldier. This, I saw, confused the chef. His puffed-out cheeks collapsed; he spat, and led me away. I walked after him, feeling foolish and looking back at the soldier. In an uneasy tone Smoury said, "That's a wild one! What do you think?"

Serge ran up to us and said breathlessly, "He's going to kill himself!"

"Where is he?" cried Smoury, running.

The soldier stood before the steward's cabin brandishing a big knife. It was the one used both to chop off the heads of chickens and split sticks for the stove, which had blunted it and notched it like a saw. He was ringed around by the passengers, twittering at the little funny man with the dripping head. His snubnosed face skittered like jelly; his mouth had a weary sag; his lips twitched; and he howled at them, "Torturers! Torturers!"

I found something to stand up on and was able to see over the heads of the people into their giggling faces, and hear them call to each other, "Look! Look!"

As he pushed his crumpled shirt into his trousers, with a hand thin as a child's, a handsome man beside me said, "He's preparing to die, and he hitches up his trousers!"

This drew a big laugh. It was obvious they didn't consider it likely that he would actually commit suicide, nor did I; but Smoury took one glance, and butting people out of the way with his paunch, shouted, "Out of the way, fools!"

He called them fools, repeatedly. Approaching one group he said, "Go where you belong, fools!"

This sounded funny, yet was true; for all of them, from morning on, had been behaving like one common fool. Having scattered the passengers, he came to the soldier, held out his hand and said, "Let's have that knife!"

"Who cares!" said the soldier, holding out the handle.

The chef handed me the knife and pushed the soldier into the cabin. "Lie down and sleep. What's bothering you, eh?"

Without a word the soldier settled down in a hammock.

"He'll fetch you something to eat and a drop of vodka. Do you take vodka?"

"A drop, sometimes."

"But watch out, don't touch him. It wasn't he made fun of you, understand? I want you to know it wasn't he."

"Why did they torture me?" the soldier asked.

Smoury paused before he replied heavily, "How do I know?"

Coming into the kitchen with me, he muttered, "It's a sad one they got their claws in this time, all right. Look at him! And there you are. My boy, a man can be driven out of his mind, that he can. They stick to him like leeches, and he's done for. There are people here like leeches —worse than leeches."

Bringing bread, meat and vodka to the soldier, I found him still in the hammock, swinging, and crying like a woman. Placing the food on the table I said, "Eat."

"Shut the door."

"Then it will be dark."

"Shut it or they'll be sneaking in."

I left him. It was hard for me to look at him. He aroused such pity as to embarrass me. Endlessly grandma had reiterated, "One must be compassionate toward people. We're all miserable. Life is hard for us all."

"Did you bring it to him?" asked the chef. "How is the soldier?"

"I feel sad about him."

"So, what's the trouble now, eh?"

"You can't help feeling sad about people."

Smoury took my arm and pulled me to him, and said, "Your pity is not misspent, but don't waste time chattering about it. When you don't know how to cook jam, you must learn." Then, giving me a push, he said, brusquely, "It's no place for you here. Have a smoke."

The behavior of the passengers depressed me. There was something indescribably unfeeling in their persecution of the soldier, in their gleeful laughter when Smoury pulled him by the ear. How could they get pleasure out of something so revolting and pitiful? What was it that gave them such pleasure?

There they were back under their awnings, sitting or lounging, having a drink, playing a hand of cards, chatting, or holding serious discussions, or taking in the scenery, as though it were not they who, an hour ago, had whistled and jeered. Now all were quiet and languid as ever. From morning to night they eddied over the deck like fluff in the wind or motes in the sun. In knots of ten they would saunter to the hatchway, cross themselves; they would disembark at the landings, while the same sort embarked, their backs stooped under the same sort of bags and boxes, and wearing the same sort of clothes.

For the constant shifting of passengers made no change in the life aboard, at all. The new arrivals spoke of the same things as those who had departed: land, work, God, women—and in identical phrases. "Our sufferings are ordained by the Lord; our part is to bear it patiently. There's nothing more we can do. It's fate."

It depressed and exasperated me to hear such phrases. I did not care to suffer dirt or any ill; I would not endure injustice or insult. I knew I had not earned maltreatment; nor had the soldier earned it. Perhaps he had wanted to amuse others.

Max, quiet and good-natured, had been fired; but spiteful Serge had been kept on. And why had people who had nearly driven a man insane allowed themselves to be so tamely herded by the shouting sailors, why had they so meekly borne abuse?

"Why are you lolling over the deck?" shouted the boatswain, rolling his handsome, but ill-natured, eyes. "If the boat dips, over you'll go, you devils!"

Placidly, the "devils" resorted to the other deck, only to be driven away again, like sheep. "Accursed ones!"

On hot nights, it was smothering under the metal sheeting which the sun had baked red hot; and the passengers swarmed over the deck like beetles, lying where they had dropped. The sailors poked them up with marlinspikes, shouting, "No sprawling around here; back where you belong!"

Standing up, they would grope like sleepwalkers wherever they were being prodded. The sailors were of the same sort as themselves; their only difference was their uniform; yet they ordered the others around like cops. What most marked these people to me was their spiritless, timid, sad submission. It was frightful, then, to see the cruel, mindless spirit of mischief that had so little of real mirth in it, break through the meek shell. It seemed to me they had no idea where they were being carried, and it did not matter to them where they were disembarked. Wherever it was, they stayed ashore only briefly, re-embarking on our boat or taking another, starting their travels anew. They seemed all astray, to be without kin, to have become strangers on earth. And every last one of them was a witless craven.

It was past midnight, once, when something went wrong in the engines, and there was a detonation like a cannon shot. Immediately, steam, pouring from the boiler room and filtering through every crack, covered the whole deck. Someone, unseen, shouted, "Gavrilov, some red lead and felt wadding!"

My bed was on the wash table in the kitchen, which was near the boiler room, and the explosion and the jolt woke me. The deck was quiet. From the engines came a hot, bubbling whisper, and the tapping of a hammer. However, a minute or two later, the quiet gave way to a pandemonium, as the passengers began their howling.

Through the white mist which was already dissipating, came women with streaming hair, and untidy men with eyes rounded into fish stares, all rushing pell-mell, colliding into each other, staggering under bundles, valises, boxes, falling, jostling each other, invoking God and St.

Nicholas. It was dreadful, yet diverting, and I followed them around to see what they would do next.

I was observing a panic for the first time in my life, yet it was immediately apparent to me that the passengers had taken needless alarm. The vessel had not slackened speed. The life belts were clearly within reach. There was a full moon and plenty of light. But the deck passengers ran wild over the deck, to be joined, soon, by milling passengers from the lower decks. One man jumped overboard, to be followed by another and then a third. Two peasants and a monk, using heavy blocks of wood, pried loose a bench screwed to the deck. A large crate of chickens was pitched overboard. At the foot of the stairway leading to the captain's bridge, in the middle of the deck, a peasant knelt, kept bowing to the people swarming past him, yelping like a wolf, "I'm an Orthodox . . . sinner . . ."

A fat citizen, who had pulled on his trousers without bothering to put on his shirt, beat himself on the chest and yelled, "To the boats, you devils!"

The sailors grabbed them by their collars, cracked their skulls together and dropped them on the deck. Smoury waddled up ponderously, his overcoat thrown over his pajamas, and harangued them in an echoing voice, "Shame on all of you! What's all this fuss about? Have we stopped? Have we slowed down? There's the shore! The idiots who jumped overboard have been tossed lifebelts and are being fished out. You see? The two boats there!" And, as he spoke, he strode among the third-class passengers, knocking them on the head with his fist; and they collapsed like sacks.

The commotion was not yet over when a lady, dressed in a cloak, lunged at Smoury, brandishing a spoon in his face, and cried, "What nerve!"

A damp gentleman sucked at his moustache and held her back, saying fretfully, "Idiot, let go of him!"

Smoury, waving his arms and blinking with embarrassment, asked me, "What's wrong, eh? What's she after me for? A nice thing! Never saw her in my life!"

A peasant with a bloody nose cried, "Call them human beings? Bandits!"

Before that summer ended, I had been through two such panics, both caused not by actual danger, but the dread of it. A third time two thieves, one in foreign dress, were caught by the passengers, who spent a solid hour mauling them, before the sailors found out and delivered the victims out of their hands; for which the passengers abused the sailors, crying, "A case of thieves covering thieves, that's clear! You're scoundrels yourselves; that's why your sympathies are with the scoundrels."

Beaten into a coma, the thieves could not stand up when they were turned over to the authorities at the next stop.

There were other times when my feelings were thus agitated, and I could not decide whether people were good or evil, whether they preferred being at peace or making trouble; nor could I explain their cruelty, their impulse to hurt others, their diffidence when showing kindness.

I asked the chef, but he covered his face with a smoke cloud, and curtly dismissed it. "What's this chatter about? Humans are humans; some are clever and some are dopes. Stop talking and read. In books, the proper kind, I mean, you'll find the answers."

To please him, I bought him books as presents, picking up in Kazan for five kopecks, *The Tale of the Soldier Who Saved Peter the Great*. The chef happened to be drinking at the time, and in a surly mood, so I read it myself. I was captivated by it; it was short, simply written, easy to follow, interesting. I was sure it would give my teacher pleasure. But he crushed it into a ball in his hand and flung it overboard.

"There's your book, dope!" he said. "I train you up like a trick dog, and all you look for is trifling tales!" He stamped and raved. "What sort of book to hand me! Am I the kind that reads nonsense? Is it true what's written there? Answer me!"

"I don't know."

"But I know! If a man's head were off, the trunk would fall down the stairs; and the other fellow wouldn't have climbed up the haystacks. Soldiers aren't dopes. He would have set the place on fire, and finished them off that way—understand?"

"Yes."

"That's it. I know all about Tsar Peter and nothing like that happened to him. Get along with you."

Though I realized the chef was right I had enjoyed the book; so I bought another copy and reread it. I was astonished to discover that it was actually a poor book. This puzzled me, but increased my respect for the chef. Meanwhile he became more irascible, and reiterated, "How much you have to learn! It's no place for you, here."

I, too, considered it no place for me. I was distressed by Serge's rotten treatment of me. More than once I saw him stealing tea things and sneaking them to passengers. I knew this was the theft Smoury had frequently cautioned me against. "Watch out. Don't let the staff have any of the cups or plates from your table."

This added to my burden, and but for Smoury I would have jumped ship and gone off into the woods. His affection for me grew every day; and besides, the boat fascinated me by its continuous movement. I grudged our stopovers; and I was ever anticipating something new, a voyage on the Kama River, the Bielaya River, and the Viatka, and then back up the Volga to see new sights, cities, people. But that was not to be. My career on the steamer was abruptly cut off. One evening, on the way to Kazan from Nizhny, I was summoned to the steward. Shutting the door behind me, he said to Smoury, who glowered from his seat on a stool, "There he is!"

Smoury gruffly asked me, "Did you give Serge any cups and plates?"

"He takes them behind my back."

Quietly the steward remarked, "He doesn't see it, yet he knows."

Smoury slapped his knee, then scratched it and said, "Hold on!"

Pondering, I looked at the steward, who returned the glance from glasses behind which there seemed to be no eyes. The man lived soundlessly. His movements were quiet; his voice was low. You would get just a glance of his colorless beard or his vacant eyes around a corner, and he would be gone. Before he went to sleep, he spent a long time on his knees in the buffet, under the icon and its lamp. The door was slightly ajar, and seen through the crack, he appeared like a black bundle. How he prayed I never found out; all he seemed to do was to stay on his knees, keep his eyes turned up to the icon, tug his beard and sigh.

Smoury broke the silence. "Ever get any money from Serge?"

"No."

"Never?"

"Never."

"He never lies," Smoury told the steward, who replied in his lifeless voice. "That makes no difference. Please——"

"Come," said the cook, and, back at my table, he tapped his fingers on my head. "Fool; and fool that I am, too. I should have taken care."

I was discharged by the steward at Nizhny. I received close to eight rubles, my first big earnings. In his farewell to me, Smoury said gruffly, "Well, that's that. Eyes open from now on, understand? Don't go around with your mouth hanging open." He took my hand and put in it a beaded tobacco pouch. "For you. It's good handiwork. Made for me by my godchild. Good-by, then. Read; there's nothing better you can do."

He lifted me under the arms, kissed me and set me down on the dock. I felt sorry for him and myself. I could hardly keep the tears back, when I saw him going off to the steamer, jostling the stevedores aside, so big, heavy and lonely. Often, since then, have I run across his kind—good-hearted solitaries, cut off from the lives of others.

Chapter Seven

GRANDPA AND GRANDMA HAD MOVED BACK TO TOWN. I WENT THERE, working up an aggressive mood; but I was heavy-hearted. Why had I been thought a thief?

Grandma's greeting was tender, and she immediately started the samovar. In his mocking way grandpa asked, "Save any money?"

"What I saved is mine," I replied, and took a seat at the window. With an air I took out a pack of cigarettes and lit up.

"So!" said grandpa, glowering at me. "It's come to that, tasting the devil's poison! Aren't you a bit hasty?"

"I've even been given a tobacco pouch," I bragged.

"A tobacco pouch!" squealed grandpa. "Are you trying to rile me?"

He lunged at me, his strong, lean hands outstretched, his green eyes blazing. I met him head on, butting him in the stomach. The old man sat on the floor, and for some tense moments, stared at me, blinking with astonishment, his mouth gaping. Then he said in a low voice, "Your own grandfather you knock down? Your mother's father?"

"You've knocked me down plenty in the past," I mumbled, not realizing how abominably I had behaved.

Dry and light, grandpa bounced up, sat beside me, flicked the cigarette out of my mouth, flung it out of the window, and said apprehensively, "You lunatic! Don't you realize God will repay you for this all your life? Mother," he turned to grandma, "did you see? He knocked me down, he knocked me down! Ask him!"

Without waiting or asking, she just reached for me, grabbed me by the hair, and slapped me, "For that, take this and this!"

I felt not pain, but humiliation, especially from grandpa's giggling. He hopped on a chair, smacked his thighs, and chirped through his laughter, "That's the way; that's the way!"

I wrenched loose and ran to the shed, where I lay in a corner, forlorn and miserable, listening to the purring samovar.

Then grandma came in, bent over, and in a just audible whisper, told me, "You have to forgive me; I took care not to hurt you. I had to do it, for grandpa's an old, old man. He has to be indulged. He's fractured some small bones, and in addition his heart's eaten up with grief. Avoid doing him any injury. You're no longer a little boy, remember that, Alex. Now, he's the child."

Her words soothed like warm water. That loving whisper made me feel ashamed, but light-hearted, too. I embraced her.

"Go to him; go. It's all right, only don't smoke in front of him for a while. Give him a chance to get used to it."

I went back to the room, and after a look at grandpa, I could hardly keep back my laughter. His satisfaction was actually like a child's. His face was blissful; he was sitting at the table, crossing and uncrossing his legs, and running his claws through his reddish hair.

"Come back to butt me, goat? Ekh, you bandit! The image of your father! Freemason! Comes home, doesn't cross himself, and starts smoking on the spot! Ekh, you Bonaparte, you kopeck's worth of stuff!"

I said nothing, and let him exhaust his stock of abuse; fatigue silenced him. But at tea he began lecturing, "The fear of God is essential to men like reins to the horse. God is our only friend; man is a bitter enemy to man." Man's hostility to me I knew to be the truth; but the rest had no interest for me.

"You can return to Aunt Matrena now, and in the spring go back on a steamer. Spend the winter with them; they don't have to know you'll be quitting in the spring."

"Why should he be deceiving people?" said grandma, who had, herself, just deceived him with her pretense of beating me.

"There's no living without deceit," asserted grandpa. "Can you name anybody who lives without deceiving somebody?"

At nightfall, while grandpa was at his prayers, grandma and I went out through the gate, into the fields. The hut with the two windows where grandpa lived, was at the edge of the town, behind Kanatnoi Street, where he had once owned his house.

"And here we are, back again," said grandma with a laugh. "The old man can't find a place to rest his soul; he's always on the move. He's not contented here, either, but it suits me."

Ahead of us stretched some two miles of stubby growth, cut up by ditches and bordered by woods, and the row of birches lining the highway to Kazan. From the ditches protruded bush tips, which the beams of a chill, setting sun reddened like bloody fingers. A mild evening breeze rumpled the dusty grass. From a nearby path, silhouetted and erect like grass blades, too, we saw the shapes of city lads and their girls. In the right distance rose the red walls of the Old Believers [10] cemetery, termed "The Bugrovsky Hermitage." On the left, beyond the raised road over the marshes, stood a dark clump of trees hedging the Jewish cemetery. There was something impoverished about it all, and everything seemed to cling to the wounded earth. The hovels on the edge of the town seemed to peer timidly out of their windows on the dusty road, on which scrawny, famished chickens sauntered. Toward the Dievichia monastery ambled a string of lowing cows. From the military post came band music, the brasses braying. A drunk stumbled along, holding an accordion in a combative attitude, and mumbling, "I'm on my way to thee, faithfully."

"Dope," said grandma, blinking in the red glare of the setting sun, "Where are you off to? You'll lose the accordion with which you console yourself."

As I looked around I described the life on the steamer. After it this was drab; it made me feel like a fish out of water. Grandma listened attentively as I used to listen to her. When I described Smoury she said, crossing herself, "That's a good man; take care of him, Mother of God, he's good!" And to me, "See that you don't forget him. Keep the good in mind and forget the bad."

It was a struggle for me to tell her why I had been discharged, but I got the courage to tell her. It did not disturb her at all. She said, calmly, "You're still young; you haven't learned how to live."

"That's what everybody tells the other, 'You haven't learned how to live'—the peasants, the sailors, Aunt Matrena to her son. Where do you learn?"

She pursed her lips and shrugged, "I, myself, don't know."

"But you say it like all the rest."

"And why shouldn't I?" grandma calmly replied. "You mustn't take offense. You're young; you're not called upon to know. And who does, when it comes down to it? Only scoundrels. There's grandpa, educated and sharp as he is, and he don't know."

"And you, have you lived well?"

"I, yes. And badly, too. Both ways."

[10] A sect that followed an older ritual of the Orthodox Church, instead of the ritual revised during the reign of Tsar Alexis.

People loitered past, their long shadows trailing after them, to be obliterated by the dust that rose from their steps like puffs of smoke. The
evening melancholy became more cramping. From the window streamed
grandpa's mutterings, "Lord, let me not be judged in Thy anger, nor
punished with Thy wrath."

Grandma smiled. "He's tired God out. Every night his tale of woe
and what about? He's old, he doesn't need anything; but he's always
complaining and working himself into a lather over this or that. I
imagine God has a laugh in the evening, hearing his voice. 'There's
Basil Kashirin, at it again!' Get to bed, now."

I decided to deal in songbirds for a living—a pleasant livelihood, I
thought it. I to catch them, and grandma to sell them. I purchased a
net, a trap and a hoop, and constructed a cage. At dawn I posted myself
in a clump of bushes in a ravine, while grandma, with sack and basket,
went to glean the last mushrooms, nuts and bulbs in the woods.

The weary September sun was just on the rise. Now a cloud snuffed
out its wan rays; now they settled over me like a veil of silver stuff. In
the pit of the ravine it was still dim with a white mist rising. It had
dark, raw, clayey edges, with the further side overgrown with grass and
scrub, and covered with fallen leaves; red, gold and brown, which a
freshening breeze whipped along the gully.

The goldfinch sang among the turnip-tops. In the dusty, tattered
grass I saw birds with animated, red-bonneted heads. Inquisitive tit-
mouses noisily fussed above me, their white cheeks ludicrously puffed
out, like the Sunday gallants on Kunavin Street. Quick, bright and
saucy, they had to know and touch everything, and, one after another,
they landed in the trap. It wrung my heart to see them flapping their
wings; but it was strictly business with me. I transferred them into a
spare cage, which I put in a sack, where the darkness quieted them
down.

A flock of finches took up perches on a hawthorn enveloped in sunlight. The finches, in enjoyment of the sun, warbled joyously, and frol-
icked like schoolboys. The tame black and white magpie, thirsty and
late for his voyage to warmer climes, clung to a swaying sweetbriar
branch, grooming his wing feathers, while his black eyes measured his
prey. The soaring lark returned with a bee, which he carefully stowed
away in a burr, and hopped to the ground, with his thievish head
cocked. The dreamed-of prize—if I could only net him—the hawfinch,
who can be taught to talk, flitted soundlessly by. A bullfinch, chased

from his flock, perched in an alder where, red and pompous as a general, his black bill shook with his wrathful chirping.

As the sun mounted, more and more birds turned up, and their singing grew livelier. The ravine, itself, hummed with autumn music, a muted, melancholy, sweet sound that could be felt through the unceasing, windy rustle of the bushes, and the rapturous bird song. In it I heard summer's farewell serenade, with whispered words meant only for my ears; and these words spontaneously grouped themselves into a song. As spontaneously, at the same time, my memory repictured scenes of the past.

Somewhere above me, I heard grandma calling, "Where are you?" She was sitting on the edge of the path. On a handkerchief was laid out bread, cucumbers, turnips and apples; and, in the center of this spread stood an exquisite little cut-glass decanter, with a crystal Napoleon head for its stopper, containing a portion of vodka, brewed from herbs. "Oh, Lord, but it's good!" exclaimed grandma, in a grateful voice.

"I made up a song." I told her.

"Yes? Let's hear it."

I recited something I thought was a poem, which began:

"Many are the signs of approaching winter; farewell to thee, oh sun of summer."

She broke in and wouldn't hear it out. "I know a song like that, and it's better." And, in a sing-song, she recited:

"Ah, gone is the summer sun into dark night behind woods far off. I am left behind, a maid and solitary, reft of the bliss of spring. In the morning I retrace the walks I took in May. Sad are the bare fields where I lost my youth. From my white breast pluck my heart and under the snow, bury it."

Though I suffered as a slighted author, I took delight in the song and pitied the girl. "That," said grandma, "is how grief sings. It was made up, you know, by a young girl. There were those walks in the springtime, but by wintertime her lover had thrown her over, for another girl, I suppose. Her heart ached, and she wept. Unless you've lived through it, yourself, you can't speak truly or well. See what a good song she made up."

The first time she sold a bird, getting forty kopecks for it, she was taken by surprise. "What do you think of that? And I thought it was foolishness, just a boy's sport! And this is how it turns out."

"You let it go too cheap."

"Is that so?"

On market days she got a ruble per bird, and was truly startled. What profitable sport! "Women wash clothes or scrub floors for days to earn a quarter of a ruble, and all you do is catch a bird! But, you know, it's not a nice thing to do, caging birds. That's enough of it, Alex."

But I got pleasure out of trapping birds. It brought me independence without trouble to anyone except the birds. I secured good equipment and learned much from old bird trappers. I covered as much as two miles, by myself, hunting birds, to the forest that lined the Volga in whose pines the crossbills, valued by collectors, lived and bred, and the Apollyon titmouse, a rare and beautiful white bird with a long tail.

I would set out at dusk, and spend all night ranging the highroad to Kazan; sometimes I hunted through the fall rains, slogging through the mire. Over my shoulder, in an oilskin sack, were my cages baited with food; in my hand a thick walnut stick. The autumn night was chill and dismaying. One would pass under birches mutilated by lightning; and dripping branches scraped my head. Below, to the left, over the black flood of the Volga, swayed solitary lights on the masts of steamers and barges, looking lost in a measureless abyss, while the wheels splashed and the sirens moaned.

From the hardened earth along the roadside jutted the village hovels. Snarling, famished dogs circled my legs; watchmen stumbled into me and chattered in fright, "Who's that? Only the devil brings people out at this hour."

Fearing lest my gear be confiscated, I kept five-kopeck pieces in my pocket to bribe the watchman. The one in the village of Fokinoi became my friend, and was always lamenting, "What, again! What a rash, restless night-bird you are!"

His name was Nifron, a little, gray man who looked like a saint. From his blouse he took a turnip, an apple, and some peas and gave them to me. "There, my friend, a present for you. Eat it with enjoyment." Escorting me to the village limits, his sendoff was, "Go, and God be with you!"

I reached the forest before dawn, set my traps, and lay down on my coat at the forest edge, waiting for daybreak. Heavy autumn sleep enfolded the earth, and everything was still. The broad meadows bordering the forest were barely visible through the gray mist. Divided by the Volga, the fields met and separated again, until they dissolved in fog. Unhurriedly the bright sun came up above the meadows. Lights spangled the dark mane of the forest and a strange, poignant pulsation began in my heart. Ever more swiftly swirled the fog off the meadows, silvering in the sunlight, and then bushes, trees, haystacks began to take form. Sunlight flooded the meadows, looking like streams of gold along the riversides. The sun, by a mere look into the still water under the bank, made the whole river seem to rise up toward it, as it mounted the sky and blessed the bare, chilled earth with warmth and joy and drew from it sweet autumn fragrances. In the air's transparency, earth looked limitlessly vast. Everything seemed to be afloat in space, beckoning one toward the world's farthest reaches. I saw ten such sunrises that fall, and with each a new world, a new beauty took shape under my eyes.

I so loved the sun that I took delight in its very name, whose sweet sound [11] seemed to reverberate like a bell.

I used to put my hands on it when a beam pierced, like a sword, through branches, or through a crack in the fence. Grandpa had repeatedly read to me the story of Prince Michael Chernigovsky [12] and Lady Theodora, who refused to worship the sun, and I pictured them as a gypsy pair, swarthy, sullen and ill-natured, with infected eyes like the poor Mordvins. A spontaneous smile came to my face with every sunrise over the meadows.

The pine forest murmured above me as, with green paws, it brushed off dew. Like silver brocade on fern leaves and on shadowed ground, gleamed the morning hoar-frost. Rain had beaten down the russet grass; stiff blades were bowed to the ground; yet, when the sun's rays touched them, a tremor seemed to run through them, stirring them to, perhaps, their last effort.

The birds rose. They rebounded from bough to bough, like balls of gray fluff. With their hooked beaks flamboyant cross-bills pecked at pine cones in the top branches. Perched on the tip of pine branch, a white Apollyon titmouse sang, wielded its long tail, like a rudder, and cast a wary glance from its jet-bead eye at my net. And, all of a sudden, the entire forest, solemnly brooding a moment ago, echoed with thousands of bird voices, with the animation of earth's purest living creatures. In their image have fairies, cherubs, seraphs and all the angels been created by man, father of earthly beauty, to console himself.

[11] The Russian word for sun is *solntse*, with the *l* almost silent.
[12] *Cherni* means black.

I felt some pangs in trapping the little singers; I regretted shutting them up in cages. I would have preferred the mere pleasure of looking at them. But the craving of the hunter and the need of money stifled these feelings.

The birds tantalized me with their shrewdness. After a cautious inspection of the trap, the blue titmouse understood what threatened, and helped herself to seed between the rungs of the trap, by pecking them from the side and thus avoiding risks. But inquisitiveness was the undoing of the titmouse. And I got whole flocks of puffed-up, but doltish, bullfinches, who ambled into the nets like fat burghers into church. On finding themselves trapped they looked amazed, rolled their eyes, and went for my fingers with their strong beaks. The crossbill came into the trap with a grave air. Unlike the rest this witless, avaricious bird contemplated the net a long time, propped back upon its long tail, with its pointed beak stuck out. He can run up a tree trunk like a woodpecker, always acting as the escort of a titmouse. There is something disagreeable about this smoke-hued songbird. It shows no love and receives none. It resembles the magpie in the way it is tempted by bright objects which it steals and hides away.

My catch was completed before noon, and I returned by way of the forest. Had I taken the road, boys and young men from the village would have waylaid me, stripped me of my cages and destroyed my gear, something I had already experienced.

I got home at dusk, tired and hungry, but with a sense of having grown that day, of having added to my knowledge and my strength. This enabled me to bear grandpa's jibes without feeling affronted, whereupon he began to reason with me.

"Quit this pointless business. Finish with it. No one ever made his mark through birding. I've never known it to happen. Hunt out another job where your wits can develop. Man isn't given life without purpose. He's God's grain and he must produce a full ear. He's like a ruble; well invested it brings in three rubles. You think life is play? No, it's not play. The world man inhabits is a darkness, and every man must light his own way through it. Everybody gets enough to fill his ten fingers, but greedily grasps for more handfuls. Be strong; but if you're weak, be crafty. The strengthless man dangles between heaven and hell. Live so that people feel you're with them, but always realize that you're alone. Trust nobody, whatever the situation may be. You'll never make a straight measure if you follow only your eye. Guard your tongue. No city, no house was constructed by the tongue; but the axe has carved out rubles. You're not a fool and you're not a Kalmuck,[13] whom wealth bothers like vermin on their sheep."

He could go on like this through the night, and I knew the phrases by heart. They interested me, but I was dubious about their sense. According to them, there were two obstacles to man's fulfillment of his desires—his God and his fellowmen.

Seated at the window, grandma worked with her lace thread, the spindle whirring in her able hands. After silently listening to grandpa's long homily, she broke in, "The smile of the Mother of God, that's what everything hangs on."

"What!" gulped grandpa. "God! I have God always in mind. I know everything about God's part. Ekh, you old fool! Did God plant fools on earth, eh?"

As I saw it, Cossacks and soldiers led the most joyful life of all—cheerful and carefree. Early on clear mornings, they were out in the valley near the house. Dispersed over the bare fields, which they dotted like white mushrooms, they started up a tricky and absorbing game. Husky and lively in their white blouses, they charged over the fields with their guns at the ready, and vanished down the ravine; then, at a bugle call, they were suddenly all over the field again, shouting their "Hurrahs!" above the menacing roll of drums. With bayonets fixed, they sometimes charged our house, apparently about to sweep it up like a haystack. I shouted "Hurrah!" too, and charged with them, in an ecstasy of movement. Under the incitation of the drums I felt a passionate urge to demolish something, pull down a fence or strike another boy. In their rest periods the soldiers enraptured me by teaching me signals, or showing me the mechanism of their artillery. Now and then a soldier would prod my belly with his bayonet and cry, with pretended excitement, "Get the cockroach!"

The bayonet glittered; it seemed to be alive, to coil like a snake about to strike. It was all rather scary, yet enjoyable.

The Mordvin drummer taught me to use the sticks. At first, manipulating my wrists, he would beat out the rhythm with my fingers, till they hurt; then he would place the sticks in my bruised fingers. "Strike it—one-two, one-two! Rum-ti-tum. Left-soft, right-loud, rum-ti," he bellowed, fixing me with his round, birdlike eyes.

I went through most of their drill with the soldiers, and when it was over, I escorted them through the streets, to their barracks, listening to

[13] The Kalmucks were mainly nomadic herdsmen.

their hearty singing, and peering up into their good-natured faces, all as fresh as newly-minted coins. The procession up the street of this jovial mass of men roused amiable feeling in me, made me wish to immerse myself into them as into a river or a forest. These men had no terrors; could overcome everything; could do anything they wished; and were all good, simple-hearted people.

One day, however, during a rest, a young corporal handed me a peculiarly thick cigarette. "Have a smoke! I wouldn't hand this out to everybody. Matter of fact, I shouldn't give one to you, they're so special!"

I lit up and he moved off a few paces. Suddenly a blinding red flame singed my fingers, my nose and eyebrows, and a corrosive smoke made me cough and retch. Blinded and in a panic, I stamped up and down, heartily amusing the soldiers who were ringed around me. I ran home, with pursuing whistles and laughter, and a sound like a snapping whip. My scorched fingers pained, my face smarted, tears ran down, but the pain did not hurt so much as my wondering, bleakly, why this should be fun to such nice chaps.

On reaching home, I secluded myself in the attic to brood over this unaccountable cruelty whose repulsive presence blocked my path. How sharp and actual was the image memory brought before me, large as life, of the skinny Sarapula soldier saying, "Now you understand?"

I also frequented Cossacks' barracks near Pechersky Square. They differed from our soldiers, not only in being such good horsemen and wearing handsomer uniforms, but in their dialect, their songs, and their accomplished dancers. At dusk, after tending to their horses, they made a ring near the stables, and a little Cossack, wagging his tufts of red hair, began singing in a soft, high voice that had the timbre of a trumpet. In the prolonged, melancholy notes flowed the Don and the blue Doonia.[14] His eyes were shut, like those of a linnet, which has been known to sing till it drops, dead, from its perch. His shirt collar was open, baring a collar bone that gleamed like a copper band. There was something metallic, coppery, about all of him. Teetering on his skinny legs, as if rocked by the earth under him, and his hands out, he seemed to be without other senses, to be all sound—a man no longer, but a horn of brass. Sometimes he appeared to me on the point of falling, about to drop prostrate and dead like the linnet, because all his spirit and vigor had been spent in his song.

Their hands in their pockets or held behind their stalwart backs,

[14] Rivers of the Cossack regions in the south of Russia.

his mates surrounded him, their grave eyes fixed on his coppery face. Or, clapping their hands, and spitting to clear their throats, they joined in, reverently, like church choristers. The bearded and shaven, all looked like icons, dignified, a race apart. The song stretched like a long street, level and wide. Listening to him, everything left my mind, the hour of the day, or whether I was man or boy. Nothing else existed. Then the voice of the singer died away. The horses were heard in long neighs, full of longing for their steppes; and, imperceptibly, but surely, the autumn night drifted up from the fields. My swelling heart almost split under pressure of many strange emotions, and I felt an encompassing, inarticulate love for all human beings and all the earth.

The coppery little Cossack seemed to be superhuman, a man of legend living in realms beyond ordinary folk. In his presence I became tongue-tied. When he asked me something, I was lost in bashful silence, and responded only with a blissful smile. I would have followed at his beck in humble, doglike silence. All I asked for was to see as much of him as I could, and hear him sing.

Chapter Eight

WITH THE FIRST SNOWFALL, GRANDPA TOOK ME BACK TO GRANDMA'S sister. "It won't hurt you," he said.

With my wonderful summer experiences behind me, I felt older and wiser, and that household seemed drearier than ever. They still poisoned themselves in their gluttony and fell sick and expatiated minutely on their ailments to each other. The old woman continued her bloodthirsty prayers to God. The boss' wife had slimmed down, but her movements were as sedate and heavy as when she was pregnant. Fussing with baby clothes, she hummed one tune: "Spiria, Spiria, Spiridon, little brother Spiria, I sit inside the sled and Spiria sits on the floorboard."

At any interruption, she would stop and ask irritably, "What do you want?" I believe she knew no other song.

Evenings I was called into the sitting room and commanded, "Tell us, now, what happened on the boat?"

Sitting near the door, I told my story. It was a pleasure to me to call up a different life from this, into which necessity had forced me. I became so absorbed, my audience was forgotten; but it soon made itself heard.

Never having been aboard a ship, the women wanted to know, "Wasn't it dangerous?" I couldn't understand; what danger was there?

"The boat could sink any minute; then everybody would drown."

The boss laughed at them, but I could not convince the women that ships did not sink in deep water. According to the old woman, the ship did not float on the water, but made its way on wheels over the riverbed, like a wagon on land.

"If they're iron, how do they float? An axe doesn't float; no chance of that!"

"But a metal cup floats."

"How can you compare them? A cup's too small to count."

My description of Smoury and his books evoked contempt. Only heretics and the witless wrote books, according to the old woman.

"How about King David and his Book of Psalms?"

"The Psalms are scriptures; besides, King David asked God's forgiveness for writing them."

"Where does it say that?"

"On the palms of my hands, that's where! My hand on your neck will show you where!"

She was the know-it-all. She had positive—and barbarous—opinions on every subject. "A Tatar died on the Pechora River and his soul was coal black when it came out of his mouth!"

"Soul or spirit?" I asked; and she said, contemptuously, "Of a Tatar, idiot!"

The boss' wife also distrusted books. "They do a lot of harm," she said, "especially to the young. At Grebeshka, where I lived, there was a girl, came of a good family too, and she read all the time; and what happened? She fell in love with a deacon, whose wife shamed her right in the street, before all the people; it was awful!"

At times I used phrases recalled from Smoury's books. For example, in one of them, an interminable volume, there was a sentence reading, "Strictly speaking, no single inventor gave us gunpowder; as, in other cases, it climaxed a succession of observations and discoveries." I don't know why this had impressed me. I particularly fancied the combination of the two phrases, "strictly speaking, no single inventor gave us gunpowder," which seemed to me very effective. These phrases were to bring a farcical misery upon me.

Once, being called upon to entertain my employers with my maritime recollections, I replied, "Strictly speaking, I have nothing left to tell."

They never got over it. "What?" they cried, "What did you say?" And all four laughed and repeated to themselves, "Strictly speaking! Oh, my!"

The boss, himself, twitted me, "That was clumsily put, old man."

And for a long time after, I'd hear, "Hey, there, Strictly Speaking, come here and wipe up the baby's mess, Strictly Speaking!"

This oafish horseplay did not offend me so much as it surprised me. I lived in a daze of stupefying misery, and it was a struggle to survive it. I had no sense of incompetence at my work. There were two babies in the house, whose nurses never satisfied the mistresses, and were regularly being replaced. I had to tend the babies, wash their diapers daily, and once a week take the linen to rinse at the Spring of the Gendarmes. Here I met with the jibes of the washerwomen, "How come you're doing woman's work?"

Sometimes their baiting infuriated me to such a pitch that I struck at them with the damp twists of linen, for which I was well repaid in kind. Yet, I found the women jolly and entertaining.

The Spring of the Gendarmes flowed alongside the causeway over the swamp and into the Oka. The causeway separated the city from a field, which still bore the name of the ancient god, Yarilo. The people of the neighboring town of Semika had laid out part of the field as a sort of park. I heard from grandma that, when she was young, the people there had still sacrificed to Yarilo. They wrapped a wheel in tow and pitch, set it ablaze, and amidst shouts and songs, started it down the hill, watching if the burning wheel rolled into the Oka. In that case, it was believed Yarilo had received the sacrifice, and they could look for a sunny and fruitful summer.

The washerwomen came mostly from the Yarilo, tough, willful women who knew the world. I enjoyed their accounts of the merchants, *chinovniks,*[15] and officers for whom they worked. Rinsing their wash in winter in the icy water was gruelling work. The hands of all of them were chapped. They toiled, stooped over the wooden trough that carried the stream, under an old, splintered shed, which kept out neither wind nor snow. Their faces were red with the pinching frost, which stiffened their wet fingers until they couldn't bend their

[15] Government officials and clerks; the word generally carries a connotation of bureaucratic behavior.

knuckles, and made their eyes tear continually. Yet they chatted incessantly, exchanging stories, and faced everybody and everything with bravado.

The best story-teller among them was Natalie Kozlovsky, a woman about thirty, fresh-faced, strong, with laughing eyes and a sharp, agile tongue. Her admiring companions consulted her in their affairs and praised her skill and her neat dress, and commended her for sending her daughter to high school. When she came down the slippery hill footpath, bowed under her two baskets of wet linen, she got warm greetings from all, "And how's your daughter?"

"In good health, thank you, and learning well, thank God!"

"There you are; that girl will be a lady!"

"That's why I'm educating her. Where do the ladies all come from, rouged faces and all? From our own kind, from the dark earth. And where else? The one with the most knowledge has the longest reach and can grasp the most; and the one who grasps the most gets the rank and the honors. God puts us into the world ignorant children, and expects to get us back wise elders; this means we all have to learn."

When she spoke, the others listened, attentive to her self-assured, fluent phrases. The women talked her up, not only to her face but behind her back, marvelling at her intellect. Yet she had no imitators. She had sewn leather cuffs, made from the uppers of old boots, over her blouse sleeves, and this spared her baring her arms to the elbows, and kept her sleeves dry. Everyone applauded the device, but no one used it. When I did they jeered me: "Imagine, learning from a woman!"

About her daughter, she said, "It's an important step. It will add one more young lady to the world. Is that a small matter? Still, she may not be able to keep it up; she may die. And students don't have it easy. But there was the Bakhilovs' daughter. She studied and studied and got to be a teacher, and she was set for life."

"Of course, if they marry, they don't need the education; provided they're good for something else."

"A woman's cleverness isn't in her head."

I found it odd and embarrassing to hear them speak of such things without reticence. I had heard sailors, soldiers and peasants on the subject of women. They always boasted of their craft in getting the best of women. I sensed a certain hostility in their attitude toward "females"; yet there was usually a hollow ring in their brag, which suggested that their tales were more invention than truth.

The washerwomen did not drool over "conquests"; but, in their comments upon men there were overtones of disdain and animosity that made me feel that women, in truth, might be the strong ones.

"Even those that don't gad about, the quiet ones, come to women!" said Natalie; and an old woman, in a snuffling voice, asked, "And where else? Even monks and hermits turn from God Himself, to us."

These talks, heard through the mournful gurgle of water and the smack of wet clothes on stone, or on grimy boards which not even the snow could cover clean, this brazenly prurient chatter about intimate things, about the life source from which all peoples spring, drove me into shocked diffidence; and it pulled my thoughts to the "romances" that simmered, irritatingly, all around me. My understanding of these "romances" drew upon smut I heard all around me.

Yet, I found the company of the washerwomen, or orderlies in kitchens, or laborers in cellars, far more exhilarating than what I had at home, where the stilted talk dwelt on the same inanities, where life was so drably routinized that I felt suffocated in constraint and resentful ennui. My employers lived as though bewitched, ringed by food, sickness and sleep, and the concern over the preparations for meals, and for bed. They were preoccupied by sin and death, of which they had a craven fear. They were in constant friction with each other, as grain kernels are in friction with the millstone that is pulverizing them.

When I had some time to myself I used to go to the shed to cut up firewood, and to enjoy being alone. But I seldom had that pleasure. I was sought here by the officers' orderlies, eager to spill the gossip of the yard. My most frequent visitors were Yermokhin and Sidorov. The former, who came from Kaluga, was tall, but stooped over; prominent, thick veins seamed his skin; and he had a little head with vacant eyes. He was sluggish and stupid to an annoying degree, and slow and clumsy in movement. At sight of a woman his eyes fluttered, and he lurched forward as if about to prostrate himself at her feet. His rapid conquests of cooks and housemaids provoked astonishment and general envy. He elicited further respect for his bearish strength. Sidorov, who hailed from Tula, was a moody, soft-spoken man who stared into corners, except when he was telling an anecdote, in his low tones.

"What are you staring at?"

"I thought there was a mouse there. I love mice, the quiet way they run."

I wrote letters home for the orderlies, love letters, mostly. I enjoyed it, especially when writing for Sidorov. Regularly, every Saturday, he had me get off a letter to his sister in Tula. He called me into his kitchen, seated himself at my side at the table, rubbed his bristly, recently-shaven skull, and gave me low-voiced instructions straight in my ear.

"So, let's get going. The regular beginning, you know. 'Dearest sister, hoping this finds you in good health'—you know how it should go. And now write, 'The ruble you sent me came. Thank you for sending it, but it was not necessary. There's nothing I lack; we live very well.' . . . We don't, as a matter of fact; we live like dogs; but there's no point letting her know. She's young, only fourteen. Why should she be burdened? Now, go on by yourself, the way you've been told."

He crowded me, spurting his hot and odorous breath into my ear. "Write this: 'If anybody tries any soft talk on you, don't believe him. He wants to fool you; his game is to ruin you.'"

The strain of repressing a cough reddened his face, and brought tears in his eyes. He leaned on the table, and crowded me still more.

"You're in my way."

"Never mind, keep on writing! 'And especially gentlemen. Never trust a gentleman. They'll mislead a girl the first look. They know just what to tell her. If you have any money saved up, let a priest, who you know to be a decent man, hold it for you. But it would be still better to bury it; only make sure you remember where.'"

It was a trial trying to follow his whispering, which was often lost in the rattle of the tin vanes in the ventilator. Before me was the oven front, sooted over, and the dish closet black with flies. The foul kitchen stank acridly of charred grease, kerosene and smoke, and swarmed with vermin, cockroaches crawling on the oven and in and out of the firewood. A melancholy mood chilled my heart. Pity for the soldier and his sister almost brought me to tears. Could people live like that, could it be right for them to live like that?

I continued writing, ignoring Sidorov's whispers; I dealt with the misery and ugliness of life until, with a sigh, he said to me, "You've written her a lot. Now she'll know what she has to look out for."

"There's nothing she has to look out for!" I retorted, although there was so much I, myself, looked out for, in dread.

The soldier chuckled and cleared his throat. "You're an odd one! What do you mean, nothing to look out for? How about gentlemen and God? Don't you have to worry about them?"

On receiving a letter from his sister, he would hurry me, "Quick, please, read it to me." And he made me read the poor, trivial and insultingly hasty scrawl three times over.

Kind and good though he was by nature, he treated women like the rest, that is, brutishly. These affairs as they came to my voluntary or involuntary notice—often they happened right under my nose—were astonishing and indecently abrupt in their beginnings and endings. I saw Sidorov excite sympathy in a women over his soldier's life, then make her swoon with false avowals, and then describe his feat to Yermokhin, scowling and spitting in disgust, as if it had been a dose of salts. I observed all this with a sinking heart and, outraged, I demanded of the soldiers why they were so false in dealings with a woman, misleading her, then deriding her among themselves; why they exposed her and often treated her to a beating, besides.

One answered with a condescending laugh, "Such things are not for you to know. It's wrong and sinful, and you have a way to go before you get to that; you're too young to understand it."

But I once got a clearer answer which has stayed in my mind. "Do you imagine," Sidorov said, "that the woman doesn't know I'm fooling? She knows, all right. She's looking to be fooled. In these games everybody cheats. It's a disgrace all around. It's not love for either; just a game. A miserable shame! The time will come, and you'll experience it, too. It got people chased out of paradise; it's the source of all unhappiness."

What he said was put so truly, yet so glumly and contritely, as to somewhat reconcile me to these "love affairs." It made me feel better disposed toward him than toward Yermokhin, whom I came to loathe, looking for occasions to annoy and ridicule him. This I managed so well as to have him frequently chasing me across the yard, intent on doing me an injury, and his clumsiness alone kept him from it.

"It's prohibited," Sidorov said of relations with women. That I knew, but that such relations were the source of man's miseries I rejected. Unhappy people I saw all around, but I could not accept his view of it, after seeing the inexpressible light in the eyes of lovers, and after having become aware of the inexpressible tenderness they felt for each other. The sight of this festival of the heart never failed to exhilarate me.

Nevertheless, as I recall it, that life grew steadily more dull and brutish, and more rutted in its ways. I could not even dream of any lightening of the dreariness that bleared my gaze.

One day I heard a story from the soldiers that affected me profoundly. There was a cutter, a mild-mannered foreigner, who worked for the most exclusive tailor in town. He was married to a dainty little childless woman, who spent the day reading books. Above the din of the yard, among drunken, roistering neighbors, these two lived, quite unseen and unheard. They never had visitors and never went out, except to theatres on holidays.

The husband was kept busy into the night. The wife, who gave the impression of an undeveloped girl, made a bi-weekly trip to the library. I used to see her, her books strapped around like a student, walking to the dike, limping as though she were a bit lame. Her little hands were gloved, and she seemed to me unaffected and gracious and fresh and neat. Her face was birdlike with its little, darting eyes; altogether she had the prettiness of a porcelain figurine. The soldiers said it was missing ribs that gave that quaint sway to her walk; but it appealed to me, and she had a place in my esteem far above the yard's other ladies, the wives of the officers. For all their confident tones, their fancy wardrobes and their affectations, they looked stale, like superfluous things long forgotten in a closet.

To the yard folk the cutter's dainty wife was a halfwit. Their theory was that books had addled her brain, and brought her to such a pass that housekeeping had got beyond her, obliging her husband to do the marketing and give instructions to the big, foreign woman who cooked and did for them. This woman was one-eyed, and that one always red and tearing; the other was just a pink slit. According to the yard folk, she had no more wits than her mistress, couldn't do a proper veal and onion fry; and had once mistaken radishes for parsley. How dreadful!

The three were as out of place there as if, accidentally, they had been cooped up with chickens. They made me think of a titmouse, seeking warmth, flying through the ventilator pane of a winter double window, and finding itself in the foul and smothering tenement of man.

And then I learned from the orderlies of the nasty and humiliating trick on the cutter's wife that was being played by the officers. Taking turns, they composed a letter to her daily, containing an avowal of love, tributes to her beauty, and lamentations over the supposed correspondent's misery. Each of her replies pleaded to her correspondent to be left in peace, regretted hurting him, and asked God to help him overcome his infatuation. He would read her reply to the rest; and then another love letter would be concocted, and dispatched to her under another signature.

As the orderlies told me this they laughed and jeered at the woman. "That hunchback's a miserable nitwit!" boomed Yermokhin, and in softer-voiced agreement, Sidorov remarked, "No matter what, a woman likes to be fooled with; she knows what's happening."

I didn't think the cutter's wife knew they were fooling, and I decided to enlighten her. Waiting till I saw her cook go down in the cellar, I skipped up the dim staircase to the cutter's apartment, and made my way into the kitchen. No one was there, and I went on into the living room, where I saw the cutter's wife at the table. She had a large, gilt cup in one hand, and a book in the other. Startled, she caught the book to her bosom, and cried out in a faint voice, "Who's that? Auguste! Who are you?"

In confused, blurted phrases, I explained why I was there, looking for her book, at any moment, to be flung at my head. She was in a pale blue robe, fringed at the bottom, and with lace trimming on collar and sleeves; and she sat in a raspberry-tinted armchair; and her flaxen hair waved over her shoulders; and she appeared to me like one of heaven's angels. Leaning back in her chair, she first stared at me, with eyes rounded with anger, then bright with smiling astonishment.

My courage spent, I turned to the door, but she stopped me. "Wait a moment."

Putting her cup on the tray and laying the book down on the table, she said in a mature, full voice. "You're a funny lad. Come here."

I edged up to her shyly, and she took my hand and stroked it with her cool, dainty fingers. "Are you sure," she asked, "no one told you to come here with this? No? Very well. It's clearly your own idea."

Letting go of my hand, she said in a low, halting voice, "So that's how the soldiers feel about me."

"Move away from here," I urged her.

"Why?"

"They'll deceive you."

This drew a cheerful laugh from her. "Are you studying? Do you like books?" she asked me.

"I have no time for them."

"If you liked them, you'd make the time. Thank you." And she held a two-greven piece out to me, between her thumb and forefinger. I accepted that cold coin with reluctance, not daring to refuse it; but on my way down, I laid it on the post of the banister.

I brought away from that woman profound new perceptions. I felt myself in the dawn of a new time. For days I lived in the elated memory of the cutter's wife in that spacious chamber, robed and like an angel in pale blue. Everything about her had a touch of exotic loveliness. I recalled the rug of dull gold under her feet. The winter light, through the silvery, frosted panes, seemed to take warmth from her presence. I longed for another sight of her and thought, Supposing I came to her to borrow a book?

I put the thought into action. Once again I saw her in the same room, and with a book in her hand; but her face was bound in a red kerchief and her eyes were swollen; and I could not make out her indistinct words, as she handed me a book bound in black. I left her sadly, with the book, which gave off a mingled tar and licorice odor. I secreted it in the attic, folded first in paper and then in a freshly laundered shirt, for fear of its being found and damaged by my employers.

They were subscribers to the magazine "Neva," [16] for the cut-out patterns and the prize offers; but they never read it. After a glance at the illustrations, they stored the copies in a bedroom cupboard, taking them out at the close of the year to the binder's, and then storing the bound volumes under the bed, where they had company with three previously bound volumes of "The Review of Painting." When I washed the room the slop water lapped around them. The boss also subscribed to "The Russian Courier," which he read, without pleasure, in the evening, muttering, "Why the hell do they publish such junk?"

On Saturday, packing away the linen in the attic, I unwrapped the book. Its first lines were, "Houses are like people; their faces are all their own." I was startled by this truth and I read on, standing at the gable window, until it got too cold. In the evening, when the rest were gone to vespers, I took the book into the kitchen and buried myself in the worn pages, yellow as autumn leaves. I was transported, in a glance, into a new life, where criteria were new, and the very names were new; I was shown exalted heroes and moody villains, utterly unlike the people I lived among.

The book was a novel by Xavier de Montepin, lengthy, like all his novels, congested with action and characters living a strange and intense life. Here everything was remarkably clear and direct, as if good and evil were illuminated by a light glowing between the lines. It took over direction of one's emotions, involving one in the complicated destinies of its characters. I trembled with sudden urges to assist one and foil another, oblivious of the fact that this life suddenly opened to me, had only a paper reality. These absorbing conflicts shut every other thing out of my mind. I was in ecstasy on one page and in despair on the next.

I read on and on until the door bell rang. I knew immediately who was ringing and why. The candle had quite burned down, dripping wax

[16] A popular magazine that took its name from the river that flows through Leningrad—then, St. Petersburg.

all down the candlestick that I had polished that very morning. The lamp had gone out, through my neglecting to adjust the wick. I ran around the kitchen, seeking to cover up the evidence of my crimes. Slipping the book under the oven, I pottered about the lamp. The nursemaid ran in, "Are you deaf? They're ringing."

I hurried to open the door. "Were you sleeping?" the boss asked, testily. Ascending the stairs with dragging steps, his wife whined that the exposure had given her a cold. The old woman scolded. Immediately noticing the burned-down candle, she demanded what I had been doing. Just hauled down from my heights, I was in a panic over their possible discovery of the book. There was danger of my setting the house afire, howled the old woman. When the boss and his wife sat down to dinner, she accused me before them. "Look how he let the candle burn down; he'll set fire to the house!"

Through that dinner I got tongue-lashings from all four of them; all my misdemeanors were reviewed, conscious or unconscious, and my ruin was prophesied. But I was well aware that neither animus on their part, nor concern over my welfare, motivated their scolding. They were merely venting their boredom. And I found it interesting to contrast their vacuous and foolish behavior with that of my literary heroes.

After dinner they became comatose and lumbered wearily to bed. After bothering God with her nagging confidences, the old woman retired to the top of the oven and lay still. Then I rose and pulled the book out of its hiding place and brought it to the window. It was a moonlit night, but not quite light enough to read such fine print. Tormented by the itch to read on, I took a polished brass pan, and held it so that it reflected light from the moon upon the page; but this produced a blur that added to the strain. Then I went to the bench in the icon corner, and standing on it, I began to read by the dim light of the icon lamp. But, overcome with weariness, I dozed and clattered down on the bench. Howls and blows by the old woman roused me. She was thumping me painfully over the shoulders with the book. She was barefoot and had nothing on but her nightgown; and her face was red with fury and her withered head shook.

All I thought of was, "She's found the book; she's going to tear it up."

My inquisition came at breakfast. Harshly, the boss asked me, "Where'd you get that book?"

The women interrupted each other. Victor sniffed it, and made a face. "What on earth is that smell?"

Hearing that the book was the priest's, they gave it another look, shocked at a priest reading novels. Nevertheless, this somewhat calmed them down, though I got a lecture from the boss on the perils and damage one incurred from books. "Readers of books are your train-robbers and murderers."

In angry dismay, his wife interrupted, "Are you crazy? Putting such things in his mind!"

I brought Montepin to Sidorov, and told him my story, and he wrapped the book in a clean towel and hid it in his trunk. "Don't pay any attention to them," he said. "Do your reading here. I'll keep it quiet. And when I'm not here, you'll find the trunk key behind the icon."

My employers' attitude toward the book made my reading a formidable secret in my mind. That readers of books had held up a train, or attempted a murder, did not trouble me; but my mind dwelt on the priest's question about banned books, at the confessional; on the reading I had witnessed by the student in the cellar; on Smoury's talk of the "right books"; and on grandpa's accounts of the black books of the Freemasons.

I had heard him say, "In the time of Tsar Alexander [17] of blessed memory, the nobles began studying the black books of the Freemasons. They meant to turn over the Russian people to the Roman pope, nothing less. But they were caught red-handed by General Arakcheyev; and, no matter what their rank was, he packed them off to Siberia; and there they perished like vermin."

And the "umbra pierced by a star" of Smoury's book came to mind, and Gervase and the grotesque verse, "Inquisitive ones, seeking to profane our secrets, never will your weak eyes penetrate them; never will you hear the music of faery."

I felt on the verge of discovering a great secret and went around like a madman. I was trembling to finish the book and terrified lest the soldier lose it or damage it. What to say to the cutter's wife, in that case?

The old woman kept a sharp eye on me to keep me back from the orderly's room. "Bookworm!" she railed at me. "Books teach corruption. Just look at that woman bookworm. She can't even do her own marketing. But she knows how to carry on with the officers! She has them coming all day. I know!"

[17] The Tsar who reigned at the time of Napoleon's invasion of Russia.

I wanted to shout out, "It's a lie; she doesn't!" But I dared not come to the defense of the cutter's wife; the old woman might guess, then, that the book belonged to her.

For some days I had a harrowing time. In my agitation, fear that Montepin might receive an injury kept me sleepless. Then the woman who cooked for the cutter's family stopped me in the yard to say, "You must return the book."

I picked the hour after the midday meal, when my employers napped. Despondent and embarrassed, I made my appearance before the cutter's wife. She looked as I had seen her at our first acquaintance, except that she had on different clothes. She was in skirt and blouse, the skirt gray, the blouse black velvet. A turquoise cross lay on her bare neck. She made me think of a female finch. When I told her I had been unable to make the time to read the book, and that I was not allowed to read, tears streamed from my eyes. They had a twofold source: my own misery and the bliss of seeing this woman.

"Pugh! What ignorant people!" she said, knitting her charming brows. "And your boss' face looks so interesting! Don't let it worry you. I'll send him a letter."

"You mustn't! Don't write!" I pleaded. "They'll laugh at you and mock you. Don't you realize, they're all against you here? They all laugh at you and call you a fool; and they say you're missing some of your ribs."

The moment I had blurted this out, I was aware I had said a word too much and a humiliating word. She bit her underlip and put her hands to her hips like a horsewoman. I lowered my head in my embarrassment, and wished to sink through the floor; but she flung herself into a chair and laughed and laughed, repeating, "How stupid! How stupid!"

Then, fixing her eyes on me, she said with a sigh, "Well, what do we do? You're a strange lad, very strange."

I stole a glance into the mirror at her side, to inspect a face with high cheekbones, a pug nose, a large welt on the brow, and hair badly in need of cutting, which stuck out in all directions. This was her "strange lad." And this strange lad had not the slightest resemblance to a porcelain figurine.

"You didn't take the money I gave you. Why not?"

"I didn't want it."

She heaved a sigh. "What can we do? Any time you're allowed to read, come here, and I'll let you have books."

On the mantelpiece were three volumes; the one I had just returned was the fattest. I gave it a sad look. The cutter's wife gave me her tiny, rosy hand. "Good-by, then!"

Timidly, I touched her hand and ran out.

So it turned out to be true, as they said, that she didn't know anything. Imagine calling two greven money! She was like a child.

But I liked her for it.

Chapter Nine

FOR CERTAIN LUGUBRIOUS REASONS I WELL REMEMBER THE MORTIFICA-tion, the indignities, the alarms I incurred in the precipitate growth of my literary appetites. The books belonging to the cutter's wife had a costly look, and since I feared their immolation in the oven by the old woman, I did my best to forget them and turned instead to small, paper-bound volumes on sale in the shop where I made my morning purchase of bread.

Its owner was an unhandsome, thick-lipped individual, whose skin was continually agleam with sweat, whose pallid, wrinkled face was sown with eruptions and their scars, whose eyes were white, and whose bloated hands terminated in stubby, clumsy fingers. His place served as a club for the grown men and the flightier girls on our street. It was my boss' brother's hangout for a nightly glass of beer and a hand of cards. Sent there to summon him to supper, I saw him, or some other young gallant, more than once, in the tiny, airless back room, with the shopkeeper's pink, coquettish wife on his knee. The shopkeeper seemed to take no offense, nor did he seem to mind that his sister, who helped tend shop, lavished her caresses on drunken soldiers, or anybody else, for that matter, who suited her whim.

Business was poor, for which the shopkeeper gave the explanation that it was a new venture, although he had actually opened in the fall. His services to his customers included exhibits of pornographic pictures, and permission to copy the salacious rhymes underneath.

I read the trivial little tales by Misha Yevstigneyev at a rental of a kopeck or so apiece. This was high, while the pleasure I got out of them was nil. As also from such literature as *Gouak, or Truth Uncon-querable, The Venetian, The Battle Between the Russians and the Khabardins,* or *The Moslem Beauty Who Died on Her Husband's Grave*—books that, in fact, annoyed me. I felt laughed at, by these books, for my gullibility; their matter was so incredible and their manner so insipid.

More satisfying were such tales as *The Marksman, Yury Miloslavsky, The Mysterious Monk, Yapancha,* and *The Tatar Raider.* Such reading enriched me. But my favorites were the *Lives of the Saints.* These had substance that made them credible, and roused responsive emotions in me. I found resemblances in all the martyrs to Good Idea, and, in the women martyrs, to grandma; and in the hermits to grandpa at his best.

My reading was done in the cold shed, when I went out to split firewood; or in the attic, which I found hardly any warmer or more convenient. When I became absorbed in a book, or had to finish it by a certain time, I would wait till the rest were asleep, and read by candle. Observing the diminution of the candles, the old woman took to measuring them with a piece of wood. And if, in the morning, I had failed to find her measuring rod and notch it to the burned-down length, her outcries would ring through the kitchen.

Once Victor stormed at her, "Cut out that yelling, mama. Sure—he uses up the candles reading books. I know where he gets them—in the store. You'll find them in his stuff in the attic."

Up to the attic the old woman leaped, hunted out a book, and burned it. As you can well understand, this made me furious, but only sharpened my appetite. I realized that if a saint strayed into that household, my employers would have gone to work on him, to tune him to their own key. And the attempt would be made just to give themselves something to do. Had they stopped making judgments on people, nagging them, deriding them, they would have lost the faculty of speech, become mutes, been themselves no longer. One becomes conscious of himself through his contacts with others. No relationship with others was possible to my employers, except that of censorious mentors. Had they educated somebody to their identical way of living, feeling, thinking, then they would have reproached him for that. That was the sort they were.

I kept up my secret reading. This meant the annihilation of several books at the hands of the old woman and I found myself the shopkeeper's debtor for the staggering sum of forty-seven kopecks. He demanded it from me, threatening to withhold it when he made change for me on purchases I made for my employers. "What'll you do then?" he scoffed.

I found him intolerably coarse. He knew it, and retaliated by tormenting me with his threats. He greeted me with a broad leer on his pustular face and the bland inquiry, "Have you come to settle your debt?"

"I can't."

He appeared startled, and frowned. "How come? Are you looking for charity from me? I see I'll have to get my money by fixing up a trip to the reformatory for you."

There was no way I could put my hands on the money, my wages being turned over to grandpa. I got into a panic. What was to become of me? To my pleas for more time, the storekeeper replied by stretching out his greasy, bladder-like hand and saying, "I'll wait if you'll kiss my hand."

Instead, I picked up a weight from the counter and aimed it at his head. He ducked and yelled, "What's the matter? I was only fooling!"

I knew very well he wasn't fooling, and to be quit of him, I decided to steal that sum.

Brushing the boss' clothes in the morning, I heard coins jingling in the trouser pockets, and some, at times, fell out and rolled over the floor. Once two had rolled under the staircase, which I forgot about. Finding them several days later, I had given them back to the boss, and his wife had remarked, "See! Better count the money you leave in your pockets."

With a smile at me he had replied, "I know he won't steal."

Having decided to steal, the recollection of these words and his confiding smile made it hard for me. Several times I took coins out of his pocket, counted them, and then put them back. For three days I kept torturing myself this way, when the problem was solved for me, simply and at once.

The boss surprised me by asking, "What's wrong with you, Peshkov? You've grown so listless, lately. Don't you feel well, or what?"

I gave him a candid report of what was on my mind. Frowning, he said, "See what your books have gotten you into? Sooner or later books are bound to get people into trouble."

He gave me a half a ruble, cautioning me, "Look, you, not a word about this to my wife or my mother, or there'll be a scandal." With a kind smile, he added, "The devil, but you're persistent! And that's good. Just the same, no books. Come New Year, I'll subscribe to a good journal, so there'll be reading for you."

Thereafter, between tea and late supper, I read aloud to my employers from "The Moscow Leaf," read them installments of novels by Bashkov, Rokshanin, Rudinkovsky, and other literary pap written to enliven people out of their deadly boredom.

I did not enjoy reading aloud, because it kept me from following what I was reading. But my employers were a good audience, paying rapt attention, heaving sighs and congratulating each other, "We lead such decent, peaceful lives, thank God; such things are beyond us!"

Nevertheless, they got everything mixed up, confused the characters' names and had the coachman, Foma Kruchin, performing the feats of the notorious bandit, Churkin. When I set them straight, they expressed surprise. "What a memory that boy has!"

From time to time "The Moscow Leaf" carried poems by Leonid Grav. I was impressed by them, and copied some of them down. My employers' comment was, "He's got very old, you know, so he writes verses. He's a rummy or a half-wit, doesn't matter which."

I also enjoyed the verses of Struzhkin and Count Memento Mori, but the two women found them clumsy, and besides, "Only clowns and actors talk in poetry!"

I found life a trial, those winter evenings in that stuffy room, with my employers' eyes on me all night long. Night lay like a corpse outside the window. Now and then there would sound the crack of frost. They sat around the table dumb as fish in ice. We heard the snowstorm rattle the windows, pound on the walls and scream down the chimney flues, making the valve clatter. From the nursery came the wail of the children. I had a longing for a corner of my own, where I could howl away like a wolf.

At one corner of the table sat the women with their sewing or knitting. At the other end sat Victor, bent over, reluctantly copying plans, and crying out, now and then, "Stop shaking the table; there's no living here! Goat hooves! Dogs after mice!"

Off to a side sat the boss at a huge embroidery frame, cross-stitching a table cloth. From his fingers grew red lobsters, blue fish, yellow butterflies and russet autumn leaves. It was his own design, and this was his third winter at it. He had wearied of it and, on afternoons, when he saw me with time on my hands, he would say, "Hey, Peshkov, come do a bit of the tablecloth."

I'd get to work at once with the thick needle. I was glad to help the boss, for whom I felt sorry. I had a notion that someday he would quit his drafting table, his embroidery frame, his card games, and turn to something else, something that really interested him, something that I could see came to his mind, and made him drop his work as he gazed at it inwardly, as at something strange. At such moments, with his lank hair dripping over forehead and cheeks, he had the appearance of a neophyte in a monastery.

Then would come the question, "What are you thinking about?" from his wife, and he would resume his work, answering, "Nothing special."

Such a question stunned me. Imagine asking anyone to give an account of his thoughts. There was no answering such a question. One's thoughts were so manifold and evanescent; they speculated on the present; and reviewed the past, yesterday or the year before. They were all so inextricably fused, so fleeting, in such constant flux and ferment.

The installment in "The Moscow Leaf" was not enough to fill the evening, and I dipped into the magazines under the bed. The boss' wife inquired, "What's there to read in them? They're all pictures."

But alongside "The Review of Painting" lay, also, the magazine, "Flames," in which we read *Count Tyatin-Baltisky*, by Salias. The boss took quite a liking to its ludicrous hero, laughing over his misadventures until his tears rained down, and shouting, "Now, that's really funny!"

To prove that she had a mind of her own, his wife exclaimed, "Nonsense!"

That library under the bed was a great help to me. It secured me the right to read in the kitchen, and thus to read at night. Once, to my joy, the old woman slept in the nursery, substituting for the drunken nursemaid. Victor did not bother me, for when the rest were asleep, he put on his clothes, slipped out, and didn't get back till morning. No candle was allotted to me; the others took theirs with them; and I had no means to buy any of my own. So I secretly collected scrapings of tallow from the candlesticks, placed them in a can, mixed in some lamp oil, fashioned a wick out of cotton thread, and thus contrived a small, sooty flame. I put this light on the oven.

Turning the pages of the thick tomes made the little red tongue of fire flicker, and the wick submerge in the charring, malodorous grease, while the smoke irritated my eyes. But all these discomforts were forgotten in the pleasure I got in the pictures and their captions. They placed in my ken a world which widened every day, a world splendid like the cities of romance. They brought me views of lofty peaks and lovely beaches. Life unfolded its marvels; earth became more enchanting, studded with towns and laden with treasures.

When I now peered into the reaches beyond the Volga, it was no longer empty space I saw, such as formerly had made me feel strangely lost. Then the meadows had appeared prostrate; then the bushes had been untidy clumps; and then, where the meadows had given way to the woods, the forest had reared its forbidding, jagged wall. And above the meadows the sky had been a stark, cold blue. All in all the earth had seemed lonely and barren, and had had its reflection in my barren heart, bruised by melancholy and emptied of desire. I had thought of nothing and wanted nothing, except to shut it all out. This vacuous melancholia had nothing to offer me, and sucked my heart dry.

But now, in ways that I could comprehend, I learned, through the captions, about different lands and peoples; I learned of great events, historical and contemporary. Yet, much of it still remained incomprehensible and I was troubled. Strange words lodged in my brain, "metaphysics," "chiliasm," "chartist." My anxiety enlarged them into monsters that obscured my view, preventing me from ever understanding anything. I could not work out their meanings; to me they were sentries barring my access to secret knowledge. In some cases phrases were driven into my mind, like splinters into my skin, making awareness of anything else impossible.

I recall these exotic lines: "Sheathed in steel, through the ravaged land, silent and somber, rides Attila, Tsar of the Huns; behind him the dark press of his warriors, calling, 'Where lies Rome, where lies Rome, the Mighty!'"

I knew Rome was a city, but who the devil were the Huns? I burned to find out.

In what I thought was a favorable moment, I asked my boss.

"The Huns?" he asked, startled. "Devil knows. Rubbishy folk, I suppose." And with a gesture of disapproval, he went on, "That head of yours is filling up with junk. That's bad, Peshkov."

Bad or not, I had to know. The regimental chaplain, Soloviev, occurred to me as a possible authority on Huns, and the next time I ran across him in the yard, I asked. That pallid, ailing, eternally grouchy man, who had a yellow beard and no perceptible brows over his red eyes, prodded his black staff into the ground and said, "What's that to you!" Lieutenant Nesterov's reply was also an irascible, "What!"

I decided that perhaps the man to ask was the druggist, who gave me

friendly looks, had a wise face, and gold-rimmed spectacles astride his
big nose.

"The Huns," the druggist told me, "were nomads, like the Kirghiz,
but there are none of them left. They died out."

And this exasperated me and made me sad, not because the Huns
had died out, but because the word that had so baffled me had turned
out to be quite commonplace and useless to me. But I was grateful to
the Huns, now that I was no longer troubled when confronted with the
word; and to Attila; through them I became acquainted with Goldberg,
the druggist.

This man could define profound words, had keys to everything know-
able. Adjusting his glasses between thumb and forefinger the better to
focus on my eyes, he drove in ideas as if he were hammering tacks into
my head. "Words, my lad, are like leaves. To discover why they are
shaped this way and not that, we must study the growth of the tree. To
understand words, my lad, we must know books. Man can be a flourishing garden where every plant is both pleasing and useful."

I was often sent to the drug store for magnesia for the adults, who
were afflicted with heartburn, and castor oil and other laxatives for the
children.

The clerk's capsule-lectures deepened my interest in books, which in
time became as essential to me as alcohol to a toper. They gave me a
view of a new life, which exalted the emotions and impulses that led
people to heroic feats and crimes. The people I lived among were clearly
neither potential heroes nor criminals. They led an existence unrelated
to anything I encountered in books; and I found it hard to imagine
how they endured their dull lives. I had no wish to lead such a life; in
fact, I was determined not to.

From the captions under the illustrations, I had discovered that
Prague, London and Paris had no open sewers in the central districts, no
gullies used as dumps. Streets were straight and broad, and houses and
churches had, each, an individuality of its own. There, no six-month
winter imprisoned people in their dwellings; and no long Lenten season
limited people to a diet of fermenting cabbage, pickled mushrooms,
oatmeal, and potatoes fried in nauseating vegetable oils.

During Lent reading is tabooed; so I was denied "The Review of
Painting," and that paltry, arid life reclaimed possession of me. With
the life portrayed in books as a contrast, its ugliness and meagreness
became more pronounced than ever. With something to read I felt fit
and strong; I did my work briskly and well, and had something to an-

ticipate. The quicker I got done, the more time I had for reading. Without my books I became apathetic and forgetful, which I had never been before.

But the somnolence of those days, I recall, was broken by a mystifying event. One night when we were all in bed, the cathedral bell suddenly began to toll, waking everybody. There was a rush of half-dressed people to the windows, a buzz of questions, "Is it an alarm? Is there a fire?"

The same scurry was audible in other apartments. Then doors slammed, and we heard a saddled horse being led across the yard. The old woman screamed that the cathedral had been robbed, but the boss quieted her, "Pipe down, mama; can't you recognize it's not the alarm bell?"

"The archbishop must have died."

Victor came down from his garret room, put on his clothes, and bragged, "I know what's the matter; I know."

The boss sent me up to the garret to see if the sky was red. I got to the roof by way of the gable window. No red glow in the sky. The slow tolling went on in the still, frosty air. The town looked sprawled, in its sleep. Unseen people could be heard in the dark streets, the snow crunching under their boots. The screech of sleigh runners cut through the portentous wailing of the bells.

I returned to the living room to report, "There's no light in the sky."

"Pugh! What, then!" exclaimed the boss, who was in his overcoat and cap. He raised his collar, and gingerly began working his feet into his galoshes.

His wife begged, "Don't go out; don't go out!"

"Ridiculous!"

Victor, also dressed, kept teasing, "I know what's the matter."

After the brothers had left, the women rushed to the window, after sending me to start the samovar. But, almost immediately, the doorbell rang, and the boss ran up the stairs in silence, shut the door, then said in a choked voice, "The Tsar's been assassinated!"

"Assassinated? How?" exclaimed the old woman.

"He's been assassinated. I was told by an officer. What's to happen now?"

Victor came in, reluctantly pulled off his coat, and said crossly, "I was sure it was a war!"

Then they sat down to tea and a discussion of the event, in controlled, but low and uneasy, tones. The streets were now quiet, and the bells had stopped.

So, for a couple of days, there was a running about and a mystified whispering all around. Visitors came to enlarge on some new item. I did all I could to understand what had occurred, but newspapers were kept from me, and when I asked Sidorov why they had killed the Tsar, he answered warily, "Speaking about it is prohibited."

But the excitement wore off. The customary vacuity returned to this life, and the next break was a highly disagreeable experience.

On a Sunday, when the adults were all in church, I started the samovar, and went to tidy up the other rooms. While I was in another room, the older child got into the kitchen, managed to unscrew the faucet of the samovar, and took it to play with under the table. The charcoal in the samovar was blazing; and, as the water drained out of the open vent, the metal began to overheat, and the solder that joined the separate parts melted. All this produced strange sounds which I heard from the other room. Running into the kitchen, I was dismayed to see the samovar roasted to a blue color, and shaking as if about to jump. The dismantled faucet hung down as though in misery; the lid had heeled over; and the molten pewter was streaming down, drop by drop. All in all the now purplish-blue samovar seemed to be in a drunken delirium. When I poured water over it, it collapsed with a sorrowful hiss, in ruins.

The doorbell rang. My employers were back, and I let them in. In reply to the old woman's question, "Is the samovar ready?" I repeated dumbly, "Yes, it's ready."

This, which was said in confusion and fright, was taken as an impertinence. It brought me a double measure of punishment, that half-killed me. The old woman laid on with a bundle of pine twigs which, though it didn't hurt very much, drove many splinters under my skin. By nightfall, my back had swollen like a pillow, and by the following noon the boss had to take me to the hospital.

On examining me, the rather ludicrously tall and cadaverous doctor said, in a flat, even tone, "Here's a case of cruelty; it calls for investigation."

My boss grew red, and whispered something to the doctor, who looked away and said, "Impossible; can't be done."

Then he asked me, "Do you want to enter a complaint?"

Though I was suffering intense pain, I said, "No; just hurry up and cure me."

I was carried to another room, stretched out on a table, and the doctor pulled out the splinters with tweezers, whose chill touch felt pleasant. "They've adorned your skin artistically, my friend; they've waterproofed you." And when he was through with his ruthless gouging, he said, "Forty-two splinters have been removed, my friend. It's something to remember, a record of a sort! Come back tomorrow, same time, to have the dressing changed. Do they beat you much?"

"Not as much as before."

His comment was a harsh laugh, and, "It'll work out for the best; it's all right."

He brought me back to the boss, to whom he said, "I turn him back to you, repaired. But be sure to have him here tomorrow. You're lucky; quite a comedian you got there!"

In the cab my boss told me, "They used to beat me, too, Peshkov, imagine that! What beatings I got, boy! And you have me to sympathize with you, while I had nobody, not a soul. People are hard on one another, everywhere; no sympathy anywhere. Ekh, wild geese!"

He went on that way. I felt a deep sympathy for him, and gratitude for his treating me as man to man.

I was welcomed back in the house as if it were my birthday. The women had to hear all the details of the treatment, and everything the doctor had said. They were all attention; they sighed; their faces emoted; they covered me with kisses. Such close interest in sicknesses, in aches and pains, in miseries of all sorts, has always puzzled me.

Seeing they were touched by my not having lodged a complaint against them, I took advantage of it to ask permission to borrow books from the cutter's wife. They didn't have the heart to say no, though the old woman fumed, "What a demon he is!"

The following day I visited the cutter's wife, who told me, "I heard you were sick and in the hospital; look what tales they spread!"

I said nothing, too embarrassed to let her know the truth. Why should she hear of such brutalities? I liked to think of her as different from the rest.

Again I was engrossed in fat tomes by Dumas père, Ponson de Teraille, Montepin, Zaconne, Gaboriau, Emar, and Bouagobert. With voracious haste I consumed them, one after another, and was blissful. I felt myself a participant in a life above the ordinary, which animated me and pricked up my courage. Again, by my makeshift light, I read on through the night, till my eyes showed the strain. The old woman cautioned me, but in a kindly manner, "Watch out, bookworm, or you'll ruin your eyes and go blind!"

I soon became aware, however, that all these entertaining and subtle books, despite their variety of incident and diversity of settings, told much the same story, how good people were abused and hurt by evil people who were cleverer than they, and managed better; yet, in the end, through some sudden turn, they overcame the evil ones and emerged the victors. The "love" on which heroes and the heroines both dilated, I found a bore. In fact, I found it somewhat silly, as well as dull.

My speculations as to who would come out on top and who on the bottom, often began in the opening chapters; as the plot took shape, I began to figure it out on my own. Even away from the books themselves, I had their plots in my mind, and kept working them out as if they were arithmetic puzzlers. Every day I acquired greater skill in forecasting who would be admitted into the paradise of the happy ending and who would be cast into the outer darkness.

Through all this welter, nevertheless, I glimpsed vital and momentous truths, shapes of another life, other criteria. It became evident to me that cabmen, workers, soldiers, and the rest of the "black people" [18] were very different from their counterparts in Nizhny, Kazan or Perm. They did not hesitate to speak to people of the upper classes, and conducted themselves toward them in a more direct and independent manner than did our folk. For example, here was a soldier who resembled none whom I knew, not Sidorov, nor the Viatkin I had met on the boat, and least of all, Yermokhin. There was more human dignity in him than in any of them. He was something like Smoury, but less rude and wild. Here, too, was a storekeeper, but a finer sort than any known to me. And the priests in the books were unlike those I knew, more sensitive, more deeply involved in the fates of their flock. All in all, life abroad, as reflected in the books, appeared more stimulating, more comfortable, and more decent than here. There, people were not so cruel; they never baited a human being as pitilessly as the soldier from Viatka had been, nor did they badger God with their prayers as did the old woman. Above all, I observed that, as portrayed in these books, even brutes, skinflints and other villains did not display the mystifying heartlessness, the derision of man, which I, myself, knew here, and which so frequently caught my attention. The cruelties of these literary villains were calculated; almost always one could see why they behaved so. But the cruelties inflicted here were inflicted without purpose, were entirely irrational; no one gained anything from them.

Every volume I read accentuated this disparity between Russian life

[18] An idiomatic Russian term for the masses.

and that of other countries, producing a mixture of annoyance and confusion in me, and leading me to suspect the truth of these pored-over
pages with their grimy "dogs' ears."

And then I came upon Edmond Goncourt's novel, *The Brothers
Zemganno.* I read it through at a sitting, and startled by that, I reread
that simple, unhappy story. There were no plot complications, nothing
arresting in it. Indeed, the opening pages seemed stiff, rather like the
Lives of the Saints. At the beginning, the diction, so precise, so devoid
of ornament, disappointed me; but soon the spare words, the solidly-
worked phrases, impressed me. The fate of the acrobat brothers was
described so feelingly, that my hands throbbed with sympathy during
the reading. Through tears I read how the ill-fated artist crawled, on his
broken legs, to the garret where his brother was secretly practicing new
turns.

When I brought this magnificent book back to the cutter's wife, I
requested another, just like it. "What do you mean, just like it?" she
asked with a laugh. Confused by her laugh, I couldn't express my wishes.
Then she said, "That's a dry story. Wait! I'll get one for you that's
more interesting."

And a day or two later she gave me Greenwood's *The True History
of a Little Waif.* The title prejudiced me against it; however, the very
first pages evoked rapturous smiles from me; and I smiled on, to the
end, rereading some pages several times.

So there were other lands where boys led hard and harassed lives!
Then my lot was not so miserable; no need to pity myself. I took heart
from Greenwood.

Soon afterwards, I got a "real" book to read, *Eugenie Grandet.* Old
Grandet brought grandpa vividly to mind. I was exasperated at the
brevity of the book, and amazed how much truth it held. Truths, familiar enough to me, and boring enough in life, now took on other
aspects, as they were seen objectively and without anger. The books I
had read before I got to Greenwood, damned people as mercilessly and
garrulously as my employers, frequently provoking me into sympathy
with the villain and annoyance with the heroes. And I always somewhat
regretted to see so much wit and resolution go to waste, as the villains
were frustrated. The heroes, immobile as stone columns, waited, from
first page to last, for events to take their course; and, though one beheld
these stone columns, beset by plotters of every evil, stones do not stir
up the emotions. The grace and solidity of a wall has no appeal to him
who wants the apple hanging on the tree, on its other side. It appears to

me that that which is most desirable and vital has always been pushed, by the "good people," into the background.

Goncourt's, Greenwood's and Balzac's people were no villains, but wonderfully living people. One never questioned anything they were reported to have said and done; nothing else could have been said and done by them. Thus I discovered what joy is to be found in a "proper" book. But how to search it out? There the cutter's wife was not much help.

"Here's a good one," she said, offering me Arsene Huissier's *Hands Filled with Roses, Gold and Blood*. She also introduced me to the novels of Henri Beyle,[19] Paul de Kock and Paul Feval, which I relished; but she recommended those of Marietta and Vernier, which I found dull. Schpielhagen did not appeal to me, but Auerbach did; and I preferred Walter Scott to Victor Hugo and Eugene Sue. I sought books which elated me as did my marvelous Balzac.

My feeling for the porcelain woman cooled down. On my visits to her I wore a fresh blouse, combed my hair, and tried to look handsome, but with little success. A better appearance, I hoped, would induce her to more natural and friendly speech and behavior toward me, and some other expression than that blank, fish-smile on her frivolous face. But all I got was that smile and that inevitable question in her sugary, limp voice, "You read it? How did you like it?"

"Not much."

With raised eyebrows, she gave me a stare, then, with an indrawn breath that made her talk through her nose, she asked, "Why?"

"I've read all about that."

"About what?"

"About love."

Her eyes sparkled as she gave her syrupy laugh. "But don't you understand every book is about love?"

She sat in her spacious armchair, her little swinging feet slippered in fur, her blue robe wrapped around her. As she yawned and tapped her pink fingertips on the book on her knee, I wanted to tell her, "Better move away! The officers keep writing you letters and making fun of you."

But I did not dare, and I went off with a tome on *Love*, disenchantment saddening my heart.

The yard gossip about this woman had increased in vileness, venom and spite. I took offense at the obscene talk, which I was sure was all

19 Stendhal.

fabrication. Away from her, I was all sympathy for her; but in her presence, observing her small, quick eyes, her catlike suppleness, and the always frivolous expression on her face, my sympathy and my concern for her evaporated.

Suddenly, in the spring, she disappeared; and a few days later, her husband moved away.

Before the advent of a new tenant, I visited the vacant rooms, looked at the bare walls and the nail scars. Bits of colored cloth, crumpled balls of paper, broken drug boxes and empty perfume bottles littered the dirty floor. Among them glittered a big brass pin.

And, all of a sudden, I had a twinge of regret and a desire to see the cutter's little wife a last time, and give her my thanks.

Chapter Ten

BEFORE THE DISAPPEARANCE OF THE CUTTER'S WIFE, THERE MOVED INTO the apartment below us a dark-eyed young lady, her young daughter, and her gray-haired mother, a chain smoker, equipped with an amber mouthpiece. The young lady was beautiful and proud, and her voice was deep and melodious. Her head was held high and her eyes were unwavering, as if she saw everybody from a distance. On most days her swarthy soldier-servant, Tufayev, led a fine-legged, brown horse to the door; and out strode the lady in a sweeping, velvet dress, steel-gray in color, her feet shod in tan riding boots, and her hands gloved in white gauntlets. In one hand she held the train of her skirt and a riding crop, with a lilac-colored gem set into the handle; with the other she petted the muzzle of the horse, who fixed his enormous eyes on her, quivered, and deliberately pawed the muddy ground with his hooves.

"Robert, Robert," she murmured (giving it the French pronunciation, *Robaire*), and stroked his handsome, arched neck with a strong hand. Then, using Tufayev's knee as a step, she vaulted deftly into the saddle, and with a proud bearing, the horse pranced through the gate. Her seat in the saddle had such ease, she might have grown from it. She had that individual type of beauty that is always fresh, and always astonishes and jubilantly intoxicates the heart. The sight of her made me think that Diane of Poitiers, Queen Margot, the young La Valliere, and other storied beauties must have been like her.

In constant attendance upon her were the officers of the local garrison division. In the evenings these visitors played the piano, the violin or the guitar, and sang and danced. Her most frequent guest was fat, gray-haired, red-faced Major Olesov, whose greasiness made me think of a steamboat engineer. He kept circling her on his stumpy legs. He was good on the guitar. And he acted up to her as the devoted, all-suffering swain.

As radiantly lovely as her mother was her plump, curly-haired five-year-old daughter. Her big, dark blue eyes looked about her with serene expectancy; she had a thoughtful air that made her seem not quite a child. The housekeeping took up all her grandmother's time, though she had the help of Tufayev, who was close-mouthed and gloomy, and a maid who was fat and crosseyed. There was no nursemaid, and the little girl was quite neglected, getting almost no adult attention. She played all day on the doorsteps, or on a pile of boards nearby. I took a liking to her, and often, toward dark, I went out and played with her. Soon she got so used to me she would fall asleep in my arms, as I told her stories, after which I carried her in to bed. In time she refused to go to sleep until I bid her good night. Holding out her chubby hand with quite an air, she would say, "Good-by, see you tomorrow. Grandma, what do I say next?"

"God keep you," recited the grandmother, puffs of dark blue smoke issuing from her mouth and bony nose.

"God keep you till tomorrow! And now I'm going to sleep," said the child, rolling up in the lace-trimmed bedclothes.

"Not till tomorrow, but always," corrected her grandmother.

"But tomorrow means always, doesn't it?"

She was in love with the word "tomorrow," reserving for it everything that delighted her. She would stick the stems of cut flowers or branches blown down by the wind into the ground, asserting, "Tomorrow it will be a garden." "Tomorrow I'll buy myself a horse and ride on his back like mama."

Though she was clever, she was not an active child. Often some passing thought would stop her in the midst of a lively game; or she would break off to surprise me with some question, like, "Why is a priest's hair long like a woman's?"

If she pricked her hand on a thorn, she would shake her fingers at it and say, "You'll see! I'll pray to God to do something very, very bad to you. God can do very bad things to anybody. He can punish mama, too."

At times, a gentle, grave mood would settle upon her; she would snuggle close to me, look up into the sky with her confiding, blue eyes and tell me, "Grandma gets mad sometimes, but not mama; because mama only laughs. Everybody loves her because she's too busy. She's so beautiful people come to look at her. Mama is so attractive, that's what Joseph says."

I enjoyed her prattle, because it echoed a world of which I knew nothing. She spoke very freely about her mother, and a new vista of life stretched before me. It brought Queen Margot back to mind, which confirmed my faith in books, and intensified my interest in life.

Once, sitting on the steps outside, waiting for my folks to return from a walk, the child dozed off in my arms, and her mother, back from a canter, lightly dismounted, gave a toss of her head, and asked, "Is she sleeping?"

"Yes."

"Good."

The soldier, Tufayev, dashed up, and led the horse away. She stuck her riding crop into her belt, said, "Let me have her," and reached out her arms.

"Let me carry her in."

"Hey, there!" the lady burst out at me, as though to her horse; and she stamped her foot on the step. This woke the little girl who, seeing her mother through her fluttering lashes, reached out her arms to her.

Accustomed though I was to being shouted at, I would rather not have had it from this lady. No matter how quietly given, one jumped to any command of hers.

A minute or two later, their crosseyed maid came out to me. The little girl was being stubborn; she wouldn't go to bed without bidding me good night. I could not avoid some cockiness when I approached her mother, who had the little girl on her knees, and was undressing her with swift, capable hands.

"He's here, that monster," she said.

"He's my boy, not a monster."

"Is that so? That's good. You'd like to give your boy something wouldn't you?"

"Yes, I would."

"That's a good idea. We'll take care of it; and now to bed."

"Good-by till tomorrow," the little girl said, giving me her hand. "God keep you till tomorrow."

"Who taught you that, grandma?" exclaimed the lady, startled.

"Yes."

When the child had gone to her room the lady called me over. "What would you like?"

I told her I wanted nothing, but would like to borrow a book.

She chucked my chin with her warm, perfumed fingers, smiled agreeably, and said, "So you like books? What have you read?"

The smile made her look still more dazzling, and in my confusion, I rambled off some titles.

"What did you see in them?" she asked, lightly tapping on the table with her fingers.

A heavy flower scent of some sort, overlaying a smell of horse sweat, came from her. She gazed at me through long eyelashes, in a penetrating, thoughtful look, such as I could not remember having got from anybody before.

The room was stuffed as full as a bird's nest with lovely, upholstered furniture. Heavy green drapes covered the windows. A pale luster, in that dim light, came from the snow-white tiles of the oven, a black luster gleamed from the piano nearby. From the walls, framed in dull gold, peered dark scrolls in large Russian script, with a big seal, suspended by a cord, from each. The very things around her seemed to share my diffidence and submission to her.

To the best of my ability, I explained how reading helped me through the darkness and drudgery of my life.

"So that's it," she said, rising. "Not a bad notion; indeed, it's a bit of all right. What to do? I'll get you some books; but right now I have none around. Just a second; take this one."

She picked up a battered, yellow-covered volume off the couch. "When you've finished this I'll give you the second volume; it's in four volumes."

I went off with Prince Meshchersky's *Petersburg Secrets*, which I started with avid interest. Before I had turned many pages, however, I realized that Petersburg's secrets interested me far less than those of London, Paris or Madrid. The only thing I took a fancy to was the dispute between *Svoboda* (freedom) and *Palka* (cane):

Svoboda asserted, "I'm your superior; I have the brains."

Palka retorted, "No, I'm your superior; I have the power."

The dispute ended in a fight, with *Palka* the victor. If my memory serves me, *Svoboda* had to be taken to the hospital, where she died of her injuries.

There were references to Nihilists in the book. To Prince Meshchersky, as I recall, a Nihilist was such a venomous character that his very glance was enough to poison a chicken. I found the comments on the Nihilists offensively coarse, but that was all that I understood, which upset me. Apparently I could not respond to good books, as I believed this one to be, since I could not conceive of so grand and beautiful a lady reading poor ones.

"Did you enjoy it?" she asked, when I returned Meshchersky's yellow book.

It was a strain to admit to her that I hadn't, for fear that she might take offense; but she merely laughed and, parting the portieres which curtained off her bedroom, she picked up a small volume in a dark blue, morocco binding.

"You'll enjoy this one," she said, "but be careful; don't soil it."

It was a collection of Pushkin's poems. I read them through in a rush, greedily drinking them in as if I had come upon some breathtaking new scene, in whose every corner I tried to be at once. It was as if, after toiling across mossy footholds in a bog, one were suddenly to see spread before him a sunny, flower-decked meadow over which, after a fascinated glance, he gambols blissfully, feeling a pulsation of joy at every touch of his foot on the resilient herbage.

The melody and the spontaneity of poetry, as I found it in Pushkin, so overwhelmed me that for long afterwards, prose seemed artificial beside it, and hard to read. The Ruslan [20] prologue recalled grandma's choicest tales, all packed into one; and some lines stunned me with their ringing truth: "There on barely visible trails, glide the invisible creatures of the wild."

Repeating these thrilling phrases to myself recalled those trails I had learned to see, that were invisible to others. I saw the obscure footprints upon the trampled grass, on which gleamed still unshed dewdrops, heavy as mercury. The round, resonant lines were easy to remember. What they spoke of took on luster as if adorned for a fête. They brought gaiety and ease into my life. Like chimes the verses rang in a new day for me. What a joy it was to have learning!

Pushkin's wonderful tales touched me more intimately, and I understood them better, than all I had read hitherto. After several rereadings, I knew them by heart; on going to bed, I repeated the lines under my breath, till sleep overcame me. I told the tales to the orderlies, who listened, laughed and kidded me about them. But Sidorov patted my head and murmured, "That's something, now, isn't it? Oh, God——"

[20] A narrative poem by Pushkin.

My employers took note of the new sense of life that I felt. The old woman scolded, "You read too much; the samovar's not been cleaned these last four days. You young ape, I'll have to get out the rolling pin for you!"

The rolling pin? Who cared? I had the verses for sanctuary. "Hag, you have given your heart to the devil!"

My esteem for the lady mounted, since such were the books she read. She was different from the cutter's little porcelain wife.

When, regretfully, I returned the book, the lady asked, in a manner that encouraged confidences, "Did you enjoy it? Have you heard about Pushkin?"

I had seen something about Pushkin in a newspaper, but, desiring to have her comment, I said, "Never." So she gave me a brief account of Pushkin's life and death,[21] and, with a smile like a day in spring, she concluded, "See the danger of loving a woman?"

What I had read had all illustrated the dangers, but also the raptures, of love, so I replied, "There's danger; but everybody falls in love, just the same; and women suffer for it, too."

She gave me one of her characteristic looks, under her lashes, and said earnestly, "You believe that? You understand it? The best thing I can wish you is to have it always in mind." And she asked which verses were my favorites.

I declaimed some from memory, with sweeping gestures. After listening in grave silence, she rose, paced about the room, and said soberly, "We must see that this wild one gets some education, I must give it some thought. Your employers—are they your relations?"

Hearing me answer, "Yes," she exclaimed, "Oh!" at me, as if I were to blame.

She lent me the *Songs of Beranger*, in a de luxe edition, illustrated, gilt-edged and bound in red leather. The odd blend of inconsolable grief and lusty gaiety in these lyrics made me a little dizzy.

It was with an icy clench at the heart that I read the sardonic challenge in the "Old Beggar":

> "Do I, the homeless worm, intrude? Then step on me; squash me! Why take pity on me? Quick, down with your crushing heel! Why did you never teach me, never provide scope for my powers; then from the worm might have come an ant; dying, I would have been content in the love of com-

[21] Pushkin was killed in a duel with an admirer of his wife.

rades. Instead, in my death, an old beggar takes a small vengeance on the world."

And immediately after, I laughed until the tears came, over "The
Weeping Husband." I particularly recall the lines: "To the simple it is
simple to master the science of a happy life."

Beranger put me into a cheerful, cocky mood, in which I dared to
be pert and even uncivil to people, to make rude and cutting remarks.
Skill in such accomplishments came quickly to me. I learned Beranger's
stanzas by heart, too, and I liked to declaim them to the orderlies, when
they dropped into the kitchen. But not for long. The lines, "But such
a hat's unsuitable to a maid of seventeen," turned the conversation to
such ribaldry on the subject of young girls, that I was provoked into
laying a saucepan over Yermokhin's head. I was delivered out of his
clumsy grip by Sidorov and the other orderlies; but from then on, I
resolved to stay away from the officers' kitchen.

Any gadding about in the street was forbidden me; and, in any case,
I lacked the time, my work had so piled up. To my chores as household
drudge, porter and errand-boy, had been added the preparation of frames
—calico nailed to boards—on which plans were tacked, copying down
my boss' architectural data, and checking his accounts with contractors.
My busy boss was at it into the night, working incessantly, like a machine.

In those days the structures of the annual Nizhny-Novgorod Fair were
in private hands. The rows of booths were put up in haste. My boss had
contracts for both reconstruction and new construction. He made plans
for altering vaults, building out gable windows, and so on. I took my
boss' plans to an elderly architect; secreted in the large envelope in
which the plans were enclosed, were twenty-five rubles in bills. He pock-
eted the money, and then signed the plans, "Tested and approved after
inspection at the site. Imiarek." Actually, he inspected nothing, being
confined indoors by his infirmity.

I brought bribes, also, to the Inspector of the Fair, and to other big
shots from whom I acquired what the boss termed, "documents," au-
thorizing certain building violations. For all this I earned the privilege
of sitting on the doorstep, waiting for the return of my employers from
a visit. The visits were infrequent, but when they occurred, they lasted
past midnight. From my seat on the top step, or on the stacked lumber
opposite, I looked up for hours into the windows of the lady's apartment, hungrily absorbing the music and the merry talk.

Through the curtains and the flowers that hedged the open window, I could see the handsome figures of the officers, the round major rolling, and she gliding about in a beautiful, but markedly simple, dress. To myself, I had named her Queen Margot, and thought, staring into the windows: This is the high life described in the French novels. And I felt melancholy as I succumbed to the pangs of a childish jealousy, watching the men swarm about her like bees around a flower.

The rarest of her visitors was a tall, moody-looking officer, whose eyes were sunken deep under worried brows. He always brought along a violin, which he played so ravishingly that passersby stopped to listen, joining the people from our street already crowding under the window. My employers, too, if they were home, would open their windows to hear it and praise it. I cannot recall their having praised any other person, unless it was the deacon's assistant at the cathedral; and a fish patty, I knew, excited them more than any music.

At other times this officer sang or recited poems to her, with his hand to his brow, and his voice choking with sighs. Once I was with the little girl under their window, when I heard Queen Margot coaxing him to sing, and he reiterated his refusals. He ended it with these lines, spoken in a distinct voice: "A song has need of beauty, but beauty has no need of a song."

I admired these lines, and sympathized with the officer.

Above all, I loved to watch my lady when she was alone, at the piano. In the intoxication of the music, only her window existed for me, and the yellow light within; and in that light, her graceful woman's figure and the imperious profile, the white hands fluttering like birds over the keys. I stared, I heard the moody music, I dreamed. If I could but dig up a treasure, she should have it all and be rich. Had I been Skobelov [22] I would have renewed the Turkish War, and with the money won in ransoms, I would have built a house for her on the Otkosa, the choicest district in town. Let her but move from this street, where she had become the butt of the vilest gossip. The neighbors and their servants, and, above all, my employers, spoke of her as filthily and maliciously as about the cutter's wife; but more warily, with muffled voices and nervous glances around them.

Her position as the widow of a man of high rank put some fear into them, I suppose. The framed inscriptions on her walls were awards bestowed on his ancestors by former Tsars—Godunov, Alexis, Peter the Great. This I learned from Tufayev, a man with some letters, who was

[22] Russian general who won victories over the Turks.

forever poring over the Gospels. Or it may have been that people feared a horsewhipping at her hands, with that riding crop inset with the lilac stone, which she was reported to have used, before, on a scandal monger. But words are not better for being muttered instead of shouted out. A cloud of enmity enveloped my lady, as disturbing as it was incomprehensible to me.

With the knowledge now of another life, of other sorts of people, emotions, thoughts, the old life became ever more distasteful and wearisome to me. It was wound around in a dirty web of shameless gossip, which left no one untouched. It converted the sickly and unhappy regimental chaplain into a dissolute toper. My employers had it that every officer and his wife were profligates. The same burden filled the soldier's talk about women, talk that had become nauseating to me. Of all the gossips, however, I found my employers the most offensive, knowing too well what value to put on their favorite diversion, ruthless judgments upon others. To spy and expatiate upon the misbehavior of others was the one entertainment which they could have without expense. They enjoyed putting everybody they knew on their verbal rack; thereby, so to speak, retaliating on others for their tedious, tabooed, toilsome lives.

On hearing their obscenities about Queen Margot, I was shaken by a paroxysm of emotion far removed from any childish feelings. My heart dilated with hatred toward the slanderers. I felt an uncontrollable urge to hurt everybody, to flout them all. And, at times, a gush of searing pity for myself and for everybody, flowed over me. That voiceless pity ached more than hatred.

As regards my queen, I knew more about her than they; my fear was that they would discover it, too.

On Sundays, when my employers were celebrating mass at the cathedral, I started the morning with a visit to her. She called me into her bedroom where, sitting in a gold silk upholstered armchair, with the little girl on my knee, I reported on my week's reading. She lay in her wide bed, her face in her small cupped hands, her body covered by a quilt, gold in color like everything else in the room. The braid in which her dark hair was coiled, hung over her shoulder and bosom, and sometimes down to the floor. Listening, she gazed at me with her luscious eyes, and with a barely perceptible smile, gave me her approval, "That's good."

To my sight her kindest smile was the condescension of a queen. Her voice was deep and gracious, and it seemed to declare in every phrase, "I realize my immeasurable superiority. I can do without anybody."

I sometimes came upon her at her looking glass, before which she sat on a low chair, dressing her hair, strands of which lay on her knees and over the back and arms of the chair, almost reaching the floor. Her hair was as long and abundant as grandma's. She put on her stockings in my presence; and I felt unembarrassed; there was something clean in her nakedness. All I felt was happy pride in her beauty; her flower-like fragrance was a defense against unruly impulses. The love discoursed in kitchen gossip was alien to her, I was sure. Hers was something else, on a higher plane.

However, one late afternoon, on entering the parlor, I heard a peal of laughter from the lady of my heart, from the bedroom, and a man's voice saying, "Just a minute! Lord, it's inconceivable——"

I should have gone, I knew, but could not.

"Who's there?" she called out. "Oh, you? Come in."

The bedroom was dim, the curtains being drawn; the air was heady with the perfume of flowers. Queen Margot was in bed, the coverlet drawn up to her chin; beside her, sitting back against the wall, was the violin-playing officer, stripped down to his shirt, and his chest showing. It was red-striped by a scar on the right side, that extended from the nipple to the shoulder, and was so distinct that I would see it clearly even in that dim light. His hair was playfully mussed, and the first smile I ever saw there lit his moody, lined face. It was a strange smile; his glowing, feminine eyes were fixed on the queen as if in a first spellbound sight of her beauty.

"My friend," Queen Margot introduced us, and I was at a loss to know whether I or he was the friend referred to. "Why that scared look?" I heard her ask me, as if from far away, "Come here!"

When I came to her she put her hands around my shoulders, and said, "You'll grow up a happy man. Now run along."

I put one book back on the shelf, and took another, and was off.

I felt a rasping in my heart. Actually, I did not believe my queen gave her love like other women, and the officer gave me no cause to feel so. I could remember his face and his smile. His face was amazingly transformed in that joyful smile, like a child who has suddenly been made happy. His love for her was inevitable. Who could help loving her? And she had good cause to lavish her love on him; he played so beautifully, and recited poetry so eloquently. But my very need for those rationalizations made it clear to me that there was something amiss in my reaction to what I had witnessed, and even to Queen Margot herself. I sensed some loss, and was thrown into a depression that lasted for days. On one of these days, I had behaved with rash and riotous truculence, and when I came to my lady for a book, she said severely, "From what I hear you're quite a desperado. That I didn't know."

I was exasperated and described the nauseating existence I had to endure; and I told her how unbearable I found it to hear her ill-spoken of. At first she listened with earnest attention, keeping her hand on my shoulder; soon she began to laugh, and playfully pushed me off. "Enough; I know all about that. Understand me? I know."

Then she took me by both hands and said affectionately, "The less thought you give to it the better. You don't wash your hands very well."

She could have spared me that. Had she had to polish brass, scrub floors and do laundry, her hands would have turned out no better.

"He who knows how to live is slandered out of envy. And he who doesn't know how to live is despised," she said soberly, pulling me to her and smiling at me. "Do you love me?"

"Yes."

"A lot?"

"Yes."

"But how much?"

"I don't know."

"Thank you. You're a good lad. I want people to love me." She said it with a smile, as if she were about to add something, but she said, instead, after a silence, during which she held me close to her, "Come to see me more often. Come as often as you can."

I presumed upon this to my great benefit. When my employers took their after-dinner siestas, I ran over, and if she was home, spent an hour or so with her.

"You'll have to read Russian books, learn about Russian life." And she began teaching me, as she pinned up her fragrant hair with her rosy fingers. She recited a list of Russian authors. "Will you try to remember them?"

Often she said, in a preoccupied and almost fretful manner, "We'll have to see to your education. The thing keeps slipping my mind. Oh, God!" And from such visits, I went off, a new book in my hand, and a new feeling inside, as if I had been cleansed within.

By that time I had already read Aksakov's *Chronicles of a Russian Family, Recollections of a Sportsman* and the magnificent Russian poem, "In the Forests," some volumes of Grebenko and Sologub and

the poems of Venevitinov, Odoyevsky and Tiuchev. These books bathed
my soul, carrying off the dregs of sterile and sour realities. I appreciated the quality of these books which had become indispensable to
me. One gain to me from their reading was the realization that I was
not all alone on this earth; a sense of not being lost in this life took hold
within me.

On grandma's visits I enjoyed telling her about Queen Margot. Taking her snuff with added gusto, grandma remarked with conviction,
"Now, that's fine; so you see there are good people around; you'll find
them if you look for them." And once, she offered, "Suppose I go to
thank her for you." But I told her, "No need of that."

"All right, if you don't want me to. Lord, how good everything is!
I feel like living forever!"

Queen Margot's educational project for me never came through,
because of an accident that occurred on Trinity Sunday, and that nearly
did for me. Some days before the holiday, I suffered such swellings
of my eyelids as to virtually close my eyes. My employers feared I was
going blind, and I shared their fear. I was taken to the famous oculist,
Rodzevich, who lanced the eyelids, after which, for several days, I lay
in torturing, gloomy shadows, my eyes covered with bandages. The day
before Trinity Sunday, the bandages were removed, and I walked like
one who had experienced burial alive. Nothing can be more dreadful
than the loss of one's sight, an incalculable injury that deprives one of
dozens of worlds.

Festive Trinity Sunday came and, excused from my chores as a con-
valescent, I made a call on the orderlies in their kitchen. They were
all drunk, including the puritanical Tufayev. During the afternoon,
Yermokhin clouted Sidorov over the head with a club. Sidorov fell
down unconscious, and the frightened Yermokhin ran away.

The alarm spread through the yard that Sidorov had been murdered,
and people crowded around to look at his body sprawled motionless in
the threshold. It was proposed that the police be called, but no one
went for them; and no one dared touch the unconscious man. At that
point, Natalie Kozlovsky, the laundress, hove in sight, all dolled out in
a new blue dress and white kerchief. She shouldered the spectators
aside, entered the kitchen doorway, bent down and shouted, "Fools,
he's alive; fetch some water!"

They upbraided her, "What are you meddling for? It's none of your
business!"

"Water!" she repeated, as loud as if the place were on fire. Picking up her new dress and spreading out her petticoat in a deft and efficient manner, she took the soldier's bleeding head upon her knees. The timorous and disapproving crowd scattered. In the dim hallway light, I could see the angry, tearful eyes of the laundress flashing in her round, pale face. I brought her a pail of water, with which she directed me to douse Sidorov's face and chest, taking care not to spill any on her. "I'm going visiting," she explained.

The soldier recovered consciousness; his bleary eyes opened, and he fetched a groan.

"Lift him up," Natalie directed, holding him from her so as not to stain her dress. We dragged him into the kitchen and got him into bed. She sponged his face with a damp cloth and gave me these instructions before she left, "Keep the cloth wet and hold it over his head, while I rout out the other fool. The devils! When they've drunk themselves into jail maybe they'll think they've had enough." Then, after slipping her stained petticoat to the floor, and kicking it into the corner, she went out, tidying her rumpled dress.

Sidorov stretched, hiccoughed and sighed. From his head, warm, sticky blood dripped on my bare feet. Unpleasant though it was, I was too rigid with fright to move my feet. Out in the yard the sun shone with a festive glow; young birch boughs decorated steps and gates and fresh boughs of maple and ash decorated the lintels. The leafage brightened the whole street; everything looked new and young. It had seemed to me, that morning, that with the holiday spring had come to stay, and that life had become more joyful, shining and clean.

The soldier felt sick. Stale vodka and scallions fumed, in a suffocating stench, through the kitchen. On the windows were gaping faces of spectators, looking hideous flattened against the pane, with hands pressed to their cheeks.

Toiling out of the fog of unconsciousness, the soldier muttered, "What's the matter with me? Yermokhin, my pal, did I fall?" Then he had a coughing fit, followed by a fit of drunken weeping, and he groaned, "Oh, sister, my little sister!"

He staggered, dripping, out of bed, then fell back again and, with his eyes rolling grotesquely, howled, "They've practically killed me," which struck me funny.

"What the hell are you giggling about?" he asked me, with a foggy look. "Here I am killed for eternity, and you laugh!" And he flailed at me with his hands, mumbling, "It was the prophet, Elijah, the first time; and St. George on his horse, the second time; and the third time—keep away from me, you wolf!"

"Don't be an idiot!" I retorted.

In witless rage, he stamped his feet and howled, "I'm killed, while you—" And he gave me a poke in the eyes with his big, grimy fist. Almost blinded, I yelled, and felt my way into the yard, where I encountered Natalie hauling Yermokhin in by the arm, yelling, "Get going, you horse!" Stopping me, she asked, "What's happened to you?"

"He's come to."

"He's come to, has he?" she exclaimed, dragging the words out in astonishment. Giving Yermokhin a tug, she said, "That's something you can thank God for, werewolf!"

I bathed my eyes. Looking in, I saw the two soldiers being reconciled, with embraces and tears. Both tried to hug Natalie, but she cuffed them off, exclaiming, "Don't you paw me, you dogs! What do you think I am? Better go to bed and sleep it off before your bosses get back, or you'll be in a worse mess!"

At her bidding, they lay down like little children, one on the floor, the other on the cot; and when they were snoring, she came out on the porch.

"What a sight I am now! And I started out, all dressed up, for my visit. So he punched you, that idiot! That's what vodka brings them to! Don't take to drink, little chap, don't ever take to drink!"

We sat down on the bench by the gate, and I asked her what made her so fearless with drunks. "I'm not scared of them sober, either. If they bother me, here's what I'll give them!" and she raised her firm, red fist. "My dead husband hit the bottle, too. I tied him up, hand and foot, once, when he was drunk; and after he'd slept if off, I gave him a thrashing—for his own good—and I told him, 'You have your wife for fun, not vodka!' I gave him such a talking-to, talked till I was tired; and he was like wax in my hands, afterward."

"You're strong," I said, thinking of the woman, Eve, who had fooled God himself.

Sighing, Natalie answered, "A woman has to be stronger than a man; she has to have the strength of two, and that's how God has made her. A man's such a flighty creature."

She spoke coolly, without rancor, as she sat there, leaning back against the fence, her arms akimbo over her massive bosom, her eyes fixed somberly on the gutter, coated with dust, and cluttered with rubbish. Listening to her shrewd comments, I lost track of the time when, sudenly, the boss hove to with his wife on his arm. Their gait was slow and sedate; they might have been a turkey cock and his hen; they gave us a close look and made some remarks to each other.

I sprang up to open the door to them. As she came up the stairs, the boss' wife said viciously, "So, you're shining up to the washer-woman? Carrying on with that kind, are you?"

I could not even feel annoyance at such stupidity, but I took offense at my boss when he laughed, and said, "It's time; that's to be expected."

Next morning, in the woodshed, I found an empty purse stuck into the hole in which the door was hooked down. Recognizing it as Sido-rov's purse, I took it to him immediately.

He felt into its vacant depths. "Where's the money; the thirty rubles? Give me them!"

His head was turbaned in a towel. He looked green and sickly; his swollen eyes twitched with wrath. He would not take my word that the purse was empty when I found it.

Yermokhin, coming in, concurred with Sidorov, with accusing wags of his head at me, "Sure, he stole it. Take him to his boss. Soldiers don't steal from each other!"

This made me think he was the thief and the one who had flung the empty purse into my woodshed. I had no hesitation in saying it to his face, "Liar; you're the one who stole it!"

I realized I was right when I saw his dull face contort with exaspera-tion and fear. He shook, and screeched, "Prove it, prove it!"

How could I? Yermokhin, bellowing, towed me over the yard, with Sidorov bellowing in accompaniment behind us. Heads appeared at win-dows, Queen Margot's mother's, with its cigarette, among them. The thought that my lady's respect for me was in decline, maddened me.

I recall standing in the grip of the two soldiers before my employers, who were nodding agreement to the soldiers' charges. The boss' wife even confirmed it. "He must have taken that money! I saw him petting with that washerwoman on the bench last night, and that took money. That kind has to be paid for it!"

"Of course!" agreed Yermokhin.

Driven into a frenzy by this, I called the boss' wife names, and got myself a thrashing. But I ached, not from the beating, but my concern over Queen Margot's reaction to the affair. How to restore myself in her esteem? What agonies of mind I suffered! I escaped strangling myself only because there was no time for it.

Luckily, through the blabbing of the soldiers, the story was soon over the yard and the street, and before the day was over I heard, from the attic where I lay, the ringing voice of Natalie Kozlovsky down below. "No! Why should I keep quiet? Let me alone, you! If you don't I'll have something to tell your officer that'll fix you!"

I sensed, immediately, that all this uproar had to do with me. It was happening practically on our doorstep; Natalie's voice was loud and exultant as she asked Yermokhin, "You showed me a wad of money yesterday; how much did it amount to? And where did it come from? Come on, tell us!"

Almost gasping with joy, I heard Sidorov's aggrieved voice, "So; Yermokhin—"

"And the boy had to suffer for it; you got him a beating for it!"

How I wanted to dash down to the yard, hop with glee, and shower the laundress with grateful kisses; but, that very moment, seemingly from the window, the boss' wife yelled down, "The boy was thrashed because he was impudent. No one thought him a thief except you, you tart!"

"Tart, yourself! Allow me to tell you, madam, you're no better than a cow!"

This exchange was like music to my ears. Scalding tears of self-pity and thankful tears for Natalie bubbled in my heart. With difficulty I choked them back.

My boss dragged himself up to the attic, and, sitting on a projecting rail, and stroking his hair, said, "So, brother Peshkov, you had no hand in it."

I turned away from him without answering. "Just the same, the language you used was inexcusable," he said; and I replied, with composure, "The minute I can get up, I'm leaving."

He pulled at his cigarette in silence, his eyes staring at its tip. Then he said in a low voice, "Well, that's up to you. You're not a little boy any longer. Look around you and decide what's best for you." He left me and, as always, I felt sorry for him.

Four days later I went away. I was aching with the desire to bid good-by to Queen Margot, but I couldn't get up the courage for it, and I must admit, I was waiting for her to invite me. When I made my farewells to her daughter, I said, "Tell your mama, will you, I thank her very much."

"Yes," she promised, and with a fond, sweet smile, she added, "Good-by till tomorrow."

Our next meeting was twenty years later; she was the wife of a gendarmes officer.

Chapter Eleven

AGAIN I WAS A MESS BOY ON A STEAMER, THE PERM, A FAST, ROOMY vessel, white as a swan. This time I served as a "black" mess boy; that is, I worked in the kitchen. My pay was seven rubles a month, and I worked under the cook.

The steward, so fat he looked bloated, was bald as a billiard ball. With his hands folded behind his back, he paced the deck all day long, like an uncomfortable bear, feeling the sultry heat, and hunting for some shade. His wife's beat was the buffet. A woman touching forty, she was still personable, though faded. Her powder makeup was so heavy it flaked off her cheeks, depositing a greasy white dust on her print dress.

Ruler of the kitchen was the fancy chef, Ivan Medveizhenok, a short, plump fellow with an arched nose, and ironic little eyes. A dandy, he shaved every morning, and wore starched collars. His cheeks had a bluish hue, and his black moustaches took an upward twirl; he devoted every spare moment to them, working on them with sooty fingers before a pocket mirror.

The boat's outstanding personality was a stoker, Jake Shumov, a stocky man with a massive chest. His face was snubnosed, and as smooth as a shovel. Thick eyebrows almost hid his coffee-colored eyes, tough, curling hair, like swamp moss, coated his cheeks; and the same sort of hair covered his head like a skullcap, through which he could barely dig his gnarled fingers.

He was a tricky card player, and greedy beyond conception. Like a famished dog, he haunted the kitchen for meat scraps and bones. He took tea with Medveizhenok, to whom he recounted fantastic memoirs. As a youth he had been apprenticed to the town shepherd of Riazan; later, having been recruited by an itinerant monk, he put in a four-year stint at a monastery.

"And I would have turned monk, one of God's black stars," he commented, in his pert, humorous way, "had not a female pilgrim from Penza happened along. That diverting creature overthrew me. 'Here you are, a nice husky lad; and here am I, a lonely, respectable widow. How about coming along with me?' she proposes, 'I've got a house of my own where I do a business in down and feathers.' That sounded all right to me, and I joined up with her. I was her boy friend, and for three years we lived as cozily as bread in the oven."

"What a liar!" Medveizhenok interjected, worriedly inspecting a boil on his nose. "If lies could earn you money, you'd have thousands in the bank."

Jake's response was an indistinct murmuring, and a slight tremor among the bristling, blue hair covering his flat face and the tips of his shaggy moustache; then, the chef's remark having been passed over, he continued his fluent recital: "Being older than me, I began to find her a bit stale; so I hooked up with her niece; and when she found out, she took me by the scruff of the neck, and showed me the door."

"Just what you deserved," commented the cook, as evenly as Jake himself.

The stoker ignored the interjection. Sucking at a lump of sugar in his cheek, he said, "I was all up in the air, but I ran into an old peddler from Vladimir. With him I tramped the roads of the world. We crossed the Balkan Mountains into Turkey, Romania, Greece and all over Austria-Hungary; a whole row of nations. Wherever we got wind of a customer, there we were to show our wares."

"And steal a thing or two?" asked the chef, seriously.

"Certainly not; I'd been warned by the old man, 'You have to be honest abroad; they're so strict there, I hear; it's off with your head for a little nothing.' I admit I tried to get away with a little something, but it didn't pay. There was a horse I succeeded in leading out of a certain merchant's yard; but I got no farther when I was caught, given a beating, and hauled to the police station. I had a partner, a real horse-thief, but I just did it for fun. I'd been doing some repairs in the merchant's house, rigging up a stove to heat his bath. He took sick and had some nightmares, in which I figured; so he took fright and said to the magistrate, 'Please let him go'—him meaning me—'please let him go; he's given me nightmares; if you don't, you'll come down sick. He must be a wizard!' That meant me, imagine!—a wizard. Now, that merchant happened to have pull, so I was let off."

"I wouldn't have let you off," remarked the chef. "I should have put you to soak in water to wash out some of your foolishness."

Jake pounced upon these words. "I know I'm full of folly—enough to stock a village."

Putting a finger under his collar with an angry jerk to ease its pressure, the chef said in vexation, "Nonsense! It's more than I can understand how a ne'er-do-well like you gets along, stuffs himself, guzzles, promenades over the whole earth! What good are you, I'd like to know?"

Calmly chewing away, the stoker replied, "I'd like to know, too. I get along, and that's all I can tell you. One man takes to his bed, and another walks, and a *chinovnik* sits all day; but everybody has to eat."

This infuriated the chef still more. "You're an unspeakable swine, really. Hog's swill——"

"What are you sore about?" asked Jake wonderingly. "Men are all acorns off the one oak. No point hollering at me; that won't improve me, you know."

I was immediately taken by this man whom I gazed at with endless amazement and listened to, open-mouthed. I sensed that his knowledge of life reached deep. He used the intimate forms of address to everybody, captain, steward, the haughtiest first-class passengers, and sailors, waiters, deck passengers, as if he were on an equal footing with everybody.

Called before the captain or the engineer, to answer for some negligence or for cheating at cards, he would stand there listening, his baboon-like hands behind his back. It was obvious, even as he listened, that he was unconcerned, and not in the least intimidated by threats of firing him at the next stop. He gave the impression of the eternal outsider, as had Good Idea. He appeared conscious of his singularity, and that he baffled people.

I cannot recall this man to have taken offense at anything, or to have held his tongue any length of time. Involuntarily, as it appeared, a constant stream of talk gushed from his coarse lips. Even when he was taking a scolding, or listening to an anecdote, his lips were in motion, either repeating what was being said to him, or just talking to himself. Regularly, when his work was done, he emerged from the stokehold barefoot, dripping perspiration and smeared with oil; no belt around his damp blouse, which was open, leaving his hairy chest exposed; and the same instant, his steady, resonant, monotonous voice would reach across the deck, his words as continuous as rain.

"Greetings to you, mother. And where are you bound? Cristopol? I know the town; been there, too. Lived there with a well-to-do Tatar;

name of Usan Gubaidulin. Had three wives, the old boy. Rugged he was, red-complexioned, and one wife was young. Amusing she was, that little Tatar wench."

He had been all over and, seemingly, had fornicated with every woman he had encountered. He spoke about people serenely, without a touch of animosity, as if he had never suffered injury or insult.

Soon after, his voice would echo from the stern, "How about it, folks; how about a game of cards? Just a shuffle, eh? Cheer you up a bit. Make money sitting down; there's a profitable occupation, eh?"

I observed that he never described things as good, bad or dreadful; his adjectives were "cheering," "amusing," "odd." A beautiful woman reduced down to "an amusing little female," and fine weather to "a cheering little day." His most frequent expression, however, was "I spit on it!"

He was considered an idler, but as far as I could see, he toiled as responsibly as the other stokers in that smothering, fetid hell-hole; and I never heard complaints from him, as from the rest, of exhaustion and heat.

One day an old woman passenger was robbed of her purse. The night was clear and still; and people's tempers were concordantly amiable. The captain contributed five rubles to make good her loss, and the passengers took up a collection. On receiving the money, the old woman crossed herself, bowed low, and explained, "But, kind friends, it's three greven (thirty kopecks) over."

"Take it, good woman. Take all there is," someone replied cheerfully. "No such thing as having anything over."

Jake, however, asked the old woman quite soberly, "Let me have the overs for a card stake." Everybody around laughed, but he kept at the bewildered woman. "Come on now, woman, let me have it; what good will the money do you? Tomorrow you'll be in the graveyard."

He was driven away with imprecations, at which he said to me, wonderingly, "How ridiculous people are! It's none of their business! Why do they have to butt in? She, herself, said she didn't want all of it. And the three greven would have been a comfort to me."

The very look of money gave him pleasure. As he talked, he would polish coins on his trousers till they gleamed; and his eyebrows twitched as he held them, between his gnarled fingers, before his snub-nose. Yet, he was not stingy.

He once got me into a card game I didn't know; and he cried out in astonishment, "How is it you don't know? And you consider yourself educated! You'll have to learn. We'll start playing for lumps of sugar."

I lost half a pound of the finest sugar to him, every lump of which went into his shaggy cheeks. As soon as he thought I knew the game, he said, "Now let's play for money. Have you got any?"

"Five rubles."

Understandably enough, my five rubles changed hands. Burning to recoup, I staked my jacket, valued at five rubles, and lost it; then, my new shoes—another loss. At this, Jake said with reluctance, and almost with irritation, "No, you don't understand the game yet; you get too excited. You have to throw in everything, down to your shoes. Here you are, take back your clothes and your money—only I'll keep a ruble as my instructor's fee. Is that a go?"

I expressed my gratitude. "I spit on it," he replied. "A game's for fun, you understand; but you want to turn it into a fight. And even in a fight, it's no good boiling over. You have to be able to measure your punches. What's the use of getting into a lather? You're a kid; you have to learn control. So you don't win the first try, or the fifth; so it's the seventh time, then you spit on it! Go and cool off, and then try it again. That's playing the game."

I took increasing pleasure in his company; nevertheless, he also grated upon me. In some of his anecdotes he reminded me of grandma; and there was much else in him that drew me to him. But his ingrained apathy filled me with aversion.

Once, near sundown, a second-class passenger, a fat, drunken business man from Perm, fell overboard, and the ruddy-gold current quickly carried the struggling man away. The steam was shut off; the ship was stopped; under the red rays of the sun the spray jetting from the wheel looked like blood. Already a good distance from the boat, the dark shape fought for life in that frothing, blood-red cauldron. His outcries were carried back to us; they shook one to the core. Answering screams came from the passengers, colliding into each other as they swarmed over the deck and crowded into the stern. The friend of the man overboard, a ruddy, bald chap who was also drunk, hit everybody within reach, bellowing, "Out of my way; I'll get him!"

Two sailors had already dived in and were swimming toward the drowning man; and boats, too, had been lowered. Through the ringing orders of the captain and the screams of the women, Jake's steady, composed, resonant voice could be heard. "He'll drown; he's bound to, seeing that he has all his clothes on. With all his clothes on, he's bound to go under. Take women, for example. Why do they always go under quicker than men? It's their petticoats. They drag a woman straight down to the bottom, like weights, when she falls in. You'll see, he'll drown."

And, in fact, the business man did drown. For two hours they kept looking for him, but he had disappeared. Now sober, his friend sat on deck, wheezing and mumbling mournfully, "We're almost home. What'll happen when we arrive? He had a family; what'll they say?"

Taking up his hands-behind-his-back stance, Jake tried to console him. "You're worrying yourself over nothing. Who knows when he's fated to die? One man eats mushrooms and is poisoned and dies; thousands of others eat mushrooms and thrive on them. But one man dies. And what about the mushrooms?"

Stocky and powerful, he stood there before the business man like a boulder, and poured words over him like grain. For a time the business man wept, without a word, brushing his tears out of his beard with his big hands; but after a time he bellowed, "Stop torturing me! Fellow Christians, there'll be a murder if you don't get him away!"

Jake went off, undisconcerted. "People are funny; you go do them a kindness and they curse you for it."

At times I considered the stoker a dimwit, but more frequently, I felt his stupidity to be put on. I tried to get a straight account from him of his youth and his trampings over the earth, with unexpected results. His head back, and his dark, coppery eyes asquint, he drew his hand across his mossy face and said, with an indolent drawl, "People all over, brother, are no wiser than ants. And where you have people you have trouble, let me tell you! The most of them, naturally, are peasants. The earth is just littered with *mujiks*, like autumn leaves, as the saying goes. I've seen the Bulgars and also the Greeks and those, what d'ye call them, the Serbs, and Romanians besides, and all sorts of Gypsies. Are there different sorts? What are they like? What do you mean? In towns, they're townspeople. They're alike in lots of ways. There are even those who speak our language, though poorly, as for instance the Tatars and the Mordvins. The Greeks can't. They jabber whatever they fancy, and it sounds like words, but what it is or what it's about, is beyond our understanding. You have to use sign language with them. But my old man could make himself understood even to the Greeks! He'd mumble something, and they got it. A sly one he was. He knew how to put it over on them. You still want to know the sort they were? You're a funny one! What sort of people are people? Dark, of course, and the Romanians, too, and they all have the same religion. The Bulgars are dark, too; but their religion is the same as ours. And the Greeks are the same as Turks, in origin."

I felt he was holding something back, something he didn't care to speak about. From the magazine pictures I knew that the capital of Greece was Athens, a town of great beauty and antiquity. But Jake shook his head and cast doubt on the idea.

"They've been filling you with lies, my friend. Athens? There's no such place; but there's a place called Athos; but that's not a town, just a hill with a monastery on top. It's called Holy Mount Athos. An old man used to sell pictures of it. There's a town on the Danube River called Belgrade; it's like Yaroslavl, or Nizhny, the way it's built. There's nothing special about their towns, but there's something different about their villages. And their women, it's enough to kill you, they're so agreeable. I nearly settled down there on account of one of them. Now, what the devil was her name?"

As he rubbed his sweating face, his bristles crackled. From somewhere deep down came a drumroll of a laugh. "Ah, how a man can forget! And, to think of it, she and I were—. When we parted she wept and I wept, too." And off-handedly, and without a trace of reticence, he gave me instruction in the ways of a man with a woman.

We were on deck. The tepid moonlight night floated toward us; the shore meadows were barely visible beyond the gleaming waters. In the heavens twinkled yellow stars—stars drawn to the earth. There was a stir all around, a quiet, but incessant, pulsing of life, real life. And, into this agreeably melancholy stillness, struck his hoarse voice, "And so, letting go of each other's hands, we parted."

Jake's tales were not to any prude's taste, yet they were not obscene, being neither vicious nor exhibitionistic, and with a naïve and mournful minor note in them. I was as touched by the innocently naked moon, which filled me with incomprehensible longings. My mind clung to what it had found good, the dearest thing that had come into my life, Queen Margot, and those lines, so true and memorable: "A song has need of beauty, but beauty has no need of song."

Shaking myself free of these reveries, as if rousing myself from a nap, I called upon the stoker again for recollections of his life and his travails.

"You're funny, you know," he responded. "What's there to tell? I've been around. Was I in a monastery? Yes. Taverns? Yes. How the peasants live and how the gentry live; I've seen both. I know what it is to be full and what it is to be hungry."

And, picking his way over his past, as if it were a precarious rickety bridge over a deep river, he went on, "Take the time I was stuck in the police station over that horse theft. 'I'm sure bound for Siberia,' I thought to myself, and then the police captain starts beefing about a smoky oven over in his house. So I said to him, 'I can fix that for you, your honor.' He waves me away. 'It has baffled the best workmen here.' So I tell him, 'It happens, sometimes, a shepherd gets the best of a general.' I felt bold; I could have faced up to anybody, with Siberia ahead of me; what did I care? 'O.K., try it,' he says, 'but I'll break your neck if it smokes worse than before!' It took me two days and wasn't that police captain stunned! 'Oh, you dummy, you dope! A master workman, and you have to go horse stealing! How come?' I explained it to him, 'That was only a prank, your honor.' 'So it seems,' he said. 'Just a prank. Too bad. Yes, too bad,' he said it over again. You see, there he was, a ruthless police captain and all that, and he sympathized with me."

"So what happened?" I asked.

"Nothing. He sympathized with me! What more?"

"What's the point of sympathizing with a stone like you?"

Jake laughed genially. "You funny guy! So it's a stone? Well, one can have sympathy for stones. There's a place for stones, too; they make paving for streets. There's no material of any sort one can't have feelings about; it has a place of its own, and not by accident. What's dirt? But out of it comes the grass."

When he went on like this, I realized the stoker understood things that were beyond my reach.

"What's your opinion of the chef?" I asked.

"Medveizhenok?" said Jake, reflectively. "What's there to think of him? Nothing."

That was a fact. Medveizhenok was so frictionlessly proper, no thought could take hold there. The only interesting thing about him was that he was fond of the stoker, though he was always reprimanding him. He was always inviting him to tea.

Once he told Jake, "If you'd been a serf of mine, you lazybones, you'd have gotten seven thrashings a week!" And Jake replied, with all seriousness, "That's too much!"

Although the chef was forever upbraiding the stoker, he nevertheless kept feeding him tidbits. He'd toss him something, and say rudely, "Here's something for you to wolf down!"

Calmly eating it, Jake would reply, "With your help, I'm building up reserves of strength."

"And what good is strength to you, you loafer?"

"What good? Why, it'll lengthen my life!"

"What for; you're no use to anybody."

"Useless people keep living, just the same. It's fun living, isn't it? Very convenient."

"What an imbecile!"

"Why say that?"

"Im-be-cile!"

"What a way to talk!" said Jake, astonished, while Medveizhenok turned to me to say, "Imagine! We stand around the stoves, in the hellish heat, our blood drying out and the marrow frying out of our bones, while this pig stuffs himself!"

"We each fulfill our destiny," said the stoker, between mouthfuls.

I was well aware that stoking furnaces was harder and hotter work than tending cook stoves, for I had made several tries; and it puzzled me that he didn't pass on this fact to the chef. It was clear this man's thinking was all his own.

He caught it from everybody—captain, engineer, mate—who must all have known he wasn't lazy. I found it baffling. How come they so misjudged him? His fellow stokers treated him better, though they kidded him about his loquaciousness and his weakness for cards.

I asked them, "What do you think of Jake? Is he a good sort?"

"Jake? Nothing wrong with him. But you can't get a rise of him, no matter if you heaped live coals on his chest."

With all his long hours in the boiler room and the horse's hunger he had to appease, the stoker did with little sleep. There were times when, not bothering to change from his work clothes, all sweaty and dirty as he was, he was up all night chatting or playing cards with the passengers.

For me he was a locked chest, secreting something I had to get at, and I stubbornly kept at him for the key.

"What are you after? I can't make it out, little brother," he would exclaim, with a glance at me from eyes almost buried under his eyebrows. "So, I've knocked around everywhere, so what? You're a funny guy. Better let me tell you what happened to me, once."

And he embarked on a tale about a tubercular young lawyer he had run across, in a town he had stopped in, whose robust, childless German wife was languishing over a drygoods dealer. But this man had a beautiful wife and three children. Learning of the German woman's infatuation for him, he decided to play a trick on her. He fixed up a rendezvous at night in the garden, and brought along two friends, whom he hid behind the hedges. Think of it! And when that German dame arrived, he announced, "Here she is; all yours." And he explained to her: "I'm no good for you; I'm a married man. But I'm making it up to you with my two friends; one's a widower and the other's a bachelor."

"Oh, did that German woman give it to him—a smack that knocked him over a bench, and then she dug her heel into his numskull and his homely mug. I'd brought her there; I was her janitor. I was peeping through a crack in the fence, and I saw how the soup was boiling over. The two in the bushes jumped out and grabbed her by the hair, so I hopped over the fence and got her clear of them. 'That's not done, misters,' I told them. The lady had gone there in good faith and he thought ill of her. I got her away, but with a hole in my head from a brick they shied at me. The woman was so mortified, she was frantic. 'The minute my husband dies, I'm going back to my own German folk.' 'That's right, you should,' I told her. 'You've got to go back to them.' And so she did, soon as the lawyer died. A good-hearted sort she was, and smart, too. And the lawyer, God rest his soul, he was a good-hearted sort, too."

I wasn't sure I had quite gotten the point of the story, so I said nothing. I had a sense of something known, something experienced before, something ruthless and blind in what he reported.

"That was a good story, eh?" asked Jake.

I made some confused protest and, in his neutral way, this is how he put it. "People who have more than they need look for amusement; but there are times when their horseplay isn't fun; doesn't come off according to plan. Business calls for brains, and business men, of course, are brainy people; but they're too clever; life becomes dull for them; so they look for amusement."

Ahead of the bow foamed the river; we could hear the rushing current and see the shores gliding alongside. Passengers snored on the deck. Silently weaving her way around benches and prostrate sleepers, a tall, sallow woman in black, her gray head bare, approached us. With a nudge the stoker whispered to me, "She's in trouble, see." And I felt that other people's troubles amused him.

I was an eager listener, and he told me many tales which I remember very well. But I don't recall one that was cheerful. He spoke more coolly than did people in books. In books I was often aware of the writer's emotions, anger, pleasure, sorrow, sarcasm; but the stoker was never sarcastic, never passed judgments. Nothing stirred him, either to rapture or disgust. He spoke like an indifferent witness in a courtroom, who felt alien to all, judge, plaintiff, and defendant alike. This insentience disappointed me increasingly, and my feeling toward him turned into active dislike.

Life was no different to him than the flame that heated the boilers. He stood before the furnace with a mallet in his pitted, coffee-colored hands, and lightly tapped the tip of the gauge to raise or lower the temperature.

"Hasn't all this hurt you?"

"Who could hurt me? I'm strong. The punches I can hand out!"

"I'm not thinking of punches. Hasn't it hurt your soul?"

"You can't hurt the soul; nothing can injure it!" he replied. "Souls are invulnerable to human powers, to anything outside them!"

In the talk of the passengers, the sailors, of everybody as a matter of fact, the word "soul" was as common as land, work, food and women. "Soul" is the tenth word in the conversation of ordinary people, a word that quivers with life and movement. But it troubled me to hear it roll so easily off slippery tongues. And when it was defiled by the peasants, in obscenities, I was cut to the heart.

I recalled with what care grandma mentioned the soul, that inner repository of love and grace and happiness. When a good person died, I thought, angels in white took up his soul to grandma's good God and he gave it a tender welcome. "Ah, my dear, immaculate one, what miseries you have borne below!" And the soul would receive from Him the pinions of a seraph, six white wings. Jake referred to the soul as circumspectly and as infrequently as grandma. When he was bawled out he never retorted blasphemously; when others prated about the soul he was silent, his red, bull neck bowed. I asked him about the nature of the soul, and he told me, "God's breath, that's what the soul is."

Not feeling much enlightened by that I wanted more; at which the stoker, with a sidelong twist of his head, told me, "Of the soul even the priests have little understanding. That, little brother, is a secret matter."

I kept thinking about him, had an exasperated determination to understand him; but to no avail. And, in the meanwhile, I could look at nothing else; his stocky frame blotted out everything else.

The stewardess showed me a dubious good will. I was assigned to fetch her hot water for her morning ablutions, although this was properly the chore of jolly little Lucy, the second-class chambermaid.

Standing near the stewardess in her cabin cubicle, where she stood bare to the waist, I looked at her yellow body, doughy like half-baked pies, and, remembering Queen Margot's supple, tawny figure, I felt nauseated. And the stewardess kept jabbering away, complaining, scoffing, scolding.

I missed the intent of her words, though I had a dim sense of its debased and pitiful character. But I remained untroubled. I was beyond her reach, beyond everything that happened on that boat. I had shut myself off from the world, behind rugged, protecting rock. Whatever transpired those days and nights drifted off into infinity.

"Our Gabriela's infatuated with you," came with Lucy's laughter, like something heard in a dream. "Open your mouth for your happiness."

And she wasn't alone in kidding me; the whole dining room staff was aware of the stewardess' frailty. The chef remarked, scowling, "The woman's had a bite of everything; now her mouth's watering for cookies. Such people! You, Peshkov, watch your step!"

And Jake also advised me like a father. "Now, if you were a bit older I'd speak to you differently; but, at your age, it's wiser to hold off. However, you must follow your own inclination."

I said, "Shut up! It's disgusting!"

"Sure it is."

But, immediately after, his fingers plucking at a hair, trying to unkink it, he said in a solemn, profound way, "Now, one should also look at it from her viewpoint. Her work is harassing. If a dog wants to be patted, think how much more people want it. And a female lives on love, the way a mushroom lives on dampness. Sure, it's a disgrace; but what can she do?"

Trying to fix his evasive eyes, I looked at him and said, "Then you'd deny her that?"

"What's she to me, my mother? And even then—you're a funny guy!" And his laugh rattled like a drum. There were times when, looking at him, I felt myself toppling through space, down to a dim, silent, bottomless pit.

"Jake, everybody except you has a wife; why did you never marry?"

"Me? A pet of all the women, thank the Lord! You see, it's this way. When you marry you have to settle down, live on one patch of earth. My patch is small and poor and even that's grabbed up by our uncle. When my younger brother gets back from his army service, he and the uncle have an argument, and he's taken to court for clouting the uncle on the head—a bit of blood was spilt in that affair; for which he gets eighteen months in jail; and from jail only one road lies ahead, which leads you right back there. Such a nice, young woman his wife was—but what's there to say? In marriage a man must be boss of the stable; but for a soldier, even his life is not his own."

"Do you pray?"

"You funny guy; of course!"

"How do you pray?"

"Lots of ways."

"What sort of prayers?"

"Well, here's the night prayer, brother. I just say, 'Lord, Jesus, have mercy on me, living; and rest me, when I die. Keep sickness from me, Lord'—and there's a couple of other things I say."

"Such as what?"

"Oh, a couple of things. Even the things you don't say reach Him."

Toward me he acted with a kindly, but amused, curiosity, as with a smart kitten that could be put through tricks. There were nights when, as I sat with him, in the reek that came from him of kerosene, burnt oil and onions, which he ate raw as others ate apples, he would suddenly demand, "Come on, Alex, my boy, some poetry."

I knew many verses by heart and, in addition, I kept a fat notebook into which I transcribed poems I fancied. I read him "Ruslan," to which he listened, motionless, like a mute, holding in his snorting breath. After it he commented, in a low voice, "Now, that's a nice, sweet little story. You didn't make it up? There's some gentleman I ran across, named Mukhin Pushkin."

"But he was killed a long time ago."

"How come?"

I told him the story briefly, as I had gotten it from Queen Margot; Jake's nonchalant comment was, "Women ruin lots of people."

I told him similar tales from books I had read. The stories fermented in my mind into one continuous, bubbling stream of tumultuous and lovely lives, illuminated by blazing passions. Acts of senseless derring-do, blue-blood hauteur, fabulous heroics, deaths, duels, purple language, and meannesses, all stream together. Rokambol got mixed up with the chivalrous Lia Molia and Hannibal; Louis XI assumed the shape of Père Grandet, Lieutenant Otletayev that of Henry IV. In this narrative world of mine, in which I transposed characters and events to suit my fancy, I had sport with people as capriciously as grandpa's God. It didn't keep me from facing reality; nor did it weaken my urge to know living people; but this nebulous book life interposed a transparent, but impervious cloud, immunizing me against much of the contagious smuts and virulent poisons of life. Books helped me to meet many evils without taking harm. My observations of human love and anguish kept me from whorehouses. Those who found debased pleasure sweet aroused my aversion and pity. Rokambol helped me to a stoical indifference to circumstance. Dumas' heroes made me seek to emulate their self-dedication to noble causes. The merry monarch, Henry IV, was my favorite, the hero, it seemed to me, of Beranger's splendid verses: "He lightened the tax load of the peasants, and he loved his glass; for when his people live merrily, may not the King drink?"

According to the novels Henry was a good sort, close to his people. I thought of him as a sun; and he made me feel that France, the world's loveliest land, the realm of chivalry, was just as glorious, whether symbolized by a man in royal robes or a peasant's homespun. Ange Pitou was no less the knight than D'Artagnan. The passages on Henry's murder brought tears to my eyes, and I gnashed my teeth in rage against Ravaillac. In my stories to the stoker, the king was generally the hero, and Jake seemed to share my affection for France and "Khenry."

"A good man, that King Khenry," he said, "putting down rebels or anything else."

No interjected comments, no questions came from him to interrupt my recital; he was a silent listener, his eyelids almost shut, his expression unchanging, like a mossy stone. But should I pause, for any reason, he would immediately inquire, "Finished?"

"Not yet."

"Then what are you stopping for?"

Of the French people he commented, sighing, "They had it easy!"

"In what way?"

"Look, you and I have to bear this heat, and work hard, while they lolled around, doing nothing but drinking and strolling—a very comfortable life."

"But they had to work too."

"Where does it say that in your stories!" demanded the stoker; and I was made suddenly aware that, in most of my reading, there had scarcely ever been a mention of toil or ordinary hardships to inconvenience the heroes.

"Now, I'm going to doze off a bit," said Jake, and, stretching out where he was, was soon placidly asnore.

In the autumn, when the shores of the Kama were reddening, leaves were turning gold, and the slanting rays of the sun were paling, Jake startled us by quitting his job. The very day previously, he had made these plans with me, "Day after tomorrow, boy, we'll be in Perm. We'll steam ourselves all we like in a bath, and afterwards we'll go off, you and I, to an inn, where there's music and things are pleasant. It's nice watching the machine play."

But at Sarapulia, a fat man with a sagging, beardless, effeminate face came aboard. His womanish look was accentuated by his cozy, voluminous cloak and his cap, with fox fur earlaps. Right off he picked himself a table where he would be enveloped in the warm gusts from the kitchen, ordered tea, and could not get at the boiling yellow fluid soon enough. He neither loosened his cloak nor took off his cap and was, consequently, soon in a heavy sweat.

A thin rain distilled from the autumnal fog. This man, as he swabbed at the perspiration with his handkerchief, gave me the impression that the rain was slackening; but as he began perspiring again, it seemed to rain harder.

Jake joined him, and they scanned a map together. The passenger pointed to something, but Jake exclaimed, "There? That's nothing! I spit on it!"

"Very well," said the passenger, and stowed the map away in a leather case he held on his knees. They had tea together and an intimate talk.

Before Jake went down to his boilers, I asked him about this man. He answered, laughing, "Might be a pigeon by his looks. A eunuch is what he is, from far off in Siberia! An amusing chap; lives in a colony."

He thumped his blackened heels, tough as hooves, on the deck, paused again, and scratched himself. "I'm taking a job with him. At Perm I'll get off and bid you good-by, my lad. We'll go part of the way by train, then by water again, and after that on horseback. It'll take us five weeks to reach the man's colony."

"Do you know him?" I asked, startled by his sudden decision.

"How could I? I've never seen him before, never lived within sight of him."

The following morning Jake came forth, togged out in a greasy fur jacket, with sandals on his bare feet, and Medveizhenok's battered and brimless straw hat on his head. He gripped my arm as with iron, and said, "How about coming along? That pigeon'll take you, too; just tell him you want to. How about it? Shall I ask him? They'll rid you of something you don't need, and pay you for it. They have a feast when they castrate a man and make it worth his while."

The eunuch,[23] a white package under his arm, stared at Jake with dull, bulging, leaden eyes, like those of a corpse pulled out of the water. I cursed him in a low voice, and once again the stoker gripped my arm. "Let him be. He's harmless. Everybody has his own belief. Is it any concern of ours? Well, so long! Good luck!"

[23] The Skoptsy, a sect of Old Believers, whose members, in order to achieve complete sexual abstinence, resorted to castration.

And Jacob Shumov went off, waddling like a bear, leaving my heart perplexed and restless. I grieved at the loss of my stoker, and resented him for it. I felt a bit of jealousy, as I recall, and I pondered, awed, "Imagine a man setting out like that, not knowing where and to what!"

Ah, what sort of man was Jacob Shumov?

Chapter Twelve

L ATER THAT AUTUMN, WHEN THE NAVIGATION SEASON ENDED, I WAS apprenticed to an icon painter. It took only a day or two to hear from the owner of the shop, a good-natured old woman, rather fond of the bottle, this announcement, in her Vladimir dialect: "Now, the days are short and the evenings grow longer; so, by day you'll help out in the shop. You'll learn at night."

And so my new boss turned out to be the manager of the shop, a young man with a handsome, calculating face. In the chill and dimness of the dawn, I used to cross the town with him, up the quiet business street, to the Fair grounds where, on the second floor of the bazaar building, set back to form a sort of arcade, the shop was located. It had formerly been a storeroom and was, consequently, dark. It had one small, iron-barred window, and an iron door. The shop was stocked with different sized icons and icon frames and books in polished yellow leather, stamped with a grape design, printed in Slavonic.[24] Next to our shop was another, dealing in the same wares, icons and religious books, and run by a black-bearded shopkeeper, related to an appraiser of such religious goods, who belonged to the sect of the Old Believers.[25] The reputation of this expert extended over the Volga region to the borders of Kerzhensk. The shopkeeper was assisted by a thin, spry son with a little, oldish face and shifty, mouselike eyes.

After opening the shop, I hurried to a nearby inn for some boiling water. Breakfast over, I had to put the shop in order, dust around, and

[24] The classic language of the church ritual.

[25] The *Raskolniki* (Old Believers) refused to accept certain revisions in the sacramental literature and in the icon imagery, instituted in the reign of Tsar Alexis by the Patriarch Nikon. Religious dissent in Russia found its chief expression in this sect which proliferated into many sub-sects.

then stand in the arcade outside, to steer customers from our competitor's store into ours.

"Customers are dopes," the young shopkeeper impressed upon me. "They don't care where they trade, so long as they get a bargain. They don't appreciate the value of the goods."

Giving the wooden edge of an icon a tap, he displayed his superficial trade knowledge for my instruction. "Here's a nice job—cheap, too—doesn't need a stand—three or four *vershoks* [26] high. And here's another, doesn't need a stand—six or seven vershoks. Are you up on the Saints? Keep in mind that Boniface helps against drunkenness, and the Holy Martyr Barbara, against toothache and fatal accidents; and Basil, The Blessed, against fevers. Are you up on the madonnas? Here's the Madonna of Sorrows, the three-armed Madonna, and the renowned Madonna of Abalatzk; and the Mourn Me Not Mother Madonna; and the Soothe My Grief Madonna, and the Madonna of Kazan, and the Madonna of Pokrov, and the Madonna of the Seven Wounds."

Soon I had by heart the prices of the icons, which were fixed according to size and detail, and I learned to distinguish between the different madonnas; but the diverse functions of the Saints were harder for me to keep in mind.

I might be standing at the shop door, daydreaming, when my boss would quiz me, "What Saint lightens the birth pangs?" And, if I replied amiss, he would fume, "What do you use your head for?"

Hardest of all was my role as puller-in. I, myself, saw nothing pleasing in the daubed icons, and had no urge to foist them on others. From grandma's stories I had brought away the image of a gentle and beautiful Madonna, similar to those represented in the art magazines; but on these icons she was a harsh, old woman with a long, hooked nose and stiff hands.

Our busy days were the market days—Wednesdays and Fridays. Peasants, old women, sometimes whole families, trooped down the arcade, all Old Believers from Zavolzh, morose and wary forest folk. I would spy a bulky man in homespun and sheepskins approaching hesitantly, or even apprehensively, and, overcoming my own embarrassment and reluctance, I would finally bring myself to accost him. I was clumsy at it, and as he twisted in his heavy boots, I would drone my spiel, "How can we serve you, your honor? We have annotated psalters and the works of Ephraim Sirin and Kyrillov, and the canonical literature and breviaries. You're welcome to browse around. And icons, a large assortment, whatever you're looking for, at different prices. All first-class work, dark colors! Or made

[26] A vershok is 1.7 inches.

to your order, any Saint or Madonna you specify; for a birthday gift or for your home. Finest shop in Russia, finest goods in town!"

Expressionless and imperturbable, the customer would make no response until suddenly, with an arm like a block of wood, he would jostle me out of his way and enter our competitor's door; and my boss, pulling at his big ears, would grumble, irritably, "So, you let him get away; a fine salesman you are!"

And from the next shop would issue a syrupy voice that had a drug-like power, "Our wares are not sheepskins or boots, my friend, but God's priceless grace, which is more precious than silver or gold."

"What a devil!" my boss would whisper, livid with envy and exasperation. "A plague on that peasant's eyes! You'll have to learn! You'll have to learn!"

I did my best to learn, for one should do whatever he must as well as he can. But I was no success, either as a puller-in or as salesman. These surly, laconic men, these ratlike old women, always so diffident and abject, somehow aroused my compassion; and my impulse was to disclose the real price and spare them the couple of greven that had been tacked on.

Their connoisseurship in books and icon art astounded me. A gray-haired old man, whom I had steered into the shop one day, informed me curtly, "No, my boy, this is not the best icon maker in Russia, Rogozhin's in Moscow is the best."

Bewildered, I stood aside to let him go and he went on, passing our competitor's shop as well.

"You let him go?" exclaimed my boss.

"You never said anything to me about the Rogozhin workshop."

He raged on. "These quiet ones! There's nothing they don't know, a plague on them! They're on to everything, the dogs!"

The sleek, overfed egotist hated the peasants. At his best moments he was all complaints. "Here I am, a man of brains, a clean person, who uses perfumes and incense and cologne water; but, though I value myself so highly, I have to bow and scrape to a peasant in order to wheedle five kopecks from him for the old woman! Is that justice? After all, what's a peasant? A parcel of smelly wool, a louse, and here—" And he lapsed into aggrieved silence.

I liked the peasants, who mystified me as Jake had done.

Sometimes a miserable-looking figure would clump into the shop, remove a shaggy cap, cross himself with two fingers, try to avoid looking at the unblessed icons, as his eyes turned to the glimmering lamp in the icon corner. And, after staring around, wordless for some time, he would finally ask for "an annotated psalter."

Tucking up his coat sleeves, he would pore over the pages, clumsily thumbing them, and gnawing at his lips.

"Nothing older?"

"An old one would come to a thousand rubles, you know."

"I know."

Moistening a finger to turn a page, his touch left a dark print on the margin. My boss, with a murderous look at the back of his head, said, "The Holy Scriptures don't age; God's word doesn't alter."

"That we know about. That we've heard before. God did not alter it, but Nikon[27] did." And, silently, shutting the book, he went out.

My boss sometimes got into disputes with these forest folk, who obviously knew the sacred writings better than he, drawing from him the exclamation, "Outlandish heathen!"

I observed that, though any new volume was in disfavor with these peasants, they nevertheless regarded it with respect, handling it like a bird that might soar up out of their grasp. This gave me pleasure to see, for a book was magic to me, too. It held the writer's soul, which spoke to me personally, when I opened the book and set it free.

Many old men and women came in to sell old books of pre-Nikon times, or beautiful copies made in the monasteries of Irgiz and Kerzhentz. They also brought missals free of the revisions by Dmitry Rostovsky; and icons bearing ancient inscriptions, and crosses, and diptych-icons, hinged and mounted in brass; and silver eucharist spoons presented as mementoes by the princes of Muscovy. These were offered furtively; they came from hoards secreted under floorboards.

Both my boss and his competitor were on the lookout for such business, and tried to lure the seller from each other. On resale, such antiques, purchased for anything up to ten rubles, would fetch hundreds from wealthy Old Believers.

"Watch for these werewolves, these sorcerers! Keep your eyes peeled for them; they're good luck!" my boss cautioned me.

When such a man turned up, my boss sent me to fetch the appraiser, Peter Vassilich, an expert in ancient volumes, icons, and antiques of all sorts. This old man was tall, and long-bearded, like Basil the Blessed, and had shrewd eyes in a genial face. A tendon had been cut in one of his

---

[27] The Patriarch Nikon, reformer of the Orthodox Church liturgy. Nikon subsequently suffered persecution for his opposition to Tsar Alexis' state control of the Church.

legs, so he walked stiffly, using a cane. Summer and winter alike, he wore the same light, cassocklike cloak, and an odd velvet hat, the shape of a saucepan. From his usually erect and brisk carriage, he changed, on entering the shop, to a professional, round-shouldered stoop, sighing and crossing himself and keeping up a continuous mumble of devotional words. This pretense of piety and frailness always made an impression on the seller.

"What's the trouble? Anything gone wrong?" he would inquire.

"Here's a man wants to sell an icon; says it's a Stroganov."

"What?"

"A Stroganov."

"Oh. My hearing's bad. Thus has the Lord shielded my ears against the defilements of the Nikonites!"

Removing his hat, he held out the icon, peered at the inscription from all sides, then at the knots in the wood, screwed up his eyes and muttered, "How the godless Nikonites, aware of our love of beautiful old work, and with the devil for teacher, have set out to confuse people with forgeries! How easy it is, nowadays, to make images, no trouble at all! At first glance this might be an authentic Stroganov, or a Ustiuzh or even a Suzdal; but examine it and it turns out a forgery."

Forgery, however, was his code word for a precious rarity. By such prearranged symbols he cued my boss as to how much to offer for book or icon. "Melancholy" and "affliction," I came to realize, signified ten rubles, "Nikon the Tiger," twenty-five. I felt ashamed, looking on, but also found it an entertaining performance, this skillful swindling by the old appraiser.

"Those Nikonites, dark progeny of Nikon the Tiger, are capable of anything, having the devil for their guide! You see, even the signature looks authentic! And the background, you'd think it was the work of one hand. But look at the face—done by a different brush. An old master, like Pimen Ushakov, heretic though he was, could do an icon all by himself; the background, the face, even the finishing, and the inscription! But the profane ones of our time can't. In the old days image-making was a sacred calling; but now they profane what should be of God into a mere art!"

Finally, laying the icon down gently, and taking up his hat, he concluded, "It's a sin!" Sin was the code word for "buy it."

Stuck in this syrupy flow and awed by the old man's erudition, the seller would ask in a deferential tone, "So what's your honor's opinion of the icon?"

"It's Nikonite handiwork."

"But it can't be! My grandfolks prayed under it."

"Nikon came before your grandfolks."

The old appraiser held the icon up in the seller's face, and exclaimed with asperity, "Just look at that unseemly expression of joy! Call that an icon! It's a soulless picture, just an art work, a Nikonite trick! Here am I, an old man, suffering persecution for the truth, and soon to face God —would I withhold the truth from you?"

And he would step from the shop out into the arcade, looking enfeebled by age, and affronted by having his judgment questioned. My boss got the image for a few rubles, and the seller, on his departure, bowed low to the old appraiser on the terrace; and I went off to the inn to fetch boiling water for tea. On my return, I would find the appraiser looking spry and chipper, and rapturously going over the fine points of the icon for my boss' benefit. "Observe with what care it's been done! This is painting, done in awe of God, with the human emotions repressed."

"What master do you attribute it to?" my boss wanted to know, smiling and capering.

"Can't say yet. Let me have it and I'll show it around."

"Oh, Peter!"

"And when I'm offered a good price, you'll get fifty rubles; everything over goes to me."

"Oh!"

"Stop oh-ing!"

And the conscienceless pair haggled through their tea, watching each other, shifty-eyed. My boss was plainly under old Peter's thumb. When the appraiser was gone, my boss would warn me, "No tattling to the old woman, now, about this business."

Having exhausted the icon as a subject, my boss would ask the old man, "What's going on in town?"

Caressing his beard with his yellow fingers and his greasy lips glistening, old Peter gossiped about business people, described big deals, banquets, wealthy invalids, society weddings and love affairs. He served up these dripping tidbits as artfully as a good cook serves up a dish of pancakes, with sputtering laughter for the sauce. My boss' round face darkened with envy and desire. His eyes went wistfully wide as he lamented, "Others live while I stew here!"

"Everybody's fate is appointed. For one it is rung out by angels with little silver mallets; for another, the devil does the ringing—with a sledgehammer!"

This robust, sinewy old man was in on everything in town. He had inside dope on business men, officials, the clergy and ordinary citizens. He was as sharp-sighted as a hawk and he added to that traits of the wolf and the fox. I would have liked to get him angry, but couldn't get at him; he seemed to see me from afar, and as though through mist. I had a sense of a man insulated by space; approaching him gave me a sensation of falling. In him, too, I felt a touch of Shumov, the stoker.

Although my boss eulogized old Peter's cleverness, both in his presence and when he was out of sight, he, too, at times, felt an impulse to bait the appraiser.

"You're a swindler!" he would exclaim, glaring at old Peter. To which the latter laughingly retorted, "Only the Lord manages without fraud; and we have to spend our lives among fools. Can you deal with fools without defrauding them? What, then, would be the purpose of fools?"

My boss would fly into a rage. "The peasants aren't all fools; and where did your business men come from, if not from the peasants?"

"We're not discussing business men. Fools and rogues are different. A fool's like a saint; his brain is in a dream."

The old man's speech was an irritating drawl. He seemed to be perched, out of reach, on a dry mound in a marsh. You could not provoke him to anger. Either he was beyond wrath, or knew how to control it. Yet it was he who often picked quarrels with me. He'd come up to me, and, grinning down into his beard, would ask, "Now, what's that French writer's name—Ponoss?"

This silly horseplay of turning names upside down infuriated me but, restraining myself, I replied, "Ponson de Tarail."

"And where'd he get lost?" [28]

"Don't fool around; you're not a child."

"True enough, I'm not a child. What writer are you reading now?"

"Ephraim Sirin."

"And who's the better writer, your foreign authors or he?"

I did not answer.

"What do the foreign authors write about, mainly?"

"About everything that happens in life."

"That is, dogs and horses, whichever happens along?"

My boss laughed, and I was exasperated. I was heavy-hearted and dejected in that atmosphere. But if I tried to get away, my boss stopped me. "Where are you off to?"

And the old man would turn to quizzing me. "Now, you scholar, here's a nut to crack. Let's suppose you're standing in front of a thousand

[28] A double pun; *ponoss* means diarrhea, and *terr yat* means to lose.

naked people, half of them men and half of them women, with Adam and Eve in their midst. How would you pick out Adam and Eve?"

He kept at me with this and, at last, triumphantly gave the answer. "Can't you see, you young fool, that since they weren't born, but created, they'd be without navels?"

The old man had a bottomless store of these nuts, on which he wore me out.

In my first days at the shop I told the boss stories from the books I had read; later they came back to me obscenely transformed. My boss regaled old Peter with them, cutting them up and giving them salacious twists. The old man expertly aided him with lewdly provocative questions. Their filthy tongues slobbered over Eugenie Grandet, Ludmilla and Henry IV.

I realized they resorted to this, not out of ill-will, but as a pastime. Nevertheless, I found it hard to take. Having spewed out the filth, they made a pig's wallow of it, grunting with delight as they soiled all that had beauty and mystery, which, by those very qualities, became laughable to them.

The whole bazaar, all its business men and shopkeepers, led an unnatural life, which they filled with oafish or childish, and always vicious, amusements. They would willfully misdirect passersby who asked the way; this, indeed, had become so habitual it no longer gave them enjoyment. Having caught a pair of rats, they would tie their tails together, and then gloat over the torments of the bewildered animals as they pulled each other or turned on each other; or they would pour kerosene over the rats and watch them burn. Or they would tie a tin can to a dog's tail, and laugh as the distraught animal whirled about, howling and snapping.

They had many varieties of this kind of entertainment; they behaved, so it seemed to me, as if every sort of people—and the peasants in particular—lived solely to provide them entertainment. In their relations with people they seemed to feel only the urge to scoff at, to cause pain to, to discommode others. I found it strange that books ignored this incessant, ingrained inclination of people to humiliate one another.

Particularly brutish and repulsive to me was the following bazaar diversion: On the street floor, just below us, was a shop selling felt boots, whose salesman had achieved city-wide notoriety for his appetite. His boss boasted of his gluttony as one might boast of the temper of a watchdog, or the endurance of a horse. He would offer bets to the neighboring shopkeepers. "Who'll lay ten rubles? Ten rubles says Misha disposes of a ten-pound ham in two hours!"

Everybody knew Misha could do it and the reply was, "We won't bet, but we'll pay for the ham to watch him eat it." And another would say, "But it must be all meat; no bones!"

After some desultory banter, there crawled forth from that dark shop a gaunt chap, with a beardless, bony face, with a long coat belted around with a band of red leather, ornamented with tassels of wool. Deferentially baring his small head, he turned his dull, expressionless, deep-set eyes on his boss' plump and ruddy face and waited in silence. The latter asked in a coarse voice, "How about eating up a ham?"

"How long will I have?"

"Two hours."

"That'll be hard."

"What's hard about it?"

"Can I have a drop of beer with it?"

"All right." And then the boss would brag to the audience, "Don't think he's filling up an empty stomach. This morning he had his two pounds of bread, and then he had his regular lunch."

The ham was fetched in, and the audience settled down for the show. The tradespeople were bundled up in their heavy fur coats, like immense parcels. They were all paunchy; some were humped with fatty growths, and all had little eyes. Incurable boredom was their common affliction. They tucked their hands into their sleeves and crowded around the performer, who had an equipment of knives and wedges of rye bread. Crossing himself, he sat down on a bale of wool, laid the ham on a box beside him, and his dull eyes fixed on it in sluggish calculation.

Slicing the ham thick and the bread thin, he took a sandwich into his two hands and held it to his mouth. His lips quivered; he moistened them with his long, doglike tongue, there was a flash of short, sharp teeth, and like a dog, he applied his muzzle to the meat.

"He's off!"

"Time him!"

All eyes fixed on the machinelike, masticating face, on the lower jaw and on the knobs near the ears; as the pointed chin went up and down, they indulged in indolent repartee.

"He's a neat feeder—like a bear!"

"Ever see a bear eating?"

"Do I live in a forest? I mean the saying, 'Gobbles like a bear.'"

"Like a pig, you mean."

"Pigs don't eat pig."

There was a reluctant snicker. Someone remarked, "Pigs eat every-thing—suckling pigs and their own sisters."

Gradually the eater's face darkened; his ears turned blue; his damp eyes almost popped out of their sockets; his breath came in gasps; but the movements of his chin continued as regular as before.

"Easy does it, Misha; you've got time."

He turned a worried, measuring glance on the remaining meat, took a sip of beer and munched on. The spectators grew livelier; took more frequent looks at the watch in the boss' hand, and cautioned each other. "He's probably set the hands back! Let somebody else hold it! Keep your eyes on Misha, or he'll slip some meat up his sleeve. He'll never finish on time."

To which Misha's boss retorted heatedly, "Bet you a ruble! Come on, Misha!" The rest argued with him, but no one covered his bet.

And Misha ate and ate; his face took on a ham tinge; his pointed, gristly nose whistled for breath. He was a horrible sight. He seemed on the point of beseeching them, "Have pity on me!"

It was over at last. Opening his swimming eyes, he pleaded in a hoarse, exhausted voice, "May I go to sleep?"

The boss, angrily eying his watch, cried, "You've gone four minutes over, you!"

And the others took digs at the boss. "We should have taken you on; you'd have got a trimming." "Just the same, that guy's a regular wild animal!" "What monsters the Lord can turn men into!" "How about some tea?" And, like barges, they floated off to the inn.

What fermented in their iron hearts, I wondered, that they should cluster round that miserable creature and find amusement in his unwholesome gluttony?

It was close and dark in that narrow arcade, heaped with wool, sheepskins, hemp, rope, felt boots and harness. Its thick brick columns were weather-stained and mud-spattered. I had counted every brick, every crack between the bricks, and every gap in the cement, a thousand times over; and their unsightly patterns were stamped on my memory.

Pedestrians loafed along the sidewalk; cabs and loaded sledges slowly creaked up the road. Across the street was a bazaar, a square, two-story affair of red brick, littered with crates, straw, paper scrap, mud and trampled snow.

And everything, people and horses, too, despite their movement, appeared immobile, or to be languidly revolving about a pivot to which each was chained by unseen links. You suddenly realized that this life was almost without sound, or the sound was so thin as to be little better than muteness. The sledge runners squeaked; shop doors slammed; piemen and honey peddlers gave their spiels, but in tones that were dismal and forced. They all sounded alike; one soon got so used to them as to no longer hear them.

The funereal church chimes kept ringing in my ears. That mournful sound seemed to hover over us from morning to night. It got into all my thoughts and emotions, coating all my impressions as with a deposit of copper.

The breath of ennui, chill and poverty exhaled from everything; from the earth raggedly sheeted in stained snow, from the gray snow lid on the roof, from the brick walls, red like chapped flesh. From the chimneys ennui floated in thick, gray smoke and crawled over the low, leaden, vacant sky. In ennui toiling horses steamed and men sighed. And the people here had a smell all their own: a dense, dull stench compounded of sweat, grease, hemp oil, ash and smoke. The smell settled over your head like a snug, warm cap; it trickled down your chest, making you feel dizzy, making you want to shut your eyes on everything, to raise desperate outcries, to run out and knock your head on a wall.

And I stared into the tradesmen's faces, the stuffed, thick-blooded, chapped faces of men as sluggish as if they slept. They were almost always yawning, their mouths gaping like stranded fish.

In winter business was dull; the shopkeepers' eyes lacked that alert, predatory glitter which lent them animation in other seasons. Their heavy furs weighed them down to the ground, and slowed their movements. Their speech dragged, but anger could give it vitality; and it seemed to me that they invited occasions for wrath, in order to demonstrate that some life lingered in them.

I could see how the burden of ennui was crushing them; the only explanation I could find for their sadism, for their victimizing others with insensate horseplay, was that they were in a hopeless struggle with their overpowering ennui.

I sometimes spoke of this with old Peter. Generally he took a mocking attitude toward me, but, because of my fondness for books, he unbent now and then, spoke seriously to me, and gave me advice.

"I despise the way shopkeepers live," I said.

Curling a lock of his beard between his long fingers, he retorted, "Do you know the way they live? Do you frequent their homes? This, my friend, is just a street; nobody lives in the street; people only do business here; and when it's done, hurry home as fast as they can. People walk about, dressed; do you know what they're like underneath? The real person is only to be seen at home, inside his own four walls—you don't know a thing about them!"

"Agreed. But don't they think the same here as at home?"

"How can you know what's in your neighbor's mind?" asked the old appraiser, rolling his eyes. "You can't count a man's thoughts any more than you can count his lice. One man, when he gets home, may drop to his knees and call on God, through his tears, 'Forgive me, dear Lord, for desecrating Thy holy day.' This man's house may be his hermitage, where he is alone with God. That's how it is! Every spider is at home in a corner of his own, spins his own web, and figures on the situation he is in, how best to fend for himself."

In serious conversation he pitched his voice lower, to a muttering bass, as if he were confiding secrets.

"Here you go, passing sentences on people; you're too young for that. A lad of your years should rely on his eyes, not his logic. You just look on, hold what you see in mind, and keep quiet. The mind has to do with business; the soul has to do with faith. Reading is fine, but the golden mean is best there as in other things; there are people who've read their way into lunacy and atheism."

I regarded him as something eternal. I found it difficult to think of him growing older or changing in any way. He was fond of telling stories of counterfeiters and notorious swindlers. I had had my belly full of these anecdotes from grandpa, who was the better raconteur. But the purport of the stories was the same in both—that the quest for millions leads to transgression against God and one's fellow men. Toward people old Peter had no feeling; but when he spoke of God his voice became soft, and he sighed and put his hand over his eyes.

"God, too, they try to swindle, and He, Lord Jesus Christ, sees through it and laments, 'Oh, people, my miserable people, they're getting hell ready for you!' "

Once I pointed out to him, "But you, yourself, swindle the peasants."

He shrugged it off. "Should I worry myself over that? I may cheat them of three or four rubles; that's what it comes to."

When he came upon me with a book in my hands, he would take it from me and quiz me on it, trying to trip me up. With astonishment and disbelief he would call out to my boss, "Think of it; the little rascal understands books!" And what he followed with stuck in my memory.

"It'll pay you to listen to this. There were two Cyrils, both bishops; Cyril of Alexandria and Cyril of Jerusalem. Cyril of Alexandria fought against the damn heretic, Nestorious, who fostered the lewd notion that the Holy Mary, having herself been conceived in original sin, could not have been God's mother; that her issue was a human being, whose name and traits were those of the Messiah; consequently she should be designated Christ-bearer, but not God-bearer. Do you follow that? That's a heresy! Cyril of Jerusalem, he dealt with the Arian heretics."

I was absorbed by his accounts of church history. Caressing his beard with hands carefully groomed, like a priest's, he boasted, "I have it all at my fingertips. In Moscow I disputed the abominable dogmas of the Nikonites, taking on their wise ones, priests and lay people. Yes, my little one, I debated with professors! And one of them found my verbal barb so sharp, he bled from the nose!"

His cheeks flushed; his eyes glittered. For him, his opponent's nosebleed had been the ultimate victory, the topmost ruby of the gold coronet of his triumph; and he took voluptuous delight in the recital.

"Handsome he was, that priest, and healthy looking. There he stands on the platform, and drip, drip from his nose plops the blood. He didn't see it, his humiliation! That priest raged like a lion in the desert. His voice clanged like a bell. But quietly, right between his ribs, my words sawed away! The man was like a furnace; the hateful fires of heresy heated him red-hot—ehk, that was something!"

From time to time other appraisers turned up. They included Pakhomy, a paunchy, one-eyed man, with a seamed and scowling face; little old Lucian, velvety as a mouse, and kind and quick. Lucian was always accompanied by a sombre giant, a coachman in appearance, a forbidding, though handsome, black-bearded man whose face was grim as death, and whose eyes had a fixed glare. Generally they came to offer for sale rare books, old icons and thuribles, or religious vessels. Sometimes they were accompanied by the seller, an elderly Volga man or woman. After they had made the deal, they perched on the counter like crows along a furrow, had rolls and tea sweetened with Lenten sugar, and tut-tutted over the evils perpetrated by the Nikonites.

In one town homes had been raided and devotional books confiscated; in another, a house used for worship had been closed by the police, and the owner prosecuted, under Article 103. This statute was constantly on their lips, but it was referred to like something inevitable, like winter frost. The words police, raids, prison, courts, Siberia, recurring in their conversation, made real the religious persecution they suffered. The words lodged in my breast like live coals, kindling sympathy and brotherliness toward these sectaries. Reading had taught me to value spiritual fortitude, to respect those who unflinchingly held to their purpose. I ignored the evil that I saw in their attitudes toward life. I let myself see only their serenity and steadfastness, which betokened, it seemed to me, an immovable devotion to their teachings, for whose sake they would make any sacrifice.

In the long run, after encounters with a great variety of these pillars of the traditional faith, both learned and unlearned, I came to see that this steadfastness was rather passivity, the rootedness of a static people who never even wanted to move from the spots they were planted on, whose outworn words and ideas served only to hold them down. Their wills were paralyzed; they could not turn from their backward-looking attitudes to meet a blow; and so, when they were struck out of their fixed place, they toppled over without resistance, like boulders down a hill. They fasted in their own way and remained in their cemeteries of outlived doctrines; their memory of the past had a sort of morbid strength that filled them with insane yearnings for suffering and persecution. Stripped of occasions of suffering, they lost cohesion, they vanished like a cloud blown out in fresh winter gusts.

Undeniably, the faith for which they were contentedly and even smugly prepared to suffer, is a strong one; but what protects it from the wear and tear of time is what often protects old clothes—incrustations of all sorts of dirt. Mind and soul become habituated to the close and oppressive confines of dogma, and finally see security and comfort in deformity and winglessness.

Our life exhibits few things more lamentable and injurious than this faith constructed on old customs. Within the reach of such ideas, as in the shadows of stone walls, new growth is slow, crippled and feeble. In that dismal faith love rarely shines; instead, humiliations, annoyances and grudges that verge on hate. Its light is the spectral glow of decay.

But before I came to this realization, I had to bear many dreary years, and shatter many icons in my soul and hurl them out. But when I first encountered these teachers of life, I was mired in dull and squalid circumstance, and they impressed me by their seeming spiritual strength. I thought them the salt of the earth. Almost to a man, they had experienced persecution, imprisonment, exile; they had been driven from place to place with convicts; they had all lived precariously.

I soon perceived, however, that these old folks who scoffed at the "confined spirit" of the Nikonites, gladly helped to keep each other confined. Hunched Pakhomy, when he was in liquor, vaunted his prodigious memory for sacerdotal details. He was at home in certain books as a Jew is in his Talmud; could lay a finger on a picked page, and, from the word his finger covered, could go on, by heart, in a bland, snuffling recitation. Almost always his one eye roamed the floor agitatedly, as if hunting some lost treasure. The book he most frequently used in this performance was Prince Mishetsky's *The Russian Vine*, and the passage he was best at was "The Endurance and Fortitude in Suffering of Our Brave and Glorious Martyrs," with old Peter ever on the alert to trip him up.

"That's wrong! It was not Cyprian the Noble, but Denis the Pure."

"Which Denis? You must be thinking of Dionysius."

"Don't twist words!"

"And don't you lecture me!"

And soon the two, blown up with wrath, would be glaring at each other, Peter bellowing, "Defiler of truth; out of my sight, shameless one!" And Pakhomy, countering, "You roué, you goat, always smelling after women!"

His hands tucked into his sleeves, my boss, excited like a boy, egged on these guardsmen of the Old Faith. "That's the stuff! Give it to him!"

Once old Peter unexpectedly slapped his adversary's face, and put him to flight, and, mopping his sweating face, called out to the fleeing man, "Remember, that sin's on your head. It was you who seduced my hand into sin, accursed one; pugh on you!"

Old Peter enjoyed badgering his comrades with concern over the slackness of their faith, and forebodings that they would slide into "Protestantism."

"It's that Aleksasha who bothers you—that cock's started crowing again!"

Protestantism caused him much concern, but my question, "What's the doctrine of that sect?" brought this not very intelligible reply, "There's no worse heresy. Its devotion is given solely to Reason; it rejects God! There's the Bible Christians for one, whose only book is the Bible, which they got from a German, Luther; of whom they say Luther's well named; you see, if you form it as a verb you get *liuto bo, liubo, liuto*.[29] And it spreads from the West, from the heretics of those regions."

And, stamping his lame foot, he would say in a cold, ponderous voice, "It's they whom the New Ritualists [30] will have to go after, whom

[29] A pun on the word *Lutui*, meaning rough or violent.
[30] Another term for the Nikonites—the established government sponsored clergy and communicants of the Orthodox Church.

they'll have to keep their eyes on—and throw into the fire!—not we who are of the true faith, Easterners of the true, Eastern faith, the original Russian faith! but those derive from the West, infected by free will! The Germans and the French—has anything good come out of them? Think of what they did in the year 12—"

In his excitement he forgot he was talking to a boy; his powerful hands gripped my belt, he pulled me toward him at one moment, pushed me from him the next, speaking, in the meanwhile, with eloquence, with ardor, with a youthful resonance, "In his own imaginings, rank as a forest, roams the mind of man; roams like a wild wolf; becomes the devil's helper; puts the soul, given by God, to torture! What have they not devised, these lackeys of Satan? The Bogomili,[31] carriers of the Protestant plague, spread this teaching: Satan they aver to be the son of God, Christ's older brother! That's what they've fallen to! Another of their teachings is to acknowledge no superiors, to refuse to work, to desert one's family! To listen to them a man can do with nothing; needs no goods at all; just lives as he fancies with the devil to give him hints. That Aleksasha's around, again!"

Called in by the boss to do some chore, I had to leave the old man, who went on, addressing space, "You wingless soul, you kitten born blind, where shall I flee to escape you!" After which he lapsed into silence, and sat motionlessly staring out upon the grisly winter sky.

He began giving me more of his attention, and took a kindlier attitude toward me. Finding me reading, he'd look over my shoulder, remarking, "Read, my boy, it will repay you. However, though you may have brains, it's no good having so little regard for your elders. You imagine yourself a match for anyone, but where will that impertinence get you? Nowhere, lad, but to jail. Yes, keep on reading, but bear in mind, books are only books; you have your own wits to use. Danilov, who started the sect of the Khlists, decided there was no need of books, old or new, made a bundle of all his books—and into the water with them! The act of a fool! And now that dog, Aleksasha, must nose around here, to make trouble."

This Aleksasha kept cropping up in his talk. Once, he entered the shop with a grim and thoughtful look, and remarked to my boss, "Aleksasha's in town; arrived yesterday. But I can't rout him out; found himself a snug hiding place."

In a snapping voice my boss replied, "I know nothing about him!"

[31] A sect of the Old Believers.

With a nod the old man said, "Which signifies that to you a man's nothing but a buyer or seller. Well, let's have some tea."

Coming in with the big copper tea pot, I found we had more company—old Lucian, with a grin on his face, and away from the door, in a dim corner, a stranger in a dark coat fastened with a green belt, wearing high felt boots and a cap pulled awkwardly over his forehead. I could hardly see his face, but it seemed decent and modest and a little dejected, like that of an unemployed clerk.

He kept pulling convulsively at his cap, as old Peter, without deigning to look at him, delivered censorious oratory. The stranger lifted his hand as though to cross himself, pushed his cap all the way back, then pulled it all the way down again; a compulsive gesture, recalling that of the idiot beggar, Igosha, Death-in-His-Pocket.

"All sorts of snakes infest our sluggish rivers, and muddy the waters," blared old Peter.

Quietly, even gently, the man who looked like a clerk asked, "Is that meant for me?"

"And what if it is?"

"And what, man, have you to say for yourself?" the stranger retorted, manfully, but not raising his voice.

"That I say to God—that's my affair."

"No, man, it's mine, too," the stranger said, in a grave and steady voice. "Don't hide your face from the truth; don't hide from yourself in calculated blindness; thereby you sin against God and your fellow men!"

It pleased me to hear him address Peter as "man"; and there was something stirring in his controlled and stately voice. His diction was like that of an eloquent priest at a reading of "Lord, Master of My Life." He leaned forward, rose from his seat, his hands outstretched, and said, "Judge me not, for my sins are no heavier than yours."

The samovar bubbled and piped; the old appraiser held to his scornful tone; but his adversary went on, undeterred. "God alone knows who pollutes the fountain of the Holy Spirit more. It may be you, you scholars, you lettered people. I have no learning or letters; I lead a simple life."

"That notorious simple life of yours—we've heard enough of it!"

"You scribes and Pharisees, it's you who perplex the people, who disrupt the true faith. About me, what's there to say, tell me?"

"Heretic!" hissed Peter. The other, holding his two hands before his face, like the sides of a book he was reading from, retorted hotly, "Is it your notion that, to herd people out of one pen into another, is an improvement? No, I say. Man be free, I say! What does house, wife or possessions count with the Lord? Let us liberate ourselves, man, from the vanities over which men contend, for which they rend each other—from gold and silver and all manner of wealth, which can but corrupt and defile. Not on fields in this world, but in the vales of Paradise, is the soul to find salvation! Pull yourself free of it all, I say; strike off all chains, all bonds; rip the nets of this world; their weaver is anti-Christ. I take the straight road; I do not play tricks with my soul; I have no part in this dark world."

"No worldly bread and water and trousers for you, eh?" jeered old Peter.

But these gibes did not affect Aleksasha. Low-pitched though his voice remained, it now pealed like a brass trumpet. "Man, what is it you hold dear? You should hold only Him, the one God, dear. With all my stains washed away I appear clean before Him. Heave the world out of your heart, and look at God; you—alone; He—alone! Only thus may you reach God; there is no other approach to Him. That's the salvation road—to give up father and mother; everything! even to lose your eye; which, if it presents temptation, tear it out! If you wrench yourself away from things for His sake, you will keep your soul; take sanctuary in the Spirit, and the soul shall gain eternal life."

"The dog returns to his vomit, that's how it is with you," said old Peter, getting up. "A year has passed, but, instead of acquiring wisdom, you've grown more hardened in your evil!" He limped out of the shop, to Aleksasha's consternation, who asked, "Did he go? Why?"

Good-natured Lucian consoled him, with a wink and a "That's all right," which brought Aleksasha's homily down upon him. "Ah, you, worldly one! Your words, too, sow chaff! What sense have they? So, a triple Hallelujah, a double——"

Lucian, grinning, also left the shop, and Aleksasha, turning to my boss, said complacently, "They can't take it! They vapor out like smoke from the flame."

My boss gave him a sidelong glance, and observed curtly, "I give no thought to it."

"What! You mean to say you give it no thought! But this matter must be thought about!" His head dropped and he sat in silence, until the two old men called him, and the three went off.

This man flared up before me like a bonfire in the dark. After his bright blaze was out, I realized that I had seen a revelation in its light, a truth in his rejection of the ordinary ways of life.

That evening, when an occasion presented itself, I raved about him to the chief icon painter. Gentle, sweet-natured Ivan heard me out and explained, "He's a Begoon; they disown all authority."

"How do they live?"

"They roam the earth, like fugitives; wherefore they're called Begoons.[32] They're against all property, land or goods. The police consider them subversive and lock them up."

With the bitterness in my life, I could not comprehend what would make one shun good things. In the life around me, there was much that interested me and that I treasured, and Aleksasha soon ebbed out of my mind.

Yet, at one time or another, in a dark hour, his image would return. I saw him crossing a field or trudging the gray forest path, pushing his cap up and down with ticlike movements of his white hands, unstained by toil, mumbling, "I take the straight road; I have no part in this dark world; I have cut all ties."

And with this image, I recalled my father, as he had appeared in grandma's dream, picking his way with a walnut stick, and a spotted dog, whose tongue hung out, at his heels.

Chapter Thirteen

The icons were painted in a two-room workshop. One room had four windows, three over a yard and the fourth over a garden; the second had two windows, one facing the garden, the other the street. The windows were small squares and their aged, iridescent panes reluctantly admitted the wan winter light. The icon painters stooped over the work tables which filled the room. From the ceiling hung glass globes filled with water; these reflected cool white rays from the lamps upon the square planes of the icons.

In these hot, stuffy workrooms some twenty men were at work, men from Palekh, Kholuya, and Mster. They wore cotton shirts, unbuttoned at the neck, and trousers made of ticking. Some were barefoot;

[32] From the word *beg*, meaning flight. The Begoons were one of the many sects of the Old Believers.

some wore sandals. Like blue gauze over their heads hung the smoke of their cheap tobacco; and the room was heavy with a stench compounded of glue, varnish and rotten eggs. Slowly, like tar, dripped their lugubrious, Vladimir tune: "How corrupt the times have become; the lad seduced the maid, nor cared who knew."

They sang other sad ditties, but this was their favorite. Its languid measures did not interrupt one's thoughts, nor the strokes of the fine, weasel-hair brush as it outlined a figure or etched in the sharp lines of suffering over a gaunt Saint's face. At the windows sat the engraver, Goloviev, a tipsy old man with a swollen blue nose, tapping away with his little hammer. Its incessant, dry, pecking sound pitted the flowing song. It had the effect of a worm gnawing in a tree.

Some evil genius had brought division of labor into the craft, to such extent as to strip each process of creativeness, leaving it incapable of inspiring love or sustaining any interest. The bad-tempered, squinting woodworker, Panfil, planed and glued together the different sized panels of cypress and lilac wood; the consumptive youth, Davidov, laid on the background colors; his comrade, Sorokin, did the inscription; Milyashin pencilled the outlines of the decorations from a pattern; old Goloviev laid on the gilt and embossed the design in gold; others painted in the landscapes; others the robes; and then the icons were stacked up, against the walls, waiting for the brushes of the painters who did the faces, hands and feet. It was weird, seeing a large icon that was to stand on an altar or to panel an altar door leaning against the wall, minus face, hands or feet—merely robes or armor or the tunics of archangels.

To me, these differently painted boards suggested death. What might have given them life was lacking; it seemed to have been there, but to have been spirited away, leaving behind nothing but voluminous cloths.

After the features had been put in by the face painter, the icon went to one who colored in the engraved design; still another worker did the lettering, and the varnishing was the job of the foreman, the taciturn Ivan Larionovich. His face was gray; his fine, silky beard was gray; and his strangely sad and sunken eyes were gray. His smile was friendly, but it was hard to return it. For some reason he made you feel awkward. He resembled the image of Simeon Stolpnik; he was similarly withered and gaunt; and his still eyes seemed fixed on something remote, with glances that penetrate people and walls, like that abstracted Saint.

A few days after I joined the workshop, its chief worker, a Don Cossack named Kapendiukhin, a strong, good-looking chap, came in drunk. His teeth were clenched, and his rather soft, feminine eyes twitched as, wordlessly, he set about demolishing everything within his reach. Though not more than medium height, he was of powerful build; and he lunged on the things in the workroom, like a cat on rats in the cellar. The other workmen took panic and, shivering in corners, each called on the other to "knock him down!"

The face painter, Eugene Sitanov, succeeded in knocking out the delirious man by a blow on the head with a stool. The prostrate Cossack was then tied up in towels, which he began to bite through, like an animal. Infuriated, Sitanov climbed on a table, and, with his hands to his sides, poised himself to jump on the Cossack. Sitanov being a tall and heavy man, this would have meant crushing Kapendiukhin's breastbone. The foreman, Larionovich, appeared just in time, and without removing overcoat or cap, motioned Sitanov back, and in a calm tone, as if it were a routine instruction, ordered the workmen, "Carry him out in the hall; let him sober up there."

The Cossack was hauled out; the chairs and tables were set in place again, and work was resumed. The workmen commented on the strength of their drunken shopmate, and predicted his death in a quarrel. "It will be hard to kill him," remarked Sitanov, in a matter-of-fact voice, as if it were something he knew by experience.

Gazing at Larionovich, I wondered at his control over these tough, pugnacious men. He gave every one of them directions, and not even the best of them took affront. Kapendiukhin received his special attention.

"Kapendiukhin, you're a real painter; I mean your work should be from life, in the Italian style. Oils call for warm coloring; you've mixed in too much white; the eyes you've given the Madonna are ice cold. The red apple cheeks you've given her don't go with them. And they're not set right; one's over her nose and the other lands on her temple; and the face isn't pure and holy; it's crafty and cold. Put more thought into your work, Kapendiukhin."

The Cossack listened with a sour expression. With a pettish smile in his feminine eyes he said, in a voice naturally sweet, but hoarse from drinking, "Ekh, father of mine, this is no calling for me. I'm a born musician, but I got stuck among monks."

"With a mind to it, anything can be learned."

"No; not my sort! I should have been a coachman, driving a team of three fast horses, eh?" And, his Adam's apple vibrating, he sang dispiritedly, "Ai-akh! had I hounds and horses, then, on gloomy, frosty nights, I'd speed to my beloved!"

With a slow smile, Ivan adjusted his glasses on his melancholy, gray nose, and went out. A dozen voices joined in the tune, and the flood of song seemed to heave the shop into the air and shake it rhythmically.

"The horses knew the way; they got there by themselves."

The apprentice, Paul Odinstov, stopped pouring off egg yolks and, eggshells in hand, led the chorus like a maestro. Lost in that intoxication of song, they seemed to breathe from one breast, and to be animated by one emotion; all kept their eyes on Kapendiukhin, the Cossack. In singing he was their acknowledged leader; they followed him as if magnetized, responding to every flutter of his hands, as his arms stretched out like wings, and he seemed poised for flight. I think if he had suddenly stopped and shouted, "Let's wreck the place!," even the most responsible workmen would have joined him, and the place would immediately have been demolished.

He didn't sing often, but then it was with an all-conquering effect. It was as if these people were light and inflammable to his touch, and he would pick them up and kindle them, as if everything became pliant when it entered the zone heated by his mighty voice.

In me the songs evoked a scalding envy of the singer, of his amazing hold upon people. An overwhelming emotion flooded my heart, till I thought it would burst. Close to tears, I had an impulse to cry out to the singers, "I love you!"

When the tubercular, sallow Davidov, strangely covered with tufts of hair, opened his mouth in song, he looked like a newly hatched crow.

Only the Cossack could get such rollicking songs going. Ordinarily they sang that mournful, dragging tune about these corrupt times, another about the forests, and another on the death of Alexander I: "How Our Alexander Went to Review His Troops." At the suggestion of Zhikharev, the best of our face painters, they sometimes started hymn tunes, but rarely with success. Zhikharev sought some special effect; he had a fixed notion of harmony; and he would keep interrupting the singers.

A man of about forty-five, dried out and bald, what was left of his hair was curly and black like a gypsy's; and his eyebrows were thick as moustaches. His swarthy, un-Russian face was handsomely adorned by a full, pointed beard; but the fierce moustaches under his prominent nose were rather a superfluity on the same face with his eyebrows. His blue eyes were ill-matched, the left being conspicuously larger.

"Paul," he would call out in a tenor voice, to my fellow apprentice, Odintsov, "Start now, 'Praise ——' The rest of you, listen!"

And Paul, wiping his hand on his apron, would lead off, "Praise——"
And several voices would come in with, ". . . the name of the Lord";
but they never satisfied Zhikharev. He would interrupt, "Lower, Eugene;
your voice should be coming from the very depths of your soul."

Sitanov, in a voice so deep it boomed like a kettle drum, bellowed,
"Slaves of the Lord!"

"Not that way. Here, it should shake the earth, it should make the
doors and the windows fly open!"

Zhikharev's excitement was quite indescribable. His astounding eyebrows would throb up and down, his voice would crack, and his fingers
would fly over an imaginary dulcimer.

" 'Slaves of the Lord!' Understand?" he would repeat, solemnly.
"You've got to feel that in your bones—all the way in! 'Slaves, praise the
Lord!' How can you, living human beings, fail to understand that?"

"We just don't seem to get it the way you want it," Sitanov quietly
said.

"Well, let it go!" And Zhikharev, annoyed, returned to his work.

He was our prize worker, being able to paint the faces both in the
Byzantine style and in the art-conscious, new Italian style. Larionovich,
on taking commissions for icon-altars, would always consult Zhikharev.
He had a comprehensive knowledge of the whole range of icon-art.
Costly copies of miracle-working icons, such as the Theodorov and Kazan, had passed through his hands. On seeing an original he would
grumble, "There's no getting away from it; they hold us down!"

Despite his top position in the shop, he was not always as aloof as the
rest, and treated the apprentices, Paul and me, with consideration. He
tried to give us some instruction, something none of the others bothered to do. But he was hard to follow. He was a cheerless sort, and
would sometimes go on for a week without a word, as if he were a mute.
He behaved toward people as if they were all strangers, and of an astounding sort, such as he had never come across before. Though he
enjoyed singing, in such moods he did not join in, did not even seem
to hear. And the others stared at him and winked at each other. Dark
and foreign-looking himself, he would bend over the icon, which rested
on his knees and against the edge of the table, and brush on the dark,
foreign face. Suddenly he would call out, as if in annoyance, "Forerunner—(predtech) what does that mean? Tech means 'go' in Slavonic;
so the forerunner is one who goes before; that's all there is to it."

The workshop was in dead silence. Covert glances were turned on
Zhikharev, and there was suppressed laughter. Then, out of the silence,

came these strange words, "He should be painted in a sheepskin and wings."

I asked him, "Whom are you talking to?"

He gave me no reply, either not having heard me, or not deigning to answer. Again his words sang out in the waiting stillness, "We ought to know more about the lives of the saints. But what do we know? Where are the wings of our lives? Where's the soul? The soul, where? The models, yes, but the souls, where?"

His thinking aloud drew derisive laughter, even from Sitanov, and there generally followed a gloating whisper, "He'll get stewed this Saturday." At that, tall and muscular Sitanov, a youth of twenty-two, round-faced, and almost hairless, would stare morosely into a corner.

I remember how, when the copy of the Theodorov Madonna was finished, Zhikharev set it up on the table and addressed it in an excited tone, "It's done! Little Mother! Shining Grail, Thou! Bottomless Vessel, in which fall tears from the hearts of the world's living!"

And, getting into his overcoat, he went off to a bar. The younger workers laughed and whistled; the older ones heaved envious sighs; Sitanov went over to take a look at the completed icon, and said, "Sure! He has to get stewed! It's a pang to him to let his work go. Not all of us are worthy of suffering such pain!"

Zhikharev's benders, which always started on Saturdays, were nothing like the usual workers' sprees. This is how it began: Saturday morning he would write a note which he would have Paul deliver. About noon he would tell Larionovich, "Today, I'm going to the baths."

"When will you be back?"

"The Lord——"

"Please get back by Tuesday."

Zhikharev made the promise with a nod of his bald skull and a flourish of his eyebrows. On his return from the baths, he dressed up, nattily, in tie and dickey and satin vest, with a silver chain strung across; and then left, without a word, except to order Paul and me, "Have the place clean by evening; have the table scraped and washed."

Then a festive stir would possess everybody. They went to the baths; they spruced up; they rushed through their suppers. Later in the evening Zhikharev reappeared, bringing snacks, beer and wine. A woman followed behind, oversize in so many ways she looked monstrous. She was nearly six and a half feet tall, making our big Sitanov look insignificant beside her, and our stools look like doll's furniture. She was well proportioned, but her bosom jetted up, like a mountain ridge, toward her chin; and she moved heavily and clumsily. She must have been forty, but her pliant face, with its big, horse eyes, was fresh, unwrinkled and lively. Its little mouth looked daubed on like a cheap doll's. She grinned at everybody, and made incessant small talk. "How goes it? It's real cold today. It's so stuffy in here! The paint smell, that's it. So, how goes it?"

She was relaxing to look at, like a placid, wide river; but her conversation, heavy with redundant phrases, was soporific. She breathed hard before she spoke, puffing out her quite livid cheeks, rounder than before. This made the younger men giggle and exchange whispers, "An engine!" "No, a steeple!"

Her lips pursed and her hands folded under her bosom, she sat at the table next to the samovar, and turned a friendly horselike eye on us all, one after the other. We were all respectful toward her, the younger ones even timid. They looked at that enormous figure with avid eyes that dropped in confusion, however, on meeting her enveloping gaze. Zhikharev treated her with respect, using the formal pronoun, calling her "little comrade," and bowing as he offered her snacks. To which she made a languid protest, "Now, don't you be putting yourself out for me; no need to fuss."

She moved through life without fluster. She raised her arms only from the elbows, which she kept at her sides. A hot scent came from her, like that of bread out of the oven. Stuttering in his ardor, old Goloviev eulogized her beauty like a deacon offering ritual praises. When he became confused, she would smile amiably and help out with autobiography, "We were no way good-looking in our youth; it's all the result of living as a woman. By thirty it got so the nobility, itself, took notice; and, actually, a garrison commander offered a coach and a team of horses."

Kapendiukhin, unkempt from drink, turned a hostile glance on her and asked, hoarsely, "What did he offer them for?"

"For our love, of course."

"Love, what kind of love?"

The woman answered simply, "I don't have to tell a handsome young fellow like you about love."

The shop resounded with laughter, but Sitanov muttered to Kapendiukhin, "She's a fool—or worse! Everybody knows it's only a great passion that brings them to that!"

He was pale from the drink; the sweat on his temples stood out in pearl-like drops; alarming lights kindled in his sensitive eyes.

Old Goloviev, however, seeming to pick tears out of his eyes with his fingers, and wrinkling his prodigious nose, asked, "How many children have you?"

"Just one."

There was a lamp over the table and another over the oven. Their light was dim and shadows clustered in the corners, from which glowered the faceless figures of unfinished icons. The blotches of dull gray where faces and hands should have been, looked eerie and disproportioned, and my usual fantasy returned to me—that the saints' bodies had stolen away from under their painted vestments. The glass bowls, now hoisted up near the ceiling, rested on hooks, in billows of smoke, and reflected a bluish light.

Zhikharev circulated around the tables, urging people to eat and drink. His broad, bald head nodded to one after the other, his skinny fingers were in incessant motion. The nose of this gaunt man, beaked like that of a bird of prey, now looked sharper than ever; and when it caught the light, it cast a big shadow over his cheek. "Drink up and eat, friends," he persisted, in his resonant tenor.

"Don't trouble yourself over us, comrade. Everyone has his own hands and his own appetite. More than his appetite allows he can't eat, not even if he sets his mind on it."

"Be at peace, friends," cried Zhikharev, in sonorous tones. "We're all slaves of the Lord; let's sing out, 'Praised be His Name!' "

The singing did not go well. People were too stupefied with food and vodka. Kapendiukhin now held a double keyboard accordion; young Victor Salautin, solemn and dark as a young crow, had a drum, and his fingers wandered over the taut skin, scrubbing up a deep rumble; and tambourines jingled.

"Now, the Russian dance!" commanded Zhikharev, "please, little comrade."

"Akh," sighed the woman. "What a bother you are!"

A space had been cleared, and there she stood, planted like a sentry, in her short brown skirt, a yellow batiste blouse, with a red kerchief over her head.

Its little bells chiming, the accordion voiced impassioned laments; the tambourines whispered; the drum uttered heavy sighs. The effect was unpleasing, as if somebody was having a tantrum and knocking his head on a wall

Zhikharev was no dancer. He merely let himself go, hopping like a goat and rapping the heels of his highly polished boots on the floor, never on

the same beat as the noisy music. His feet seemed not to belong to him;
his movements were an uncouth writhing, as of a wasp in a spider's web,
or a fish in a net. Hardly a cheering sight, yet they all, even those who
were drunk, seemed awed by these convulsions, silently following the
changes of his arms and face, whose shifts of expression were astounding.
From a diffident and ingratiating look, he would turn to frowning hauteur;
then to a look of surprise; then, sighing and shutting his eyes, he would
open them and look bowed with grief. With clenched fists he furtively
approached the woman, but when he reached her, stamped his foot,
dropped to his knees, flung out his arms, and from upraised eyebrows
flashed her a rapt smile. She smiled back, and affably bid him, "Get up,
friend." Her eyes sought to close, but the gap was too much for the
lids, and the result was an unpleasing grimace. She, too, was a poor
dancer, doing nothing but waddle to and fro, silently shifting the weight
of her ponderous body from leg to leg. From her limp left hand hung a
handkerchief, and her right arm was crooked around her hip, giving her
the shape of a gigantic pitcher.

As Zhikharev circled around this massive woman, his expression underwent so many changes, he might have been ten dancing men, not one.
Now he was all hushed humility; now he was all pride and defiance; in
a third mood he was all timidity and deprecating sighs, as if anxious
to steal away, unobserved, from this formidable creature. Then, another
person made his appearance, one who gnashed his teeth and thrashed
convulsively about like a hurt dog. This uncouth and joyless performance
brought to mind the squalid affairs I had witnessed in that backyard
among the soldiers, washerwomen and cooks.

Sitanov made a quiet remark that dinned in my memory, "Everybody
cheats in these affairs; it's part of the game. There's no love; it's just a
diversion; and everybody's ashamed of it."

I was loathe to believe that everybody cheated in these affairs. What
about Queen Margot? And Zhikharev, here, certainly was sincere. And
Sitanov, himself, as I knew, had been deceived by a girl of the streets
with whom he had fallen in love; yet he had treated her kindly, and had
not given her a beating, as he had been urged to.

The big woman continued to sway and, with a fixed, corpselike smile,
to wave her handkerchief; and Zhikharev kept up his contortions around
her; and, watching them, I thought, had Eve, who succeeded in deceiving God, in any way resembled this horse? And suddenly, she became
repugnant to me.

The faceless images stared from the shadowy walls. The black night bulged upon the windows. The lamps were dim; the workshop was stifling; if you listened for it, the drips of water from the copper pan into the wooden bucket could be heard above the shuffle of feet and chatter of voices. How little this resembled the life presented in books—so painfully little!

Finally, everybody had had enough of it, and Kapendiukhin turned the accordion over to Salautin and said, "Come on! Let's have it!"

He reminded me of Tsigan; like him, he danced as if he were whirling in air. Paul and Sorokin followed after him, in fleet and ardent steps. The tubercular Davidov also slid his feet over the floor, coughing all the while from the dust, the smoke, and the reek of vodka and smoked sausage, which has a tannery smell. They danced, yelled and sang, as if conscious that this was a holiday on which they offered and met challenges to skill and endurance.

Sitanov, drunk, and looking as if about to burst into tears, inquired of one after another, "Think anybody really can love such a woman?"

Larionovich, with a shrug of his bony shoulders, replied, "A woman's a woman, what more is there to look for?"

The pair under discussion, had gone off, unobserved; Zhikharev not to turn up in the workshop for two or three days, and then, after a trip to the bath, to work, speechless, in his corner, sedate and aloof for the next fortnight.

"Are they gone?" Sitanov asked himself, peering all through the workshop with his mournful, gray-blue eyes. He had a plain face, rather prematurely old, but he had kind and candid eyes. His friendliness to me was due to my scrapbooks filled with copied verses. He was an outright non-believer, though, aside from Larionovich, it was hard to think of anyone in the workshop as having faith in or love of God. All their references to Him were mocking, like their remarks about their mistresses. Yet, they crossed themselves at meals, and said prayers before going to sleep, and were at church Sundays and other holy days. Sitanov, however, abstained from all this, and was regarded an atheist.

"There's no God," he asserted.

"Then, where do we come from?"

"I don't know."

How was it possible that God did not exist? I asked him, and he replied, raising his long arm above his head, "God is high, you see." Then, lowering his arm to about two feet off the floor, he said, "And man is low! Right? But it's written, you know, that man is created in the image of God. Now, what's Goloviev the image of?"

This bowled me over. That slovenly and besotted old man, for all his years, was addicted to an unmentionable vice. People like the Viatkan soldier, Yermokhin and grandma's sister came to mind. Was that God's image in them?

"Human beings are swine, you know," declared Sitanov, and then added, consolingly, "but, Alex, there are some good people, really."

It was easy to get along with him; he was so open. When there was something he didn't know, he was frank to say so. In that he was unique. Up to my meeting him, I had encountered only people who were omniscient, and discussed everything.

I was puzzled to find in Sitanov's scrapbook, along with much good poetry that reached into the soul, salacious verse that could only make one ashamed. When I mentioned Pushkin, he showed me the "Gavriliad," which he had copied down. "Pushkin? Just a clown! But Benediktov— he's worth talking about!" And, with shut eyes, and in a rapt whisper, he recited: "Oh, the witchery of a beautiful woman's breast!"

His favorite lines, which he recited with elated pride, were: "Even the eagle's eye cannot penetrate that warm sanctuary and unriddle that heart!"

"Understand?" And it embarrassed me to have to admit that I couldn't understand something that gave him so much pleasure.

Chapter Fourteen

MY WORK WAS SIMPLE ENOUGH. I ROSE WHILE THE MEN WERE STILL IN bed to get the samovar ready for them; while they were having their tea in the kitchen, Paul and I cleaned up the workrooms and set out the paints, after which I went over to the store. My evening chores were to prepare the colors and to learn by looking on. For a time, looking on absorbed me, but it was soon apparent to me that the operations of this handicraft, so minutely divided, gave no joy to the craftsmen, who were bored by it to the point of torture.

Soon I was using my evenings as leisure time. I told the craftsmen of my experiences on the steamers, and tales from books. Imperceptibly, I took on the role of storyteller and reader to the men. I discovered that they had seen less of the world than I, having been caged in such workshops from childhood. Of them all, only Zhikharev had seen Moscow, of which he reported, "There they don't cry; they know how to look after themselves."

Of the rest, none had been farther than Shuya or Vladimir. They asked me were there Russians and churches in Kazan. To them Perm was off in Siberia; and they could not take in the fact that Siberia lay beyond the Urals. They spoke of sea fish coming from the Urals. "Where do they get sturgeon? From the Caspian Sea? So the Urals come down to the sea?" It was hard for me to realize they were not joking, when they located England across the Atlantic, and gave Napoleon a genealogy that linked him with the aristocracy of Kaluga.

They questioned my reports of what I had seen with my own eyes; they preferred macabre tales seasoned with a little of the historical. Even the older men preferred fantasy to reality. The more unreal and incredible the story, the more absorbed they became. They sought an escape from reality into a dream future, a refuge from the squalor and privation of their daily life.

This startled me the more, since I was becoming more aware how life contradicted the books. In the books there were no people like Smoury, Jake the Stoker, Aleksasha the wanderer, Zhikharev, or the laundress, Natalie.

Davidov fished a tattered copy of Golitsinsky's stories out of his trunk, Ivan Vyzhigin, the Bulgarian, and a volume of Baron Brambusse. They enjoyed having me read them aloud, Larionovich remarking, "Good. It keeps us from quarreling and making a racket."

I hunted out books from everywhere; and the readings occurred almost nightly. They were pleasant, those evenings. It became quiet as the night itself in the workrooms. Above the tables, like chill, white stars, the glass globes cast their rays on heads, tousled or bald. Serene, thoughtful faces were turned toward me. Every now and then words of praise for the author or the hero were interjected. The men were interested and amiable then, quite different from their ordinary selves. I was fond of them, then, and they treated me well. I felt contented to be there.

"With books," remarked Sitanov, "it becomes like spring, when the winter double windows are removed, and we can breathe the fresh air."

Books were hard to get, since we could not afford the rentals. I got hold of them, somehow, by begging or borrowing. From an officer of the fire patrol I received a volume of Lermontov. This gave me my first awareness of the power of poetry over people. Even now I can see Sitanov, after hearing the opening lines of "The Demon," looking at the book, then at my lips, then putting his brush down, cradling his knees in his long arms, and rocking himself with a blissful look on his face.

"Quiet, brothers!" said Larionovich, and, also dropping his work, drew his chair up to Sitanov's table, where I was doing the reading. The poem brought us both pain and delight. My voice broke till I could scarcely read, and the tears gushed from my eyes. But I was stirred still more, by the absorption of the workers; everything seemed to have veered from its customary orbit; all were drawn to me as by a magnet. When I had finished reading the first part, nearly everybody in the room was crowding around the table, arms around each other's shoulders, faces smiling or lost in thought. And Zhikharev pushed my head back into the book, ordering me, "Read further!"

When I had finished the book, he took it from me, studied the title, put it under his arm, and said, "We'll have it again, tomorrow. I'll keep the book safe."

Having put Lermontov under lock and key, he returned to his table. The stillness in the workrooms continued, as the men quietly resumed their posts. Sitanov went to the window where, his brow against the glass, he stood as though frozen. Zhikharev, putting his brush down again, said solemnly, "So, that's life; slaves of God—ah, yes!" Shrugging and covering his face, he added, "I can do the devil, make him dark and shaggy, the wings all flames, done in red lead; but face, hands, feet, they have to be a blue-white, like snow under moonlight."

Until it was nearly time for our late supper, he fidgeted on his stool, with an agitation strange in him, his fingers tapping on the table, and holding forth in a rambling monologue on the devil, women, Eve, Paradise, and sins of the saints, concluding, "It's the truth. If the saints yielded to lewd women, certainly the devil might be tempted by a pure soul."

He was heard in silence. Like me, probably the rest had no inclination to speak. The work dragged; they kept looking at their watches; and at the stroke of ten they stopped. Sitanov, Zhikharev and I went out into the yard. Looking up at the stars, Sitanov recited, "They shone, like a caravan, wandering in space," adding his comment, "That's something your ordinary eye don't see!"

Shivering in the frost, Zhikharev said, "I can't carry lines in my mind. I have no memory. But he . . . astounding . . . a man who even pities the devil! Makes you sorry for him, doesn't he?"

"He does," Sitanov agreed.

"That's a man for you!" exclaimed Zhikharev. In the doorway, he stopped to caution me, "Don't talk about the book in the store; it must be one of the banned books." I was overjoyed; I thought it must be one of the books my confessor had referred to.

Everybody was meditative at supper. The usual din and chatter was lacking, as if we were preoccupied with some important occurrence. As we were undressing for bed, Zhikharev pulled out the book, and commanded me, "Let's have it again!" A number of the men got out of bed to hear it, sitting around me, cross-legged and in their bed clothes. And again, when I had finished, Zhikharev's fingers drummed on the table, and he said, "A living picture, that devil; and that's what he's like, eh, brothers?"

Sitanov, looking over my shoulder, read some lines, and laughed. "I'll copy that down in my notebook."

Zhikharev strode to his own table with the book; then returned and said, in a cracked and indignant voice, "We're no better than blind puppies, living for a purpose we don't know. Neither God nor the devil needs us; what sort of slaves of the Lord are we? Jehovah, Himself, is God's slave; God spoke with Him. And with Moses, too. And He named Moses—'He's mine—a man of God!' But what are we?"

Shutting the book, he started putting on his clothes, and said to Sitanov, "Come on out for a drink."

"At my bar," said Sitanov, quietly.

After they had gone, I stretched out on the floor beside Paul.

I heard him turning, snoring, then weeping.

"What's the matter?"

"I feel so sorry for them it makes me ill," he explained. "I've been with them four years; I know them through and through."

I, too, pitied them. We stayed awake a long time, discussing them in whispers, discovering good traits in each, something to feed our adolescent sympathy.

Paul and I were friends. They turned him, finally, into a competent craftsman; but not for long. Before the end of the third year, he had become an alcoholic; later, in the Khitrov market place in Moscow, I ran across him and found him in rags and recently, I heard that typhoid had done for him. It gives me pain to think of the number of decent people I have seen gone to ruin. People in all lands go to pieces; self-destruction comes easy to all; but nowhere do people wreck themselves with such headlong, senseless speed, as in our Russia.

At that time he was a round-headed youth, a couple of years older than I, gay, bright, honest and talented. He did excellent drawings of birds, cats and dogs; and clever cartoons of the craftsmen, each of whom he pictured in a feathered incarnation; Sitanov as a melancholy wood-cock teetering on one leg; Zhikharev as a cock with a plucked head and a ripped comb; sickly Davidov as a crippled lapwing; and—his master-piece—the engraver, Goloviev, as a bearded bat, with a sneering nose, and four feet armed with six nails apiece. From the round, dark face glared white, round eyes, with pupils small as lentils; in addition they were crossed, imparting an expression at once lifelike and monstrous.

The workers took no offense at the cartoons of themselves, but were disturbed by the one of Goloviev, and warned the artist, "Better tear it up; if the old man sees it, he'll murder you!"

The filthy, corrupt, constantly tipsy old man was cloyingly pious and unwearying in malice. He kept traducing his shopmates to the store manager, to whom the owner had betrothed her niece, and who, on that account, had come to consider the business as his, and to boss the craftsmen who hated, but feared him, and therefore feared his toady, Goloviev, too.

Paul, in turn, harassed the old engraver with such persistence and resourcefulness, one would think he had set that as his life's work. In this I collaborated with ardor; and the workers enjoyed our usually coarse and heedless horseplay, though they cautioned us, "It'll get you into trouble, kids! Kuzka-Zhuchok will murder you!" Kuzka-Zhuchok was our secret nickname for the store manager.

Untroubled by these warnings, we took advantage of Goloviev's drunken stupors, once, to paint his face, another time to gild his nose; and it took him three days to dig the gold out of the pores of that spongy organ. But with each such success, I could not help recollecting the little Viatkan soldier on the steamer, and I was uneasy in my soul. But, despite his age, Goloviev was strong enough to pay us back with a beating, which he would follow with complaints to the owner.

This woman, who was also a habitual drunk, but whom drink only made more amiable, would do her best to scare us. Pounding on the table with her puffy hands, she would exclaim, "Misbehaving again, you animals! Where's your respect for the old? Now, which of you poured the chemical in his vodka glass?"

"We both did it."

The astounded woman cried out, "Good heavens! They flaunt it! You accursed ones, have respect for an old man!"

She sent us off and let the store manager deal with us. To me he said wrathfully, "You read books, the Holy Scriptures, no less, and then be-have like that. Watch your step, brother!"

The owner was lonely and melancholy. After tippling syrup brandies, she would sing at her window, "No sympathetic heart turns to me; no pity is shown; to none can I speak my sorrow; I must grieve alone." And ended it with the quavering long drawn sob of the old, "Oo-oo."

I saw her, once, carrying a pitcher of warm milk down stairs, and suddenly collapsing, continuing her descent, seated, with a bump on each step, but never letting go of the pitcher. As the milk splashed over her, she held the pitcher out at arm's length, and scolded it, "What's come over you, satyr? Where are you bound for?"

Though she was not fat, she was flabby, resembling an old cat past her mouse-hunting days, sluggish from overeating, who now could only purr over memories of past hunts and frolics.

"This shop," said Sitanov, with a preoccupied frown, "used to do a big business. It used to be a first-class place, with clever craftsmen at the tables; but since Kuzka-Zhuchok got his paws on it, it's gone to pot! You feel you're slaving away for strangers, and when you think of it, something seems to snap in your head, like a broken spring; and you feel like loafing—to thumb your nose at any kind of job—just to stretch out on the roof, all summer through, and look at the sky."

Paul aped Sitanov; puffing at a cigarette given him by one of the men, he too held forth on the subjects of God, drink and women, and especially the mortality of the products of labor, created by one only to be destroyed by another, and neither able to understand or appreciate it. And then his alert, pleasant face would age and take on shadows. Sitting on his bedding on the floor, he would stare through the blue quadrangle of the window at the snow-covered roof of the shed below, and the stars above in the wintry sky.

The workers' sleep was noisy with snoring or dream-mumbling. One of them had a nightmare. Above, Davidov kept coughing out the residue of his life. In the corner, alongside each other, bound together in the iron sleep of drunkenness, sprawled the "slaves of God," Kapendiukhin, Sorokin and Pershin. From the walls glowered the faceless stares of unfinished icons. From the floor, where they had fermented in the cracks, came the fetid reek of rotten eggs and dirt.

"Lord, how pitiable they are!" whispered Paul.

I found this feeling sorry for ourselves and the others, more and more disquieting. As I have observed before, both of us thought of the workers as good people, who led lives unworthy of them, tedious and evil. During the winter storms, under which everything—trees, houses, and earth, itself—shivered and moaned, and during Lent with its sombre bells, tedium submerged the workshop like a tide, weighed on it like lead, prostrating the craftsmen, deadening them, forcing them to the taverns and to women who served, like vodka, to induce forgetfulness.

On such nights books had no power; and Paul and I provided other entertainment, dressing up for improvised comic roles and coating our faces with soot or paint, carrying on the battle against boredom, until their laughter brought us victory. I dramatized my recollections of the story of the soldier who saved the life of Peter the Great; and using Davidov's cot for our stage, we decapitated the supposititious Swede, to uproarious laughter from our audience. We got a particularly big hand when we enacted the mishaps of the Chinese devil, Tsing-Yu-Tong, when, for a change, he sought to do good. Paul played the title role, and I all the other parts—the peasants, the crowds, the good soul, and the stones, too, whereon the poor devil, bruised and exhausted, after his vain efforts to practice virtue, rested up.

This drew loud laughter, and the ease with which it could be so evoked astounded and irritated me. "You clowns!" they yelled at us, "you devils!" The more I saw of it, the more pained I was to realize that sorrow brought quicker responses than joy. In itself, joy seemed to have no value to them as not belonging to their lives; only as a relief to the burdened, as a contrast to the Russian melancholy, did it have a place. What innate vigor can there be in a joy that has no life of its own, nor will to live for itself, but only as surcease from miseries? Much too frequently the Russian gaiety takes a sudden turn to cruelty and tragedy. Suddenly, in a dancer who appears to be soaring out of his chains, a wild beast breaks loose, and with the frenzy of anguish, he leaps upon all whom he encounters, rending, biting, destroying.

This hysterical elation, to which they were driven by outer pressures, troubled me; and disregarding what might be thought of me, I improvised fantasies that I hoped would evoke a pure, free, spontaneous gaiety in them; and in a measure I succeeded. I astonished them and won their praises; yet, the misery I had almost managed to rid them of slipped back, and regained its grip.

Gray Larionovich remarked, "God bless you! You're a cheering sort." And Zhikharev joined in with, "We're lucky to have him. You know, Alex, you ought to join a circus or theater; you'd make a fine clown." Only two of the workers there, Kapendiukhin and Sitanov, went to the theater on Christmas or carnival week; and the older workers were earnest in advising them, afterward, to purify themselves by washing themselves in baptismal Jordan water. Sitanov was persistent in urging me, "Better drop this and become an actor." And, as illustration, he would give me a fervid recital of the sad life of the actor, Yakovlev. "You see what can happen!"

Sitanov liked to tell stories of Marie Stuart, "the wanton," as he named her; and particularly of "the Spanish knight." "Don Cezar de Bazan was a real knight, Alex, a wonderful guy." And there was a bit of "the Spanish knight" in Sitanov, himself.

Once he came upon three firemen in the market place, beating up a peasant for amusement, with a crowd of about forty onlookers enjoying the spectacle. Sitanov lunged through, his long arms swinging; he beat off the firemen, carried the peasant to safety through the mob, crying, "Get him away!" and then returned, one against three. The firehouse was only a few steps away; it would have been simple for the three to have summoned their mates and killed Sitanov. Fortunately, he had so terrified them that they ran away, with Sitanov calling, "You dogs!" after them.

A Sunday diversion for the younger workers were the bouts held in the Tyesny yard beyond the Peter and Paul churchyard, where carters and peasants from the nearby villages gathered to watch their champions fighting it out with champions put up by Nizhny workmen. One of the carters' champions was a celebrated bruiser, a Mordvin giant with a little head, and incessantly tearing eyes. Smearing the tears on his filthy coat sleeve, he stood in front of his backers, his feet wide apart, and called out in genial challenge, "Come on out! What's the matter? Turned cold?"

Kapendiukhin, our champion, always lost. The breathless, bleeding Cossack would gasp out, "I'll beat that Mordvin yet, if it costs me my life." And that became his life's purpose. For it he even gave up vodka; he massaged himself in snow before going to bed; he ate more meat; and exercised with two-pound weights to build his muscles; but all to no avail. Finally he stitched a lead weight into his glove, and gloated to Sitanov, "Now we'll finish off that Mordvin!"

"Throw that away!" warned Sitanov, "or I'll expose you!"

Kapendiukhin refused to believe him; but just as the bout was about to start, Sitanov told the Mordvin, "One side, please; there's something I have to say to Kapendiukhin."

Reddening, the Cossack shouted, "Beat it! I have nothing to do with you!"

"You know you have!" said Sitanov, with a significant look. Kapendiukhin stamped his feet, pulled off his boxing gloves, tucked them into his blouse, and left the yard.

Both groups were disconcerted, and a man of prestige in these circles berated Sitanov, "It's against the rules, brothers, to intrude private matters in the ring." And Sitanov was beset on all sides and vilified. At last he broke his silence to say to the ring authority, "Was I to stand aside and let murder be done?"

Then the expert understood, and doffing his cap to Sitanov, said, "We're grateful to you!"

"But please keep this to yourself, uncle; don't spread it around."

"What for? Kapendiukhin hardly ever wins, and always being the loser makes a man desperate. That's understandable. But from now on when they fight, the gloves will first be inspected."

"That's up to you."

When the expert went away, our side began to abuse Sitanov. "Now you've spoiled it. Our Cossack would have beat him this time; so you have to see to it that our side stays on the loser's end!" They kept this up until Sitanov cried out, "Oh, you dopes!" and startled everybody by himself challenging the Mordvin. The latter, jokingly brandishing his fists, said, "Come, let's kill each other!"

A ring was formed by people linking hands and spreading out in a wide circle. The boxers faced each other, right hand out and left to their breasts. The more knowing in the audience took note that Sitanov's arms had a longer reach than the Mordvin's. It was very still; all that was audible was the crunching of snow under the boxers' feet. One impatient onlooker demanded, "Start mixing it!"

Sitanov probed with his right; the Mordvin blocked with his left, and Sitanov got in a left under the Mordvin's right arm that made the latter grunt. As he drew back, he said good-naturedly, "He's young, but he's no fool."

Now they waded in, trading heavy punches on the chest. Before long, even people on the other side were rooting for Sitanov, "That's the stuff, icon painter! Give it to him, engraver!"

The Mordvin was heavier and slower and took two or three punches to one of his; but he was the stronger and well-seasoned, and did not suffer much, and laughed and bantered, and suddenly with an upswinging punch, dislocated Sitanov's right arm at the shoulder.

"It's a draw; separate them," came from the onlookers, as they broke their circle and crowded around the contestants. The good-natured

Mordvin said, "The icon painter's not too strong; but he's smart. I'll tell the world, he'll be a good ringman."

While the rest got into a free-for-all wrestling match, I took Sitanov to the *feldsher*.[33] What he had done had increased my respect and affection for him. A straightforward and honorable man, he had done what he had considered his duty; but the sloven-soul, Kapendiukhin, ridiculed him, "Showoff! Shining up that soul of yours like a samovar on holiday eve, bragging, 'See how bright it shines!' But it's nothing but brass, that soul of yours, and rusty at that!"

Sitanov ignored the taunts, sticking to his work and using his spare time to copy Lermontov into his scrapbook. When I asked him, "Since you have the money, why don't you buy the book?" he replied, "I prefer having it in my own handwriting."

When a page had been filled in his minute and graceful script, he would recite in a low voice, till the ink dried, "Having no part in it, feeling no regret, you will look down upon this earth where happiness is a mirage, and beauty is fleeting."

With eyes half-shut, he said, "How true! That man knew!"

Sitanov's forbearance toward Kapendiukhin astonished me. When he was drunk the Cossack became quarrelsome, and Sitanov would fend off provocations with placating words, "Enough; let me be." Yet, in the end, he would turn on the drunkard so savagely that the other workmen, who enjoyed such brawls among themselves as spectacles, would intervene, explaining, "If we didn't stop Eugene, he would kill Kapendiukhin or anyone, and then he'd never forgive himself."

When sober, Kapendiukhin baited Sitanov incessantly, jeering at Sitanov's interest in poetry, making coarse allusions to his unhappy love affair, and attempting vainly to incite him to jealous rages. Sitanov took it all silently, seemingly without resentment, sometimes even joining Kapendiukhin in self-mocking laughter.

They slept beside each other, spending part of the night in whispers and keeping me awake as well, consumed as I was with curiosity over what could be the mutual interest of such an ill-matched pair. But whenever I edged closer, the Cossack would push me off with, "What are you after?" Sitanov didn't even seem to notice.

Once, however, they summoned me over, and the Cossack inquired, "What would you do if you had a lot of money?"

[33] A medical practitioner without degree who performed simple medication and surgery.

"I'd buy books."

"And then what?"

"I don't know."

Kapendiukhin gave an exclamation of disgust and turned away, while Sitanov remarked, "You see, young or old, nobody can say. In itself, money's nothing except where it's put to some use."

"What are you discussing?" I asked.

"We just prefer talking to sleeping," the Cossack replied shortly.

After hearing more of their conversations, I found that they were no different from daytime conversations, that they had the usual subjects of God, truth, happiness, the wiles and follies of women, the cupidity of the wealthy, and the complexity and mystery of life. I was an eager listener-in, getting great stimulation out of such conversation. And I observed with satisfaction that almost everybody came to the same conclusions about our life, namely, that it was evil and should be made better. I observed, too, that their desire for a better life was futile, would lead to no improvement of their conditions, or in their dealings with one another. These discussions, at the same time as they illuminated the life around me, lit up an empty and gloomy horizon beyond; and, across this vacant horizon drifted, like dust particles on a windswept pond, grotesque and irritable people, among them the very ones who called the people an insensate crowd. Opinions came so easy to them, they were so ready to condemn others, to show off, to repeat commonplaces, to rush into quarrels over nothing, to insult each other. They speculated on conditions after death, while the flooring under the washstand where they stood, rotted through, and up the hole rose a chill damp that froze our feet, and a sour, fetid earth smell. Paul and I did what we could to stop up the hole with straw and rags, but the hole gained on us, and, in bad weather, the smell was like sewer fumes. Everybody agreed new flooring should be laid there, but in the meanwhile, the draft gave us all colds and coughs. Then the tin mechanism of the little ventilator panel in one of our winter windows began rasping, and everybody complained. But after it had been oiled, Zhikharev grumbled, "It's more boring now that the ventilator's quiet."

To return from a bath to a dirty bed, and lie there in dust and stenches, seemed not to distress any of them. Many little things, whose accumulation made for intolerable conditions, could have been altered with little trouble, but no one bothered to. I heard them say, "No one cares about human beings; God doesn't; and not human beings themselves."

When Paul and I took the trouble to bathe Davidov, who was on the point of death and whose body was being consumed by parasites and filth, our efforts brought us hosts of laughter from the others. They pulled off their shirts and offered them to us for delousing. From their jibes, you'd think we were doing a silly thing, something to be ashamed of.

From Christmas till Lent, Davidov coughed and spat blood which, if he missed the wash basin, spattered the floor. At night he kept us awake with delirious shrieks. And every day, the talk went, "Let's get him to the hospital!" But one obstacle was that Davidov's passport had lapsed. Then his condition eased a bit, and they said, "It's nothing; and he'll die any day now, anyway." Davidov himself said, "I'll be off soon." He had a dry humor with which he sought to break the tedium. He would stick out his shadowy and emaciated face, and wheeze out such songs as: "Hear ye, people, to the voice of one above; the attic's my home; my day begins early; and cockroaches feed on me, awake or asleep."

"He keeps chipper," applauded his audience.

When Paul and I went to him he joked, no matter what the effort cost him. "What'll you have, dear guests; how about a fresh little spider?"

His death was slow and he wearied of it, remarking with frank exasperation, "It's an affliction! I don't seem to be able to die!"

His indifference to death awed Paul. One night Paul roused me to whisper, "Alex, looks like he's dying now; supposing he dies, right there above us. God, I'm scared of dead people!" Or he'd comment, "He was born—but what for? He's not reached twenty-two, and here he's dying!"

One moonlit night he got up and, with eyes wide with fright, called to me, "Listen!" Davidov, in the garret, was croaking out, "Give me it, give——" And then went into a fit of hiccoughs.

"By God, see? Now he's dying," said Paul, trembling.

I had been shoveling snow out of the yard all day and was exhausted, but Paul pleaded, "Please, for God's sake, don't sleep." And suddenly, getting up on his knees, he gave a frantic cry, "Get up! Davidov is dead!"

Some of the workers awoke; some stumbled out of bed; there were questions from growling voices. Kapendiukhin climbed into the loft and said, astonished, "He's dead, all right, though he's still warm."

In the ensuing stillness Zhikharev, wrapping himself in a blanket, said, "Now he's in the kingdom of heaven."

Someone suggested, "Let's put him out in the hallway."

Kapendiukhin climbed down from the loft and looked out of the window. "Let him be till in the morning. He was no harm to anybody when he was alive."

Paul lay sobbing, his head hid under his pillow.

Through it all, Sitanov slept.

Chapter Fifteen

THE SNOW THAWED OFF THE FIELDS; THE WINTER CLOUDS LEFT THE sky. Now, when snow fell, it was damp, and alternated with rain. The sun loitered on his day's journey. The air grew mild. Gay spring seemed to be hiding flirtatiously in the fields, before bursting into town. The streets became brown with mud, and the gutters streamed. Over the thaws on Arestansky Square giddy sparrows skipped. And, like the sparrows, human beings livened up. The almost continuous Lenten chimes outvoiced the other spring sounds, their hollow beats striking on one's heart. In that tolling, as in the tones of the elderly, there was a note of reproach, as if the bells were saying, sad and aloof, "Been-o, all has been, been-o."

On my name day [34] the craftsmen gave me an exquisitely done icon of Alexei, Man of God; and well I remember Zhikharev's solemn presentation speech. "What are you?" he began, wagging fingers and eyebrows, "just a kid, a thirteen-year-old orphan; and I, a man about four times your age, speak your praises and commend you for standing with your face toward people and not aloof. Stay like that toward people and you'll be all right!" He went on about people and about slaves of God, but I could not distinguish between his "slaves" and his "people," and neither, I think, could he. He rambled on till the others began laughing at him, while I stood there, holding my gift, deeply stirred but embarrassed. Finally Kapendiukhin broke in, exasperated, "Oh, quit that gush! You're turning his ears blue."

Giving me a whack on my back, he launched on praises of his own. "Where you're worth praising is where you're like other people; not what makes it hard to give you a scolding or a beating when you've earned it!"

[34] The name day, or saint's day, was celebrated in Russian custom, like the birthday.

They were all kind to me, taking advantage of my embarrassment with gentle ribbing. I could barely keep from bursting into tears of joy over finding myself esteemed by them. Only that morning the shop manager had remarked to the appraiser, with a gesture toward me, "There's an unlikely, worthless lad for you!"

I had gone off to the store that morning, as usual. At noon the manager ordered, "Go back to the house; clear off the snow from the storehouse roof and get the cellar clean!"

He didn't know it was my name day and I wasn't aware that anyone else knew. When the felicitations were over in the workrooms, I got into work clothes, and climbed up the roof of the shed to shovel off the snow winter had piled on it. In my excitement I forgot to shut the cellar door, and later found that I had filled the cellar with snow. When I got down and saw it, I immediately set to clearing the cellar doorway. The thawing snow was heavy; it made slow work for my wooden shovel—we had no metal one. I broke the shovel just as the manager was opening the yard gate. There and then the aptness of the Russian proverb, "Misery dogs the heels of joy," was demonstrated to me.

"So!" jeered the manager. "What a worker you are, damn you! Just let me get my hands on you, you numskull!" and he threatened me with the broken part of the shovel.

Backing away I retorted, "I wasn't hired as a porter!"

He threw the piece of wood at my shins and I retaliated with a snowball smack in his face. He went off snorting; I dropped my shoveling and returned to the workrooms. In no time his fiancée, a noisy girl with a vacant, pimply face, burst in. "Alex, you're wanted upstairs!"

"I'm not going," I replied.

"Not going?" asked Larionovich, astounded. "What do you mean?"

I told him what had happened and he went upstairs, frowning anxiously, and grumbling at me, "Impertinent kid!"

The workrooms echoed with curses at the manager. Kapendiukhin said, "They'll certainly kick you out for this!"

I felt no uneasiness on that score. My relations with the manager had reached the breaking point. He took no trouble to hide his animosity, which grew sharper every day, while my aversion toward him kept pace. But his absurd behavior toward me mystified me. He would scatter small coins over the floor which I found when sweeping, and put into the cup kept on the counter for beggars. Guessing that he did this to catch me, I said, "You're dropping the coins at my feet on purpose."

Flaring up, he gave himself away. "Don't you dare tell me what to do!

I know what I'm doing!" Immediately he corrected himself, "What do you mean, my throwing money around on purpose? It just drops by accident."

I was forbidden to read the books in the store. "That's nothing for you to bother your head about. Thinking of becoming an appraiser, you loafer?"

He persisted in trying to frame me in a theft of a coin. It was clear to me that, should I happen to sweep one of the dropped coins into a crack, he would accuse me of stealing it; and I reminded him that I was onto his game. That very day, however, on returning from the tavern with the hot water for tea, I overheard him prompting a new salesman in the shop next door, "Get him to steal some psalters; we're putting in a new stock." From their constrained look as I came in, it was obvious that I had been the subject of their conversation; and, from other signs, I had additional reasons for suspecting them of some idiotic plot against me.

That salesman, as a matter of fact, was not really a new man there. He was considered a shrewd salesman; but he had a weakness for drink. After one of his sprees, he had been discharged, but his boss had recently taken him back. He was a frail, bloodless fellow with crafty eyes. Slavishly subservient to his boss, he went about, smiling secretly and cleverly into his beard, and uttering ironic remarks. From him, though his own teeth were white and strong, came the characteristic odor of dental decay.

He gave me a shock one day, by approaching me with an amiable smile, then suddenly knocking off my cap and grabbing me by the hair. I did my best to twist out of his grip, but was dragged from the arcade into the store, where he tried to get me to knock against the icons. Had he managed it, I would have cracked a glass frame, or damaged the embossing, or scratched up some expensive item. But he was too feeble, and I was soon on top when, to my astonishment, this grown man sat on the floor, rubbed his skinned nose, and wept.

The next morning, when we happened to be alone, still nursing battle bruises on his nose and around his eye, he told me amicably, "D'you think I wanted to attack you yesterday? I'm not such a fool. I knew you'd get the better of me. I have no strength. I'm a souse. Your boss made me do it. 'Fix it so he'll break something while you're fighting.' I'd never have done it on my own. Look what decorations you've given my mug."

I believed him and felt sorry for him. I knew the poor, half-starved wretch was also knocked about by the woman he lived with. But I asked him, "And if he asked you to poison somebody, would you do it?"

"He might, at that," said the salesman with a pallid smile, "that's not beyond him." Later he asked me, "Look, I'm broke. There isn't a crust of bread in the house, and my missus is carrying on. Couldn't you slip me a piece out of your stock, an icon or a breviary, and let me have it to sell on the side? Just as a favor to a friend, what?"

This recalled to me the shoe store and the church beadle, and I wondered, "Will he give me away?" But I couldn't refuse him, and gave him a cheap icon. A breviary worth several rubles seemed too much, made the crime seem too big. Arithmetic always lies hidden in morality. The sanctimonious naïvete of the "Regulations for the Punishment of Criminals" bares the pretenses behind which the big lie of property masks itself.

So, overhearing my boss urging this man to get me to steal psalters, I felt frightened. He must have known of my previous charity; the salesman must have blabbed about the icon. Realizing the unseemliness of dispensing charity with somebody else's goods, and the foul trap that was being prepared for me, made me sick of myself and of them all. I was in torment until the consignment of breviaries was delivered. When I was storing them away, the salesman from next door came in to beg for one.

"You told the boss about the icon, didn't you?" I asked him.

"Yes," he replied, in a mournful tone. "I just can't hold anything back."

Completely at a loss, I sat down and turned a stupefied stare upon him. In miserable, desperate, uncontrollable frankness he continued, "You see, your boss, I mean mine, guessed it, and he told your boss——"

I thought it was all up with me; I was in the plotter's trap and could expect my next lodging to be at the reformatory. So, what did it matter? If you drowned, it was less humiliating to drown where it was deep. I put a breviary in the salesman's hands. He tucked it into a coat sleeve and went off; but suddenly, he was back; the breviary tumbled on my feet; and he went away again, exclaiming, "No! If I took it, you'd be finished."

This mystified me. Why would I be finished? Nevertheless, I was relieved that he had left without the breviary. But the incident intensified my boss' antagonism toward me.

All this was in my mind when Larionovich went to intervene. He was there only a short time, and returned, dejected and silent. Just before

our evening meal he took me aside and told me, "I tried to fix it for
you to put in all your time here, and not go to the store, but Kuzka
won't hear of it. He's certainly got it in for you!"

The fact was, I had an enemy here, too, the loose wench who was
the boss' fiancée. The younger workmen all took liberties with her.
Catching her in the hallway, they handled her; and all the objection
she made was to squeal with delight, like a puppy. This wench kept
stuffing herself day and night, her jaws going incessantly and her pockets
crammed with sweets. The look of her shifty eyes on her vacuous face
was repellent. She was always plaguing Paul and me with riddles, the
answers to which implied something indecent; and she was always repeating phrases which, when rapidly spoken, formed lewd words.

Once, one of the older men remarked to her, "You're nothing but a
tart!" To which she promptly replied, in a vulgar couplet then current,
"The maid who's a prude won't be wooed."

It was my first contact with that kind of a girl. Her crude frisking disgusted and embarrassed me. This distaste for her capers won me her
hostility. Once, Paul and I were in the cellar with her, helping her steam
out pickling tubs, when she proposed, "How about my teaching you
boys how to kiss?"

Paul answered, "I'm as good at it as you," while I suggested that she
save her kisses for her husband-to-be; and I did not put it in very formal
terms. Enraged, she said, "You animal! A young lady tries to be nice to
him and he turns squeamish, the dope!" And, shaking a warning finger
at me, she added, "I'll remember this, you see!"

Paul took my part. He said, "You'd get it from your intended if he
knew how you were carrying on."

She made a face. "I'm not scared of him. I got a dowry. I'm better
class than he is. Besides, a girl can have fun only till she's married."

From then on, she horsed around with Paul, while toward me she
showed a tireless malice.

In the store, life became steadily more burdensome. I read church
books whenever I could; but religious disputation had lost its savor for
me; the same arguments were repeated in the same phrases. Only old
Peter continued to interest me, for his perceptions into the depths of
human behavior, and his way of making things interesting and vivid.
There were moments when I thought he might be the prophet Elijah,
revisiting the earth and condemning it. Every time, however, that I was
candid with the old man about the people around me, or gave any free

expression to my ideas, he passed it on to my boss, and won me a scolding or a ribbing.

Once I remarked to the old man that I had copied some of his sayings into my scrapbook. He was greatly disturbed by this, quietly limped over to me and plied me with anxious questions, "What for, my boy? It's a waste of time. You want to remember that? Forget it. What a queer one you are! You're going to let me have what you've written, eh?" And he persisted in attempts to induce me either to let him have my scrapbook, or to destroy it myself; and he spoke about it, in agitated whispers, to my boss.

On our way home the latter remarked, "This note-taking of yours has got to stop, understand? That's something only sleuths do."

Heedlessly I said, "What about Sitanov? He keeps a scrapbook, too!"

"That stringbean, too?" After a silence he said, with an amiability foreign to him, "Look here; if you let me see your scrapbook, and Sitanov's as well—on the quiet, naturally, so he won't know—I'll give you half a ruble."

He must have counted on my doing it, for he had nothing more to say to me, and trotted ahead on his stubby legs. On reaching the house I told Sitanov what the boss had plotted. With a scowl, Sitanov said, "That's what your blabbing gets us. Now he'll have somebody sneak away both our scrapbooks. Let me have yours. I'll hide them. And see if he doesn't send you packing soon!"

I had no doubt about that, myself, and made up my mind to quit when grandma got back to town. She had spent the winter at Balakhaya, teaching lace-making to girl apprentices. Grandpa had moved back to Kunavin Street, but I didn't visit him; and when he came out our way, he never stopped in to see me. Once we met in the street. He was in his raccoon coat and his gait was slow and pompous. I greeted him and he put up his hands to shade his eyes, so he could see me better, squinted at me and said, weightily, "Oh, it's you; so now, you're an icon painter. Well, that's good; run along." And, nudging me aside, he went his slow, self-important way.

I saw little of grandma. She was working herself to the bone, not only to support grandpa, who had become helplessly senile, but my Uncle Mike's neglected children as well. Of the latter, Sascha was her chief care. He had turned out a handsome youth, but a dreamy book-lover. He worked in dye-shops, shifting from place to place, and between changes, loaded himself onto grandma's shoulders, leaving it to her to get him a new job. Fastened on her shoulders, too, was Sascha's sister, who had married a drunkard who beat her, and drove her out of the house.

Every time I met grandma, I was more conscious of the charm of her personality. But I realized that her gorgeous soul, bedazzled with fantasies, was incapable of clear vision, could not comprehend life's harsh realities; therefore my tension and unease mystified her.

"Patience, Alex!" This was all she could offer when I told her of the revolting conditions, of the miseries, of the agonies I saw around me, and which astounded me and made me boil. I was not the patient kind, however, and on the occasions I practiced that virtue of cattle, trees and stones, it was to discipline myself, or to test my endurance or stability. In their ignorant youth people sometimes attempt feats that overstrain their muscles and bones; they will seek enviously, in tests with heavy weights, to match fully-developed adults, known for their strength.

I had a double share of this weakness—I strained my spiritual, as well as my physical, powers, and it was a matter of luck that I did not overstrain myself and blast my life with some deformity. Nevertheless, worse disfigurements of one's life are incurred by patience, by submitting one's powers to the pressures about one. If I wind up a disfigured corpse, I can take pride that, to the very end, good people, despite all their efforts, failed to mutilate my soul.

My ungovernable impulses toward wild pranks, to entertain people and extort their laughter, became ever stronger. And I had successes. In my descriptions of a business day among the icons, I impersonated the shopkeepers, the peasant customers, the wrangling appraisers; I showed how all plied the tricks of their trade. Laughter echoed through the workrooms; and some of the craftsmen would leave their tables to have a better look; and then Larionovich would say, "Better wait till after supper to do your acting, or you'll keep us all from our work."

After a performance I felt relaxed, as if I had thrown off a load. For upwards of an hour my head felt clear and light; but then the sensation of small, pointed nails moving in my skin would return; and I would feel as though I was stewing in some stinking mess, in which I was slowly being boiled down. Is this what life is, I wondered? Was I doomed to live like these people, never to reach, never to see anything beyond?

Zhikharev would stare at me. "Why the sulks?" And Sitanov would ask, "What's bothering you?" And I had no answers.

The turbulent and incessant waters of life splashed at the most sensitive inscriptions in my soul, blurring them into wishful nonsense; and, wrathful and resolute, I resisted the violation. We were all afloat on that stream; but for me the current was icier and I was less buoyant in it; so that, at times, I felt pulled down into measureless abysses.

Not that I suffered from ill treatment. I was not shouted at or nagged as Paul was; I was always properly addressed by name, to emphasize the respect in which I was held. This was satisfying. But it tormented me to see so many of the people taking to drink and becoming repulsive; and to see them make their relations with women a noxious thing; yet I realized that women and vodka were the relaxation life offered them.

It grieved me to realize that that warm-hearted, fearless, and clear-minded woman, Natalie Kozlovsky, was also dismissed as a loose woman. And what of grandma? And Queen Margot? The latter, when I thought of her, filled me with awe. She had become as remote as a dream.

Women, in fact, were too much on my mind, and I was considering the question, shall I accompany the others on their next holiday dissipation? Not out of physical desire. I was robust, but choosy; the desire with which I burned was to hold close someone who was tender and understanding, to whom I could spontaneously and freely, as to a mother, pour out the ferments in my soul.

Paul had taken up with a housemaid who worked in the building across the way, and his reports made me envious. "It's funny, pal. A while ago I didn't like her at all, and I snowballed her; now we sit on a bench together; and I hug her and love her more than anybody."

"What do you talk about?"

"About everything; she tells me about herself, and I tell her about myself; then we kiss; only she's decent. To tell you the truth, pal, that's the trouble; she's too good. Man, you're smoking like an old campaigner."

I smoked heavily; tobacco drugged me, was sedative to my agitation and restlessness. Vodka, however, only made me nauseated with my own smell and taste. Paul, however, took to it. When he got drunk he bawled, "I want to go home; let me go home!" though, so far as I knew, he was an orphan, without brother or sister. His parents had died years ago, and for eight years he had lived with strangers.

Spring's calls were particularly potent to me in this state of agitation and discontent. I resolved to take a job on a ship again, and if there was a stop at Astrakhan, to run off to Persia. Why Persia, I cannot now recall. Perhaps, because I had been impressed by the Persian merchants at the Fair grounds, placid as marble images, their dyed beards spread in the sun, serenely smoking their bubble pipes, and looking around them with big, black, knowing eyes.

I would surely have run off somewhere; but one Easter day, when some of the craftsmen had gone off to their homes and the rest were in the taverns, I was sunning myself along the banks of the Oka, when my old boss, grandma's nephew, came along. He was in a gray topcoat, his hands in his pocket, a cigarette between his lips, his hat back on his head. On seeing me a warm smile immediately overspread his amiable face. He had the look of a free and happy man. "Ah, Peshkov, Christ is risen!" [35] he greeted me.

After we had given each other the Easter kiss he asked how I was getting on, and I made no bones about my disgust with my job, the town, and everything, and spoke of my plans to go to Persia. "Get that out of your mind," he advised me. "What on earth do you think you'll find in Persia? I know just how you feel, brother; at your age I, too, had the wanderlust."

I liked him for talking to me in this manner. His natural goodness was freshened by the touch of spring; he was different from the rest. "Smoke?" he asked, holding out a silver cigarette case stuffed with plump cigarettes. And that sealed his victory.

"Better come back to a job with me," he proposed. "This year I have contracts for new Fair buildings. I can use you there, a sort of overseer. You can check on the material as it's delivered, see that it's stacked properly, and keep an eye on it so the sub-contractors don't make off with it. How about it? I'll pay you five rubles a month, and five kopecks for your meals. The women won't bother you. You'll leave in the morning, and come back at night. Pay no attention to them. But don't let them know about this talk; just drop in Sunday, at Fonin Street. I think it'll work out fine!"

We parted like old friends, with a warm handshake, and he waved his hat to me when I looked back.

When I let it be known in the workrooms that I was leaving, most of the craftsmen expressed flattering regrets. Paul, particularly, was dejected. He tried to dissuade me. "Living among all those boors, after us! Carpenters and house painters! Ah, you! That's going from bad to worse!"

Zhikharev grumbled, "A fish finds the deepest place; this clever one hunts up a worse place!"

I was given a mournful sendoff. "Naturally, one must try every-

[35] The customary Russian Easter greeting.

thing," said Zhikharev, whose last spree had left him looking jaundiced. "And it's better to do it right away, before you get too tied down."

"Tied down for life!" said Larionovich, in a low voice.

Nevertheless, I felt that what they said was prompted by constraint and a sense of obligation. The thread by which I had been bound to them, had somehow rotted through.

In the loft above, the drunken Goloviev thrashed about and ranted, "I'd stick them all in jail! I know all about them. Who's a believer here? Aah——!"

And the usual unfinished icons stared, faceless, from the wall. The glass globes were high up under the ceiling. For some time we had been working in natural light, and the unused globes had acquired a grayish film of soot and dust. This setting is all so vivid in my memory that, with my eyes shut, I can see it all, every table, the paint jars on the sills, the brushes tied in bunches, the icons, the refuse can shaped like a fireman's helmet under the brass washstand, and dangling from the loft, Goloviev's bare foot, blue like that of a corpse pulled out of the water.

I tried to shorten the parting, but Russians love to prolong sad occasions. Their good-bys have the solemnity of requiems.

Zhikharev, with a flick of his brows, said to me, "That book—the devil book—I can't return it to you. I'll give you two greven for it."

The book was mine; the old fire-patrol officer had made me a gift of it, and I wanted to take Lermontov with me. But when I showed offense at being offered money, Zhikharev coolly put the coins in his pocket and said, positively, "Money or not, I won't let you have it back. It's not good for you. A book like that would smooth your way to sin."

"But it's on sale in the stores; I've seen it."

However, this only increased his obstinacy. "So what? They sell revolvers in stores, too." And I never got Lermontov back from him.

On my way upstairs to say good-by to the woman who owned the workshop, I ran into her niece.

"Are you really leaving, as I'm told?"

"Yes."

"If you hadn't gone by yourself, you'd have been kicked out, anyway," she said, with candor if not with kindness.

And the drunken owner said, "Good-by; God be with you, you bad, impertinent boy. I've never found you so, but that's what they tell me." Suddenly she broke into tears and blubbered, "If my dead husband, the good, dear soul, had been here he would have known how to handle you. He would have beat you and we could have kept you. We shouldn't have had to fire you! But nowadays, things are awry. If everything isn't to your taste, off you go! Akh, boy; where will you land? What's the good of knocking around?"

Chapter Sixteen

I WAS ROWING MY BOSS THROUGH THE FLOODED FAIR GROUNDS WHERE the water had risen to the second story. His paddle made a poor rudder, and we zigzagged through the sleepy streets over the muddy, still water.

"Damn it, the flood's still rising! It's holding up the work!" my boss grumbled, as he smoked a cigar that gave off the aroma of scorched rags. "Careful!" he exclaimed, "we're going into a lamppost!"

Righting the boat he cursed. "Some boat the bastards gave us!"

He showed me the site of his construction job. His face close-shaved until it was blue, his moustache trimmed, and a cigar between his lips, he did not look like an architect. He was in a leather jacket; he was booted to the knees; a game-bag hung from his shoulder, and at his feet lay a costly double-barreled gun of the famous Lebel make. He was restless. Every now and then he pulled his leather cap over his eyes, pursed his lips and cautiously looked around; then he'd push his cap back on his head and smile as if diverted by a pleasant thought. He looked years younger. No one would have imagined him then as a man burdened with responsibilities, concerned over the failure of the flood waters to subside. It was clear that the thoughts flitting through his mind had no connection with business.

As for myself, I was mute with astonishment. It was strange to see that dead community, its submerged blocks with all the windows down. The flooded city seemed afloat. The sun was deep in the clouds of the gray sky, but here and there, in broad, silvery patches of wintry light, it broke through.

Gray and chill, too, was the water, whose current was imperceptible. It seemed to have jelled, to have been pasted down, like the vacant houses in dirty yellow paint, that stood beside the stores. When the pallid sun peered out of a cloud, everything brightened. The gray water reflected the gray sky, with our boat seemingly suspended between the two. Even the rearing stone buildings seemed to be afloat toward the Volga or the Oka River. Around the boat drifted broken barrels, crates, baskets, wood fragments and straw. Some wooden rods or limbs, afloat on the surface, looked like dead snakes.

At intervals an open window would be seen. On the roofs of arcades, wash was drying, or felt boots protruded. From one of the open windows a woman stared into the gray water. Moored to one of the submerged iron pillars of an arcade was a red boat, whose reflections in the water looked like greasy cuts of meat.

Nodding toward these manifestations of life, my boss explained, "Here's where the market watchman lives. From the window he climbs out on the roof; from the roof he boards his boat; he rows around looking for thieves; and if there are none around, he does the stealing."

His phrases idled, his mind on something else. Everything around us was silent, vacant, unreal, like something in a dream. The confluence of the Volga and the Oka had broadened into an enormous lake. On the higher ground the city gleamed in varied colors. Gardens were still bare, but the trees were budding, and warm mantles of young green enfolded churches and houses. Over the water stole the muffled Easter chimes. The sounds from the town drifted here as living sounds drift into a cemetery.

Now our boat threaded between rows of dark trees. We were over the highway to the cathedral, the wind now against us and blowing the acrid cigar smoke back in my boss' face, and into his eyes; he lost control of the boat, which rammed a tree; and, startled and vexed, he cried out, "Some boat!"

"But you're not steering!"

"How can I?" he complained. "When there are two in a boat, one rows and the other steers—if he can. Look, there's the Chinese block!"

I knew the Fair grounds thoroughly; especially that absurd block with a grotesque roof where plaster Chinese sat cross-legged. Many a time my pals and I had stoned the figures, and some had had their faces and limbs nicked by me. But I no longer vaunted such exploits.

Pointing to it, my boss said, "What crap! If the designs—" He whistled and pushed his cap back on his head. But I felt that, if it had been up to him, that stone town would have been just as drab, there on the low ground, flooded every year by two rivers. He would have provided the Chinese block, too.

Pitching his cigar over the side, he spat after it disgustedly. "Life's a bore, Peshkov, a bore. There are no cultivated people to talk to. You want to display your talents—but to whom? Who've you got here? Carpenters, bricklayers, clods——"

He stared at the white mosque, which perched on a small hill. He spoke as if probing his memory for something forgotten. "I took to beer and cigars when I was working for a German. They're a practical race, the wild geese! Beer's a good drink, but I've never got used to the cigars. After you've had one, your wife nags, 'What's that smell? You reek like a harness-maker!' I tell you, brother, the longer we live the worse cheats we become. But—true to yourself——"

Resting his paddle he took up his gun and fired at one of the Chinese figures. It suffered no harm; the pellets lodged in the roof and the wall, and raised dust. "I missed," he admitted without hesitation, and reloaded. "Getting along with the girls? Don't you chase them? I was in love at thirteen!" And, as if telling me a dream, he recalled his first love, a servant girl in the household of the architect where he had served his apprenticeship. The gray water washed softly against the protuberances of the buildings; past the cathedral stretched a desert of water with outcrops of black twigs. I recalled the seminarist's song, which we had often sung in the icon shop. "Oh, stormy blue sea . . ." That blue sea must have been a bore.

"I couldn't sleep," my boss went on. "Sometimes I got out of bed and stood shivering outside her door, like a dog. How cold that house was! My boss came to her at night. He might have caught me but I didn't care." He spoke in a preoccupied way, like someone examining an old coat to see if it were good for another season. "She knew and was sorry for me, and called to me, 'Little fool, come in!' "

How many such stories I had heard; and how banal, though they had one virtue in common: stories of "first love" were all told without brag or lewdness, and usually with such tender melancholy that I gathered that first loves are the best.

Laughing and tossing his head, my boss wondered aloud, "But can you tell such a thing to your wife? No. What harm is there in it? But you never do. That's a tale . . ."

He was telling himself the story, not me. Had he stopped I would have started talking. In that stillness and desert, one had to speak, sing, play the accordion—or risk falling into leaden, lasting sleep in the center of a drowned city, lying under icy, gray water.

"Above all, don't marry early," my boss advised. "Marriage settles you for life. Now you can live at will, where and how you please. You can be a Mohammedan in Persia, or raise hell in Moscow. You can plan your life to suit your own preferences. You can have a taste of everything. But, brother, when you marry, you marry the weather; there's no way to control a wife. And you can't get rid of a wife like an old shoe!" A change had come into his face. His face was drawn, now, as he looked into the gray water. He scratched his long nose and said, "Yes, indeed, brother, look before you leap. Suppose you're harassed on all sides, yet you stand firm. You think you've ridden out the danger? But there's a special trap for you—one for each of us."

We were now in the reeds of Meshchersky Lake, a backwater of the Volga. "Sh-sh!" whispered the boss, leveling his gun at the bushes. After he had bagged a few famished woodcocks, he proposed, "Let's go to Kunavin Street. I'll stay there overnight. You go on home and tell them I was detained by contractors."

He got out in a street on the outskirts, which was also flooded; and I went back to the Fair ground on the Stravelka, where I tied up the boat, and sat in it, gazing at the point where the two rivers met, at the moored steamers, at the sky which was like a gigantic, beautiful bird-wing—all white, feathery clouds. Between blue rifts gleamed the sun, each glance transfiguring the earth and everything upon it. Here, things were lively. The currents were swifter. In the flotsam they carried along were floats of timber, poled by peasants, who shouted warnings to one another or to passing steamers. A tug was hauling an empty barge upstream, with the river pulling back at it, shaking it, while it forced its nose like a pike, panted, and gritted its wheels against the onrushing tide. On a barge, their legs dangling over its side, four peasants sat huddled together, one, in a red blouse singing a tune I recognized, though I could not hear the words.

I felt that here on the living river, I knew everything, was in contact with everything, understood everything. The flooded town behind me was only a bad dream, one of my boss' fantasies, as impossible to account for as himself. When I was sated with what I saw, I went home, feeling grownup and competent for any task. On my way back, I stopped on the Kremlin [36] hill for its view of the Volga. As seen from the hill the earth seemed infinite, and to promise satisfaction of every desire.

At home I now had books. Queen Margot's apartment was now tenanted by a large family, five young ladies, each prettier than the other,

[36] The central citadel, usually walled, of most ancient Russian cities, was called the Kremlin.

and two schoolboys from whom I borrowed books. I was enraptured with Turgenev, enjoying his directness, his intelligibility, his autumnal clarity, the purity of his characters, the nobility of his observations. I read Pomyalovsky's *The Stockmarket*, and found the operations it depicted startlingly like those in the icon store. I was reminded both of the malicious practical jokes I had seen played there and the suffocating boredom which provoked them. The Russian books absorbed me. They had the intimate melancholy I knew; it was as if, on opening the book, I immediately heard muted, frosty Lenten bells, concealed within.

Dead Souls I turned to with reluctance, as well as *The House of the Dead*. Books with such titles—*Dead Souls, Dead Houses, Three Deaths, Living Relics*—though they won unwilling attention from me, were read with a sort of torpid antipathy toward them all. From *Signs of the Times, Step by Step, What to Do, Chronicles of the Village of Smurin*, and other such tendentious works, I got little pleasure. Dickens and Scott delighted me, and I reread their works many times. The latter made me think of festival services in wealthy cathedrals, a little overlong and wearying, but always impressive. To Dickens I continue to bow for his astounding facility in that most difficult of artistic achievements —a loving understanding of human nature.

At night there were gatherings on the roof. They included the brothers K. and their grown-up sisters and Vyacheslav Semashko, the schoolboy with the turned-up nose. At times Miss Ptitzin, daughter of a high-ranking official, joined us. The talk was literary, which I enjoyed, and was within my province, since I was better read than any of them. When the talk turned to school and the tyrannical teachers I felt freer than they and was astounded at their submission. At the same time I envied them their schooling.

Though my companions were older, I felt more mature. I was more experienced and more alert. This somewhat distressed me; I would have preferred to feel in closer rapport. I got home late, work-grimed and filled with impressions of a different life from theirs—mostly dreary. They spoke about young ladies, of being in love, and made attempts at poetry in which they sought my help. To this I willingly acceded; rhyming came easy to me though, for some reason, my verses always slipped into the comic; and I found myself irresistibly associating Miss Ptitzin, the customary subject of these verses, with fruits and vegetables.

Semashko exclaimed, "Call that poetry! It's no more poetry than carpet tacks!"

Determined to keep up with them in everything, I too, paid court to

Miss Ptitzin. I do not recall all the terms of my declaration, but it had a bad ending. In stagnant Zviezdin Pond there was a log on which I offered the lady a ride. I managed to pull the log ashore; it bore my weight well. However, when the fashionable Miss Ptitzin boarded it and I, with a flourish of my pole, pushed off, the cursed log tipped over, sending her headfirst into the water. Gallantly I dove in after her and quickly fished her out. The shock and the pond's green slime both marred her beauty. Shaking her dripping fist at me, she screamed, "You deliberately pushed me into the water!" She brushed all my protestations aside, and from then on, was my declared enemy.

All in all, I didn't find life in the town exciting. The old woman's hostility to me was undiminished; the boss' wife held me in contempt. Victor, with a new crop of freckles, bristled at everybody, nurturing a seemingly perpetual grudge.

My boss had more work than he and his brother could handle, and took on my stepfather. Coming home early one day, and stepping into the dining room, I was startled to see this man, who had passed out of my life, sitting beside my boss, at the table. He offered me his hand, "Hello!"

I recoiled. The fire of the past, suddenly rekindled, scorched my heart. I saw a smile on a fearfully wasted face, whose dark eyes looked larger than ever. He seemed utterly spent. I put my hand in his hot, bony fingers. "So we meet again," he said, with a cough. And I went out, feeling as limp as after a flogging.

We were reserved with each other. He spoke to me as an adult and an equal. "When you go to the store, would you mind getting me a pound of La Fern tobacco, a hundred Victorson cigarette tubes, and a pound of boiled sausage?" The money I got from him was always unpleasantly warm from his hot hands. He was clearly a consumptive on his way out of this earth. This he knew and, pulling at his pointed beard, he would remark, in his deep, composed voice, "I'm quite incurable. Still, if I get plenty of meat, I may recover, I may."

And he ate incredible quantities. And cigarettes were never out of his mouth, except mealtimes. Day after day I bought him sausage, ham and sardines; at which the old woman would make opinionated and insulting comments, "What's the point—treating death to such snacks; you can't fool him."

The boss' wife also had it in for my stepfather and, with a curious note of indignation, pressed him to take this or that medicine, meanwhile ridiculing him behind his back, "Such a dainty gentleman! We should sweep up crumbs more carefully in the dining room; they breed flies, he says."

To which the old woman chimed in, "Such a gentleman with his coat worn to a gloss, and his forever brushing it, so fussy, can't stand a speck of dust!"

The boss would say indulgently, "Patience, you wild geese! He'll soon be in his grave!"

Their blind middle-class antipathy to him, as a man of birth, somehow drew my stepfather and me together. The crimson agaric may be a parasite, but it is beautiful. Stifling among these people, my stepfather was like a fish accidentally dropped into a chicken coop—an absurd simile; but that life was all absurdity.

I began to see resemblances in him to Good Idea—whom I had never forgotten. The finest impressions I drew from books went to adorn him and my queen. What was purest in me, distilled through my reading, I lavished on them. And so my stepfather became another alien and unloved man like Good Idea. He was impartially well-mannered to all, never interrupted, and gave brief but courteous replies when questioned. I was always tickled when he suggested changes to the boss. Bent over the table and tapping the drafting paper with his brittle nails, he would propose, "You'll have to put in a keystone here to distribute the pressure or the pillar will come through the walls."

"The devil; that's so!" the boss would exclaim. When my stepfather would step out, the boss' wife would scold, "How can you let him act the teacher toward you, like that?"

What particularly annoyed her was my stepfather's habit of brushing his teeth and gargling after supper, something which caused his Adam's apple to protrude. "I don't think it's good for you to bend your head so far back," she nagged.

"Why?" he asked, with a polite smile.

"Because . . . I just know it is."

When he started grooming his bluish nails with a small bone pick, she bridled, "There he goes, cleaning his nails again. He's dying, but he's still fussy!"

"Ekh," sighed my boss, "how stupidity fattens in you, you wild goose!" And, astonished, his wife exclaimed, "What's that for?"

At night the old woman importuned God, "Lord, now they've laid that putrefying one on my back and they've edged Victor aside, again!"

As for Victor, he ridiculed my stepfather's manners, his easy gait, the assured movement of his aristocratic hands, his deft knotting of his ties, his fastidious table habits. Victor would ask, "How would you say, 'knee' in French?" deliberately using an overfamiliar form of address; and imperturbably, as if he were correcting a child, my stepfather would remind him of the proper form of address. "All right," Victor replied, "then how do you say 'chest'?" And he would turn to his mother, "Ma mère, donnez-moi encore du pickles!" and she would play to him with, "Oh, you Frenchman!" And my stepfather chewed on, without a sign, as if he had heard and seen nothing.

Once my boss said to his brother, "Since you're acquiring French, I suppose you'll be acquiring a mistress."

My stepfather smiled, the first time I saw him do so. But the boss' wife, flustered, dropped her spoon on the table, "What a disgusting remark to make in my presence!"

Now and then my stepfather came to me in the corner, where my bed was, behind the stairs leading to the attic. Usually he found me sitting on the stairs, reading under the window.

He would exhale a puff of smoke, a whistling breath following it, like the hiss of fireworks. "Reading? What's the book?"

He glanced at the title and said, "I think I've read it. Have a smoke?"

We smoked together. Staring out of the window upon the cluttered yard, he said, "A pity you're not in college. You appear to have abilities."

"I'm reading; that's studying, too."

"That's not enough. You need systematic study in school."

I suppressed an inclination to retort "You had that advantage, old man, and to what effect?" And, as if reading my mind, he followed, "A school education can be valuable to one who's responsive. Only with a good education does a person make his mark."

Once he advised me, "You'd be better off out of this dump. I see no point, no value, in your staying here."

"I enjoy the work."

"What's there to enjoy in it?"

"It's interesting working with these people."

"You may be right."

But he remarked to me, once, "What trash these bosses of yours are!"

Recalling how and when my mother had used that word, I involunarily recoiled. Smiling, he wanted to know, "Don't you think so?"

"I don't know."

"But they are; it's plain that they are."

"Just the same, I like the boss."

"It's true; he's a decent sort—odd, though."

I would have liked to get his opinion of books, which, however, he evidently didn't care for. Once he told me, "Don't be carried away. Things are fancied up in books, misrepresented in some ways. Writers generally are limited people, like our boss."

Opinions like these sounded bold to me, and had a demoralizing effect. During that talk, he asked, "Have you read Goncharov?"

"*The Frigate Pallada.*"

"A dull book. Yet Goncharov's our keenest writer. You ought to read his *Oblomov;* his truest and boldest book, by far; indeed, the best book Russian literature has to show."

On Dickens' novels his comment was, "Muck, I tell you," and added, " 'Nova Vremya's' serializing something interesting, *The Temptation of St. Anthony.* Have you seen it? You seem to go in for stuff about the church, and you may find *The Temptation* worth looking into."

He brought me the issues containing Flaubert's erudite work, which recalled to me the endless lives of the holy men, and odds and ends of religious history I had gotten from the icon appraisers. I got more out of *The Memoirs of Upilio Famali, Lion Tamer* which appeared alongside.

When I admitted this to my stepfather, he said in his imperturbable way, "That only means you've not yet grown up to that sort of thing. Keep that book in mind."

Sometimes he would sit with me for hours, in utter silence, smoking and coughing. I could see the consuming fire behind his beautiful eyes; and, in my surreptitious glances at this man, who was meeting death so candidly and uncomplainingly, I forgot his relationship to my mother, and how he had maltreated her. I was aware that he was living with a seamstress, for whom I felt a wondering compassion. How could she bear his cadaverous embraces, his kisses that exhaled his body's decay?

Like Good Idea, my stepfather made odd observations, "I'm crazy about hounds; they're stupid, but so beautiful; as, often, beautiful women are stupid."

With a flash of pride, I thought, "If he only knew Queen Margot!"

An observation of his that I jotted down in my scrapbook was, "When people live long in the same house, their faces all get to look the same." I waited for such observations as one waits for desserts. To hear unhackneyed, cultivated language in a house where everything said was a colorless commonplace, was refreshing.

My stepfather never referred to my mother, never even mentioning her name; and this heightened my sympathy for him.

I don't recall how the subject came up, but one day I questioned him about God. Matter-of-factly he replied, "I don't know. I have no belief in God."

This brought Sitanov to mind, and I described him to my stepfather. In the same matter-of-fact way, he said, "He has doubts; but those who doubt need something to believe. I just don't believe."

"Then, can that be?"

"But why not? You're looking at someone who doesn't believe."

I could not see anything except a dying man; and what I felt at the sight was something different from compassion. Uppermost in my feelings was a sharp and earnest interest in a man through whom I could come closer to the mystery of death.

A man sat so close to me our knees touched, warm and sentient, coolly commenting on people as he observed them in their behavior toward him, commenting in the manner of one fully competent to make decisive judgments; a man in whom I sensed something necessary or good for me, mixed in with what was of no consequence to me. In this unfathomably complex person thoughts spun in an incessant maelstrom. I felt more than contact with him; I felt an identity with him, as if he were, somehow, living inside of me. I had him constantly on my mind; my soul felt itself under the shadow of his. Yet, in a day he would vanish, with all the riches stored in his heart and mind, with all there was to decipher in his spell-binding eyes. With his going, there would break another of my living links with life. The memory he would leave in me would be reduced to a limited and fixed thing; whereas, that which lives is infinite movement and change. And under these perceptions were incommunicable words, those which generate and nurture ideas, which tap life to its roots, peremptorily demanding, why?

One rainy day my stepfather said, "Probably I'll have to take to my bed soon. This absurd weakness. It leaves me without the will to do a thing!"

Next day, after evening tea, he took particular trouble to dispose of crumbs from his place at the table, and from his clothes, from which he seemed to be brushing off something unseen. The old woman, with a surreptitious glance, whispered to her daughter-in-law, "Look at him primping and tidying himself!"

After I had missed him from the work bench a couple of days, the old woman handed me a large, white envelope, remarking, "Here. I forgot to give it to you. It came yesterday, around noon. A woman brought it; a cute little thing, she was. What she wants with the likes of you is beyond me."

I took out a slip of paper, stamped with the name of a hospital, on which I read this, in a scrawling script: "When you can spare the time, pay me a visit. I'm in the Martinovsky Hospital. E. M."

Next morning I was in a hospital ward, sitting on a long bed in which my stepfather lay, his feet in gray, threadbare socks, sticking out between the posts. His beautiful eyes uncomprehendingly traversed the yellow walls to rest, alternately, on my face, and on the little hands, lying on his pillow, of a girl who sat on a stool at the head of his bed. My stepfather, his mouth hanging open, rubbed his cheek against her hands. She was a plump girl in a silky, dark dress. Tears rolled slowly down her oval face; her damp blue eyes never left my stepfather's face, with its jutting cheekbones, its sharp, prominent nose and shadowed mouth.

"There ought to be a priest here," she whispered, "but he refuses, he doesn't realize." And, lifting her hands from the pillow, she laid them on her breast as though in prayer.

My stepfather recovered and looked at the ceiling with a frown, as if straining to remember something. He held out his gaunt hand to me.

"You? Thanks. And so here I am, as you see. I feel so foolish!"

Fatigued by the exertion, he shut his eyes. I touched his long, cold, blue-nailed fingers. The girl whispered, "Eugene, please introduce us."

"You must become acquainted," he said, "She's dear——"

He stopped; his mouth widened; then, suddenly, he gave a hoarse caw, like a crow. Flinging herself on the bed, clawing at the blanket, her bare arms shuddering, the girl screamed into the pillow in which she buried her head.

It was a quick death, and immediately it was over, my stepfather's good looks were restored. I left the hospital with the girl on my arm. She staggered like an invalid, weeping. Her handkerchief, balled into her hand, was alternately dabbed to her eyes, then held off and examined, as if it were her last and most prized possession. She stopped suddenly, and pressing close to me, as though for protection, she said, "I shall not live out the year. Lord, Lord! What's the meaning of it all?"

Then, holding out her hand, moist with tears, she added, "Good-by. He esteemed you. The burial is tomorrow."

"Shall I walk you home?"

"Why? It's not night."

From the corner I followed her with my eyes. Her pace was slow, like that of a person with no one to hurry to. Is was August, and the leaves had begun to fall. I was unable to attend the funeral, and that was the last I saw of her.

Chapter Seventeen

M Y WORKDAY ON THE FAIR GROUNDS BEGAN AT SIX. I WORKED WITH interesting people—gray-haired Osip, head of the carpenters' gang, who looked like Santa Claus, a deft workman with a ready wit; Yefim, the hunchback slater; pious Peter, who bossed the bricklayers, a rather solemn man who also made me think of saints; and the boss plasterer, Gregory Shishlin, a handsome, blue-eyed man with flaxen hair, who quietly radiated good will.

I had become quite well acquainted with them before. Every Sunday these peasant sub-contractors had assembled in the kitchen. I had been impressed by their appearance and manner, finding their speech pleasing, because of expressions that had a flavor new to me. These sturdy looking peasants had seemed straightforward, thoroughly good people, a wholesome change from the thievish, back-biting, drunken sort I had lived among in nearby Kunavin village.

I had been most taken with the boss plasterer, Shishlin, and had gone so far as to ask him to enroll me in his gang. But, stroking his tanned brow with a white finger, he had gently dismissed the idea. "Not yet," he had said, "the work's too hard; let it go another year." And, with a toss of his handsome head, he had said, "You don't care for the way you live here? Don't let it get you down. Make a life of your own apart from it, and you'll find it easier." Just how profitably I applied this wise counsel, I can't say, but I recall it with gratitude.

On their Sunday morning calls these people, sitting on benches around the table, had had interesting chats while waiting for the boss. His greetings, when he came in, had always been boisterous, and after handshakes all around, he had taken a seat at the head. The workers had laid their tattered ledgers and sheafs of memoranda on the table, and the accounting for the week began. Arguing back and forth, in a stream of good-humored repartee, that only on rare occasions sharpened into

acrimony, being more frequently marked by friendly laughter, my boss
and they challenged each other's figures.

"Ah, for such a nice chap to be born a rascal," I heard them tell him,
and he, with an embarrassed laugh, replied, "And what about your
rascality, you wild geese! There's as much of it among you!"

"And what else should there be among us," Yefim said, nodding in
agreement, and solemn Peter would add, "It's what we steal that we
live on. What we actually earn we have to turn over to God and the
Tsar."

"In that case, I'll gladly part with you as a burnt offering."

Good-humoredly they stretched out the joke, "You mean set us
ablaze? Toss us into a furnace?"

And Gregory Shishlin, stroking his flowing beard down over his chest,
said in a sort of chant, "Oh, brothers, let's get our business transacted
without swindling. Just let's live honestly and see what peace and joy
it will bring us. How about it, good people?"

At that moment, as his blue eyes glistened, and grew more intense,
he appeared amazingly attractive. Apparently rocked off their balance
by his appeal, the rest turned away in embarrassment.

"Peasants don't swindle much," handsome Osip remarked, sighing, as
if commiserating with them.

Peter, the swarthy bricklayer, stooping over the table, said in a thick
voice, "Sin's like a swamp; the further you go, the deeper you sink."

And the boss orated, "And how do I get in it? I'm lured in!"

The philosophizing over, they got back to their haggling. When it
was done, fatigued and sweaty with the strain, they trooped over to the
tavern for tea, taking the boss in tow as their guest.

The job I was given was to keep an eye on these sub-contractors, to
see that they didn't make away with any lumber, bricks, or nails. In
addition to his work for the boss, each had contracted for other construction jobs, where they could use this building material; and they
managed to move it off right under my nose.

I received a warm welcome from them, Shishlin remarking, "Remember, you wanted me to take you into my gang? And, now look at you,
you're my overseer." And Osip kidded me, "Keep your eye on the water
and trust in God." But Peter said sourly, "So, to catch the old mice they
send this young crane."

I found my task a torture. I felt embarrassed before these people,
whose special knowledges seemed to set them apart, yet whom I had to
watch as if they were robbers and swindlers. I took it so hard at first

that the observant Osip led me aside and said, "Be sensible, now, you won't get anywhere taking it so hard, understand?"

I didn't, of course, but realizing that he was aware of the absurdity of my position, we had a candid talk. "Get this, now, the man to watch is Peter, the bricklayer. He has a large family to provide for; and he's grasping by nature, besides. Anything he can lay his hands on, no matter how small, a pound of nails, a dozen bricks, a bag of cement, everything's good pickings to him. There he is, an upright, God-fearing man, with a strict code, yet he has this weakness for other people's goods! As for Yefim, he's like a woman, passive and harmless; you don't have to concern yourself about him, though, like other hunchbacks, he's no fool. Then you have Gregory Shishlin, whose peculiarity is that he neither takes nor gives. He gets practically nothing for his work; he's constantly being cheated, and he never cheats to make it up. He doesn't behave rationally."

"Then, he's a moral man?"

Osip stared at me as if from a distance, and made his comment, which has fastened itself in my mind, "He's a moral man, that's true. Being moral comes easy to the lazy. Morality requires no brains."

"And you?" I asked.

Osip laughingly replied, "Me? I'll answer like a young girl. Wait till I'm a grandmother, then I'll tell you everything. And, meanwhile, use your brains and hunt out the real me; it's up to you to find it."

And so all my notions about them collapsed. I could not question Osip's judgments, since Yefim, Peter and Gregory, themselves, referred to the stately old man as keener and more worldly wise than they. They came to him for advice and showed him every mark of respect. "Be so good as to advise us," they would begin, and were all attention.

Yet, afterwards, Peter would hiss to Gregory, "The heretic!" and with a laugh, Gregory would add, "The clown!"

Gregory's friendly warning to me was, "Watch yourself when you're with the old man, Alex. Before you know it, he'll have you twisted around his finger. The old man is gone sour. God keep you from harm from him."

"What harm?"

The handsome plasterer blinked. "I don't know how to tell you!"

I was now mystified about all of them. To all appearances, Peter, the bricklayer, was the most pious and upright of the lot. His remarks were brief and pithy, and his mind dwelt on God, death and the hereafter.

"Ekh, children, brethren, don't be so rash! How can you ignore what's ahead of you? There's no detour past the cemetery."

He suffered from stomach trouble. On some days he could not eat at all, a morsel of bread causing him such agony as to bring on convulsions.

The humpbacked slater, Yefim, had also seemed thoroughly honest, though eccentric. There were times when his amiability seemed to border on imbecility. He was forever falling in love and he used the same expressions about each woman, "I tell you right out, she's not just a woman, she's peaches and cream. Oh, boy!"

When the vivacious Kunavin Street washerwomen came to the Fair grounds to do odd jobs, Yefim left the roof, watched them from a corner, his bright, gray eyes winking, his mouth stretched wide in a grin, intoning, "What a butterfly the Lord has favored me with; what bliss is my portion! Look at her—peaches and cream! I should offer thanksgivings for this gift of chance. Beauty like this revives me, inflames me!"

In the beginning, the women laughed at him. "Lordy, listen to that hunchback raving!"

But, ignoring their laughter, the slater raved on. A rapt expression covered his face, with its prominent cheekbones; and his flow of honeyed speech had an intoxication that finally worked on the women. An older one remarked to her companion, "Listen to that man carrying on; but he's not a bad young fellow!"

"It's like a bird singing!"

"You mean a beggar croaking on the church steps," said an obstinate one.

But Yefim was far from a beggar. He had a solid stance, like a wellrooted tree. His voice had a challenging ring; his words were spellbinding, and they lulled the women to silence. Indeed, his whole being seemed to stream toward them in soft, hypnotic speech.

And, in the end, shaking his big, pointed head as though the incident amazed him, as well, he reported to his fellow workmen over the supper table or on the Sabbath, "What a honey, what a darling, that little woman was! I haven't met up with her like, before!"

In these recitals of his conquests, Yefim did not brag about his powers, or gloat over the woman as his victim, as other men did. What he expressed, above all, with his wide, astonished eyes, was joy and gratitude.

Osip, with a reproachful shake of his head, exclaimed, "You're incorrigible. How old are you?"

"Forty-four, but what's that? I threw off five years today; it's as if I bathed in rejuvenating waters. My heart's at rest, and I feel good all over. That's the effect some women have, eh?"

Sour Peter lectured him, "You're heading toward your fifties. Take care or your dissolute ways will have a bitter ending."

And Gregory sighed, "You ought to be ashamed of yourself!" And I could see that that good-looking man was envious of the hunchback.

Old Osip looked about him from under his straight, silvered eyebrows, and jibed, "Every Mashka has her quirks. One covets cups and spoons, another pins and earrings; yet every Mashka turns into a grandma."

Gregory had a wife, but she lived on a farm. He, too, had his eyes on the approachable washerwomen, who had no qualms about "earning something" to supplement their income. They regarded that, in their poverty-stricken circumstances, as no different a means to a livelihood from other work. But the handsome plasterer contented himself with looking. His gaze was oddly pitying, as if sorry for them, or for himself. When they flirted with him, he would give a bashful laugh, and walk off. "Ah, you—"

"What's there stopping you, you goof?" Yefim would ask, astounded.

"I have a wife," Gregory reminded him.

"So what? She doesn't have to know a thing about it!"

"She'd know it if I was unfaithful. She wouldn't miss it, brother."

"How could she?"

"I couldn't tell you how, but she's bound to know so long as she keeps chaste, and as long as I keep chaste, I'd know if she was unfaithful."

"But how?" persisted Yefim, and Gregory reiterated quietly, "I couldn't tell you."

The slater waved his hands, "So! Chaste and knows what? You're a sap!"

Shishlin's gang of seven bricklayers did not defer to him as their boss, but regarded him as one of themselves and, among themselves, referred to him as their "calf." When he saw them dawdling, he would pitch in himself, and with an artistic bit of work as an example, would coax them, "Come on now, boys—get to work!"

Once, delivering a wrathful message to him from my boss, I remarked, "What slow workers they are!"

"Why?" he asked, apparently surprised.

"They should have been through with what they're on now, yesterday; but it won't be done today, either."

"That's so," he agreed, "They won't make it, today." He was silent for a while, then added, "I know I ought to fire them, but you see, they're my own, they come from my village. And, besides, it's God's punishment on man to eat his bread in the sweat of his brow; but the punishment must be borne by all, by you and me, as well. But you and I don't have it as hard—the fact is, I can't fire them!"

He went around like a man in a dream. At times he would walk through the deserted Fair ground streets and, lingering at the railing of one of the canal bridges, would stare down into the water, or up into the clouds, or off into the distance, beyond the Oka. And if one came up to him and inquired, "What are you doing here?" he would reply, "What?" and coming to himself, would return an embarrassed smile. "Just looking around."

Often he would say, "God's put things together very properly, brother —sky, earth, the rivers, the steamers. You can board one and off you go, wherever you want—Ryazan, Rybinsk, Perm, Astrakhan. I took a trip to Ryazan, not a bad little spot, but dead, not like our wonderful, gay Nizhny. And Astrakhan's deader still. It's filled with Kalmucks for whom I've got no use. I don't care for any of those outlandish peoples— Mordvins, Kalmucks, Persians, Germans."

His speech was slow, as if probing for a responsive feeling in others, and always finding it in the bricklayer, Peter.

"They're not settled people, they're nomads," said Peter, sternly, as if imposing a sentence. "They were here before Christ came, but they'll be gone before His second advent."

His face alight, Gregory's voice gained animation. "That's so, isn't it? A people that can look you straight in the face, an honest people like the Russians, that's what I like. I can't stand the Jews, either; and it beats me how they came to be God's people. But I suppose there was wisdom in that."

Portentously the slater added, "Wisdom in it—but much that's super-fluous, too."

"Much that's superfluous, indeed," Osip interjected, acidly, "and that fits your talk, you gabblers. You could all use a flogging!"

Osip stood apart and it was impossible to anticipate what his comments would express, agreement or dissent. Though he might go along with them, at times, in their notions, it was clear that he thought them dullards, if not halfwits; and he would growl at them, "Ekh, you sow's litter!" At which they grinned, involuntarily and sourly, but grin they did.

My boss' daily food allotment of five kopecks was not enough to fill me, and I went around hungry. Observing this, the men had me join them at their meals; and sometimes they would have me along when they went to the taverns for tea. I readily accepted their invitations. I enjoyed sitting with them, hearing their rambling talk, their anecdotes; and I made a return which they seemed to enjoy—readings from church books.

"You're stuffed with these books of yours; your crop's swollen with them," Osip remarked, studying me with eyes blue as cornflowers. It was not easy to read their expression; the pupils seemed to dissolve and to be afloat. "Better do your reading, bit by bit. You can become a monk when you grow up and be a help to people with your teaching, and end up a millionaire."

"A missionary," Peter, the bricklayer, corrected, in a voice that had a curious overtone of indignation.

"What?" asked Osip.

"You mean missionary! You're not deaf, are you?"

"Well, then, a missionary, and confute the heretics. But those who are reckoned heretics have a right to their bread. A discreet person can get along even with heretics."

Gregory uttered an embarrassed laugh and Peter snorted into his beard, "And those who practice spells get along well enough, and all sorts of godless ones."

Osip retorted, "One who practices spells is an uneducated man; education is not a customary part of their equipment."

And to me he said, "Consider this; listen. A peasant named Tushek lived in our neighborhood, a skinny little tramp, going wherever chance blew him, like a feather—neither a worker, nor altogether an idler. Finally he took to prayer, having nothing else to do; and wandered off, praying, and turned up two years later, his hair down to his shoulders, a skull cap over his head, and a brown leather cassock over his shoulders, and gave us all the condemning eye and howled at us, 'Repent, ye doomed ones!' And why not have fun repenting, particularly if you're a woman? And, as the repenting went on, Tushek ate and drank his fill and over, and had his pick of the women——"

Wrathfully, the bricklayer cut him short, "What's his overeating and drinking got to do with it?"

"What else?"

"It's what he had to say that counts."

"His words? I didn't bother with them. I have enough of my own."

"We've heard all we want about your Tushek!" roared Peter, while Gregory, silent, his head lowered, stared into his glass.

"No argument there," said Osip placatingly, "All I wanted to do was to show our Alex the different roads to the morsel——"

"Some take you straight to jail!"

"Sometimes," Osip agreed. "But priests you run into on all the roads; the point is to know where to make a turn."

He enjoyed ribbing the pious plasterer and bricklayer. He may have disliked them, but if so, he managed to hide it. You could not pin down any positive attitude in him. He showed Yefim more indulgence, more good will, than the rest. The slater stayed out of their discussions about God, the eternal verities, the miseries of mankind, religious dogmas, etc. In a chair placed sideways, so that he could sit at the table without the chairback jolting his hump, he would silently sip his tea until, suddenly on the alert, he would peer through the smoke and hold his ear cocked for a certain voice he had picked out of the din, and then he was up and out in a flash. That meant that someone he owed money to had come in—Yefim's creditors were many. Since some had taken to beating him on sight, he fled to keep them from that temptation.

"The cranks get furious!" was his surprised comment. "Don't they realize I'd pay them the money if I had it?"

"Oh, the bitterness of poverty!" Osip would call after him.

There were times when Yefim, lost in reveries, would seem insensible to sight or sound. A soft look that made his amiable eyes glow more amiably still, suffused his face.

"A penny for your thoughts!" he would be offered.

"I was thinking how I'd marry a lady, a noblewoman, by God! If I was rich, maybe a colonel's daughter. God, how I'd love her! Because, brothers, once there was a colonel whose house I was roofing——"

"Yes, and we've heard all about his widowed daughter," Peter interrupted irritably.

But Yefim, putting his hands on his knees, and rocking himself till his hump seemed to be hammering the air, went on, "She'd come into the garden, sometimes, all in white, gorgeous she was. I looked at her from the roof, and felt sunstruck. Where did that white ray come from, like a white dove flying up from the ground! Peaches and cream she was! With a lady like that you'd not want any days, only nights!"

"And what would you do for meals?" taunted Peter.

But Yefim, undisturbed, said, "We wouldn't need much. And then, she's so rich!"

"And when are you starting this high life, you rascal?" laughed Osip.

Yefim never talked of anything but women, and was an undependable worker. After a stretch of good work, he would go lax, his mallet tapping at random and leaving gaps. He had a tarry smell, but a wholesome, pleasant smell as well, like that of fresh-cut lumber.

With Osip, the carpenter, you could discuss anything you were interested in. His words always reached inward, though you couldn't tell his banter from his serious talk.

Gregory's favorite topic was God, of Whom he spoke with serious confidence.

"Some people don't believe in God, did you know that?" I asked him.

"What do you mean?" he replied, with a gentle laugh.

"They deny the existence of God."

"Oh, you mean that! I know." And, as if he were fanning off invisible insects, he went on, "Remember what King David said long ago, 'The fool hath said in his heart, "There is no God." ' That's how David put it. Without God, where would we be?"

As if in corroboration, Osip said, "Just try to take God away from our Peter. He'd give it to you!"

Gregory's good-looking face set into a solemn look. With fingers whose nails were crusted with lime, he stroked his beard, and said loftily, "There's God in every animate thing; conscience, our whole spiritual life, derives from God."

"What about sin?"

"Sin is from the carnal part, from Satan! It's external, a sort of smallpox, that's all. The more one thinks of sin, the more sinner one is! If you don't dwell on sin, you don't sin. It's Satan, the tempter, ruler of the flesh, from whom come sinful thoughts."

This, Peter the bricklayer disputed. "That's where you're wrong."

"Certainly not! God's without sin, and man's both His image and His resemblance. The image, which is the flesh, sins; but his resemblance is spirit and is beyond sin." And his face took on a triumphant smile.

Still Peter muttered, "You're wrong!"

"I suppose your view," Osip cut in, "is that without sin there can be no repentance and without repentance, no salvation?"

"That way there's hope. As our Father said, "Fear of the devil maintains the love of God.""

Gregory was no drinker; two glasses, and he was off. His cheeks would flush, his eyes take on an infantile expression, and he would sing out, "Brothers, how well we live; we do a bit of work, we eat our fill; praise

God! How good it all is!" And tears would trickle down and stud his silky beard like paste pearls.

I found his lachrymose praise of our life unseemly. Grandma's praises of life had been more human, warmer, and more convincing.

These arguments, which aroused emotions in me too vague to define, kept me in a perturbed state. By that time I had read much that had been written about peasants; and saw no resemblance between those in the books and those to be encountered in the real world. In the books their talk was less of God, of sectarian dogma, of churches, than of government, law and the land; in the books their talk was less about women and, then, though coarse, was less hostile. In the real world women were the peasants' pastime—albeit a risky one. A man had to be clever to get the best of a woman; and if he failed, his life was a failure. The book *muzhik* [37] might be good or bad, but too entirely one or the other. The real *muzhik* is neither wholly good nor bad, but a remarkably interesting character. Among peasants, if a man doesn't blurt out everything, you have the impression that he is holding something back, reserved for himself alone; and the concealed and unexpressed thing is the key to him.

Of all the book peasants, I preferred Peter in the book, *The Carpenters' Society*. I brought the book to the Fair grounds to read to the men, on one of the many nights I slept over in one of the workshops, because I was too exhausted to plod home. On hearing I had a book about carpenters, they showed keen interest, Osip in particular. Taking the book from me, he leafed through it dubiously, with questioning shakes of his head. "It's really about us? You rascal! Who's the writer? A gentleman? That's what I guessed! Gentlemen and *chinovniks*, they're your universal authorities. Where God won't risk a guess, a *chinovnik's* mind is all made up. That's their whole life!"

"Bringing God in that way smacks of blasphemy," warned Peter.

"Never mind; what are my words to God? Less than a snowflake or a raindrop to me. Don't fret; you and I don't trouble God."

And from him came a sudden spurt of talk, bright little sayings, sharp as sparks from a flint, with which he snipped, as if they were scissors, whatever was not to his liking. And, several times a day, he asked me, "Will we have a reading, Alex? That's the idea!"

After supper, which I had in Osip's shop, Peter came in with his helper, Ardalon, and Gregory with a boy named Tom. In the shed, where the workers' bunks were, there was a lamp, and I did my reading in its light. They did not interrupt, but they were restless; and at least Ardalon pro-

[37] A common term for peasant, sometimes derogatory.

tested, "I've had enough of it!" and went out. Gregory was the first who napped off, his mouth open as if sleep had taken him by surprise. All the carpenters followed; but Peter, Osip and Tom drew closer to me, with intent expressions. The reading finished, Osip turned out the lamp. By the position of the stars, we knew it was about midnight.

In the dark, Peter asked, "Why was this written? Against whom?"

"Time to sleep," said Osip, pulling off his boots.

"I'm asking, whom was that written against?" Peter insisted.

"That's their concern," said Osip, stretching out on a trestle bed.

"If it's against stepmothers, there's no point to it; it won't reform them," insisted the bricklayer. "And if it's against people, it's just as pointless; his sin's the answer. Siberia for murderers; that's all there is to it. Can books stop such sins, eh?"

Osip kept silent and the bricklayer went on, "They can't do a piece of work themselves, so they gab about the work of others; like women at a meeting. Let's get some sleep; good night."

But he paused in the deep blue rectangle of the open door and asked, "Asleep yet, Osip? What's your opinion?"

"What?" asked the carpenter, drowsily.

"Never mind; go back to sleep."

Gregory had dropped off on his side; Tom was stretched out on trampled straw at my side. Sleep had the whole neighborhood in its grip. From far off came the sounds of a passing train; the blast from the engine, the grinding of wheels on rails, the clank of the couplings. Snoring, in different keys, filled the shed. I felt restless. I was disappointed not to hear the discussion I had expected.

Suddenly Osip's voice came upon me, quietly and evenly, "Son, don't take any of that seriously. You're young; you have a long life ahead of you. Trust to your own thoughts. What you feel for yourself is worth twice what anyone else can tell you. Are you asleep, Tom?"

"No," said Tom, eagerly.

"Good! The two of you've been taught to read. Keep it up. But don't believe everything in print. Anything can be printed, you know. Printing things is a business."

He sat up, and with his hands gripping the edge of the board, bent toward us and went on. "Books?—How should you look at them? A book denounces somebody, that's what a book does. See the sort of man he is, a carpenter, or what have you—and contrast him with what gentleman —quite another sort, eh? A book's written with some purpose and about somebody."

In a choked voice Tom said, "Peter had a right to kill that contractor!"

"No. Nobody has a right to take a human life. I know you hate Gregory, but get that idea out of your head. There are no magnates here. Today I'm a boss, tomorrow back at my bench."

"I wasn't thinking of you, Uncle Osip."

"It's all one."

"You're fair——"

"Hold it. Let me show you why they write books," Osip caught up the overwrought Tom. "They had a clever idea, there. On the one hand, you have a gentleman without a muzhik, and on the other a muzhik without a gentleman. Watch them. Both are in trouble. The gentleman loses his strength and goes out of his mind; the muzhik struts and takes to drink and gets sick and nasty. That's how it goes. It went better in the lord's castle; the muzhik was protected by his master, and the master by the muzhik; and so it went between them, and they all ate well and lived in peace. Certainly it was more peaceful living under the nobility. A muzhik who was too poor was no good to the master; it was to his advantage if the muzhik was intelligent and well off; it was as if he was armed with a good weapon. I know; some forty years, you see, I lived on a nobleman's estate. A lot of experience is scored over my hide!"

I recalled similar views of the nobility from the carter who had cut his throat; and it troubled me that Osip should think along the same lines as that crooked-minded old man.

Osip put his hand on my knee and went on, "So you must know how to interpret books and writings of whatever sort. Nothing's done without a reason. They don't write books for nothing, or just to puzzle people. Every being in creation is given the power to think; and without it you couldn't lift an axe or cobble a shoe." After going on so for a long time, he lay down. But, soon, he was up again, his individual and neatly-turned phrases playing deftly through the still darkness.

"It's said the nobility is a different breed than the peasantry, but that's not so. We're the same stock as the nobility; only by chance, we're born on the lower rungs. Certainly, a nobleman has the advantage of books, while I have to learn with my own skull; and his skin hasn't got my callouses; that's all the difference. Well, boys, it's time for a new way of life; they ought to scrap all those writings! Everyone should ask himself, 'What am I?' 'A man!' 'And what's he?' 'A man, too!' Then what? Does a rich man's superfluity count with God? No. In the sight of God, our endowments are equal!"

And by the time dawn had extinguished the stars, Osip told me, "See, now, what writing I could do? I've talked of things I've never thought of till now. But don't take me too seriously. I was talking because I couldn't sleep, not because I meant anything by it. Lie down and think of something entertaining. Once there was a crow, and it flew across the fields and over the hills and from frontier to frontier and lived past its time; and the Lord finished it. The crow is dead and dusty. What's the meaning? There's no meaning whatsoever. Just get some sleep; soon it will be time to go to work."

Chapter Eighteen

As IN THE CASE OF JAKE THE STOKER, OSIP GREW UPON ME, TILL HE blotted all others from my eyes. He somehow resembled the stoker, but there were touches in him, as well, of grandpa, of the old appraiser, and of the chef, Smoury. Among the people engraved in my memory, he has cut the deepest, bitten in as an oxide into a brass bell. What set him apart was his two-sided mind. By day, at work and among people, his brisk, clear ideas were practical and far easier to comprehend than those he expressed in the evening among his cronies, or talking to fill a sleepless night. His night thoughts changed their shape like a lamp flame. They burned so brightly; but what was their actual form? And in which form did the idea reflect the real, inward Osip?

He seemed to me quite the cleverest man I had ever met, and I was always at his heels, as I had been with the stoker, studying him, trying to understand him. But he slipped out of my grasp; there was no way to hold him. If there was anything real in him, where was it hidden? What dare I believe? And I recalled his remark, "The real me? It's up to you to find it!"

My self-esteem was challenged; in fact, it had become almost a life-and-death matter for me to track down that elusive old man who, nevertheless, was so formidably solid. It seemed to me he could live another hundred years without change, so invulnerably did he preserve his individuality in the flux of unstable people around him. The appraiser had given me a similar expression of stability, but it had not had the same attraction for me. Osip's was of a different sort, and in a way I can't define, more attractive.

Human inconsistency impinges only too forcefully on one's notice; I was bewildered by the acrobatic hopping of people from one perch to another. I had long wearied of the surprises in these incomprehensible somersaults, which had exhausted my interest in people and lessened my love for them.

Thus, one early June day, a rickety cab pulled up at our work site. The bearded, hatless cabman was drunk; his lip was cut, and he sat hiccoughing on the driver's seat; and inside was Gregory Shishlin, drunk and rolling on the arm of a plum, red-cheeked girl. She was equipped with a straw bonnet trimmed with glass cherries and a red band, a parasol in her fist, and rubbers on bare feet. Flirting her parasol, and swaying her hips, she said, in a blend of screams and giggles, "What the hell! The Fair's not open; there isn't any Fair; and that's how he takes me to the Fair! Holy Mother——!"

Gregory, tattered and crestfallen, tottered out of the cab and collapsed on the ground, where he proclaimed to all the spectators, tearfully, "Down on my knees I go! I have sinned! I had sinful thoughts and I sinned! Yefim says 'Come on, Gregory!' And he's right, too; so you people will forgive me; let's all have something; it's on me. He's right; we live only once; and that's the long and the short of it."

The girl shrieked with laughter and swung her legs in the cab, kicking off her rubbers; the cabman growled, "Let's get on; the horse wants to be off!"

The horse, an aged, worn animal, lathered with foam, stood as if he had landed in his grave. There was something wildly ludicrous in the scene. Gregory's workmen were doubled up with laughter, as they watched their boss, his lady, and the besotted cabman. Tom alone was not laughing. He stood beside me, in the shop door, muttering, "The swine! Devil take him! And his wife's a real beauty!"

The cabman kept calling on them to get going. The girl got out, pulled Gregory to his feet, and, directing the driver with her parasol, cried, "Drive on!"

With good-natured laughter and looks of disguised envy at the boss, the men went back to work at Tom's order. The latter, it was obvious, hated to see Gregory an object of ridicule. "Call that a business man!" he grumbled. "I've got just about a month to finish up here. Then I'll go back to the village. This is more than I can take."

I felt upset for Gregory's sake; that cherry-festooned girl had looked so cheap beside him.

It puzzled me how Gregory had come to be boss, and Tom Tuchkov his workman. A powerfully-built youth with curly hair, an eaglelike nose, and shrewd, gray eyes lighting up his round face, Tom did not have a peasant look. In good clothes he would be taken for a merchant's son, a man of good family. He was sober, sparing of words, and practical. Having received an education, he kept Gregory's books and drew up estimates; and, though a reluctant worker himself, knew how to keep his workmates on the job. "You can't stretch the work out to eternity," he remarked coolly.

He despised books. "Let them print anything they care to," he said, "but I'm doing my own thinking. Books are all bunk."

He was interested in everything, and when something took his attention, would pursue it, adding detail upon detail, but giving it the color of his own thoughts, assessing it by his own standards.

When I told him he ought to be a contractor on his own, his answer was, "Yes, if it meant a business in thousands. But to fret myself over kopecks, that's not worth my while. I'm keeping my eyes open; then I'll join a monastery in Oranko. I've got looks and a strong build; I may catch the eye of a rich widow. Things like that happen. I knew a chap from Sergatsk who struck it rich in a couple of years, got himself a city wife, from these parts, too. Delivered an icon to her house and caught her eye."

The idea obsessed him. He was full of stories of how work in a monastery had been the foundation of an easy life. Such stories and this drift of Tom's mind repelled me; but I took his going to a monastery for granted. And so, when the Fair opened and Tom took a job as a waiter in a tavern, he surprised everybody. Perhaps it was no surprise to his workmates, but they all scoffed at him. On holidays they would troop out for tea, saying, "Let's have a look at our Tommy." And, when they arrived, they would bawl out, "Hi, there, you with the curls, some service here!"

He'd come up, his nose up in the air. "What can I do for you?"

"Don't you remember faces?"

"I never remember faces."

He was aware of the scorn of his mates, their ridicule, and his look was defensive. His face might have been carved out of wood, but its expression said, "Get it over with. Laugh, and have it over with."

"Shall we tip him?" they would say, and after deliberately fussing with their wallets, they would leave him nothing.

I asked Tom how come he had taken the waiter's job instead of a job in the monastery. "I never meant it about the monastery, and I won't be a waiter for long."

He was a waiter still when I ran across him, four years afterward, in Tsarytsyn; [38] and some time later, I saw an item in the paper about the arrest of Thomas Tuchkov, on a burglary charge.

I was also moved and mystified by what became of the bricklayer, Ardalon, Peter's oldest and best workman. This man, too, black-bearded and cheerful, made one wonder, Why is Peter the boss and not he? He rarely touched vodka and then usually in moderation. He knew his work well and seemed to love it, the bricks soaring in his hands like red birds. Alongside him the skinny, sickly Peter seemed valueless to the gang. Peter said of their work, "For others I build houses of stone; for myself I build a wooden coffin."

In contrast, Ardalon, jovial at his bricklaying, told me, "Work is for God's glory, my boy!" Next spring, he said, would see him in Tomsk, in Siberia, as overseer in the construction of a church his brother-in-law had the contract for. "I've got my mind set on that. I love building churches!" And he urged me to join him. "Siberia's made for a man with an education; that's where it's a big advantage!"

I agreed, and delighted as if over a personal triumph, he crowed, "It's a deal. I'm not joking!"

Toward Peter and Gregory, his attitude was jestingly good-natured, as toward a pair of children. To Osip he said of them, "Showoffs—always making big claims to each other, like card players, 'I hold the ace,' 'And I'm trumping it!' "

Osip immediately rejoined, "That's how it's bound to be. It's natural to show off. Don't girls walk with their tits out?"

"That's right. God's always on their tongue, but their money these guys keep to themselves," said Ardalon.

"Can't say that about Gregory, though."

"Aah—I'm talking about myself. I want to be with God in the deep forests, in the wilderness. I'm tired of it here. In the spring it'll be Siberia for me."

Ardalon's workmates said enviously, "Give us a break like that, such a brother-in-law, and we'd risk Siberia, too."

Suddenly Ardalon dropped out of sight. After leaving his workshop on Sunday, three days went by without a sign of him. "He might have been murdered," "He might have drowned," were among our worried guesses. But Yefim came to announce sheepishly, "He's on a bat."

[38] Now Stalingrad.

"What do you want to lie for?" exclaimed Peter.

"He's drinking; he's hitting it hard. He's going like a kiln on fire in the center. Maybe the wife he loved so much just died."

"Go on; he's a widower. Where is he?" And Peter started out to Ardalon's rescue only to be fought off.

Then Osip, with a determined set to his lips, and his hands in his pockets, said, "How about my taking a look into it? A guy like that's worth the trouble."

I went along. On the way Osip said to me, "Here's a chap, quiet, well-behaved, no peep out of him for years; then, suddenly he cuts loose and he's all over the place. Watch, Alex, and learn."

Our destination was one of the Kunavin village dives, where we were met by a predatory old madam. After a whispered confab with Osip, she brought us to a small, bare room, as dim and reeking as a stable. There on a cot, lay a hulking woman, who, even in sleep, thrust herself into suggestive postures. The old madam prodded her with her fist, bawling, "Up, frog, get up!"

"Heavens! Who's there? What's up?"

"Detectives!" shouted Osip. The woman moaned, and scuttled out. Osip spat after her and enlightened me: "Detectives scare them worse than the devil."

The old madam removed a small mirror from the wall, and folded away a loose strip of wallpaper and asked, "Take a look. Is that your man?"

Osip looked through what turned out to be a crack in the wall, and replied, "That's the man. Get the woman out!"

I, too, took a look and, through the crack, beheld a companion stable stall to ours. Beside a window with drawn shutters, on whose sill burned a tin lamp, was a naked, cross-eyed Tatar woman mending a chemise. The bed was behind her and on its pillows we could make out Ardalon's puffy face and black, matted, outthrust beard.

With a shudder the woman slipped on the chemise, walked past the bed and, suddenly, was in our room.

Osip glared at her, spat, and muttered, "Pugh, you tart!"

With a laugh she retorted, "Pugh on you, old dodo!" Laughing, Osip wagged his finger at her.

We made our way into the Tatar woman's stall. It took some time for old Osip, sitting at the foot of the bed, to rouse Ardalon out of his stupor. "Hold on," he mumbled, "wait a while. We'll be along."

Finally he came to, gave a wild look at us, shut his bloodshot eyes again, and mumbled, "Well, now."

"What's come over you?" asked Osip, more in pity than reproach.

"I was pushed into it!" said Ardalon, with a grating cough.

"How so?"

"I had a reason."

"You were dissatisfied, I suppose."

"What's the use!" And Ardalon picked an uncorked vodka bottle off the table and took a swallow, inviting Osip, "How about a nip? We ought to be able to rustle up a bite to eat, too."

Old Osip took a gulp, frowning as the liquor went down, and chewed thoughtfully at a bite of bread, while Ardalon mumbled foggily, "So I've come to this, holing up with a she-Tatar. Pure Tatar, according to Yefim, a young one, an orphan from Kasimov, getting all set for the Fair."

From the other side of the wall, the woman called out in halting Russian, "The prize ones are the Tatars, you know; game like young hens. Tell him to beat it. He's not your father!"

"That's her," said Ardalon, gawking at the wall.

"I've had a look at her," said Osip.

To me Ardalon said, "Well, brother. So you see the sort I am!"

I awaited a storm of reproaches, a biting homily from Osip, that would drive Ardalon to cringing repentance. Nothing of the sort. The two sat side by side, their shoulders touching, and spoke in quiet monosyllables. They were a melancholy pair in that dingy stall. The woman kept up a ridiculous tirade through the wall, but was ignored. Osip took a walnut from the table, cracked it under his heel, neatly picked out the kernel, and disposed of the shell, and asked, "Money all gone?"

"No. Peter has some of it."

"So. Aren't you going away? If you went to Tomsk——"

"What for?"

"So, you've had a change of mind?"

"If it was with strangers it would be another matter."

"What are you talking about?"

"But it's with my sister and my brother-in-law."

"So what?"

"It's no holiday, making a new beginning among your own folks."

"It's no holiday anywhere."

"Just the same——"

And their talk, though serious, was so amiable that the Tatar woman stopped railing at them, came in to get her dress, and left them.

"A young one," remarked Osip.

Ardalon looked at him and continued affably, "Yefim's a nitwit. He has nothing on his mind except women. But the Tatar woman's a joy; she sets you on fire."

"Watch out, or you won't get away from her," warned Osip, and having masticated the walnut, he made his farewell.

On the way back I asked Osip, "Why did you go there?"

"Just to have a look. I've known him for years, and he's not the first case I've seen of your good citizen suddenly carrying on like an escaped convict." And Osip repeated a former warning, "Steer clear of the vodka," adding, a moment later, "though life without it would be a bore."

"Without vodka?"

"Yes. You drink, and it's like slipping into another world."

There was no real coming back for Ardalon. He was back at work several days later, but only for a couple of days. In the spring, I ran across him among the casual dock laborers. He was one of a gang that was breaking up the ice around the moored barges. We exchanged friendly greetings and had tea together in a tavern where he boasted, "Remember what a hand I was—A, number one! I could have made my pile."

"But you didn't."

"No, I didn't," he agreed jauntily. "Work? I spit on it!" The people, listening in around us, were impressed by his swagger.

"Remember what that crook, Peter, says about work? Stone mansions for others and a coffin for himself; that's what work is!"

I said, "Peter's a sick man and he's got death on his mind."

"I'm a sick man, too; my heart's out of whack."

On holidays I sauntered out to the waterside, to "Million" Street, where the longshoremen hung out, and was amazed at how quickly Ardalon had adapted himself to that rough crew. A year before he had been a serene, sober man; now he was one of the most boisterous of them, had acquired their odd, shambling gait, their pugnacious look, as if daring everybody to a fight, and bragged, "See how I have it here! I'm a leader here!"

He was free with his money, standing treat whenever he had it. In fights he was always on the side of the under-dog; and you'd often hear his cry, "That's not fair, boys; keep it fair!" And this won him the nickname, "Fair-play," which thrilled him.

To these people, crammed into that noisome sack of a street, I gave impassioned study. All had broken away from conventional ways, and had improvised jollier ways of their own, without grace of bosses. Bold and carefree, they brought to mind grandpa's bargemen pals who had so readily turned hermit or bandit. When work was slack, they did not hesitate to lift something from barge or steamer holds, which gave me no shock, since, so far as I could see, life was held together by the thread of robbery, like a worn coat stitched together with gray thread. I observed, however, that they were lackadaisical workers except in emergencies, such as fires or the break of the river-ice, when they threw in all their energies. On the whole their life had a more festive character than that of other people.

Osip, observing how I had gravitated to Ardalon, gave me fatherly counsel. "Take care, son; why find your pals in 'Million' Street? See that you don't get hurt!"

I did my best to explain my attraction toward these poeple, who led such a lively, workfree existence.

"Birds of the air!" he broke in, laughing. "Idle, useless people, who look on work as a calamity!"

"But, after all, what is work? As they put it, 'Honest labor provides no stone mansions!' " Out came this facile saying which I had heard so often, and seemed so true to me.

It only incensed Osip, who stormed at me, "Where did you hear that? From fools and wastrels! A snipper your age shouldn't swallow such things. You—! It's the failures who spew out such envious drivel. Hold off flying, son, until your feathers grow in. I'm going to let your boss know about your new pals."

He did and the boss added his warnings. "Keep away from 'Million' Street. It's a hangout for crooks and whores; and it's next door to the jail and the hospital. Keep away, I tell you!"

From then on, my visits to "Million" Street were surreptitious; and they soon came to an end. I was with Ardalon and Robenok, a pal of his, one day, on the roof of a shed in a boarding house yard. Robenok, whose soldiering had included service both as cavalryman and sapper, was giving a humorous account of a hoboing trip from Rostov-on-Don to Moscow. A wound in the knee, received during the Turkish War, had left him lame. Thus, the power in his unusually powerful arms was no help in getting him jobs. As the result of some other affliction he had become hairless, and his head was like that of a new-born babe.

His brown eyes flashed as he narrated, "And at Serpukhov I ran across a priest in a sleigh, and I said, 'Alms, Father, for a Turkish hero.' "

"That's a lie," said Ardalon, shaking his head.

"Why should I lie?" asked Robenok, not put out at all.

In indolent reproach my friend muttered, "You're incorrigible. You could get a job as a watchman; any cripple can get a job like that; but you'd rather mooch and lie."

"All I do it for is to amuse people; I lie to make them laugh."

We were having dry, sunny weather, but it was dark and damp here in the yard. Suddenly a woman came in, waving a rag before her, and crying, "Friends, who wants to buy a petticoat?"

Women crawled out of their holes, and surounded the seller, whom I had immediately recognized as the laundress, Natalie. She made her sale to the first bidder, and by the time I got down from the roof, was gone. But I caught up with her at the gate and greeted her rapturously, "How are you?"

"What nerve!" was her return greeting, as she gave me an irritated glance. Then, recognizing me, she stood stock still and exclaimed, "God save us! What brings you here?"

Her reaction disturbed me; she was clearly upset on my account. Astonishment and dismay were only too clear on her wise face. I explained that I did not live here, that I came here only as an onlooker.

"An onlooker!" she burst out, in angry mockery. "What sort of place is this for sight-seeing? You're after the women!"

Her face had grown withered; there were rings under her eyes; and her lips had a feeble droop. At a tavern door she said, "Come in for a glass of tea. I don't believe you, though you dress differently from the people hereabouts."

In the tavern, however, her doubts began to disappear. As she poured the tea, she told me that she had got up only a little while ago and had not yet breakfasted. "And last night I got to bed dead drunk, and where I had been drinking and with whom, I couldn't tell you."

I couldn't help feeling awkward with her and full of sorrow. My chief concern was to find out about her daughter. After she had had some vodka and hot tea, her talk took on the coarse, lively familiarity of the women of this street; but my question about her daughter immediately sobered her. "What are you so curious for? No, my lad; you won't get your hands on her. Get that out of your mind." And after she had had some more drink, she said, "My daughter and I have nothing to do with each other. Who am I? A washerwoman; what kind of mother is that for an educated girl? And that's just what she is, brother! She's gone off to be a teacher, and she lives with a rich friend, just like—" A pause, and then she concluded, "And that's how it goes. You don't care for the washerwoman, but the street walker——?"

It was obvious she had become a street walker; no other sort frequented that alley. But to have her admit it brought tears of shame and pity to my eyes. I felt seared, as by a flame, by that admission from one once so courageous, bright and free.

With a sigh, after giving me a long look, she said, "Now, you get out of this place, I beg you. Please stay away from here, or you'll go under!" And in a gentle, broken voice, as if to herself, her head bowed and her fingers scrabbling on the tray, she said, "But how can I expect you to listen, no matter how I advise you and beg you. My own daughter wouldn't hear me. I cried to her, 'You can't throw your own mother off! How can you think of that?' 'I'll choke myself!' said she. That's what she said. And she went to Kazan, to study for a midwife, but how about me? What did I have to do? And this is what I've come to; I've gone on the street!"

Then she was silent a long time, though her lips fluttered with the soundless motion of her thoughts. It was clear she had forgotten about me. Her mouth sagged at the corners; it was a torture to see the trembling of her lips and to read the wordless writing of the twitching furrows on her face, which seemed to me like that of a heartbroken child. Strands of her hair had escaped from her kerchief and lay over her cheek or around her dainty ear. Observing that her tears were splashing into her cold tea, she pushed it away and shut her eyes, the pressure forcing out more tears. Then she dried her face on her handkerchief. I could stand it no longer and got up and bid her "Good-by."

"What? Oh, go to the devil!" she replied, waving me off without a look, having forgotten, apparently, whom she was with.

I returned to look for Ardalon, with whom I was to have gone crabbing; and I was eager, too, to talk to him about Natalie. But both he and Robenok had left the shed roof; and while I was hunting him through the slovenly yard, the street began to ring with the sort of brawl common in that quarter.

Coming out of the gate, I bumped into Natalie, who was weeping and dabbing her handkerchief at bruises on her face. She was also trying to fix her hair, as she staggered, almost blindly, down the sidewalk. After her came Ardalon, with Robenok following behind and egging him on: "Come on; let her have another one!"

Overtaking the woman, Ardalon brandished his fist. Turning on them, her bosom heaving, her eyes blazing hatred out of her awful face, Natalie cried out, "Come on, hit me!"

I grabbed Ardalon's arm and he turned an astonished look upon me.

"What's come over you?"

I barely managed to blurt out, "Don't you touch her!"

He burst into laughter. "So, that's your sweetie! Damn that Natalie; she's caught our little saint!"

Robenok joined in the laughter, holding his sides. I stood there, frying in the heat of their obscenities; but while they were at it, Natalie got away. Finding them unbearable, I butted Robenok with my head, knocked him over, and ran from them.

After that I kept away from "Million" Street. However, I came upon Ardalon on the ferry, and he gave me a jovial greeting. "Where've you been keeping yourself?"

When I let him know how offended I had been by his cruelties toward Natalie and his lewd conjectures about me, he dismissed it all with good-natured laughter.

"So you took all that seriously? We were only ribbing you, smearing it on for fun! And as for that tart, what's wrong with giving a street walker a beating? Men beat their wives, so do you expect us to have more consideration for that sort? But the whole business was a joke. And would you have it that the fist isn't a good teacher?"

"Who are you to instruct her? How are you any better?"

He put his hands on my shoulders, gave me a shake, and said in a jesting tone, "Among the disgraced, who's better than the other?" Then, with a laugh, he boasted, "But, brother, I understand it inside out. I'm on to it all. I'm not a block of wood!"

He had been drinking, but had not yet got beyond the happy stage. His glance at me was that of the indulgent and sympathetic teacher to the uncomprehending disciple.

I sometimes ran into Paul Odnitzov. He was quite the dandy, and, if anything, livelier than before. His manner toward me was rather condescending and even a bit resentful. "Wasting your time in this sort of work! Living with muzhiks!"

But when he gave me news of the workshop, he became sad. "Zhikharev's still doting on that cow of his. Sitanov's discontented and he's hitting the bottle. Goloviev's made a meal for the wolves. He was reeling home, dead drunk, from Sviatka, and the wolves made a meal of him." He laughed as he added, "After they ate him, they got tipsy, too. They got up on their hind legs, like trick dogs, and waltzed through the woods. But then they took to quarreling and before the end of the day, they'd finished each other off."

I joined in his laughter; yet, the workshop and my experiences in it seemed very remote from me now, and it made me melancholy to realize it.

Chapter Nineteen

SINCE THERE WAS PRACTICALLY NOTHING TO DO AT THE FAIR GROUNDS in winter, the countless house chores became my occupation. These devoured my day, but my evenings were free. Again I read aloud to the boss' family, the tasteless serials in "Neva" and "The Moscow Gazette"; but at night I divided my time between reading books of my own choice and composing verses.

On a day when the women were at church and my master was confined to the house by illness, he asked me, "Is it true you're writing poetry? Victor's been making cracks about it. So? Well, read me some of it."

I could not refuse, and read him some pieces which apparently did not impress him. However, he was kind enough to say, "Stick at it! You might turn out a Pushkin. Have you read him?" And he quoted the lines, "Do elves hold solemn funerals? Do witches marry in state?" adding, "In his time people still believed in demons and witchcraft, but not he; he was only playing with it. It's a fact, brother, you should have been given an education, but it's too late for that, now. If I were you I'd keep that scrapbook out of sight of the women. If they get their hands on it, they'll ride you. Women, I tell you, brother," he concluded, with a meditative slowing down of his words, "women have a way of stinging at one's sore spots."

Recently the boss had become noticeably preoccupied. He took quick, uneasy looks about him; and every time the doorbell rang, he jumped. He would sometimes flare up over trifles, find fault with everybody, then slam out of the house, to get home late and drunk. You could feel he was hiding something that had come into his life and was cutting him to the heart; and that his daily life was now involuntary, hardly conscious even, that it went on out of habit.

Sundays, after the midday meal and up to nine o'clock was my free time, and I used it to roam around, winding up in the early evening at a tavern on Yamsky Street. Its stout, sweaty proprietor was a devotee of music, a fact known to choir singers, and of which they took advantage by congregating at his bar. Their vodka, beer or tea was on the house when they sang for him. I found the singers a dull and sottish sort who sang not for the love of it, but for the free drink—and seldom anything but church music. Since some of the more pious sots were squeamish about being seen in a tavern, the proprietor had them in a back room; and their performances I had to enjoy, muted, as it came through the door. Often country people and peasant laborers came in to show off their voices. The tavern keeper broadcast his invitations to singers through the town, especially on market days when the peasants flocked in.

The performer was seated at the bar, with the bottom of a vodka keg behind him, making a circular frame for his head. The best of them—and they were all good—was the skinny, squeezed-in little harness-maker, Kleshchov, whose head was crowned with red tufts, whose little nose was shiny like a corpse's, and whose eyes had a serene, dreamy, immobile stare. Shutting his eyes and leaning back till his head touched the vodka keg, and swelling out his chest, he would let go with his soft, yet overwhelming, tenor, singing the staccato "Ah, how the fog descends, to stain the clean fields and blot out the roads." After a pause, and bending farther back till he was resting on the bar, while his face was turned up to the ceiling, he went on, "Ah, where then, where shall I go, where find the broad, high road?"

His was a small voice, suited to his small body, but it was tireless. He filled the dim, bleary depths of the tavern with chords of silver, with sighing words. His plaintive singing captivated everybody. Even the drunks were silenced and sat with their heads bowed. And my heart was flooded with those overwhelming emotions that always well up when good music, in its miraculous way, plumbs the very sources of the soul.

Then a churchlike quiet descended over the tavern and the singer was like a benevolent priest who did not arraign, but simply and with all his heart, prayed for the whole family of mankind, meditating aloud, one might say, on the tribulations that afflict man. Bearded men turned rapt stares upon him; in hard faces, eyes blinked like those of children; and involuntary sighs testified to the power of music. It seemed to me, then, that it was the ordinary life of people that was insignificant and unreal; that it was here that one came upon reality.

Blowsy Liza, the old clothes dealer, a dissolute, repellent creature who sat in a corner by herself, hung her head down to her fat shoulder and wept, surreptitiously dabbing at tears in her usually shameless eyes. Near her sat the sullen choir singer, Mitropolsky, a hairy young man with round eyes set deep in his sodden face, who looked like an unfrocked deacon. He stared into his vodka glass, lifted it to his lips, then carefully set it down again, but with a clatter. At that moment he couldn't bear to drink.

His song over, Kleshchov made himself comfortable in his chair, and the tavern keeper, handing him a drink, said with a smug smile, "Ah, that was certainly well done, though it's hardly what I'd call singing. I'd call it declamation. But you're a master at it, they can say what they like. Nobody can deny that."

Kleshchov sipped his drink, and with a throat-clearing cough, said in a matter-of-fact way, "Whoever has a voice can sing, but it's my particular gift to project the very soul of the song."

"Why brag about it?"

"He doesn't brag who has nothing to brag about," replied the singer with even calmer self-assurance.

"What conceit, Kleshchov!" exclaimed his annoyed host.

"I don't go beyond what my conscience permits."

From his corner the sullen Mitropolsky growled, "Oh, you dirt and worms, a fallen angel sings, and what do you know about it?"

Mitropolsky was the eternal adversary, arguing with everybody, arraigning everybody, incurring cruel retribution every Sunday from a singer or anybody else who decided to pay him off.

The host could not abide the singer, though he adored the song. He ran him down, and took every opportunity that offered, to direct ridicule upon the singer, a fact that was no secret to the customers, nor to Kleshchov himself. "A good singer—that he is," acknowledged the host, "but vain; he needs to be taken down a peg." And not a few of the guests nodded agreement. "Yes, he's too conceited."

"What's he so vain about? His voice? He got that from God, not by any act of his own. And it's lacking in volume, isn't it?" his host went on.

And his auditors amplified, "It's not his voice, it's his mind."

Once, when the singer had left, after having swallowed his drink, the host began to incite Liza, "How about having a bit of fun with Kleshchov, eh? How about stirring him up? What'll you ask for a job like that?"

"I would if I could shed a few years," she said, with a laugh.

The host persisted. "What are the young ones good for? I'm sure you'll hook him. You'll have him prancing around you. And when you've got him down, then how he'll sing out of misery! Come on, do me a favor, will you; take him on!"

But she refused. The blowsy old creature looked down, toyed with the fringes of the kerchief that was pinned over her breast and reiterated, in

a drawling monotone, "That's for a young one to do. I wo[...]
a second if I could shed a few years."

Time after time, the host tried to get Kleshchov drunk; but [...]
done his couple of songs and had his glass after each, he would draw [...]
wool scarf around his throat, and adjust his cap over his tufted head, each
operation being performed very precisely, and would make his departure.

In his attempts to get Kleshchov down, the persevering host sought to
find a rival. After applauding the harness-maker's performance, the host
would hopefully present a competitor. "Now, let's hear this other singer.
Come on, show your stuff!"

Sometimes a really good voice would turn up; but I can't recall the
time that a rival of Kleshchov's could match his simple, but profound,
renderings. "Ahem," said the disappointed host, "that's not bad. You have
a voice, certainly; but the soul isn't in it."

The auditors jeered, "You can't beat the harness-maker!" And Kleshchov, looking down on them all, from beneath his tufted brows, said with
icy politeness, "Why waste your time? You'll find no one to rival me; my
endowments come from God."

"We all come from God."

"You may hand out drinks till you're ruined; but you'll not find my
rival."

The host reddened with rage. "Well, we'll see, we'll see!"

"This is singing," said Kleshchov pointedly, "not a cock fight."

"Of course. You don't have to harp on that!"

"It's not harping; I'm only trying to get the matter clear. The song
that's meant just for entertainment comes from the devil."

"O.K. Cut the talk and let's have another song, instead."

"I can sing anytime, even when I sleep," said Kleshchov, and clearing
his throat, he sang.

And, miraculously, the trivialities, the stupid wrangling, the conceit,
vanished as if in smoke. Over us flowed refreshing streams of another life,
meditative, loving and melancholy. How I envied him, his gifts, his power
over others, of which he made remarkable use. Though I yearned to become acquainted with the harness-maker and have long talks with him, I
could not get up the nerve to do it.

The look he gave everybody out of his pallid eyes had an annihilating
effect, as if those in front of him did not exist. Something about him
offended me and short-circuited the attraction I felt toward him. I would
have preferred to admire him for his own personality, not merely for his

singing. I felt repelled by the way he tucked his cap over his head like an old man, by the way he swaddled his neck so conspicuously with that red woolen scarf, saying, "It was knitted by my little one, my own daughter."

When not singing, his face puffed out and he massaged his cold, corpse-like nose with two fingers, answering queries in reluctant monosyllables. When I came up to him to put some question, he gave me a chilling look and said, "Be off, boy."

My preference went to the choir singer, Mitropolsky. He swayed into the tavern with the gait of a heavily burdened man, hooked a chair over to him with the toe of his shoe, and sat down, his elbows on the table, and his heavy, shaggy head supported in his hands. After silently downing two or three glasses, he would emit a resounding bellow. With a start everybody would turn toward him, and, chin in hands, he would return their stare with defiant eyes, his mane of unkempt hair forming a wild halo around his pale, bloated face.

"What're you gawking at, what?" he would demand.

"Looking at a werewolf!" would sometimes be the answer.

Evenings would pass without a sound from him, and as he had drunk in silence, so he would shuffle heavily off in silence. Other times he would play the prophet, howling denunciations at people. "I, the incorruptible servitor of God denounce you! Behold, Isaiah! Woe to the city of Ariel.[39] Beware, ye sinners, ye evildoers, ye wicked ones, ye abominations in every form, sunk in the slime of your depravity. Woe to the worldly ships, for they carry sinners to lewd destinations. I know ye, ye sots and gluttons, ye scum of the earth; your day is not set; you live because earth shrinks from admitting such cursed ones into her womb."

His voice was so resonant that it made the window panes rattle, something which always titillated his audience. They honored the prophet thus, "What a bark the shaggy dog has!"

Acquaintance with him came easily. All it cost was your hospitality to the extent of a bottle of vodka and a slice of beef liver. To my question, what books would he recommend, he replied with a fierce counter-question, "Why any?" But, observing my confusion, he softened down and asked, "Have you read Ecclesiastes?"

"Yes."

"Then keep on reading it. There's nothing more you need to read. There's all the wisdom of the world in it, though the sheep, of course, can't follow it; which means no one does. Can you sing anything?"

[39] Symbolic name for Jerusalem, as possessed by an evil spirit, as used by Isaiah.

"No."

"Why not? You should sing. There's no more absurd way to pass the time."

From an adjoining table someone observed, "But you sing, too?"

"It's all right for me. I'm a tramp. So what?"

"Nothing."

"That's nothing new. We all know there's nothing in that blockhead of yours. And there will never be more than nothing there. Amen!"

This was his way with everybody, but after I had stood him to several liver-and-vodkas, he softened toward me. One day he observed, with a note of actual surprise in his voice, "I look at you and I can't make you out, who or what or why you are! Devil take you, whatever you may be!"

Toward Kleshchov his behavior was mystifying. He accorded him obviously delighted attention; yet he avoided acquaintanceship and his expressed opinions of him were rude and derisive. "That dummy! He has breath control and some understanding of what he's singing, but beyond that—an ass!"

"Why?"

"Like the rest of them."

I would have preferred talks with him in sober moments, but in those moments all he could do was growl and stare out of dim, fogged eyes. I was told that this alcoholic had been a divinity student at Kazan Academy. I doubted it, but once, talking about myself, I mentioned Bishop Khrisanph. With a nod he said, "Khrisanph? Him I know. I was a protégé of his at the Kazan Academy. Khrisanph means 'flower of gold.' Ah, Paul Berynd was correct when he wrote, 'Khrisanph was truly a flower of gold!' "

"Who's Paul Berynd?" I asked, but Mitropolsky cut me short, "None of your business."

At home that night, I jotted into my notebook, "Must read the works of Paul Berynd." For some reason I decided that there I would find answers to questions that were troubling me.

Mitropolsky had an annoying way of interjecting names I did not know and words of his own coinage.

"Life's no anisio," he said.

"What's anisio?"

"Something good for you!" he replied, enjoying my befuddlement.

From his epigrammatic remarks and the knowledge of his Academic studies, I concluded that he was a learned man, and I resented his unwillingness to share his wisdom, or his imparting it in such unintelligible forms. Or had I no right to expect so much of him? At any rate, he was one of those who left their mark on my mind. I relished the alcoholic audacity of his diatribes, in which he patterned himself on Isaiah. "Oh, ye unclean and debased worldlings!" he roared, "among you it is the worst who are acclaimed and the best who are reviled. But the Day of Judgment advances. Then, you will repent, but the time for repentance will be gone, will be past!"

Listening to his tirade, Good Idea came to mind, Natalie the laundress, so suddenly and directly plunged into hideous ruin, Queen Margot blurred over in foul scandal. What memories I had heaped up!

A strange incident brought my acquaintance with this man to an end. One spring day I met him in the fields adjoining the garrison encampment. He shambled like a camel, his bloated head wagging from side to side. He looked lonely. "Taking a walk?" he asked hoarsely. "I'll join you. I also came out for a walk. Brother, I'm one sick man!"

After taking a few steps together, without speaking, we came upon a pit which had been dug under a tent. In the pit we saw a man sprawled on the bottom, seemingly resting his shoulders against the side. His coat was pulled up over one ear as if he had tried to take it off and given up.

"Drunk," conjectured Mitropolsky, coming to a halt.

However, on the new grass beside the man lay a pistol, and nearby a cap and a bottle of vodka, barely started, with the neck knocked off and tossed into the high grass. The pulled-up overcoat covered his face as if he had hid under it in shame. For a moment neither of us spoke; then Mitropolsky, standing with his legs apart as if to steady himself, said, "He's shot himself!"

The realization that the man was not drunk, but dead, came upon me so suddenly that I couldn't quite accept it. I recall feeling neither fear nor sympathy as I stared at that big, shaven skull and that pallid ear. Incredible that a man would take his life on such a vivid spring day.

Mitropolsky stroked his stubby cheek and, in a shaking voice, as if he felt a chill, said, "He's on in years. His wife must have left him or he might be an embezzler."

He dispatched me to fetch the police while he sat down at the edge of the pit to wait, his feet dangling over and his threadbare overcoat swathed around him. Having informed the police, I hurried back, to be met on the way by Mitropolsky who had finished the dead man's vodka, and was waving the empty bottle. "That's what ruined him!" he cried, and dashed the bottle to smithereens on the ground.

The policeman who had followed behind me, after a glance in the pit, bared his head and worriedly crossed himself. Then he asked Mitropolsky, "Who are you?"

"None of your business!"

The policeman paused, then tried to sound reasonable. "How can you account for yourself? There's a man dead and you're drunk!"

Slapping himself on the chest, with a proud air, Mitropolsky said, "I've been drunk these twenty years!"

I feared he would be arrested for drinking the liquor. In the meanwhile a crowd gathered. A stern police inspector, who had arrived in a cab, let himself down in the pit, lifted the dead man's overcoat and peered at his face.

"Who was the first to see him?"

"I," claimed Mitropolsky.

The inspector stared at him and said with portentous irony, "Congratulations, your lordship!"

There were about a dozen people there by now, including spectators and police, clustered around the pit, looking down and panting with excitement. From one of them came the outcry, "I know the man! He's in civil service; lives down our street."

Mitropolsky, hatless now, confronted the inspector, swaying unsteadily, and engaged him in inarticulate argument. The inspector knocked him down with a blow in the chest and the policeman unhurriedly brought some cord out of his pocket and bound the wrists of Mitropolsky who had arranged them, docilely, behind his back, as if quite used to it. The inspector, shouting, "Beat it, now!" dispersed the crowd.

Now an older cop arrived, a man with red-rimmed, watering eyes, his mouth gaping with fatigue. He took up the end of the cord which made up Mitropolsky's bonds and quietly led him off. I, too, left the place, feeling dejected, with the singer's arraignment, "Woe to the city of Ariel!" echoing in my mind's ear. Nor could I keep out of my mind's eye that melancholy scene of the policeman unhurriedly pulling the cord out of his pocket, and the thundering prophet submissively crossing his hairy red hands behind his back, wrist over wrist, as though it were by habit.

Shortly afterward I learned that the prophet had been banished from the town. Kleshchov also vanished. He had made a good marriage and had moved to another quarter and to another harness shop.

I had sung Kleshchov's praises so ardently that my boss said, "I must hear him!" And thus, one night, he sat with me and I saw his brows lift

and his eyes go round with awe. On the way over he had ribbed me
and had kept up the ribbing in the tavern, deriding its frequenters and
complaining of the stuffiness. As the harness-maker began, a contemptuous smile was still on his lips. But he was so taken by the singing that
he stopped midway, while pouring a bottle of beer, exclaiming, "What
the devil!" With a reverent hand he put the bottle down and settled
back, absorbed. "Yes, indeed, brother," he acknowledged, sighing, when
Kleshchov had finished. "That man can sing! Devil take him, he's
heated up the whole room!"

The harness-maker resumed, his head back, his eyes on the ceiling.
"On the path from the thriving village, a maid tripped over the dewy
meadows."

"He sure can sing," repeated my boss, with a smile and a contented
nod.

And clear as reed notes came Kleshchov's cadences, "And to him,
the lovely maid replied, 'An orphan, I, by no one wanted.' "

"How good!" my boss said, his eyes suffusing, "damn good!"

It delighted me to have him enjoying it. The lamentation in that song
overcame the tavern din, and gained in strength, in beauty, in pathos,
with every note. "Solitary am I in the village; no invitations come to
me; poor am I, alas; my dress is plain. No young hero will come for me.
A widower will take me to work for him. Such is my fate, but I shall
not submit."

Making no effort to restrain them, tears dripped from the boss' eyes
down to his knees, as he sat with his head bowed and his big nose
snuffing. After the third song, looking nervous and rumpled, he exclaimed, "Let's start home. I'll stifle in this reek. I can't stand it any
longer!" But when we were outside he said, "Let's not go home, Peshkov; let's have supper in a restaurant."

He hailed a cab and, without stopping to haggle down the fare, got
in and was silent all the way. In the restaurant, however, where we took
a corner table, he started off wrathfully, though in a low voice, abusing
the singer, "That goat's bowled me over, driven me into a black melancholia! Tell me—you do a lot of reading and thinking—what the hell
sort of sense does it make? You live; forty years go by; you're married,
have children, and not a soul to talk to! Sometimes I feel I must un-
burden my soul to someone, talk out the things on my mind, but I
have no one. My wife? We have nothing in common. What is my wife?
She has her children and the house to occupy her. To all that's in my
soul she's alien. One's intimacy with one's wife lasts only till the first

child arrives. Altogether, in fact, she's— Well, I don't know how to tell you, it's not to my tune that she dances. Damn it, flesh without a soul!"

Feverishly he guzzled down the chill and bitter beer. After a silence, he ran his hand through his long hair and said, "All in all, what scum people are, brother! Take my sub-contractors. You've been talking to them. I know there's underhand work going on; they're all thieves! And does anything you say matter an atom to them? No! They spill everything you say to me—all of them, Peter, and Osip, too. They're a gang of crooks. They talk about me—you speak up for me—and what's it all about, brother?"

I was too dumbfounded to say a word.

"There you are," said my boss with a sudden smile. "That Persian trip of yours wasn't such a cockeyed idea, after all. You'd understand nothing they say there, not knowing their language. In your own tongue you can count on hearing nothing but filth."

"Has Osip been telling you things about me?"

"Mm—yes! But that shouldn't surprise you. He's the gabbiest of the lot; a real gossip; and a sly article, brother! No, Peshkov, you won't get at them with your words. Don't you see that? What the devil is it all about? And what the hell difference does anything make? Nothing. Autumn snow, it lands in the mud; it melts; it makes more mud. Better keep mum."

He had one beer after another without getting drunk, though his talk grew fiercer and more staccato. "You know the proverb, 'Speech is silver but silence is golden.' Brother, brother, life's all misery! That was true what he sang. 'Solitary am I in my village.' Man's a lonesome animal!"

With a furtive glance around him, he confided to me, in a lowered voice, "I'd found myself a friend, someone really compatible, a woman who lived alone, practically a widow; her husband had been sent to prison in Siberia for counterfeiting. I made her acquaintance. She hadn't a cent. In fact, that was how our acquaintance began. 'What a sweet little thing!' I thought. She was young, pretty—really a wonderful little woman. I saw her a couple of times, and I told her, 'Your husband's a no-good. You yourself are living a disreputable life. So what's all this talk about following him to Siberia?' But that was her decision. 'No matter what he is, I love him,' she told me. 'He's good to me. Probably it was for my sake that he committed the crime. And it's for his sake that I'm sinning with you. I need the money for him. He's a gentleman, used to a good living. If I were unmarried, I'd lead a chaste life. You're a good man, too,' she told me, 'and I'm very fond of you; but please don't bring this up again.' Damn, I gave her all the money I had—eighty rubles or so—and I told her, 'Forgive me, but I can't see you any more. No more!' And I went away—and so——"

He stopped and the next I knew he was drunk. He sat huddled up, muttering, "Six times I went to her apartment. You couldn't begin to understand what I went through. I might have paid her six visits more; but I couldn't get up the courage, just couldn't. Now she's gone."

He put his hands on the table, drummed with his fingers, and whispered, "I pray God never to come upon her again! God grant me that! Otherwise, the devil would have me. Come on, let's go home!"

As he staggered along, he mumbled, "And that's how it goes, brother!"

His story was no surprise. I had long suspected that something out of the way had occurred. Yet, I was depressed by his conclusions about life, and still more by what he had revealed about Osip.

Chapter Twenty

I SPENT THREE YEARS OF MY YOUTH AS OVERSEER IN THAT DEAD AND empty town, watching workmen dismantle the ill-proportioned stone bazaars in the autumn and reconstruct them in the spring. The boss saw to it that I earned every kopeck of the five rubles he paid me. If a foundation had to be relaid, it was my job to excavate the whole site to a depth of over two feet. Day workers were paid a ruble a week for such labor, but I received nothing, being held accountable for my regular work, as well. But while I was digging away, the carpenters unscrewed door knobs and locks and got off with whatever else was detachable.

Workmen and contractors both used every deception to make off with something; and took little trouble to hide it, going about it as if it were just another chore. They were amazed, rather than outraged, at my remonstrances. "Making a twenty-ruble fuss over a mere five. You're comical!"

I pointed out to the boss that for the ruble he saved on my labor he was losing ten in stolen goods, but he blinked and dismissed it with, "Go on! You're imagining things!"

I realized he suspected me of being in collusion with them, but I did not react to this—though it alienated me from him—with any sense of personal injury. In that world theft is universal; the boss himself gloated over picking up a piece of unguarded property. When the Fair was over and he was inspecting booths that were to be reconstructed and came upon forgotten articles—a samovar, kitchen utensils, a mat, a pair of scissors, or even a case of merchandise—he would smile and order me to "List the articles and carry them to the supply room." From there he would take them home, sometimes without bothering to remove them from the list.

I had no such itch for possessions; even books I found hindrances. I had kept only the little volume of Beranger and the lyrics of Heine. I would have added Pushkin if the bookseller, an avaricious old man, had not overpriced his copies. Furniture, mirrors, rugs cluttered my boss' home, and far from affording me any pleasure, their graceless bulk and the smell of varnish they exuded, was an irritant to me. The most disagreeable room of all belonged to the boss' wife; it made me think of a trunk crammed with useless articles. And I could not help thinking less of the boss for adding the lifted stuff to all this clutter. Queen Margot's apartment had also been crowded, but had nevertheless been exquisite.

On the whole, life seemed a ridiculous mess; too much of it was obvious stupidity. Here we were constructing bazaars, knowing that the spring floods would waterlog the floors, warp the doors, and rot the beams. The Fair grounds had been inundated all these past ten years, with huge damage to bridges and buildings; but no move was made to divert the flood waters, as if they were expected to find their own spillways. Each spring, too, the ice-pack, as it broke up, slashed and cracked barges and other vessels; and with resigned groans the people built new ones, only to have them destroyed again by the ice. It was ludicrously like a treadmill, where all one's motion serves to pin one down.

When I spoke to Osip, he laughed and expressed amazement. "You young heron! What a perky heron we have here! What've you got to do with it? What's your stake in it?" Then his voice sobered, though a humorous gleam still flickered in his pale blue eyes, which had a clarity unusual for his age. "But that's a very keen perception. Conceding that it's no business of yours, still it may be of some use to you to look into it. Here's a case that bears upon it." And in a flow of talk, lavish with pithy proverbs, odd images and witty turns of all sorts, he went on: "Here, the people deserve sympathy. They have little enough land, but in the spring the Volga floods off the topsoil and deposits it on sandbanks, bringing suffering to others who complain that this silts up the channel. Other streams in the spring flood stages tear gullies through the soil and carry off still more of the topsoil into the river."

All this was spoken without a trace of fellow-feeling for the sufferers, almost as if this knowledge of life's privations gave him some satisfaction. Although what he said was in corroboration of my ideas, I could take no pleasure in it.

"When there are fires——."

I can't recall a summer without forest fires veiling the sky with muddy, yellowish smoke, through which the leaden sun, its radiance dimmed, stared down like a sick eye.

"Who gives a hang about the forests?" continued Osip. "They're the property of the gentry, or the crown. The peasants have no stake in them. And if a town burns down that's not so terrible, either; it's the rich, mostly, who live in towns, so why waste pity on them! But it's a different matter when a village burns; and how many burn each summer? At least a hundred, I suppose. Now, that's serious." And he gave a soft laugh. "Some who have property mismanage it; so, as we see, a man labors less for his own profit, on the land, than against fire and water."

"Why are you laughing, then?"

"What's wrong with that? Tears won't put out a fire or make any difference in a flood."

I considered this personable old man the cleverest I had run across, but what did he actually love or hate? That question was always on my mind as he provided me sere little sayings to add to my collection.

"Watch and take note how spendthrift people are of their own or other people's energies. Your boss, how he wastes yours! And what's the price of water in a village? Such things will bring you a richer wisdom than schools can provide. If a peasant's hut burns down it can be rebuilt; but when a good peasant goes blind you can't build him a new eye. Ardalon or Gregory, for example; that'll show you how a man can cut loose! The first one's a fool but Gregory's a man of intelligence. But he smolders like straw. Women swarm over him as worms swarm over a corpse in a forest."

Not out of anger, but out of curiosity, I asked, "Why did you report to my boss what I told you in our talks?"

His reply was unembarrassed, and in fact kindly. "To let him know what dangerous ideas are cooking in your head. He has to know to be able to teach you better; who's there to teach you otherwise? I didn't tell

him to make trouble for you, but for your own good. You're certainly
no fool, but the devil's at your brain. If it were just stealing, or skirt-
chasing or liquor, I'd have kept mum; but any wild talk I hear out of
you will go right back to your boss; so now that's clear."

"Then I won't talk to you any more."

He said nothing, picking off resin that had crusted on his hands. Then,
with an affectionate look at me, he said, "Oh, yes you will. Whom
will you talk to otherwise? You have nobody else."

Spruce and tidy, Osip sometimes made me think of the stoker, Jake,
in his indifference to others; or the icon appraiser, or the carter, Peter;
now and then, something in him reminded me of grandpa; in fact, in
some ways, he recalled every old man I knew. They were all wonderfully interesting, but I felt living with them would be out of the question, would be a strain and a nuisance. There was a spiritual rot in them;
their worldly wisdom covered hearts brown with rust. Was Osip a man
of good will? No. Of ill will? Not that, either. All I could be sure of was
his shrewdness. And, while I could applaud his intelligence for its dex-
terity, it did not stir me; and in the long run I felt it as a hostile force.

There was a seethe of dark thoughts in my mind: All men are alien to
one another no matter how much they smile at each other and exchange compliments. Furthermore, we are all aliens to Nature, to whom
few feel the bond of love. Grandma alone actually enjoyed life and was
fond of other creatures—grandma and sweet Queen Margot.

Such thoughts deepened the mist around me, in which I choked and
felt overpowered. But what other life could I live? And where could I
find it? I had no one to confide to, except Osip, to whom I spilled more
and more. He heard out my feverish chatter, with obviously piqued interest, drew me out with his questioning, made revealing points and concluded, matter-of-factly, "The woodpecker taps away and alarms nobody. From the bottom of my heart I urge you to settle down in a
monastery till you come of age. Talks with the holy men will clear things
up for you and soothe you and you'll feel at peace; and you won't be a
financial burden to them. That's my truest word to you. The world
is not for you; that's clear."

But the monastery had no attraction for me, though I felt lost and
confused and miserable here in the bewitched maze of the world. I lived
as in an autumn forest, with the mushrooms gone, the woods empty,
and nothing more to discover there.

I did not drink and I kept away from girls, books substituting for
the intoxications they might have afforded me. Yet reading made the

empty, useless life I saw around me rather more unbearable. I had barely rounded fifteen, yet there were moments when I felt elderly. It was as though I had inwardly grown heavy and aged with what I had experienced, and read about or thought about. In my self-examination I realized I had allowed my field of impressions to clutter up like a cellar bin, till it was beyond my strength or understanding to clear it out. And the clutter was not packed down, but seemed to churn about, with my mind eddying in it, like a piece of floatsam.

I had a distaste for troubles, sickness, injustices. The sight of blood, brawls and the infliction of cruelty of any kind, even when no more than verbal assaults, aroused a physical repulsion in me which soon passed into cold fury and made me hurl myself into brawls, like an animal, and left me afterwards sore with shame. To see a bully in action precipitated me into blind charges, which I recall to this day with dismay, as expressions of my despair and helplessness.

I was a dual personality. In one I was sensitive to the perversions and violations of the dignity of life, and depressed to timorousness for that reason, and bowed down by the awareness of the daily horror of existence; and then I looked at life and people warily and with a touch of scorn, though expending a frail compassion toward all, myself included. In this personality I contemplated a withdrawn, hermit-like existence of books, a monastery, a forest ranger's hut, a railroad signal-man's shed, Persia, a night watchman's post somewhere out of town— in any case, somewhere away from people. The essential was to see fewer people, to be removed from the human animal.

In the other personality I had received my knighthood in the vigils of profound and elevated reading. I had perceived the overpowering might of the daily evils of life, how it could wear away the mind's strength, how it could muddy and trample the heart with its dirty feet; I had set myself in unremitting opposition to it, and taken a belligerent stance, with gnashing teeth and raised fists. Here love and pity were of the active sort; and like the heroes of chivalrous romance, I was always poised for battle; my sword flashed from its scabbard, on the first occasion.

In that period, I had an implacable foe in the porter of a Maly Pokrovsky Street brothel. I encountered him, one morning, on my way to the Fair grounds, dragging a girl, torpid with drink, out of a cab, before the gateway. His hands were clamped around her rumpled stockings; and holding her thus by the legs, bared to the waist, he was gloating over what he had exposed. After spitting on her bare body, he gave her a tug that yanked her out of the cab; and bedraggled, unseeing, her mouth gaping open, and her limp arms trailing behind as if they were without joints, she jolted out, her spine, the nape of her neck and then her bluish face bumping in turn against the cab seat, then the step, and finally on the pavement, her head banging on the stones.

The cabman drove off and the doorman, one of her feet in each hand, hauled her after him as if she were inanimate. In a blind rage, I lunged at him, but by a mischance, overturned a rainwater barrel, something which spared us both much unpleasantness. On the rebound I bowled him over, sprang up the steps, pulled the bell-rope and brought out some furious people to whom I was unable to give any articulate explanation; and I went off, stopping to right the upset barrel. I overtook the cabman, who looked down from his seat and said, "Nice, the way you bowled him over."

I vented my rage on him. How could he have permitted the porter to so vilely maltreat the girl! His reply was cool and supercilious, "On my part, they can all go hang. A gentleman engaged me to drive her here. I don't give a damn who beats whom!"

"Supposing he had killed her!"

"Aah, that sort you kill off sooner or later," said the cabman, quite as if it were his habit to murder drunken prostitutes.

From then on, I ran into that porter practically every day. He would be sweeping out his gateway, or straddling the banister as if awaiting me. At my approach he would get up, roll up his sleeves, and favor me with the announcement, "Now, I'm going to chop you up in little pieces." The man was over forty, paunchy, small and bowlegged. It was rather horrifying to observe a cheerful and even amiable expression in the laughing look he gave me. It was no match because I had a big advantage in reach. After absorbing a few punches, he would look puzzled, call it a round, and send me off with, "Never mind, I'll show you yet, smarty!"

Bored by all this, I asked him, "See here, you fool, why do you have to bother me?"

"Then, why do you fight me?"

In turn, I asked him why he had abused the girl.

"What business is it of yours? Do you pity her?"

"Naturally!"

He stroked his lips, then, after a silence, asked, "Would you pity a cat?"

"Yes."

"Then you're a dope, you rascal," he said. "I'll give it to you, yet!"
I could not go another way and so, in order to avoid these encounters, I got up earlier. After a few days, however, there he was waiting for me with a gray cat on his knee. When I was just a few steps
away he cracked its head on the stone balustrade so that its warm blood
spattered me, and threw its body at my feet, crying, "What are you going to do about that?"

What indeed? We thrashed about the yard like two dogs; and, later,
sitting in the grass, nearly demented with inexpressible anguish, I bit my
lips to keep from bawling. Every time I recall it, a sickening shudder
convulses me, and I wonder that I did not go mad and kill someone.

Why do I speak of these enormities? Just to let you know, gentle
readers, that they are by no means a thing of the past. You have a taste
for the macabre, perhaps; you enjoy horror stories artistically told; you
get pleasurable thrills from the grotesque and the terrible? But I can
match them with real, daily horrors; and it is certainly in place for me
to provide you with these unwelcome chills to remind you of the way
we live, under what actual conditions. Let the truth be told, ours is a
debased and squalid life!

I love mankind, and have no wish to add to anybody's misery; but
sentimentality must not be served at all costs; one must not cover up
dreary reality with rainbow verbiage. Let us see life for what it is. What
is good and human in heart and mind needs to be refreshed by knowledge of the truth.

What disturbed me most at the time was the common masculine attitude toward women. From my reading I had come to look upon
women as all that gave life beauty and meaning. Grandma had nourished this in me with her accounts of the Madonna and the wise Saint
Vasillissa. And I had been helped by what I knew of the forlorn
Natalie, the laundress, and by those countless smiles and loving looks
with which women, the source of life, offset this sordid existence.

Turgenev's novels gave loving regard to women; and my memory
image of Queen Margot was wreathed with all that I had learned about
women's excellences. For that I drew mainly on Heine and Turgenev.

On my return from the Fair grounds in the evening, it was my habit
to stop on the hill beside the Kremlin wall and gaze at the sunset over
the Volga. Torrents of fire streamed across the skies; the river, on the
earth below, had turned purple and blue. There were moments then
when the land had the appearance of a colossal convict barge or pig,
on a towline behind a slow steamer.

But my mind veered more and more to the world beyond, to cities I had read about, to peoples abroad and the differences in their customs. The life described by foreign writers was more wholesome and pleasing, less burdensome than the viscid, tedious life that clung about me. And this soothed my spirit with the horizons it projected of a possible different life ahead of me. And I anticipated, with some confidence, a meeting with some wise but unsophisticated man who would guide me there.

Sitting one day on a park bench under the Kremlin, my Uncle Jake took a seat beside me. I had not observed him approaching, and I did not immediately recognize him. Though we had both been living in the city, we had seldom met, except by chance, and then for no more than a glimpse and a greeting.

"My," he remarked jokingly, "you've certainly stretched out!" In the conversation that followed, we spoke like people well, but not intimately, acquainted.

From grandma's accounts, I knew that Uncle Jake's recent course had consisted mainly of idling and quarreling. Also, that he had been assistant warden at the jail, but had had an ignominious fall from that eminence. The head warden, having been indisposed, Uncle Jake had taken command. He had gone so far as to entertain the convicts in his own room. In addition, he had allowed some of them to take airings outside the jail gates, the chief charge in the indictment against him, when the episode was investigated. None of the convicts had gotten away, but one had been apprehended in an attempt to choke a deacon. The affair hung over a long time, but never came to trial. The testimony of both wardens and prisoners exonerated my uncle sufficiently to keep him out of the courts. Now he was jobless and living on his son, one of the singers in the currently modish Rukavishnikov church choir.

Of this son he made some curious remarks, "He's turned hoity-toity, just because he's one of the soloists. He flares up if the samovar's not ready just when he wants it, or if I miss a speck of dust when I brush his clothes. Quite the dandy, he is!"

Uncle Jake himself was prematurely aged; he looked run down and seedy. His former mass of curly hair was quite gone, making his rather small ears look conspicuous. Heavy, purple veins seamed the whites of his eyes and his leathery cheeks. He seemed to have good teeth, yet his kidding talk was thickly enunciated as if he suffered some impediment.

I welcomed the opportunity to talk to a man who knew something about good living, whose experience was wide and who therefore ought to know a good deal. My recollections of him included sprightly songs and grandpa's characterization of him, "In singing he's a King David, but in business matters he's a plotter like the evil Absalom."

The promenaders who passed up and down included gentlemen in fashionable attire, military officers and officials. The contrast of Uncle Jake's threadbare topcoat, ragged cap and discolored boots obviously put him out. We therefore went to a tavern on the Pochainsky causeway, where we took a window table from which we could look out on the Fair grounds.

"Remember how you sang, 'When the beggar hung out his socks another beggar stole them'?" As soon as I said this, the cynical sense of the verse became clear to me for the first time, and I felt confirmed in my impression of my uncle as a man whose wit had a tincture of animosity in it. As if answering unspoken questions he remarked, as he poured himself some vodka, "The truth is, I'm getting old and I know I've done very little with my life. That song's none of mine; a seminary teacher was the composer. Now, what was his name? I can't remember, though we were bosom friends. He's dead and gone now. He was a bachelor and he died of a stroke in his sleep. Ah, how many I've known of, who've gone asleep—beyond counting! You don't drink? Good; keep away from it. See much of grandpa? He isn't having a happy old age; in fact, I think he's losing his mind."

Reanimated by the vodka, he straightened up and looked like his old self once more, and his conversation became lively. I took the opportunity to ask him about the convicts.

"So you've heard of that?" he said, and followed, after a cautious look about him, in a hushed voice, "The convicts? Who was I to judge them! To me, they were human beings, that's all, and I told them, 'Let's see if we can be happy here; let's see if we can live in harmony.' There's a song which goes, 'Happiness laughs at prison bars; no matter how they deal with us, laughter's still what we live for; only a fool lives for other things.'"

He laughed, stroked his beard, and looked out upon the gathering evening shadows on the causeway. "Naturally, they were bored, lying there in jail; and after roll call, they visited me. We had vodka and snacks; on some occasions they were provided by me, on others by them. I'm fond of singing and dancing and there were some grand singers and dancers among them. Now it all seems unbelievable. Some were chained, and they don't malign me who say that I unchained them. But Lord, they know how to manage that themselves without a locksmith. Remarkably handy they are, those people. But those who say I let them roam around and hold people up, they're spreading nonsense; no evidence of that was presented."

He fell silent again, looking through the window, watching shop-keepers locking up showcases. There was a clatter of iron bars, a creaking of rusty hinges, a thump of wooden shutters being let down. Then, with a wink, he resumed, but still in a hushed voice, "To be honest, a convict did get out, but not one of the chained ones; just a neighborhood thief from that part of town. His girl lived nearby, on the Pechorka. And the trouble with the deacon was an accident. He mistook the deacon for a businessman. It was a snowy night, with everybody bundled up in winter clothes. He was in a hurry; how was he to tell, rushed as he was, the deacon wasn't a businessman?"

This struck me funny; and he joined in the laughter. "By God! What a hell of a thing——"

But here, my uncle was seized by an unaccountable fit of anger. He pushed away his dish of refreshments, frowned, and his eyes darkened with disgust. Puffing belligerently at his cigarette, he growled, "They swindle each other, then they catch each other; then they put each other away in jail, in Siberia, and in the mines. What's that to me? I spit on the whole business. I'll take care of my own soul!"

And he seemed to me, then, another incarnation of that shaggy stoker, also named Jake, who had also, defiantly, "spit upon" people.

"Now, what are you thinking?" asked my uncle in a low voice. "Did you feel sorry for the convicts?"

"It's natural to feel sympathy for them; they're children; really it would surprise you. I'd look at one of them sometimes and I'd think, 'I have authority over him, when the truth is, I'm not fit to shine his shoes!' What handy fellows they were, those devils!"

Once again, with his recollections seemingly spiking his drink, his manner livened up. He rested his elbow on the window sill, flourished his cigarette in his cigarette-stained fingers, and said, in a now ringing voice, "Among them was a twisted little man, a watchmaker and engraver who was in for counterfeiting. You should have heard him talk! It was like a song, no, like a flame! 'Explain if you can,' he'd say, 'why the treasury can mint money and not I? Explain that!' And no one could explain it. I, the person in authority, couldn't. Then there was a famous Moscow pickpocket, a well-mannered chap, rather dandified, but neat as a whistle; and in his well-bred way, he'd say, 'People dull their senses with work. I'll have no part of it. I've given it a try. You work and work until you're too tired to think straight; and then two kopecks of vodka makes your brain swim; you take a hand at cards and drop seven kopecks; five kopecks goes to a woman for a minute or two of kindness; and back to the bench you go, shivering and famished. Not for me,' he says, 'that game's not for me.' "

Uncle Jake bent over the table, his face red to his small ears, which quivered, along with the rest of him, with excitement: "And let me tell you, brother, they made sense. They knew what's what! To hell with formalities! Take me. What account can I give of myself? The life I can look back on fills me with disgust. Its joys? Fragmentary and underhand. My sorrows I could claim openly, but my joys I had to take by stealth. My father on one side, my wife on the other, both yelling, 'You can't this!' and 'Don't that!' I didn't dare spend a ruble on my own. And that's how my life dribbled away. And now, what I've come to, lackey to my own son! I won't attempt to fool myself. I'm his humble servant, brother, that's all, and he's as sharp with me as any gentleman with his servant. He calls to me, 'Father!' and up I bounce like any man in livery. Is this what I came into this life for? Is it for this that I struggled against poverty—to become my son's servant? But, apart from that, why was I born? What good have I got out of life?"

My attention had wandered. When he stopped, however, I asked, merely as a rhetorical question and not looking for an answer, "I wonder how my life will turn out."

He burst into laughter. "Does anybody know? I've yet to meet the man who does! People just hang on; and the one who can take whatever comes——"

And again his tone became caustic and resentful, "One of the men was in for assault, a gentleman from Orla who happened to be a good dancer. He used to amuse us with a song he called 'Johnny.' 'Johnny would pass the cemetery; a simple matter you think; but, whoa, Johnny; you'll never get past the grave!' It don't sound so funny to me now, because that truth's too close to home. You can't go back in life; and you can't get past the grave. So, what's the difference, convict or warden!"

He had talked himself to weariness, finished his vodka, and stared into the empty decanter with one eye, quite like a bird. In silence he lit yet another cigarette, the smoke billowing out of his moustaches.

"There's no sense striving, or hoping for anything, for no man gets past the grave and the cemetery." That I had heard from Peter the mason, who was nothing like my Uncle Jake. How many such sayings I knew by now!

I had nothing more to talk about with my uncle. It was rather dismal being with a man you pitied. There kept coming back to my mind his jolly tunes, and the sound of his guitar on which he had converted a soft melancholy into happiness. But neither had I forgotten the jovial Tsigan. No, I recalled him, too; and, looking at Uncle Jake's beat-up face, the thought leaped into my mind, "Does he ever think of how he killed Tsigan, crushed him under the cross?"

But I had no wish to remind him. I looked out on the causeway on which one of the gray fogs of August was settling. There streamed in fragrances of ripening apples and melons. Down the converging streets the night lamps began to glimmer. And at that moment the Rybinsk steamer whistled, to be followed by the siren of the Perm steamer. It was all so familiar.

"Well, we better get going," my uncle said. And, at the tavern door, as we shook hands, he said jestingly, "Don't give way to your moods. You're a little on the gloomy side, aren't you? Spit on it. You have youth. Just bear in mind that Fate is no bar to happiness. Well, so long, I'm off to Uspen!" And away went my jovial uncle, leaving me more confused than before.

I walked through the town and out to the fields. It was midnight now, and there was a heavy scud of clouds whose shadows blotted out mine. Walking on, I came to the banks of the Volga where I lay down in the dry grass to gaze at the river and the fields and the still earth. Slowly across the Volga drifted cloud shadows which, when they reached the opposite bank, seemed to glisten as if they had bathed in the river. Everything around me seemed sleepy, in a sort of torpor; every movement seemed to be forced and unwilling, lacking the animation, the energy of movement that came out of desire.

And I was overcome with the wish to liberate the whole world and myself, by some magical act, so that I and everyone would whirl with joy in a mass carnival dance, so that people would give their love to each other here on earth, so that they would live for each other, and their lives be courageous, exalted and beautiful.

But I thought also, "I must do something for myself or it will be all up with me."

Often on scowling autumn days in the past, when there was no sight of the sun, and no sense even of his warm presence, when one almost forgot there was sunlight—more than once on such days, I walked into the forest, off the highroad, past even the dimmest trails, until I was too fatigued even to look for them. Then, gritting my teeth, I would go straight ahead, clambering over rotting logs, over the almost jelly-like mounds on swampy ground; and, sooner or later, I would strike the road. And it was in such a way I reached my decision.

That autumn I went to Kazan, secretly purposing somehow to become a student.

My Universities

Chapter One

ERE I AM, ON MY WAY TO THE UNIVERSITY OF KAZAN, NO LESS. THE gymnasium [1] student, Nicholas Yevreinov, had talked me into it. This handsome youth, whose soft eyes had an almost feminine charm, had made my acquaintance as a boarder in grandma's attic. Seeing books so often in my hand, he had taken an interest in me and we had become friends. Convinced that I had exceptional scholarly potentialities, he had done what he could to pass on this conviction to me.

Tossing his mane of hair he would say, "You're made to serve knowledge!"

Yevreinov could be so convincing! Besides, I wasn't then aware that one could serve knowledge in the role of guinea pig. Yevreinov, of course, likened me to the great Lomonosov,[2] who had been self-taught like myself, and had come from as humble a background. The universities, continued Yevreinov, needed men like me.

Yevreinov's suggestion was that I join him in his native Kazan to which he was returning to finish his studies. He assured me a "few" examinations, as he put it, would bring me a scholarship, and in five years I would be an educated man. It was that simple to Yevreinov because he was only nineteen and had a sanguine heart.

Two weeks after Yevreinov's departure I followed him. Grandma saw me off with this parting advice, "Now don't show your temper with people. You're so angry and demanding and quarrelsome. You take after your grandpa, and look what it brought him. Lived a fool and ended up a fool, a bitter old man. Remember this: God doesn't judge men; that's the devil's specialty. Well, good-by."

Wiping some tears from her faded, sunken cheeks, she added, "We won't see each other again. You're a restless one. You'll wander off and I—shall die."

Lately I had neglected the good old woman, seldom coming to see her. And now the realization came suddenly to me that I should never

[1] A college preparatory school more advanced than the American high school, more like a junior college.

[2] Mikhail V. Lomonosov (1711–65), generally considered the founder of Russian literature, and famous also for his achievements in science.

know another person so intimately; and no other would be so dear to me.

From the rail of the steamer I saw her on the dock making the sign of the cross with one hand while, with the other, she wiped her cheeks with a corner of her threadbare shawl. In her eyes shone her unquenchable love for people.

And now I'm in half-Tatar Kazan, in a crowded, one-story house. The little dwelling was the last on a narrow, impoverished street. Perched on a rise, it overlooked a burned-over, weed-cluttered lot. From a tangle of wormwood, burdock, sorrel grass and elderberry bushes protruded the remains of a brick building. Well do I remember its capacious cellar, in which homeless dogs and alley cats lived and died. That was one of my universities.

The Yevreinovs, mother and two sons, lived on her meagre widow's pension. On her first return from marketing I understood her plight. As she spread out her purchases on the kitchen table, I could see on her worried face the hopeless problem she had to solve—how to turn the meat scraps she had purchased into a meal to satisfy three growing youths—to say nothing of herself. She was a quiet little woman. In her gray eyes one could see the hopeless, shrinking, yet stubborn, will with which an exhausted mare pulls a wagon uphill, knowing she will never make the top, but pulling on!

One morning, some three days after my arrival, while the other two boys were still in bed, I joined her in the kitchen to help her prepare vegetables.

Guardedly she asked me, "Why did you come to Kazan?"

"To enter the university."

Her eyebrows and the yellow skin of her forehead wrinkled irritably upward, and she cut herself with the paring knife. Sucking her finger, she sat down on a chair, but immediately jumped up again, exclaiming, "The devil!" As she wrapped a handkerchief around her finger she said, ironically, "You're good at peeling potatoes!"

And how! I boasted of my ship-kitchen training.

"And that, you think, will get you into the university?"

In those days I was too raw to take such things humorously. In all seriousness I told her of my plans, fostered by Nick, to storm the temple of knowledge.

"Akh, Nick, Nick!" she sighed.

And Nick entered the kitchen, at that very moment, to wash up.

Sleepy and disheveled though he was, his gaiety was wide awake.
"Mama, how about some of your wonderful meat dumplings?"
"Yes, wonderful!" said the mother.

To show what a connoisseur I was, I said, "But this meat won't do
for dumplings." I might have added there was not enough of it.
My thoughtless remark threw Mrs. Yevreinov into a rage. Her
epithets made my ears burn. Flinging the bunch of carrots she was
fixing on the table, she stamped out of the kitchen.

Nick winked at me, "A touch of temperament, that's all!"

Sitting down he observed that, in general, women have touchier
nerves than men. Some Swiss scholar had proved it beyond question
and the Englishman, John Stuart Mill, had arrived at similar conclusions.

How Nick loved to play teacher to me. He seized every available
moment to tuck some new, essential item into my brain. And I received it all gratefully, though Foucault, La Rochefoucauld, and La
Rochejaquelain merged into a single being in my mind. As to who
cut off whose head, Dumouriez Lavoisier's, or vice versa, I never got
that straight.

Good-hearted Nick was intent on making a man of me, as he
promised over and over, but he lacked the time and, alas, other requi-
sites. With the self-absorption and irresponsibility of youth, he gave
no heed to the desperate struggle which it cost his mother to carry
on the household. His phlegmatic, high-school-student brother gave it
even less heed. But I understood the chemical feats and desperate econ-
omies she achieved in her kitchen. I understood the resourcefulness
with which she daily deceived her sons' stomachs, and managed to find
food, too, for me, a young tramp not particularly appealing in appearance and behavior. This knowledge made every morsel of bread apportioned to me fall like a stone on my soul. I went out looking for work.

I left early in the morning to avoid having to take their food. In
bad weather my refuge was the cellar of the burned-out house. There,
in the stench of cat and dog corpses and under the pounding of wind
and rain, I came to the conclusion that my university career was a
fantasy, that a voyage to Persia would have made more sense. My plans
vapored off into daydreams of myself as a savant who bred grain
with kernels the size of apples, and potatoes the size of bushel baskets,
a great-hearted savant who thought not only of himself, but made the
whole world his concern and eased its hard lot with other stupendous
inventions.

In other daydreams I performed phenomenal feats. This life of visions helped me through many despairing days. Deeper and deeper I took refuge in these grandiose dreams. I jealously ruled out anybody's help and any stroke of luck. The worse things got for me, the stronger and even wiser I felt. And in this stubborn independence, I acquired at that early age my first knowledge that man becomes man through his resistance to his environment.

To keep from starving I went to the docks on the Volga. There, in the summer, one could earn fifteen to twenty kopecks a day. Among the dockworkers, hoboes and drifters there I felt like a scrap of iron tossed into a furnace. A thousand fiery impressions filled my day. Before me rough lives, fulfilling primitive instincts, swirled like a cyclone! Their harshness pleased me, their jeering defiance of the conventional world, their irresponsibility. What I had lived through attracted me to them, impelled me into their acid circle. My reading of Bret Harte and other fiction of adventurous outcasts predisposed me to their company.

Bashkin, once a Teachers' College student, now a professional crook in the cruel throes of consumption, would eloquently reprimand me. "Why do you cover up like a young girl? Afraid to lose your honor? For a girl it's all her wealth, but to you it's only a hindrance. The ox may be honest but he has to be content with hay."

Clean-shaven like an actor, graceful and light in his movements, little, red-headed Bashkin made me think of a kitten. He put me under his tutelage, and I knew he sought my success and happiness with all his heart. He was clever and well read. His favorite book was *The Count of Monte Cristo,* which, as he put it, "has a soul and a purpose."

Bashkin adored women. Talking of them he smacked his lips and his racked body quivered. Though this sickened me, I listened to his talk, nevertheless, for the beauty I saw in it.

"Woman, woman," he would rhapsodize; and a flush would redden his yellow skin and rapture shine in his eyes. "For a woman—anything! For her, as for the devil, there's no sin. Live and love. Nothing . . . nothing better has been invented."

Story-telling was only one of Bashkin's talents. For the prostitutes he composed lamentations over the miseries of unrequited love. They were sung up and down the Volga. One of them, incidentally, was the widely circulated, "Badly dressed, poor and no beauty . . . Who'd marry such a one . . ."

I was decently treated also by the illiterate Trusov, a mysterious, handsome and exceptionally well-groomed personage, who had the slim fingers of a musician. His little shop in the suburb bore the sign, "Expert Watch Repairing." Actually his business was disposing of stolen goods.

His counsel to me was, "Avoid thievery." Shaking his graying beard and with a sly squint in his bold eyes, he said, "I see a different road ahead for you, Peshkov. You're one of the inspired."

"Inspired? What do you mean?"

"One who is led on not by envy, but by curiosity."

But this was hardly the case with me. I coveted many things, I envied a great many people. I was even jealous of Bashkin for the fresh similies, the poetic turns of phrase in his speech.

I recall how I envied this luscious opening of one of his yarns of love: "Through the foggy-eyed night I sit like an owl in an oak tree, in an inn in the poor town of Sviyazhsk. It is autumn. The wind snuffles like one of those sad Tatars, singing alone, his song without beginning or end, 'aw—aw—aw . . . oo—oo—oo.' Then she trips in, light and rosy like a puff of cloud at a sunrise. In her eyes there is a deceptive purity of soul. 'Darling,' she says, and her voice rings true, 'I haven't deceived you.' She's lying, I know, yet I accept it as the truth. My mind knows it to be a lie but my heart . . . believes."

And, as he told his story, Bashkin marked a rhythm with his swaying body, closed his eyes and his right hand gracefully pointed to his heart. Actually, he spoke in a monotone, but his vivid words gave it the effect of a nightingale.

And I envied Trusov, too. He had fascinating stories to tell of Siberia, Khiva and Bokhara,[3] and with indignant irony he scored the lives of the church hierarchy. Like one in the know, he said to me of Tsar Alexander III,[4] "This one knows his business." Trusov thrilled me like the villain in a romance who, to the astonishment of the reader, turns out to be the real hero at the end.

Sometimes, on hot summer nights, the group would picnic on the meadow across the little Kazanka River, and the talk would be about their doings, but more frequently about the complications of life and its tangled human relations, and most frequently about women. What was said was a composite of bitterness and pitiable yearning, and came

[3] Central Asian moslem emirates, tributary to tsarist Russia. Now parts of the Uzbek, Tajik and Kazakh Soviet Republics.
[4] The liberal Tsar who freed the serfs, but later became reactionary and was assassinated by terrorists.

to little more than a frightened look into the dark, in dread of dangerous surprises.

I spent a couple of nights there with them, under the dark sky with
its brooding stars, in the stifling warmth of a ravine, thickly overgrown
with tall brush. Being close to the Volga, we could see through the
humid darkness the lights on the ship masts, like golden spiders, swaying
in all directions. Atop the steep, dark river bank were the saloons and
houses of the rich village of Uslon, shining like a cluster of illuminated
hives. One heard the muffled thud of paddle wheels on the water; the
wolfish sounds of bargemen; distant hammer strokes on iron; and someone's heart smoldered over a plaintive song, whose sound strewed a
layer of ashes over the heart.

Even sadder to hear was the softly flowing talk of the men expressing
their thoughts about life, each preoccupied with his own as if what
had just been spoken had gone unheard. Sitting or sprawling under
the bushes, smoking or drinking—never to excess—vodka or beer, they
retraced their paths through memory.

"Here's what happened to me . . ." began a voice from someone
flattened to the ground by the darkness. And at the end of his tale there
were confirming murmurs, "Yes, it may be so, such things often
happen."

And hearing all about me, "it was, it may be, it might have been,"
it seemed to me, that night, mankind had reached the final hour.
Everything had happened, how could there be more!

And this sense of no further reach to their lives alienated me from
Bashkin and Trusov. Nevertheless, I continued to like them and, following the logic of my situation, I should have gone along with them.
The frustration of my hopes of becoming a student and elevating myself, pushed me upon them. And stretches of hunger and yearning made
me feel capable of crimes, and not alone against "the sacred institu-
tion of property." A youthful romanticism, however, held me to the
path to which I felt destined. In my reading, a goodly number of serious books had joined the kindly Bret Harte and other adventure
hunters. These aroused in me vague ambitions transcending what I
saw around me.

At the same time I made new acquaintances and found new horizons.
On the vacant lot beside the Yevreinov hut came high school students
to play a game resembling shuffleboard. To one of them, George
Pletnev, I was strongly attracted. His hair was blue-black like a Japanese,
his dark face thickly spotted as if gunpowder had been rubbed into it.

Ever cheerful, sharp-witted, and adept in games, George had a store of embryonic talents. But he made no effort to strengthen and develop them, satisfied, like all talented Russians, to live by his natural wit. His fine ear and his magnificent feeling and love for music did not take him further than the balalaika, the psaltery, and the accordion, all of which he played with great skill, but he made no effort to master any higher instrument.

The sweep of his audacious gestures and the dashing movements of his muscular body made his crumpled shirt and torn and patched trousers and worn shoes seem glamorous on him. He enjoyed life as if everything in it was new, like a man just out after long confinement to a sickbed, or a prison cell. He responded to everything with exuberant joy, popping over the ground like a string of exploding firecrackers.

Learning of my difficulties in making a living, he took me in with him and set about preparing me for the career of a rural teacher. This move brought me into a dilapidated, but strange and ebullient slum house, called Marusovka, on Ribnoriadskaya (Fishmonger) Street. It was known, I am sure, to more than one generation of Kazan students. It looked as if it had been taken by storm by the starved students, prostitutes and wraithlike men who lived there. George occupied the corridor under the attic stairs, where stood his camp cot beside a window at the end of the corridor. A table and chair completed his furnishings. Three rooms opened on the corridor, two occupied by prostitutes and the third by a consumptive mathematician, tall and cadaverous, and topped with coarse, red hair. Through holes in the dirty rags that barely covered him, one shuddered to see his corpselike ribs and bluish skin.

It would appear that the mathematician sustained himself chiefly on his own nails, which he chewed down till they bled. Day and night he was at his formulas, mumbling numbers, and coughing with dry rasps. The prostitutes were uneasy about him, considering him insane, but out of pity they put bread, tea and sugar outside his door. As he carried them in he snorted like a tired horse. If, for some reason, these gifts failed to appear he would stand in the doorway croaking indignantly, "Bread! Bread!"

In their dark caverns his eyes gleamed with maniac pride, happy in the assurance of his greatness. He had an occasional visitor, a humpbacked cripple with a gray beard, thick lenses straddling his swollen nose, and a sharp smile on his yellow, eunuch's face. Behind the shut door the two would sit for hours in an incomprehensible silence. But

once, late in the night, I was awakened by mad screams from the
mathematician, "A prison! I say, a cage, a mousetrap! Geometry is a
prison!"

The humpbacked dwarf's retort was a shrill giggle and a word I
could not make out, repeated several times.

"Damn you! Get out!" the mathematician roared.

His expelled visitor stood in the corridor, sputtering and pulling his
cape about him, while the mathematician, gaunt and terrifying, in the
doorway, his fingers writhing in his hair, shouted, "Euclid's a fool! A
fool! God's wiser than the Greek. I'll show you!" And he banged the
door so hard things in his room crashed down.

The mathematician's aim, I discovered, was to prove God's existence
mathematically. He died with the task unfinished.

George earned his livelihood reading proof at a newspaper, at twelve
kopecks a night. On days when I earned nothing this meant our making
three meals on some four pounds of bread and sweetened tea. My
studies left me little time for paying work. Mastery of the sciences
came difficult to me. Grammar, with its narrow, rigid forms, particularly oppressed me. The lively, protean, capricious Russian language defied my efforts to confine it into these forms. It satisfied rather
than disappointed me, to learn that, even had I passed the examinations, I could not have qualified as a rural teacher because of my youth.

The same cot served both George and me. He slept on it by day, I
by night. Early each morning he arrived from his night work with
inflamed eyes and haggard face. We had no samovar of our own, of
course, and I rushed out to a restaurant to fetch some boiling water.
Sitting by the window we had our bread and tea. George recapitulated
for me the news he had proof-read, and recited the jingles of the
drunken columnist "Red Domino." George's debonair attitude toward
life seemed to me to fit his dealings with his moon-faced landlady,
Galkina, who traded in ladies' second-hand clothes and less reputable
articles. Unable to find the rent for his "apartment"—the space under
the staircase—he paid with jokes, sentimental songs and performances
on the accordion. A mocking smile lit his eyes as he sang in his thin
tenor. In her youth Galkina had sung in opera choruses, which had left
her with an affection for music. From her brazen eyes, down the purple,
puffed cheeks of a glutton, tears would frequently glide. She would
brush them off with greasy fingers, which she then dried on a dirty
handkerchief.

"What an artist you are, George," she would sigh. "If you had a bit of good looks I'd have fixed you up something good. Many's the youth I've found a well provided lonelyheart."

One of her well provided "youths" lived above us. He was a student, son of a furrier. Of medium stature with a broad chest and hips narrow to the point of deformity, he resembled a triangle resting on a blunted angle. His ankles were as delicate as a woman's. A disproportionately small head, set deep into his shoulders, was topped with a mat of red hair. From his bloodless face two bulging, green eyes leveled a sullen stare at you.

In defiance of his father, and under tremendous hardships, famished most of the time like a homeless dog, he had managed to make his way into the university. Discovering himself in possession of a deep and plaintive bass, he decided to take up singing. With this as pretext, Galkina "provided" him with a merchant's wife, a woman in her forties, who had a son and a daughter in preparatory school. She was thin and flat, and her gait was like that of a soldier on parade. She had the arid face of an old man, and her large, gray eyes were sunk in dark cavities. She was always in black; her hat was out of fashion; and poisonously green gems wagged from her ears.

Her visits to the student occurred at dusk or early morning. Pletnev and I would remark how she seemed to break through the gate, then march across the yard with a determined stride. Her face seemed terrible to us, with the lips so tightly pressed together they were almost invisible, and her eyes staring, with a doomed glance, as if she had become blind. It was not that she was hideous, but that her yearning disfigured her, tensing her body and gnarling her face. "She has the look of a maniac," remarked George.

The student loathed her and hid from her, but she kept after him like an implacable creditor or a detective.

"I'm a goner," he would say despondently, when a little drink loosened him up. "Who am I to think of a singer's career? My face and figure's enough to bar me from the stage."

"Then why not stop this nonsense?" said Pletnev.

"But I'm sorry for her. I can't stand her, but I pity her. If you only knew what she . . . but never mind."

We knew well enough. Often we heard her, standing on the steps, pleading, "For God's sake, darling, for God's sake——"

She, the owner of a factory, and many houses and horses, a philanthropist who gave thousands to foster obstetrics, begged in this hole for a caress!

After our meal of bread and tea, George went to bed and I went out looking for a day's work. If I had luck I brought home bread and sausage or boiled fish. I had my share at home while Pletnev took his share, wrapped up, to the print shop.

Left alone, I explored the passages and corners of Marusovka, observing the life of its inhabitants, a species new to me. The house swarmed like an ant heap. It was sodden with acrid smells of decomposition; and the shadows in its corners were menacing like ambushes. An unbroken hum, from morning till the small hours of night, filled the place. The sewing machines of the seamstresses rattled, the operetta singers rehearsed their songs, the student drove his bass voice up and down the scale, a half-mad and ever-tipsy actor loudly rehearsed his part, hysterical and drunken screams came from the prostitutes. The inevitable and insoluble question recurred to my mind, What is it all about?

Among the famished youths ambled a balding, red-haired chap with high cheekbones. He had a big belly which looked all the more unnatural above his skinny legs. His huge mouth, armed with horselike teeth, had won him the nickname, "Red Horse." He was involved in endless litigation with some merchant relations in Simbirsk. "If it kills me I'll ruin them," he announced to everybody. "After they've had three years of begging in the streets, I'll return everything to them and ask them, 'Well, how was it, you monsters!' "

"So that's your life goal, Horse?"

"Yes," he replied, "till that's done, I can't think of anything else."

After hours in the courts and his lawyer's office, he often brought home food and drink and invited students and seamstresses, anyone, in fact, who wanted a meal, to noisy banquets in his dirty room with its cracked ceiling and its sagging floor. Red Horse's only drink was "Rhum," a beverage whose red stains spotted napkins, gowns and floor.

After tippling his "Rhum," he shouted, "I love you all, my sweet birds. Such honest folk and I, crocodile, evil monster that I am, I'm out to ruin my kinsmen. And I will, by God, if it kills me . . . !"

The maudlin glitter in his eyes was pitiful; his strange face with its high cheekbones was streaked with tears, which he wiped with the palm of his hand and which he then dried on his knee, caked from such greasy rubbings.

"How do you live? Hunger, cold, rags—is that right?" he shouted.

"How can you become educated leading such a life? If the Tsar only knew!"

And he pulled money out of his pockets and held it out. "Here, take it, you need it."

The singers and seamstresses snatched at it, but he laughed at them. "Not for you, the students!"

But none of the students would take it.

The furrier's son angrily consigned "The money to the devil!"

One day Red Horse brought a roll of ten-ruble notes to George, slapped it down on the table and said, "Do you want it? I don't."

Lying down on our cot, he had a hysterical crying fit. We cooled him off with water. After he fell asleep Pletnev tried in vain to straighten out the money; the bills were so matted together we had to soak them in water to separate them.

His smoky, filthy room, whose windows had the bleak walls of the next house for a view, was always mobbed, close, noisy and revolting. The Horse's shouts grew deafening. I asked him, "Why live here when you can live in a hotel?"

"For my soul's sake, friend. At your hearth my soul warms itself."

"That's right," agreed the furrier's son. "Anywhere else I'd have gone to the dogs."

"Let's have some music. Give us a song," the Horse begged Pletnev. And plucking the zither on his knee, George sang "Rise, you red sun, rise." His soft voice seeped into the soul.

Everybody sat still in pensive attention. Only the moody words and the plaintive twang of the strings were heard.

"You sing devilishly well!" enviously grumbled the unhappy soother of the merchant's wife.

Acting on the wisdom called gaiety, Pletnev played the consoling role of the wonder-working elf of the fairy tales to the odd folk who tenanted the dilapidated house. Bright with the tints of youth, his soul glowed into their lives. It set off a continuous fireworks of jokes, songs, raillery on the habits of people, dashing ironies on the brutal deceptions of life. Though but twenty years old, a mere youth even in appearance, every one there turned to him when in trouble, and his advice was shrewd and his help never failing. Good people were drawn to him, the bad-hearted feared him; even old Nikiforich, the Law in our parts, reserved a special smile for him.

Marusovka's backyard was also an alley. It abutted on two streets, the Ribnoriadskaya and Staro-Gorshechnoy. Occupying a cozy corner of the

latter was Nikiforich's booth. This tall, dried-up old man was the
police captain of our district and his breast was aglitter with medals.
He was polite; and his shrewd, smiling eyes gave his face a clever look.
He kept close watch on our tumultuous colony of people with a past
and questers of the future. At intervals during the day we had this neat
visitor in our yard. At an unhurried pace he would walk by, peering into
our windows, with the air of a zoo attendant examining his charges.

That winter a flock of Marusovka's tenants were arrested, among them
the one-armed officer, Smirnov, and the soldier Muratov, both decorated with the Order of St. George and veterans of Skobelev's Akhal-
Tekke [5] campaign; also Zobnin, Ovsiankin, Grigoriev, Krylov and somebody else, all charged with attempts to start an illegal printing press.
Another of the arrested was one whom I had nicknamed the "leaning
tower." In the morning when I told George of his arrest, he ran his
hand excitedly through his hair and said, "Run, Maxim, quick as you
can, to—" and gave me an address and instructions, cautioning me,
"Take care, they may have spies planted there."

I got a pleasant excitement out of this mysterious commission, and
flew straight as a bird to the Admiralty suburb. The place was a
coppersmith's shop, where I found a curly-haired young man, with remarkable blue eyes, soldering a pot. He did not have the appearance of
a workman. In a corner, working at a vise, was a little old man with a
leather band around his gray hair.

"Got some work for me?" I asked.

The old coppersmith answered irascibly, "Not for you!"

The young man looked up at me, then returned to his pot. I gave his
foot a little kick. Amazement and anger flashed from his blue eyes and
he swung the pot by the handle as if about to bring it down on my
head. But seeing me wink at him, he said, "Get out!"

With another wink I made my exit, but waited outside the door. Soon
the young man joined me, lit a cigarette and looked me up and down.

"You're Tikhon?" I asked.

"M—yes."

"Peter's been arrested."

He frowned at me. "What Peter?"

"The tall one who walks like a deacon."

"So what?"

"That's all."

[5] Skobelev's campaigns helped to reduce Turkestan in Central Asia to a colony
of the Tsarist's Empire.

"What's that to me, your Peter who walks like a deacon?" The way he put it made me sure he wasn't a workman. I hurried home, pleased with myself for having carried out my assignment.

That was my first piece of conspiratorial work. George Pletnev was right in the midst of it, but when I asked to be drawn in he put me off with, "Don't rush it, boy. You have a lot to learn yet."

It was at this time that, through Yevreinov, I became acquainted with a most mysterious person. This acquaintance was given ominous importance to me by the complications with which Yevreinov surrounded the meeting. The place was Askoye Field, a barren stretch outside the city. On the way Yevreinov kept cautioning me to be prudent, and repeating that the meeting must be kept a secret. When we reached the field, Yevreinov pointed to a small, gray figure slowly walking across it. Looking all around, Yevreinov then whispered to me, "That's him. Catch up with him and when he stops, say, " 'I'm the new one!' "

Mysteries are always exciting, but this one was a little funny. A bright day, a little man crossing the field like a gray speck—and that's all. When I caught up with him at the cemetery gates, the little gray figure turned into a dry sort of youth, with a severe look in eyes that were round as a bird's. He wore the gray overcoat of a school boy's uniform, but black steel buttons had replaced the bright brass ones. The worn cap still bore the marks of the school insignia. Physically he gave the impression of an untimely plucked bird; in manner he was a boy trying to impersonate, to himself at any rate, a full-grown man.

Thick bushes cast shadows over the spot, among the graves, where we sat. His talk was dry and matter-of-fact, and aroused my dislike. After searching questions about my reading, he invited me to join a group he had organized. I consented and we separated, he walking off first, with cautious glances, over the bare field.

In that circle of five or six youths, to which Pletnev also belonged, I was the youngest, and completely unequipped for the task they had set themselves: the study of Adam Smith with Chernyshevsky's commentaries.[6] Our meeting place was in the room of Milovsky, a student at the Teachers' Institute, who later published short stories under the pen name of Yeleonsky. After some five volumes of them, this career was ended by the author's suicide. How many men I came to know chose to part with life by their own will!

[6] Adam Smith, British economist, author of *The Wealth of Nations*. Chernyshevsky, Russian radical and critic.

Milovsky was rather timorous in his thinking, and fussy with words. He lived in a filthy cellar room and sought to acquire "equilibrium of body and soul," at a carpenter's workbench. He was boring company. Nor did I find Adam Smith stimulating. His economic theses were no revelation to me. Direct experience had engraved them on my flesh. It struck me as pointless to have filled a thick book with long words to demonstrate what was self-evident to anyone whose life forces were being used up for the advantage and profit of "Uncle Stranger." [7] It was a strain for me to sit through the two or three hours of daily study in that hole, breathing sewer stenches and watching beetles on their journeys over the foul walls.

Once our teacher was late, and thinking he would not come at all, we decided to celebrate and bought some vodka, bread and cucumbers. Just as we were falling to, his gray legs flashed across the window, and we barely had time to hide the vodka under the table and resume our consideration of Chernyshevsky's wise commentaries. We held ourselves rigid as idols to keep from knocking the vodka bottle over. But the bottle was doomed; the teacher himself upset it. After a glance under the table, he went on without a mention of it. A good bawling out would have been easier to bear. That silence, that taut face, those screwed-up, indignant eyes filled me with chagrin. Turning sidelong glances toward my comrades' blushing faces, I felt as guilty as if I had committed a criminal act against him, though it was not I who had proposed buying the vodka. At the same time I felt genuinely sorry for him.

In the boredom of these readings, I longed to visit the Tatar quarter where gentle, kindly people led a different and more wholesome life. The Russian they spoke was quaintly distorted. In the evening the muezzin wailed from the minarets to summon them to pray. This Tatar life, founded on other concepts, seemed so different from our drab ways.

The Volga also seduced me, and the rhythms of labor, a music that continues to this day to be a pleasant intoxicant to me. How clear in my memory stands the day when the epic poetry of labor first revealed itself to me.

A big barge, laden with Persian goods, stove in its bottom on a submerged rock below the harbor. A gang of stevedores enlisted me to help take out of the cargo. It was September. Angry waves roughened

[7] A term for exploiter. The title Uncle is used familiarly or satirically in Russian to stand for any symbolic relationship.

the gray river. The wind, skimming their crests, drove the spray like a cold rain. Our gang, numbering about fifty, were muffled in mats and tarpaulins, spread out over the bare deck of an empty barge that was to take on the salvaged cargo. The small tugboat that towed us belched out red gusts of sparks with each snort of its engines.

Dusk coming on, the damp, leaden, darkening sky seemed to descend on the river. The grumbling stevedores cursed the rain, the wind and their hard life, and crawled about the deck seeking shelter. These half-numbed men seemed unfit for any work, not to speak of salvaging the submerged cargo.

Before midnight we reached the stranded barge and moored alongside it. The gang boss, a poisonous-looking old man, pitted with small-pox and with the sharp eyes and beaked nose of a hawk, tore his wet cap off his skull and in a voice shrill as a woman's, cried out, "To your prayers, boys!"

From that black heap, gathered in the darkness, the prayers sounded like the growling of bears. His prayers finished before the rest, the gang boss yelled, "Get the lanterns! Show how you can work, and no bluffing. God's help, to get us started!"

And the chilled, drenched men showed how they could work. With whoops and cheers, they charged upon the flooded barge as if they were going into battle. Soon sacks of rice, crates of raisins, bales of hides and caracul fleeces were flying about me as light as cushions, and the thickset, racing men cheered each other on with howls, whistles and slangy challenges. Hard to believe that these men, working with such verve and efficiency, were the lifeless, dispirited fellows who, a little while back, had sullenly cursed the rain, and cold and life itself. Yet the rain had grown heavier and colder and the wind stronger. The wind blew their shirts over their heads, and lashed their exposed bellies. The thud of their feet resounded on the deck as, in the dim light of six lanterns, scarcely penetrating the damp darkness, the men heaved about. They worked as if they had been thirsting for it, as if it were play for them to toss 150-pound sacks from hand to hand, and as if they were running obstacle races with the bales on their backs. They worked with the gaiety and ardor of children, with that intoxicating rapture of accomplishment which is surpassed, for a man, only in the embrace of a woman.

A tall, bearded man, in a sticky, dripping jacket, the owner of the cargo or his agent, yelled to the men, "I'll put up a pailful, boys, two pailfuls, my little buccaneers! Lively now!"

Hoarse voices from all sides barked back, "Three pailfuls!"
"All right. I'll make it three. So, lively, boys!"
The hurricane of work became stormier. I, too, grabbing sacks and tossing them about, seemed to be whirling with the others in a wild dance. These men, working with such fierce and uninterrupted intensity and joy, looked as if they could go on for months and years, as if they could move the city itself, lifting it up by its steeples and minarets.

Such rapture as I lived through that night I had never before experienced. My soul was inflamed with longing to live out my life in such half-mad orgies of activity. The waves surged against the barge, the rain scourged the deck, the wind howled down the river, while in the gray mist of the dawn, drenched men dashed about, half-naked, eager and untiring, shouting, laughing, exulting in the power expressed in their work. Then the dense cloud masses were parted by the wind and the rosy dawn light glowed through the bright, blue rift of sky, and was greeted in unison with a cheerful roar by these good-natured beasts, shaking the wet hair from their muzzles. These two-legged animals, so drawn to their work, so intelligent and adept—one had the impulse to kiss them and hug them.

The onset of such a joyous frenzy of energy appeared irresistible, appeared capable of miraculously transforming the earth, covering, in one night, the whole globe with palatial cities, as in fairy tales.

The sunbeam that, for a minute or two, had witnessed this miracle of man's labor, proved too futile to overcome the massed clouds. It drowned like a child washed overboard, and the rain became a torrent.

"Let's stop," a voice suggested, but was met with an angry, "I'll stop you!"

And, till two that afternoon, when every last bale had been transferred, the half-naked men worked without rest, in the biting wind and pouring rain; and I had to pay tribute, in reverent awe, to the richness and power of man's earth.

The work done, we boarded a steamboat, falling asleep on the deck like drunkards. Back in Kazan we gushed out on the sandy riverbank like a discharge of gray bilge; then off to the tavern to drink down the promised three pails of vodka.

Bashkin the thief was there. Looking me up and down he asked, "What did they do to you?"

Enthusiastically I described what we had done. "Fool!" he snorted contemptuously. "Worse than a fool, an idiot!"

With a mocking whistle, his body wriggling like a fish, he swam dexterously around the tables clustered with the carousing stevedores. In a corner, a tenor voice launched an obscene song:

> "On a dark night, so it is told,
> The lady in the garden strolled . . ."

To which a dozen men, clapping on the table, deafeningly roared the refrain,

> "And the watchman of the town
> Finds the lady lying down."

Then laughter, howls and thunderous cynicism which is probably un-equaled, in violence, anywhere on earth.

Chapter Two

I WAS INTRODUCED TO ANDREW DERENKOV, OWNER OF A SMALL GROCERY, tucked away at the end of a miserable little lane above an open sewer. A man with a withered arm, Derenkov had intelligent eyes and a kind face framed in a fair beard. He owned the fullest collection of banned books in town, and made them available to the Kazan students and others interested in the revolutionary movement.

Derenkov's grocery occupied a wing of the house of a Skoptsy [8] money-changer. The back door of the shop led into a large room, dimly lit by a window opening on the courtyard. That room opened, in turn, into a small kitchen beyond which, in the passageway that connected the wing with the main structure, was a storeroom where the illegal library was kept. A number of its volumes were handwritten copies, in thick note-books, of such books as Lavrov's [9] *Historical Letters*, Chernyshevsky's [10] *What Must Be Done*, and Pisarev's [10] *Tsar Hunger and Complex Devices*. They were worn and shabby from constant use.

[8] Member of a religious sect whose members considered all sexual intercourse sin and, in some cases, castrated themselves.

[9] A Populist leader who charged the intellectuals to go among the people as propagandists and teachers.

[10] Chernyshevsky and Pisarev were famous Russian sociological critics.

The first time I came into the grocery, Derenkov, who was serving some customers, indicated the next room with a gesture of his head. Entering it, I saw this: In a dim corner, absorbed in his devotions, knelt a little old man, very like the portraits of St. Seraphim of Sarov.[11] He seemed out of place here; Derenkov, I had heard, was a Narodnik.[12]

As I understood the term, that meant he was a revolutionary, and therefore a non-believer, so what was this worshiper doing here? His prayers done, the old man slicked back his hair and stroked his beard. Having looked me over he said, "I'm Andrew's father. Who are you? So. I thought you were a disguised student."

"Why should a student disguise himself?" I asked.

"Why, indeed!" answered the old man. "God sees through all their disguises."

Going to the kitchen, he left me sitting at the window, occupied with my own thoughts. I was roused by the exclamation, "So that's him!"

I saw a young girl standing in the kitchen doorway. She was all in white; her fair hair was bobbed; and a pair of deep blue eyes shone, smilingly, in a pale round face. She resembled a Christmas postcard angel.

"Startled you? Am I so terrifying?" she asked in a thin, tremulous voice; and she made her way toward me, feeling along the wall, as though it were not firm flooring she was on, but a swaying rope in mid-air. The inability to walk normally accentuated the other worldly impression she gave. Her body shuddered as though she were stepping on nails, and the wall were burning her soft, childlike hands, whose fingers were unaccountably stiff and still.

In a confused mixture of compassion and uneasiness, I stood silent before her. How strange everything was in this shadowy room!

Carefully, as if she feared it might slide from under her, the girl felt her way into a chair. This was only her fifth day up, she told me, after about three months in bed with paralyzed hands and legs. With a smile she explained, "It's some nerve disease."

I remember wishing for some other explanation. Nerves seemed too ordinary for such a girl in so eerie a room, where everything shrank so diffidently to the walls, and where even the light of the icon lamp, swinging in the corner, seemed overbright, and the random shadows of its brass chains seemed too sharp on the white cloth on the big table.

---

[11] The relics of this saint were discovered at the Tsar's orders and in his presence in 1906.

[12] A group of intellectuals who sought to educate and uplift the peasantry.

"I've heard so much about you," she said, in her thin child's voice. "I wanted to see what you're like."

I could not stand her scrutiny, the piercing quality of her deep blue eyes; and talking was hard for me; I didn't know how to begin. I looked at the portraits of Herzen, Darwin and Garibaldi on the walls, pretending to be lost in silent reverence. A youth of about my own age, with blond hair and confident eyes, came in from the grocery and went into the kitchen, calling out on the way, in the cracked voice of an adolescent, "What're you about, Maria?"

"That's Alex, my younger brother," she said. "When I fell ill I was studying obstetrics. Why don't you say something? You needn't feel shy here."

Then Andrew Derenkov appeared, his withered hand hidden in a pocket. Stroking and ruffling his sister's fine hair, he asked me what kind of work I wanted. After him came a slim, red-haired girl with greenish eyes. Giving me a severe look she said, "That's enough for today, Maria," and led the girl in white away. That name, Maria, did not suit her; it was too common.

I, too, left, and in a strange agitation; but the next evening saw me back trying to account for the life these people led and what was in their souls. Certainly theirs were peculiar ways.

The gentle, meek old father, so pale as to seem almost transparent, looked out from his corner, his lips in continuous motion over a defensive smile, as if pleading, "Don't touch me, please." Clearly he was obsessed with presentiments of misfortune; he had the fears of a hunted hare.

One-handed Andrew, in a gray jacket, so caked in front with oil and flour that it had the toughness of bark, leaned to one side as he paced the room, in a sort of guilty self-consciousness, smiling like a child who had just been forgiven a prank. His lazy and brutish brother, Alex, helped out in the shop; a third student brother stayed in the Teachers' Institute dormitory, and made his appearance here only on Sundays. A neat little man, he had the air of an elderly official. The invalid sister seldom came down from the attic and always upset me when she did. The house was run by the money-changer's housekeeper, a tall woman with the expressionless features of a doll, except for the hard eyes. Redhead Nastya, her daughter, also bossed around; when her green eyes settled on a man the nostrils of her sharp nose quivered.

However, the real masters in the Derenkov apartment were the seminarians and veterinary students from the university who lived in a state of incessant and noisy solicitude over the Russian peasant and the future of the nation. In an endless seethe of ideas drawn from newspaper articles and newly read books, and re-agitated by events in the town and the university, they swarmed from all the Kazan streets to Derenkov's grocery, to engage in feverish arguments or in whispered discussions in corners. They all carried thick books; and each disputant poked his fingers in the pages, shouting at his adversary the truth he chose to affirm.

My comprehension of these discussions was deficient, of course; the truths floated beyond me in the wallow of words, like the tiny stars of nourishing fat in the thin soup of the poor. I was reminded of the Old Believers in the icon store; but I realized that these people sought to transform life, that their sincerity might be muffled in the verbal, but was not drowned in it. The problems they wrestled with were real by me; and I knew their successful solution would affect me personally. Often my own mute thoughts seemed to ring out in their words; and I regarded them with the exaltation of a prisoner promised his freedom. In turn, I was to them the block of wood out of which the carpenter might construct an unusual piece of furniture.

"Unspoiled!" they would say of me, to each other, with the pride of kids in the street showing off a coin they had found.

But to be thought "unspoiled," or called "a son of the people" did not appeal to me for some reason; quite the contrary, I felt myself to be one of life's stepsons, and I chafed at their restrictions on the development of my mind. For example, seeing in a bookshop window a volume mysteriously entitled *Aphorisms and Maxims*, I burned to read it and sought to borrow it from a Seminary student.

"What next?" asked the future bishop, sarcastically, a chap with kinky black hair and thick lips over gleaming white teeth. "Nonsense, boy! You read what you're told to and keep your nose out of matters that don't concern you."

His rudeness provoked me, and I bought the book with money partly earned by work on the docks and part a loan from Andrew Derenkov. That was the first serious book I bought and I still own it. Altogether I was rather arrogantly treated. In *The A. B. C. of Social Sciences*, which I had read, the role of the shepherd tribes in the development of culture seemed to me to have been exaggerated by the author, while that of the adventurous hunters was scanted. I ventured this opinion to a philologist who, trying a patriarchal look on his womanish face, lectured me a whole hour on the "responsibilities of criticism." "Only a belief in some basic truth can give you the right to criticize—what is your basic truth?"

That chap buried himself in a book even when he was out walking. His face invisible behind the covers, he felt his way, shoving passersby aside. Once, stretched out on his attic bed with typhoid, he kept howling, "Morality must unite freedom and violence in harmony, in har-har-harm . . ."

Hunger and his unremitting quest for basic truths kept him frail. Reading was the sole joy of his life; and when he thought he had resolved the differences between two powerful minds, a childlike happiness would radiate out of his pleasant, dark eyes. Some ten years after I left Kazan I ran across him in Kharkov. He was again studying at a university after having put in five years in exile at Kem.[13] He was still on his ant heap of contradictory ideas. Spitting blood, and speaking with the hoarse whisper of the dying consumptive, he was now "reconciling" Nietzsche with Marx. Clawing at my hands with his clammy fingers he said, "Life's impossible without a synthesis."

He died on a street-car on his way to the university. I have encountered many such martyrs to learning, and I hold their memory sacred.

About a dozen of his kind gathered in the Derenkov flat, including even a Japanese, Panteleimon Sato, a Seminary student. Sometimes, too, a large broad-shouldered man appeared, conspicuous for his huge spade beard and his Tatar-style, shaven head. His tight-fitting gray jacket, buttoned up to his neck, made him look corseted. His usual place was in a corner where he smoked a stubby pipe and watched the rest with gray, serene, but penetrating eyes.

When his glance rested on my face, I felt myself being mentally weighed and he made me feel uneasy without knowing why. His silence puzzled me. Everybody else was loud, positive and fulsome in his speech; and at that time, the more pretentious the words the more impressed I was—it was a long time before I conceived what pettiness and deceit are masked in pretentious words. Why no word from this bearded Hercules?

They called him the Khokhol,[14] and I believe only Andrew knew his real name. I learned that he was just back from a ten-year exile in Yakutsk.[15] This intensified my interest in him but still left me short of the courage to make his acquaintance, though timidity and shyness were not among my afflictions. Inquisitiveness was my failing, a hunger to know everything and at once. Throughout my life it has kept me from applying myself to any particular study.

When the talk was of the people, I felt on uncertain ground; I could

[13] A town in Karelia, and a station on the Murmansk railroad.
[14] A term for Ukrainians used by the Russians.
[15] In Eastern Siberia.

not get myself to think in the same terms as the rest. To them the people were wisdom, spirituality, and loving-kindness incarnate, a quite godlike entity, containing everything that was upright, stately and beautiful. Such a people, however, was unknown to me. I knew carpenters, dockhands, bricklayers. I knew Jake, Osip and Gregory; but I didn't know this "unified" People whom they put above themselves, and to whose will they submitted themselves. It was they, however, who embodied for me the beauty and strength of the mind; in them I could feel surging the will to life, the striving for freedom, the ambition to raise a new world, founded on mutuality. It was just this mutuality that I had failed to find among men with whom I had lived hitherto; whereas, here it vibrated in every word, it shone in every face.

What the people-worshipers said penetrated my heart like a refreshing rain. Their naïve literature on the martyr-life of the peasants had a like effect on me. Only from such a passionate and overpowering love for man, I realized, came the impetus to pierce to the core of life. No longer did my thoughts center on myself; I gave greater attention to others.

Andrew Derenkov confided to me that his modest profits all went for the benefit of these men who "put the welfare of the people above everything." He flitted about among them like a reverent acolyte at services presided over by a bishop, responding to the agile intellect of these bookworms with unconcealed rapture. With his withered hand in his breast, and the other pulling at his beard, he asked me with a happy smile, "Magnificent, eh?"

And when Lavrov, the veterinary, in a voice grotesquely like the honk of a goose, inveighed against the Narodniks, to whom these people-lovers belonged, Derenkov, blinking his eyes in agitation, muttered, "The hooligan!"

His attitude toward the Narodniks was like mine; but the students treated him with the unfeeling manner of a grand gentleman toward a valet. He did not notice it, however. Frequently, after having seen his guests out, he talked me into spending the night there. We tidied up the room, and then, lying on mats on the floor, we kept up friendly, whispered talk through a darkness assuaged by the light from the icon lamp.

With the serene assurance of the devotee he said, "These splendid people in hundreds and thousands will come together, take the key posts in Russia and, at once, make over our life."

He was some ten years my senior. I realized that he was infatuated with the redhead, Nastya. He tried to avoid her provocative eyes. In the presence of others he put on a commanding manner to her. But he followed her movements with yearning looks; and when he talked to her alone his manner was shy; he kept pulling at his beard and he smiled a diffident smile.

Sitting in a corner, his little sister also followed the verbal affrays with wide-eyed awe. The effort puckered her childlike face into a funny pout. If the discussion sharpened and harsh words were spoken, she gave shuddering gasps as if she had been sprayed with icy water. A red-haired medical student strutted before her like a cock, stopping to impart mysterious whispers and to put on impressive frowns. How frightfully interesting it all was!

With the return of autumn, life without a regular job became impossible for me. Enthralled by what went on around me, I had been working less steadily and eating the bread of others, which has a way of sticking in your throat. I looked about for a job for the winter and found it at Basil Semenov's bakeshop.

I have described my life at this period in the stories, "The Boss," "Konovalov," Twenty-six and One." It was a hard time for me, but instructive. And it was hard spiritually as well as physically.

Buried in that cellar bakeshop, the "wall of forgetfulness" rose between me and those whose intellectual company had become a necessity to me. None of them paid me a visit; and, working fourteen hours a day, I could not make Derenkov's on weekdays, and holidays I stayed in bed or spent the time with my shopmates, for some of whom I was a clown, while others treated me with the simple-hearted affection children have for an adult who tells them stories. What I told them the devil alone knows exactly; but it was intended to raise hope in them of another, easier and saner life. Sometimes it did, and seeing the sodden faces light to an angry consciousness of their lot, their eyes flaring with indignation, I felt my soul at peace, proud to be working "among the people," "instructing" them.

Oftener, however, I only became more aware of my own helplessness, ignorance, and unfitness to answer the simplest questions. Then I seemed to flounder in a pit where men wriggled like blind worms, searching refuge from reality in the bottle or in the embraces of streetwalkers. Attendance at the "houses of joy" was obligatory every monthly pay day. A week before that paradisiacal day the men day-dreamed aloud about its delights; and, later, relived them in drawn-out reminiscence. Those recitals were full of cynical boasts about their sexual feats and sneers at the women, of whom they spoke with disgust. Yet through it all, strangely enough I heard, or imagined that I heard, undertones of contrition and sorrow. In the "houses of joy" where one could have a woman all night for a ruble, I noticed that my friends' behavior was backward and shamefaced, which seemed natural to me. Where the attitude was aggressive and bold, its very exaggeration betrayed that it was put on. There was a strange thrill for me in the relation of the sexes—and I looked on with avid interest.

Doing without the caresses of a woman there, put me in an unpleasant position; both the women and the men made me their butt. Soon they asked me to stay away.

"Why?"

"It's no fun with you around."

These words, in which I sensed great significance, impressed me, though I felt the need of further explanation. "We don't want you," they repeated. "Keep away. You spoil it for us when you come along." And, laughingly, Artyom added, "It's like having your father or a priest around you!"

At first the girls, too, kidded me; but later, they took offense: "You find us disgusting?"

Forty-year-old Theresa Boruta, who ran the house, a plump and comely Polish woman, looking me over with the sharp eyes of a thoroughbred hound, told the girls, "Hands off him. He must have a bride—eh? Only a bride could hold in such a champion!"

She drank heavily and when she was drunk was unbearably repulsive. In her sober moments, however, she amazed me by her thoughtful observation of people, of whose actions she tried to make some sense.

"The Seminary students are the oddest," she said. "What they won't do with a girl! They have her wax the floor, then get down on all fours, with her hands and her feet on platters, and give her a push to see how far she'll slide. They do it with all the girls, one after the other. Why?"

"Liar," I said.

"Oh, no!" exclaimed Theresa, without offense, and in a voice whose quiet tone had a curiously crushing effect.

"You must be making it up," I insisted.

"Would any girl make up things like that? Think I'm crazy?"

The men gave close attention to our discussion, as Theresa went on about these high jinks, talking in the passionless tone of a person who only wants to know the why of it all.

With savage oaths the men voiced their disgust with the students. Seeing that Theresa was rousing antagonism toward the people I had come to love, I said that the students were on the side of the people and only sought their good.

"You're thinking of the lads from Voskresensky Street, but I'm talking about the Seminary students from the Arskoe Polye. They're all orphans, these spiritual ones, and orphans turn into crooks, and no-goods; they've got nobody to hang on to."

Theresa's off-hand tales and the girls' complaints of the nastiness of students and officials roused the men not only to resentment and disgust, but to a certain satisfaction. "The educated ones don't seem to be any better than us!"

All this was hard for me to bear. The town's filth seemed to discharge into these small, dank rooms as into a sewer, simmer there over a smoky fire, and then, steaming with hatred and evil, flow back into the town. Yet, moving songs of wistful and anguished love were shaped out of unsuitable words in these pits, into which instinct and boredom dragged people down. It was thus, I saw, that the vile myths about "educated people" arose, thus hostility and contempt toward whatever was beyond them were nourished in people. I realized that these "houses of consolation" were universities where my friends imbibed a most venomous knowledge. I watched the "daughters of joy" as they slovened across the filthy floor, dragging their feet; as their flabby bodies shimmied revoltingly to the horrible squeal of the accordion or the cracked chords of a dilapidated piano. For me they distilled a vague anguish. Here rose a boredom that sickened the soul with impotent desires to escape. When I spoke to my shopmates of the disinterested men who were pioneering paths of freedom, who worked for the happiness of people, I was challenged, "But the girls have a different story to tell."

With cynical, unsparing rancor they jeered at me. And I, like an aggressive kitten who thinks himself fit to stand off full-grown dogs—I returned their anger! Understanding life, I realized, is as hard as life itself, and at times, hatred flamed in my soul against these stubborn, though forbearing, shopmates. What especially roused my indignation was their submissiveness, the meekness with which they endured the delirious cruelties of the drunken boss.

And, as if it had been planned, I came, in those hard days, upon a dismal new set of ideas which greatly agitated me; they, too, were something I had to overcome.

On one of those wild nights when the howling wind seems to be pulverizing the gray sky, which sifts down and buries the earth in drifts of icy dust, when life appears to be at its last gasp and the light of the sun to be put out forever, on such a night I was returning from the Derenkovs' to the bakery, walking against the wind with my eyes shut—when open, there was nothing to see but seething gray chaos. Suddenly I tripped

over a man sprawled on the pavement. The same oath, "The devil!" came
from both of us—but mine in Russian, his in French.

My curiosity roused, I lifted him to his feet, finding him short and
hardly any weight at all. Pushing me he cried angrily, "Damn you, where's
my hat! I want my hat back. I'm freezing." I found it for him, picking
it out of the snow, shook it dry, and put it on his unkempt head. But he
pulled it off again, waved it at me, and swearing at me in two languages
and howling, "Get away from me!" he tried to drive me off.

And then suddenly, running ahead, he slipped and plunged into the
frothing mush. Going after him I found him embracing a wooden lamp-
post, whose light was out, pleading, "Lena, I'm dying, Lena!"

Seeing that he was drunk and realizing that, left there on the street,
he might freeze to death, I asked him where he lived.

With sobs in his voice he cried, "I don't know how to go. What street
are we on?"

As I steered him off with my arm around his waist, I tried to fish out
his address from him.

"Bulak Street," he mumbled, "Bulak Street; there's a bathhouse, and
a house."

I couldn't make any progress, he was shaking so. I actually heard his
teeth click together.

"*Si tu savais!*" (If you know) he muttered, shoving me aside.

"What?"

He stopped, and lifting his hand, said distinctly and with apparent
pride, "*Si tu savais, ou je te me mene.*" (If you know where I'm bound.)

He put his fingers in his mouth to warm them, which made it still
harder for him to keep his balance.

I put him on my back and carried him along, his chin pressed against
my skull. He kept mumbling, "*Si tu savais ou*" (If you know where) . . .
God, I'm freezing."

Reaching Bulak Street, it was some time before I located his house.
Finally, under snowdrifts at the end of the yard, I found a hut. Groping
for the door and hushing me, "Sh—sh—quiet," he knocked lightly.

A woman in a red housedress, with a candle in her hand, let us in.
Standing off, she put on glasses and looked me up and down.

The man's hands were rigid with cold; I told her he should be undressed and put to bed.

"Yes?"

"His hands should be soaked in cold water."

Saying nothing, she pointed with her glasses to the corner where, on

an easel, stood a painting of some trees over a riverbank. The eerily immobile face of the woman astonished me; still more, her going off to the
other end of the room, sitting down at a table lit by a kerosene lamp with
a rose-tinted shade, and taking up a card, the knave of hearts, and staring
at it.

"Have you any alcohol?" I demanded. She did not answer, but began
to lay cards out on the table. The man sat on a chair, his head sunk on
his chest, and his frostbitten red arms dangling. I carried him to the couch
and began undressing him, doing it mechanically, moving as in a dream,
unable to comprehend what was going on in this strange house.

Among the photographs covering the opposite wall was a dully glowing
gold wreath from which hung white ribbons, lettered in gold, "To Gilda,
the Incomparable."

"Easy!" complained the man when I began massaging his hands. The
woman remained preoccupied with her cards. Down her sharp-featured,
birdlike face, peered her still eyes. Suddenly, putting hands small as a
child's into gray hair fluffed like a wig, she asked in a voice low but distinct, "Georges, did you see Mischa?"

Georges pushed me away, sat up and said, "But he's gone to Kiev."

"To Kiev," the woman repeated, not looking up from the cards. I was
struck by the monotone of her inexpressive voice.

"He'll be back soon."

"Yes?"

"Sure, soon."

"Yes?" she repeated.

Half-undressed, Georges jumped from the couch and got on his knees
to the woman, pleading something in French. She answered in Russian,
"But I'm quiet."

"You see, I lost my way. It's storming outside, an awful wind. I thought
I'd freeze to death. We didn't have much to drink." He rushed out the
words, and caressed the hand that lay on her knee.

He was a man of about forty. Black moustaches over thick lips crossed
a red face tense with anxiety and fright. He rubbed the gray bristles on
his round skull, seeming to sober up that way.

"Tomorrow we go to Kiev," she said, half as a command, half as a
question.

"Tomorrow of course—you need some sleep. It's late. Why don't you
go to bed?"

"Mischa won't come today?"

"Not in this snowstorm! Come to bed." Taking up the lamp from the table, he led her through a small door beside a bookcase. Left alone, I sat still, not thinking of anything, listening to his hoarse, urgent voice. Across the window panes scraped his hairy hands. From a pool of melted snow came a hesitant reflection of the candle-flame. The room was cluttered with furniture, and gave off an odd, warm smell that had a narcotic effect on me.

Georges teetered back, holding the lamp so unsteadily, the shade kept knocking the glass. "She's gone to sleep."

He stood the lamp on the table, and standing in the middle of the room, but looking aside, said to me, "What's there to say? But for you I'd probably be dead. Thank you—whoever you are."

Shivering and anxious, he kept his ears cocked to the sounds from the next room.

"Your wife?" I asked him hesitantly.

"My wife, yes. My whole life," he said distinctly, but in a low voice, his head hanging. He rubbed his hand, hard, over his head.

"Care for some tea?"

Absent-mindedly he went to the kitchen door to call in to the servant, then recalled, aloud, that she had gorged on spoiled fish and had been taken to the hospital.

I offered to put the kettle on. He nodded, and unaware that he was undressed, led me into the kitchen, his bare feet slapping on the damp floor. Leaning against the stove he repeated, "But for you I'd have frozen to death. Thanks!" Then, with a start, and with a terrified, round-eyed stare he added, "And what would have happened to her. My God!"

In a hurried whisper, and with an anxious glance toward the bedroom, he explained, "She's sick. She's still waiting for her son. Two years. He was a musician in Moscow. He committed suicide two years ago."

Over our tea he told me in odd, incoherent phrases that the woman owned a country house, that he had tutored her son, that he had fallen in love with her and got her to leave her husband, a German baron, and that she had become an opera singer. Her first husband had done everything he could to thwart them but they had been happy together.

He told me this, staring fixedly through squinted eyes at something in the dark, sloppy kitchen where the floor rotted around the stove. He gulped his tea so hastily he burnt his mouth; his face puckered with pain and his round eyes blinked.

"And you?" he asked. "Oh, I see; a baker, a workman. Strange. You don't look like it. Why?"

His manner was uneasy. His look became suspicious like that of a hunted man. I told him something of my life.

He offered sympathetic exclamations, such as, "Indeed?" "Is that so?" In sudden animation he asked me, "Do you know the story of the Ugly Duckling? Ever read that?" and his face became distorted, his tone shrill with anger, giving his voice an unnatural timbre that startled me.

"It fascinates me, that tale! When I was your age I, too, thought myself a swan. I was to enter the seminary but went to the university instead. My father, a clergyman, disowned me. In Paris I steeped myself in the history of human misery, of human progress. And I spent my time writing. How it all . . ." He turned in his chair, stopped to listen, then went on. "Progress is something we have invented to console ourselves. Life makes no sense, it has nothing to do with reason. Without slavery there's no progress; the majority must submit to the minority if it's to get ahead. We set out to simplify our lives and our work and we only complicate them, we only multiply our tasks. Factories and machines only produce more machines—how senseless! The number of workmen grows, when it's the peasant, after all, the food producer, who is really necessary to society. Bread's the one thing you must labor to wrest from nature. The fewer a man's desires the happier he is; the less he wants the freer he is."

These may not be his exact words, but I had never heard these dismal thoughts before, and I was hearing them now in a brutally stark form.

He gave me these thoughts in shrieks, as, in his agitation, he kept looking apprehensively at the door opening on the other rooms; finally he lowered his voice to a frenzied whisper, "Understand me? A man needs very little. A slice of bread, a woman."

On the theme of women his whisper became mysterious; I heard words new to me, unfamiliar verses, and I was suddenly reminded of the thief, Bashkin.

"Beatrice, Fiametta, Laura, Ninon." These strange names reached me in reverent murmurs, in tales of the loves of kings and poets, in French verses, whose rhythm he chopped out with his thin bare arm.

"Love and hunger are the rulers of the world."

These words of his feverish whisper recalled to me the revolutionary pamphlet *Tsar Hunger*, and this magnified their impression on my mind. "People seek to forget, seek not to know. They need consolation." That idea struck me numb.

When I left the little kitchen in the morning, the small wall clock showed a few minutes after six. The wailing of the storm, as I walked in

458 Autobiography of Maxim Gorky

the shadowy snowdrifts, recalled to me Georges' screaming whispers, and I felt his words sticking in my throat, choking me. Feeling disinclined to meet people in this mood, I did not go straight to the bakery. I stumbled about in the streets of the Tatar suburb, dragging clods of snow behind me until it was light, and the dark figures of people were visible among the billows of snow.

I never met the painter again, nor did I wish to. But often, after that, I heard the same views of the senselessness of life and the futility of work, usually from illiterate hoboes, or sophisticates. I have heard such ideas from a priest, a theosophist, a chemist specializing in explosives, a neo-vitalist, a biologist, and so on. But none gave me the shock I got that first time. Two years ago, that is, thirty years after, I heard those thoughts in almost the identical words, spoken by an old worker friend of mine.

We were in the midst of one of those "soul to soul" talks when this "political leader," as he claimed to be, said with an unflinching candor which only we Russians are capable of: "My dear Maxim, what's the point of all these academies, sciences, airplanes—they're all excess baggage. All one needs is a cozy corner and a woman to embrace when he likes, and who'll respond decently, body and soul. That's all. You think like an intellectual now, you're no longer one of us. You think like a Jew—the idea above the people—the man is made for the Sabbath——"

"Jews don't think like that."

"Devil knows what they think. We're such ignoramuses!" Throwing his cigarette into the river he watched it snuff out.

We were on one of the Neva quays, sitting on a granite bench, on a moonlit night in the fall. Both of us were emotionally spent after a day of stubborn, but futile, seeking to do some good, to be of some service.

"What I mean is you're with us, but not one of us," he went on, with a gentle, thoughtful expression. "The Intelligentsia enjoys worrying; always in revolt. Christ, the idealist, had heavenly goals for His rebellion; the Intelligentsia has Utopia. The idealist rebels—and finds at his side scoundrels, no-goods, a mob who act out of malice, feeling themselves outlaws in the world. The workman rebels to bring about the proper distribution of the tools and produce of labor. When he has seized control, do you think he will want to bother administrating? Not for the whole world. The workers will scatter. Every one will avoid responsibility, look to himself, dig himself a cave. Talk about technical progress? That only tightens the collar around our necks, fastens our chains tighter. No. We must be liberated from unnecessary toil. The human being needs rest. He won't get it from science and factories. A human being needs so little.

Why heap up a whole town when all I need is a hut? Where people live in swarms, there you get such inventions as aqueducts, canals, electricity. And suppose you live without all that? How much simpler it would be! The truth is, we're surrounded with unnecessary things—and the Intelligentsia is the source of them all; that's why I find the Intelligentsia unwholesome!"

"No one manages so profoundly and persistently to strip life of sense," I replied, "as we Russians do."

"But the nation freest in spirit," he said smiling. "Don't be offended with me, because what I say is right; millions of us think the same way and we're right—though we may express ourselves badly. Life must be made simple—then it will prove kind to people."

This man was no Tolstoyan, and he never showed any Anarchist tendencies. I knew all that had gone into his spirit's growth. Thus, talk with him compelled me to think: Suppose millions of Russian peasants endure the agonies of the revolution with only this hope in the abysses of their souls, that they will be liberated from labor! A minimum of labor and a maximum of pleasure, alluring temptation, like everything visionary, like all Utopias. And I recalled Ibsen's lines:

"I'm no conservative, not I. What I am I've always been. I wouldn't like to distress the players; just to foul up the game. The one revolution I recall with approval, wiser than all that came after, the one that could have done away with everything, was the flood, of course. But even then the devil was outsmarted. Noah was made dictator. If only it could be done more sensibly I'd gladly give you a hand; while you're pouring on the flood, I'd torpedo the ark."

Chapter Three

DERENKOV'S SHOP WAS NO MONEY-MAKER; BUT PEOPLE AND CAUSES that called on him for material support kept growing all the time.

"We must find a way," Andrew would say, tugging at his beard with a guilty smile. Apparently this man held himself under a life sentence to help others; and, although resigned to it, the punishment sometimes weighed on him.

On various occasions I asked him, "Why do you do it?"

Not understanding the real purport of my question, he answered as if I wanted the dress-occasion reasons. His answers were bookish, unconvincing—the miseries of the people, the need for knowledge and enlightenment. "But who wants knowledge; who searches for it?" "But don't they? You know they do. Don't you want it?" I did, of course. But my memory echoed the little history teacher's words, "People seek to forget, seek not to know. They need consolation." It is unwholesome for seventeen-year-olds to be confronted with such edged ideas. The ideas lose their edges, while for youth there is nothing there to hold on to. I began to connect with them former observations that people like a thriller which brings an hour or so of forgetfulness into their drab, hard lives. The more "imagination" there's in it, the more avidly the story is listened to; the more "fantasy" it contains the more it is to the popular taste. In brief, these ideas set me adrift in billowing fog.

Derenkov's solution was to open a bakery. I remember how precisely he figured it to bring him a minimum profit of thirty-five percent. I was to come on as assistant; and being "in the family," was to see that the master baker didn't steal flour, eggs, butter and baked goods.

And that was how I came to move from a large and filthy cellar to a smaller and somewhat cleaner one—its condition was my responsibility. Instead of a gang of forty to deal with, I had only one, a gray-haired man with a small, pointed beard, whose face looked as if it had been smoked. His eyes were black and brooding, yet with mockery in their depths; and he had a small, smug fish mouth, pursed out, as though inwardly he was kissing himself.

And he was an unashamed thief. On the first night of our working together his loot was ten eggs, three pounds or so of flour, and a slab of butter.

"What's that for?"

"For a little girl," he said in an ingratiating tone. Wrinkling up his nose he added, "Such a nice little girl."

I did my best to make him feel the heinousness of stealing. Either I was unconvinced myself, or lacked eloquence—at any rate my sermon was without effect.

From the pastry bin in which he was lying, looking through the window up at the stars he said, as if in a revery, "My teacher he wants to be! The first time he sees me and, look, he's lecturing me! And about a third my age! That is funny."

After further contemplation of the stars he asked me, "Where did you work before? Seems to me I've run into you somewhere before. Was it

Semyonov's? Where there was a bit of a riot, remember? No? Then you must have appeared in my dreams."

I soon noticed his remarkable capacity for sleep, for any length of time and in any posture, even leaning on a shovel. In sleep his face assumed an expression of ironic wonder. His favorite conversation pieces were treasure trove and dreams. There was real conviction in his voice as he told me, "I can see right into the earth. It's stuffed with treasure like a big pudding; boilers, trunks, iron pots are down there all full of money. In my dreams I often find myself in a familiar spot, the bathhouse, let's say, with a trunk full of silver buried under one end of it. I wake up and keep it in mind, and at night I go and dig there. Once I dug more than two feet down and found—what do you think? Coals and the skull of a dog. There was my treasure! And on top of it, I hear a crack—the bathhouse window is smashed and a woman screams, 'Help! Robbers!' And I have to chase off or I'd have caught it! Funny, eh?"

Funny—the word was one of his favorites, though Ivan Latonin never laughed. He half-closed his eyes and a smile wrinkled up his nose and distended his nostrils.

There was no fantasy in his dreams; they were dull and trivial as his reality, and I couldn't see why he preferred them as his themes, to what was going on around him.

There was a great commotion in town over the suicide, immediately after her wedding, of a rich tea merchant's daughter, who had been forced into a loveless marriage. Thousands of young people marched after her coffin; the police dispersed students who tried to make speeches over her grave; crowds in the next-door shop shouted their opinions. The excited voices of students reached down to us in the cellar.

Latonin's comment was, "That girl could have taken a little more of the rod in her upbringing," and went on, "I was out fishing when a policeman turned up. 'Stop!' he hollered. 'What right have you got!' There was no place to run so I plopped into the water and—woke up."

Yet, though reality extended beyond the range of his comprehension, he became aware of the unusual reality of the shop. The two girls who tended it, Derenkov's sister and her friend, a big, pink-cheeked girl with cozy eyes, were not suited to this work—they were more apt to be reading books. Students passed in and out of a non-stop, shout-and-whisper discussion in the room behind the shop. Derenkov himself was rarely seen; I, the baker's assistant, was at the same time a sort of manager.

"Are you a relative of the owner," Latonin asked me, "or are you being considered for his son-in-law? No? That's funny. And why are all these students here? It's possible they're after the girls, but they're nothing special to look at. I'd say these hungry ones come more for the fresh rolls."

On most mornings, at about five or six, a stump-legged young woman arrived opposite the shop. She had the look of a bag of melons, seeming to be constructed of hemispheres of varying dimensions. Seated on the edge of the ditch with her feet hanging over, between yawns, she called out, "Ivan."

A polka-dot kerchief covered her head, and her face peeped out under it. Her curls fell over her low forehead and her red cheeks puffed like balloons, and tickled her eyes. She brushed the curls out of her eyes indolently, with little hands, whose fingers rayed out like those of an infant. I couldn't make out what one could talk of to a girl like that.

I roused the baker, who asked her, "You're here?"

"You see."

"Did you sleep?"

"What d'ye think I did?"

"Dream anything?"

"I can't remember."

The city was still, except for the scrape of the janitor's broom on the sidewalk and the chirping of the awakening sparrows. The cozy little rays of the rising sun hugged the windowpanes. These dreamy beginnings of the day pleased me. Stretching a hairy hand out of the window, the baker plucked at the girl's leg. Unsmiling, blinking her sleepy eyes, she submitted with indifference.

"Peshkov, it's time to take out the bread."

From the trays I pulled out of the oven the baker snatched a dozen or so rolls and other stuff and tossed them into her lap. Flipping one of the rolls from hand to hand, she bit into it with her sheep teeth, burned her tongue and emitted an angry groan.

As an expression of admiration he said, "Pull your skirt down, you hussy."

When she was gone he boasted to me, "Did you see? Looks like a ewe lamb in her curls. I want them clean; I never do it with women, only girls. She's my thirteenth. She's Nikiforich's god-daughter."

Listening to such ecstasies I wondered, Is this how I, too, will have to live?

Drawing the long loaves of white bread out of the oven, I arranged about a dozen of them in a row on the board, and raced with them to Derenkov's grocery. Returning, I filled an eighty-pound basket with rolls and hurried with them to the Academy for the students' breakfast. Standing there in the big dining room, I handed out the rolls on credit or for cash while trying to follow a discussion on Tolstoy. Gusev, one of the professors, was a violent antagonist of Tolstoy. At times there were notes, concealed under the rolls, that I was to put into certain students' hands, while books and notes from them went in hiding at the bottom of the basket.

Once a week I had a still longer run, to the "Mad House" where, with patients as exhibits, Professor Bekhterev delivered lectures. One day his exhibit was to be a case of "mania grandiosa." I could not help smiling at a tall man in a white robe and a sort of stocking cap who appeared at the door. Stopping for a moment in front of me, he looked into my eyes. I recoiled as if the flaming dark spear of his glance had aimed at my heart. And all the while Bekhterev, stroking his beard, talked to him, and I, with the palm of my hand, touched my cheek, which felt as if scorched by cinders.

That patient's voice was a low bass. Pulling his long hand with long fingers menacingly out of the sleeve of his robe, he made some demand. His body seemed to me to elongate unnaturally, to undergo visible and continual growth. It seemed to me he would get at me with this dark hand, and take me by the throat, without moving a step from where he stood. Out of the dim pits of his skull-like face gleamed the piercing glance of his ominous and commanding black eyes. Some twenty students gazed at the man in the funny cap, some with a smile, most of them with an absorbed, moody look. How banal the look in their eyes alongside his flaming glances. Frightening though he was, he carried himself with majesty.

The students kept as silent as fish and the professor's voice reverberated. Every question of his drew a menacing retort from the low voice, that seemed to issue from the floor or the dead-white walls. He was as solemn and slow in his movements as a bishop. That night I composed verses about the madman, naming him "Lord of lords, friend and Adviser of God." His memory image became one of the burdens of my life.

Working from dusk till about noon, I slept through the afternoon. My reading time was between kneadings of the dough, and after the bread had gone into the oven. Observing that I had mastered the secrets of the profession, the baker idled more and more. For this reason he was generous with his praise when "instructing" me. "You're getting the knack of it. In a year or two you'll be a baker. Funny! You're young, so people won't pay any attention to what you say; they'll have no regard for you."

He disparaged my preoccupation with books. "Sleep'll do you more good." He said this with some concern; but never asked what I was reading.

His treasure dreams and his globular girl took all his attention. When she visited him at night, he would take her to a heap of flour sacks in the hallway. If it was too cold there he would pucker up his nose and tell me, "Take off about half an hour."

I left them, thinking how horribly different this was from the love portrayed in books.

Derenkov's sister lived in the little room behind the shop. It was my task to put her kettle to boil, but I avoided any encounter, feeling ill at ease with her. I found the stare of her childlike eyes as unbearable as ever. I suspected a smile in the depths of those eyes, and a derisive one.

I was bursting with excess energy and this made my movements clumsy. Watching me drag and lift two-hundred-pound bags of flour, the baker would commiserate, "You've got strength enough for three but no knack! You're a tall fellow, yet you carry yourself like a bull."

Though I had read many books by then and had developed a taste for poetry—had even tried versifying myself—I used my "own" vocabulary in speech. My words felt leaden and coarse to me, but only with them, I felt, could I express the thick tangles of my thoughts.

Sometimes the coarseness was deliberate, as if in rebellion against something in me that was alien and disturbing. An annoyed mathematics student who gave me lessons burst out, "What a queer way of speaking. They're not words you use; they're iron weights!"

On the whole, as is frequently the case with adolescents, I had little self-esteem. I felt clumsy and clownish. My face with the high, Mongol cheekbones, my voice which I could not control; neither were to my liking.

In contrast, the movements of Derenkov's sister were swift and light like the glidings of a swallow. They seemed out of keeping with her pudgy, little body. They gave a certain unreality to her gait and her gestures. Her voice had a gay ring; she laughed most of the time. Listening to it I thought, She wants me to forget how she was the first time I saw her. But I held on to that memory. I valued everything out of the ordinary; I wanted to make sure of its existence.

Sometimes she asked me, "What are you reading?"

My replies were curt; I felt like answering in return, "What do you want to know for?"

Once, the baker, fondling his stumpy darling, said to me in a choked voice, "Go away, will you? Why the hell don't you go to the boss' sister, instead of wasting your time around here?"

I threatened to split his head with one of the iron weights if I ever heard another word from him on this theme; then I went out into the hallway where the bags of flour were stacked. Through the crack left by the unshut door I heard Latonin saying, "Why am I angry with him? He's stuffed up with book knowledge and lives like a lunatic."

In the hallway the rats provided the disagreeable noises; in the bakery it was the moaning girl. Going out into the yard I found myself in a thin rain, falling listlessly and soundlessly. Despite the rain the air was oppressive and had a faint burnt flavor from a wood fire nearby. The hour was long past midnight. In the house opposite the windows were open and from the dim rooms came the sound of singing. Picturing Maria Derenkova in my arms, like the girl in the baker's arms, my whole being recoiled as from something unthinkable and even terrifying.

"And through the night, He stays so tight, And does strange things—"

Provocatively, a deep bass voice lingered on "strange things." I bent down and took a look into an open window in the house opposite. Through a gap in the lace curtain I saw gray walls lit by a small, blue-shaded lamp. Before it, her face toward the window, sat a girl writing. Lifting her head she reset a curl on her temple with a red penholder. Her half-closed eyes were smiling. Slowly she folded a letter into an envelope, passed her tongue over the flap, sealed it, tossed it on the table, and shook her forefinger at it, a forefinger thinner than my little finger.

Picking it up again, she ripped it open, read through the letter, put it into another envelope, and leaning over the table, wrote the address. Then she waved it over her head like a pennant, did a little jig, clapped her hands, marched to the end of the room where her bed was and, having taken off her blouse, marched forward again. Her shoulders were round like bubbles. Then she took up the lamp from the table and vanished.

Watched when he is alone, a man's behavior always resembles that of a maniac. I thought as I walked up and down the yard, how queerly this girl lives, alone in her cell. But when that red-headed student visited her and whispered something, she shriveled up, appearing to diminish as she looked at him, with a timid smile, not knowing what to do with her hands, hide them behind her or under the table. I didn't like that man; not for a moment.

Stumbling and tugging a shawl around her, the stump-legged beauty mumbled to me, "He wants you in the bakery."

And as the baker emptied the dough bin he described the consolation he received from his long-enduring inamorata. I thought, What is to become of me? And I had a feeling that close by, awaiting me around a corner, stood misfortune.

The bakery did so well that Derenkov looked for a bigger place and decided to take on another helper. I was glad, for I was overworked. "You'll be chief helper in the new place," the baker promised me, "and I'll ask them to raise you, ten rubles a month, I will." I knew it was to his advantage to have me as his chief helper. He had no inclination to work, whereas I went at it willingly, knowing that fatigue brought me relief, smothered my spiritual torment and repressed the stubborn demands of the sexual instinct. However, it kept me from reading.

The baker's comment was, "You've stopped reading; that's good. But is it possible you have no dreams? You must have; but you keep everything back. You're a funny one! To tell one's dreams, there's nothing wrong in that, nothing to worry about."

The man was friendly to me; I think he was even respectful; if he had any fear of me as a protégé of the owner, it did not keep him from steady pilfering.

Death took grandma. The news came to me seven weeks after the burial, in a letter from my cousin. This brief missive, composed without punctuation, told how she had broken her leg in a fall while begging on a church porch. "Anthony's Fire" (gangrene) came upon her on the eighth day. I learned later, that the two Saschas and a girl cousin, as well, had all ridden on the old woman's back, living on the alms she brought home. They lacked the sense to call in a doctor. The letter said: "We buried her in the Petropavlovsk (cemetery) all of us were there also the beggars they cried they liked her Grandpa cried too he chased us away and he stayed on the grave behind the bushes we watched how he cried he is soon going to die too."

I did not cry, but I remember how like an icy wind the knowledge crossed my soul. That night, sitting in the yard on the wood pile I yearned to talk to somebody about grandma, about her kindness and understanding, and what a mother she had been to all. That yearning remained with me a long time, but I had no one to confide in and it burned itself out. Many years afterward, reading Chekhov's marvelously true story of the coachman who told his horse about his son's death, these days came back to me. The misery of that period sharpened in my memory with the thought that I had not had even a dog or horse beside me then, that I had not thought of confiding my grief to the rats in the bakery with whom I had gotten on quite friendly terms.

It was at this time that Nikiforich, the policeman, began circling me like a hawk. He was a broad-shouldered, stately man, his hair standing upon his head like silver bristles, his face set off by a neatly trimmed spade beard. Watching me as if I were a goose being fattened for Christmas, he licked his lips.

"You're quite a reader, I hear," he said. "What kind of books do you read? *The Lives of Saints* or maybe the Bible?"

I told him I read both these books. This news surprised and disappointed Nikiforich.

"Ah yes, wholesome reading is lawful. But what about Count Tolstoy? Did you take a look into his books?"

I had also read Tolstoy, but not the writing of his that the policeman was interested in. "Those are the ordinary kind of books, such as anyone might write," said the policeman, "but I've heard that he stirs people up against the priests in some of his writings. If one could get hold of those books. . . ."

I had looked into those "writings," too, which had been run off on mimeographs; but had found them dull. Moreover, I knew better than to discuss such literature with a policeman.

After a few such passages in the street, the old man invited me to "have a bit of tea" with him in his post.

What he was after was no mystery, but I had reasons of my own for wanting to see him. I had consulted some people, and it had been decided that if I declined his cordial invitations it would only intensify his suspicions against the bakery.

And so I was a guest at Nikiforich's. One third of the wretched place was taken up by the oven, another third by a double bed curtained off with cotton print, and bulbous with pillows. The remaining space was occupied by a cupboard adorned with crockery, a table, two chairs, and a bench under the window, on which Nikiforich, his uniform unbuttoned, sat, blocking off the light and air. Next to me sat his wife, a roly-poly little woman of about twenty, with a bounteous bosom, pink cheeks, red pouting lips, and eyes of a curious violet tint that had a shrewd and corrupt look. Her voice had a sharp, petulant note.

"My godchild, Secheta, I hear, comes often to your shop," said the policeman. "She's a spiteful, depraved girl. All women are spiteful!"

"All of them?" asked his wife.

"There's no exception," Nikiforich insisted, and jingled his medals like a horse shaking his harness. He sucked up his tea and with equal relish, continued, "They're spiteful and depraved, all of them, from the lowest prostitute up to the queens. Take the Queen of Sheba who rode thousands of miles across the deserts to get into depravity with King Solomon. And the same with our Catherine, though they call her the Great." Then he went into the particulars of a stove-tender who rose, after one night with Catherine, to the rank of general. His wife, listening avidly, kept licking her lips and caressing my leg with hers under the table.

Nikiforich went on and on, from topic to topic, finding words savory to his wife.

"For instance, there's the student Pletnev."

His wife interjected, dreamily, "Not handsome, but nice!"

"Who?"

"Mr. Pletnev."

"He's no Mister to begin with. He'll get to be a Mister on graduation. Till then he's only a student and we've got those by the thousands. And what do you mean he's nice?"

"He's young and gay."

"So is a clown at the fair."

"A clown is paid to laugh."

"Hold your tongue. As for his being young every dog was once a pup."

"A clown is like a monkey."

"Hold your tongue. We've been through that already. Why don't you listen?"

"I've listened."

"That's better."

Having dealt with his wife he gave me the benefit of his advice. "Supposing you try and pick up an acquaintance with Pletnev—he's an interesting chap."

Realizing that he must have often seen me with Pletnev on the street, I said, "Oh, I know him."

"Is that so?"

It was clear that he was vexed by that. He jerked about and his medals jingled. On my part I was all ears because I knew Pletnev had been running off leaflets.

Nudging me under the table, the woman incited the old man, who puffed up like a peacock and fanned out the gaudy feathers of his oratory.

The nudges of his spouse distracted me, and before I could notice the change his voice lowered and became heavy with significance. "An invisible thread—get it?" and stared into my face, his eyes round with awe.

"We might compare the Emperor to a spider——"

"Heavens, what are you saying!" exclaimed his wife.

"Hold your tongue, dope. I'm saying this only to make something clear, you mare, not to slander! Take off the kettle."

And knitting his eyebrows, and narrowing his eyes, he continued, "An invisible thread, like a spider's, issues from the heart of His Imperial Majesty, the Emperor Alexander III. It winds, through all the ministers, through His Most High Excellency, the governor, and down the ranks to me and even the soldier in the ranks. Everything is bound together by this thread. In this invisible strength the kingdom of the Tsar is held together for all time. But the scheming English queen is bribing the Poles, the Jews and Russians, too, to cut this thread wherever they can, saying they are doing it for the sake of the 'people.'"

Leaning toward me across the table, he said in an impressive whisper, "Get me? That's it. Why am I telling you all this? Your baker thinks you're a right guy, and clever; he says you live by yourself. But the students are in and out of the place all the time and they sit up all hours of the night with the Derenkovs. If it were one visitor, that I could understand. But so many! Eh? I've got nothing against students. Today one of them is a student, tomorrow a district attorney. Students are generally a nice sort, but they're in a hurry to be somebodies, so the Tsar's enemies set them against the law. Get me? And this, further . . ."

But he got no further, for the door opened wide and a little, red-nosed old man with a bottle of vodka in his hand, the effects of which were already apparent, came in.

"How about shoving the chessmen around?" he said cheerily, and precipitated an immediate shower of small talk.

"My father-in-law," Nikiforich introduced him, sullenly.

In a few minutes I was making my farewells. The sly woman got in a pinch as she closed the door, saying to me, "Look how red the clouds are, like fire!" But there was only one cloud, and it was small and golden and vaporing out.

With no offense to my teachers intended, I must admit that the policeman explained the machine of state and its processes more clearly and factually to me than they did. Somewhere squats the spider; the spider reels out the invisible thread; that thread binds together the whole of life. The tough little loops of that thread were soon to be felt by me everywhere.

After the bakery closed that night, Derenkov's sister summoned me to her room, and in a matter-of-fact tone told me she had been instructed to query me about my talk with the policeman. "Oh dear, oh dear," she exclaimed in agitation over the account I gave her, and shaking her head, ran restlessly back and forth, like a mouse. "Does the baker try to pump you? Isn't his mistress related to Nikiforich? We must fire him . . ."

I leaned at the doorpost and looked at her furtively. The word "mistress" came too easily to her lips; I didn't like that. Nor did I like the idea of firing the baker.

"Watch yourself," she cautioned, and, as usual, she bewildered me with her clinging glance which seemed to ask questions I did not comprehend. She stopped now, faced me, and with her hands folded behind her back, asked me, "Why have you been so morose?"

"My grandmother died."

This seemed to amuse her and she smiled as she asked me, "Were you very fond of her?"

"Yes. Is there anything else?"

"No."

I left her, and stayed up working on verses of which I recall one defiant line: "That which you would appear, you are not!"

It was decided to cut down the students' visits to the bakery as much as possible. Not seeing them anymore, I could not consult them about unclear passages in the books I read, and I wrote down my questions in a notebook. Once, dropping off to sleep while I was writing, the baker read my notes. Nudging me awake, he asked, "What's this you've been scribbling? 'Why didn't Garibaldi chase out the King?' Who's Garibaldi? And when was it permitted to chase out kings?"

He slammed the notebook on the bin, found himself a cozy spot on the stove, and from there growled at me, "A fine business! Funny! You cut out that nonsense. So, a bookworm! In Saratov, such bookworms were caught by the cops, like mice, about five years ago . . . yes, sir. As if Nikiforich hasn't got his eye on you already! You stop chasing kings!"

His feeling for me was friendly, but I couldn't answer as I wished, having been instructed not to talk to him on "dangerous subjects."

Chapter Four

Aт THAT TIME A BOOK WAS BEING PASSED AROUND THAT WAS EXCITING a lot of controversy. I asked the veterinary, Lavrov, for a copy, but he said that was impossible. "But," he added, "I think there'll be a reading from it before a group and I may be able to take you along."

And at midnight, on Assumption Day, I tramped over Arskoye Field, trying to make out, in the darkness, the silhouette of Lavrov, who kept about fifty paces ahead of me. The field was empty, but just the same, I conducted myself with the "precautions" suggested by Lavrov, that is I whistled and sang, pretending to be a worker who'd had a drop too much. Among lazily gliding puffs of black cloud whirled the moon like a golden ball. Shadows mantled the earth. I passed puddles that gleamed like steel or silver. The sound of the town receded behind me to a sullen din.

At a garden gate behind the Seminary my guide stopped and I hastened to catch up with him. Silently we vaulted over the hedge, and crossed an overgrown garden, with the branches of trees, as we caught on them, showering large drops of rain on us. At the wall of a house we knocked at a shuttered window, which was opened by a bearded man who had been standing there silent, in the darkness.

"Who's there?" he asked.

"Jake sent us."

"Come in."

In the pitch darkness one felt the presence of a lot of people; one heard, besides, the rustle of clothes, the scrape of feet, the muted cough and whisper. A match flared up before my face. In its light I perceived some dark figures stretched along the wall.

"All here?"

"Yes."

"Pull down the curtains; make sure no light gets through the cracks in the shutters."

There was an angry grumble, "Whose idea was it to pick an abandoned house to meet in?"

"Sh—sh—quiet!"

A lamp in a corner was lit. The room was without furnishings except for two crates, straddled by a board on which five persons perched like crows; another upended crate served as the lamp stand. On the floor near the wall, three more were seated, with another one on the window sill, a long-haired young fellow, slim and very blond. Except for him and a man with a beard, I knew them all. In a low voice the bearded one announced that he would read from the pamphlet, *Our Dissensions* by George Plekhanov, "an ex-Narodnik." A muffled voice from the floor protested, "We know!"

All this mystification gave me a thrill—what is secret is always poetically exciting. I felt like a worshiper at early mass; I recalled the first Christians in the catacombs. The reader's low bass filled the room. He enunciated every word distinctly.

Another growl from the corner, "Rub-bish!"

Something glowed dully off in the darkness, a circle of copper. It called to mind a warrior's helmet. I realized it was the stove ventilator.

There were the reverberations of whispered conversation; in the ferment of heated words the speaker's words were lost. Above me, from the window sill, came the ironic question, "Is this a reading or not?"

It was the long-haired youth speaking. It silenced everybody and only the reader's basso was heard. There were flashes of matches; the red gleams of cigarettes lit up pensive faces, some with eyes half-shut, some wide open.

The reading seemed endless, it tired me, though I had been fascinated by the sharp words as they meshed easily and deftly into ideas that carried conviction. As the reader's voice broke off suddenly, the room immediately seethed with angry outcries,

"Renegade."

"A jingling of dross!"

"Heroes shed their blood and he spits into it!"

"This, after the execution of Generalov and Ulianov!" [16]

Again from the window sill the voice of the youth, "Gentlemen, instead of this swearing, how about some serious discussion?"

Discussions were not to my taste; I didn't know how to follow them. I found it hard to keep up with the antic leaps of excited minds, and debaters repelled me by their naked egotism.

Bending toward me from the window sill, the youth asked, "Aren't you Peshkov, the baker? I'm Fedosev. Let's get acquainted. There's nothing more here for us. This uproar will go on for a long while; and it won't amount to anything. Let's go, eh?"

[16] Brother of Lenin.

Fedosev was known to me as the organizer of a youth circle; his pale, intense face and his deep eyes attracted me. In our walk across the field, he wanted to know what friends I had among the workers, what books I had read, what free time I had. "I've heard about this bakery of yours. Strange to see you messing up your life like that."

I, myself, I told him, was fed up with it. He shook my hand warmly, as if pleased to hear this, told me he was leaving tomorrow, for three weeks or so, and would let me know when he got back, so we could meet again.

The truth was that as the bakery prospered my lot grew worse. My work piled up in the new building. In addition to my baking, it was I who made deliveries to the Seminary and to the Finishing School For Noble Maidens. As they fished rolls out of my baskets, the maidens fished in little notes, providing me with choice reading—sophisticated phrases set down in childish scrawls on dainty sheets of paper. It flustered me to be beset by this gay crowd of neat, clear-eyed girls, making cute faces as they burrowed into my heap of rolls. Watching them I tried to pick out the ones who had written the indecent expressions, perhaps, without understanding their lascivious sense. Recalling the squalid "houses of consolation" I wondered, Does that unseen thread, perhaps, reach from those houses, here?

Once I was stopped in the corner by a high-bosomed brunette with hair in a thick braid. In a hurried whisper she said, "Deliver this note for me and I'll give you ten kopecks."

Tears filled her dark, sentimental eyes, and she blushed to her ears and bit her lips as she waited for my decision. I refused the ten kopecks, but I delivered the note to the son of a judge, a gangling student whose cheeks had a consumptive flush. Absent-mindedly counting out half a ruble in change, he offered it to me and when I wouldn't take it carried it back to his trousers pocket, but missed, and the coins jingled on the floor. Looking distractedly at the rolling coppers, he wrung his fingers until the joints cracked, and mumbled with a sigh, "What should I do? I must think about it; good-by."

What he had to think over and to what conclusions that thinking brought him I don't know, but I pitied the poor girl. Not long after she was missing from the school. I ran into her again fifteen years later, teaching in the Crimea. She was consumptive and in her conversation on anything I sensed the bitterness of a cruelly thwarted life.

After delivering the rolls in the morning, I turned in for a nap. In the evening I had to be in the bakery to help to prepare and then deliver fresh pastries, just before midnight, to the shop opposite the theatre, to be ready for the crowd that swarmed in after the performance for snacks. After that back to the bakery to prepare the French bread, and kneading six to eight hundred pounds of dough is no joke! Another two to three hour nap; and up to make other deliveries. And this was my life—day after day.

Yet, my consuming purpose continued to be to spread goodness, reason, and enduring truth. Being a sociable soul, I wanted to share with others the harvest of my imagination, drawn from what I had experienced. I needed very little to turn a commonplace incident into an eventful story, taking for my starting point some unexpected twist of the "invisible thread." I had friends among the factory hands, Krestovnikov and Alafusov among them, and especially the old weaver, Nick Rubzov, a keen, nomadic sort who had worked in nearly every weaving mill in Russia.

"Today is the fifty-seventh year of my journey on this earth, Maxim, my boy, you little fresh loaf!" he would exclaim in a thick voice, his swollen eyes smiling behind glasses untidily fastened together by brass wires that left green lines of tarnish behind his ears and over the bridge of his nose. He was nicknamed "the German" by the weavers because he shaved his moustache down to a wisp and his beard to a gray tuft. He was of medium height but broad of shoulder. A sort of commiserating gladness radiated from him. He would cock his bald, bumpy skull to one side and say, "I like the circus. Think what they teach the animals, the horses! Makes me feel good. I esteem those beasts. I think that proves one may be able to teach man some sense, too. A lump of sugar is what the circus people use to inspire the beast; there's some at the grocer's for us, too. Sugar for the soul, a little love. So it's a pat on the head, my boy, not a club, that we should offer to people, not the club we're so used to."

However, he himself shunned kindness; he spoke to people with mockery and disdain. In discussions his expressions were curt and rude and obviously intended to wound his adversary. I first came upon him in a brewery where men had started to beat him; he had already received two blows. I intervened and escorted him to safety.

"Are you hurt?" I asked him, as we walked off in the dusk through an autumn drizzle.

"That! That wasn't anything," he replied. "But I say, why this respectful tone toward me?"

And so our friendship began. In the beginning I got only smart-aleck ridicule from him; but when I went into the part played in our lives by the "invisible thread," he said soberly, "You've got a head on you, you know! Imagine thinking that up!" And he took on a fatherly regard for me while showing me increased respect. "Your ideas, Maxim, you dear old owl, are right enough, but who's going to take stock in them? They're unprofitable."

"You take stock in them, don't you?"

"Me? I'm a homeless cur with a skimpy tail, but the others are watchdogs who pick up heaps of such weeds on their tails, as wives, children, accordions, hip boots; and they're devoted to their kennels. No, they won't take stock in anything else. We've seen something like that at the Morozov factory. The one in front gets his forehead whacked; and the forehead isn't like the behind; it aches for a long time."

He spoke differently after meeting up with Jake Shaposhnikov, the consumptive carpenter who worked for Krestovnikov. Jake, who played the guitar well, was still more accomplished as a Bible authority, and he dumbfounded Rubzov by his savage rejection of God. Spitting bloody shreds of his disintegrating lungs right and left, he exclaimed hoarsely, "First, I'm no image and copy of God; I know nothing; I do nothing; I'm not a good man. Secondly, either God doesn't know the misery of my life, or He knows and hasn't the power to help me; or He has the power and won't. Thirdly, God is not all-knowing, not all-powerful; He's no merciful one, either. In short, He is not! It's all a fraud; all life is a fraud; you won't take me in."

After his first benumbed surprise, Rubzov grew pale with rage and swore at him, but Jake silenced him with Bible citations and left him mute and hunched-up in thought.

Jake Shaposhnikov, when he got going, was frightening to look at. His face was dark and skinny; his black hair curled like a gypsy's. From between his blue lips flashed wolfish teeth. His black fixed eyes glared at his opponent. It was difficult to withstand those grim, unyielding eyes; he always made me think of the "mania grandiosa" case.

On the way back from Jake's, Rubzov said moodily, "I've never heard such a going against God. I've heard every kind of talk, but never anything like that! That man won't last long, poor chap. What a red-hot temper he's got!"

"But you found it interesting, eh?"

In no time he was fast friends with Jake. Now I found him agitated and restless, and continually poking at his swollen eyes. "So God's to be sent packing, hm," he said, with a leer. "As for the Tsar, my dear, the way it looks to me, he don't bother me. The trouble's not the Tsars, but the bosses! I can get along with a Tsar, even an Ivan the Terrible for that matter; he can squat on the throne as long as he likes; just give me a free hand otherwise. Do that and I'll weld you to the throne with gold chains; I'll give you my prayers."

After reading *Tsar Hunger* he exclaimed, "It's right, all of it."

The first time he saw a lithographed pamphlet he was deeply impressed. "Who sent you this? What clear handwriting. You must thank him!"

His thirst for knowledge was unslakable. He gave equally absorbed attention to Jake's devastating blasphemies and to my accounts from books. He'd laugh, his head back and his Adam's apple protruding, and comment admiringly, "What a wonder man's brain is!"

He read little, his eye trouble kept him from it, but he amazed me with his knowledge.

"There's a German carpenter who's so intelligent the king himself asks his advice." And it turned out he was referring to Bebel.[17]

"How'd you hear of him?"

He scratched his lumpy skull with his finger and said, "I know."

Jake ignored the rest of life, concentrating on his anti-God, anti-clergy diatribes, giving special attention to the monks. One day, Rubzov asked him mildly, "Why do you spend all your time growling against God, Jake?"

More savagely than before, Jake yelled in reply, "What else stands in my way? For nearly twenty years I was a believer; I endured everything. I lived in awe of Him. This and that was not for me to discuss. Everything was settled for us up there. I lived in chains. Then I began to read what's actually in the Bible and I saw through the put-up job it is. Man, it's all a put-up job!"

He made a gesture of tearing something in the air, tearing the "invisible thread," and concluded, "By all that, I'm hauled to an early grave!"

I had other friends to go to, among them my old comrades at the Semyonov bakery who always gave me a cheerful welcome and listened to me with absorbed attention. Rubzov, as it happened, lived in the Admiralty district, Shaposhnikov in the Tatar district, about three miles apart, which made visits to them something I could manage only infrequently. Since I had no place to invite them to, they could not

17 August Bebel, German Socialist leader and writer.

come to me. Moreover, the new baker, a retired soldier, hobnobbed with the police. Our yard abutted on the backyard of the police station and the "blue uniforms" were often over our hedge to fetch rolls for their captain and something for themselves. I was instructed, in addition, to stay out of sight in order to keep suspicion off the bakery. I could no longer consider my work here necessary. It also happened that the cash was drawn upon without consideration of the needs of the business. Often there was no money for the flour. Derenkov, gloomily pulling at his beard, said, "Bankruptcy ahead!"

Things were not going well for him. Red-haired Nastya was now "filled up"—as pregnancy was termed. Spitting like a cat, she cast at everyone and everything her green, irritated glance. She'd stalk upon Derenkov as if he weren't there and he, guiltily, would scramble, sighing, out of her way.

At times he sought my sympathy, "It's not proper. They walk off with everything. Only lately I bought myself half a dozen pairs of socks—and they're gone." This might have amused me as an anecdote were I not concerned over the efforts of this unassuming man who was trying to run a business in the interests of people who were heedlessly looting it. Derenkov did not look for their gratitude, but he was entitled to their friendly consideration and he was not getting it. In the meantime his family was rapidly collapsing about him. Suddenly his father fell into a religious mania; his younger brother became a habitué of saloons and brothels; his sister acted like a stranger in the house. She appeared to be launched on a dismal love affair with the red-haired student. Her eyes were often noticeably swollen with tears, and I fell to hating the student.

I thought I was in love with her, and at the same time, with the girl behind the counter in the bakery, Hope Shcherbatova, who was plump and red-cheeked, with a perennial smile abloom on her red lips. I was in love all over. My nature, my youth and all the conditions of my life impelled me toward a woman. I desperately needed a woman's fondness, or at least her friendly interest. To such a one I ached to talk unrestrainedly about myself, and thereby to make a clearing through my tangle of disconnected ideas, the wilderness of my impressions.

I missed real friends. There were those who looked on me as "raw material worth cultivating"; they had no real appeal to me; I could not be openhearted with them. If I touched on things that did not interest them, they curtly advised me to "leave that alone."

George Pletnev was arrested and hauled away to St. Petersburg, to the Kresti prison. I heard it first from Nikiforich, whom I ran into one morning. He was solemn about it. All his medals were on his breast, as though he had just come from a parade. He put his hand to his cap and passed me; then he stopped and called back to me, "Pletnev was arrested last night." He made a despairing gesture, and said in a lowered voice, "That boy's done for." And tears seemed to glisten in his deceitful eyes.

I knew Pletnev had expected to be arrested—he had warned me and Rubzov, whom he also knew, to keep away from him. Looking down, pensively, at his feet, Nikiforich added, "Why don't you come to see me any more?"

I paid him a visit that evening. He had just had a nap and was sitting up in bed drinking Kvass. His wife was at the window mending his trousers.

Scratching his broad chest, bristling with raccoon-like hairs, and looking at me calculatingly, he said, "So it goes. They arrested him. They found the pot in his room in which they prepared the ink to print their leaflets against the Tsar!"

He spat on the floor and shouted to his wife, "Give me my trousers!"

Without raising her head she said, "Just a minute."

Pointing to his wife, the old man went on, "She's sorry for him. She cries over him. I'm sorry for him, too; but what does a student set himself against the Tsar for?"

While dressing himself he said, "I'll be gone a minute . . . the pot, you—!"

His wife stared unheedingly out of the window until he was gone; then she brandished her fist at the door and hissed wrathfully, "Skunk!"

Tears had swollen her face and her left eye was blackened and closed. Jumping up, she went to the stove and bent over the kettle, and screamed, "I'll give it to him yet! I'll have him howling like a wounded wolf. Don't trust him, don't trust a word of his; he's out to trap you. He's a liar, and he has no heart. He knows about all of you. That's his life, trapping people."

She came close to me, and with a pleading voice said, "Give us a kiss, will you?" I found her repulsive, but there was such hungry longing in her eyes I put an arm around her and caressed her coarse hair, tangled and grimy.

"Who's he after now?"

"A roomer on Fisher Street. You want names, too! Watch yourself or I'll tell him you're pumping me! He's coming back—the only one I know by name is Pletnev." And she hurried back to the stove.

Nikiforich brought out a bottle of vodka, some bread and jam. We sat down to tea. Marina, beside me, served me with exaggerated solicitude, her good eye searching my face, while her husband declaimed, "That invisible thread goes deep in the heart, in one's bones. Try to snap it! The Tsar's a God to people!"

Then he turned to me, "Now, you're a well-read man. You've read the Bible, eh? Do you think everything it says there is right?"

"I don't know."

"To my mind there's much there that's superfluous. A good deal of it. About beggars, for example. Blessed are the beggars, it says. What are they blessed with? That could go out. And all the stuff about the poor. You have to see the difference between the poor and those who become poor. The one who's poor is no good, but with the one who becomes poor it might be a case of hard luck. That's the way to look at it. That's the best way."

"Why?"

He was silent for awhile, studying me. Then he said, distinctly and with conviction, as if he had thought it all out, "Compassion is an unhealthy feeling and there's too much of it in the Bible. That's my opinion. Compassion puts us to big expense for useless people who even infect others. Poorhouses, jails, asylums. The help should go to strong, healthy people so their strength shouldn't be wasted. Instead our help goes to the weak, as if a dwarf could be made over into a giant! Because of this foolishness the strong are weakened and the feeble sit on their backs. That's what ought to be looked into. Change that! It must be acknowledged that the course of life and the notions of the Bible have nothing in common. That's how Pletnev ruined himself. Compassion; give to the poor and the students go under. Where's the sense in that?"

I hadn't yet heard these ideas put in such direct terms, though I had come across them before. Such ideas are stronger and more widespread than we realize. Some seven years afterwards, coming upon Nietzsche, I was reminded of the Kazan policeman. As a matter of fact, I seldom came upon an idea in books that I have not previously encountered in life.

The old trapper of men went on, rapping his finger on the desk in cadence with his words. His face wore a frown, and he looked intently, not at me, but into the mirrorlike brass of the kettle.

"Better start now. It's late," his wife interrupted, several times. He did not heed her, but winding word after word on the spool of his thought, he suddenly set a new one turning. "You're a clever chap, you can read; is it right for you to be a baker? You could have done much better serving the Tsar's realm in another manner."

Through his talk I kept thinking, how to get word to the people on Fisher Street that Nikiforich was after them. The roomer was a certain Serge Somov, a man just back from exile in Yalutorovsk, of whom I'd heard enough to excite my interest.

"Clever people must swarm together, like bees in a hive or wasps. The Tsar's realm——"

"It's nine o'clock already," said the woman.

"Damn it!" said Nikiforich and got up, buttoning his uniform. "I'll take a cab to save time. Good-by. Remember, you're welcome here any time."

Leaving his house, I resolved never to have tea again with Nikiforich. He revolted me despite the intriguing turns of his ideas. His views of the sickliness of compassion boiled in me and penetrated deep into my mind. Feeling some truth in them, it was repugnant to have them come from a policeman.

Ethical discussions were frequent; one of them, particularly, put me into a ferment. A Tolstoyan appeared in town, the first I had ever met, a tall, sinewy, swarthy man with a black goat beard and thick lips. He had a stooping walk, and his eyes sought the ground. Sometimes, brusquely throwing back his bald head and with a passionate glitter in his dark, moist eyes, he would start ranting. His glance snapped with rancorous flames.

There was a gathering in a professor's apartment, young people mostly, and among them a slender, fastidious little priest whose black silk robes showed off his handsome pale face to advantage. An aloof little smile flickered from his cold gray eyes.

The Tolstoyan went on at length, about the unchanging and eternal truths of the Bible. His voice was somewhat choked up, his sentences were clipped; and the words had a harsh ring, though one felt the intensity of a true faith in them. A didactic, rhythmic gesture of his hairy left hand timed his words; his right hand was deep in his trousers pocket.

"An actor," someone whispered to me.

"Yes, histrionic, true enough."

I had just finished reading a book by Draper, I think, on the Catholic offensive against science. The man before me seemed to me another of those violent believers in the salvation of the world through overpowering love, who are prepared, in their passion to save people, to flay them and burn them alive.

His clerical dress set him apart from the others. He ended his sermon with the cry, "Are you on the side of Christ or on the side of Darwin, tell me!"

He pitched his question, like a stone, into the group of young people who looked at him with a sort of frightened admiration. His speech seemed to have startled everybody; they sat silent with bent heads. Looking around him with a burning glance, he added sternly, "Only Pharisees can seek to reconcile these two opposed ideas, shamelessly lying to themselves and corrupting others."

At this the priest got up, daintily threw back the sleeves of his cassock, and with a condescending smile and a venomous sweetness said, "Evidently you hold to the vulgar notions of the Pharisees, that are as unfair as they are vulgar——"

To my amazement, he set up the Pharisees as honorable men, the true guardians of the sacred Hebrew scriptures and argued that the people had always been with them. "For instance, take Flavius Josephus——"

The Tolstoyan leaped to his feet, cut Josephus down with his gesture, and shouted, "Now, too, the people march in the ranks of their enemies against their friends, but they march against their will, driven and betrayed. Who cares about your Josephus!"

The discussion had now been scattered in unrelated bits by the little priest and the others. "Truth is *Love*," shouted the Tolstoyan, his eyes gleaming with hatred and contempt.

These words intoxicated me, left me too shaken to grasp the concepts they reflected; the earth seemed to reel under me in this tornado of words; and in my despair it seemed to me nobody could be duller and stupider than I. I saw the Tolstoyan mop the sweat off his purpling face; I heard him shout, "Cast off the Bible, ignore it. That way you will not lie! Re-crucify Christ! That would be more sincere!"

And all this set before me the contradiction: If life is an unending struggle for happiness on earth, do not compassion and love stand in the way?

I learned the name of the Tolstoyan—Klopsky—and where he lived, and went to see him the very next evening. He lived in a nearby country house owned by two young girls. I found him in the garden, sitting with the two girls at a table under a huge, shady lime tree. He was in white—white trousers and white shirt, out of which bristled a swarthy chest. This long, weathered, awkward figure in white fitted my notion of the wandering apostle, the bearer of truth.

From a silver spoon he was swallowing milk and raspberries, showing how he relished them by smacking his thick lips and puffing the white drops, after each spoonful, from whiskers as sparse as a cat's. One of the girls stood at the table serving him; the other, her hands folded to her breast, leaned against the tree dreamily staring into the dry, hot sky. In identical lilac dresses the girls looked remarkably alike.

Willingly and even graciously he dilated to me upon the creative powers of love. That feeling ought to be nourished in one's soul as the only one capable of "fusing man with the spirit of the world"—with the love which permeates all life.

"Only by this can a man be won. Without love life is incomprehensible. Those who say struggle is the law of life are blind and doomed. Fire is not overcome by fire, evil is not overcome by the powers of evil."

However, as soon as the girls went off, arm in arm, toward the house, he asked me, looking after them through half-shut eyes, "But tell me, who are you?"

On hearing my story, he drummed on the table with his fingers, and said, a man was a man in any station of life, he should not strive to change it; instead he should foster in himself love for people. "The lower a man's status the nearer he is to the roots of truth, to life's holy wisdom."

I had my doubts about his share of the holy wisdom, but was silent. It was clear that I bored him. The look he gave me was one of distaste, he yawned, he stretched his arms behind his head, he stretched out his feet, he shut his eyes as if ready to drop off with exhaustion, and muttered sleepily, "Complete submission to love is the law of life."

He came to with a start, put out his hands as if clutching at something in the air, and looked at me almost in fright. "Forgive me. I'm tired."

Again he shut his eyes. His teeth came together in what looked like a grimace of pain. His lower lip hung down, and the upper lip rose up and his thin, bluish whiskers stiffened.

I left him feeling inimical toward him and suspicious of his sincerity.

Some days later, delivering rolls to a doctor friend of mine, a drunken bachelor, I came across Klopsky again. He must have had no sleep the night before, because his cheeks were ashen and his eyes puffed and red. He appeared drunk. The fat little doctor, dissolved in a crying jag, was on the floor in his underclothes, in a litter of displaced furniture, beer bottles and clothing. He had a guitar in his hands and, rocking to and fro, howled, "Let the gates of mercy be opened to us."

Klopsky's angry response was, "Mercy, bah! Love will turn us to stones; or we will be crushed struggling for it. Just the same, we're doomed."

Hauling me into the room by the shoulder, he said to the little doctor, "Ask him what's he after! Ask him, is he looking for love for people?"

The doctor laughed, as his watery eyes recognized me. "He's the baker. I owe him money." Striving to keep his balance, he fumbled for a key and handed it to me. "Open up and take what you want."

But the Tolstoyan snatched it from me and showed me to the door, and saying, "You'll get what's coming to you later," he flung the rolls I had brought upon a couch in the corner.

I was glad he didn't recognize me. From that encounter the memory I brought away, in addition to my revulsion, was his idea of man doomed by love. I heard, shortly after, that he had declared his love, in turn, to each of the two girls in whose house he lived. Confiding a joy to each other that turned immediately into hatred for the lover, the sisters, through their servant, ordered him out of the house and he vanished from town.

The meaning of pity and love in human existence, this complex and tormenting problem confronted me early in life, first as a vague, but corroding, sensation of spiritual disharmony, then in a question whose terms were definite and distinct: What role does love play?

All my reading had been filled with Christian and humanist ideas, calls for brotherly feelings toward others, urged by the best people I knew at the time, with eloquence and fervor. But what passed before my eyes was far from brotherly. The life that stretched before me was an unbroken chain of hatred and cruelty, an unending, sordid struggle for trifles. For myself I only needed books; no other possessions had value in my eyes.

I had only to sit in the doorway for an hour to discover that cab-men, porters, workers, officials, merchants and so on, led a life different from mine and from that led by the people I esteemed; that they had other goals and walked different paths. Those whom I esteemed and trusted in were shoved aside and unwanted in the squalid, cunning, bustling ant life of the majority; a life that struck me as irrational to the point of absurdity and deadly dull. And I observed that compassion and love in people were often voiced, but seldom acted upon, in daily life.

I was taking all this rather painfully. One day the veterinary, Lavrov, jaundiced and bloated with dropsy, panted, "Cruelty should be made so familiar that it becomes a bore, like this unbearable autumn." Autumn had come early and wet and cold, thriving with diseases and suicides. Lavrov was poisoning himself with drugs in preference to being suffocated by dropsy.

"He healed animals and died like one!" was the epitaph pronounced upon him by the tailor, Mednikov, with whom he roomed. A wizened little devotee, who knew all the apostrophes to the Virgin by heart, Mednikov used to flog his seven-year-old girl and eleven-year-old boy and crack his wife on the shins with a bamboo cane, and then protest, "The judge who sentenced me said I smuggled this system from the Chinese, and I never saw a Chinese in my life except in pictures."

An apprentice of his, a morose, bandy-legged man for whom "Doon-kina's husband" sufficed for a name, used to say of his boss, "It's these meek, pious ones I'm leery of. The man who lets himself fly into a temper reveals himself and you can get out of his way; but the meek one creeps up on you like a snake in the grass and gets his fangs into the exposed part of your soul. It's the meek who are dangerous." And "Doonkina's husband," himself a meek, cunning spy, and Mednikov's pet, spoke a truth he exemplified.

Occasionally, it seemed to me, the meek and mild ones soften the petrified core of life and make it fruitful; but oftener, contemplating their numbers, their pliant adaptability to evil, the fickle elasticity of their changeable souls, and their whinings, I felt like a horse tethered under a swarm of gnats. All this came to my mind as I walked off from the policeman's.

The wind moaned; the light flickered in the street lamps; but it seemed to be the dark, shuddering, gray sky that sowed over the earth an October drizzle as fine as dust. A soaked streetwalker was hauling a tearful drunk by the hand, who was muttering something woeful; and

the woman was replying mechanically, in a tired voice, "Such is fate."
And I thought, "I, too, am hauled into corners, into mess and
misery, and am confronted with confused people. How tired I am of
it all!"

Probably those were not the words that then came into my mind,
but I know that this idea entered my mind on that dismal night and I
felt then, for the first time, weariness of soul and a corrosive mold
over my heart. How I suffered after that hour, with what a cold, hostile,
alien, sidelong glance I looked at myself thereafter!

On nearly every man I saw the awkward, shapeless huddle, not
merely of contradictory actions, but of contradictory feelings; and this
witless game depressed me. What made it worse was that I felt it overcoming me. I was being pulled in all directions, toward women, toward books, toward workmen, toward roistering students; and I was
getting nowhere; I was "neither here nor there." I felt myself turning
somersaults to an invisible smoking whip, cracked over me by a strong,
invisible hand.

Jake Shaposhnikov, I heard, had been taken to a hospital, and I
went to visit him. As I entered a fat, spectacled, crooked-mouthed
woman in white from under whose white kerchief large red ears protruded, told me off-handedly, "He's dead."

When I did not leave at once, but stared at her, she flew into a
temper and yelled at me, "What more do you want?"

I fell into a rage, too, and called her a dope.

"Nikolai, come put this man out."

Nikolai, who had been polishing some brass rods, laid one of them
across my back. I toted him by the scruff of the neck out to the street,
and deposited him in a puddle before the door. He remained unsur-
prised and calm through this treatment; and giving me an intent stare,
he rose and said, "You dog."

I went to Derzhavin Park,[18] and on a bench under the poet's statue
I felt an overpowering desire to commit some foul and shameless act
for which people would rush at me, giving me a pretext to punch somebody. But though it was a holiday the park was deserted; it was left
to the wind, which was swirling the dead leaves and flapping the unglued
edges of the poster on the lamppost. A blue, translucent, icy twilight
descended on the park. The towering bronze image loomed above me.
As I looked at it I thought: Here on earth lived a lonely man, Shaposhnikov, devoting all his spiritual powers to the extermination of

[18] Named after the poet, Gabriel Derzhavin, a precursor of Pushkin.

God. Now he is no more, having died a common, ordinary death. There is something in this offensive and unbearable. And that idiot, Nikolai, ought to have put up a fight and called the police and had me stuck in jail.

I went to see Rubzov. I found him at a table mending his vest in the light of a small lamp.

"Jake just died," I told him.

The old man raised his hand in which he held a needle, as if to cross himself, but only gave a little wave of despair. He looped the thread around something, swore some indistinct, but expressive, oaths, and muttered, "We'll all die; that's the foolish custom, my boy. He's dead, and another man I know, a brass worker, is done for, crossed out. It was last Sunday, a cop got him. I met him through George. A bright chap. Used to pal with the students. I hear the students are on strike; are they? Could you put some stitches into this vest? I can't see a thing."

He handed me the ragged vest and the needle and thread, and folding his hands behind him, marched up and down the room, coughing and growling, "Now and then, in one spot or another, a light flares up. The devil blows it out and things are dull again. What a miserable town! I'll get away from it while the ships still navigate." Stopping and scratching his head, he asked, "But where to? I've been all over; I'm worn out."

He spat on the floor and said, "What a confounded life! You search and you find nothing to please body or soul!"

He stood in silence in the corner by the door, as if he expected to hear something. Then he came back to the table and sat at the edge.

"Maxim, my boy, Jake was wrong to use up his big heart reviling God. Neither God nor king will reform if I renounce them; one should rather be furious with himself and repudiate this odious life. Were I young—I'm going blind, it's terrible! You've fixed it? Thanks. Let's go out for tea."

On the way, stumbling as he held on to my shoulder in the darkness, he said, "Take my word for it, some day the people will come to the end of their patience and in their rage they'll finish with everything, they'll grind all this trash into the dust. They'll come to the end of their patience."

We never had our tea. We ran into a siege of a "house of consolation" by a gang of sailors, who were being kept off by factory workers guarding the gates.

"Every holiday there's a free-for-all, here," said Rubzov, with animation. Recognizing some friends among the factory workers, he took off his glasses and plunged into the fray with them, cheering them on with, "Steady there, you factory boys. Crush these frogs, come on, finish these cockroaches!"

It both alarmed and amused me to watch the agility and ardor of the old man as he shouldered his way through the sailors and longshoremen, parrying their blows and butting them over with his shoulder. The brawl was carried on for the joy of it, as an outlet for overflowing strength; there was no rancor in it.

At last, under the impact of the massed, struggling bodies at the gates, there was a sound of cracking timber and above it the cry, "Beat up the bald one!"

Two men climbed to the roof where they sang lustily:

> "No robbers, thieves or tramps are we
> But men of the river and the sea "

Police whistles blew and brass buttons flashed and mud spattered, and from the roof came:

> "We dry our nets on river shores,
> On merchant sheds and coachhouse doors."

"Hey, you don't hit a man when he's down!"
"Watch yourself, old man! What bruisers!"

Rubzov and I and five others, enemies and friends, were hauled off to the police station, and from the pacified shadows of that autumn night, these cheerful strains escorted us:

> "Now the forty beasts are trapped,
> In whose furs the rich are wrapped."

"What swell people the Volga folks are," exclaimed Rubzov rapturously, and spat and blew his nose. Then he whispered to me, "Make a breakaway. Pick the right time and beat it. No need to stew in the police station!"

Along with a tall sailor we broke away in a side street, scrambling over hedge after hedge. That was the last I saw of my dear, clever, old friend, Nick Rubzov.

Life got still more grim. The student riots were beginning, but I could not make out what for. There was bustle and spirit in it, but the drama of it escaped me. It seemed to me that in return for the joy of studying at the university one could endure anything. Had I been told, "Go and study but every Sunday, on Nicholas Square, you'll have to take a beating with wooden clubs!" I would readily have agreed.

One day I overheard the workers at the Semyonov bakery planning a raid on the students. "We'll give it to them with the balance-weights!" they said, with sadistic glee. I argued and swore at them, and suddenly felt spent. I was drained of the wish and the words to defend the students. I stumbled out of the cellar like a cripple, a mortal grief and yearning in my heart. That night I sat on the banks of the lake pitching stones into the black water, with four words incessantly repeating themselves in my mind, What shall I do?

In my despair I began practicing on the violin, sawing away in the shop at night and incensing the watchman and the mice. I was fond of music and went at my lessons with enthusiasm. But one day my teacher, who played in the theatre orchestra, took advantage of my stepping out of the shop a moment and opened a drawer of the cash-register that I had neglected to lock, and stuffed his pockets with money. I came back in time to catch him. Submissively turning to me his out-stretched, dull, clean-shaven face, he said in a low voice, "Go on and slap me." Big, oily tears dripped from his colorless eyes and his lips quivered.

To prevent myself from striking him, as I wanted to, I sat down on my fists. Sitting thus I ordered him to return the money to the drawer. Having emptied his pockets, he stopped at the door, and in a high-pitched voice that had a desperate and idiotic sound, begged for ten rubles.

I gave them to him and that ended my music study.

In December I decided on suicide. I have tried to visualize my motives in the story, "An Incident in the Life of Makar." The attempt was unsuccessful. The story turned out awkward, unpleasing and without inward truth. All the data are there but they sound as though they were told by and had happened to somebody else.

Chapter Five

I BOUGHT THE REVOLVER FROM A REGIMENTAL DRUMMER. IT WAS loaded with four cartridges. I aimed at what I thought was my heart, but struck a lung. Within a month, feeling ashamed and foolish, I was back at the bakery. But not for long. One late March evening, returning from the bakery I found a man called the Khokhol (Ukrainian) in my room, sitting at the window drawing on a cigarette and watching the smoke coils that he exhaled.

Wasting no time on salutations, he asked, "Have you some time?"

"About twenty minutes."

"Sit down. Let's talk."

As always he wore a tight, black, leather jacket. His fair beard sprayed over his broad chest and his short-cropped hair hedged a stubborn forehead. From his thick peasant boots came a strong tar smell.

"How about coming along with me?" he said a cool, quiet voice. "I'm at the village of Krasnovidovo, about thirty miles down the Volga. I run a shop there and you can help me; it won't take much of your time. There's a good collection of books, and I'll help you in your studies. How about it?"

"Yes."

"I'll expect you on Friday at the Kurbatov pier. Ask for Vassily Pankov's boat from Krasnovidovo. I'll meet you there. So long!"

Getting up, he stretched his broad palm to me. With the other he pulled a large silver watch out of his breast pocket. "We've taken only six minutes. By the way, my name's Michael Romass."

And without another gesture, out he went, his firm tread carrying his powerful, well-built body with ease.

Two days later I was on my way to Krasnovidovo. The Volga ice had just broken. Gray rounded blocks of it coasted on the heaving water. Rammed by the flat-bottomed ship, they splintered into jagged crystals. A strong wind rolled a high surf over the shores. The sun's radiance rebounded from the bluish mirrors of the ice. The ship had its set; it carried a heavy cargo in barrels, sacks and crates. At the wheel sat the young peasant Pankov, smart in a sheepskin coat with a multi-colored braid facing. Silent, looking out with cool, steady eyes, his calm face had little of the muzhik in it. At the ship's prow, with legs spraddled, stood his workman, Kukushkin, a tattered little peasant whose ragged overcoat was belted in with string and who wore a soiled priest's hat. His cheeks were seamed and spotted with scratches and welts. As he prodded ice blocks off with his long boat hook he roared, "Hey you, scram!"

Sitting beside me on crates under the sail, Romass said to me, in a low voice, "I'm no pet of the peasants, especially the kulaks.[19] And of course you'll come in for a share of that ill feeling."

Kukushkin, resting his hook across the bows, commented, "It's the priest who's the worst."

"Right," agreed Pankov.

"You're like a bone in the throat of a bad-tempered dog."

"But I have friends, too, and you'll make friends too," the Khokhol reassured me.

I shivered. It was cold. The March sun gave little warmth. Kukushkin filled his pipe and started philosophizing, "You're not the priest's wife, of course. According to the motto of his profession it's one's duty to love everybody."

"Who gave you that beating?" asked Romass. "Some skunks had it in for you!"

Kukushkin gave a contemptuous snort. "Nuts!" he said. "But once the artillerymen got me alone and beat me. That was some scrap, I can tell you. Don't know how I came out of it alive."

"Why did they beat you?"

"When? Do you mean yesterday or that time with the artillerymen?"

"Yesterday."

"Who knows? Our people are like goats. They go for you if you only touch them. You'd think they were all prize fighters."

"Your tongue probably got you the beating. Watch yourself."

"I'm an inquisitive man; I ask questions. I get a thrill hearing anything new."

The ship creaked in all its timbers as it took a hard blow, head on, from an ice floe. Kukushkin picked up his hook as Pankov exclaimed angrily, "Tend to business!"

A good-natured bickering between them followed while Romass told me, "This soil is poorer than our Ukrainian soil but the people are superior. A handy lot!"

I gave him rapt attention, trusting his every word. I was calmed by

[19] The wealthier peasants who employed others and lent money at usury.

his serenity, his extraordinarily balanced way of speaking, so plain, yet so weighty. I felt myself in the presence of a man of experience and independent judgment. I appreciated his sensitiveness in avoiding any questions about my suicide attempt, though that would have been one of the first questions any other man would have put to me, and the matter had become a bore to me. The question was hard to answer. Why had I wanted to kill myself? The devil knows! My explanation to the Khokhol would probably have turned out devious and ridiculous. I preferred not to think of it anymore.

It was so nice on the Volga, everything shining and free. We sailed downriver. The spring waters flooded the lower left bank, covering the sandy shores of the pastureland. The water topped the bushes and merged with the clear spring torrents, coursing down the gullies and slopes of the earth. Young rooks reflected the rays of the smiling sun from feathers like black steel and croaked noisily as they worked at their nests. Where unobscured spots had caught the loving force of the sun, bright green shoots of grass pierced sunward through the earth. One's body is chilled, but one's soul hums with a restrained joy budding with luminous hopes. How resplendent earth is in spring!

As through a dream the voice of the Khokhol reached me, "There's a fisherman there whom I'm sure you'll like."

We arrived at Krasnovidovo at noon. On a steep hilltop rose the blue dome of a church and from it, sturdy, well-built huts, spread along the ridge their yellow planks gleaming and looking decorative under their embroidery of thatch. It was simple and lovely. Sailing past it on ship I had often admired that village.

Joining Kukushkin in unloading, Romass passing the sacks to me, said, "You're a hefty one, boy," and added, looking away, "Chest give you any trouble?"

"Nothing at all."

I was grateful for the tact behind this question; the last thing I would have wanted was to have the peasants hear of my suicide attempt.

A tall, thin peasant, taking long, sliding strides through pools that sparkled like silver, came down the slope. He was barefoot; a shirt and trousers were all his clothes. His beard was curled like an apostle's and his hair was matted into a thick, red cap. At the shore he raised a friendly shout, "Welcome!"

He picked up two thick poles, leaned them against the moored ship, and leaping aboard, took charge. "Bear hard on the rods so they don't

slip under," he said, and beckoned to me, "Here, lad, give us a hand."
Strong and handsome, he made a picturesque figure. On his ruddy
face above his large straight nose his blue eyes flashed authoritatively.
"You'll catch cold, Isot," said Romass.
"Don't worry, not me."
As we rolled a barrel of kerosene to the shore, Isot looked me over
and asked, "A clerk?"
"Trade a few punches with him!" Kukushkin suggested.
"I see someone's been pecking at your nose again!"
"What can one do about them?"
"About whom?"
"Those bullies——"
"You're hopeless," sighed Isot and turned to the Khokhol.

It was noticeable that Isot treated him with friendly, but slightly
patronizing concern, though Romass could have been ten years his
senior.

Half an hour later, I was at my ease in a neat, homey room in a new
hut whose planks were still odorous of resin. An agile, bright-eyed
woman was setting the table. Romass unpacked some boxes of books
and stood them on a shelf near the stove.

"Your room's in the attic," he said to me.

From the attic window a section of the village was visible, and the
tops of the bathhouses among the bushes in the ravine above which
our hut perched. Beyond stretched the gardens and plowed fields merg-
ing in velvety folds as the eye rested on the blue forest that crowned
the horizon. Astride one of the bathhouse roofs was a peasant in blue,
one hand holding his axe, the other shading his eyes as he looked
absorbed into the Volga waters below. There was the creak of a cart on
the path, the far-off lowing of a cow, the lisp of brooks. An old woman
in black came through the gate and cried, vehemently, "I hope you
croak!"

Hearing her, two boys, damming a brook with stones and mud, ran
away and she, picking up a sliver of wood, spit on it and flung it into
the water. She wore high boots and with one of them kicked over the
boys' engineering and strode down to the river.

How am I going to live here?

We were called to supper. Isot, sitting at the table with his long,
red feet outstretched, stopped talking when I entered.

"Go on!" said Romass frowning.

"That's all. You've heard everything. It's our decision to take matters in our own hands. You must have a revolver on you, or at least carry a stick. We must keep secrets from Barinov; he and Kukushkin are as loose-tongued as women. And do you care for fishing, boy?"

"No."

Romass talked about organizing the peasants and small orchard owners to break the grip of the produce speculators.

Isot took it all in, then said, "You'll have trouble with the 'men of peace,' you can be sure."

"That remains to be seen."

"No doubt of it!"

Watching Isot I thought: He is the sort of peasant the writers Karonin and Zlatovratsky deal with.

Had I come upon something real; would I have men of action to work with at last?

Isot, his meal finished, said, "Mike, take it easy. Nothing good can be hurried. It must be done in its own good time."

After he left, Romass said ponderingly, "A sharp, straightforward fellow. What a pity he had no education. He can just barely read. But he sticks at it. You must help him with it."

We stayed up far in the night while he showed me his stock and listed the prices. "I undersell the two other shopkeepers in the village. Naturally they resent it. They use dirty tactics and mean to maim me, if necessary, to get me out. I stay on not because I like it or am making any money; I have other reasons. My idea is something like the one at the bakeshop."

I had guessed as much, I replied.

"What's there better to do than spread the light of reason?"

The shop was locked, but on the street someone, seeing our lamp, was tramping about in the mud and, now and then, mounting our doorstep.

"Do you hear that? That's Migun, a boozer and a beggar, a vicious beast to whom mischief comes as naturally as flirting to a pretty girl. Careful what you say when he's around."

Afterwards, having lit his pipe, leaning against the stove, with his eyes half-shut, he blew smoke rings through his beard and with slow, deliberate words told me that he had been watching me misspending my young years. "You have gifts," he said, "you have high ambitions and a determined nature. You should be learning but not in such a way that books shut you off from people. A little old religious dissenter once said to me and correctly, 'All knowledge comes from man.'

The teaching done by people is harsher and more painful than the teaching in books, but such teaching sinks in."

He mentioned the idea, now familiar to me, that our first duty was to activate the mind of the country. Yet, the familiar words, as he spoke them, had a new and deeper meaning.

"They're so full of love for the people, your student chaps. What I'd say to them is, 'You can't love the people.' Phrases, that's all it is. Love for the people!" His laugh rippled in his beard, he took a sharp look at me, then rose and paced up and down as he spoke to me very earnestly. "To love is to acquiesce to everything, to indulge the beloved, to resent nothing. That is womanish. With the people, can one overlook ignorance, condone their mistakes, indulge all their pettinesses, absolve them of all their cruelties? Can you?"

"No."

"So. There you all sit reading and chanting Nekrasov,[20] but you won't get far, you know, with Nekrasov. Here's how to stir up the peasant. My dear chap, you're not a bad guy as you look at it; but you're living a hell of a life. You can't do anything by yourself to improve it, make it something worthwhile. There's something more rational in the way an animal looks after himself; he's certainly more independent than you are. Everything comes out of you, out of the simple peasant; the aristocracy, the bishops, the professors, the tsars—peasants once, all of them. See? Understand? Learn how to live so that no one can put anything over you."

Going into the kitchen he asked the woman to put on the kettle, then showed me his books—works on science, most of them, Buckle, Lyell, Hartpool, Lecky, Lubbock, Taylor, Mill, Spencer, Darwin, and the Russians Pissarev, Dobroliubov, Chernychevsky, Pushkin, Goncharov's *The Frigate Pallas* and Nekrasov.

His broad palm over them, he gently stroked them like kittens. With animation he said, "These are good ones. Here's a rare one—ordered burned by the censor! Read it if you want to know what makes a state."

The book he handed me was Hobbes' *Leviathan*.

"Here's another about the state, but done more lightly, in a gayer style." It turned out to be Machiavelli's *The Prince*.

Over the tea he gave me a brief sketch of himself. His father was a blacksmith at Chernigov. His first work was at the Kiev Railroad

[20] A poet, author of *Who Can Be Happy or Free in Russia*, very popular with the Narodniks, or Populist Party.

depot, as an oiler. There he fell in with some revolutionists. His first activity was organizing a workers' study circle. He was caught, jailed two years, then exiled to Yakutsk [21] for ten years.

"At first living among the nomad Yakuts I thought it was all up with me. The winter there is enough to literally freeze your brains. But brains there are no use for anything. Then I learned that other Russians, a few, were also marooned there. And to keep them from getting homesick the government was kind enough to send in others for company. One of them was the student Korolenko; he's also back by now. We were together for awhile, then separated. We're alike in too many ways and friendships don't thrive on similarities. He was earnest, persistent and good at all kinds of work. He even painted icons, which I couldn't stomach. Now I hear he writes for the magazines, and writes well."

We talked on till midnight. I gathered his aim was to win me immediately and solidly to his side. It was the first time I felt so soberly at ease with anyone. My suicide attempt had lowered my self-esteem. I considered myself a nonentity. My guilty conscience made me ashamed to live. I think Romass divined this and simply and humanly invited me into his own life, and thereby helped me to get adjusted. I shall never forget it.

On Sunday, after church, we opened the shop and immediately peasants crowded our door. Matthew Barinov was the first to arrive, an unwashed, unkempt man with the long arms of an ape, but handsome, almost feminine, eyes that had a romantic, faraway look.

"What's the word in town?" he asked after the greetings, but wouldn't wait for an answer. He railed at Kukushkin, "Your cats have made a meal of another rooster." He went on to say that the governor had gone to Petersburg to petition the Tsar to transport the Tatars to the Caucasus or to Turkestan. He commended the governor. "A clever chap. He knows the score."

"You're making that up," Romass exclaimed.

"Me? You have no faith in people," and Barinov shook his head reproachfully. "I sympathize with the Tatars. It's no cinch in the Caucasus."

A skinny, timid little man approached in an obviously borrowed, ragged coat. A tic distorted his face, pulling his lips open on a sickly smile, and plaguing his left eye with an incessant wink that made the gray, scarred eyebrow above throb.

[21] A remote district in Northeast Asia.

"Welcome, Migun," mocked Barinov, "What did you steal tonight?"

"Your money," Migun answered in a singing voice, and doffed his cap to Romass.

Our landlord joined us and our neighbor Pankov in a red neckerchief, a vest, spanned by a silver chain as long as a harness, and sport shoes on his feet. Measuring Migun with an angry glare, he said, "You old devil, if you keep plundering my orchard I'll stick a pole into you."

"There it goes again, the same old talk," replied Migun, unabashed. "We can't live without knocking each other!"

As Pankov continued reviling him, he said, "Old devil you call me. I'm only forty-six."

"Last Christmas you were fifty-three," said Barinov. "You yourself said you were fifty-three. Why these lies?"

The grave, bearded old peasant Suslov came along and the fisherman Isot—about ten people altogether. The Khokhol sat on the doorstep smoking his pipe, listening to the talk of the peasants perched on benches and steps.

Migun and Kukushkin were now amicably arguing the profound question, who was the tougher fighter, landowner or merchant. Kukushkin favored the merchant, Migun the landowner, and his vibrant tenor silenced the stuttering speech of Kukushkin.

"There was old Fingerov who gave Napoleon Bonaparte's beard a yank. And young Fingerov, why, he could grab two men by the scruff of their necks, and knock their foreheads together. And that did it. The two were out cold."

"Sure, that'll make anyone lie down," said Kukushkin. "But, anyhow, the merchant eats more than the nobleman."

Good-looking Suslov, from the top step, complained, "The peasant has lost his balance. They had to be steady when they had masters—everybody tied down to his job."

"How about a petition to return you to serfdom?" answered Isot.

Romass looked up, but was silent. He knocked the ash out of his pipe, against the stair rail.

It was for what he would say that I was waiting. I carefully followed the disconnected remarks of the peasants, and tried to anticipate what he would reply. It seemed to me he had already missed several good openings. But he heard them out without comment, sitting as still as an icon, and watching the wind wrinkle the puddles and sweep up the clouds into one dense, gray pack. A ship was straining up river; from below girls shrilled a song to the notes of an accordion. A drunkard, staggering down the street, hiccoughed and grunted. His legs kept crossing each other, tripping him into the puddles. Slower became the speech of the peasants; sadness came into it like an undertone. The gentle melancholy infected me, too, perhaps because the bleak sky forbode rain and I was nostalgic for the many-toned hum of the city, the flood of people in the streets, their energetic speech and the pour of words that stimulated the mind.

Over tea I asked the Khokhol when he found time to speak to the peasants. "What about?" he asked. And having heard me, replied, "Why, man, if I talked on that subject I'd be on my way back to Yakutsk."

He filled his pipe, lit it, puffed a cloud around him, and spoke quiet words that I carried in my memory. He found the peasant discreet and suspicious. The peasant is doubtful of himself, of his neighbor, and above all, of every stranger, he said. It's scarcely thirty years since he's been granted his freedom. Every forty-year-old peasant was born a serf and has only too fresh a memory of it. What freedom is, he finds hard to comprehend. One's first notion of freedom is to live as you like. But soon you're aware that life is hedged around by the authorities, that everyone stands in the way. The Tsar took the peasantry away from the landowner, and now he's the boss. So what then does freedom mean? Someday the Tsar will explain. The peasant has a strong faith in a Tsar who commands the earth and its riches. In the same way as he took the peasants from the landowners he may take the ships and shops of the traders. The peasant is a Tsarist to the extent that he knows too many cooks spoil the broth. He looks forward to the day when the Tsar will proclaim the meaning of freedom! *Take all you can!* The peasants wait for that moment, yet dread its arrival. So they live in anxiety, worried lest they miss the chosen day of a general confiscation. And he has inner fears. He wants so much, there is so much to reach for, and how is he to get at it? They're all out for it. And all around are the numberless bureaucrats, inimical to the peasant, and for that matter, to the Tsar. But they must be put up with for without them what a brawl there would be!

The wind dashed a spring shower against the windows. The street filled with gray mist, and something as dim and gray settled over my mind. The low, even voice continued:

"It should be suggested to the peasant that he can take the power, in time, out of the Tsar's hands into his own; that the people should get the right to choose officials from among themselves, the whole lot of them, policemen, governor, Tsar . . ."

"But that might take a century."

"So what! Did you think you'd have it all settled by Christmas?"

Later he went out. About eleven I heard a shot fired nearby. I rushed out in the rain and darkness and saw Romass' burly, black figure approaching the gate, taking his time as he avoided stepping into puddles.

"I did the firing," he replied to my question.

"At whom?"

"Some people came at me with sticks. I said let me go or I'll shoot. They wouldn't leave off so I fired into the air, which harmed nobody."

Standing in the anteroom, taking off his clothes, wringing his dripping beard and snorting like a horse he said, "My shoes are going to pieces, damn it! I must change them. Do you know how to clean a revolver? Do it for me or it will rust. Rub some oil over it."

His impregnable serenity and the resolute, yet gentle, look in his gray eyes filled me with admiration. Combing his hair at the mirror in the adjoining room he warned me, "Careful when you're out in the village, especially at night and on holidays. They may go after you, too. But no stick; that's a challenge to the bullies and may be taken for fear. There's nothing to fear. They're a rather cowardly lot."

I began a splendid life in which every day brought something fresh and significant. Greedily I absorbed books on natural history, of which Romass used to say, "Fix this in your mind before anything else and better than anything else; the best of man's intellect is contained in this science."

Isot came to me three evenings a week for reading lessons. Mistrustful and sarcastic at first, he paid me the compliment, after a few lessons, "Your explanations are clear. You ought to become a teacher, my boy."

One day he suggested, "They talk about your strength. Let's get a stick and see who's got more muscle."

We got a stick in the kitchen and sitting on the floor, sole to sole, tugged at the stick, each trying without success to pull the other up. The Khokhol looked on, smiling and urging us on.

Isot applied himself and did quite well, and expressed himself, strikingly, about what he was discovering. Sometimes, in the midst of the lesson, he'd reach up, take a book down from the shelves, toil through a couple of lines, his eyebrows tense with the strain. Then with a flush, he'd look up at me, saying with amusement, "Damn it, here I am, reading!"

He was charmingly and touchingly ingenuous, even childlike; and I found in him, more and more, the good-souled peasant of the books. There was a strain of poetry in him as in all fishermen. He loved the Volga and the still nights; he enjoyed solitude and revery. Looking at the stars he asked, "The Khokhol says that up there, there may be life. What's your opinion? Suppose we signaled them and asked how they live? Perhaps they have a happier and better life . . ."

On the whole he appeared to be a contented man. Though he was an orphan and a pauper, his fisherman's life was a secure and independent one. But he had an animus against the peasants and counseled me, "Don't be taken in; they're not good-natured; they're shrewd and deceitful. They'll show one face to you today, another tomorrow. None of them cares for anything outside his own skin; and each one tries to get out of his social obligations." With a rancor strange in this warm-hearted man, he cursed the rich, the devourers.

Women ran after this sturdy, handsome man. "I'm lucky there," he confided. "It makes the husbands sore; and if I was in their boots I'd swear, too. But how can you hold off a little kindness to a woman who can be a second soul to you? Her husband lets her live without a heart, without a sign of feeling; he lets her work like a horse—that's her life; he has no time to give her—while I have all the time in the world. In their first year of marriage she has already felt his fist. I know it's a sin to play with her . . . 'Just don't let it make hard feelings among you,' that's one thing I beg the women. 'Don't be jealous of each other; there's enough of me to go round. I play no favorites; I'm good to all alike.' "

With a jovial smile, through his beard, he went on, "Once, you know, I nearly had a lady. She was a summer vacationer from the city. What a beauty; skin white as milk, hair fair as flax, and such kind, blue eyes. I sold her fish, and I couldn't help staring at her."

" 'What do you want?' she asked.

" 'That's easy to guess,' I answered.

" 'Wait till tonight. I'll come to you,' she said.

"And she did. Only the mosquitoes interfered. They were at her all the time, and it was no go. 'I can't,' she said. 'They bite me all over,' and she was nearly in tears over it. The next day her husband, a judge, arrived.

"And that's your ladies," he concluded reproachfully, "letting mosquitoes get in their way!"

Isot was full of praise for Kukushkin. "You'll see—he's a good sort! They're wrong not to like him. He lets his tongue wag—that's true, but then, who doesn't?"

Kukushkin had no land. His wife drank. She was a workingwoman, a small, but strong and evil, little beast. He had rented his own hut to the smith, and lived at the bathhouse. Newsmongering was his passion. When there was none to pass around he invented it, unbelievable yarns all strung on the same thread. "Have you heard, the Tinkov cop is joining a monastery. 'Damned if I'll go on hounding the peasants,' he says, 'if that's to go on, to hell with being a cop!'"

Gravely the Khokhol commented, "Watch out, there won't be enough officials to take care of you." Kukushkin pondered this dilemma, scratching hay, straw and seeds out of his tousled flaxen hair.

To the village Kukushkin was a nobody. His eccentricities and his fabrications incited the peasants to curses and mockery. Nevertheless they listened to him and their attention showed that they divined some truth behind his fantasies. The steady people called him "beggar" and "empty head," but Pankov, the fashionplate, regarded him as "a mystery."

Kukushkin was a good all-around workman, a cooper, a stove-mender, a beekeeper. He could also carpenter cleverly and give women pointers on the breeding of chickens. And though he resisted work and was slow, whatever he took on turned out well. A cat-lover, he kept about ten fat ones, of all sizes, in his bathhouse.

He once used to read but forgot how and didn't bother to re-learn it. Naturally keen, he was always the first to get Khokhol's point. "So," he said, with the puckered face of a child receiving a dose of bitter medicine, "So Ivan the Terrible wasn't bad to ordinary folk."

He, Isot and Pankov used to drop in, evenings, often staying on till midnight, listening to the Khokhol's accounts of the origins of the earth, of life in foreign parts, of revolutionary upheavals. Pankov's favorite was the French Revolution. "Life took a real turn there," he said.

Pankov had rented his hut to Romass and defied the village Croesuses by adding the shop to it. He was indifferent to their resentment and spoke of them with contempt. He found the country life irksome. "Had I any kind of profession I'd live in the city."

Very tidy, always carefully groomed, he bore himself with self-conscious dignity. He had a wary and suspicious mind.

Pankov's first feeling toward me was cool, even hostile. Sometimes he used sharp, bossy language to me. He soon stopped but I felt in him a hidden residue of distrust. On my part, I cared little for him.

Well can I recall the evenings in the neat little room with whitewashed walls. Windows shuttered, a lamp on the table, and sitting before it a man with a high forehead, close-cropped hair and a full beard, saying serenely: "Man should get as far away as he can from the beast; in that idea you have the meaning of life."

Three peasants sat around turning sharp eyes and shrewd faces upon him. Isot sat still as if following an inner meaning communicated to him alone. Kukushkin fidgeted as though beset by mosquitoes. Pankov, twisting his blond moustache meditated, "So, no matter what, the people had to separate into classes."

I was touched that Pankov never had a rough word for his workman, Kukushkhin, and listened to that dreamer's fantasies.

After the discussion I went up to my attic and sat at the open window, gazing at the sleeping village and the silent fields. The stars that pierced the night's darkness were further from me the nearer they approached the earth. The quiet constricted my heart with awe, while my mind floated in infinite space and brought to my vision thousands of villages hugged as tightly as this, to the earth. Everything around me was still and serene!

All the joylessness of village life became clear to me. I have read and been told that country people lead a more wholesome and honest life than townspeople. But what I saw was unending drudgery that wasted and exhausted the peasants. Few were happy. The city workers' life was no less toilsome but there was more gaiety in it, and their grievances were not given such dreary and savage expressions. The peasant's life appeared far from simple to me. It called for close attention to the soil and wary subtlety in their relations with others. There was heartiness in their life; and the cultural level was low. The villagers seemed to live like the blind. Groping in shadows, they were in perpetual fear, and they distrusted each other. The touch of the wolf was in them.

I found it hard to understand their stubborn hostility to the Khokhol, Pankov, all "our people" who tried to live rationally. I became keenly conscious of the superiority of the town, of its urge toward happiness, of its bold quests for knowledge, of the abundance of its ambitions and hopes. And on nights like that two townsmen reappeared in my memory:

F. KALUGIN and Z. NEBEY

Watchmakers; Also repairs on all kinds of surgical instruments, sewing machines, music boxes, all makes, and other mechanisms.

The legend could be seen over the narrow doorway of a little shop. The door was flanked by two windows coated with dust, and inside one of them sat F. Kalugin, with a yellow swelling on his bald pate and a magnifying glass cupped over his eye. He was corpulent and had a moon face creased with an untiring smile or open in song, disclosing a round mouth concealed beneath a bristling gray moustache; all this as he probed into watchworks with tiny pincers. Inside the other window sat Z. Nebey, whose hair was curly and black, and who had a big beaked nose, eyes like big plums, and a goatee. Stringy and tall he looked like Mephistopheles.

He too was busy putting miniatures together, and surprised you with sudden outbursts, in a low bass voice, of "Tra-la-la-la-la." Back of them loomed a chaos of chests of drawers, mechanisms, curious wheels, globes, instruments; the shelves were piled with metal articles of varied shapes; and the walls were hung with clocks, their pendulums swinging away.

I could have spent all day watching them but my tall frame cut off their light and they grimaced at me and waved me away. I used to leave with the envious thought, What happiness there is in knowledge! Such people command my respect. To be adept in the mysteries of any mechanical apparatus, to be able to repair anything on earth—that's people for you!

But the country did not appeal to me and the peasants were beyond me. Their illnesses were the chief theme of the women. "Something" within them, "rises up to the heart" or "presses on the chest" or "gripes the stomach." They told you all without reticence as, on holidays, they sat before their huts, or on the riverbank. They were bad-tempered and on edge and cursed each other. Over a twelve-kopeck jug three families wielded poles on each other, broke an old woman's arm and a boy's shoulder. Such rows were a weekly affair.

The boys fooled around with the girls openly and cynically. Getting hold of a girl in the field they tied up her skirts over her head. It was called "making her a flower." Naked to the waist, the girls cursed and howled, but they obviously relished the game since they were slow to untie their skirts. At evening mass the boys pinched the girls' behinds, as though that was what churchgoing was for. One Sunday the priest yelled from the pulpit, "You swine. Pick another place for your indecencies!"

"I suppose people in the Ukraine have a more poetic feeling for religion," said Romass. "What goes under the name of faith in God, here, is only the crude instincts of greed and fear,—no real love of God, no adoration of His power and grace. That may be all the better, make it easier for them to rid themselves of religion which, you may be sure, is all unhealthy fantasy."

The boys here were braggarts and cowards. They already had had three tries at beating me, without success. Once they managed to hit my foot with a stick. I said nothing about it to Romass, of course, but seeing me limping, he understood what had happened.

"So you got a little surprise, as I told you."

Though he had advised me against going out at night, I sometimes walked to the Volga through the orchards and, sitting under the willows, I watched the river below and the pastures beyond, through the transparent web of night. The gold of the invisible sun, reflected from the deserts of the moon, gilded the slow and majestic current. I had no fondness for the moon. Something sinister in it provoked me, like a dog, to a howling melancholia. The knowledge that its light is not its own, that it is a dead planet on which there is not nor ever can be life, gave me pleasure. Up to then I had imagined it to be populated with a metalplated species, made of linked triangles, who gyrate like compasses, and sound like crashing churchbells rung at Lent.

Watching the embroidered band of light quivering in the current till it was borne off into the darkness, disappearing in the black shadows under the steep bank, I felt my mind growing firmer and keener. It made me feel strangely light as my mind filled with thoughts inexpressible in words, and unrelated to the events of my day. The stately current was almost soundless. On its broad dim path glided a ship, like an enormous bird with feathers of fire. It passed with a deep murmur, like a flutter of great wings. A spark seemed to float beside the low bank where the pastures lay and toward which it cast a long, red ray. It was a fisherman and his tow line but it had the look of a homeless star, lost from the sky, hanging over the water like a burning flower. What one has found in books has a fantastic growth in fanciful ideas. The tireless imagination weaves design after design of matchless beauty. One feels the soft air to be a part of the river and feels himself afloat in it. Usually Isot joined me. In the night he loomed larger than by day and even more attractive.

"Here again?" he asked, seated himself beside me and lapsed into a long silence, absorbedly watching the water and the sky and stroking the fine silk of his golden beard.

"I'll learn all I can, read all I can; then go up and down the rivers, and everything will come clear to me. And I'll teach it to others, I will. Boy, it's a good thing to share one's soul with others! Even women understand, some of them, if it's soul to soul you talk with them. A while ago one of them I had in my boat asks me: 'What'll happen to us when we die? I don't believe in heaven or hell.' Hear that? Boy, they too are . . ." Searching the right word he was silent a moment, then concluded, "living souls."

Isot was a nocturnal soul. He was remarkably responsive to beauty everywhere and he gave expression to it, magically, in the manner of a wondering child. He had an untroubled belief in the God of the church, imagined Him as a stalwart, handsome old man, a wise and kind-hearted master to the world, Who fails to overcome all the evil in it only because "there's too much He's got to do; too many folk to take care of. Just the same

He'll get around to it. As to Christ, He's beyond me. What can I do about Him? There's God, so what more do I need? And there's the Son besides. Why the Son? God isn't dead yet."

Generally Isot sat perfectly silent, deep in his thoughts, now and then murmuring with a sigh, "That's how it is."

"What?"

"Oh, about myself."

Another sigh, another absorbed glance into the depths of space. "How wonderful life is."

I agreed, "Wonderful!"

With velvety power the dark waters streamed past. Over it arched the silver bow of the Milky Way, the stars flashed like golden birds and gently the heart, defying reason, chanted its surmises on life's mystery. Far off, beyond the farthest fields, the light of the sun rayed out from ruddy clouds. There it was, the peacock tail spread across the sky.

"Wonderful thing, the sun!" exclaimed Isot, with a happy smile.

Chapter Six

THE APPLE TREES BEING IN BLOSSOM, THE VILLAGE WAS BANKED IN ROSY drifts whose sharp fragrance, penetrating everywhere, overbore for a time the odors of tar and manure. The hundreds of flowering trees seemed swathed in pink satin for a party. The rows stretched straight from hut to field. Under the moonlight, in the gentle breeze, the mothlike blossoms rustled delicately, and the whole village seemed to be washed by rolling, gold-blue billows. The nightingales poured out their passionate and continuous melody while by day, the starlings teased, and the unseen larks serenaded the earth, with their tender and tireless chant. On holidays girls and young women promenaded, singing, opening their mouths like fledgling birds, and intoxicating men with their languorous smiles. Isot's smile also appeared drunken; he looked emaciated, his eyes sunken inward; and his face turned handsomer as it became graver and more saintly. He slept all day, venturing out only toward evening, a gentle and preoccupied look on his face. With coarse but affectionate humor Kukushkin railed at him and Isot, with a shy smile, begged him to stop, and then went on, rapturously:

"How delicious life is! How good to be alive! What things the heart can say! Things that will remain with you till death; that will come forth first from your memory, on resurrection day!"

"Look out or those 'things' will get you a beating from the husbands," smilingly cautioned the Khokhol.

"They have a right to that," said Isot, nodding.

Joining the nightingales, every evening, the high-pitched, nervous voice of Migun rose from gardens, fields and riverbanks. His were good songs, beautifully rendered, and on that account the peasants forgave him much.

Our shop became a Saturday night rendezvous for him and old Suslov, Barinov and the smith Krotov, who would soon be deep in discussions. When one left, another took his seat, and so it went on till midnight. Some would drink too much and start rows, particularly the war veteran, Kostin, who had lost an eye and two fingers. Rolling up his sleeves and waving his fists, he swaggered up like a fighting cock, shouting: "Hey, you Khokhol, you son of the Turkish heathen! You soul of a heretic! You tramp! Answer me, what's in your heart?"

In reply he heard, "Why did you blow off your fingers? Got scared of the Turk?"

As Kostin rushed in to the attack, the laughing, shouting men picked him up, and pitched him, head first, down the ravine; from there he howled, "Help! Murder!"

Crawling out, covered with dust, he demanded vodka from the Khokhol. "What for?"

"For the fun you got out of me," replied Kostin, raising a hearty round of laughter.

Once, on a holiday, the cook had gone out in the yard after having started the oven.[22] I was sitting in the shop when I suddenly heard a sound like a giant's sob, from the kitchen; the whole place shook; tin caramel boxes slid from the shelves; glass tinkled from broken windowpanes and the floor throbbed like a drum. I rushed into the kitchen, from which black clouds of smoke were eddying and where something was hissing and crackling.

"Stand back!" shouted the Khokhol, grabbing me by the shoulder.

In the doorway the cook howled, "The idiot!"

Romass plunged in through the smoke; there was a rumbling sound; then we heard him swearing, "Stop that confounded racket! Fetch some water!"

On the kitchen floor were smoldering firewood, one still brightly aflame,

22 Most ovens were wood burning.

and scattered stove bricks. The black mouth of the stove was bare as if it had been swept out with a broom. Groping through the smoke for a bucket of water, I doused the burning stick on the floor and pitched the wood back into the stove.

"Careful!" said the Khokhol, pulling the cook back into the room. "Lock up the shop!" he ordered. "Careful, Alex; it might go off again!"

Kneeling down, he examined the round pine pieces, plucking them out of the stove where I had pushed them.

"What are you doing?" I asked him.

"Here it is!" he exclaimed, handing me a log, hollowed out and blackened within.

"You see! The devils filled it with gunpowder! But the idiots! As if a pound of the stuff can do any damage."

He put the wood aside. Washing his hands he said, "A good thing Axinia went out or she'd have got hurt."

Through the thinning smoke we could see that the glass of the shelves and the windowpanes had been shattered, and some bricks had been torn out of the mouth of the stove. At the sight of this damage Khokhol's serenity rather shocked me. He showed no indignation over this stupid joke, while, out in the street, boys were bawling, "Fire! Fire at the Khokhol's!"

A woman's shriek came from somewhere, outside, while from the shop Axinia cried, "They're breaking in!"

"Take it easy," replied Romass, drying his beard on a towel. We could see through the shattered window, hairy faces wild with fear and anger, their eyes screwed up against the smarting smoke. A shrill, hysterical voice was urging, "Let's run them out of the village. One scandal after another!"

Mumbling and making the sign of the cross, a small red-headed peasant was trying to work himself through the window. An axe was in his right hand and his left hand was convulsively grabbing at and slipping from the window sill.

"Where are you going?" asked Romass, holding the hollow log in his hand.

"To put out the fire."

"But there's no fire."

The peasant, gulping, disappeared. Romass went to the doorway, and exhibiting the log, said, "One of you stuffed gunpowder in this and put it in our woodpile. But there was too little to do any damage."

Watching the crowd, I heard the peasant with the axe saying, "And when he waved the log at me . . ."

The tipsy Kostin shouted, "Away with him, the heretic! Take him to the judge!"

The rest were listening to Romass in skeptical silence.

"To blow up a place like this you need more gunpowder, about forty pounds. Now get out of here."

There were cries of, "Where's the sheriff?" "Get the police."

The crowd took its time scattering, hanging back as if leaving something cherished behind. We sat down to tea and, as she poured it, Axinia, in an unusually soft mood and giving him a sympathetic look, said to Romass, "As long as you don't complain they'll keep up with their mischief!"

"Doesn't it infuriate you?" I joined in.

"Why let this nonsense upset you!"

If everybody took things so serenely!

The next thing he was telling me of his plans to go to Kazan and asking me what books I wanted him to bring me. There were times when I thought the man had clockwork instead of a soul, and wound up to go for life. My love and admiration for the Khokhol were deep, but I longed to see him get into a temper with me or anyone, to hear him shout with fury and stamp his feet. But he was incapable of such rages. When some meanness or softishness annoyed him, he contracted his gray eyes to a mocking squint and made a curt and cutting remark. Once he asked Suslov, "How is it that you, a grandfather, haven't yet learned to play an honest game of cards?"

The old man's sallow forehead and cheeks slowly flushed to a purplish tinge; even the white hairs of his beard seemed to blush to the roots.

"You don't really gain by it; and you forfeit the respect of people."

With bowed head Suslov admitted, "I gain nothing by it; that's true."

And later he said to Isot, "There's a spiritual leader for you! If only we had such people in the government!"

Briefly and clearly, Romass counseled me on what to do in his absence. He appeared already to have forgotten the explosion, as another man would have forgotten the bite of a fly.

A visitor, Pankov, looked at the stove, and asked concernedly, "Did you get a fright?"

"What of?"

"It's a declaration of war, isn't it?"

"Sit down; have some tea."

"Can't; my wife's waiting."

"Where have you been?"

"With Isot. Fishing."

On his way out through the kitchen he repeated gloomily, "It's a declaration of war."

His conversation with the Khokhol was always in short sentences, as though they had long ago talked themselves out of weighty subjects. I remember a conversation about Ivan the Terrible.

"A gloomy Tsar," Isot began.

"A butcher," said Kukushkin.

"Nor much brains," said Pankov. "So he killed all the princes. But he put mobs of small noblemen in their place. And what's worse, foreigners. No sense to that. A small landowner's worse than a big one. You can't shoot a fly with a rifle, so a fly can annoy you more than a wolf can."

Kukushkin brought in a bucket of wet clay to mend the stove. While smearing the loosened bricks back in place, he muttered, "They've got no brains, these devils. Their lice they can't get rid of, but they're always ready to exterminate a man. Better not bring in a large stock of goods at once. Better a little at a time. Otherwise they'll set fire to your stuff. There's bound to be trouble over the thing you've arranged."

To the Kulaks in the village the "thing" was a great irritant. It was a cooperative of the fruit growers. The Khokhol had organized it; and Pankov, Suslov and several others of the more alert peasants had come in with him. As a result, Romass' stock had risen in the village; more customers came to the shop. Even "good-for-nothings" like Barinov and Migun gave the Khokhol a hand in the venture.

I was drawn to Migun, drawn by his melancholy but beautiful songs. Singing them he shut his eyes and peace came to his martyr-like face, relieving its distorting tic. The dark of the night was the time he felt at his best, moonless nights when thick layers of cloud hid the sky. Some evenings he would whisper to me, "Let's go to the Volga." There, after setting forbidden fishlines off the stern of his boat, he dipped his deformed, stained feet in the dark waters. Then he would mumble his complaints: "When somebody important pushes me around, I take it. He's a big shot and knows more than I know. But when he's a peasant, no better than I am, can I take it? What's the difference between us? He counts rubles, I count kopecks—that's about all."

His face contorted, his eyebrows twitched, and his fingers ran over the tackle, feeling the lines, and filing the hooks. Then he went on:

"'I'hey take me for a thief, and I admit that's what I am. But who isn't? They all plunder each other, suck and gnaw at each other. It's not God, it's the devil who loves us!"

The black river crawled below; the black clouds floated above; and the shores with their meadows were lost from sight between them. Discreetly the waves fingered the sandy shore; my feet felt their pull toward the fathomless flood of darkness. And I heard Migun's plaintive protest, "One must live!"

A dog's mournful howl descended from the hill. As in a dream I pondered, Why do you live as you do?

On the river everything was still, dark and eerie. The warm darkness seemed infinite.

"They'll kill the Khokhol, and you, with him, if you don't watch your step!" muttered Migun and, suddenly, gently, started singing, "My mother, she loved me; my mother, she said, 'Live in peace, darling, and keep your head.' "

His eyes shut, his voice grew sadder as it rose, and his fingers in the tackle moved more slowly: "I did not listen, I gave no heed . . ."

A strange sensation overwhelmed me, as if earth, unbalanced by the movement of black and fluid space, had overturned, and I had slid off into the darkness, where the sun has set forever.

Having ended his song as suddenly as he had begun it Migun soundlessly launched his boat in the water, and, sitting down in it, vanished without a sound in the shadows. I looked after him, thinking again, To what end do such people live?

I was on good terms, too, with Barinov, a lazy, absurd, bragging, scandalmongering, restless vagabond. Of Moscow, where he had lived, he spoke with loathing. "A hell of a place; a mockery! It has fourteen thousand and six churches and a population of swindlers! And they all have the itch; on my word, they all twitch like horses! Merchants and officers and ordinary folk, every man of them, walk about scratching. And it's true they have a big gun there, they call the Tsar-Cannon, and a huge piece it is. Peter the Great, he cast it himself to fire at rioters. A noblewoman raised a revolt against him, driven by disappointed love. After he lived with her seven years, to the day, he went off, leaving her with three children. It made her mad and a rebellion started. And didn't he give them what-for, with that cannon. One shot and down went nine thousand three hundred and eight of them! It frightened Peter himself and he said to the Archbishop, Philaret, 'Let's plug up the damn thing!' to avoid temptation. And they plugged it up."

When I told him "that's nonsense," he became resentful. "What crust you have! I got this straight from a learned man, and you . . ."

This is how he described Kiev, where he had gone to see the saints: "That town's like our village. It's also up on a hill, and it's on a river, but I can't recall its name. A puddle compared to our Volga. It's a tangled-up town, I tell you. The streets are all crooked and they all go uphill. The people are Khokhols, not of the true blood like Romass, but a half-Polish, half-Tatar race. They don't talk, they cackle. An uncombed, unwashed folk. The frogs there weigh about ten pounds apiece and the Khokhols eat them. They ride on oxen and they plow with them, besides. Remarkable beasts they are; the smallest is about four times the size of ours—seven tons each, in weight. The monks there number fifty-seven thousand, and the bishops two hundred and seventy-three—How can you contradict me, you fool? I've seen it with my own eyes; and you, were you ever there? No! that's enough. My dear chap, I put accuracy above everything!"

Barinov liked figuring. I had taught him to add and multiply, but he hated division. He did complicated multiplications with ardor, boldly disregarding errors. Having carved a long line of ciphers in the sand with a stick, he contemplated it with awe, with round, childlike eyes. "Who can even say such a number!" he exclaimed.

Though he was clumsy, unkempt and tattered, his face was almost handsome and his blue eyes, above his roguishly curling beard, had a child's open smile. He reminded me of Kukushkin and probably because of the resemblance they kept apart.

Barinov raved about the Caspian Sea where he had fished. "It's like nothing else, the sea. Next to it you're a speck. You look at it and you feel yourself disappear. Life is good there. All kinds of people, once even an archbishop was there, and he workd, too, along with the rest. There was a cook there, who'd been a judge's mistress. You'd think that would satisfy her. But, no. She couldn't stand being away from the sea. 'I'm really fond of you, your honor,' she told the judge, 'but good-by, just the same.' And back she went to the sea. Whoever's been to the sea is pulled back to it. There's room there. You don't feel crowded. It's like the sky. I'll be going back there, to stay. I feel crowded out with so many people around. I ought to have gone off to the desert, like a hermit. But where have you got a decent desert around here!"

In the village Barinov was despised like a homeless dog, but his stories were a delight to listen to, like Migun's songs.

His stories even mixed up practical people like Pankov. That suspicious peasant told the Khokhol one day, "Barinov says a lot about Ivan the

Terrible has been kept out of the books. He says Ivan the Terrible could turn himself into anything. He turned himself into an eagle and ever since they've stamped the figure of an eagle on money, to commemorate it."

How often I've observed that the strange and the fantastic—the further from reality the better—has a far greater appeal to people than any account of sober reality.

The Khokhol, when I told him that, laughed and said, "But they get over that. Let them learn to think and they'll find their way to the truth. And the dreamers, the odd ones like Barinov and Kukushkin, you have to understand them. They're artists, inventors. Christ must have been one like that. And some of the things he made up, you must admit, weren't bad."

To my surprise, all these people made little mention, and then hesitantly, of God. Old Suslov alone used to interject with conviction, "Everything is from God!" For me those words always sounded a note of helplessness.

It was good living among these people, and there was much I learned from our nights of talk. Every question put by the Khokhol seemed to root itself in the substance of life, like a strong tree in earth, and in these living depths, to entwine with the roots of other trees; and ideas blossomed on the boughs and memorable words flourished like fine leaves. I felt myself growing, stimulated by the intoxicating nectar of books. I could speak with more assurance and won the Khokhol's smiling praise, "Bravo, Alex, you're getting there."

Sometimes Pankov brought his wife, a little woman with a demure face, but a shrewd look in her deep blue eyes. She wore a store dress. She sat unobtrusively in a corner, her lips modestly pursed, at the beginning. But soon her mouth and her eyes would open wide in wonder and apprehension. At a spicy remark she would cover her face with her hands and laugh in embarrassment. Then Pankov would wink at the Khokhol, "You see, she got that!"

Sometimes there would be mysterious guests whom Romass would confer with in the attic. There Axinia served them food and drink. They slept there, too, unseen by anybody but myself and the cook, whose devotion and worship for Romass were doglike. Isot and Pankov would ferry them in their boats by night, to a passing ship, or to the port of Lobishki. From the hilltop I watched the beanlike boat gliding on the black, or when there was a moon, silvery river. A lantern hung aloft to signal the captain of the ship. Watching thus, I felt myself to be a participant in some weighty and mysterious enterprise.

Sometimes Maria Derenkova also came in from the town. I did not now find the look in her eyes which had formerly so troubled me. Now her eyes were those of a young girl, confident of her charm and pleased that the big bearded man was in love with her. His words to her were as quiet and as ironic as to the others; but he gave his beard more frequent strokes and a warmer light gleamed from his eyes. She was all in blue, with a blue ribbon in her blond hair, and her lovely voice had a merry ring. Her hands were like a child's and strangely restless, as though seeking something to grasp. As she fanned her soft, rosy face with a handkerchief, she kept humming wordless music. Something in her disturbed me anew, angered me and roused my hostility. I avoided her whenever possible.

In mid-July Isot disappeared. The talk was that he was drowned, and this was confirmed a few days later. About five miles below the village his boat drifted ashore. Its bottom was stove in and its stern was smashed. The explanation given of the accident was that Isot must have fallen asleep in the boat, which, as it floated down, was sucked into the wash of the three barges that rode at anchor some four miles from the village.

At that time Romass was in Kazan. In the evening Kukushkin came to the shop, sat gloomily on some sacks, staring at his feet. Then, lighting a cigarette, he asked, "When is the Khokhol due back?"

"I don't know."

Uttering curses of unusual violence in a voice that sounded like the growl of a dog with a bone in his throat, he rubbed his bruised face hard with his palm.

"What's the matter?"

He gave me a strange look and bit his lips. His eyes were bloodshot, his jaws quivered. Seeing that emotion prevented him from speaking, I knew he had bad news and awaited it with anxiety. At last, with an effort, stumbling over the words and staring into the street, he said, "I've been to the boat, with Migun—Isot's boat. The hole in the bottom was made with an axe. Understand? That means Isot was murdered. Murdered. Murdered, I'm convinced of it!"

His head shook, he strung one curse upon another, and was scalded within, with boiling, unshed tears. Growing silent, he crossed himself. To see his need to sob and his inability to satisfy it was unbearable to watch. Unable to let go, he sat trembling, suffocating with grief and rage. Then, shaking his head, he got up and bolted away.

The next day some boys, swimming at that point, came upon Isot under the broken barge, which had been beached near the village. Half of it was lying on the boulders of the shore; the other half was still in the water. Under it, hanging face down from the arc of the rudder, was the long body. The stove-in skull was hollow, the water having washed out the gray matter. The fisherman had been dealt a blow from behind; the nape of the neck was hewed in as with a hatchet stroke. His body moved with the stream, which tugged his dangling arms and legs toward the shore, making him appear to be exerting all his energies to scramble up the bank.

Some twenty of the richer peasants, the poor ones still being in the fields, stood around in gruff and solemn attitudes. The sheriff, a grafting, cowardly little old man in a rose-colored smock, bustled about, snorting, wiping his nose on his sleeve and brandishing a staff. With his feet spread apart to accommodate his paunch, the dumpy little shopkeeper Kuzmin watched the tragic scene, his frowning eyes darting from Kukushkin to me. Grief had misted over his dull eyes and made his pock-marked face pitiful.

"What a blow!" croaked the sheriff, pattering around on his misshapen feet. "Look, peasants, at this crime!"

A plump young woman, his daughter-in-law, sat on a stone, and looking blankly into the water, kept crossing herself with a shaking hand, her lips working, the thick, red lower one hanging down like a dog's, exposing yellow, sheeplike teeth. From the hills, like masses of tinted snow, crowds of girls and children rolled down; in from the fields swarmed dusty peasants.

A low, uneasy muttering came from the crowd, "He was a trouble-maker . . ." "How so?" "You must be thinking of Kukushkin." "That man was killed for nothing." "Isot was a peaceful sort."

Kukushkin rushed at them, roaring, "A peaceful sort! Why kill him, then?"

There was a sudden hysterical laugh from a woman. The sound lashed the crowd like a whip. The peasants pressed upon each other, gave him a hard slap on the cheek, "That's for you, you dog."

He shouted at me, as, with flailing fists, he got himself clear, "Get out, there's going to be a free-for-all."

He had already taken some blows and was spitting blood from a torn lip, but his face glowed with pleasure, "Did you see me give it to Kuzmin?"

Barinov came up to us, looking back with terror at the crowd around the barge. From the thick of it shrilled the reedy voice of the sheriff, "You're going to prove to me whom I'm covering up! Let's have your proof!"

"We better clear out," muttered Barinov, and began ascending the hill. It was a sultry evening; one could hardly breathe in the oppressive heat.

As the purple sun set behind blue cloudbanks it cast red reflections on the green foliage. There was a crackle of distant thunder.

Before me floated Isot's body; on his broken skull the hairs, brushed up by the stream, stood straight. His low, hushed voice, his well-phrased talk, came back to me, "There's a good deal of the child in every man. That's what to reach for. The Khokhol, too, has the soul of a child, though he appears to be made of iron."

At my side, Kukushkin exclaimed fiercely, "That's how we'll all be done in! God, how stupid it is!"

Two days later the Khokhol arrived, late, looking pleased over something, showing it in his particularly affectionate manner. Slapping my shoulder he said, "You don't get enough sleep, Maxim."

"Isot has been killed."

"Wha-at?"

Swellings appeared over his cheekbones, the beard flowing over his chest quivered like a roiled stream. He stopped in the middle of the room, his cap still on, his eyes narrowed, and shaking his head, "Do they know who did it? Of course not . . ."

He walked slowly to the window, sat down and stretched his legs, "I warned him. Have the police come?"

"Yesterday."

"Well?" And then answered his own question, "Nothing, naturally!"

I told him the policeman had paid his usual call at the house of Kuzmin, and had then gone on to arrest Kukushkin for the slap he'd given the shopkeeper.

"So—well, what's there to say?"

I went into the kitchen to put the kettle to boil.

At tea Romass said, "These poor people! They kill off their best. You'd think good people frightened them. 'This is no place for them,' they say. On my march to Siberia I heard this story from a convict who commanded a gang of five thieves:

"One of his five said, 'Boys, how about going straight? Thieving brings us nothing that lasts, except trouble.' And for that they strangled him, one day, when he was sleeping off a drunk. The man from whom I got the story admitted three more murders after this one, but felt no remorse. To this day, however, he praises his murdered comrade. 'He was a real pal, good-natured, clever and honest. But what could you do?' he asked me, 'You couldn't have him among us, one straight among the crooked. It was no go!' "

The Khokhol began pacing the room, his pipe between his teeth, his hands behind his back, and his long Tatar shirt flapping over his bare feet, saying in low, meditative tones, as though to himself, "How often I've encountered this feeling against the upright man, this urge to drive a good man out of this life. The good are dealt with in two ways: either methodically hunted down and destroyed, or adored, people crawling on their bellies before them, like dogs—by far the rarer case. But to learn to live by their example—no, sir! They can't, or is it that they don't want to?"

Lifting his glass of cold tea, he said, "They can, of course, but they won't. It's like this: people have fixed this kind of life for themselves; they've struggled to get used to it. Suddenly someone comes along and wants to change it. 'Your ways are all wrong.' 'Wrong? But, damn you, we've put our best efforts and all our strength into this. So down with you. Don't come bothering us!' Yet, surely, the living truth is in those who tell us, 'Your ways are wrong.' Ah, the truth is in them. It is they who point out the perfect life."

With a gesture toward his bookshelf, he went on, "These, above all! Ah, if I only could write! But that's not for me. My thoughts are too heavy and clumsy."

Sitting down at the table, resting his weight on his elbows, and his head in his hands, he said, "Poor Isot, what a pity!" And after remaining in that position a long time in silence, he finally said, "Well, now to bed."

Up in my attic I sat at the window. Heat lightning played over the fields, illuminating half the sky with each flash. The moon seemed to shudder when the reddish bolts pierced the clouds. They drew frenzies of barking from the dogs, but for whose howling one might have thought himself stranded on a desert island. With the rumble of thunder streams of hot, suffocating air poured in through the window.

In my mind's eye I again saw Isot's body on the shore, shaded by the willow thicket, his blue face turned to the sky, his glassy eyes turned into their own depths, the golden beard clotted into tufts and almost covering the mouth, half open as if in astonishment. It seemed to me he was saying, "Be considerate and gentle, Alex; that's what's needed above all. I love Easter because it's the year's gentlest feast." His blue trousers, clean from their washing in the Volga, and drying in the hot sun, clung to his bluish legs. Flies buzzed over the fisherman's face and his body gave off a nauseating, overpowering odor.

Heavy steps sounded on the stairs. Romass, bending down to get into the doorway, entered, sat on my cot and, holding up his beard in his hand, announced abruptly, "I'm getting married, you know!"

"Rather hard for a woman to live here," I said.

Romass stared at me, waiting for me to add something. But I had nothing more to say. The wraithlike glimmer of reflected heat lightnings filled the room.

"I'm going to marry Mary Derenkova."

I could not help smiling. Till that minute it never occurred to me that Maria could be called Mary. It struck me as funny. I could not recall her father or brothers ever calling her that.

"Why the smile?"

"Nothing, really."

"Think I'm too old for her?"

"Not at all."

"You've been in love with her, she told me."

"Yes, I think I was."

"Has it passed?"

"Yes, I think it has."

He stopped stroking his beard and said quietly, "At your age, love can be a thought, but at mine, it's no longer in the thinking; the feeling gets you and won't leave you time or strength for anything else."

His strong, white teeth flashed as he went on, "At Actium Antony lost to Octavius, running after Cleopatra who took fright and went sailing off. That's what things can happen through love!"

Standing up and straightening himself he repeated, as if speaking of something he was doing against his will: "That's how it is. I'm getting married."

"Soon?"

"In the fall, after I've laid in the apples."

He went out, bending lower in the doorway than was necessary, and I went to bed thinking I'd better be gone by the fall. Why had he said that about Antony? It was not to my liking.

Early in August, Romass returned from Kazan with two cargo boats, one loaded with goods to sell, the other with household gear. It was a weekday morning, about eight. The Khokhol had barely had time to wash and change and sit down for some tea. He was remarking, "It's fine sailing on the river at night," when he interrupted himself, sniffed and asked, "Do you smell smoke?" At the same moment Axinia cried out, "Fire!"

We rushed into the yard. The shed where we stored kerosene, tar and oil, was ablaze, on the side facing the orchard. For a moment we were stunned by the sight, the yellow flames, dingy in the glare of the sun, but already reaching to the roof.

The Khokhol doused the burning wall with a bucket of water brought up by Axinia, then threw the bucket down and said, "Confound it, Alex, roll out the barrels! Axinia, you get back in the shop."

I got out a barrel of tar and went back for the kerosene barrel, but as I grabbed at it I saw that the spigot had been unscrewed and the kerosene was flowing out. The fire did not hold off while I hunted it. Its sharp flames slashed through the boards; the roof cracked, and about me there was a mocking hiss. When I got the half-empty barrel out on the street, a crowd of women and children had already collected, milling about and making a racket. The Khokhol and Axinia were carrying goods out of the shop, and unloading them into the ravine. In mid-street a swarthy, gray-haired old woman shook her fist and screamed, "Oh, the devils!"

Back in the shed I found it filled with smoke, through which I heard steaming and crackling sounds. Crimson ribbons unwound from the roof and the wall looked like a stove grate. Blinded and smothered by the smoke, I hardly had the strength to roll the barrel to the door where it got stuck. I could not push it out for the sparks raining from the roof and singeing my skin. I called for help and the Khokhol grabbed my arm and dragged me into the yard.

"Run, it'll explode any minute!"

I followed him into the house, and rushed into the attic to save my books, which I tossed out of the window. I wanted to toss out a crate of caps that proved to be too large to get through. I was wedging out the sides of the window with a balance-weight when I heard something drop and streak across the roof. I understood that the kerosene barrel had blown up. The roof took fire and I heard a menacing crackle above me. Flames streamed red across the window and the room became sizzling hot. I rushed to the staircase to find smoke billowing up and purple flames snaking up the steps. The jagged crackling below sounded as though iron teeth were gnawing the wood. I got into a panic. Blinded and suffocating with the smoke I stood there stunned. A face with a red beard and a yellow snout leered in through the dormer window, grimaced at me, then vanished; and blood-red spears of flame lacerated the roof. I remember feeling that the hair on my head was frizzling; it was the only sound I was conscious of. I thought I was dying; my legs grew heavy as lead and, though I covered them with my hands, my eyes ached.

The sole way to safety was pointed out to me by the wise instinct of life. Wrapping my head in the Khokhol's sheepskin coat and grabbing my mattress, my pillow and a heap of bast, I dived out of the window.

I recovered consciousness on the edge of the ravine. At my side was Romass, shouting, "Well?"

Staggering to my feet, and with dazed eyes, I watched our hut melting away in crimson streamlets, in angry tongues licking the black earth. The windows exhaled black smoke; and yellow flowers came to a wavering growth on the roof.

"What now?" cried the Khokhol. Down his sooty, sweaty face streaked dirty tears; his eyes blinked with fright; and some bast fibers were caught in his beard. I felt a refreshing and overpowering wave of joy, when a stab of pain in my left foot so weakened me I had to lie down. "I've sprained my foot," I told the Khokhol.

He examined it, and gave a sudden pull. I felt a sharp pain but a minute later, my elation returned; and though I still limped, I was soon carrying the goods we had saved to the bathhouse.

Romass, his pipe between his teeth, said, "I was sure you'd be fried alive when the barrel exploded, and sent the burning kerosene up the roof. The blaze built up in the air like a column; then it spread out like a mushroom, and then it swallowed the whole hut. So I thought, poor Alex, he's done for!"

His usual calm had returned. Heaping things together he told the disheveled and slovenly Axinia, "You stay here and watch. I don't want it all stolen. I'll go help put out the fire."

Over the ravine, white leaves of paper swirled in the smoke. "Ah," mourned Romass, "there go the books. How dear to me were those books!"

Four huts were now afire. There was no wind, and the fire went ahead, unhurriedly, to right and left, hooking, as though involuntarily, at fences and roofs. The red flame tips clawed at the thatch; the crooked, blood-red fingers brushed over hedges as though over the strings of a dulcimer. Ringing through the smoky air came the cruel, shrieking song of the flames, and the soft crackle of consuming wood. Blazing cinders dropped out of the smoke clouds; there was an aimless darting hither and thither by men and women, frantic about their goods, and crying everywhere, "Water! Water!"

Far away, at the foot of the hill, in the Volga, was the needed water. Romas got the peasants organized, taking them by the shoulder and pushing them into some order. He divided them into two groups and set them to clearing away the hedges and sheds in the tow paths of the spreading fire. Under his command the fire-fighting became a more rational counter-offensive against the fire that sought to destroy all "order," to level the whole street. Even so the people worked in a scared and dispirited manner, as if on somebody else's job.

I was in inexpressibly high spirits and felt at the peak of my strength. I observed a group of well-to-do peasants, headed by Kuzmin and the sheriff, at the foot of the street. They themselves did nothing, but they waved their hands or their sticks, and shouted advice. More peasants came in from the fields, atop their horses, and were met by clamoring women and children running to them with shrill cries.

The sheds of still another yard were invaded by the fire and there was a rush to pull down the wattle wall of the stable already ornamented with red fire ribbons. As the men sawed at the wall, sparks and cinders showered over them and they jumped away, slapping the blaze out of their kindled shirts.

"Don't run away," cried the Khokhol. This did not hold them. Grabbing off someone's cap he clapped it on my head and said, "You saw on the other side while I take it here."

When I had sawed through a second stake, the wall began to sway. I scrambled to the top, and the Khokhol pulled at me to bring the wall down with me. As it fell it nearly covered me entirely. The peasants dragged it into the street.

"Are you hurt?" Romass asked. His concern spurred me on to greater vigor. I was eager to please this man, so dear to me, and I worked with frantic energy to earn his praise. And through the clouds of smoke the pages of our books flew in and out, like pigeons.

On the right side we succeeded in stopping the fire but on the other side it burned on, reaching the tenth yard. Leaving a few peasants on the right side to see that the red snakes there did not uncoil again, Romass moved the rest of the men to the left. As we passed the knot of idle, weathy peasants, I heard a malicious exclamation: "It's arson!"

And Kuzmin the shopkeeper added, "How about taking a look into his bathhouse."

This left an unpleasant impression in my mind.

When one is stimulated, particularly when the stimulus is a joyous one, it increases his strength, as everyone knows. In my fervor I worked at top pitch for a long time, then, suddenly I broke down in complete exhaustion. I remember sitting on the ground leaning against something hot. Romass was dousing me from a bucket and I heard the peasants around me saying, with respect, "The lad's a strong one!"

"He's no slacker."

Pressing my head to Romass' leg, I burst into tears, without shame. Romass stroked my wet hair and said, "You've done enough, now you must rest."

Kukushkin and Barinov, smoke-black like devils, helped me to the edge of the ravine, cheering me up by the way, "It's all right, my boy. It's over now. Don't be scared."

Before I caught my full breath, I saw about ten of the "Croesuses," led by the sheriff, moving toward our bathhouse, followed by Romass, between two policemen who were gripping his arms.

He was without a hat, and the sleeve of his wet shirt was torn off. With his teeth gritted over his pipe and his brows knitted, his face had a terrifying look.

Kostin brandished a stick and cried out, "Into the fire with this heretic."

"Open the bathhouse."

"Break the lock," shouted Romass, "the key's been lost."

I picked up a stick from the ground, jumped to my feet and stood beside him. The policemen swerved aside and the sheriff complained: "Breaking locks! That's forbidden!"

Kuzmin pointed to me and shouted, "This one, too. Who's he?"

"Keep cool," Romass said to me. "They think I've hid goods in the bathhouse and set fire to the shop . . ."

"The two of you!"

"Break it open!"

"Christians!"

"We'll answer for it!"

"Let's stand back to back," Romass whispered to me, "so they won't be able to get us from behind."

The lock was broken, a number of people ducked in and right out again. I made use of this diversion to hand my stick to Romass and pick up another.

"It's empty."

"Nothing there?"

"They're devils."

Someone said hesitantly, "That's all, peasants. Break this up."

In answer fierce, drunken voices bellowed, "Why!" "Into the fire with him!" "The hooligans!" "Start labor cooperatives!" "Robbers, the whole lot of them."

"Quiet!" shouted Romass. "You've had your look. You've seen that I've got nothing hidden away in the bathhouse. What more do you want? You see everything is in ashes; you see all that's left? Why would I destroy my own property?"

"It's insured!"

And once more about a dozen voices roared in a furious chorus. "Enough! We've had enough to bear from him!"

A dimness passed before my eyes and a trembling came into my legs. Through a reddish mist I saw savage muzzles with the hairy holes of their mouths gaping open. I had to fight off an impulse to club these people to death.

As they leaped around us they roared, "Look out; they've got sticks."

"Sticks, eh?"

"They'll surely be pulling off my beard," said the Khokhol, and I felt that he said it with a smile. "And they'll hand you a licking too, Alex. But keep cool, just keep cool."

"Look out for the young one. He's got a hatchet!"

This reminded me that I had a carpenter's hatchet tucked under my belt.

"That seems to be cooling them down," said Romass. "But don't do anything with that hatchet whatever comes."

A lame little peasant, unknown to me, hopping about on one leg, yelped, "Stone them! Drive them out!"

He went as far as picking up a piece of brick and heaving it at my stomach, but before I could retaliate Kukushkin pounced on him like a hawk and the two rolled down into the ravine. Behind Kukushkin came Pankov, Barinov, the smith and about a dozen others. At that Kuzmin began taking a reasonable tone. "You're a clever chap," he said to Romass, "you know how it is, a fire drives a peasant mad."

"Come on, Alex," Romass said to me, "let's go to the cafe on the beach." Taking the pipe out of his mouth he thrust it into a trousers pocket. Using his stick he picked his way up the ravine. To Kuzmin who was at his side, saying something placating, he replied, without deigning to look at him, "Beat it, you idiot."

On the site of our hut we saw a golden heap of smoldering coals, with the oven in the midst of it, its chimney emitting a bluish wisp of smoke into the heated air. The red-hot rods of our beds curled out like spider legs. The gateposts, reduced to charcoal, stood beside the woodpile like black sentries, one of them with a crimson crest rayed with sparks like a cock's comb.

"All the books are destroyed," sighed the Khokhol. "What a shame!"

Prodding them with sticks, boys drove large embers through the street mud, as they drove pigs. Hissing and aglow, the embers emitted a thick, steamy smoke. A towheaded and blue-eyed boy of about five was sitting in a warm black pool, drumming with a stick on a bucket, enchanted with the sound of wood on iron. The victims of the fire were glumly pacing before the wreckage picking up whatever was salvageable. In the nearby orchards the leaves of the trees were reddened from the heat, or burnt off and the pink apples were visible.

We went down to the river, washed ourselves in it, and then sat down peacefully to a glass of tea in the cafe on the beach.

"Just the same," said Romass, "the apple dealers didn't get their way."

Pankov, more thoughtful and gentler than usual, joined us.

"How is it with you?" asked the Khokhol.

With a shrug, Pankov replied, "My place was insured."

We sat there, not saying much, eying each other like strangers.

"What are your plans, Romass?"

"Still thinking it over."

"Better get away from here."

"I'll see."

"Come outside," said Pankov. "I've got an idea I'd like to talk over with you."

As they left, Pankov turned to me from the doorway, "No one will be calling you a sissy. You can stay; they'll be scared of you."

I also went out. Under some bushes on the river bank I stretched out and watched the flowing water. It was hot, though the sun was setting. My life in this village unrolled before me, as if painted in bright colors on the surface of the river. A strange sadness flooded my heart. But, overcome by fatigue, I was soon fast asleep.

As in a dream I felt myself being shaken and pulled, and heard, "Hey! Are you dead? Wake up!"

Over the meadows, across the river, gleamed a moon as wide as a wheel. Barinov was bending over me, his head on my shoulder.

"The Khokhol's worried; he's looking for you; come on!"

Grumbling as he walked behind me, he said, "You can't just nap off like that, anywhere. Someone passing by might trip over you and pay you back with a stone. Might mean to do it, too. Boy, people are always set on evil. What else have they got to think of?"

There was a rustling in the bushes and Migun's voice echoed, "D'you find him?"

"He's with me here," replied Barinov. As we passed Migun, Barinov said with a sigh, "He's stealing fish, Migun. His life isn't an easy one, either."

Romass was angry with me. "What were you hunting for? Were you looking for a thrashing?" When we were alone he said in a low and depressed voice, "Pankov's idea is for you to stay with him. He's thinking of opening a shop here. I'd advise you against it. As for me, I've sold him whatever I had left. I'll go to Viatka and I'll soon send for you. Is that agreeable to you?"

"I'll think it over."

"Good."

He stretched out on the floor, tossed about awhile and then was silent. Sitting by the window I looked at the Volga.

"Do you feel mad at the peasants?" Romass asked sleepily. "You mustn't. They were foolish. To be angry is foolish, too."

This gave me no consolation; the words could smooth down neither my rage nor their offense. I kept seeing the bestial, hairy mouths spewing the vicious howls, "Stone them!"

I had not yet acquired the ability to forget what it was not good to remember. I understood, of course, that in each of them, as individuals, there was little viciousness, perhaps none. Beasts they might be, but good-natured beasts; it was no trouble to make one of them smile like a child, listen like a confiding child to your tales of the human quest for wisdom and happiness, of great and self-sacrificing deeds. Dear to their souls is anything that sets them to dreaming of an easy life whose law is one's own will.

But at the village meetings where they collect into a gray huddle, or in the dives on the beach, they cover up the good in them, they go around like priests, robed in falsehood and pretense. Their doglike fawning to the strong makes them repulsive to watch. Or, turning on each other, they show a wolfish ferocity, bristling and baring their fangs, snarling at each other and prepared to fight—and too often they do—over trifles. They're terrifying then, capable of tearing down the church into which, only the night before, they had meekly trotted like sheep into their fold. Among them are poets and story-tellers, but their lot is to be the laughing stock of the village, everybody's helpless butt. I don't know how to live with such people, I can't live with them.

I made these bitter observations to Romass on the day of our parting and he reproached me, "These are the thoughts of an immature mind!"

"But what am I to do if these are the thoughts that form in my mind?"

"But they're not right, they have no foundation!"

And he tried to show me my mistakes and to talk me over to his fine sentiments.

"Don't be in such a hurry to condemn people," he said. "Condemnation is easy. It can run away with you. Whatever comes keep your head. Remember one thing: there's an end to everything; and there's a constant change for the better. Not fast enough for you? But when the change is slow it's the more lasting. For yourself look into every corner of a thing; overlook nothing of what comes before you; don't let any of it scare you; and—don't rush to condemn! Good-by, my friend! We'll be seeing each other soon."

But it was fifteen years before we saw each other again, in Sedlets, after Romass had lived out ten years more of exile in Yakutsk for the sake of "the people's truth."

A leaden melancholy weighed me down after Romass left Krasnovidovo—I sniffed about like a puppy that had lost its master. With Barinov, in whose bathhouse I lived, I worked for the well-to-do peasants, threshed grain, dug potatoes, weeded gardens.

One rainy night he asked me, "Alex, you general without an army,—shall we go to the sea tomorrow? By God, that's the thing for us to do. What are we doing here? They don't fancy folks like us. If we don't look out, a brawl might start . . ."

It wasn't the first time he spoke to me like this. He, too, had fallen into a melancholy mood; his apelike hands hung slack; and he looked about him uneasily like a traveler in a forest.

The rain beat on the panes of the bathhouse, water trickled into the room and out again and down the ravine. Pallid lightning from a spent thunderstorm flickered on the sky.

Barinov coaxed, "How about it, Alex? Shall we go tomorrow?"

And we went.

Sailing down the Volga on a fall night, seated in the stern of a barge, though a hairy monster with a huge head handles the rudder, emits loud sighs, and clumps heavily whenever he moves—that can be an indescribably satisfying experience.

Under the stern the sound was a gentle splash, the water seemed boundless and thick as jelly, and rippled like silk. Above glided black autumn clouds. Around us the flooding darkness, in which the shores had disappeared, into which the whole earth seemed to have fused, turning into smoky liquid, flowing into a desert space, sunless, moonless, starless. The tug hauling us strained against this elastic force, panting and shaking. Three lights, close to the water and the third high aloft, followed it; nearer to me, seeming to swim in the clouds, were four other lights—one the lantern over our stern.

I had the feeling of being stuck, like a fly, in a cold bubble of oil that was gently rolling down a slope, with momentum slowing to a stop, the next moment. Then the ship would cease its creaking; the blades of its wheel would stop slapping the viscid water; sounds would whisk off like the leaves of a tree; things would be erased like chalk marks and I would be swathed in immobility and silence.

The huge steersman in his torn sheepskin and shaggy cap would stop stamping as he handled the rudder, would become motionless, forever, as under a spell, and his growl would be stilled.

I asked him his name. His reply, given in a choked voice, was, "Why do you want to know?"

Seeing him when we sailed out of Kazan at sunset, I saw that this hulking bear-like man had a hairy and nearly eyeless face. Taking his stand at the rudder he emptied a bottle of vodka into a wooden mug, swilled it down in two gulps like water, and finished off with an apple. As soon as he felt the pull of the tugboat, he took hold of the rudder arm, and staring at the red disc of the sun, dropped his head with a thud, and emitted a solemn, "God bless us!"

The haul was from the Nizhny Fair to Astrakhan; the tugboat was towing a string of four barges loaded with iron ore, barrels of sugar and some heavy crates consigned to Persia.

Barinov kicked at the crates, then sniffed at them, pondered a few moments, then said, "Why, it's a crate of Izhev rifles."

The man at the rudder planted his fist on Barinov's belly, "What concern is it of yours?"

"I was just thinking."

"Maybe you'd like one in your face!"

We had paid no fare; we had been allowed on "in kindness." It didn't matter that we kept watch just like the crew; they treated us like beggars. "And you romanticize about people!" Barinov sneered at me. "It all depends on who's saddled first."

The darkness was so thick the barge ends were out of sight; all one could see were the mast lights, outlined against the smoky clouds, which seemed to smell of kerosene. I was exasperated by the sullen silence of the steersman. I had been ordered to keep watch beside this animal and to help him.

Guided by the movement of the lights he said, "Watch out!"

Up I jumped and gave the rudder a twist.

"Good!" he growls.

Again I sit down on the deck. Talk is impossible with this man whose answer to everything is, "What concern is it of yours?"

What's in this man's head, I wondered. At the point where the yellow Kama waters turn upon the steel rail of the Volga he faced north and growled, "Skunk!"

"Who?"

No answer.

From far off, in the abyss of darkness, came the sounds of dogs. Their howls called up fragments from one's past, rescued from the darkness, but unattainably distant and purposeless.

"Bad dogs here," came suddenly from the steersman.

"Where?"

"All around. The one we have is a monster."

"Where are you from?"

"Vologda."

And like potatoes from a torn sack gray, heavy words tumbled out. "That man an uncle of yours? In my opinion he's a dope. Have I got a smart uncle! Amounts to something. Owns a wharf in Simbirsk, and a waterfront saloon."

He got all this out with an effort, then stared with his specklike eyes at the mast lantern, watching it climb over the web of darkness like a golden spider.

"Give it a twist, you . . . " he continued. "Can you read? Know who make the laws?" Giving me no time to answer he went on, "Some say it's the Tsar. Others say it's Archbishop Senate. If I knew I'd go and tell him, 'You write a law like this: that I mustn't even raise my hand to anyone, let alone hit him.' A law must be like iron, like a key. It must lock up my heart, and period! Then I'd know where I am. But this way where am I?"

He finished with incoherent mutterings, knocking his fist on the wooden rudder bar. Someone from the tugboat called through a megaphone, but the voice came to us dull and wordless, like the barking of the dogs, not yet smothered in the greasy night. On the black water under the stern, the reflected lights from the lantern floated like patches of oil, and dimmed away, incapable of lighting anything. And so thick and clammy were the dark, pulpy clouds it was as though we were in a river of muck, above. Deeper and deeper we glide along the silent cave of the darkness. The steersman rumbled, "What have I come to? My heart can't beat."

But I had become indifferent. My own heart was heavy with apathy and chill with melancholy. All I wanted was to sleep.

Making its way with difficulty through the clouds, timidly and furtively, a drab, sickly, sunless dawn emerged. It gave the water a leaden tinge, it revealed the yellow scrub on the shore, the rusty pine trees, the dark claws of thin branches, the rows of village huts, the peasants silhouetted as if carved out of stone. Above glided a seagull on crooked wings.

As others came to relieve us, I crawled under a tarpaulin and went to sleep, only to be awakened by outcries and trampling feet. Peering out, I saw three crewmen holding the steersman against the wall of the hold. They shouted at him, "None of that, Pete!"

"But it's nothing!"

"Now, none of that!"

The steersman stood quietly, with crossed hands gripping his own shoulders. His foot was on a bundle. Looking from one to the other of the three men he coaxed, "Let me preserve myself from sin!"

He was barefoot and hatless and wore only a shirt and trousers. A mat of unkempt hair fell over his bulging, stubborn forehead, from beneath which glittered the small bloodshot eyes of a mole. Their look was agonized and pleading.

"You'll drown," the men warned.

"No, I won't. Let me go, boys! If you don't, I'll murder him. When we land in Simbirsk I'll——"

"Now quit it."

"Come on, boys."

He kneeled, spread out his hands on the deck like a man crucified, and repeated, "Let me preserve myself from sin!"

The tone of his strange, bass voice made me anxious; his outspread hands, broad as oars, with the palms turned in appeal to the other men, quivered. His bear's face could be seen twitching within his shaggy beard; the little molelike eyes rolled in their sockets like little black marbles. An unseen hand might have had him by the throat.

The three men silently backed away from him as he clumsily rose to his feet. Picking up his bundle he said, "Thank you!" Then, with unexpected agility, he dashed to the stern and overboard.

Following him to the stern I saw him, his bundle on his bobbing head, swimming toward the sandy bank where he was met by bushes, swaying in the wind and scattering their yellow leaves on the water.

The men said, "Well, he did it."

"Is he crazy?" I asked.

"Crazy? No. He did it to preserve his soul."

Still up to his chest in the water, he waved to us with his bundle.

"Good-by!" shouted his bargemates.

At Simbirsk the barge crew put us ashore. "You're not the kind we need," they told us.

They rowed us into Simbirsk harbor, where we sat on the shore to dry ourselves. There were thirty-seven kopecks in our pockets. We had tea at an inn.

"What do we do now?"

"What do we do? Why, we just go on," said Barinov, nonchalantly.

And we did. We sailed as "hares" [23] on a steamer to Samara; there we got work as barge hands, work that, in seven days, brought us to our destination, the shores of the Caspian where we joined a crew at the Kalmuck [24] fishery, Kabankul-bai.

Chapter Seven

I WAS NIGHT WATCHMAN AT DOBRINKA DEPOT. FROM SIX IN THE EVENING to six in the morning I patrolled the baggage rooms swinging a club. The thousand-mouthed steppe wind howled, herding huge flocks of snow clouds through whose gray folds locomotives painfully made their way, in slow proddings back and forth, with heavy sighs, and tugging the dark links of their trains. It was as though someone was heedlessly getting the world entangled in an endless chain and hauling it through skies pulverized to a cold white powder. Over the snow sounded a screech of iron, the clank of the links, a low howling and weird creaking sounds. Two dim figures hovered in the eddying snow around the baggage room—Cossack flour thieves. They plunged into a snow bank to hide from me. Through the flurries and howls of the

[23] A term used for passengers who work out their fares.

[24] The Kalmuck were a Mongolian people, descended from the people, part of whom escaped from Russia in the journey immortalized in DeQuincy's *Flight of a Tatar Tribe.*

storm, a few moments later, came their whining pleas, their offers of bribes, their curses. "None of that," I tell them.

They bored me. I had no inclination to listen to them, knowing they were not poor driven to theft, by need, but by the itch for money, drink, or women. At times they sent me, as their go-between, the pretty grass widow, Louise Grafova, wife of a Cossack stationed in St. Petersburg. To the watchmen, she unbared firm, yet supple, breasts.

"See, they point straight out like cannons," she boasted. "Well, make it one sack of wheat, second grade. Agreed? No? Well, a sack of third grade."

Baikov, the pious lad from Tambov, and the crippled Ibrahim, the Tatar from Usman, haggled with her.

She stood there with bared breasts, the snow thawing down her warm skin. She shrugged her shoulders and berated them, "Come on, you damn Katzaps,[25] you skunks, you mud breeds, make up your mind. Where are you going to find a honey like me, you dog shit!"

She loathed the Russian peasants. Her voice was deep and strong, and in her attractive face gleamed arrogant cat's eyes. While her companions heaped sacks on the sleigh Ibrahim took her up into the loft.

The woman's shamelessness revolted me and I felt compassion for her strong and beautiful abused body. Ibrahim spat on the memory of her embraces and called her "the bitch," and Baikov muttered, meditatively, "that sort ought to be killed."

On holidays she dressed up, put on squeaking kid boots, tied a crimson kerchief round her thick, russet hair, and went to town, to solicit among "the intelligentsia," whom she treated with the same offhand disdain.

When she tried her spells on me I drove her off. One warm, moonlight night, however, having dozed off on the warehouse steps, I woke up to find Louise before me. Her fine figure clearly outlined in the moonlight, she stood with her hands in her coat pockets and her brows knitted, "Don't worry," she said, "I'm not going to pinch anything. I'm just out for a walk."

From the position of the stars it was well past midnight. "Isn't it late for a walk?"

"A woman is a creature of night," replied Louise, sitting beside me. "And why are you asleep? Is that what you're hired for?"

She took a handful of sunflower seeds out of her pocket and, as she chewed, said, "They say you're literate. Where's the city of Obolak?"

[25] Colloquial Ukrainian term for Russians.

"I don't know."

"It's the place where the Virgin Mary appeared. On the icons she's painted with the Child in her lap and her arms over her head."

"You mean Abalatzk."

"Where's that?"

"In the Urals or Siberia."

She licked her lips and said, "Suppose I went there. But it's so far. I suppose I'll have to."

"Why?"

"For penance. I'm a sinner. You men lead me into it. Have you a smoke?"

As she lit a cigarette she warned me, "Don't mention it to the Cossacks. They're against a woman smoking." Her face in the winter air was rosily beautiful. Within the opal ovals of her eyeballs the dark pupils gleamed.

A falling star left a momentary golden ray in the sky. Crossing herself she said, "God rest his soul. One day mine will fall that way, too. When do you feel lonelier, on bright nights or dark ones? It's the bright ones that get me." Spitting on the cigarette she threw it on the ground, gave a wide yawn, and offered, "How about some fun?"

When I refused she said, "People all say I give them a good time."

Gently I spoke to her of her immodesty that scandalized people. Looking aside, she said in a matter-of-fact way, "It's boredom that drove me to it. Man, how bored I am!"

The word "man" was strange on her lips, took on a different meaning. Leaning her head back to look at the sky she continued, meditatively, "It's no fault of mine. There's something in what they say that it's God's will to have a woman judged by her legs. I'm not to blame for that."

After a few minutes of silence she got up, peered about her and said, "I'll look in on the station-master."

I saw her move slowly along the tracks, silvered by the moonlight, while I sat under the crushing weight of her words, "Man, how bored I am!"

I could not then comprehend the "boredom" of the steppe people, whose life is cast in immense spaces, in bright emptiness under the sun and the moon, where a man is depressed by the clear evidence of his minuteness and nonentity, where there is little to support his will to live.

People who were strangers to all I believed and acted on passed before me, each thrusting his shadow into my soul. The incessant flickering of these shadows doomed me to the torment of trying to comprehend the incomprehensible. A tornado seemed to whirl before me—the station-master, Afrikan Petrovsky, broad-shouldered and long-armed and an athlete. He had a lobster's protruding, black eyes; his beard was thick and black and he was shaggy all over like an animal. Oddly enough he spoke in a high tenor. In anger he whistled through his huge, swelling Kalmuck nostrils. He stole, ordering the handlers to jimmy open the freight cars shipped from the Caspian Sea. The handlers brought him Oriental silks and confections, whose sale provided the means for the "monastic orgies" he held in his apartment. A cruel man, rumored to have beaten his wife to death, he maltreated the watchmen. After office hours he sported about in a shirt of red silk, trousers of black velvet, Tatar boots of green Morocco and, atop his mat of curly black hair, a Tatar cap of lilac and gold embroidery. In this getup he looked like a cabaret singer impersonating a nobleman of the past.

He had a frequent visitor in the police lieutenant, Maslov, a bald, close-shaven, priestly looking chap with little fox eyes and a hawk nose. He was nicknamed "the actress." Another frequent visitor was the soap manufacturer, Tikhon Stepakhin, a good-looking, red-haired peasant, slow and somnolent like an ox. Workers in his plant were slowly being poisoned; they rotted alive; and several times he had been brought to trial and made to pay damages. A third crony was the deacon, Voroshilov, a drunkard, small and slovenly, the high cheekbones of whose pockmarked face were topped by gray hairs thick as porcupine quills. He was a virtuoso on the guitar and the accordion, and his hands were delicately cared for like a girl's. He had beautiful glowing blue eyes which had been nicknamed "stolen eyes."

Farm girls and Cossack village women, Louise often among them, usually accompanied them. In a crowded little room overfurnished with couches, they sat down at a heavy round table to a feast of smoked fowl, ham, baked apples, jams, melon and sauerkraut, with a big bottle of vodka to crown this magnificence. In complete silence, Petrovsky and his companions swallowed, masticated and guzzled the vodka out of a silver "brotherly" flagon that held a quarter of the bottle. When they were stuffed, Stepakhin, continuously crossing himself, belched like a Bashkir; the deacon, with a smile on his lips, caressingly tuned the guitar. They went into another room, unfurnished except for some chairs, and the singing began.

It was beautiful singing. Petrovsky was a tenor; the deacon a baritone, Stepakhin, a bass. Maslov expertly accompanied the host. The women's voices were fine, too. Notable for its purity was the contralto of the Cossack's wife, Kubassova. Louise was the shrill one and the deacon often pointed an accusing finger at her. They looked at each other solemnly as if they were a church choir, all except Stepakhin, whose head was bent down. There was a wondering look in his face, as though he found it hard to believe that the unceasing, velvety sound was streaming from his own throat. The songs were melancholy. Some were church songs which they sang with gravity, usually, the "Penance" hymn.

The whites of Petrovsky's lobster eyes grew bloodshot, he straightened up like a soldier at drill and bellowed, "Hey, deacon, dance! Come on Tikhon! Liven up boys!"

"Ready!" replied the deacon, with a deft run of his fingers up the guitar strings. With the agility of a juggler, he began playing a trepak.[26] Stepakhin stepped up. A dreamy smile lit the soapmaker's cloddish face; a graceful, feline, elasticity possessed his heavy frame. Like a fish in a shadowed pool, he moved with swift glides around the room, his limbs in beautiful, rhythmic tremors, his almost soundless feet tracing out intricate figures, meanwhile gazing blissfully on the others. His dancing fascinated and although Kubassova, with little cries, flirted around him, in seductive and luring motions, he went far beyond her in the beautiful vigor of his body. Everyone was intoxicated with motion. In a joyous frenzy Petrovsky yelled, whistled, shook his head, spattered tears from his ecstatic eyes. The deacon stopped playing, embraced Stepakhin, and in a voice choked with emotion exclaimed, "Tikhon . . . it's heavenly, it's like the church. . . . My dear chap, you'll be absolved from everything."

And Maslov circled around them, crying, "Tikhon, you're a tsar, a genius, you murder us!"

Only now did these people who had downed a big bottle of vodka become drunk but their intoxication appeared to come from happiness, from mutual esteem and affection. The women were drunk, too. Their eyes had an avid gleam, their cheeks were flushed, they fanned themselves, they were excited like unexercised mares led out of dark stables on a spring day, into a large sunny yard.

Louise, her mouth half-open and her eyes humid and cruel, looked at Stepakhin, rocked in her chair and slapped the floor with her soles.

We heard the wind screeching outside and humming in the chimney;

[26] A Russian national dance measure.

wings of snow scraped the window panes. Stepakhin, mopping his sweating face, said with plaintive guilt, "It's for this dancing that your good people look down on me."

Petrovsky spieled out a fierce, thick stream of obscene invectives against the "good people"; the women uttered affected outcries, pretending to be shocked. In their combinations the licentious phrases beautifully displayed the flexibility of the Russian tongue.

The deacon resumed his playing and it was Petrovsky's turn on the floor. Aggressively he charged about, crashing and stamping with harsh cries, as though kicking and ripping to pieces something in his way. Louise joined him; and Maslov, like one possessed, made clumsy leaps. The room heaved and shimmered with trampling feet, whistles, yells, and women's flashing skirts and, above it all, Petrovsky's heels beating out the time and his belligerent shout, "Hey, hey! It's ruining me!" You could hear his teeth gnashing.

But in this frantic hilarity there was no gaiety, nothing of the light-winged elation that lifts a man above earth. It was closer to religious transports. It reminded one of revival meetings, of dervish dances in the Caucasus. In this cyclone of whirling bodies there was destructive power; in its unappeased unrest there was something akin to despair. Each of the men was talented, in his own eerie way; each intoxicated the other, with a mutual ecstasy for music, for the dance, for the body of woman, for triumphant and beautiful motion and sound. Yet it resembled a ritual of savages.

Petrovsky excused me from duty to enable me to take part in the "monastic life," because I had a large repertory of songs, rendered them well, and managed to stay sober after downing quantities of vodka which I didn't enjoy.

"Shoot, Peshkov!" he roared—he roared even when kissing women. It was a necessity to him to make the sounds of a beast.

Leaning against the wall I "shot." By deliberate choice I sang touching songs, trying to lay bare the beauty and the emotion in the words. I surrendered to their ineffable sadness which hostile reason denied but my soul held close.

"Dear God!" exclaimed the deacon, his head in his hands, their small puffy palms disappearing in his gray mat of hair. Stepakhin's amazed look had a touch of envy and I observed an unpleasant twitch in his face. Petrovsky's teeth were so clamped together as to make his cheekbones bulge. Maslov, who had maneuvered Kubassova onto his knee, forgot her and had a downcast stare like a sick dog.

I don't know what I looked for in these people. Sometimes it seemed to me that if their souls were saturated with music it would somehow change them and bring them closer to me. Now they crowded around me in admiration, rapturously hugging and kissing me.

"You rascal," said Maslov and stroked my hand. Stepakhin, kissing me, said nothing.

"Drink up. It'll all come out the same, whatever you do," said Petrovsky.

Louise, waving her hands, cried, "I've fallen in love with him. I declare it openly. I'm in love with him. I tremble to my feet with love."

Insatiably they called for more and more.

Outside the windows, in a gloom gashed by the station lamps, the serpent trains, red-eyed and ponderous, rumbled past with an iron creaking attended by engineers and oilers, padded till they resembled globes, and waving their lanterns. The smoke and steam misted the window panes which, when the engine whistled, responded with a plaintive vibration. Out there, in the night, life plodded its hard road unrelated, in any way, to the rapturous devotions here paid to beauty.

I knew these people to be worthless—still they worshiped beauty with religious ardor, they served it self-denyingly; they poisoned themselves with it, they were capable of dying for it. These paradoxes brewed a misty longing in which I suffocated, as their ecstasy mounted to its climax. All the songs had been sung; all the dances performed.

"Undress the women," ordered Petrovsky.

The disrobing was done by Stepakhin who never hurried it. Carefully he undid the straps, unfastened the hooks, and folded the separate garments neatly and heaped them in a corner.

The men circled the women, breathing delighted gasps, giving the nude bodies as delirious praise as, some moments ago, they had given to the singing and dancing. Then they returned to the table in the other room, swallowed and swilled—preliminaries to nightmarish orgy, beyond description, beyond words.

I was not surprised by the animal vigor of the men but it was a shock to watch their cruel handling of the women to whose beauty they had just given religious adoration. Their sensuality seemed to be part vengeance, and the vengeance was the rage of their despair over their inability to spend themselves, to relax from the mutilating load that burdened them.

I remember Stepakhin and his nerve-wracking cry. Catching sight of his reflection in a mirror, he saw that his red face had purpled, that his eyes bulged unnaturally. "My God, look at this, men," he roared. "My face is inhuman. It's inhuman!" And grabbing a bottle he hurled it into the glass. "That's for you, you devil's mug!"

He had had a good deal to drink but he wasn't drunk, and when the deacon tried to calm him down, he said, rationally enough, "Let me be, deacon. It's no use. What else? I don't live like a human being. Am I human at all? In place of a soul there's a hairy devil inside me. Go away. There's nothing you can do!"

Some dreadful abysmal thing writhed within them all. The women howled with pain, yet seemed to welcome the torment as something natural, as pleasure of a sort. Louise inflamed Petrovsky with her cries, "Another one, now. Pinch me harder now." The catlike pupils of her eyes enlarged, and at those moments she resembled the martyrs on icons. I was terrified lest Petrovsky kill her.

Once, at dawn, walking away with her from the station master's, I asked her why she permitted it.

"But it's themselves they torture," she said, "all of them. Take the deacon, he weeps over it."

"Why?"

"The deacon? Because he's old, because his strength is giving out. And the others, Afrikan and Stepakhin—you wouldn't understand. I couldn't find the words for it, but I know. There's a lot I know that I haven't got the words for. When I hunt for the words the thoughts stray away, and when I have the thoughts again, the words run out."

There was some actual understanding in her, of these frantic energies. Well I recall her grieving cry to me, on a spring night, "How I pity you! You'll burn out here, like a bird in fire and smoke. How I pity you all!"

With the soothing words of a mother, with the understanding of one who has looked, unterrified, into the most terrifying depths of the soul, she dwelt on things that were terrible beyond shame.

As it looks to me now I was lending a hand in the fierce conflict of two natures—those of the animal and the man. The man seeks, once and for all, to satiate the animal within him, so to be freed of the overmastering animal desires which, however, grow in the struggle, acquiring added strength to subdue the man to their rule. Those frantic feasts of the flesh revolted me and brought me anguish, at the same time that I felt compassion for the people, particularly the women. Though steeped in that sorrowful feeling, I did not abjure these delirious "monastic" pleasures. I suffered for what is pompously called "fanaticism for knowledge." My mentor was that arch-fanatic of knowledge, Satan himself.

"You must know, you must understand everything," Romass used to tell me, barely opening his mouth, bemused with his pipe and the blue smoke rings that hung on the gray hairs of his beard. "To justify your life, to avoid living uselessly, get used to looking into the cracks and pits. Understand that there you may come upon your hidden truth. Don't turn away from the frightening and unpleasant; live without fear. Only what you fail to understand frightens and repels you."

So I poked into everything; I spared myself nothing; and I learned much that might have been better for me, personally, to be ignorant of, though it is necessary to exhibit to people the harsh drama of man's conflict with the beast, his attempts to overcome Nature within and outside himself, that is part of their lives. If anything on earth may really be considered noble and holy it is man's continuous development, in which even his hateful moments have value. And having entered so deep into the play of life I lost the capacity to hate, not because it is hard—hating comes easy—but because it is purposeless and degrading—the hated thing, after all, is part of oneself.

Philosophy—and especially ethical philosophy, is a dull matter indeed; but when the soul bleeds from the bruises of life, when it sobs out of its inexhaustible love for that "tremendous trifle, man," it seeks consolation in philosophy.

Three or four months at Dobrinka Station was more than I could stand. Apart from the orgies at Petrovsky's I began to be tyrannized over by his cook, Marian, a six-foot woman in her forties who tipped our Fairbanks baggage scales at two hundred and fifty-three pounds. On her swarthy moonlike face angry rays shot from her spherical green eyes, that reminded one of oxidized copper. A mountainous mole under her left eye pulled it down into a watchful frown. She was literate and read, with ecstatic absorption, *The Lives of the Saints*; and with all the might of her giant heart she hated the emperors Diocletian and Decius. "If I'd got hold of them I'd have scratched their eyes out," she said fiercely. But this fury toward ancient emperors did not keep her from tremulous enslavement to "Actress" Maslov. At the drunken suppers she served him devotedly, gazing into his hypocritical eyes with the look of a contented dog. At times, pretending to be overcome, he sprawled on the floor, beat his breast, and moaned, "I'm sick, I'm dying." Terrified, she picked him up in her arms, and rocked him, like a child. Maslov's name was Martin, and on such occasions she confused it, in her fears, with her master's, calling him Martikan. At that he would leap up and howl, "What? What was that you said?"

Her hands humbly crossed over her middle, she would bow low to him and in hoarse, trembling tones, plead, "Forgiveness, for God's sake!"

To distress her still more, he would utter a shrill whistling and yelping sound while the poor woman stood stock still, her eyes fluttering guiltily and dropping small greenish tears. They all laughed, and Maslov, butting her playfully in the belly, said in a relaxed voice, "It's all right, you scarecrow, run along now."

As she left, timidly, he would comment, with some pride, "She's an ox but she has a heart of gold."

At first Marian was like a good-natured mother to me, but one day I reproached her for her submissiveness to the "actress." She recoiled as if I had scalded her with boiling water. Her green eyeballs purpled and became bloodshot. She sagged down on a bench, almost suffocated with indignation, her whole body quivering, and gasped out, "What are you imagining, you heel! The nerve of you, saying things like that about him! Such words! You ought to be torn to pieces for that! You must be insane! That man—more of a saint than the saints— And you, who are you?" and ended with a sudden outcry, "You ought to be poisoned like a wolf, you soul of a wolf; get out!"

I was dismayed by this wrathful explosion. Young as I was, I perceived that I had put a callous hand on something sacred and tender. But how was I to guess that this mound of meat and suet covering her giant skeleton bore deep within its heart something so treasured and inviolable. In such ways life revealed to me what it was that gave people balance, taught me to respect their mysteries.

From then on Marian treated me with unforgiving hatred. She imposed many of the station-master's household chores upon me. After my sleepless night of watching, she made me prepare firewood, carry it to the stoves in all the rooms, clean the grates, start the fires, tend to Petrovsky's horse, and do other jobs which took nearly half my day and kept me from my books and my bed. She did not hide her motives: "I'll persecute you till you'll run to the Caucasus!" Recalling Barinov's remark, "One has to get used to the Caucasus," I sent off a petition in verse to the district office in Borissoglebsk in which I described Marian's despotism. It won me a transfer to the baggage station at Borissoglebsk, where I was charged with the care and repair of bags and tarpaulins.

I made the acquaintance there of a considerable circle of the intelligentsia. Nearly all were "unreliable,"[27] had sampled jail and exile, were well read, knew foreign languages—expelled students, theologians, statisticians, and one naval and two army officers.

They had been collected, about sixty of them, from the Volga cities, by a business man named Adadurov, who had undertaken to the directors of the Griaz-Tsaritsyn Railroad, to put an end to the looting of freight shipments. The sixty applied themselves to this task; they exposed the dodges of the station-masters, loaders, trainmen and others involved; and they bragged to each other of their successes in tracking down the thieves. I felt that this work was hardly suitable to their dignity, talents and background for, at that time, I was only dimly aware that to "plant the good, the wise and the immortal," was banned in Russia. My work kept me midway between these curious "culture bearers" and the ordinary townspeople and the incompatibilities of the two groups were diverting. The "Adadurovtsy" were notorious as "politicals"[28] and they were looked at with animosity and fear. The craven but hate-filled looks the townsmen gave the Adadurovtsy were noxious to see; they shunned the Adadurovtsy both as personal enemies and as foes of the "Tsar and Country."

My friend Paul Kriukov, the turner, said to me as we sat in the saloon, over our beers, "How can they give jobs to such people! They should be sent to desert islands. Let them be Robinson Crusoes all of them! Or better, hang them all! They used to be hung in Petersburg, not long ago!"

Kriukov was well read, made a hobby of geography, knew Zhukovsky's verses, owned twenty-odd books, among them an anti-revolutionary tract, which he made a mystery of as he handed it to me, "This will show you what they are! But don't let them see you with it or you'll be a goner!"

He was by no means alone in that way of thinking. I became acquainted with the writer Starostin-Manenkov, who was an accountant for the freight department of the railway. Middle-aged and obese, with a pouchy, hairless face and drab, expressionless eyes, he made one think of a eunuch, and his waddling gait and gestures strengthened this impression. Illnesses remarkable for their number and variety nested in his bloated body, encouraged by his hypochondriac nature. He

[27] The official characterization of people suspected of revolutionary activity.
[28] Revolutionaries were called "Politicals" to distinguish them from other law breakers.

wheezed, hawked, coughed continually and spat all about him, into the empty macaroni box which he used as a wastebasket, into flowerpots, into the ashtrays, and on the floor. In spitting he arched his whole body, inspected the blob and mournfully shaking his bald head, said, "That's dangerous!"

His room was small; it was curtained with coarse-woven cloths and decorated with flowerpots on the sill, and an icon of the martyrs Kiril and Ulita; there, in the evenings, he sat at a littered table, sipping vodka and chewing on an onion, and, if he had company, complaining in a high-pitched voice, "Gleb Uspensky [29] mocks the peasantry while I write with my heart's blood. Tell me, as a reader, what has Uspensky got? Yet he gets published in the big magazines, while I . . ."

His stories came out in provincial journals, and once or twice he appeared in the national magazine, "Dielo." Starostin liked to be reminded of it; I reminded him.

"So what," he retorted, but not so plaintively, "That's a little thing, considering how I . . ."

He dropped to the floor, on all fours, crawled under the bed and drew out a manuscript bundle tied in a gray shawl which, as he pulled at it, sent up a cloud of dust. Coughing from the dust, he cried, "There! Written with my heart's juices, my very blood!"

His face purpled, drunken tears flooded his eyes. On a more sober occasion he read me a story he had just composed, about a peasant who ran through flames to save the pet horse of a policeman who, barely an hour before, had knocked out a couple of the peasant's teeth for taking a pole. The peasant had to go to the hospital for his burns. Starostin declaimed this sentimental tale with outcries and ecstatic murmurings, "How well written it is, how inward! Indeed, my friend, learn from it how to penetrate the soul."

I didn't care for the story at all, but the joy the author took in it moved me almost to tears. What made this ludicrous man weep? I asked him for the manuscript to read at home. I saw that the writing was filled with the pathos of begging letters to rich widows. So what was it that evoked these genuine tears, which left the author refreshed like a child after crying?

I admitted to him that I didn't care for the story. Picking up the pages with fondling hands, he said, "Shows how coarse you are, what little understanding you have!"

"What's in it that you think so stirring?"

[29] A successful writer of the period.

"The soul," he retorted, "The soul glows there."

After giving me a scolding that left him feeling better, he drew further consolation from vodka and urged me, "Apply yourself to learning something. Foolish to write verses. You're no Nadson.[30] You haven't got the stuff. You lack a heart; you're coarse-grained. Besides, even Pushkin wasted his gifts on verse. For authentic, holy literature, stick to honest prose."

For me he was this holy prose incarnate and I felt smothered in it as in smoke.

His landlady was his mistress. She was a woman with massive breasts and a backside no ordinary chair could accommodate. Starostin, with great solemnity, gave her a wide, cane-seated armchair as a birthday gift. Deeply moved, she kissed her lover thrice on the lips, and turning to me said, "See, young man, take a lesson from him, on how to treat a woman." Happy Starostin, beside me, grinned and stroked his pale ears, limp as a dog's.

It was a clear day in late March. Flowers bloomed in the window sills; and the sound of spring freshets streamed into the room, redolent with baking odors, soap and tobacco. My youth and ignorance did not keep me from an anguished perception of the squalid and confused drama hidden behind "the holy prose."

In reveries of heroic achievement and dazzling joys, I kept watch over the bags and tarpaulins and other equipment against free-booting Cossacks of the next station; I read Shakespeare and Heine until, suddenly aware of the corroding realities about me, I would sink into a stupor for hours as though stunned by a rap over the head.

In this town, malodorous with grease, soap and decayed meat, the mayor got the priests to hold a *Te Deum* in his yard to exorcise devils from his well. Every Saturday the teacher gave his wife a whipping in the bathhouse. His neighbors invited their friends in to watch the performance through the hedge, since the fat wife sometimes got away and, stark naked, dodged about the garden to escape her husband. I was there, too, to peep at the peepers. Once I got into a fight with one of them and nearly got hauled to the police station. Someone in the crowd sought to pacify me by saying, "What are you getting in such a stew about? Everybody likes to have a look at such goings on. Moscow itself can't furnish a sight like this."

The railway clerk from whom I rented a corner of a room at a ruble a month, tried to convert me to his faith that Jews were hermaphrodites

[30] A popular poet of the period.

besides being swindlers. Following an argument with him he, together with his wife and brother, came to my bed during the night to investigate whether I was a Jew. This cost him a dislocated arm and his brother a couple of teeth before I was rid of them. It was these people, who lived merely to eat, whose greatest pleasure was to accumulate varieties of food, as if a universal famine were on the way, who imprisoned life in close and sordid cells.

After all I had seen, the enlightened "intelligentsia" seemed to me to lead a drab life, though its current detoured that confused, hectic turbulence that was the diseased reality of general everyday existence. The closer I looked, the greater grew my anxiety. The intelligentsia did not appear to be aware of its isolation in this slovenly little town where they are looked at as aliens, where there is no interest in Mikhailovsky or Spencer and no concern over the role of the individual in historical developments.

At their parties, the "intelligentsia" were diffidently gallant to anonymous, drab, little women, two of whom, sisters, had a remarkable likeness to bats. I recall the stocky, bow-legged Mazin, an ex-naval officer, a Schopenhauerian who rhapsodized affectedly over the "metaphysics of love" and the "instinct for race preservation." The bats drew up their legs and hunched themselves more deeply into their gray capes as though the philosopher's words might strip them. And, indeed, Mazin received a note from the bats' brother, a railroad official, "My dear sir, if you keep talking about the metaphysics of love in the presence of my sisters, I'll box your ears and enter charges against you to the Director."

I contrasted to this the nights at Petrovsky's where, frankly naked, the stark drama of instinct was given its hour, and reason was blinded in delirious and desperate amorous play. Semisavages, crooks, sots managed to achieve ecstasy. Skilled and beautiful was their singing of the folk songs, while "philosophers," "radicals" and "Narodniki" clumsily rendered mewling little tunes like "Not the Autumn Rain," "There Where the Slow Bulak Flows"; or

> "Old Copernicus sweated off a pound
> To demonstrate that the earth is round,
> —the fool."

I lacked the intellect, the imagination and the energy required to join these two worlds together, riven apart by a deep, ingrained split.

Writing now of what happened over thirty years ago, and seeing again, distinctly before me, both these types, I find myself powerless to picture in words, the spectacled bookworms in their blowing trousers and bohemian vests and their dull, checkered mantle of erudite words. And this not because the others are rugged and therefore easy to grasp while these have been smoothed to slipperiness under the laundering of learning. No, I find the cause in a deep, I might call it racial, and certainly inner, moral separation.[31]

On one side the ceaseless and senseless writhings of the powers of instinct; on the other the fluttering of the wingless bird of reason, in the foul cage of reality. In no other land, I think, have the creative forces of life been so cruelly sundered as in Russia. When I spoke of the Petrovsky orgies, expressing a certain anxiety over them, I sensed the repressed envy on the part of the "cultured" ones for those primitive delights and I gathered that their condemnation was a formality, a bow to the "sense of decency."

Only Bazhenov, with a heavy sigh, after exclaiming, "Phew, how awful!" admitted, "I'd have been sunk there like a bull in a marsh. I can see how your sort would be drawn to them; our life is the flat, unleavened, everyday existence, while theirs touches the epic. Petrovsky, you know, should have had some action taken against him, but he has a protector on the Board. Some time ago his house was searched on another matter—a missing consignment of tea. Taking a sheet out of a table drawer, he handed it to the inspector, "Here's everything I've honestly stolen, itemized!" Bazhenov fell silent, frowned, rubbed the back of his head and then continued, smiling, "Honestly stolen—only a Russian, I tell you, could say such a thing. We feel called upon to reconcile the irreconcilable. Our jollity can be fearsome, our love cruelty. Just the same—" getting up out of his chair, stretching and waving his hands, "we Russians are a noble people. That's probably why our misery is so measureless."

Bazhenov was among the few who aroused my fellow-feeling and respect. A divinity student from Tomsk, he had succeeded, with great difficulty, in entering Kiev University where he was found "unreliable," expelled, and given a prison term of several months. His long hair made him look like a priest in mufti; his motions had the precision of an athlete, adding to his tall and robust figure a dignity seldom found in

---

[31] (Author's note): A worried perception of the moral alienation of the "intelligentsia," that is the schism between the intellectual and the popular, has persistently troubled me all my life. I have often touched upon it in my literary work. It inspired my story, "My Companion" and others. The perception has grown into a presentiment of doom.

the shambling Seminary students. He had a remarkably soft voice, but no ear at all, and despised music which, according to him, "seduces one into chaos."

His squinting gray eyes, glancing out of a pocked, square face framed in a black spade beard, had a gentle look. There was something wise-acreish and superior in his attitude toward me and the rest. The account he gave me of the development of Christianity was captivating, particularly of the clashing sects in the Dark Ages. He also coached me through the *History of Inductive Sciences*. When talking he paced, almost soundlessly, up and down. He kept his hands in his pocket, and his only gestures to emphasize important points in what he was saying were a raising of the eyebrows and a shake of his head. Sometimes he would stop midway in a sentence, which he would never complete, and fall into a revery, during which he chewed on his beard, scraped his little finger across his steep forehead pitted with smallpox, and remained so in a long, tranced silence. Always at those moments, I don't know why, I felt a vague anguish. I once asked him what he was thinking of.

"So much intellect misspent," he replied softly, "and what intellect!"

He often dwelt, persuasively, on the power, the beauty of the mind. "After all, boy, reason decides everything. That lever, in time, will sway the world."

"On what pivot?" I asked.

"The people," he replied, with conviction. "Above all you—your mind."

I shared his conviction and it reinforced a strong mutual affection. Sprawled on the grass, on a still twilight, out on the steppe, I repeated to him the policeman Nikiforich's remarks about compassion and the Tolstoyan's about the Bible and Darwin.

After a meditative silence he replied, "Darwin is the truth that repels me just as Hell would repel me had it been the truth. In a machine, the less friction, the better it works. In life, on the contrary, the greater the friction the quicker the achievement of goals and the attainment of wisdom. And wisdom is justice, harmony of interests. Struggle, therefore, must be acknowledged, the law of life. In that your cop is right; if struggle's the law, there's no place for compassion."

And lying on his back, staring up into the sky with wide-open eyes, he sank into thoughtful silence. The sun had set fire to the clouds behind which it was setting, and had fused into a huge pile of glowing coals, scattering red rays over the steppe. The stubble of last year's grass seemed drenched with rosy dew. The perfume of the spring grass and flowers strengthened to the point of intoxication. Bazhenov sat up, lit a cigarette, but immediately cast it away, saying with a frown, "In my opinion humanitarianism has come too late in history, about three thousand years too late. I have to get back to town—coming along?"

Toward the end of May I was transferred to the Krutaya station on the Volga-Don branch, where I was promoted to weigher. There on the first of June I received a letter from a bookbinder friend in Borissoglebsk, telling me that Bazhenov had shot himself in the field adjoining the cemetery. This note from Bazhenov was enclosed, "Misha, sell my things and give the landlord seven rubles, thirty kopecks. Bind the volumes of Whewell and send them to "Oldhead" Peshkov, in Krutaya. My Spencer is also for him. The rest are yours, except those in Greek and Latin which go to Kiev to the address you will find enclosed. Farewell, my friend. B."

The note left me stunned as if I had been pierced to the heart. I found it hard to reconcile myself to the departure from life of this man, seemingly so stable and strong-spirited.

What had brought him to his death? I recalled how once, in a saloon, when he was a little beery, he suddenly remarked, "You know, Alex, what's the best song in the world?" Looking at me across the table, with the eyes of a gentle bear, he sang this little French ditty in a low, sad voice: "When I was small I wasn't tall; I went to school with the other tots."

Singing it, tears misted his eyes. "A charming song, I tell you. It's so simple, it's filled with such sad humor." He translated it into Russian, but it remained incomprehensible to me how it could bring tears and a glow of rapture into the eyes of this robust and shaggy man. I was to meet not a few others destroyed by this same "sad humor."

Within a few months life, so stern and precise in educating me, forced a review of the Petrovsky lesson upon me, one of the most depressing experiences I have had to endure.

In a dingy saloon in the Sukharev district in Moscow, a tall, cadaverous man in spectacles took a chair opposite me, at my table. His bony face, and wispy beard and moustaches could have come from one of Doré's Don Quixote drawings. He wore an obviously borrowed blue shirt and gray cotton trousers, patched at the knees and too short for him. One shoe was rubber-soled, the other leather. Working his moustaches to needle points, he fixed me with dim, but avid, eyes; then stood up, adjusted the eyeglasses on his ashen brows, and quivering and walking gropingly with his hands out like a blind man, he introduced himself as "Lawyer Gladkov."

With dirty finger he inscribed his signature in the air and then enunciated solemnly, "Alexis Gladkov."

His voice was choked and he twisted his neck as if it were in an invisible noose.

He turned out, of course, to be one of the great-hearted who had been dragged down to the depths by the enemies of truth, because he had served at its altar. Now he had won new eminence as the Grand Master of the "Order of St. Aquavita"; his new services included composing theatre notices, defending oppressed innocents and probing the hearts—and purses—of sympathetic merchants' wives. "The Russian, especially the woman, enjoys being miserable. Suffering or recitals of suffering act as the emotional mustard by which the heart can be reached through the fat deposited by the overrich food of the flesh."

I had come across many of his sort. I usually treated them with suspicion, but they also interested me. An interest in those fallen from the heights, is logical in a man making his way up. Besides the "fallen," the sinners, are frequently richer spiritually and finer-grained than the accepted, goodly ones whom I had already, in my youth, come to think of as no more real than waxwork figures.

Two hours later, or thereabouts, I was sprawled out beside Gladkov on a wooden pallet in a flophouse. Pillowing his head on his arms, his body stretched rigid, the lawyer regaled me with ferocious aphorisms suitable to wolves. His little devil's-tail beard wagged with every cough. He was pitiful in his impotent fury. He was hedged in his barbed words like a porcupine in quills.

Over our heads hung the cavernous basement ceiling. A nauseous drip stained the walls. The earthen floor exhaled acid odors of putrefaction. In the shadows nameless bodies writhed and snored, with rags for bedclothes. The iron-barred window looked like a bricked-in hole. A cat lay there, emitting a sickly mewing. On a wooden bench, underneath, sitting cross-legged like a Turk, was a repulsively obese and shaggy creature, mending trousers by the light of a candle end. He was bawling a hymn to the Virgin Mary at the end of which he smacked his bloated lips and started all over again.

"Pimen Maslov, chemist and genius," Gladkov introduced him. Other geniuses swarmed in this hole, among them the "illustrious" pianist Bragin, a sharp little fellow who looked like a boy, though his wavy hair was threaded with silver and blue pouches hung under his eyes. I was startled by that contradiction carried out in his expression—an evil smile, that seemed immovably fixed on his thin lips, denied by the melancholy loveliness of his feminine eyes.

In the morning Gladkov told me, "We will now bestow the Knighthood of the Order of St. Aquavita on this new acolyte. Watch it. It's a marvelous ritual."

He pointed to a curly-headed, trouserless youth, sitting in his shirt. He was purple from his unending drunk and the blue pupils of his eyes were frozen into his bloodshot eyeballs. The corpulent chemist stood over him, painting his cheeks, and blackening his brows and beard with burnt cork.

"Don't," mumbled the curly-head, his bare lifeless legs dangling. Gladkov, twirling his moustaches explained, "He's a student, a merchant's son. It's his fifth week of drinking with us. He's drunk up all his money and his clothes."

A dumpy, fat woman appeared. The bridge of her nose had either fallen or been knocked in. She had impudent, provocative eyes. Throwing a bundle of fibre mats she had brought in with her on the benches, she said, "The vestments are ready."

"Let's dress him," said Gladkov.

Five people, gray and shaggy, moved like phantoms among the basement shadows. The "pianist" puffed industriously on some coals on a grill. They threw brief exclamations at each other, "Quiet down," "Move over," "What're you up to?"

They dragged the benches into the middle of the basement. Maslov draped the fibre mats over him like a chasuble and put on a cardboard mitre. Gladkov robed himself like a deacon. Four men seized the curly-headed student by the arms and legs.

"Don't, please," he moaned as they laid him out on the bench.

"Choir ready?" asked the lawyer as he brandished a pan of crackling coals, from which rose the blue smoke of smoldering leaves, which he fanned upon the prostrate man. The initiate wrinkled his nose, shut his smarting eyes, coughed, rubbed his feet across each other like a fly, slapping the board with his soles.

"Hearken!" cried Gladkov, swaddled in the fibre mats, a shocking, living caricature, in the writhings of his neck, the jerks of his head, and his grimaces. Maslov, at the feet of the student, began a nasal declamation, "Brethren, let us call on the devil to rest the soul of the youth, Jacob, newly deceased from drink and Babylonian vice. May Satan welcome him with joy and esteem to the abominations of everlasting Hell!"

Five shaggy hoboes clustering on one side sullenly intoned a blasphemous hymn, their hoarse voices fusing into a toneless smother in the stony pit. Bragin led the singing with graceful flourishes of his right hand, while his left was held stiff in warning.

By this time I had become shockproof against such obscenity, I had seen so much of it and in such variety. But the chant of these people was a special abomination, its shameless images ingeniously expressed in shameless words, exhibited a truly Satanic fancy, a bottomless viciousness. Never before or since have I heard its equal for sophisticated and desperate depravity. From five throats streams of venomous filth were spat on one man. And done without gusto, as like a duty; done, not jestingly, but ceremoniously. Clearly it had often been done before; this rite, solemnizing a man's spiritual extinction, was as smoothly, harmoniously and gravely performed as church ritual.

Overcome with horror, I heard Gladkov's nasal responses, the cynical drone of the chemist, the choir's suffocated chant, at this funeral of a living man, this blasphemous ritual over a breathing corpse. He lay with his hands crossed on his breast; his lips moved in an inarticulate mumble; his wide-open eyes fluttered and he smiled vapidly; at moments, a frightened tremor convulsed his body and he tried to escape, but the choir, with silent, gentle pressures, clamped him back on the bench.

I would probably have found the ceremony less odious had these squalid phantoms done it in fun, had it evoked from them even a cynical laughter or the despairing laughter of the "has been," the life-thwarted, the life-mutilated ones. But not they. They went about it with the sullen preoccupation of assassins, with the solemnity of pagan priests making sacrifices to hallucinations of a diseased, vengeful and irresponsible imagination.

I felt limp and stunned, an overpowering weight pressing upon me and pulling me under in an impassible swamp; I felt that I, too, was being interred. With a stupefied and chagrined smile I looked on, and was on the point of beseeching them, "Stop, it's wrong; it's horrible; this isn't joking."

It was the "pianist's" shrill voice, more than anything, that pierced my ear. In venting his ecstatic yells he shut his eyes, and bent his head far back on his neck. These yells soared above the hoarse voices of the others and, in the smoky murk, they gave a peculiarly sensual emphasis to the dissolute words. I, too, felt a brutish urge to howl out.

"The grave!" cried Gladkov, waving the pan of coals that served him as censer. The choir roared out in full voice: "Grave, come hither!"

And the broken-nosed woman, almost stark nude, entered, dancing. Her flabby flesh quivered. Purple bruises, scars, and swollen blue veins covered her stumpy legs. Maslov greeted her with a lascivious gesture which Gladkov imitated. Shouting out indecencies she embraced each in turn. The choir then heaved her by the arms and legs alongside the "deceased."

"No, don't!" he shrieked, and once more tried to squirm off the bench, but was pushed back. To a tune, dismal despite its dance tempo and its leering words, the woman, bending over him, the dirty wallets of her breasts wagging, performed a disgusting parody of intercourse.

At this point "Queen Margot," the sustaining dream of loveliness in my life, came to my mind. A swelling in my breast burst. I rushed at these broken relics of men, my fists knocking their teeth out. And toward evening I found myself under a railway embankment, on a heap of railway ties, both my hands bruised and bleeding and my left eye puffed and tender. From the sky, foul as the earth, dripped an autumn drizzle. I pulled out tufts of wet, dead grass with which I wiped my face and hands and reflected on the exhibition I had just seen.

I was a robust and unusually muscular lad. I could cross myself nine times without a pause, with an eighty-pound weight in my hand. I carried two-hundred-pound sacks of flour with ease. At that moment, however, I felt spent and feeble, like a sick child. I was on the point of tears with a sense of humiliation. Avidly I had sought communion with the beauty so seductively described in books. I was ready to give rapturous reverence to anything that inspired strength for life. It was time for me to taste the pleasures of life; therefore, more frequently, I experienced the purges of rage. Hotly it flooded my breast, blotting out my reason. It turned my eager interest in people to loathing and contempt. It was a painful frustration to encounter, over and over again, things so foul, idiotic, pathetic and alien.

The ritual in the flophouse cellar became an agonizing memory, with Gladkov's yell, "The grave!" perforating my ear, and the repulsive body of the woman floating before my eyes—that mound of lusts shoveled over a human being. And this brought to mind the orgies at Petrovsky's, and I understood how clean is the fury of the flesh in healthy people in comparison with the ferment of corruption that retains an outward human semblance.

There, semi-savages pouring out their overflow of strength in devotions to beauty, regarding the overflow as sin and punishment, rebelling in a phantasmal hope of liberation, dreading to consume their souls in the insatiable hunger of their bodies. Here impotence, in the abyss of despair, revenging itself by mocking that instinct that continually resows the fields of life devastated by death and the spring of all the beauty of the world. Here life was sickened to the root, its mysterious and beautiful sources infected with the pus of a diseased imagination.

What, then, was life up there from which people fall so terribly low?

Chapter Eight

ON A GLOOMY, BLUSTERING MAY MORNING I LEFT TSARITSYN, PLANning to reach Nizhny in September. It was the year I was supposed to put in my army service. I hitched rides on freight cars at night, but most of the way I went on foot. I got my bread working in Cossack villages, in monasteries and on farms. I roamed over the Don steppes, over the districts of Tambov and Ryazan. From Ryazan I followed the Oka River, then wheeled toward Moscow. On the way I paid a visit to the Tolstoy home, but found Tolstoy himself gone. Madame Tolstoy told me he was at the Troitz-Sergeievsk monastery.

She stood in the courtyard at the door of a hut brimful of books. She conducted me into the kitchen and gave me a roll and coffee. I learned from her, among other things, of the hordes of no-goods who surrounded Tolstoy, of whom Russia had a superfluity. I had had that impression, myself, and it was with a good conscience that I corroborated this shrewd woman's observations.

September was almost over. The ground was lush with autumn rain; a cold wind combed the stubble fields; the woods were in their most fetching autumn colors; really a beautiful time of the year but not the most suitable for a traveler on foot, whose shoe leather happened to be in shreds.

At the Moscow freight yards I persuaded a trainman to accommodate me in a cattle car occupied by eight bulls from Cherkassk, who were on their way to a Nizhny abattoir. The behavior of five of them was good-neighborly, but the other three somehow resented my company and did their best, all the way, to discommode me. When they saw they were succeeding they emitted complacent snorts and bellows. The trainman, a bandy-legged little rummy with tousled whiskers, gave me the job of feeding my fellow-travelers. At the way stations he pushed in armfuls of hay to me with the order, "Give it to them!"

I spent thirty-four hours of my life in the company of the bulls. They brought me to the naïve belief that I had come upon the most brutish of beasts.

In my bag I had a notebook full of my writings, among them a phenomenon, in prose and verse, called "The Song of the Ancient Oak." Though I have never suffered from conceit and considered myself at that time an ignoramus, I was, nevertheless, confident that it was a masterpiece. Into it I had crammed every idea that had strayed into my head during my past, hard and varied ten years. I was sure the whole reading public, on making its acquaintance, would acclaim its originality. The truth I revealed in it would, I was convinced, open the hearts of all and usher in a dignified, virtuous and happy life. More than that I did not look for.

At that time Karonin lived in Nizhny. I paid him some visits, but did not venture to show him my philosophic oak. Karonin was in poor health, and my compassion toward him was increased by my feeling that he was in the grip of an obsession.

"It might be so," he would say, expelling clots of smoke from his nostrils, and sighing despondently; then he would brighten and say, "and then again it might not."

His conversation confused and troubled me. I had a feeling that it was his right to speak, but his duty to be more exact. This, together with personal affection, made me behave circumspectly with this hero of Petropavlovsk [32] to avoid hurting his feelings.

I had met him in Kazan where he had stopped over on his return from exile. He left with me an ineradicable impression of a man headed for a destination he would never reach.

"It was hardly necessary for me to come here, after all." These were the first words I heard him say on entering a dismal room in a shed in the filthy yard of a truckmen's tavern. I saw a tall, stooped man in the middle of the room, abstractedly studying the dial of a large watch in his hand. In the fingers of his other hand a cigarette smoldered. He began pacing the room in giant strides, giving short answers to questions about the revolutionary movement put by a man named Somov, a landlord. His eyes, nearsighted but clear as a child's, looked burdened

[32] Dungeon for political prisoners, in St. Petersburg.

and weary. A downy beard coated his chin and cheeks unevenly. On his pointed skull bristled the stiff, unkempt hair of a priest.

As he paced the room he jingled coins in the pocket of his crumpled trousers, while his right hand flourished his cigarette like a conductor's wand. He breathed through clouds of smoke, coughed, moistened his lips, and kept glancing moodily at his watch. It was apparent from the ill-coordinated movements of his gangling body, that he was exhausted. The room filled gradually with some dozen, dreary-looking students, with a glazier and a baker added.

In his choked consumptive's voice, Karonin spoke of his life in exile and of the morale of the exiles. He looked at nobody as he spoke. He might have been talking to himself. There were frequent pauses. Sometimes, sitting down for a moment on the window sill, his head would recoil from the gust of cold air that came in from the little winter ventilator, a gust that brought in not only the cold but the reek of manure and horse piss. He brushed his hair back with bony fingers and replied to the torrent of questions, "Possibly, but I'm not sure. I don't know. I can't say."

Karonin made no hit with the youth. They were used to know-it-alls who had an answer to everything. And his conscientious admission of a lack of knowledge only led to the judgment, "a scared rabbit."

My glazier friend, Anatol, had another explanation for the honest concern in Karonin's childlike eyes and his reiterated "I don't know," as the hesitation of a man who knows life and is fearful of leading these timid kittens too far into it. Life-tried people like Anatol and me had little confidence in the bookworms. We knew the students well and that their present gravity was all put on.

About midnight Karonin brought his speech to a sudden stop, took a position in the middle of the room, in a stance in which he soon resembled a pillar of smoke. He chafed his cheek with the palm of his hand, as if washing it with invisible water, got his watch out again from some nook under his belt, brought it up under his nose and said, in a startled tone, "So? I have to go now. My daughter is ill in bed. Good night."

He pressed the hands thrust out to him, in his humid palms and virtually staggered out of the room. We were left to the "riot" that is the inevitable and seemingly obligatory conclusion to all such occasions.

At Nizhny Karonin kept a nursing eye on the growth of the Tolstoyan movement among its intelligentsia. He also assisted in organizing a colony in Simbirsk. He described the speedy collapse of that enterprise in his story, "The Borsk Colony."

He tried to recruit me. "Why not establish yourself on the soil here? You might find it what you're looking for."

But my experiences with these devotees of self-torment had left me unattracted. In Moscow, I had come upon one of the pioneer Tolstoyans, Novoselov, organizer of workmen's associations in Tver and Smolensk, who had become a Tolstoyan renegade, a contributor to the "Orthodox Review" [33] and an embittered enemy of Tolstoy.

A tall man, he seemed to have considerable physical vigor. His affected simplicity bordered on rudeness. Behind it I sensed the ill-masked resentments of an ambitious man. He brusquely rejected all culture. This did not go well with me, for I was painfully making my way into the domain of culture, determined to overcome all obstacles to it.

I first encountered him in the apartment of a follower of Nechayev, [34] a man named Orlov, translator of Leopardi and Flaubert, and one of the founders of that splendid library of classics, "The Literary Pantheon." I found Novoselov a man of wit and erudition which, all that evening, he employed in pulling the Tolstoyan movement into grotesque pieces. That movement happened, at that time, to have some appeal to me as a place where I might find a secluded philosophic nook, in which I could review the lessons of my life, up to that moment.

I was, of course, aware that the celebrated writer, Korolenko, was then living in Nizhny. For some obscure reason I did not care for his famous *Makar's Dream*. A friend with whom I was walking in the rain suddenly nudged me and said, "Korolenko!"

I saw a stocky man walking with a vigorous gait. I could see only the curls of his beard under his dripping umbrella. He reminded me of a Tambov sexton, a breed I had sufficient reason to waste no friendship on, which lessened still further any desire I might have had to become acquainted. Nor was there anything to stimulate the desire in the advice I received from a chief of the secret police—one of the prime jokes of our curious Russian system.

A few days after my look at Korolenko, I was arrested and given quarters in one of the four towers of the Nizhny jail. In my circular cell there was nothing of interest except this inscription scratched into the steel-lined door: "Everything living comes from a cell."

---

[33] Organ of the church hierarchy.

[34] Nechayev, a leader of the Nihilists, the most extreme of the terrorist groups.

I meditated over this, wondering what the carver of that inscription had meant. Not recognizing this biological axiom, I assumed he had intended it humorously.

My examination was conducted by the head of the secret police, General Poznansky himself. He snorted, pounded his purple fist on the papers they had taken from me and said, "So, you write poems. Well, keep on writing them. It's a pleasure to read nice poems." I didn't think the epithet "nice" applicable to my verses. Yet, at that time, few of the intelligentsia shared the police chief's good opinion of verses.

For example, Sverdentzov, a writer who published sombre stories in the serious magazines, and an ex-Guards officer who had suffered exile for his Narodnik leanings and worshipped Vera Figner,[35] remarked, when I recited these lines from Fofanov: "What you said I did not hear, But that 'twas tender, well I know." "What rubbish! Most likely she asked him the time. And the ass felt exalted!"

As for General Poznansky, he was a lumbering fellow, whose waistcoat gaped from missing buttons, and whose gray-striped trousers were mottled with stains. His puffy face was rimmed with white hair and blotched with purple veins, and his swimming eyes looked confused and weary. He impressd me as lonely and wearily good-natured, like an old hound who has become bored with barking. I had seen references, in a collection of Koni's speeches, to Poznansky's tragedy. I knew he was a drug addict; that his daughter was a gifted pianist; that he had organized and served as president of the local Technical Society; that he had advocated home crafts at its meetings and had opened a shop on the town's busiest street for the sale of craftsmen's goods from various regions; finally, that he had sent off to St. Petersburg police reports on Zemstvo officials, on Korolenko and on the governor of the province, Baranov, who was, himself, not above that sort of thing.

Everything connected with the general was slovenly. Edges of dirty bed linen dragged behind his leather couch. From beneath emerged a muddy shoe and a seventy-five-pound chip of alabaster. The windows were jungles of bird cages in which a dizzy hopping went on. His desk was cluttered with laboratory apparatus. Opposite me lay a thick French volume on *The Theory of Electricity* and Sechenov's *Reflexes of the Brain*. He chain-smoked short, stubby cigarettes, whose thick smoke troubled me with the thought that the tobacco in them was doped.

"You a revolutionist!" he said, in an indignant voice. "You're not a

[35] A terrorist involved in several attempts on the life of Tsar Alexander II, which finally succeeded.

Jew or a Pole. You're a writer. When I let you off take your manuscripts to Korolenko to look over. Do you know him? No? Quite a
writer, on a level with Turgenev . . ."

A strong smell came from him. He didn't feel like going on and each
word was dragged out with an effort. It was a bore. For distraction I
looked into a showcase, beside the desk, in which there was a display
of commemorative medals.

The general, following my sideward glance, labored up out of his
chair and asked me, "Interested?"

Pulling his chair to the showcase, which he opened, he said, "These
medals commemorate great events and personalities. This one com-
memorates the seizure of the Bastille, this one Nelson's victory at
Aboukir—know something about French history? This one was struck
for an anniversary of the confederation of the Swiss cantons; this one
honors Galvani.[36] This one—an inferior piece, by the way—was struck
in honor of Cuvier." [37]

His eyeglass jiggled on his purple nose; a glow came into his watery
eyes. He handled them one by one, in his stubby fingers, as if they were
not metal, but glass.

"What consummate art!" he mumbled, blowing the dust off each
piece with comically pursed lips.

I offered sincere homage to the beauty of the little metal discs; it
was clear that they were one of the old man's passions. Sighing, as he
locked the showcase, he asked did I like singing birds? On that subject
I knew more than three generals put together, and we launched on an
animated discussion. It happened that the old man had already summoned a policeman to escort me back to jail. He stood imposingly
erect in the doorway while his chief rambled on, clucking with regret as
he concluded, "I've had no luck getting hold of one of those wonderful
bee-eaters. Birds are a marvelous race, don't you think? Well, off with
you, and God bless you! By the way," he added, "apply yourself to
learning how to write; not this."

Several days later I was again before the general, who grumbled,
"Of course you know where Somov's hiding; you should have told me
and I would have let you off at once. And there was no need to insult
the officer who was making the search." Then, leaning toward me suddenly, he asked jovially, "You don't snare birds any more?"

Some ten years after this humorous interview with the general, I

[36] Galvani, Italian scientist noted for his discoveries in electricity.
[37] French naturalist famous for his researches in anatomy.

was again under arrest at the Nizhny police station and about to be examined, when a young adjutant came up to me. "Remember General Poznansky?" he asked, "He died in Tomsk. He followed your literary career, was pleased over your successes and used to remark that he had been the first to recognize your talent. Shortly before his death he asked me to give you some medals that you had admired; that is, if you care to have them."

I was touched by this. On my discharge from prison I gave the medals to the Nizhny museum.

I was rejected as a soldier. A stout, jovial doctor who looked rather like a butcher and handled the recruits as if they were steers in a slaughterhouse, imparted to me these findings of his examination: "Unfit. You're full of holes, young chap. A perforated lung and a varicose vein in your leg."

I was chagrined. Not long before this I had met an engineering officer named Paskhin or Paskhalov, I don't recall which. He had been in the battle of Kushka and gave picturesque accounts of life on the Afghan border. That spring he was to go to the Pamirs [38] to map the frontiers. He was tall, sinewy and high-strung. He did oil paintings in the style of Fedotov, little genre scenes of camp life. I sensed something clashing and off-balance in him, what is usually called "abnormal."

He kept after me, "Join our engineers' corps and I'll take you to the Pamirs. And then—the most beautiful sight in the world—the desert! Mountains are a chaos—for harmony you must go to the desert!" Narrowing his large gray, unquiet eyes and dropping his voice to a caressing whisper, he went on and on about the mysterious attractions of the desert; and I listened dumbfounded, that one could make so alluring a void of endless sand and unbroken silence, of withering heat and torturing thirst.

Hearing that I had been rejected, he shrugged it off. "No matter. Just write out a petition to join our engineering company as a volunteer and offer to take the required examinations. I'll take care of the rest."

I composed the petition, turned it in and awaited a reply. A few days later the embarrassed Paskhalov stammered, "You're considered politically unreliable, so there's nothing to be done." He looked down and said, a little reproachfully, "Too bad you hid that from me." I told him it was as much a surprise to me as to him, but I don't think he

[38] High mountain range in Central Asia.

believed me. He left Nizhny shortly after. Later an item in a Moscow paper reported his suicide; he had slit his throat, with a razor, in his bath.

My life continued to be full of difficulty and confusion. I worked in a small brewery, rolling beer kegs in a damp cellar and washing and corking bottles. That wasted my whole day. After that I took a desk job in a distillery, but the very first day a greyhound belonging to the manager's wife jumped me. I killed him with a blow on the skull, and that ended the job.

Finally, on a particularly difficult day, I decided to show Korolenko my work. There had been a three-day blizzard. Snowdrifts hedged the streets. Every roof had a sumptuous white headdress; every window box was laced and tasselled. A sun of white ice shone in the pale sky.

Korolenko lived in the outskirts, on the upper floor of a wooden cottage. In front of it a solidly built man, dressed in a short, clumsily cut sheepskin and big Viatka boots, and a queerly shaped fur hat with earlaps was skillfully wielding a snow shovel.

As I vaulted over the snowpile to the doorway he asked me, "Who are you looking for?"

"Korolenko."

"That's me."

Above a thick, curly beard, fringed with hoarfrost, were kind, brown eyes. I did not recognize him, for, when he had been pointed out to me in the street before, his face had been covered up. Leaning on his shovel, he heard me explain my visit, then squinted as if with an effort to recall something.

"Your name's familiar. Must have been you I heard about a couple of years ago, from Romass. Of course."

He led the way up the stairs. "Aren't you cold, dressed so lightly?" adding in a mumble, as if to himself, "What a stubborn old *muzhik,* Romass. A clever Ukrainian. Where's he now? In Viatka, I think."

In a little corner room, with the windows facing on the garden, a room, over-furnished with two desks, bookcases and three chairs, he dried his streaming beard with a handkerchief, while leafing through the pages of my thick manuscript.

"Of course I'll read it," he said. "What a curious handwriting. It looks clear and legible, yet it's hard to read."

He kept glancing from my manuscript in his lap to me, in a manner that confused me. "You have 'ziz-gag' here—a slip of the pen obviously—the word's 'zigzag.' "

His pause before he found the word "slip" showed me that Korolenko knew how to salve a man's pride.

"Romass wrote me the peasants tried to blow him up and then burn down his house; was that how it turned out? You were living with him then, weren't you?"

As he spoke he kept turning the pages. "No foreign expressions except where absolutely necessary. As a rule, it's best to avoid them. The Russian language is rich enough to express any subtlety of feeling and any shade of thought."

He interspersed such comments with questions about Romass and the countryside.

"What a grim face you have," he said suddenly, adding, with a smile, "Finding life hard?"

His soft accent was nothing like the coarse Volga dialect with its heavy stress on the "O," yet he had a marked resemblance, to my eyes, to the Volga pilots, not alone in his sturdy frame and keen, intelligent eyes, but in the relaxed good humor characteristic of those for whom lives and rivers flow in tortuous beds in which dangerous rocks and sandbars lie hidden.

"You use coarse expressions—because you consider them stronger?"

I knew that coarseness came naturally to me. I acknowledged it; but I attributed it to my lack of time and opportunity to acquire a gentler vocabulary and finer sensibilities.

With an anxious look at me and in a kindly manner he observed, "You say here—'that is like that'—a harsh, clumsy expression. Why not 'that's so'? Do you feel the difference?"

It was the first time I had experienced such analytical criticism; I was awed by its precision.

Further along in my poem someone sat "like a hawk" on a temple ruin. Korolenko, smiling, found the simile unsuitable, the attitude repellent rather than majestic. "Slips" turned up again and again; their profusion crushed me. I must have reddened like a burning coal. Korolenko hastened to laugh my embarrassment away with anecdotes of "slips" in the writings of Uspensky. The intention was kindly, but I was too mortified by now to heed or even understand anything more. All I wanted was release from this humiliating scene.

Literary men and actors, as is well known, are as vain as poodles. I was in a state of utter depression the next few days. I had come in contact with a rare kind of writer—vastly different from the softhearted but unstable Karonin, not to speak of the clownish Starostin;

and from the grumpy Svedentsov Ivanovich, composer of heavy-handed stories, whose motto was, "A story must strike like a club at the reader's soul, to make him realize what a beast he is," a feeling with which I was in sympathy at that time.

Korolenko's freighted words were the first to impress upon me the importance of literary structure, of the turn of a sentence—comments whose simplicity and aptness startled me. Hearing him I realized, with a certain pang, that writing was a responsible undertaking.

I was with him more than two hours. Yet not a word on the meaning, the content of my poem. I knew the judgment on that would be unfavorable.

A fortnight or so later, the little, red-headed professor of statistics, Deriagin, a witty and gracious man, brought me the manuscript with this message, "Korolenko is worried that he might have seemed overbearing. He says you have ability but ought to stop philosophizing and draw more upon your observations from nature. Your stuff has humor but it veers on coarseness, but not to worry about that. As for the poetry, he thinks it's mad."

On the folder covering the manuscript there was a pencil notation in a precise, angular script, "It's not easy to estimate your powers from 'The Song,' but I think you have talent. Write about something you have actually experienced and let me see it. I'm no judge of poetry. Yours seems to be confused in its sense, but I found some lines that were powerful and alive. V. Kor." Still no word about the ideas. This strange man did not even give me a clue as to his reactions to it.

Two sheets slipped out of the manuscript, one a poem entitled, "The Mountain Speaks to the Climber," the other, "Dialogue Between Satan and the Wheel." I don't recall the theme of that dialogue— probably the whirl and circling of life; nor do I recall the remarks of the mountain. I tore up the verses; I tore up the entire manuscript; I tossed them into the stove. What could it mean, I pondered, to write something I had actually experienced? I had experienced everything I had set down in my manuscript.

As for the verses, they had got into the manuscript by mistake. My poetry was my secret: I had not shown it around; I did not particularly understand it myself. Among my friends the stiff translations by Barikov and Likhachev of minor foreign poets were valued above Pushkin. Nekrasov [39] then was the reigning poet though the young

[39] Populist poet, author of *Who Can Be Happy Or Free in Russia?*

were taking to Nadson,[40] whom their elders, if they accepted him at all, did so condescendingly.

I was held to be a sober soul. Solemn people whom I sincerely respected gave me serial lectures on the significance of handicrafts industry, on programs for the people, on the responsibilities of the intelligentsia, on the corrupting contagion of capitalism which never, nay, never!—will infect the Russia of peasants and socialists.

And now I would be gossiped about as the author of mad verses! I was sorry for those who would be compelled to alter their good opinion of me. I resolved to write no more, neither poetry nor prose. And actually, for the rest of that period in Nizhny, a matter of nearly two years, I didn't write a line, though sometimes the urge was strong.

Nevertheless, it was with grief that I brought the fruit of my wisdom to the altar of "all-purifying fire."

Korolenko stood apart from the local "intelligentsia," which considered itself radical and in which I felt like a goldfinch in a flock of sedate blackbirds. Their favorite author was Zlatovratsky, of whom they said, "He purifies and elevates the soul"; and who was thus recommended to me by one of the guides of my youth, "Read Zlatovratsky; he's a personal acquaintance of mine, a man of integrity."

Uspensky was another of their favorites, though he was suspected of a regrettable skepticism toward the peasant world. They also read Karonin, Machtet, Zasodimsky, and looked into Potapenko who "seems to be all right." Mamin-Siberiak was highly regarded, though his "vague tendencies" were deplored. Turgenev, Dostoyevsky and Tolstoy were outsiders.

My friends did not know what to make of Korolenko. Having suffered exile, having written *The Dream of Makar*, he compelled respect. But the content of his stories confused them; was alien to minds that had restricted themselves to literature on peasant life.

"His work comes from the brain," said one, "but the people respond only to what comes from the soul." They were especially outraged by his fine story, *In the Night*, wherein they detected a "metaphysical tendency," to them something criminal. Someone in that circle—I think it was Bogdanovich, attacked the story in a savage and rather witty pamphlet.

Somov, a man not quite in his right mind, yet with considerable influence among the young, said in an indignant stutter, "T-t-trash, the

[40] Lyric poet.

d-description of the physiology of b-birth is a t-task for s-s-scientific litera-t-ture and has n-no-thing to do with c-cockroaches. He's an im-m-mitator of T-Tolstoy, that K-Korolenko!"

But Korolenko's name reverberated in all the intellectual centers of the town. Cultural life circled around him, attracting or repelling everybody like a magnet.

"He likes to shine," said those who could produce no other indictment.

At that time an embezzlement had been uncovered in one of the city's banks and this very ordinary tale had extraordinary and tragic sequels. The chief figure in the case, a provincial salon lion, died in jail. His wife took poison. She had just been buried when her lover committed suicide on her grave. Two other people who had been involved in the scandal died before the excitement over the last suicide had subsided, and it was said they, too, had taken their lives. Korolenko had published some articles on the bank in "The Volga Herald" about the time these tragedies occurred. Superstitious people muttered that "Korolenko kills people with his pen." Lanin, for whom I was then working, defended him, "Everything is rightfully within the province of a writer."

Calumny, as we know, is a cheap commodity, easy to come by. And the poor of spirit saw to it that Korolenko got a generous and varied helping of it.

In these stagnant years, as Russian life slowly and imperceptibly spiraled upward toward uncomprehended goals, the thickset figure of a man resembling a pilot took clear shape in the sluggish whorls. Some Skoptsy (religious fanatics who castrated themselves) came to trial; and there was Korolenko, in the courtroom, sketching the almost inanimate, stunned faces of the fanatics; he was to be seen at Zemstvo meetings; he was perpetually on crusade. No significant event passed without receiving his sober attention.

An influential group of diverse, but remarkable, personalities surrounded him. Anensky, a man of profound but witty mind, Elpatievsky, a distinguished physician with passionate literary interests, a man drawn toward people with inexhaustible patience and genial affection, Bogdanovich, meditative, caustic, the "gentleman revolutionist," the critic Pisarev, Saveliev, chairman of the Zemstvo, Karelin, author of the most succinct and eloquent manifesto I have ever read—"Demand a Constitution!"—three words which he posted on the Nizhny fences after the March 1881 events.[41]

[41] The assassination of Tsar Alexander II.

Korolenko's circle had been jocularly nicknamed the Society of Sober Philosophers. On occasion a member would read a paper. I recall Karelin's brilliant study of Saint-Just and Elpatievsky's on the New Poetry—the work of the then young Fofanov, Frug, Korinfsky, Medvedsky, Minsky and Merezlikovsky. Among the Sober Philosophers should also be counted the Zemstvo statisticians, Driaguin, Kisliakov, Plotnikov, Konstantinov, Schmidt and other conscientious investigators of peasant economy, each of whom played a distinguished part in the task of clearing up the confusion surrounding the life of the peasantry. Each, furthermore, was the center of a peripheral circle concerned with the same problems, and there was something to learn in each. To me, personally, their serious attitude, free of pretense, was of great moment. Through them the impact of Korolenko's circle was spread wide, penetrating into quarters otherwise inaccessible to cultural influences.

I had a friend, Pimen Vlasov, porter to the magnate Markov, the virtual monopolist of the Caspian fish trade. Pimen, an ordinary, plain, slapped-together, snub-nosed muzhik confided to me some racketeer plans of his boss. In a hushed voice he added, "He'd go ahead, only he's scared of Korolenko. That one's a mystery man they sent down from Petersburg. They say he's a relative of some foreign ruler—hired from abroad, you know, to look into things here; they don't trust the Governor. This Korolenko, he's already got his hooks into some of the higher-ups, haven't you heard about it?" [42]

The illiterate Pimen was nevertheless a philosopher of sorts. He was possessed of an uncommonly cheerful faith in God and, with confident expectations, awaited an early approaching Judgment Day when "all lies" would come to their end. "Don't fret yourselves, dear friends," he would say, "Soon the lies will be no more; they will be drowned; they will consume each other." And saying this his gray lack-lustre eyes would grow strangely blue, burn and shine with such glowing happiness that it seemed, any moment, they might flare up and burn to ashes in that stream of blue sparks.

One Saturday Pimen and I spruced up at a bathhouse and went to a tavern. Suddenly Pimen gazed at me with his gentle eyes. "Hold on there," he said, and his hand around the tea glass trembled. He put the glass down, listened to something and crossed himself.

[42] (Author's note): In printed references to the legend that Korolenko was an English prince, S. Elionsky commented that the legend had some factual basis. I wrote him that he was in error. The legend originated in Nizhny. Pimen, I believe, was its begettor. It spread throughout the Nizhny region. In 1903 I heard it from a carpenter in Vladikavkaz.

"What's come over you?" I asked him.

"Dear friend, just this moment a corner of a little pillow of Heaven brushed my soul. That signifies the Lord will soon be calling me to His work."

"Nonsense, you're as healthy as they come."

"Sh!" he commanded, with a proud and joyous glance, "Don't say that! I know!"

The following Thursday he was run over and killed.

Without exaggerating, one may call the decade between 1886 and 1896 the Korolenko epoch, in Nizhny. That characterization of the period, by the way, has frequently appeared in print.

One of the town's eccentrics, A. A. Zarubin, the vodka distiller, who ended a career of carousing and speculation as a Tolstoyan and a teetotaler, told me in 1901, "It was in the Korolenko period that I first realized how badly I was living." Zarubin was a bit belated in setting his life to rights in the Korolenko period. He had passed fifty by then. Nevertheless he did remake or, more correctly, resurrect himself.

"I was sick in bed," he told me, "when my nephew Simon—you know, the one that was sent into exile—came to see me. 'Let me read to you,' he said, and then, brother of mine, he read me *Makar's Dream*. It was so good it brought tears to my eyes. That shows you how a man can feel for other men. From that hour I was a changed soul. I called in the chap I used to go out drinking with. 'Here, you son-of-a-bitch,' I told him, 'read this!' He read it and gave me as his opinion, that it was blasphemous. That infuriated me; we quarreled; I insulted him; and we parted for good. He happened to hold some of my promissory notes and he began to squeeze me. Didn't bother me. I was all set to get out of business anyway; my soul wasn't in it any longer. Well, they forced me into bankruptcy; they put me in jail for a three-year term. And it was there, I said to myself, an end to playing the fool. The minute I got out I headed straight for Korolenko's. He happened to be out of town so off I went, instead, to see Tolstoy. 'That's how it is,' I told him; and he replied, 'You did absolutely right!' There you are, brother. And how did Gorinov come to his senses? Also through Korolenko. And I know lots of others who subsist on his spirit. We magnates may live behind high fences, but the truth manages to search us out, too!"

I value such stories. They have great significance. They give us glimpses of the tortuous paths along which culture penetrates the tribes of men.

Zarubin was a corpulent graybeard with tiny, dull eyes in a pink, obese face, the pupils dark and sharp like inset beads. There was obstinacy in those eyes. He won notoriety as "the defender of the kopeck." Should the police extort a kopeck from anyone Zarubin would charge to the attack. In two court actions in Nizhny the cases went against him; whereupon he journeyed to Petersburg, appeared before the Senate and got a ruling prohibiting police exaction of kopecks from the citizenry. Returning to Nizhny in triumph he brought the text of the ruling to the editor of the Nizhny Gazette for publication. By the governor's order the censor deleted it. Zarubin promptly called on the governor.

"What's the matter with you?" he said, without ceremony. "Don't you acknowledge the law?"

And that ruling of the Senate saw print.

Zarubin ambled through the streets in velvet-topped leather boots, a long, black padded coat, an absurd hat on his silver hair, and a fat briefcase under his arm stuffed with copies of the constitution of the Temperance Society and petitions and complaints of citizens whose causes he had taken up. Among his movements was the reform of the language of hack-drivers. Zarubin looked into every scandal and kept constant watch on the conduct of the police. All these activities were summed up under the heading, "Pursuit of Truth."

A revivalist about whom a furor was being made at that time, Ivan of Kronstadt, came to Nizhny, and there was an overflow at the church where he was to preach. Zarubin walked over and asked, "What's going on?"

"They're waiting for Ivan of Kronstadt."

"What! For that clown of the Imperial Church!" he exclaimed.

And they did him no harm for that. A townsman simply led him aside, imploring him, "Please get away from here as fast as you can; do it for the sake of the Lord!"

He was generally accorded respect, mingled with curiosity. Some considered him a fake but most looked to him as a sort of spiritual protector and expected miracles from him, especially miracles such as might embarrass the authorities.

In 1901 I was jailed. Zarubin had not yet made my acquaintance then. He called on the prosecutor and demanded to see me.

"Are you related to him?"

"Never set eyes on him in my life."

"Then you're not entitled to visit him."

"Have you read the Gospels, man? What does it say there? How is it, man, that you govern over people, yet you have no knowledge of the Gospels?"

But the prosecutor held to a gospel of his own by whose precepts he felt justified in barring him from seeing me.

Zarubin was one of those—no rarity in Russia—who, having lived out a tumultuous life and having nothing left to experience, become "lovers of truth"—in brief, cranks.

More significant to me was the reaction to Korolenko of Bugrov, the Old Believer millionaire philanthropist, who was a power in Nizhny and a very shrewd man. "We magnates," he said, "are not nearly clever, or mighty or resourceful enough. Look, we've not yet shaken off the nobility and already others have fastened themselves around our necks—these Zemstvos, these Korolenkos! Especially Korolenko! He's a nuisance! That ignoramus has to stick his nose in everything!"

I heard this testimonial to Korolenko in the spring of 1893, after my return to Nizhny from a long tramping trip that had taken me deep into the Caucasus. In the three years or so that I had been away, Korolenko, as a civic figure and as an artist, had grown to even greater stature. His famine-relief work, his steadfast and effective opposition to the capricious governor Baranov, his influence among the "Zemstvo folk" were universally acknowledged. I think his book, *The Famine Year*, had already appeared.

The comments of still another Nizhnian, a very odd character, comes to my mind. "This leader of the loyal opposition," he said of Korolenko, "would have organized something big and international, if he were working in a cultured country, something like the Red Cross or the Salvation Army. But here, even under the most favorable conditions, his energies must go to waste. How bitter it is for us paupers, to be denied his precious alms. The like of this phenomenal new figure or, more correctly, his equal, has not shown himself in all our history."

"What's your opinion of him as a writer?"

"Too bad he's unsure of his powers. He's a typical reformer in his thinking and feeling; and that, I think, militates against a proper self-evaluation as an artist. Yet his reforming drive, conjoined to his talent, ought to give him greater artistic boldness and assurance. I'm afraid he considers himself as a writer only 'incidentally' instead of 'above all.' "

The man who told me this might have been one of the heroes of Boborykin's novel, *On the Wave*. He was drunken, dissolute, but erudite and keen. For this misanthrope it was usually quite impossible to speak well, or even indulgently, of anyone. All the more highly did I rate his judgment of Korolenko.

But to return to the years 1889-90. I did not visit him, since, as I have already noted, I had given up writing. Sometimes I caught a casual glimpse of him, on the street or at gatherings, where he figured merely as listener to the discussions. His placidity, on such occasions, disturbed me. Everything under me was swaying and tottering; it was apparent to me that my agitation was part of a general intellectual ferment; everyone around me was excited, everyone argued, where, then, did he stand? Yet I could not get up the nerve to ask him, "How about you? Why do you keep still?"

My friends acquired new books, a thick tome by Redkin, the even thicker *History of Social Systems* by Shoheglov, *Das Kapital*, Lokhvitzky's volume on political constitutions, lithographed transcripts of lectures by the historian Kliuchevsky, and Korkunov and Sergeievich.

A considerable section of our youth had turned to the steel-like logic of Marx; but the majority were deep in tendentious novels, Bourget's *The Disciple*, Sienkiewicz's *Without Dogma*, Dedlov's *Sashenka* and stories about the "new people"—the new in these people being their self-expression as individuals. This newish tendency leaped from theory to practice; the youth became aggressive in their "individualism," they ridiculed, assailed such concepts as "the responsibilities of the intellectual"; and ridiculed the efforts to solve social problems. Some of these new-fledged individualists sought justification in the determinism of the Marxist system.

The Yaroslav Seminary student, A. F. Troitsky, later to practice medicine in France, but then an eloquent and passionate controversialist, asserted, " 'Historical necessity' smacks of the mystical predestination of church dogma; it's the same nonsense as the folk notion of 'fate.' Materialism marks the bankruptcy of the mind which cannot take in the multiform phenomena of life and wants to devaluate them to the paltry integer, one; to explain everything with one simple explanation. But such simplification is materialism's set course,—from the simple to the intricate and then on to the most complex. The need to simplify is an infantile malady; such a need demonstrates that our helpless reason has not yet developed the power to comprehend the whole, to harmonize the chaos of phenomena."

Some of the youth took to the *laissez-faire* doctrine of Adam Smith with gusto. In it they found support for a materialism of the most mundane sort. Their reasoning ran something like this: "If historical

necessity exists and, by its own momentum, carries mankind forward
on the path of progress, what need is there for us to exert ourselves?"
And, hands in pockets, they stood apart, whistling unconcernedly. In
the role of spectators they looked on at the verbal battles, as crows,
perched on a barnyard fence, watch cock-fights.

Increasingly, and ever more brashly, the youth aimed their ridicule
at the "preservers of the heroic folk heritage." My sympathies happened to be with the "preservers," eccentric, but pure-hearted, people
who seemed to me close to the saints in their devotion to "the
people"—the object of their love, the beneficiary of their labors, and
the incentive for their achievements. Heroico-comic though they appeared to me, their romanticism or, more precisely, their social idealism
appealed to me. Their "people" were limned in colors far too refined.
No such "people," I was well aware, existed in reality. It was the myopic,
the sly, the self-seeking muzhik, casting a hostile and suspicious eye on
everything that does not serve his immediate interests, who inhabits
this earth; along with the dull, rascally townsman, crammed with superstitions and prejudices even more noxious than those of the muzhik,
and the hairy, powerful business man, secure under his jungle law of
profit.

In the chaos and clash of controversy arising out of the conflict of
feeling and reason, in these battles out of which any truth, it seemed
to me, had to flee headlong or come out maimed, in that roaring fire
of ideas I found nothing soothing to my spirit.

Back from these norms I sifted down ideas and aphorisms that my
memory had retained either for their content or phrasing. Recalling, at
the same time, the gestures and attitudes of the orators, the contorted
faces and the glowering eyes, I would recoil from the joy they expressed at striking down supposed fellow-seekers of the truth, their joy
over verbal blows that "prostrated" the other's "soul." Strange to have
those who mouth words like "goodness," "beauty," "humanity,"
"justice," set traps of logic for others, not hesitating to wound each
other's self-esteem, displaying, in fact, a panting eagerness to humiliate
each other, to vent irritation and spite.

I did not possess the "discipline" or, more correctly, the technique
of thinking that formal schooling provides. I had collected material,
to master which required earnest study for which I lacked the requisite
leisure. I was tortured by the contradictions between books in which I
quite unshakably believed, and life, which, by then, I knew something
of. I understood that I was gaining in sophistication; but I was aware,

also, that sophistication spoils one. Like an ill-loaded ship I listed to one side. Not to break the harmony of the philosophical choristers among whom I found myself, I, who possessed a cheery tenor, tried, like the rest, to sing an austere bass. Not only was this a strain but it put me in the false position of a man who, eager to be considerate to others, commits injustices against himself.

As in Kazan, Boris-oblebsk and Tsaritsyn, here too, I observed the situation of intellectuals with perplexity and alarm. Most cultivated people led a hard, mean, half-starved existence; overspent of their precious strength to procure a crust of bread; while about them life was famished for the sanity they could have brought to it. It agitated me still more to observe what aliens our intellectuals were in their own land. A hostile environment ringed them around in suspicion and scorn. Yet this environment, itself, rotted in the stagnant, idiotically paltry conditions of its existence.

Again it was not clear to me why the intellectuals failed to penetrate the masses of people, whose vacuous lives made so little sense, appalling me by its spiritual poverty, its excruciating boredom and especially, the callousness of personal relations. Evidences of the good, the unselfish, the beautiful were as rare as nuggets; I hoarded them; and, to this day, the spark of happiness over seeing humanity in a man, flames up clearly in my memory. Nevertheless I was spiritually oppressed; and the sedatives of books no longer relaxed me. I sought more sentient words; I sought achievements and revolts. From time to time I cried, "broaden out!"

"Better open your pockets wider," replied N. F. Annenberg, who always came through with the opposite remark.

A significant discussion with Korolenko belongs to those days. One summer night I sat on a bench on "the slope," that perch on the bluff over the Volga which commands a fine view of the expanse of meadow rolling from the opposite shore, and down, through the lace of trees, upon the current of the river. Soundlessly Korolenko seated himself at my side. I became aware of his presence only when he put his hand on my shoulder.

"How deep in thought you were," he said. "I had a mind to give your hat a pull, but I was afraid of giving you a shock."

Korolenko lived at the other end of town. It was late, well past two in the morning, and I could see that he was tired. His head was bare; he was perspiring and mopped his face with a handkerchief.

"You're a late promenader," he said.

"So are you."

Autobiography of Maxim Gorky

He nodded. "Well, how are things with you? What have you been doing?" After further random phrases he asked, "I hear you've joined Skvortsov's study circle. What's he like?"

Skvortsov was known as a Marxist scholar. He eschewed all books except *Das Kapital*—he made a boast of that. About two years before Struve published his "Critical Notes," I heard Skvortsov read a paper to a gathering at the lawyer, Shcheglov's, house where he not only advanced the same ideas but expressed them in sharper terms. They were held to be heretical but that did not keep the youth from flocking around him. Members of his circle were later to become the builders of the Social Democratic Party.[44]

Skvortsov was, almost literally, "out of this world." An ascetic, he went through winter and summer in the same clothes, a light overcoat and thin shoes. He subsisted on almost nothing and studied to reduce that still further. For some weeks he lived on nothing but sugar, and less than seven ounces of it, a day. Wasting away under this experimental "rational" diet, he contracted a grave kidney ailment.

A short man with a grayish complexion, his light blue eyes smiled, however, the triumphant smile of the lucky man who has reached a truth inaccessible to others. Toward those who differed from him he bore himself with a compassionate, yet never offensive, disdain.

He smoked thick, cheap cigarettes in a long bamboo holder. This he carried, stuck under his belt, like a dagger.

I saw Skvortsov among a drove of students who were paying collective court to a new arrival, a girl of striking beauty. Skvortsov competed with the young dandies in his own fashion. His ludicrous, shabby figure, armed with the long cigarette holder, sharply outlined against the tiles of the oven, he discharged salvos of smoke and argument at the beauty. He interdicted poetry, music, drama, the dance, with the complacency of an erudite Old Believer whose faith remains unscarred by books. "The harm of such frivolities," said Skvortsov, "was pointed out by Socrates."

As she listened to him, the elegant brunette, dressed in a white gauze blouse, coquettishly swung her well-turned leg. She regarded the wise man with a glance of her wonderful, dark eyes such as the beauties of Athens must have turned upon Socrates. This glance silently but expressively inquired, "When will you stop; when will we be rid of you?"

On that occasion Skvortsov inveighed against Korolenko as an ideal-

[44] Later to split into two groups, Bolsheviks (Majority) and Mensheviks (Minority).

ist lost in a fog of metaphysics and asserted that his writings—which he had not read—were meant to "galvanize the corpse of Populism." Having made this pronouncement, he stuck his cigarette holder under his belt, with a triumphant gesture, and went off. After using her remaining energies to see him graciously to the door, the exhausted hostess collapsed on a divan and exclaimed, "Lord, that's not a man, that's a spell of bad weather!"

Korolenko, on now hearing of this from me, smiled, then took on a preoccupied look. Then he said to me, "What's the rush to pick a creed? Materialism is becoming the fashion. Its simplicity makes it tempting. Its pull is particularly strong on those who won't take the trouble to think for themselves. And the dilettantes are taking to it, those who affect every novelty, however incongruous with their own nature, tendencies and obligations."

He spoke meditatively as if he were carrying on a discussion with himself, breaking off, from time to time, to listen to the snort of an exhaust pipe below, or the whistle of a passing steamer. "Every attempt at a rational explanation of life," he went on, "deserves a hearing. Life is made up of innumerable, intersecting circles; it defies all attempts to enclose it in the square of a logical system. It defies attempts to bring these circles into even relative order—these intersecting lines of human actions and relationships." He sighed and fanned himself with his hat.

I was impressed with the candor of his words; and with the gentle, thoughtful smile which accompanied his remarks. Such comments on Marxism, however, were familiar to me. When he stopped, I asked him how he managed to preserve his serenity through all this ferment.

He put on his hat, looked me in the face and smilingly replied, "I know what I have to do and I'm convinced that it serves a purpose. Why do you ask?"

I then confided to him all my confusions and fears. He listened in attentive silence, almost contorting himself in order to follow the expressions in my face. When I finished he said quietly, "There's much truth in your observations and they're uncommonly keen." Smiling fondly at me, he put his hand on my shoulder. "I had no idea these questions were working on you. You've been pictured to me as quite a different sort, carefree, simple, even anti-intellectual."

He then spoke with great earnestness about the role of the intellectual as always and everywhere, separated from the people, necessarily so, since he is always in advance, to forge ahead is the intellectual's historic mission. "He's the yeast" in every popular ferment, the foundation stone in every new structure. Socrates, Giordano Bruno, Galileo, Robespierre, the Decembrists, Perovskaya, Zheliabov, along with everyone now starving in exile, and those still at their textbooks yet making preparations for their struggle for justice, a struggle that begins with a prison term; this is the vital force of life, "its most sensitive and powerful organ."

In his agitation he got to his feet and paced back and forth beside the bench. "Mankind began creating history when its first intellectual appeared. The Prometheus myth honors him who obtained fire and thereby enabled man to rise above the beast. You've analyzed the shortcomings of the intellectuals accurately enough—their bookishness, their remoteness from life. But it's questionable whether even these are shortcomings. For a proper perspective it may be necessary to move away rather than come closer. My advice to you, given in friendship, and in consideration of the fact that I have had the greater experience, is to acknowledge the virtues of the intellectuals. To dwell on their shortcomings is easy and deludes one by seeming to give him a personal vantage point. Voltaire who, despite his genius, was in some ways a petty man, nevertheless did a great thing in coming out in defense of the unjustly condemned. I'm not speaking of the many dour superstitions and prejudices overthrown by him but merely of his steadfast devotion to what seemed hopeless causes. That was greatness! He understood that man must, first of all, be humane; that justice is a necessity. When it is heaped together, bit by bit, spark upon spark, it will become a conflagration that will purify earth of lies and filth and transform life from its present melancholy and onerous state. Stubbornly and relentlessly, sparing neither oneself nor others, deterred by nothing, thus to serve justice—that's the substance of my thinking."

I could see that he was now exhausted. He had been talking a long time. He sat down, and glanced at the sky. "Why, it's late—or shall we say early. It's dawning; and I think we'll have rain. Time to go home."

I lived nearby, he about two miles off. I offered to walk him home and we tramped through the streets of the sleeping city, under an overcast sky.

"Are you writing again?"

"No."

"Why?"

"I haven't the time."

"Too bad. A misfortune, really. But I think when you want to write you'll find the time. I'm convinced of your talent. You just happen to be in low spirits now." Then he spoke of the fidgety Gleb Uspensky.

Suddenly a torrential summer rain poured down, enfolding the city in a gray net. We stopped inside the gates for a few minutes; but, seeing that the rain would keep up, we parted.

Chapter Nine

I HAD LONG FELT THE NEED TO KNOW SOMETHING OF THE ORIGIN OF THE world I lived in and to clear up my own notions of it. This rather modest and understandable need gradually developed into an obsession, and with all the impetuousness of youth I beset my friends with "childish" questions. Some were frankly at a loss, and put me off with books by Lyell and Lubbock; others made me the butt of callous banter for having "such nonsense" on my mind. George Henry Lewes' *History of Philosophy* was given to me as a cure-all but I had to drop it as unreadably dull.

It was at this time that an eccentric student joined our circle. He wore a shabby overcoat and a short blue blouse that he often had to yank down in back to cover certain deficiencies in his trousers. He was nearsighted and wore glasses. He parted his beard in the middle, and his hair, which he wore in the "Nihilist" fashion, was red, long and remarkably thick, reaching his shoulders in a severe, even line. His expression made me think of an icon Christ. His motions were slow and involuntary as if he were under a spell. He gave curt and half-jeering answers to questions, yet he, himself, spoke through questions, in the Socratic manner.

He was disliked and shunned. Nevertheless, we became great friends, though he was some four years older. His name was Nicholas Vasiliev and he was studying chemistry.

I found him an admirable fellow, intelligent and very well read but, like most gifted Russians, eccentric. For example, he spread quinine over bread and smacked his lips when he ate it, to persuade me quinine was a delicacy; further, that it was good for one's health, mollifying the "racial urge." He subjected his own skin to considerable risks with his experiments. One day he followed a dose of bromides with a pull at an opium pipe and nearly died of it in excruciating agonies. Another time he nearly finished himself off with an experimental taste of some metallic acid. The surly old doctor who was called in, examining the residue of the dose said, "It would have killed a horse, perhaps two horses. You'll have to pay for it, I assure you." Turning his body into an experimental laboratory cost him his teeth, which became green and fell out, one by one. Poisoning, whether accidental or intentional I don't know, finally did for him in Kiev, where he was assisting Professor Konovalov in researches on indigo. That was in 1901.

But in the years 1889–1890 he was a strong, stocky man, good-humored with me, though rancorous with others. We had undertaken to do some reports for the local Zemstvo (district) board, for which we earned a ruble a day. I can remember Nick at his desk singing in a deliberately vulgar tenor, to the French tune, "Look here, Look there," "Twice forty-four plus twenty-two, a hundred ten, a hundred ten." He would keep that up for ten minutes or half an hour. If I held out he would start over again.

When, at the end of my endurance, I would exclaim, "Cut that racket!" he would look at the clock and say, "You've quite a good nervous system. Few can take this sort of torture for forty-seven minutes. Once I rendered the Hallelujah to a friend of mine but in thirteen minutes he was heaving brass ashtrays; and he had the gall to be studying psychiatry!"

He was deep in the German philosophers and planned a dissertation on Hegel and Swedenborg. He managed to get fun out of the latter's *Phenomenology of the Spirit*. Stretched on the bumpy couch, which we had named the "Caucasus Range," he often slapped the book face down on his chest, kicked his legs into the air and howled with laughter.

When I wanted to know what the joke was he answered haltingly, "I wouldn't know how to put it to you; it's too involved. I can't explain it to you; but it's a joke, really." When I insisted, the explanations would draw out into interminable though ardent "mysticisms of reason," of which, to my great chagrin, I got very little. Concerning his own philosophical studies he would remark, "Gives you about as much entertainment as chewing gum and just about as much use."

On his return from Moscow, where he had been for the holidays, I met him with questions, to which he gave a warm welcome. "A call for philosophy? Fine. I'll serve you all the spiritual food you need"; and offered to have some talks with me on the subject. "It'll ease your way; you'll find it pleasanter than sweating over Lewes."

Several days afterwards I was sitting, at dusk, in a dilapidated summer house in a neglected garden. Apple and cherry trees spotted with fungus, and raspberry, currant and gooseberry bushes in chaotic growth clogged the paths where Nick's father, a church official, walked aimlessly in his gray house robe, spastically muttering and coughing. He was in his dotage.

Tall sheds on all four sides loomed over the garden, giving it the appearance of a square pit, deepening as the night advanced. To the sultriness of the air was added the reek of garbage, steamed by the June sun and wafted in from the yard.

"Let's philosophize," said Nikolai, licking his lips as if he relished the very word. He sat in a corner at a table whose legs were imbedded in the ground. His eerie face was illuminated by the flashes of his cigarette, whose reflection glittered on his glasses. He was feverish and, feeling chilled, had turned up the collar of his threadbare coat. In his fidgeting his feet scraped the dirt floor and the table complained with angry creaks.

With tense absorption I followed my friend's lowered voice as he gave a simple and fascinating explanation of the system of Democritus, and his theory of the atom, now accorded scientific acceptance. Then he said, "Wait a moment"; and consumed cigarette after cigarette through a prolonged silence.

It was now full night, with a black, moonless sky. The air had become still more humid. From the house next door, occupied by the psychiatrist, Kashchenko, came the gentle singing of a violin; from the open garret window, an old man's cough.

Nick resumed, his voice still lower, through his heavy smoking. "You see, you must give these things careful thought. Someone said—I can't exactly remember who—that the convictions of the educated are just as hidebound as those of the illiterate and superstitious. A bitter truth is hidden in this heresy. In fact I would call his statement restrained. Think it over and keep it in mind."

Well do I remember his words, the best and truest advice, I think, I have ever gotten. They drove through me, their echoes reverberated in my soul and brought my thoughts to a greater pitch of concentration.

"I wouldn't have you become any other than you are now, to the end of your life. Hold always to what I know you feel now; that freedom of thought is man's only and most precious freedom. And it belongs only to him who takes nothing on faith, who looks into everything himself; only to him who comprehends the continuity of life, its flow, and the infinite fluctuation of reality."

Leaving his own chair he went round the table to seat himself at my side. "All I have said to you can be reduced to a few words. Live with your own mind. That's the thing. I don't want to stuff my opinions into your head. Actually the only thing I care to teach anybody is mathematics. Particularly you, I want you to realize that. What I'm telling you is to make that clear. I think it's revolting to try to make others over in one's own likeness. Certainly I don't want you to think as I do; it wouldn't do at all, because my thinking's faulty."

He dashed his cigarette on the floor and stamped it out. Immediately lighting another and warming his thumbnail over the matchflame he went on, with a melancholy smile, "You see, I think humanity will go on to the end setting down data and drawing from them more or less lucky surmises about their essential significance; or, ignoring the data, will keep on shaping fantasies. Then there's God, outside or above this all; but God's something I reject. Possibly he exists but not for me. You see how bad my thinking is! Indeed, there are those who consider both materialism and idealism errors of the Reason. They're like the imps who have had their fill of Hell but dread the dull orderliness of Paradise."

Sighing, he sat back to listen to the violin, then continued, "There are the smart alecks who say we only know our own thoughts about what we see; but we can't tell if what we think, or the way we do our thinking, is correct. That's another thing you must avoid. Don't take stock in that, either, just . . . take care of yourself."

These words, which I understood well enough to feel the spiritual anguish behind them, moved me deeply. Shaking hands, we stood together for some time, in silence. There was goodness in that moment, one of the happiest, probably, in all my life, which has been varied enough to have afforded me more of them. But human nature is greedy; that is to its credit, though through misunderstanding, or more likely hypocrisy, it is termed a vice.

We went into the street and stopped at the gate to hear the thunder in the distance. Lightning flashes crossed the black sky; in the east the clouds were already flaming in the smelters of the dawn.

"Thanks, Nick."

"Nonsense."

As I started off Nick's voice reached after me, with a gay ring, "Look, there's a Nechayev [45] man, Orlov, in Moscow, a grand old man. He's known for his saying: 'The truth is what you perceive.' Think that over. So long, see you tomorrow."

After walking a few paces I looked back. Nick was leaning against the lamp-post gazing at the eastern sky. Blue curls of smoke eddied over his mane of hair. I was in a state of lyric rapture as I left him; the "gates of mystery" seemed to have opened to me at last.

The next day, however, Nick dismayed me with his picture of the world as conceived in the mind of Empedocles. That fantastic world had a special fascination to my mentor, for his exposition of it was rapt and vivid, something he licked his lips over with unwonted relish. Again it was dusk, about the same hour as the night before. It had rained hard; between the damp trees shadows skulked and the wind moaned. I felt chaos and gloom,

[45] A terrorist and proponent of Nihilism.

bodies dismembered and strewn into a mindless whirlwind in which Hate and Love, so similar as to be indistinguishable, contended against each other and triumphed together. Around them shone a spectral bluish radiance, recalling a winter sky on a sunny day and casting a deathly, unchanging light on all that moves. My attention wandered from Nick, fastening on this vision, which made me feel that I, too, was caught in this world of destruction, slowly breaking apart, exploding outwards, my ruins spiralling down in the chill blue radiance. I was so stunned by this vision that I could barely make the effort to answer Nikolai's questions, "Are you asleep? You're not listening to me."

"I can't."

"Why?"

I explained.

"My dear boy, your imagination needs a halter," he said, lighting a cigarette. "It mustn't be indulged. How about a walk?"

We walked along "The Slope," a street of gleaming puddles. Our shadows spanned the street and dodged up the walls of houses to the roofs. Nick was talking about a new chemical treatment for the rags used in making paper, that would lower the cost and improve the quality. He also described the researches of a professor who sought to increase the length of wood fibres. But on my eyes were still imprinted floating hands and a pair of sad eyes.

Next day a telegram took Nick back to Moscow University. At our parting he counselled me to leave off philosophy until he returned.

My head remained crammed with uneasy thoughts; my soul remained disturbed. In a few days I began to feel that my brains were molten and bubbling and giving off the most fantastic thoughts, spectral visions and images. It was accompanied by an anguished depression which sapped my vitality and made me fear for my reason. But I had the courage to want to explore the limits of my terror, and this, very likely, was my salvation. I went through nights of terrible anxiety. Sometimes, sitting on "The Slope," staring at the pastures fading into distance beyond the Volga, and into the sky spangled with the golden rain of stars. I would await the moment when, all of a sudden, out of the blue darkness above, there should open a deep, circular blot like the mouth of a bottomless well, out of which would thrust a flaming finger in warning.

God, too, Almighty God, appeared to me exactly as on icons and pictures, a kindly, gray-bearded face with serene eyes. All alone He sat on a massive throne and with a golden needle, sewed at a horribly long white shirt which billowed down over the earth as a transparent cloud. He was surrounded by emptiness that you watched with terror for it seemed to grow ever deeper and wider. Behind the river, rising up to the sky, was a human ear, an ordinary ear with bristly hair inside the lobes. It loomed over me and heard all my thoughts. I had slain countless numbers of people with a long, double-edged sword, elastic as a whip, inherited from an executioner from the Middle Ages. From right and left, bowing and submissively offering their necks, men and women swarmed at me. Behind me the unknown being, at whose command I slew them all, breathed icicles into my brain.

In these visions a naked woman visited me. Instead of feet she had bird claws. From her breasts streamed rays of gold. Her hand sprinkled drops of blazing oil over my head, and I flared up like a tuft of cotton and vanished.

Ibrahim Gubaidulian, the night watchman, took my arm several times on the top of "The Slope" and led me home, coaxing me in his Armenian accent, "Why go walk when you be sick? A sick man, he be home in bed."

At times, exhausted by these deliriums, I plunged into the river and came out somewhat refreshed. Back home two trained mice waited up for me. They lived behind the wooden wall posts. They had gnawed out a hole at the level of the table. They stepped straight onto the cloth when they heard me seat myself to the supper my landlady had laid out for me. And, before my eyes, the odd little creatures were transformed into little imps. They sat on the tobacco canister swinging their hairy legs and, as they cast grave glances at me, a low voice—whose it was I did not know—addressed me in a whisper as barely audible as the fall of light rain on soft earth: "Devils are different types, but their common function is to help people find miseries."

"A lie!" I would cry out heatedly. "No one seeks miseries."

At this "No One" made his appearance. I heard him try the bolt and open all the doors and, presto, there he was in my room. Globular as a soap bubble, he had no hands, and a clock dial was his face. The dial hands were carrots, for which I have had a predilection ever since childhood. I recognized him as the husband of the woman I was in love with, though he had put on this disguise to baffle me. He turned into a real person, a plump little fellow with a flaxen goatee and mild eyes. With a smile he repeated to me all the secret, resentful thoughts I had toward his wife which could be known only to me.

"Get out!" I shouted.

Then I heard a muffled thump on the wall behind me. It was my kind and resourceful landlady, Felicia Tikhomirova. Her knock shook me back into the real world. I doused my head in cold water. Not to disturb the sleeping, I crawled out of the window into the garden where I stayed till dawn.

At breakfast my landlady said, "You had a nightmare again!" It embarrassed me; I despised myself.

I was then clerking for the lawyer, A. I. Lanin, a good man to whom I feel much indebted. One day my arrival at the office was greeted with angry outcries and a brandishing of papers, "Are you mad! Look what you've written in this application. Copy out a new form, today's the last day. If it's a joke, it's a bad one, I tell you."

Looking over the papers I found this verse written all too legibly:

"The good is eternal
But my soul is a wraith;
Let me know prayer
And the bliss of faith."

This disconcerted me as it had my boss. I stared at it uncomprehendingly, hardly able to believe that I had composed it.

Toward the end of the day, Lanin came to me and said, "Forgive me for that scolding, but, you see, it took me by surprise. What's the trouble? Lately you've been out of sorts; you look thin."

"Insomnia," I told him.

"There must be something to do for it," he said.

Indeed, something had to be done. There had to be an end to those hallucinations, those nightly talks with visitors who came and went, unseen, in the intervals in which I lost contact with reality; there had to be an end to this overstimulated life on the edge of madness. I had reached the stage of anxious anticipation of marvels in broad daylight.

Had a house on the street leap-frogged over my head, it would scarcely have startled me. I would have seen nothing unreasonable in a cart horse rearing up on his hind legs and, in a bass voice, pronouncing "Anathema!"

Sometimes I would approach a woman in a straw hat and yellow gloves on a bench along the fortress wall. Should I say to her, "There is no God!" she would exclaim, with a hurt glance, "What about me?" and immediately metamorphose into a winged creature, and fly away. The world would suddenly be overgrown with large, leafless trees from whose branches would drip blue slime. For my crimes I would be sentenced to live as a frog for twenty-three years and ring the huge, clanging bell of the Veskresensky Church without a stop. My urge to inform the lady that there was no God was pressing, but fear of these consequences kept me from it and as soon as I could I slipped away.

Everything was possible; also, nothing had a real existence. Therefore I was under a compulsion to touch each fence, wall, tree to reassure myself that it existed. And I was reassured. If you keep pounding your fist on something solid you're convinced that it's there.

The earth would play you mean tricks. You stepped on her confidently like all the rest and suddenly she was no longer solid; she was penetrable as the air. Yet she stayed opaque and your soul was steeped in her darkness for a period that seemed eternity though its duration was but a couple of seconds.

The sky was equally unreliable. At any moment it could transform itself from dome to inverted pyramid with its point pivoted on my skull, nailing me to one fixed spot till the iron stars that fastened the sky together rusted through. Then, everything would crumble and I would be buried under reddish rust. Everything was possible, except existence in a world of such possibilities.

My soul was in torment. Had I not personally experienced the folly and vileness of a suicide attempt, I would certainly have tried that cure.

The psychiatrist who lived by himself, a swarthy little hunchback with a keen, skeptical mind, put me through a long questioning. He patted my knee with his curiously pale hand and said, "To begin with, my boy, consign all those tomes you've been reading to the devil, along with the rest of the mess around you. What a shame to let yourself get into such a state, a lad with a strong constitution like yours. Physical exercise is what you need. And what about women? Oh, that's no good. Abstinence you can leave to others. You find yourself a girl who knows how to play; she'll be good for you."

He gave me additional and equally repellent advice; he wrote out a couple of prescriptions; and I can recall his concluding remarks, word for word, "I've heard certain things about you. You may not like what I'm going to say, so I ask you to forgive me. I think of you as what is called a primitive. With such the imagination generally rules over the reason. The reading you've done, the things you've seen, have all stimulated your imagination, which can't reconcile them with reality; reality is fantasy, too, but a special sort."

He added, "According to one of the old sages, 'He who stops to argue never gets anything finished.' That's well said; because it's only when you've come to the end of a matter that you're in a position to refute it." And seeing me out, he concluded, with the smirk of a man-about-town, "And remember that little girl!"

A few days later I left Nizhny for the Tolstoyan colony at Simbirsk. The peasants there regaled me with the tragi-comedy of its dissolution.

Chapter Ten

AND THEN, SEEMINGLY AS A STEP IN MY EDUCATION, FATE PUT ME through a tragi-comedy of first love. Some friends had planned a boat picnic on the Oka River, and I was charged with inviting the C——'s, a couple newly returned from France whom I had not yet met. That evening was the first time I went to their apartment. They had a cellar apartment in an old house, whose doorway was ornamented by an enormous puddle that never dried all through the spring, and sometimes not even through the summer. For crows and dogs it served as a mirror, for pigs as a bathtub.

In a somewhat wistful mood I rolled down upon these people, like a boulder down a hill. A stout man of medium height confronted me at the door and in a surly manner barred my way. But his eyes were kind above his trim, flaxen beard. Irritably he asked, "What do you want?" and added, pointedly, "One usually knocks at a door before entering."

In the dimness behind him, something fluttering that gave the impression of a large white bird was astir; a gay, clear voice sang out, "Particularly when you call on married people."

With some annoyance I asked were they the C——'s, and getting an affirmative answer from the man, who looked like a well-to-do shopkeeper, I delivered my message.

"V—— sent you?" he asked, and abstractedly folded his hands; but suddenly he turned around and, as if in pain; cried out, "Oh, Olga!"

From that and a mincing movement of his hand, I deduced that he had received a pinch in that unmentionable part of the body situated below the spine.

A slender young girl took the man's place. Leaning against the doorpost, she flashed me a smile from her blue eyes. "Are you a cop?"

"No," I replied, politely, "that's only my trousers," which made her laugh.

Her laugh did not offend me, for in her eyes shone the smile I had been awaiting a long time. It was my clothing that stirred her to laughter.

Over blue cop's trousers I wore the white outfit of a chef, a practical garment which buttoned up to the neck served as blouse and jacket together.
Cast-off hunting boots and a broad-brimmed hat suitable for an Italian
bandit finished off my attire.

Drawing me into the room, then depositing me into a chair, she asked
me, "How come this funny getup?"

"Why funny?"

"Don't take offense," she said in a friendly tone. And who could take
offense with such a strange girl?

Sitting on the bed, the bearded gentleman kept rolling cigarettes.
Looking in his direction I asked her, "Your father or your brother?"

"Husband," he exclaimed demonstratively.

Staring at her I said, after a silence, "Forgive me, please."

Of such laconic interjections was the conversation, which lasted but a
few minutes, made up; but I could have sat still in that basement for
hours, days, and years gazing at her oval face and her tender eyes. Her
little lower lip was somewhat fuller than the upper, looking just a trifle
swollen. Her bobbed, yet abundant, chestnut hair fell in soft curls over
her rosy ears and framed her flushed young cheeks like a sumptuous headdress. She had pretty hands and, since they were raised above the doorpost, I could see up her bare arm to the shoulder. She was dressed with
a strange simplicity—a white lace blouse and a trim white skirt. Most
wonderful of all were her eyes, which glowed with a friendly, affectionate
interest. I could not doubt it. Hers was the smile so necessary to the
twenty-year-old whose heart, bruised by the harshness of life, famished
for affection.

"There'll be a pouring rain any minute," declared her husband, smoke
eddying through his beard. I looked out of the window into a cloudless
sky bright with stars. Realizing that my presence was unwelcome to the
man, I left them, my soul filled with serene contentment, as one encounters something which, hardly known to himself, one has long been seeking.

All night long I roamed the fields, accompanied by my adoring memory of those blue, fondling, radiant eyes. By dawn I had assured myself
that she was ill-mated to that bearded old bear with the placid eyes of a
well-fed cat. I pitied her. Poor thing! Having to live with a man with
breadcrumbs in his whiskers!

Next day we rowed down the turbulent waters of the Oka, beside the
bluff formed of striated, multi-colored marl. The day was as fine as any
since Creation. The sun had an extraordinary brilliance; the sky seemed
decked out for a feast. The air was fragrant with ripening strawberries.

The people seemed to consider each other as quite perfect, and this too made me feel a joyous affection for them. Even milady's husband was transformed into a paragon, mostly, perhaps, because he did not get into the boat with his wife but left me at the oars, where I could blissfully demonstrate my accomplishments. Before we set out he amused us with anecdotes about old Gladstone. Then, having drunk a jug of rich milk, he slipped under a bush and slept until nightfall, as placidly as an infant. I got my boat to the picnic grounds ahead of the others. I carried my lady ashore, and she exclaimed, "How strong you are!"

That made me feel fit to pull down battlements and I told her I could carry her in my arms all the way to the city, some five miles away. She laughed sweetly; her eyes petted me; I saw them before me all day, certain that they beamed for me alone.

The matter raced on with the momentum to be expected in a woman who comes upon an interesting male specimen, and a youth who comes upon the woman-tenderness for which he is famished. I soon discovered that, despite her youthful appearance, she was ten years my senior, had graduated from a finishing school for "noble maidens" in Bialystock, had been engaged to the Guards commander at the Winter Palace and had studied obstetrics and lived in Paris. It turned out that had been her mother's profession and that, as the midwife on that occasion, she had officiated at my arrival on earth. I thrilled over this as a good omen.

Her life among the bohemians and emigrés, with one of whom she had a brief affair, a nomadic existence at or near the starvation level, in cellars and attics in Paris, Vienna and Petersburg, had matured the schoolgirl into a complex and fascinating oddment of humanity. Agile as a bird, she followed life and people with the perceptive inquisitiveness of a clever young animal. She had a repertoire of provocative French ditties; she smoked with graceful gestures; she drew well; she was charming in parlor theatricals; and she made her own gowns and trimmed her own hats. Obstetrics had been forgotten.

"The mortality rate of my four cases," she said, "was seventy-five per cent."

This terminated her career as facilitator in the increase of mankind. That she had taken a direct part in this honorable activity was demonstrated by a winsome and beautiful four-year-old daughter.

Milady spoke of herself in the tone used of a person with whom one is overfamiliar to the point of boredom. But sometimes it would change to a wondering tone. Then her eyes would brighten, out of their depths a hesitant smile would emerge, the diffident smile of a child.

Her quick and confident mind made me acutely conscious that she had a richer culture than mine. I was aware of her understanding, but slightly condescending, way with other people. She was, incomparably, the most attractive woman I knew. Her casual manner in conversation startled me. I thought: She knows all that my revolutionist friends know and something more valuable besides; but her attitude is detached, as if she were giving an adult's smiling indulgence to the headlong play of youth.

Her cellar apartment was divided into two rooms, a tiny kitchen which also served as a foyer and a big room with five windows, three on the street and two on a littered yard. It would have made a cozy spot for a shoemaker, but hardly for such a refined little lady who had dwelt in Paris, the shrine of the Revolution, the city of Molière, Beaumarchais, Hugo and other titans. There were other incongruities in the picture and its setting. I was upset by them, and, added to my other emotions, was sympathetic suffering on her account. She, however, seemed not to notice what I felt as hardship and indignities for her.

She worked from early morning into the night, first at her housework, and when that was done, at work for her husband, who was making statistical surveys for the Zemstvo.[46] She sat at a table, under a window, making drawings from photographs of local notables, tracing maps, doing charts, and other such work. Street dust swirled through the open window into her hair. The chunky shadows of passersby stalked over her papers. But she sang at her work. Now and then, to uncramp herself, she would hop up, waltz with her chair or romp with her child. And despite the messy work she had to do, she stayed as clean as a cat.

Her easygoing husband stayed in bed most of the day, reading foreign novels, usually the work of the elder Dumas. "This airs the cells of the brain," he said. He made much of the "strictly scientific viewpoint" which, it pleased him to think, he applied to all of life. Dining, in his lingo, was "the ingestion of food." Having eaten, he would say, "The distribution of digestive secretions of the stomach to the cells of the different organs calls for complete relaxation." And, neglecting to brush the crumbs out of his beard, he would lie down, dip into the elder Dumas or Xavier de Montepin and then, for two or three hours, render songs through his nose, his blond moustache heaving as if something submerged were trying to rise. On awakening, he would stare at the cracks in the ceiling, then recalling something, would say, "Just the same, Kuzma misinterprets Parnell's idea!" And he would go off to start an argument with Kuzma,

---

[46] A local administrative body set up to administer relief and perform other limited functions; one of Alexander II's reform measures.

asking his wife, "Could you get that survey of the Maidan district peasants who have no horses? I'll be back soon."

At midnight, or later, he returned in a jovial frame of mind. "Today I put it all over Kuzma, I tell you. The rascal has a good stock of quotations but even there he has no advantage over me. What's more, he has no understanding of Gladstone's Eastern policy."

His conversation was full of references to Binet[47] and Richet[48] and mental hygiene. In bad weather he took to educating his wife's daughter, a child born, by accident, between two love stories.

"Chew carefully, Helen, when you eat; this stimulates the digestion and assists the stomach in transforming the digestive fluid into chemical constituents easier to assimilate."

On attaining his after-dinner "complete relaxation," he would put the child to sleep with such tales, "And then when the sanguinary and presumptuous usurper Napoleon——"

He did not resent his wife's laughter at these lectures and was soon fast asleep, himself. The little girl played with his beard a little, drowsed and was soon curled up like a ball.

I made friends with her, and finding her more attentive to my stories than to his lectures on the bloody usurper and Josephine's tragic love, Boleslav, as he was called, had a strange reaction of jealousy.

"Peshkov, I must protest," he would exclaim. "Human relations must be demonstrated to the child in their basic reality. If you had a knowledge of English and could read *The Hygiene of a Child's Soul* . . ."

His own command of English, I believe, was restricted to one word, "Good-by." Though twice my age, he was as inquisitive as a puppy. He relished gossip and liked to appear as an insider not only in Russian revolutionary circles, but in such circles abroad. He might even have been well informed in these matters. He had numbers of mysterious visitors who behaved like tragic actors in the roles of ingénues and buffoons. At his house I met the revolutionist Sabunayev in an ill-fitting red wig and a checked suit several sizes too small for him.

One day, at Boleslav's, I found a lively little man with a small head who looked like a barber. He wore checked trousers, a gray vest and squeaking shoes. Pushing me into the kitchen Boleslav whispered to me, "He's just back from Paris; has to deliver a message to Korolenko. Please arrange a meeting."

I undertook to do so, but someone had already pointed out the new

[47] Binet, noted psychologist who devised the first intelligence tests.
[48] Pioneer in psychiatry.

arrival to Korolenko, who wisely refused to have anything to do with "that fop!" Boleslav took offense, both for the sake of his Parisian friend and for "the sake of the revolution." He spent two days on a letter to Korolenko using every approach from the indignant and haughty to the affectionately reproachful—and ended by tossing them all into the fire. Not long after a wave of arrests struck Moscow, Nizhny, Vladimir, and other centers. The man in the checked trousers turned out to be Landeson Harding, the first agent provocateur I ran into.

Aside from this, my first love's husband was a good fellow, a sentimentalist, particularly about science with which he ludicrously overloaded himself. One of his sayings was, "The life task of a member of the intelligentsia should be the continuous accumulation of scientific goods for distribution among the masses."

As my love deepened it turned to agony. I'd sit in the cellar watching the chosen of my heart bent over her work, kindling myself into a smoldering fever with the thought of taking her into my arms and carrying her off, rescuing her from this congested basement, with its double bed, its sagging bulky couch on which the child slept, its tables cluttered with dusty books and papers. The feet of strangers scuffed past the window; sometimes the head of a stray dog would stare in. The air was stuffy. An odor of mud, baking in the sun, would waft in from the street. Slender and girlish, she sat humming while she dug on, at her paper, with pencil or pen; and her eyes, blue as cornflowers, had for me their fondling smile. My love for that woman was a delirium; my solicitude for her was an evil yearning.

"Tell me some more about yourself," she would prompt me. But after a few minutes she would stop me. "That's not about yourself."

And I realized that what I was saying was not about myself but about the trap I was in. I felt I must somehow find myself in this chaos of events and impressions I was struggling in, but I felt too lost and frightened to know what to do. Who am I? What am I? These questions tormented me. I had a resentment against life for having already driven me to the humiliation of attempted suicide. And I could not understand the people about me whose lives seemed to me awry, inexcusably foul and stupid. I was ridden by a restless curiosity, that of a man driven, by some reason or other, to probe into life's dark corners, into its mysterious abysses, driven so hard that I sometimes felt capable of crime to satisfy my curiosity; of murdering someone in order to know what would follow.

I feared that the man of this self-discovery would turn out a loathsome sort snared in weird and uncouth emotions and fancies; in which case she would shrink from that delirious apparition in terrified revulsion. It was necessary for me first to undergo some inner change. I was convinced that she alone could lead me to self-awareness; and, still more, that she could work the magic which would liberate me from the prison darkness of my fantasies; I would rid myself, for good, of some obstruction in my soul, which would thereupon blaze up with a powerful and joyous fire.

The negligent way she spoke of herself and the superior way she had with other people gave me the firm conviction that she was possessed of a wisdom beyond the common human range; that she had a key to the riddles of life and this was a secret of her unfailing gaiety and self assurance. Perhaps it was for what I could not understand in her that I loved her most; at any rate, I loved her with all the intensity and fervor of youth. It tortured me to repress this passion, and my strength drained as it consumed me. I would have borne it better had I been of a more direct and animal turn of mind. But I believed that a man's relations with a woman should involve more than the physical union with which I had made an acquaintance in its basest and crudest forms. Though I was a robust and sensual youth with an ardent imagination, the sexual act repelled me.

A dream whose origin and whose life in my mind I cannot explain had for me the force of a conviction, namely, that, in something yet unknown to me, would be revealed the mystery of the communion between man and woman. Something tremendous, charged with ecstasy and terror, would be released by the first embrace, and living through its rapture, a man would be transformed. These fancies were not drawn from the novels I had read, I believe, but were a natural growth out of a contradictory spirit for, "I have not come into the world to agree."

Besides, I had a strange feeling that was like a vague memory, as though somewhere beyond current reality, sometime in earliest childhood, my soul had experienced an explosion of joy, a shudder of rapture born of the perception, or rather the anticipation, of harmony; and this brought a joy more glowing than the rising sun. Perhaps it was in the days when I was still lying under my mother's breast, and it was an ecstatic spasm of her nervous energy that, communicated to me, created my soul and kindled it into life. And this bliss, felt through my mother might have left me with a quivering expectation of reaching, through a woman, something of transcending beauty.

What one doesn't know one imagines. The most perfect knowledge a man can obtain comes in his love of woman, in his admiration of her beauty. All the beauty there is for man in the world is born in his love of the woman.

Out swimming one day, I dove from the stern of a barge, scraped my chest on a hawser, got my foot caught in the lines, and hung there help-less, choking, my head in the water. A truckman pulled me out. They chafed the skin off my body shaking me back to life. I suffered a hemor-rhage of the throat and had to stay in bed swallowing ice.

My lady visited me, sat at my bedside, asked for the whole story. As she stroked my head with her soft, dear hand, her eyes grew dark and troubled. Had she seen that I loved her, I asked?

"Yes," she replied with a hesitant smile. "I have seen it and it shouldn't be, but I've come to love you, too."

At these words, of course, the earth shook, the trees in the garden madly pirouetted. So unexpected was this, so blissfully stunned was I, that I could only bury my face in her lap. Had I not caught her around, at the same time, and pressed her to me hard, I might have blown out of the window like a soap bubble.

"Don't move, it's bad for you," she scolded me, trying to get my head back on the pillow. "And stop fidgeting like that or I'll have to go. You're quite mad. I didn't think there were such people. We'll talk everything over as soon as you're up and around."

And several days later, I was sitting in the grass over a ravine, the wind rustling in the bushes below. A gray sky threatened rain. There, clear, matter-of-fact words were spoken to me by a woman, about our age dif-ference, about the importance of my getting on with my studies and not taking on, untimely, the burdens of a wife and child. These depressing truths were spoken in the tone of a mother, which intensified my love and reverence for the dear woman. I felt both unutterable sorrow and happiness on hearing her tender voice; it was the first time such words had been said to me.

I stared into the depths of the ravine where the bushes streamed, in the wind, like a green river; and I pledged all the strength of my soul to the repayment of her tenderness. "Before we come to any decision, we must think everything over very carefully," said her gentle voice. She was tapping her knees with a hazel branch and looking back at the town nestled in green hills. "Naturally, I must also talk it over with Boleslav. He senses something is amiss and has become touchy. I hate scenes."

It was all sad and beautiful; therefore something ludicrous was bound to happen. My trousers were too large at the waist and were held together by a three-inch pin. Its sharp end had been pricking me and an awkward movement suddenly drove it in under a rib. I managed to pull it out, unnoticed, but, to my horror, blood from the wound was coming out on my trousers. I had no underclothes and my chef's jacket did not reach below the waist.

How was I to get up and walk with soaked trousers stuck to my body? The drama had taken a comedy turn offensive to my exalted mood, and I launched on agitated speech-making with the clumsy artificiality of an actor who has forgotten his lines. Attentive at first, then astonished, she finally burst out, "What pomposity! Be yourself!"

This was the finishing blow. I shut my mouth and felt my emotions strangling me.

"It's time to get back. It'll be raining soon," she said.

"I'll stay here," I replied.

"Why?"

I had no answer to give her.

"Angry with me?" she asked, tenderly.

"No, with myself."

"There's no reason for that either," she said, and got up. I remained there seated helplessly in a tepid pool. It seemed to me that my blood, gushing from my side, splashed like a brook, and in a moment, hearing it she would ask, "What's that?"

I prayed inwardly for her to go. In her kindness she gave me a few more tender words, then left me. She walked along the edge of the ravine, a graceful figure on shapely legs. As it diminished, and the space of our separation grew, I was stunned by the consciousness that my first love was doomed to unhappiness.

And so it was. Her husband emitted a piteous stream of tearful pleas and sentimentality and she lacked the courage to swim to my side through that muddy flood. With tears in her eyes she explained, "You're so strong and he's so helpless. 'If you leave me,' he said, 'I will die like a flower kept from the sun.' "

The picture came to my mind of the stubby legs, the womanish hips and the potbelly of that flower, and I could not help laughing. Flies lived on the food to be found in his beard.

She, too, smiled. "I know it sounds funny; but he *is* miserable."

"So am I."

"But you're young, and strong."

I think it was then that I began to hate weak natures. Later on and on graver occasions I was to observe the helplessness of the strong in relations with the weak, what rich stores of emotional and intellectual energy go to waste maintaining the useless and the doomed.

In a state verging on insanity, I left town soon after and spent two years tramping the roads of Russia, aimless as a will-o'-the-wisp. I wandered over the Povolzhe,[49] the Don, the Ukraine, the Crimea, the Caucasus. A wide range of experiences left me calloused and embittered. But I kept the image of the woman I loved unmarred in my soul, though some women I met were her betters, intellectually and spiritually.

In Tiflis, after more than two years had passed, I learned that she was there, having just got back from Paris; and that she had expressed joy at the news that I was in town. I, a husky young man of twenty-three, fainted away for the first time in my life. Some friends brought me the message that she wanted to see me; I had not been able to go to her myself.

I found her lovelier and sweeter than I remembered, her figure as girlish, her cheeks as delicately flushed, her cornflower eyes as glowingly tender as ever. Her daughter, agile and graceful as a young kid, was with her; her husband had remained behind in France.

A thunderstorm blew up the day I went to see her. The rain roared and a torrent cascaded down St. David's hill so powerful that it carried away paving stones. The shrieks of the wind, the furious surge of the water, the crashes of things breaking and collapsing, beat against the house; the windows rattled; blue lightning flashes streaked across the room; everything seemed to be plunging into a liquid abyss. With the terrified child buried in pillows, we stood at the window, blinded by the exploding sky and, though there was no need, spoke in whispers.

"I've never seen such a storm," were the words that dropped from the woman I loved, and then, suddenly, "Have you gotten over your feeling for me?"

"No."

This seemed to surprise her and she whispered on, "How different you are. You're a changed man." And she sank into a chair beside the window. As she did so a blinding lightning flash made her cover her eyes. Still whispering, she said, "They talk about you here. Why are you here? What have you been doing all these years?"

And I kept thinking, how slim she is, how perfect! I was with her till midnight pouring out everything as at confessional. I always react boisterously to Nature displaying its might; it serves me as a stimulant. I must have spoken well, for her eyes were wide open, her glance was one of eager and concentrated attention, and she would break in with exclamatory whispers, "That's terrible!" And when I parted from her, her farewell was without that protective, adult smile, at last, which had always rather

[49] The lower Volga region, near the Caspian Sea.

disconcerted me. Down the damp streets I went, watching the sharp disc of the moon shearing the ragged clouds, my head dizzy with joy. The following day I sent her these semblances of verse which she afterwards used to recite, and which I still retain in my memory.

"My lady, for a pat of your hand, for a glance of your soft eyes, a conjurer denies his skill, surrenders himself to chains in your hand, adept at creating bits of bliss out of trifles, out of nothing.

"Receive the eager prisoner! Perhaps he will build a great happiness with the little blisses. Is not the creation of the world a gathering of the grains of matter? Indeed! But the world's a cheerless creation; meagre and miserly are its joys. Though it provides some amusements, your humble servant, for one; and some things of beauty, such as you!

"But hush! I will drop these blunt nails of words, so unsuited to your heart, most beautiful of the flowers of earth, and so rare!"

This can hardly be termed poetry but it was written in joy and sincerity.

And here I was, again, facing one who seemed to me the choicest being in the world, and therefore my greatest need. Her blue dress enveloped her like scented cloud without submerging the lovely lines of her figure. Playing with the tassels of her belt she spoke words that transcended their common meanings. I doted on every movement of her little rose-nailed fingers; I was like a violin tuned by a consummate player. Now I could die. I wanted somehow to breathe this woman into my soul, to have her forever. A tension, that was both languorous and painfully sharp, vibrated in my body like a song. I felt that I would know in a moment what it was for a heart to burst. I read her my first published story. I don't recall what she thought of it. It surprised her, I think.

"So you've taken to prose?"

And seeming to reach me through a dream, I can hear her, "I have often thought of you through these years. Can it be on my account that you've undergone such hardships?"

And I replied that with her in it the world cannot be terrible or hard.

"You're a dear."

I had a mad longing to take her into my arms, but they had become clumsy, overgrown lumps, so that I dared not touch her for fear of bruising her. I shook with the spasms of my heart and I mumbled, "Come live with me, please come live with me!"

A diffident soft laugh, a dazzling glance—then she retreated to the other end of the room and said, "Let's do this; you go on to Nizhny; I'll stay here and think it over and write to you."

Like the hero of a novel I had read, I made a gallant bow, then went off cloud walking.

She came to me in Nizhny that winter, with her daughter. "At a poor man's wedding even the night is too short," runs the proverb with sad, wise irony. I confirmed its truth through personal experience.

For two rubles a month we rented a palace—a bathhouse in a priest's backyard. I took the anteroom while my wife set up house in the one big room that also served as our living room. The palace was hardly suitable for married life. Frost attacked us from every corner. In order to work at night I had to swathe myself in all the clothes I owned and added a carpet. Nevertheless, I suffered severe rheumatic attacks which I found harder to bear because of my pride in my strength and endurance.

The living room could be warmed up, but when the stove was going it thawed back all the putrid, old bathhouse odors of sweat, soap and swill water. The little girl who had looked like an exquisite, blue-eyed porcelain doll grew nervous and was afflicted with headaches.

Spring followed with an invasion of spiders and beetles, which sent both mother and daughter into hysterics, and I spent hours trying to exterminate them with a rubber-soled shoe. And our room continued gloomy, because the windows were overgrown with wild berry bushes which the besotted priest did not let me clear away.

There were more comfortable dwelling places, of course, but we were in arrears to the priest, who, furthermore, was fond of me, and wanted me to stay on. "You'll get used to it," he said, "and if you don't, then you'll pay up and go where the devil you please, even to the English."

For the latter he had great dislike, calling them, "A lazy folk; the only thing they ever invented is the game of patience, and they can't fight."

He was a giant of a man with a face like a red balloon, and a red spade beard. His drinking kept him from officiating in church. In addition, he had a maudlin infatuation for a little, sharp-nosed, brunette dressmaker who looked like a crow. He told me about her infidelities, and wiping the tears from his beard he would say, "I suppose she's just a tart but she reminds me of Holy Saint Thymia; that's why I love her." I could not find any trace of that saint in the calendar.

My being an unbeliever filled him with indignation, and he assailed my soul with these arguments, "Look at it from the practical side. There are so few unbelievers as against the millions of believers! And why? As the fish cannot live out of the water so the soul cannot live out of the church. You cannot deny that, so let's have a drink on it."

"I don't drink. I have rheumatism."

He would impale a herring on his fork, wave it at me and say, "It's your lack of faith brings it on you."

Shame over this bathhouse residence I had provided my wife, over the frequent impossibility of my buying meat for our dinner or a toy for the child, over this damnable and ridiculous poverty, gave me sleepless nights. I personally could bear poverty, at its most vicious, without distress, but for this delicate woman, and even more for her daughter, it made existence a hell.

At night, sitting at a table in a corner, copying out legal papers or working on stories, I ground my teeth and damned myself, mankind, fate, love and destiny.

She behaved with the concern of a mother hiding her troubles from her son. No complaint over this desolate existence ever came from her lips; the harder our life grew the freer rang her voice, the clearer her laugh. From morning to night she drew portraits of priests and their dead wives and sketched maps of the district. The local Zemstvo won a gold medal for them at an exhibition. When commissions for portraits slacked off she made Paris hats out of scraps, straw and wire. I was no connoisseur of ladies' hats, but my guess that she had worked private jokes into them was confirmed by the milliner herself, who gagged with laughter as she stood at the mirror trying on her creations. Yet the hats, I observed, had a strange influence on their purchasers, who, when they crowned themselves with these motley birdnests, paraded the streets with arrogantly inflated bosoms.

I worked for a lawyer and wrote stories for the local newspapers at two kopecks a line. In the evening at tea, when we had no guests, my wife would entertain me with descriptions of Alexander Second's visits to the Bielostock Girls' School where he handed out bonbons to the "noble maidens." [50] She was enthusiastic over Paris, which I already knew from books, especially DuCamps's. Her Paris was the Montmartre and the hectic Latin Quarter. Her reminiscences stimulated me more than wine. I composed apostrophes to woman through love of whom is born all life's beauty. I got most delight out of her own love stories which she told me with great charm, and a candor that at times mystified me. Humorously, with a few light words like the strokes of a sharpened pencil, she would sketch her clownish suitor, the general,

[50] (Author's note): By which some of them were brought miraculously into an "interesting condition." Now and then a pretty girl would accompany the Tsar on a hunting expedition in the nearby forest and disappear to be heard of again in accounts of a fashionable Petersburg marriage. Those visits nourished legends.

who once, during a royal hunt, brought down the game before the Tsar had time to fire, and, in his confusion, cried out to the wounded beast, "I beg your Imperial pardon."

In her talk of the Russian emigrés, I sensed a smile of disdain ambushed in her words. Her candor often had a quality of naïve cynicism. Then her sharp pink tongue would flick over her lips with relish like a cat's, and her eyes would take on an added sparkle. Sometimes the light in her eyes appeared to me to take on a fastidious sharpness; at other times it reflected the excitement of a little girl absorbed in play with dolls.

One day she said, "A Russian in love tends to be talky and ponderous. He can get repulsively oratorical. Only the French, for whom it is close to religion, achieve beauty when they love." My behavior with her observed some restraints after that.

Of Frenchwomen she said, "When they lack passion they provide a welcome substitute in elaborate and playful sensuality. They make love an art." On this she was serious, even a little preachy. It was knowledge, though not exactly the knowledge I had been seeking, and I took it in avidly. "You could compare Russian women with fruits, and Frenchwomen with conserves made from the fruits." To me, as she told me this one moonlight night in a garden, she was the conserve.

I startled her with my romantic notions of the relations of man and woman, which I disclosed to her on one of the first nights of our married life. "Do you mean that? Do you really believe that?" she asked as she lay in my arms, in blue moonlight.

From her pink, seemingly translucent, body rose an intoxicating odor of bitter almonds. Her slender fingers toyed abstractedly with my hair; she looked at me with wide, anxious eyes and an uncertain smile. Then she jumped off the bed, exclaimed, "Dear God," and began pacing the room, passing between shadow and light, the satin of her skin gleaming with the moon rays and her bare feet soundless. Returning to me, she stroked my cheeks and said with maternal undertones, "You ought to have begun with a girl, not me."

And when I pulled her to me she wept. "You must know how I love you," she said. "I've never known greater joy than with you. Believe me, that is the truth. Never has love been so tender, so simple, so lighthearted for me. I have a marvelous happiness with you. Just the same, I tell you, we've made a mistake. I'm not what you need. And I'm the one to blame."

This was incomprehensible to me; it frightened me, and I intensified my caresses to storm her out of that mood. However, the terrible thought lodged in my mind. Some days later, after raptures that excited her to tears, she said yearningly, "If only I were young!"

As I recall, a storm tossed in the garden that night; the vine branches scratched on the windows; the wind bawled in the chimney like a trapped wolf. Cold and gloom, and the depressing rustle of wallpaper peeling off in the corners, made our room mournful.

When a few rubles came in we entertained friends with lavish suppers of meat, vodka, beer and desserts, and had a marvelous time. My Parisienne had a good appetite; she liked Russian dishes; beef intestines stuffed with Kasha [51] and goose fat, fish pies and potato soup with mutton.

She founded "The Order of Greedy Guts" with a membership of about twelve would-be gourmets, who were endlessly and esthetically eloquent over kitchen mysteries. My taste ran to mysteries of another range. I ate very little and the achievement of satiety had no allurements for me, and remained outside my esthetic needs. "Futile people," I characterized the "greedy guts." "As everyone is when shaken," she retorted. "Heine said, 'We're naked underneath.'"

She had a store of sophisticated quotations, which she did not always use in place. She had a knack of giving her neighbors of the opposite sex a good "shaking," and she thought it fun. Unfailingly good-humored, witty, lithe as a snake, she quickly generated a boisterous spirit, releasing what were hardly edifying emotions. In a few minutes' talk with her, a man's ears would redden, then turn purple, and his eyes would mist over like a goat contemplating a cabbage.

"A regal woman," was the opinion of the lawyer's assistant, a declassed nobleman with moles like the False Dmitri's, [52] and a belly like a bay window. And a blond student from Yaroslav wrote poems to her, always in dactyls. I found them dreadful but she enjoyed laughing over them.

"Why do you lead them on?" I asked her.

"It's as much fun as fishing," she replied. "It's called flirting. No self-respecting woman goes without it." And she sometimes added, smiling into my eyes, "Jealous?"

I did not happen to be jealous, but all this was an intrusion upon my life. I could not endure vulgar and petty people. I was a cheerful man myself who considered laughter one of man's great accomplishments.

[51] Buckwheat porridge.
[52] A pretender to the throne, supported by the Poles during the "Time of Troubles," following the reign of Ivan the Terrible.

Clowns and other professional comics distressed me only by their incompetence; I was sure I could do better. And I frequently had our guests aching with laughter, tears gushing from their eyes. And she would exclaim, "What a wonderful comedian you could make. You must go on the stage."

She herself was a success in private theatricals and had received bids from several theatre managers. "I love the stage," she told me, "but what goes on behind the scenes terrifies me." She was direct and truthful in thought, word and wish.

Her preachment to me was this, "You philosophize far too much. Life is simple to the point of brutality. Why confuse yourself by looking for profundities in it? Learn how to lessen its brutality; that's the most you can aim for."

Her philosophy, I felt, was mostly gynecology; her obstetrics course served as her testament. She had described to me how overwhelmed she had been by her first scientific book, read after leaving school.

"I was a naïve child and its impact was like that of a brick on my head; I felt as if I had slipped from a cloud into the mud. I wept over my loss of faith. But soon I felt the ground, stony but firm, under my feet. I missed God most of all. I had felt so completely united with Him, and suddenly, pouf, He was gone like cigarette smoke and, with Him, my visions of sanctification in Love. And in school we had all given so much eager and clever thought to Love."

I was distressed by her gushing Parisian nihilism. At night I would get up from my work to take a look at her, sleeping, when she looked daintier and lovelier than ever. And as I watched, bitter reflections passed through my mind regarding the distortions of her spirit and the confusions in her life. And pity intensified my love.

We were also at odds in our literary tastes. I raved over Balzac and Flaubert while her favorites were Paul Feval, Octave Feuillet, Paul de Kock—above all his La Fille Girot, Ma Femme. This she regarded the wittiest book she had ever read, but I found it as dull as a law book. Nevertheless, our relationship was a fine one. Our passion never dulled and we remained interesting to each other. However, in our third year I began to hear my soul creaking, as it were; and the creaking became louder and more evident, it seemed to me, as time went on. I turned more avidly to study, I read more and tolerated fewer interruptions. I devoted myself more seriously to writing; our social circle palled on me the larger it grew; for both I and my wife were earning more money, which went to more and larger feasts.

Life seemed to her like a wax-works show, and since men did not carry placards "do not touch," she was often incautious in her approaches and they interpreted her interest according to their desires. This led to misunderstandings which always fell to me to resolve. My solutions were at times lacking in finesse and restraint. A man whose ears I once boxed complained, "I'll admit I was wrong, but to treat me like a boy. That's too much! I'm twice the age of that hooligan and he dares to pull my ears! It would have been more decent for him to punch me!"

It appeared that I lacked the knowledge to mete out punishment to people suitable to their position.

My wife paid little attention to my writing, but I was unaffected by her indifference, up to a point. I did not regard myself yet as a serious writer, and looked upon my pieces for the paper as hackwork, although I had begun to feel the tidal pull of a new emotion. One morning, reading to her, "The Old Woman Isergil," which I had written off in a single draft the night before, she fell asleep. At first I felt no offense. I stopped reading and watched her, bemused by my own thoughts.

Her small, dear head had fallen back on the sofa pillow; her mouth was half-open and her breathing was as placid and gentle as a child's. The morning sun peeped in through the net of branches outside the window. The golden dapples it left on her breast and knees lay there like petals of air.

Then I rose and went out into the yard, smarting with the barb of her indifference, and depressed with doubts about my abilities.

All my life I had watched women toiling like slaves, enduring filth and depravity, living in want or in smug surfeit. One beautiful memory was left from my childhood, Queen Margot, from which I was parted by a multitude of intervening impressions. It seemed to me women would respond to the story of Isergil, that it would inspire them to reach toward beauty and freedom. But it had failed to move the woman closest to me; she had fallen asleep over it!

Why? Did the bell life had cast in my breast lack resonance?

I had taken this woman to my heart, to replace my mother. I had looked to her to nourish me with a rich honey that would stimulate my creative power. I had looked to her to offset the brutalizing harshness of life.

That was thirty years ago and now my heart smiles at the recollections. But then man's inalienable right to sleep when he pleases aroused intense suffering and resentment in me.

I believed that cheerful talk about sad things would dispel their sadness. I also suspected the presence in the world of an artful Somebody whose pleasure it was to see people suffer; that a certain evil spirit composed human dramas, exhibiting particular skill in making them tragedies. This invisible playwright I held to be my particular foe, and did my best to keep out of his plots.

I recall with what indignation I read in Oldenburgh's book on Buddha that "existence is suffering." I had experienced few of the joys of life, but its cruelties and hardships I had considered the accidents, not the norms, of life. A careful reading of Archbishop Khrisanph's substantial *The Religion of the East* left me still more revolted with the idea, which I refused to accept, that fear, anguish and grief constituted the substance of the world. Having come through a period of religious intoxication, I resented its emptiness. Seeing no virtue in suffering, I had a distaste for "scenes" and developed considerable skill in turning them from heavy drama to comedy.

But it is hardly necessary to go into all this to explain that a "domestic crisis" developed, though we did our mutual best to avert it. My bit of philosophizing about it was only to indicate the detours on my road of self-discovery.

My light-hearted wife was also averse to scenes, which our superpsychological Russians are usually so ready to enact. However, the flaxen-lashed student's melancholy dactyls affected her like autumn rain. He would pen the verses neatly in script rich in curves and flourishes, on slips of paper which he secreted in whatever he got hold of—in books, hats and even the sugar bowl. On finding these neatly folded papers, I handed them to her saying, "Prepare for the latest attempt upon your heart."

At first these paper Cupid's darts drew no reaction from her. She read the interminable verses aloud and we had a hearty laugh together over such lines as,

> All that you do, in my heart is imprinted,
> The touch of your hand, the turn of your head.
> Your voice like a turtle dove's is sweet
> While like a hawk in my dreams, my wings around you beat.

One day, however, after one of these adolescent effusions she said, "Really, I'm sorry for him." I felt sorry, I recall, for somebody else. From that moment she no longer read the verses aloud.

The poet, a youth about four years my senior, was a silent person with a fondness for drink and a phenomenal ability to remain rooted to one spot. Arriving for Sunday dinner at two o'clock, he sat until two in the morning, silent and immobile. Like myself, he was a law clerk. He was slovenly in his work and astounded his good-natured boss by his absent-mindedness.

"It's all trash!" he would exclaim hoarsely.

"And what's not trash?"

"How do I know."

Then he raised his bovine eyes to the ceiling, and that was the extent of his conversation. It was this phenomenal dullness of his that I found most unendurable. When he was drunk, a slow process with him, he was elevated to the pitch of sounding ironic snuffles through his nose. Other than that, I observed nothing to distinguish him, not even evil; for, in common law, the man who tries to steal your wife must be an evil man.

Rich relatives in the Ukraine sent him fifty rubles a month, a small fortune at that time. He brought my wife sweets every Sunday. For her birthday present he brought her an alarm clock inset into a bronze tree trunk on which an owl was finishing off an adder. This instrument of torture cost me an hour and seven minutes sleep every morning.

In her treatment of this student, my wife proceeded from flirtation to the remorse of a woman who feels that she has broken the peace of a man's soul. How did she think this lugubrious story would end, I asked her?

"I don't know," she replied. "I have no clear feeling for him, but I want to stir him. Something has gone to sleep in his heart, and I think I can stir it awake again."

That was true and I knew it. She wanted to wake up everyone and everything. She succeeded, but on waking a man up the beast would stretch. I recalled the case of Circe to her, but that did not dampen her desire to waken men up; and numerous grew the herds of rams, bulls and boars in my house.

Friends who considered themselves kind came to me with tales affecting my marital honor. I was crudely direct with them, proposing to repay such stories with a beating. Some lied to justify themselves; a few were injured by my response to their kindness. And my wife said, "You'll gain nothing by such roughness; it will make their gossip more exhilarating. You're not jealous, are you?"

I was too young and confident for that. Yet, there are emotions, ideas, speculations which one shares only with the woman one loves and no one else. There is a time in a man's communing with a woman when he turns himself inside out and bares his heart, like a believer to his God. And the thought that this most intimate self of mine might be exhibited by her, to another man, drove me into frenzies. This I felt to be treason. That feeling, probably, is at the core of all jealousy. I began to feel that living with such thoughts might turn me from my chosen road. I was convinced, by now, there was no place in life for me outside of literature; and this situation made writing impossible for me. I was able to keep the matter from degenerating into scandal, because I had learned to be tolerant toward people without killing my respect or interest in them. In the sight of divine, absolute Truth I knew that all men are sinners; furthermore that, in the understanding of men, the worst sinners are the self-elected, godly ones, those bastards sprung from the union of vice and virtue. Their union, it should be noted, is not a rape of virtue, or contrariwise. The bastards are the issue of their law· ful wedlock, in which necessity ironically officiates as the priest. The marriage sacrament conjoins two distinct opposites; but what is begotten of them is, with rare exceptions, a species of dour mediocrity. In that period I was tempted by paradoxes as a boy is tempted by ice cream. Their tang stimulated me like vintage wines. The verbal paradoxes pleas· urably coated the brutal paradoxes of reality.

I told my wife, "I think I'd better go."

She gave it a moment's thought and agreed. "You're right. This is no life for you."

We embraced silently and sadly. I left town, and not long after she went on the stage. That ended the story of my first love; a fine story despite its unsatisfactory ending. Recently this woman died.

This I will say for her: she was genuinely a woman. She could live on the little she had, perhaps, because every day was Christmas Eve to her. Tomorrow would always, in her expectations, open on a brave new world abloom with magnificent new flowers, thronged with exceptional people and ringing with great events. She laughed off the troubles of life, brushed them off like gnats. Her soul was poised and eager, always ready for marvels. Hers, moreover, were not the naïve transports of a schoolgirl, but the healthy gustos of an adult reveling in the fascinating traffic of life, the tragi-comedies of emotional entanglements, the small incidents, glittering like motes in the sun.

I can't say she liked people, but she watched them, fascinated. Sometimes she injected complications of stimulants in marriages and love affairs of others, by provoking jealousy here, and raising ardors there. She delighted in this risky game.

"Love and hunger—they rule the world," she would say, "and philosophy plagues it. Love, that's all there is to live for; it's man's major occupation."

A state bank official, a long lanky chap who walked with the slow, sober movements of a crane, frequented our circle. His clothes were one of his grave concerns.' With his long, bony fingers he would flake off grains of dust discernible only to him. And he flicked off from his mind any new idea, any epigrammatic word, as well. They offended his own mental habit, which was solemn and precise. He always spoke as if he weighed every ponderous word; and before uttering a sentence, which was never to be contradicted, he would tidy his sparse reddish whiskers with his icicle-like fingers. "Chemistry, as it develops, will assume importance in industries making use of raw materials. That women are ruled by caprice is undeniable. As between a wife and a mistress the distinction is juridical, not physiological."

I would say, as solemnly, to my wife, "Will you grant, my dear, that lawyers have wings, all of them?"

With a mournful and guilty look she would reply, "Of course not. I wouldn't venture to say that; however I insist that it's absurd to feed elephants hard-boiled eggs."

And our friend's comment upon this dialogue would be, "It seems to me you're incapable of serious discussion."

Wincing from a knock he had given his knee against a table leg, he said as if he had just become convinced of it. "Density is positively a property of matter."

After his departures, my wife would take a perch on my lap and say, "How perfectly, how completely stupid he is. Stupid in everything, his walk, his gestures. That's what I like about him—his unadulterated stupidity. Now, pet me, darling."

She liked to have me stroke her cheek gently, following the barely perceptible lines under her dear eyes. She would shut them, stretch and purr like a cat. "How diverting people are. Nobody else may find a man interesting, but I can get some excitement out of him. I want to have a look into him the way you want to look into a closed box. Perhaps something's there, hidden from others, seen by nobody else before me; and I, I will discover it."

There was no pretense in these explorations of hers into the human unknown. Her quests had the inquisitiveness and wonder of a child entering a new room. There were times when all this actually kindled flickers of consciousness in the vacuous eyes of a dullard, but usually the response was an animal urge to possess her.

She delighted in her own body. Standing naked before a mirror, she would rhapsodize, "How wonderful a woman is. What harmony her body is." And she used to say, "In good clothes I feel smarter and healthier." And it was so. She became wittier and gayer; her eyes had a conquering gleam. As she wore them, the pretty cotton print dresses she made had the distinction of silks and velvets. She had a way of making simplicity seem magnificence. Women praised her clothes, if not always sincerely, always enviously. I heard one of them say to her, in a mortified way, "My dress cost three times what yours cost but yours makes it look worthless. I feel injured when I look at you."

Naturally, she was no favorite among the women, who gossiped furiously about us. A woman doctor of our acquaintance, very beautiful and very stupid, gave me this magnanimous warning, "She'll suck the last drop of your blood!"

Life with my first lady love was certainly an education. But despair consumed me, nevertheless, over our irreconcilable differences.

I took life seriously. I had seen too much, lived too intensely in my mind and was in a state of constant concern. A discordant chorus of problems that could not touch the spirit of this fine woman, boomed in the recesses of my soul.

One day I saw a policeman in the market place beating an old one-eyed Jew, a fine-looking man, whom he accused of stealing a bunch of radishes. I saw the old man again, in the street. Covered with dust, his appearance was quite majestic as he walked on slowly. His large, dark eye looked solemnly into the silent, sultry sky, while trickles of blood from his injured mouth ran into his white beard, dyeing the silver strands a bright red.

Thirty years ago it was; yet I can still see the glance of the old man raised, in mute reproach, to the still sky. I can still see the eyebrows quivering on the wrinkled face, like plucked silver threads. No, one does not forget such outrages upon a human being; let them never be forgotten!

I came home depressed and inarticulate with rage and pity. Such incidents somehow shoulder me out of life, make me alien to it, an alien whom they torment by exhibiting to him the filth, misery and madness of the world, all that can inflict incurable wounds upon his soul. At such times, I felt how distant from me was the being nearest to me.

My emotion over the beaten Jew startled her. "And it's this that drives you out of your mind? What weak nerves you have!" And she added, "A fine-looking man you call him; but how could he be with only one eye?"

She shunned all suffering as an enemy. She had no interest in hearing about people's misery. Elegiac verses were not to her taste. Her heart was too small and cheerful for compassion. Her favorite poets were Beranger and Heine, that man who laughed in his agonies.

Something of the faith of a child in the infinite power of a conjurer, characterized her attitude toward life. The tricks already performed were wonderful, but more wonderful still are those to come. They will be performed in an hour or two, or tomorrow perhaps—at any rate they will be performed.

I think that at the moment of her death she was looking forward to this last, most wonderful and perfectly mysterious trick.

Chapter Eleven

WHEN I RETURNED TO NIZHNY FROM TIFLIS,[53] KOROLENKO HAD GONE off to St. Petersburg.[54]

Having no other work to apply myself to, I wrote some short stories and sent them to "The Volga Herald," published by Reinhardt. Korolenko's regular contributions made it the outstanding periodical of the district.

I signed my stories, M. G. or G—y. Reinhardt published them promptly, sent me a flattering note and a large sum, about thirty rubles. For reasons I have forgotten, I took pains to mask my authorship, even from such good friends as Vasiliev and Lanin. I attached little importance to these stories and had no idea that they would have any measurable consequences for me. Reinhardt, however, disclosed my pen names to Korolenko, who invited me to visit him on his return to Nizhny.

He still lived in the wooden house in the suburbs, a house owned by the architect, Lembke. I found Korolenko at tea in a small room whose

[53] Now Tbilisi, capital of the Georgian Soviet Republic.
[54] Now Leningrad.

windows looked out on the street. There were flowers on the window
sills and in other parts of the room, and books and papers all over. His
wife and children had had their tea and gone out for a walk. Korolenko's
manner was even more self-assured than before; even his hair seemed
to have a more confident curl in it.

"I've just read your story, 'The Bird,'" was his greeting to me. "So
you've started publishing your pieces? Congratulations! But you're a stubborn one. Still allegorizing. However, allegory has its points, and persistence is not a bad trait, either."

He continued this affectionate banter, looking at me through half-
shut eyes. His skin was blackened and his beard almost bleached by the
sun. He wore a dark blue linen shirt gathered under a broad leather belt.
His black trousers were tucked into high boots. I had the impression
that he had just arrived from a long journey and was about to go off on
another. His steadfast, intelligent eyes had a brave glow. I told him I'd
written some other stories one of which had come out in the magazine,
"The Caucasus."

"You've brought nothing? A pity! You have a very individual way of
writing—jerky and rough, but very individual. I've heard you've done a
lot of tramping about. I've been hiking too, this summer, beyond the
Volga, along the Kerzhentz and Vetluga Rivers. And where have you
been?"

I gave an account of my roving and he exclaimed, "That's hiking!
That's what's given you your virility. You must have stored up prodigious
strength."

I had just read his story "River at Play," with admiration for its finished structure, and its insights, for which I felt grateful to the author. I
spoke of it rhapsodically. For me Korolenko's portrayal of the ferryman
Tiulin was an accurately and beautifully shaped image of the average
man who is "hero for an hour," the sort of man who, after a noble and
self-sacrificing act, can turn around and club his wife to death or skewer
a neighbor. After captivating you with smiles and words as gorgeous as
flowers, he can, without any fathomable cause, stamp his muddy boot
on your face. Like Kuzma Minin,[55] he is capable of leading a national
resurgence but ends up a vermin-ridden sot who drinks himself into the
grave.

Korolenko heard out my incoherent praises, listening attentively and
without a word. This embarrassed me. Finally, he shut his eyes and

[55] Organizer of the national revolt that drove out the Poles who seized Moscow
after the death of Boris Godunov.

smacked the table with his palm. Then he got up, leaned against the wall and said, with a good-natured laugh, "You're exaggerating. Let's say it's a successful story and leave it at that. I'll not deny I like it, myself. But whether my ferryman's so typical, I'm not sure. But you know, you speak very well; your words are vigorous and free. That's my return for your compliments. It's clear that you've seen a lot and done a lot of thinking. I congratulate you with all my heart."

He gave me his hand, calloused from the axe or from the oars. He enjoyed every form of physical exertion.

"Now let's hear what you've met up with," he said.

In the course of my recital I touched on my encounters with the "truth seekers" who crowd the tangled roads of Russia, ambling from town to town and from monastery to monastery.

Korolenko, staring out of the window said, "They're no-goods, most of them. Unfulfilled heroes, full of loathsome self-love. Haven't you observed how vile-minded they generally are? Most of them aren't after 'holy truth' at all, but an easy life on the backs of others."

Those words, spoken without heat, startled me and made clear something I had vaguely felt before.

"What orators, though, you'll see among them," he went on. "What rich language they use! As if they were weaving silk brocades."

The "truth seekers" the "summoners," were the pets of the Narodnik writers, and here was Korolenko calling them vile-minded no-goods! It sounded blasphemous but, clearly, Korolenko had thought about it and this was his conclusion. And these words strengthened my impression of his integrity.

"Were you in the Volhynia or in the Podolia? [56] That's beautiful country."

I told him of a conversation I had had with John of Kronstadt,[57] and he asked me, almost breathlessly, "What do you think of him? What's he like?"

"He's sincere, like a naïve village priest. He seems distressed by his notoriety. It burdens him. You feel that things are happening by accident in him, as though his actions are involuntary. He's continually appealing to God, 'Is this right, dear God Almighty?' He's terrified over making some mistake."

"Strange," mused Korolenko; and he told me of talks he had had with the peasants of Lukoyanov, who belonged to one of the dissident

[56] West Ukrainian districts.
[57] A famous religious recluse.

sects in the Kerzhentz region. With a warm, fondling humor he characterized the mixture of innocence and craft in their talk, the common sense of the peasant and his reserve with strangers.

"It seems to me that in no other land is the spiritual life so richly varied as in Russia. At any rate the nature of our believers and thinkers is multiform as nowhere else." And he stressed the necessity of studying this spiritual side of our life.

"But it must not be disposed of as an ethnographic issue; it needs a deeper kind of study. We're all growths from this soil, thistles and weeds with the rest. To sow 'the rational, the eternal, and the good,' on our ground requires discretion as well as energy. This summer I ran across a sharp young fellow who seriously maintained that the Kulak usurers in the village represent progress since, don't you see, theirs is a form of capital accumulation and Russia is headed for a capitalist future! With such an agitator among the peasants . . ." and he laughed.

Seeing me to the door, he again heaped me with good wishes.

"So you really feel I can write?" I asked.

"Of course!" he exclaimed, with surprise. "You are writing; you're getting published. What else? If it's advice you want, bring me your manuscripts and we'll have a session."

I left him refreshed, like a man who, after a sultry and fatiguing day, has bathed in a cool forest stream.

Korolenko won my respect, but it grieved me that I did not really feel drawn toward him. I think it was because, by this time, I was weary of the instructor-pupil relationship. I wanted some rest from teachers. I wanted simple, friendly, heart-to-heart talk in which I could speak out what was troubling my mind without embarrassment. The teachers, when I brought them what I had distilled from my experiences, trimmed it and shaped it according to their own political or philosophical patterns. They had no other patterns, I realized, to fit it to; and their intentions were honest; but it was nevertheless painful to watch them messing up my material.

About a fortnight later, I brought Korolenko some manuscripts, among them, "The Fisherman and the Fairy," in verse, and "The Old Woman Isergil," the latter a rewritten version. Korolenko was out and I left the manuscripts.

The next day I found this note from him: "Come this evening and we'll have a talk."

He had an axe in his hand when I met him.

"Don't think this is my critic's tool," he said, hefting the axe. "I've just been working on some shelving. Just the same, you're in for a decapitation, sir."

There was good-natured animation in his face, a gay smile in his eyes, and he was perfumed, like a healthy, Russian farm woman, with the smell of fresh bread.

"I wrote all through the night," he said, "took a nap after lunch and when I got up felt I needed to stretch my muscles a bit."

He was not at all, now, the man I had seen two weeks back. I no longer felt the instructor in him; just a simple-hearted man with a friendly interest in people.

He took the manuscripts from the table and slapped them on his knee. "I've read your fairy tale. If the author were a young lady, stuffed with de Musset, especially in the genteel translation of dear old Madame Misovsky, I'd tell her, 'Not at all bad, my dear; but just the same, hurry up and get married!' But for a rampaging, young giant like you to write delicate verses! It's indecent, it's criminal. When did they afflict you?"

"In Tiflis, I——"

"So, that's it. There's where the pessimistic note creeps in. Bear in mind, to be tragic about love is an adolescent ailment. Tragic love is a theory more contradicted in practice than all others. You old pessimist! We've heard about you!"

He gave me a knowing wink and went on, "Out of these funeral wreaths only the lyrics are publishable. I'll arrange that for you. 'The Old Woman' is better than the rest, but you keep on ringing in the allegories. That won't do you any good. Have you been in jail? You'll get there again, I assure you." After a pause, as he leafed through the manuscripts, he said, "A curious thing, all this is sheer romanticism which has been dead for years. And I doubt that this Lazarus deserves a resurrection. To my ears this voice you're singing in is not yours. You're not a romanticist, you're a realist, understand? Now, to get down to details. There's something here about a Pole. That's personal, eh?"

"Possibly."

"There you are. So we do know something about you! But that's not permitted. Delete everything personal, everything trivially personal, I mean."

There was gaiety and enthusiasm in his words; his eyes shone. He amazed me, and I felt that I was seeing him for the first time. Tossing the manuscripts back on the table, and pulling his chair up closer, he put his hand on my knee.

"May I speak frankly to you? I hardly know you but you're the subject of a lot of talk, and some things I have seen for myself. You're not living well. You haven't found the right place. Go away and marry a nice, bright girl."

"But I have a wife."

"That's the trouble, exactly."

I told him I would rather not discuss that. "Forgive me, then," he said, and turned to humorous banter, which he interrupted suddenly to say, "Have you heard that Romass is in jail?"

"I heard about it only yesterday. Where was it, in Smolensk? What was he doing there?"

"The police made quite a haul in his flat—the entire printing plant and office equipment of 'The People's Truth.' "

"What a nomad he is," mused Korolenko. "He'll be sent into exile again, somewhere. Is he bearing up? He had the stamina of a peasant." Korolenko sighed, shrugged his shoulders and went on. "No, that's not what's needed. You won't get anywhere on that path. Astirev's case should teach us. Its lesson is that we must get down to the hard grind of legal work,[58] the everyday work of education. Autocracy is a decaying but powerful reality. Its roots are deep and branching. Our generation will not manage to drag it all up. Our first task is to loosen it and that will take more than a decade of legal work."

He went on, at length, in this vein, and it was evident that he was expressing the great conviction of his life.

His family returned. The children filled the house with their racket. I took my leave. My heart was at rest.

Provincial life, as everyone knows, is a life under glass. People all learn about you; they know what was on your mind at two o'clock, Wednesday afternoon, and after evening mass on Saturday; they know your innermost desires and are indignant if your life fails to comply with their forecasts.

It was soon all over town that Korolenko was well disposed toward me, and I had to listen to warnings of this sort, "Be on your guard. This 'wise' crowd will mislead you." The reference was to Bobrikin's then much-talked-of, story, "The Man Who Became Wise," whose hero was a revolutionist who took to "legal work" within the Zemstvo, after he had lost his umbrella and his wife. "You're a democrat, a son of the people," they urged. "There's nothing you can learn from these leaders."

[58] Educational and propaganda work permitted by the authorities.

However, for a long time I had been feeling my relationship to the people to be rather that of a stepson. This feeling was confirmed by experience and by what I saw of the people-worshipers who seemed to me to be stepsons, too. When I voiced that opinion they yelled, "See, they've already infected you!"

A group of Yarloslav Lyceum students invited me to give them a reading at one of their get-togethers. During the reading they stealthily mixed vodka and beer in my glass. I caught them at this trick. I realized that they wanted to see me drunk as a sailor, but I couldn't understand what for. A narcissistic consumptive among them urged me to consign "ideas, ideals, and all that trash to the dead. Write simply. To hell with ideas!"

I found all this "advice" an unmitigated bore.

Korolenko, like all prominent people, became a town target. Some people, aware of his sympathetic nature, sought to involve him in their personal problems. The slanderous went after him. My friends were contemptuous of his writing. "That Korolenko of yours," they said, "seems to be religious." For some reason they particularly objected to the story, "Behind the Image," which they dismissed as "mere ethnography," something "Pavel Yakushkin might have written." Korolenko's shoemaker hero, they insisted, was plagiarized from the story of Uspensky.

The critics reminded me of a Voronezh monk who commented, testily, after a description of Miklukha Maklay's South Sea Island voyages, "Ridiculous; so he brought back a Papuan to Russia. But why a Papuan? And why only one?"

Early one morning I was returning from a field where I had been wandering through the night and I ran into Korolenko just as he was leaving his house. "Where do you come from?" he asked, "I'm just starting off on a walk. What a glorious night it's been! Come along."

He, too, evidently, had gone without a night's sleep. His eyes looked inflamed and gritty. Their glance revealed weariness. His beard was uncombed and his clothes untidily thrown on.

"I've read your 'Grandpa Arhip' in the 'Volga.' It's not bad; it's suitable for a national magazine. But why didn't you let me see it? And why don't you come around any more?"

I explained that I had felt repulsed by his manner when I had come to borrow three rubles. He had turned his back on me and said not a word when he handed me the money. This had offended me, since I resorted to the painful recourse of borrowing money only under desperate necessity.

He frowned and grew thoughtful. "It must be so since you say so, but I don't recall it. Forgive me; something must have been troubling me to make me so rude. It's been happening often to me, these days. I suddenly become preoccupied as though I had dropped into a well. I'm all tense, yet I see nothing and hear nothing."

He took my arm and looked into my eyes. "Please forget this. Really there's no reason for offense, for I have only the friendliest feelings toward you. Yet it's good that you felt offended. Usually we take no offense when we should; that's the matter with us. But, let's forget it. What I want to tell you is this. You're prolific, but you rush it; and often your stories seem a bit unfinished and sometimes unclear. In the 'Arhip,' for example, in your description of the rain, the writing is neither in verse nor rhythmical prose. It fumbles."

And he spoke at length, and in great detail, about everything I had published, making it clear that he had given it close attention. I was deeply touched, of course, and when I voiced my gratitude he answered, "We must all help one another; we're a few, and we're all in straits."

Lowering his voice he asked me: "Is it true, have you heard about it, that a young girl named Istomina was mixed up in the Nathanson-Romass case?"

I knew the girl. My acquaintance with her included dragging her out of the Volga into which she had jumped from a scow. It had been no trouble, for she had chosen a shallow to drown in. She was a drab little fool, a hysteric given to pathological lying. Later she became a governess, I think in the Stolypin household, and was one of those killed by the terrorist's bomb that demolished the premier's house on Aptekarsky Island.[59]

Korolenko heard me out but said, with great heat, "It's criminal to involve children in such risks. I, too, have met this girl, about four years ago, and my impressions of her don't fit your portrait. I found her a sensitive little thing, reacting to the obvious lies of life. She might have turned into a good village teacher. She's being accused of spilling things under the police questioning. But how much could she have had to tell? I can't condone this sacrifice of children to the gods of politics."

He was walking at a rapid pace. My feet hurt, I stumbled and fell behind.

[59] An island off St. Petersburg in the Neva River on which medicinal plants were grown.

"What's the trouble?"

"A touch of rheumatism."

"You're starting early. In my opinion," he went on, "you did the girl an injustice, but you told the story well. Why don't you try something more ambitious that you could send to one of the big reviews? It's time for you to take a crack at it. You'll be printed there; and I hope, then, you'll take yourself more seriously."

I don't recall his ever speaking to me with more charm than on that fine morning in a field, green and refreshed after two days of steady rain.

We sat over the ravine near the Jewish cemetery, admiring the emerald glitter the dew brought to leaf and grassblade. He spoke of the grotesque pathos of Jewish life in the Pale.[60] The shadows of fatigue gathered under his eyes. It was nine when we got back to town. In his leavetaking he reminded me, "So you'll try your hand on a long story, eh?"

At home I sat down and immediately set to work on "Chelkash,"[61] the story of an Odessa hobo who was my ward mate in the Nikolayev hospital. I finished it in a couple of days and sent the first draft to Korolenko. A few days later he brought some injured peasants to the lawyer whom I worked for and took the occasion to congratulate me, with a warmth only he was capable of. "It's good! Quite a story; all of a piece."

I was put into quite a flutter by his praise. That evening, straddling a chair in his workroom, he told me with animation: "Not bad at all! You know how to do character. Your people speak and act out of their own sources. You manage not to confuse thought with the play of feeling. It's not everyone who can manage that! Best of all you feel for a man as he is. I told you you're a realist!"

But he added, meditatively, "and a romanticist at the same time! And, say! You've been here a quarter of an hour and you're on your fourth cigarette!"

"I'm excited."

"That's not called for. You're always in an excited state. I suppose that's what makes people say you drink. You're all bones. You smoke without enjoying it. What's wrong?"

"I don't know."

"Do you drink, really?"

"No. They lie."

[60] The restricted area in Southwest Russia where Jews were permitted to live.
[61] One of Gorky's most famous short stories.

"No orgies at your place?" and laughed, as he looked at me and passed on to me some of the elaborate slanders circulating about me. And he concluded with remarks I long remembered, "When a man gets a little ahead of others he gets a club on the skull to hold him up. That's a phrase I heard from a Petersburg student. Now, all that nonsense aside, however much it may titillate you. We'll print your 'Chelkash' in the 'Russian Treasury.' [62] We'll lead off with it; give it the place of honor. I've made a few repairs in the manuscript, where you had some collisions with grammar; but I've touched nothing else. Do you want to see what I've done?"

Of course I said, "No."

Pacing up and down and rubbing his hands, he said, "I'm elated over your success!"

It was this endearing sincerity of feeling in him that I responded to. I was full of admiration for this man who felt for literature the strong, serene lifelong affection one may feel toward a beloved woman. That happy moment with "the pilot," was unforgettable. With mute intentness I looked at his eyes, so full of affectionate joy in human beings. How rare is this joy in human beings! Yet there is no greater joy.

Korolenko came up and laid his massive hands on my shoulders. "Wouldn't you like to get away from this town? To Samara, for instance? I have a friend on the Samara paper. If you'd like I'll write him to give you a job. How about it?"

"Am I in anybody's way here?"

"No, but some people are in yours."

I could see that he had not been left untouched by the tales about my drinking, about the bathhouse "debauches," about my "vices," the worst of which was poverty. This insistence on the part of Korolenko, on getting me out of town hurt me, but touched me also as evidence of his concern over the depths in which he supposed I had fallen. Moved by this concern, I bared my entire life. He heard me in tense silence, frowning and shrugging, saying, at the end, "But don't you see how impossible this is for you, that you must get out of this phantasmagoria? Now, do as I say. It's imperative that you get away and change the course of your life."

I let myself be persuaded.

Under the pretentious pen-name of Yehudi Khlamida, I became a second-rate columnist for the "Samara Gazette." My columns drew

[62] One of the most important literary reviews in Russia.

bantering, but severe criticism from Korolenko, but his comments were always charged with friendly concern.

I particularly recall this episode. I was bored beyond endurance by a poet fatally named Skukin.[63] Reams of his verse arrived for me at the editorial office. They were distinguished for their utter ignorance and unforgivable paltriness. Lust for notoriety inspired him to this contrivance. He printed his verses on rose-colored sheets which he handed out to the town grocers. Tea, bonbons, sausages and other dainties were wrapped in them. Thus, with every purchase, the customer received a bonus, some half-yard of poetry apostrophizing the town notables, the police chief, the mayor, the local gentry and the bishop.

These were characters, in their own way, and deserving of notice. The bishop, particularly, commanded attention. He had forced baptism on a young Tatar girl and almost provoked a Tatar uprising. He had framed a case against some Khlisti [64] involving a number of totally innocent people, whom I knew, and had secured their conviction. His most sensational achievement was the following: Driving in bad weather his carriage broke down near an out-of-the-way village and he had to stop over in a peasant hut. On a shelf near the icons he saw to his surprise a clay figurine of Jove. Investigation disclosed such images of the Lord of Olympus, along with statuettes of Venus, in other peasant huts, though no one would tell where they came from.

This was the basis for a criminal case he started against the pagans of Samara for worshipping the gods of ancient Rome. The pagans were sent to jail and rotted there until further, long-drawn-out examination revealed that the clay figurines had been the stock of a murdered merchant, and the gods had been shared out among the peasants.

In brief, I was disgusted with the mayor, the bishop, the town, the world, and myself. In my irritation I called the poet who hymned the praises of these notables so odious to me, Skukin-Sin.[65]

Korolenko immediately communicated his disapproval. One should show restraint, he said, even in justified abuse. This fine letter, taken from me during a police search, disappeared along with other correspondence from Korolenko.

Here a few words about police are in order.

[63] The word *skuka* means boredom.
[64] Members of a dissident religious sect.
[65] Making it resemble *sukin-sin*, which meant son-of-a-bitch.

In the spring of 1897 I was arrested in Nizhny and transported, without much concern for my comfort or my feelings, to Tiflis. In an examination held in the Palace of Metekh Colonel Konisky, later Police Chief of St. Petersburg, said in an envious tone, "What letters Korolenko writes you! He's our best writer now."

A strange man, Konisky; small, his movements cautious and hesitant, his monstrosity of a nose guiltily curved downward. His eyes did not seem at home on his face; the pupils seemed to want to go in hiding under the arch of that enormous nose.

"I'm a countryman of Korolenko's—we're both from the Volhynia. I'm a descendant of Bishop Konisky, who—do you recall him now?—made that celebrated address to Catherine the Great,—'Let's take leave of the sun.' I take pride in it."

I inquired politely, who of the two aroused greater pride in him, ancestor or countryman.

"Both, both, of course," he said. The pupils of his eyes seemed about to bore into his nose, but failed and returned to their places. Illness sharpened my temper and I made some remarks about the pride of a man, intruded upon by such paragons of courtesy as the police.

Konisky unctuously replied, "We each carry out the will of the Almighty, every one of us! Let's continue. You state, although we have contrary information . . ."

We were in a small room over the castle gate. From a window just under the ceiling, a bright ray dove upon the table heaped with papers, illuminating among others, to my great embarrassment, a slip of paper on which I had written down some silly phrases punning on the word for salmon.

Looking at the ridculous paper I wondered, What am I going to say if he asks me what that means?

For six years, from 1895 to 1901, I did not see Korolenko, and our correspondence was sporadic. In 1901 I made my first appearance in St. Petersburg, that city of straight lines and crooked hearts. I was "the rage"; "glory" beset me. I recall, one night, crossing the Anichkov bridge on my way home, being overtaken by two men, barbers from their appearance, one of whom, peering into my face, turned to his companion with awe and reported, "There's Gorky!" The other stopped, took a long look at me up and down, and after he got out of my way, said with rapt contentment, "The devil, walks around in galoshes!"

In addition to other diversions, I was photographed with the editors of "Nachalo," [66] one of whom, Gurovich, as it turned out, was a police agent. I'll not deny that I enjoyed the indulgent smiles of women and the adoring glances of girls. Probably, like all young men winged in premature glory, I strutted like an Indian cock.

But alone, at night, I felt like a fugitive surrounded by detectives and judges who all assumed me guilty through a mishap, a "youthful error," which, when confessed, would be generously forgiven. However, in their secret hearts they yearn to take the criminal in the act, to be able to crow over him, "We've caught you!"

At times, I had to undergo quizzes like a schoolboy in a science class, "What do you believe in?" I was asked, both by the faithful and the dissenters. Having an amiable disposition, I submitted with a patience that amazed me, too. However, after such verbal ordeals, I felt an urge to pierce the St. Izaac's cathedral dome with the Admiralty Needle,[67] or something that would cause a comparable scandal.

Beneath their usually affected good nature, Russians hide a certain caddishness. This characteristic—is it perhaps a vagary of the exploring instinct?—has varied expressions, but chiefly as a tour of your neighbor's soul, as one tours a fair, gapes at the sleights of hand and commits a little breakage, in fun, of course; then, like doubting Thomas, pokes one's fingers in the wounds, on the presumption that one can equate the curiosity of monkeys with the skepticism of the apostle.

Even in stony Petersburg Korolenko managed to hunt out a wooden house, small, old, cozily rural, with whitewashed ceiling and antiquely mellow. He had grown gray; almost white at the temples; wrinkles had formed around his eyes, whose look had become weary and abstracted. It was at once apparent that the serenity which had formerly made him so attractive to me had given way to the agitation of a man under continual tension.

It was clear that his involvement in the Multan case,[68] along with the other chains he had dragged around like a bear through these troubled years, had worn him out.

"I have insomnia, a terrible bore; and though I've become consumptive I keep on smoking. How are your lungs? I'm going to the Black Sea. Come along with me!"

Sitting down at the table and peering at me from around the samovar,

[66] A literary review, whose name means Beginning.
[67] The tall, pointed spire of the Admiralty Building, one of the landmarks of the city.
[68] A case involving a city in The Indian Punjab.

he began a discussion of my work. "You do things like *Varenka Olesova* better than *Foma Gordeyev*. That book is hard going; the material is rich but it's unfinished and formless."

Straightening out so suddenly that I heard his spine crack, he asked me, "And have you turned Marxist?"

When I said I was moving in that direction he remarked, with a wistful smile, "I can't make it out. I just can't make out socialism stripped of idealism. I can't conceive of an ethics based on co-ordinated material interests. And what's one to do without ethics?"

Sipping his tea he asked, "And how do you find Petersburg?"

"There's more to see in the town than in the people."

"The people here—" he raised his eyebrows and rubbed his tired eyes—"the people here are more European than in Moscow or along the Volga. I'm told Moscow has more individuality, but I can't say. I've found the Moscow individuality notably crude, tough, reactionary. The spirit is that of the Slavophiles,[69] Katkov [70] and the rest; while here you have the spirit of the Decembrists,[71] the Petrashevskys, the Cherneshevskys." [72]

"And Pobiedonostzev," [73] I interjected.

"And Marxists," added Korolenko with a smile. "And every kind of thinking edged with progress which means revolution. And whatever you say, Pobiedonostzev is a man of talent. Have you looked into his 'Moscow Review'? Take note that it labels itself Muscovite."

He fell into a nervous animation, and joked about the spats of the literary coteries and the controversies of the Narodniks and the Marxists.

I knew something about that for, on the first day after my arrival in Petersburg, I had become involved in an "issue," which, to this day, it angers me to recall.

V. A. Posse, editor of "Zhisn" (Life), had arranged a literary evening to honor the memory of Cherneshevsky. He had invited, among other Marxists and Narodniks, Korolenko, Mikhailovsky, Melshin, Struve and Tugan-Baranovsky. The speakers had accepted and police authorization had been secured for the evening.

The day after my arrival in Petersburg I received a call from three students, two young cleverish males and a young coquette. They de-

---

[69] A group that advocated turning from Western influences to the Slavic tradition.
[70] A reactionary official.
[71] Group involved in the unsuccessful revolution of 1820.
[72] A critic and writer whose novel, *What Is to Be Done*, had a great influence on revolutionaries.
[73] Procurator of the Holy Synod, Slavophil, and one of the chief reactionary influences at the court.

clared that they would not permit Posse to participate in any celebration honoring Cherneshevsky. "Posse, the exploiter of the staff of
'Zhisn,' is inacceptable to the student youth!"

I had known Posse for about a year, and among his varied accomplishments I had never observed any talent for exploiting editors. I knew
he was on amicable terms with them; that he worked like a horse; and,
being underpaid himself, lived with his sizable family on the verge of
starvation.

When I mentioned this to the youths they accused Posse of wavering
between the Narodniks and the Marxists. I reminded them that Posse
himself acknowledged this, and for that reason signed the *nom-de-plume*,
Wilde, under his articles. I succeeded only in irritating these precocious
Catos, and they left me with the threat that they would urge all the
speakers to withdraw from the meeting.

As it turned out, the "significance" of this incident was not so
much personal animosity against Posse as "a collision of two conflicting
political tendencies." The young Marxists were opposed to having their
representatives seen in public with representatives of the "effete," the
"watered-down" Narodniks.

This information came to me in a letter as formal as an administrative report and in a terminology that made me think I was reading a
foreign language. Along with the communication from my unknown
correspondents came a note from Struve, informing me of his withdrawal
from the meeting. A few hours later another note from him withdrew his
withdrawal. The next day Tugan-Baranovsky withdrew and Struve
changed his mind again and finally dissociated himself from the meeting.
As in his previous notes Struve did not trouble to explain his decision.

Korolenko smiled and said with wry humor, "You see; you can be
called to the stage to give a reading; but once you're there they'll pull
down your pants, and give you a glorious whipping." He paced the
room, his hands behind his back, speaking in a low, musing voice,
"We've fallen upon bad times. Something alien and deforming has come
among us. I can't make out the mind of our youth. A certain nihilism
has again cropped out among them; a new breed of career socialists is
arising. Autocracy is undermining itself in Russia; but the power that
should take over is not in sight."

It was the first time I saw Korolenko looking so discouraged and
weary and it saddened me. Some Zemstvo people arrived to see him
and I went away. In a day or two he was gone seeking rest. So far
as I can recall, this was our last meeting.

My meetings with him had been infrequent. I had never had him under day-to-day observation.

Every talk with Korolenko, however, strengthened my impression of him as a humanist. Among cultured Russian people I had not met one who was so concerned to embody truth in their lives.

When Tolstoy died, Korolenko wrote me, "Like no other before him Tolstoy enlarged the number of thinking and believing people. You're mistaken, I think, to feel that this comes at the expense of action. Man's thinking is action, too. Rouse it and it will direct him toward justice and truth."

I have had abundant evidence that Korolenko's cultural work stirred up the slumbering truth consciousness of a vast number of Russians. He has given himelf to the cause of justice with that rare, whole intensity in which the emotional and the rational fuse into religious passion. It was as if he had, himself, seen and sensed the abstraction "justice"; like all our better dreams, that phantom, cheated by man's spirit, sought a tangible incarnation.

To the detriment of his course as an artist, Korolenko spent his energies on the unending struggle against the hundred-headed monsters nurtured by our fantastic Russian life.

The austerities of revolutionary thinking cast vexation and apprehension over his heart, a heart that warmly loved beauty as well as justice and sought to merge them into a humane unity. However, he had a resolute conviction that the country's creative forces were to have their dawn. And he had a premonition that the miracle of the resurrection of the people from their inanimate state would be an awesome one.

In 1908 he wrote: "In a few years everything done today will have a consequence in a volcanic explosion. Terrible will be those days. But come they will if the spirit of the people lives—and it does live!"

In 1887 he had ended his story, "In the Eclipse," with this couplet of Berg's:

> "In Holy Rus the cocks crow;
> Soon the holy day with glow."

All his life Korolenko strode the hard path toward that outcome with the resolution of a hero; and his contributions toward hastening it are incalculable.